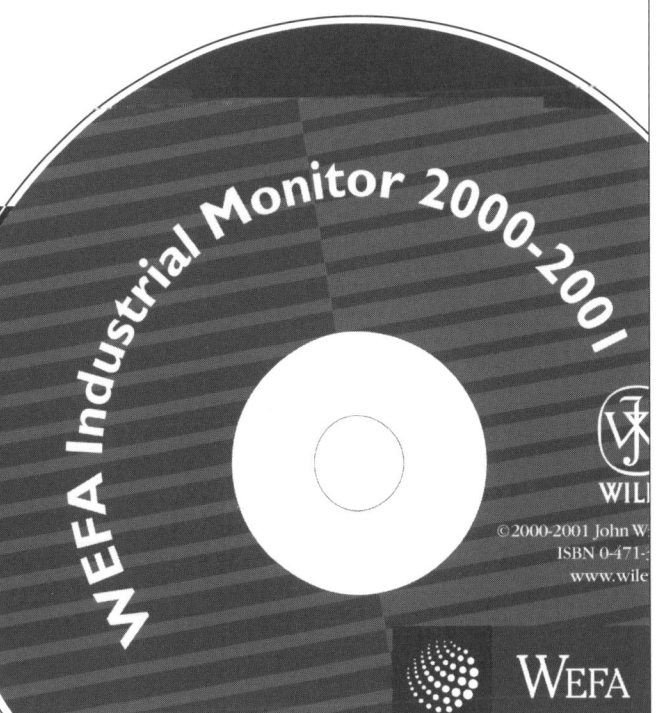

WEFA
Industrial
Monitor
2000–2001

Subscriber Update Service

BECOME A SUBSCRIBER!

Did you purchase this product from a bookstore?

If you did, it's important for you to become a subscriber. John Wiley & Sons, Inc. may publish, on a periodic basis, supplements and new editions to reflect the latest changes in the subject matter that you **need to know** in order to stay competitive in this ever-changing industry. By contacting the Wiley office nearest you, you'll receive any current update at no additional charge. In addition, you'll receive future updates and revised or related volumes on a 30-day examination review.

If you purchased this product directly from John Wiley & Sons, Inc., we have already recorded your subscription for this update service.

To become a subscriber, please call **1-800-225-5945** or send your name, company name (if applicable), address, and the title of the product to:

mailing address: **Supplement Department**
John Wiley & Sons, Inc.
One Wiley Drive
Somerset, NJ 08875

e-mail: **subscriber@wiley.com**
fax: **1-732-302-2300**
online: **www.wiley.com**

For customers outside the United States, please contact the Wiley office nearest you:

Professional & Reference Division
John Wiley & Sons Canada, Ltd.
22 Worcester Road
Rexdale, Ontario M9W 1L1
CANADA
(416) 675-3580
Phone: 1-800-567-4797
Fax: 1-800-565-6802
canada@jwiley.com

Jacaranda Wiley Ltd.
PRT Division
P.O. Box 174
North Ryde, NSW 2113
AUSTRALIA
Phone: (02) 805-1100
Fax: (02) 805-1597
headoffice@jwiley.com.au

John Wiley & Sons, Ltd.
Baffins Lane
Chichester
West Sussex, PO19 1UD
ENGLAND
Phone: (44) 1243 779777
Fax: (44) 1243 770638
cs-books@wiley.co.uk

John Wiley & Sons (SEA) Pte. Ltd.
2 Clementi Loop #02-01
SINGAPORE 129809
Phone: (65) 463-2400
Fax: (65) 463-4605, (65) 463-4604
wiley@signet.com.sg

WEFA Industrial Monitor 2000–2001

Edited by Frantz R. Price
and
Margaret M. Regester

JOHN WILEY & SONS, INC.
New York • Chichester • Weinheim • Brisbane • Singapore • Toronto

This book is printed on acid-free paper. ∞

Copyright © 2000 by John Wiley & Sons, Inc. All rights reserved.

Published simultaneously in Canada.

This publication is designed to provide accurate and authoritative information in regard to the subject matter covered. It is sold with the understanding that the publisher is not engaged in rendering legal, accounting, or other professional services. If legal advice or other expert assistance is required, the services of a competent professional person should be sought.

Library of Congress Cataloging-in-Publication Data:
ISBN 0-471-38306-6
ISSN 1093-6580

Printed in the United States of America

10 9 8 7 6 5 4 3 2 1

About the Editors

Frantz R. Price is Senior Vice President of Industry Services at WEFA. His responsibilities include the overall management of a broad range of industrial forecasting and consulting services. He advises line and staff managers of Fortune 1000 companies on the strategic implications for their markets and operations of changes in the global economic environment. His clientele ranges from the major aerospace, automotive, chemicals, metals, telecommunications, and railroad companies to energy utilities, commercial banks, and multinational consumer product groups.

He has 25 years of experience in market and cost analysis, economic forecasting, and planning. He has written extensively about the industrial sector and on the topic of industrial inflation. He speaks frequently to business audiences and is widely quoted in the trade press and leading journals.

Mr. Price has been with WEFA since 1982, and is a regular contributor to the company's macroeconomic forecast. Prior to joining WEFA, he held managerial positions at Ingersoll-Rand Company and Union Carbide. His responsibilities there included strategic planning, economic analysis, product line modeling and forecasting, competitive intelligence, and acquisition search. He also held engineering positions at American Can Company and Diamond Shamrock Corporation. He has a Bachelor's degree in Chemical Engineering from Pratt Institute and a Master's degree in Economics from the City University of New York.

Margaret M. Regester is Senior Editor at WEFA. Her responsibilities include all aspects of the editing process for WEFA documents.

Ms. Regester has over 15 years of experience in editing having worked in various business-to-business trade publications in the instrumentation, automation, automotive, and electronics fields.

She has been with WEFA since June 1999. Prior to joining WEFA, she was managing editor at Cahners Business Information, a member of Reed Elsevier Inc. Her undergraduate work was divided between Lynchburg College and West Chester University. She received a bachelor's degree in English with a minor concentration in Earth Sciences. She has also pursued graduate coursework at Villanova University.

List of Contributors

Priscilla Trumbull is responsible for all Forecasting Operations at WEFA. She has more than 20 years of experience in consulting, analysis, and modeling, much of it concentrated in industry analysis.

Harry S. Baumes is Senior Vice President of Industry and Agriculture Services at WEFA. He has over 21 years of experience in analysis of agricultural policy, commodity, price and trade analysis, and the fertilizer, pesticides, and farm equipment (manufactured input) sectors.

Mohsen Bonakdarpour is Vice President of Special Projects in WEFA's Resource Planning group. He has more than fifteen years of experience in statistical and input-output modeling.

Kate Corini is an Administrative Assistant at WEFA responsible for production and coordination of the forecast documents.

Jocelyn A. Hansell covers U.S. industrial activity as an Associate Economist at WEFA. She provides analysis for industry consulting project work.

Michael Helmar is Director of International Agricultural Services at WEFA. He has over 15 years of experience in modeling and analysis of U.S. and international agricultural policy and agricultural commodities, prices, and trade.

Andrew Hodge is Senior Vice President of U.S. Macroeconomics and Financial Markets. He has over 30 years experience with the U.S. Treasury and major corporations and banks.

Muhammed Hossain is an Associate Economist in WEFA's Foreign Exchange Service. He holds an MA in Economics and an MS in Statistics.

Kurt E. Karl is Executive Vice President of Global Services at WEFA. Before becoming the manager of Global Services, Dr. Karl was the head of the U.S. Forecasting Services. He is an expert on the U.S. and global economies with extensive experience and knowledge of foreign markets and has lived and worked in Europe, Africa, and Asia.

Kenneth J. Kremar is Director of Capital Goods and Freight Transportation for WEFA. He has more than 25 years of experience in monitoring and analyzing these markets.

Shirley Lau is an Economist in WEFA's Industry Services group. She has more than 20 years of experience in building and managing economic data bases.

George M. Magliano has been a professional economist for almost 30 years and is Director of WEFA's Automotive Research. Prior to joining WEFA, he was Chief Economist at J.P. Stevens and Director of Consumer and Automotive Research for Economic Consulting & Planning.

Robert Prybolsky covers the U.S. housing and construction markets for WEFA as a Senior economist in Regional Services. He is a panel member of the American Institute of Architects Concensus Construction Forecast.

Thomas Runiewicz, CPA, is Director of WEFA's World Steel Services and Senior Economist for other industry services at WEFA. He has more than 20 years of experience in economic modeling, forecasting, and consulting.

Adam Sacks directs WEFA's Tourism & Hospitality group and is responsible for forecasting visitor arrivals and expenditures on a global basis. He has conducted tourism impact studies for countries around the world and is responsible for WEFA's recent launch of Global Tourism Monitor, an interactive tourism research tool.

Marlene Scargill is an Administrative Assistant, and has responsibility for coordinating and preparing forecast documents and proposals for WEFA's Industry and Agricultural Services department.

Ted Semesnyei is an Associate Economist in the Industry Services group at WEFA, providing support and analysis for industrial inflation, steel, and non-ferrous metals.

Genio Staranczak is Director, U.S. Macro Long-Term Forecasting. Dr. Staranczak is responsible for producing a 25-year forecast of the U.S. economy. He also contributes to a monthly executive summary that analyzes recent developments, provides general client support, and consults on U.S. macro projects.

Christopher Swann is Director of WEFA's World Service. He is currently responsible for the U.S. Macro Short Term forecast and for coordinating the development of WEFA's World Economic Outlook. He has over 15 years of applied experience in the telecommunications industry.

Ronald J. Talley, Ph.D., is Director of Global Financial Services at WEFA. He has more than 25 years of experience as a professional economist, including positions with the Federal Reserve, a major commercial bank, and as an independent consultant.

Contents

CONTENTS

Part 6: Finance, Insurance, Real Estate, and Services

Preface

This book is a comprehensive review of the major industries in the U.S. economy, prepared by the industry analysts at WEFA, the top economic forecasting and consulting firm in the world. Each of its sections is designed to paint a picture of the economic health of an industry over the last ten years, in the very near term future, and looking forward to the year 2008.

The industries are evaluated in terms of: demand, both from domestic customers and export markets; supply conditions, including the structure of the domestic producing sector and imports; the links of the industry to the economy and to product and technology trends; pressures and opportunities in product pricing and production costs; profitability; and issues such as business cycle sensitivity, environmental issues, and consolidation trends that shape each industry and its companies. The issues discussed are key to the formulation of WEFA's forecast for the industries' sales and other activity measures, and are vital to the reader's understanding of the forces driving the companies in each segment of the economy. The information will be useful for researchers, financial analysts, portfolio managers, market researchers, corporate planners and strategists, lending officers, purchasing managers, and a host of other people who need information about industry trends. The articles were written in August and September of 1999. The actual data available at that time was complete year for 1998, full first quarter of 1999, and two to three months of the second quarter (depending on the specific indicator).

The book is organized into seven main parts. The introductory material provides the overall economic framework in which the industry forecasts have been developed, with chapters describing WEFA's U.S. macroeconomic forecast, the global economic outlook, and a brief ranking of the top performers of the various industry sectors in the United States. Parts 1 through 6 serve to organize the chapters into broad industry groups: Agriculture, Mining, and Construction; Non-Durable Goods Manufacturing; Durable Goods Manufacturing; Transportation, Communications, and Utilities; Wholesale and Retail Trade; and Finance, Insurance, Real Estate, and Services.

Close to twenty analysts at WEFA directly contributed sections to this book, and many others contributed indirectly through their ongoing analysis and projects. While we have not designated authors' names for the specific sections, each of them brings a rich blend of training, experience, and information sources to their analysis. In addition, they have all developed their forecasts in the framework of WEFA's overall economic view — each contributes to that view and each evaluates the economic environment for an industry from the WEFA forecast for the macroeconomy and for related industries. This consistency of assumptions and approach is critical for virtually all applications of the forecasts, and it is an advantage derived from producing this work from within a single, tightly-knit organization.

WEFA is pleased to continue to work with John Wiley & Sons on editions of this book. Sheck Cho and Rachael Leiserson at John Wiley & Sons have been instrumental in bringing it to completion. A special note of recognition for Ken Kremar of WEFA whose dedication to this project has been truly remarkable: his intricate knowledge of the industrial sector is reflected in the broad range of industries that he has written about in this book.

Readers who would like further information on WEFA's economic analysis and forecasting, strategic and tactical project consulting, detailed industry analysis, historical and forecast databases, or other capabilities are encouraged to contact our sales organization by fax at (610) 490-2848 or by e-mail at wefahelp@wefa.com. Continued updates for the Industry Monitor are planned, and we welcome suggestions for future editions.

Priscilla Trumbull and Frantz R. Price
November 1999

Introduction: Economic Review and Forecasts

U.S. Economic Outlook

World Economic Outlook

Forecast Highlights: The High Growth Industries

U.S. Economic Outlook

Real gross domestic product (GDP) growth will average 3.8% in 1999 and 2.3% in 2000. Slower growth in 2000 will be followed by average annual GDP gains of about 2.5%. Consumption and investment gains remain strong near term, but will slow from unsustainable levels. Inventory accumulation accelerates in the second half of 1999, as businesses stock up in preparation for possible Y2K disruptions. It then falls off in 2000, adding to other weaknesses such as housing. Solid economic growth in the long term combined with moderate increases in general spending result in government budget surpluses for the foreseeable future.

The outlook for inflation remains moderate. Core CPI inflation (the consumer price index excluding the volatile food and energy categories) will average 2.3% per year from 1999 to 2004 and 2.4% thereafter. Broader measures of inflation, such as the consumer price index, should average 2.4% per year through 2008.

The productivity performance of the U.S. economy should be fairly healthy over the forecast period. Continued growth in investment and a more slowly growing labor force should result in a rate of productivity growth during the next 25 years that is somewhat faster than the previous 25 years.

Short-Term Forecast Summary

Real economic expansion continues its surge at 3.8% for 1999 as a whole, but moderates to 2.3% in 2000.

- Housing is slowing from the extreme peaks in early 1999.

- Consumption and investment gains remain strong near term, but will slow from unsustainable levels.

- Government spending growth should hold up in 2000, led by state and local governments flush with revenue.

- Inventory accumulation accelerates in the second half of 1999 as businesses stock up in preparation for possible Y2K supply disruptions, and then falls off in 2000.

- Inflation will rise gradually through 2001, as increasing wage settlements and commodity prices combine with decelerating productivity growth to cause costs to rise.

- The Federal Reserve Board has raised interest rates in 1999 as a preemptive measure against inflation. It is expected to increase rates again in response to any strong inflation data.

Long-Term Forecast Summary

Population and Demographics Population growth is a primary long-run determinant of the potential expansion path of the economy. Population growth affects both the supply and demand sides of the economy. The growth of the population and its composition have profound impacts on the labor force, demand for consumer durables (especially light vehicles), housing, and demand for medical services. WEFA is basing its population projections on the Census Bureau's latest middle series assumptions for fertility, life expectancy, and net immigration, which were released in February 1996.

The U.S. population is projected to expand at an annual rate of 0.8% between 1998 and 2003, when the population is forecast to reach 281.3 million. Population growth will then continue at about 0.8% per year. Population growth will not be distributed evenly across the population cohorts. Rather, growth in the older age cohorts will be stronger as the baby boomers age.

Productivity and Aggregate Supply It is the economy's ability to increase supply in the long run that determines its potential growth path. Growth in aggregate supply depends on the increase in the labor force, the growth of the capital stock, and improvements in productivity.

Productivity improvement depends on several key factors:

- Advancement in the education, training, and skills of the work force;

- The amount that is saved and invested for equipping the labor force with productive capital (tools, machinery, transportation equipment, and other manufactured means of production); and

- The speed with which new technology and improved techniques are introduced into the production, transportation, and distribution of goods and services.

Potential GDP growth will slow in the long term from a 2.6% annual average over the next five years and slowing to about 2.4% by 2025. This is in stark contrast to the potential growth path of more than 3.0% that prevailed in the 1960s. Potential growth has been slowing for the past 30 years, and this slowdown is expected to continue.

The 1960s witnessed stellar growth in output per man-hour, which averaged 2.9% per year. Productivity growth slumped in the 1970s. Since that time productivity growth has averaged 1.1% per year. WEFA believes productivity growth will accelerate above its recent historical average and come in at 1.3% from 1998 to 2025. The productivity growth is due to faster growth in equipment spending, particularly for information processing machinery.

Government Policy The government sector share of GDP will decline over the forecast period. Total public purchases (including state and local) as a share of GDP will decrease to 16.7% in 2003 from 17.5% in 1998 and fall to 15.4% by 2025. This reduction in the government's share of the economy is concentrated in the federal sector. The reduction in federal spending as a percentage of GDP will largely be the result of a declining defense share which will drop from 4.0% of GDP in 1998 to 2.7% in 2025. In contrast, state and local spending as a share of GDP will decrease only slightly from 11.4% in 1998 to 11.1% in 2025.

Real GDP Growth

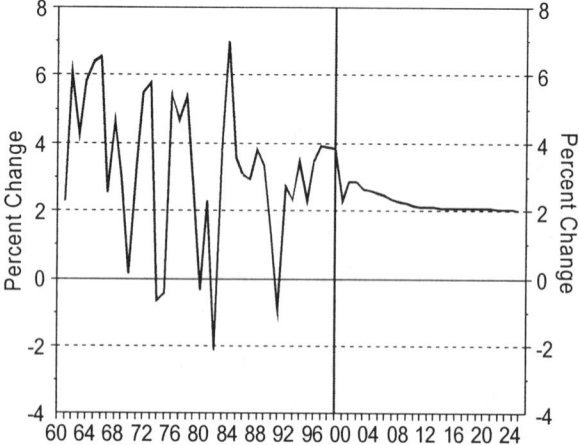

WEFA expects the federal government to record a surplus throughout the forecast period. Washington's budget balance will reach $134 billion in 1999, decline to $61 billion in 2009, but rise again to $110 billion by the year 2025. Nevertheless, the federal surplus will average less than 1% of GDP over the entire forecast period.

These projections are based upon the belief that Congress and the Executive government will find it politically more expedient to increase spending and decrease taxes rather than let the budget surplus grow over time. In particular, WEFA anticipates that the temptation to cut taxes will be too hard to resist.

On the state and local level, WEFA expects the combined surplus will rise from $150.2 billion in 1998 to $259.6 billion in 2025. The state and local governments need to run surpluses to fund pension plans for state and local employees.

Federal Budget Surplus

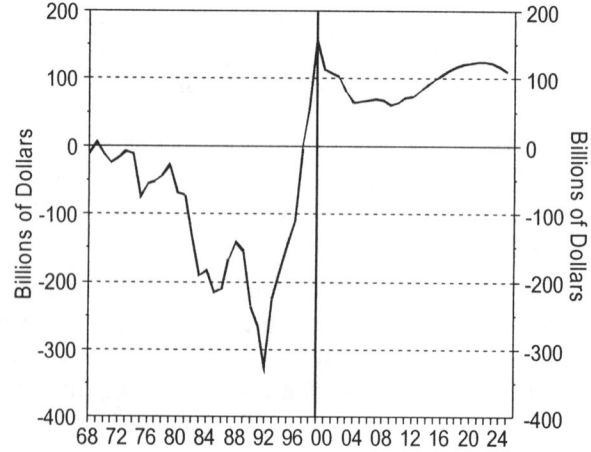

Monetary Policy and Financial Markets The Fed will continue to pursue a monetary policy that maintains vigilance against inflation and provides sufficient growth in the money supply to ensure moderate economic growth. A stricter monetary regime would lead to lower inflation, but at the expense of lost output. In order to achieve the "zero inflation rate" that some members of the Federal Reserve Board have advocated, deflation in goods markets would be necessary to offset rising prices of services in such areas as health care. It seems unlikely that the Fed will attempt to implement such a restrictive policy.

Oil Prices Because of plentiful energy supplies, oil prices, as proxied by a barrel of West Texas Intermediate, declined by 7.0% in 1997. Continued oversupply, combined with a decrease in demand from Asia led to a further drop of 30.1% in 1998. The situation has turned around, however, as prices have surged in 1999 by more than 80% on a year-over-year basis through August. The pace of escalation is expected to moderate afterward. U.S. oil production will decline steadily over the long term, but other non-OPEC production will remain strong, moderating the ability of OPEC to push oil prices significantly higher.

The Dollar On the basis of the real Morgan Guaranty index of 18 trade-weighted currencies, the dollar fell almost 30% between its 1985 peak and 1991. By 1995, the dollar had dropped another 6.9% from its 1991 level. Virtually all of this was recovered in 1996, however, as the dollar rose 4.9%. From 1996 to 1998 the dollar appreciated an additional 14%. In 1999 the dollar is expected to rise modestly again. But beyond 1999, WEFA expects the dollar to decline against foreign currencies. The dollar needs to fall to correct the large current account deficit the country is presently running.

Employment Slower long-run increases in the labor force indicate more moderate long-run employment growth in the future. Total civilian employment will rise at an average annual rate of 1.3% from 1998 to 2003, and will moderate to an average growth rate of 0.9% for the rest of the forecast period. Manufacturing's share of total employment will continue to decline over the forecast period, falling to 10.8% in 2025 from 14.9% in 1998. The broad service sector will generate an increasing share of employment growth in the forecast period, although the share of employment accounted by the federal government will decline.

Productivity Growth (Output per man-hour)

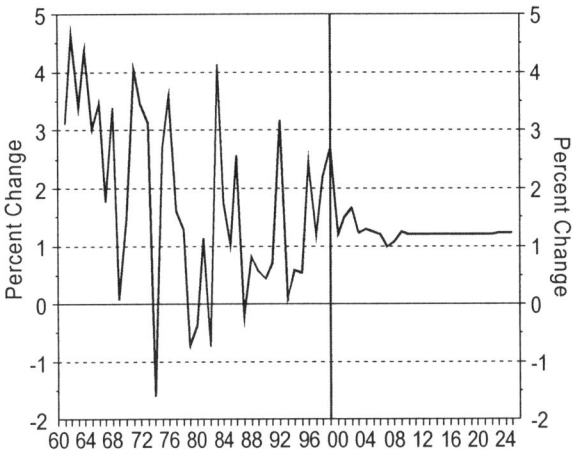

Inflation After accelerating in the 1970s and early 1980s, inflation has slowed significantly in recent years. Even with a long-lived expansion inflation has remained moderate. Although the economy is close to full employment, changes in the labor market have prevented any significant acceleration of wages. Wage pressures have remained remarkably modest. Even with some pickup in wages, inflation will remain moderate for the next several years. WEFA believes inflation will average 2.4% over the long run. The absence of a major exogenous shock, such as another oil price crisis, should permit inflation to remain in check. In the long run, inflation is primarily under the control of the central bank. Central banks have become more committed to controlling inflation, as many policy makers are advocating a "zero inflation rate" as a long-term goal.

Consumption Consumer expenditures in the long term are primarily determined by the growth of real permanent income, demographic influences, and changes in relative prices. The share of personal consumption expenditures in GDP will rise slightly over the forecast interval. Consumer spending as a share of GDP has increased since the early 1980s, reaching 68.2% in 1998. Consumer spending should account for 70.9% of the overall economy by the end of the forecast horizon. Real consumption expenditure growth will average 3.0% per year through 2003, then will slow to 2.0%.

The share of consumption devoted to services will rise, while that for goods falls. The long-term outlook for auto and light truck sales calls for a slowdown in the rate of increase relative to past performance. Vehicle sales growth will average only about 1% on a long-run trend basis. Although the number of vehicles per person has increased significantly in the past 20 years, the United States is approaching a saturation point in the rate of vehicle ownership. Future growth in vehicle sales will be primarily driven by growth in population and demand for replacement vehicles.

Housing The long-term outlook for housing is based on demographic factors. Underpinning the demand for housing is the growth in the number of households (as opposed to simply population growth). Despite slower population growth, housing starts will rise in the long run, as the number of households increases faster than the overall population does. Housing starts peaked in 1972, at 2.36 million units. The underlying level of starts has moderated to the 1.4 to 1.6 million range in the last several years as a result of the slower growth in the prime home-buying, 25–34 age population cohort. Housing starts are projected to average 1.46 million units from 1998 to 2003, then slow to 1.39 million units in 2008.

Business Fixed Investment The long-run prospects for business fixed investment are very positive. Business continues to strive toward reducing the labor portion of total costs and enhancing pro-

ductivity growth in order to remain competitive in international markets. Real business fixed investment is projected to rise by average annual rates of 4.1% from 1998 to 2003 and 2.7% between 2003 and 2008.

The composition of investment will continue to change in the forecast period: structures' share of investment will decline modestly, while equipment's share rises. This is a continuation of a long-standing trend. One of the fastest growing sectors of the U.S. economy will be producers' durable equipment, concentrated in information processing equipment. The development of advanced electronics, which promise a high rate of return on investment, has led to a massive change in business' priorities for investment.

International Trade A decline in the exchange rate combined with modest unit labor cost growth will stimulate U.S. exports abroad, and result in an eventual improvement in the U.S. current account balance. WEFA projects real exports will expand at an average annual rate of 6.0% between 1998 and 2003 and at an average rate of 4.7% thereafter. Real imports will grow at an average annual rate of 5.9% between 1998 and 2003 and an average annual rate of 3.8% thereafter. The faster growth of exports relative to imports will eventually result in an improving current account balance, which will peak at $329 billion in 2000 before dropping steadily.

FORECAST SUMMARY

	II 99	III 99	IV 99	I 00	II 00	III 00	IV 00	1998	1999	2000	2001	2002	2003	2004
ECONOMIC ACTIVITY														
Real GDP, Bil Chained $92	7794	7871	7942	7932	8001	8050	8103	7552	7842	8022	8251	8487	8711	8939
% Change, SAAR	1.8	4.0	3.7	-0.5	3.5	2.5	2.7	3.9	3.8	2.3	2.9	2.9	2.6	2.6
% Change, Year Ago	3.9	4.0	3.4	2.2	2.6	2.3	2.0							
GDP, Bil $	8882	9008	9139	9178	9287	9383	9493	8511	8959	9335	9798	10271	10734	11218
% Change, SAAR	3.4	5.8	6.0	1.7	4.9	4.2	4.8	4.9	5.3	4.2	5.0	4.8	4.5	4.5
% Change, Year Ago	5.2	5.5	5.3	4.2	4.6	4.2	3.9							
Final Sales, Bil Chained $92	7773	7824	7866	7926	7967	8016	8069	7491	7795	7994	8216	8453	8676	8906
% Change, SAAR	3.0	2.6	2.2	3.1	2.1	2.5	2.6	4.0	4.0	2.6	2.8	2.9	2.6	2.6
Industrial Prod, 1992=100	134.0	135.6	136.5	136.1	136.2	136.8	137.8	131.4	134.7	136.7	141.0	145.1	149.6	154.3
% Change, SAAR	3.8	4.9	2.7	-1.1	0.2	2.0	3.0	3.7	2.5	1.5	3.1	2.9	3.1	3.1
% Change, Year Ago	2.0	3.0	3.1	2.5	1.6	0.9	1.0							
Employment, Estab, Mil	128.2	128.6	129.0	128.8	129.1	129.4	129.8	125.80	128.37	129.26	130.86	132.48	134.03	135.46
% Change, SAAR	1.9	1.2	1.1	-0.4	0.7	1.0	1.2	2.6	2.0	0.7	1.2	1.2	1.2	1.1
Capacity Utilization, Mfg, %	79.5	79.7	79.8	78.3	78.3	78.1	78.0	80.8	79.6	78.2	78.9	80.2	81.1	82.2
Civilian Unemployment Rate, %	4.3	4.4	4.4	4.8	4.9	4.8	4.7	4.5	4.3	4.8	4.7	4.8	4.9	5.1
Lt Vehicle Sales, Mil, BEA	16.7	16.9	16.7	16.0	15.3	14.9	15.5	15.6	16.6	15.4	15.5	15.6	15.6	15.8
Auto Sales, Mil, BEA	8.7	8.8	8.3	7.8	7.9	7.5	7.8	8.2	8.5	7.8	7.8	7.9	7.8	8.0
Lt Truck Sales, Mil, BEA	8.0	8.1	8.3	8.2	7.5	7.4	7.7	7.3	8.1	7.7	7.7	7.7	7.8	7.8
Housing Starts, Mil	1.61	1.59	1.54	1.48	1.46	1.44	1.40	1.62	1.63	1.45	1.40	1.41	1.40	1.40
Disp Pers Income, Bil $92	5500.2	5533.5	5598.6	5655.7	5702.3	5745.8	5794.1	5348.5	5525.1	5724.5	5903.4	6066.8	6215.2	6364.5
% Change, SAAR	2.4	2.4	4.8	4.1	3.3	3.1	3.4	3.2	3.3	3.6	3.1	2.8	2.4	2.4
Personal Saving Rate, %	-1.3	-1.6	-1.3	-1.0	-0.7	-0.5	-0.3	0.5	-1.2	-0.6	-0.0	0.3	0.5	0.7
After-Tax Corp Profits, Bil $	510.7	486.1	509.1	472.2	494.4	496.7	494.9	477.7	502.0	489.6	505.8	525.0	534.5	543.2
% Change, Year Ago	6.0	1.9	7.7	-5.9	-3.2	2.2	-2.8	-2.2	5.1	-2.5	3.3	3.8	1.8	1.6
Fed Cur Surplus, NIPA, Bil $	140.8	135.6	138.9	120.8	118.0	110.9	104.2	72.8	134.5	113.5	102.1	102.2	88.2	76.4
Fed Surplus, Unified, Bil $	572.2	76.4	-44.4	-56.5	536.5	51.8	-79.1	54.4	156.8	113.2	107.4	102.1	79.5	63.9
COMPONENTS OF GDP														
Consumption Expend, Bil $92	5391.8	5445.0	5490.6	5526.9	5558.2	5590.2	5623.8	5153.3	5414.8	5574.8	5715.2	5853.7	5978.0	6109.5
% Change, SAAR	4.6	4.0	3.4	2.7	2.3	2.3	2.4	4.9	5.1	3.0	2.5	2.4	2.1	2.2
Nonres Fixed Invest, Bil $92	1039.4	1053.6	1056.0	1059.3	1062.7	1068.3	1074.8	960.7	1040.3	1066.3	1097.5	1135.9	1171.3	1206.6
% Change, SAAR	11.2	5.6	0.9	1.3	1.3	2.1	2.5	11.8	8.3	2.5	2.9	3.5	3.1	3.0
Prod Dur Equip, Bil $92	850.6	867.7	870.4	874.4	878.0	884.1	890.9	770.2	852.1	881.8	913.7	951.3	986.4	1022.3
% Change, SAAR	15.9	8.3	1.2	1.8	1.7	2.8	3.1	16.5	10.6	3.5	3.6	4.1	3.7	3.6
Structures, Bil $92	207.2	206.2	206.2	206.0	206.1	206.2	206.5	203.0	206.8	206.2	208.3	212.0	215.3	218.1
% Change, SAAR	-1.1	-1.9	-0.0	-0.3	0.2	0.1	0.6	-0.1	1.9	-0.3	1.0	1.8	1.5	1.3
Residential Invest, Bil $92	342.2	343.0	344.2	345.8	347.3	349.4	352.5	312.1	341.3	348.7	357.5	361.1	365.1	368.7
% Change, SAAR	7.7	1.0	1.4	1.9	1.7	2.5	3.5	10.4	9.4	2.2	2.5	1.0	1.1	1.0
Chg Bus Inventories, Bil $92	12.1	38.2	66.9	-2.5	24.9	25.2	25.7	57.4	39.0	18.3	26.1	25.0	26.1	24.0
Farm	2.9	-0.3	-0.4	-0.1	0.9	0.5	0.4	7.6	1.4	0.4	-0.3	-0.1	-0.1	-0.1
Nonfarm	9.4	38.6	67.6	-2.2	24.2	24.8	25.5	50.1	37.7	18.1	26.6	25.3	26.4	24.3
Gov Cons & Invest, Bil $92	1318.4	1321.4	1329.7	1338.8	1344.8	1355.8	1365.1	1296.9	1323.4	1351.1	1386.6	1421.4	1459.3	1494.7
% Change, SAAR	-1.7	0.9	2.5	2.8	1.8	3.3	2.8	0.9	2.0	2.1	2.6	2.5	2.7	2.4
Net Exports, Bil $92	-337.4	-357.5	-373.6	-369.9	-368.3	-371.4	-372.7	-238.2	-343.0	-370.7	-364.8	-336.5	-309.5	-281.0
Exports, Bil $92	1007.1	1014.7	1029.5	1040.5	1060.1	1078.2	1090.0	984.7	1011.9	1069.4	1146.1	1231.8	1319.3	1414.0
% Change, SAAR	4.3	3.0	6.0	4.4	7.7	7.0	7.8	1.5	2.8	5.7	7.2	7.5	7.1	7.2
Imports, Bil $92	1344.5	1372.2	1403.1	1410.4	1428.9	1449.6	1471.4	1222.9	1355.0	1440.1	1510.9	1568.3	1628.7	1695.1
% Change, SAAR	14.4	8.5	9.3	2.1	5.3	5.9	6.2	10.6	10.8	6.3	4.9	3.8	3.9	4.1
$ Exch Rate, MG18, % Chg, SAAR	10.0	-0.7	4.3	0.4	-0.7	-0.9	-1.6	5.0	-0.9	1.0	-1.3	-1.3	-0.4	-0.4
Real Exch Rate, % Chg, SAAR	11.8	5.4	5.0	-0.9	-1.0	-1.4	-2.2	4.8	2.2	1.5	-1.9	-2.2	-1.3	-0.6
% Change, Year Ago	1.2	0.8	6.8	5.2	2.1	0.4	-1.4							
Current Account Bal, Bil $	-287.3	-353.5	-355.4	-339.3	-330.8	-325.1	-320.9	-220.6	-317.6	-329.0	-307.1	-276.4	-246.1	-213.5
INFLATION AND PRODUCTIVITY														
GDP Price Index, % Chg, SAAR	1.5	1.7	2.2	2.2	1.3	1.6	2.1	1.0	1.4	1.9	2.0	1.9	1.8	1.8
% Change, Year Ago	1.2	1.4	1.8	1.9	1.9	1.8	1.8							
CPI, All Urban, % Chg, SAAR	3.5	3.0	2.2	2.3	2.4	2.5	2.5	1.6	2.2	2.5	2.6	2.3	2.4	2.4
% Change, Year Ago	2.1	2.4	2.5	2.8	2.5	2.4	2.4							
CPI, Core, % Chg, SAAR	2.4	2.4	2.6	2.4	2.5	2.6	2.6	2.3	2.2	2.5	2.5	2.3	2.1	2.2
% Change, Year Ago	2.1	2.2	2.2	2.4	2.5	2.5	2.5							
PPI, Fin Gds, % Chg, Year Ago	1.3	0.1	1.1	1.4	0.3	2.1	1.3	-0.9	0.8	1.3	1.1	2.8	2.3	2.1
PPI, Core, % Chg, Year Ago	1.6	1.3	0.5	0.5	0.9	1.4	1.4	0.9	1.4	1.1	1.5	1.6	1.7	1.8
PPI, Ind Comm, % Chg, Year Ago	0.0	0.7	1.7	2.3	0.5	0.6	0.3	-2.3	0.1	0.9	0.9	2.1	1.7	1.9
ECI, W & S, % Chg, SAAR	4.5	4.3	4.2	4.0	4.0	3.9	3.7	4.0	3.5	4.1	3.5	3.2	3.1	3.4
Comp per Hour, % Chg, SAAR	5.0	4.0	3.7	3.8	3.9	3.9	3.9	4.2	4.2	3.9	3.8	3.8	3.9	3.9
Output per Hour, % Chg, SAAR	1.1	2.2	2.5	0.4	0.4	0.9	1.4	2.2	2.7	1.2	1.5	1.7	1.2	1.3
Unit Labor Cost, % Chg, SAAR	4.0	1.6	1.3	3.4	3.4	2.9	2.4	2.0	1.5	2.7	2.3	2.1	2.6	2.6
FINANCIAL MARKETS														
Treasury Rates														
T-Bill Rate, 3-Month, %	4.5	4.7	4.9	4.9	4.9	4.9	4.9	4.8	4.6	4.9	4.9	4.9	4.9	4.9
T-Note Rate, 10-Year, %	5.5	5.9	5.9	5.9	5.9	6.0	6.2	5.3	5.6	6.0	6.1	6.0	6.0	6.0
T-Bond Rate, 30-Year, %	5.8	6.0	5.9	5.9	6.0	6.1	6.3	5.6	5.8	6.1	6.2	6.1	6.1	6.2

World Economic Outlook

The world economy continues to improve. The U.S. economy is robust, Asia continues to gain strength and Europe is healthier. Only Latin America has major problems in many countries. The United States, Canada, and Mexico have remained strong during the recent financial crisis, with the U.S. economy absorbing much of the rest of the world's exports. As the world gathers economic strength, the U.S. will be slowing down in 2000.

In Western Europe, economic growth is picking up. Low inflation and interest rates, good income growth, and a more stimulative fiscal policy will continue to boost the region's economies.

Asia's recovery has continued to gather strength. Across the region, growing external trade fueled industrial production, while rising incomes finally revived domestic demand. Stable currencies and asset prices have increased foreign and domestic confidence. The uncertainty in Indonesia notwithstanding, real GDP for the region, as a whole, is now expected to grow by more than 3.0% in both 1999 and 2000. In 1998, it contracted by 0.8%. In Japan, a small increase in output in the second quarter of 1999 confirmed WEFA's view of a sustainable recovery. Though government stimulus will decrease sharply in 2000, private sector growth will pick up strongly as deregulation, reduced debt, and improvements to profits stimulate growth.

The outlook for Latin America continues to depend on political actions rather than economic fundamentals. In particular, the Brazilian Congress needs to pass constitutionally acceptable pension reforms to improve the fiscal and economic outlook. The only two major Latin American countries that will experience growth during 1999 will be Peru and Mexico. In 2000, we expect all the economies to recover, but the recovery will not be strong. Mexico and Chile will be the leading growth economies.

The Russian economy has been performing much better in 1999 than expected. Of the three largest Eastern European economies, Hungary remains the strongest and should grow at least 4%. The recovery in oil prices continues to give a big boost to growth in the Middle East and oil-exporting countries in Africa.

Canada: Moderation Ahead

WEFA's forecast for the Canadian economy calls for growth of 3.5% in 1999 and 2.6% in 2000, a pattern that is quite similar to the United States. Strength in domestic demand will be broad based, although business investment in machinery and equipment and construction (residential and non-residential) will be important contributors to growth. Conversely, a decreasing real trade balance is expected to be a drag on growth over the medium term. Employment growth will be strong in 1999, but the unemployment rate will remain near 8% until the end of 2000. Short-term interest rates are expected to drift up from their current 4.7% rate to 5.4% by 2001, while the Canadian dollar is expected to rise from its current value of 68 cents to about 70 cents by year-end 2001.

The most significant risk to Canada's economic performance now is the possibility of further interest rate increases in the United States. Given the high level of unemployment in Canada and the level of excess capacity, the Bank of Canada is unlikely to follow U.S. rates upward. Only if there were strong and increasing downward pressure on the Canadian dollar, would the Bank of Canada, reluctantly, increase interest rates to defend it.

Japan: Recovery Is Underway

The Japanese economy is now expanding modestly. Real Gross Domestic Product (GDP) rose slightly, by 0.9% at an annual rate, in the second quarter of 1999. Though this is not rapid growth, it was much stronger than expected — the consensus was close to -1%.

In 2000, public investment is expected to begin declining rapidly as the stimulus programs end. The decline in government spending—which continues into 2001—will not derail the Japanese recovery. At this time, private sector profits have improved and sufficient deregulation of the economy has occurred to sustain business investment and support the recovery. Consumer spending, fueled by tax cuts this year and next, and rising employment and wages in 2001 will also contribute to growth. The Japanese economy is expected to grow by 1.3% in 1999 and 1.4% in 2000.

Despite official intervention, the yen has risen from near 120 yen/dollar to as high as 104 yen/dollar. Given the yen market's propensity to follow a trend for prolonged periods of time, 90 yen/dollar in the near term cannot be ruled out. With the yen at 90 yen/dollar, however, the nascent economic recovery could falter.

Western Europe: Positive Times Ahead

Real GDP growth in the Eurozone rose by 1.5%, at an annual rate, in the second quarter of 1999—slightly less than in the previous three months. The performances of the individual economies continue to diverge. Of those that have released second-quarter figures, France and The Netherlands posted encouragingly strong growth rates as anticipated, and Italian growth continued to pick up, but the German economy put in a very lackluster performance with growth almost unchanged from the previous three months. The poor German performance explains the weaker Eurozone figures in the second quarter, although we do expect some upward revision as other high-growth economies, such as Spain, report their numbers.

The current policy environment, the strength of domestic demand, and positive trends in the global economy are supporting Eurozone economic recovery. We currently expect Eurozone growth to be about 2.0% in 1999, and surpass 2.5% in 2000. Domestic demand will remain firm as real disposable incomes continue to rise. Also, further improvements in the labor market, the low-interest rate environment, a less restrictive fiscal policy stance, and an increase in exports as the global economy improves will all contribute to growth. These trends are supported by the survey data, which continue to register increased business and consumer optimism and stronger export order books. Eurozone inflation is expected to remain relatively low, although higher oil and commodity prices, some moderate increases in wages, and the weak euro are increasing inflation.

Second-quarter 1999 GDP growth in the United Kingdom was 1.2% at an annual rate, stronger than expected. The economy is clearly benefiting from the 250 basis point reduction in rates through June. Manufacturing growth is still weak due to the global downturn as well as the high value of U.K. sterling. Consumer demand has remained more buoyant than expected and investment continues to perform well. WEFA forecasts the U.K. economy to grow by 1.6% in 1999 and 2.4% in 2000. Tight monetary policy in 2000 will constrain growth somewhat, but exporters will benefit from stronger world growth, particularly in the Eurozone.

Asia: Improvements Continue

Asia's recovery continues to gather strength. Across the region, growing external trade is fueling industrial production, while rising incomes are finally reliving domestic demand. At the same time, stable currencies and asset prices have increased foreign and domestic confidence. The uncertainty in Indonesia notwithstanding, there is good reason to be optimistic about Asia's prospects. Low inflation, current account surpluses, and the resumption of capital inflows have given central banks the confidence to keep interest rates low, even with the recent hike in U.S. rates. The only exception is Hong Kong, which is vulnerable because of its pegged exchange rate and open capital account.

The sustainability of the current growth rebound depends critically on economic reforms remaining on track. A reduction in corporate-debt overhang, more progress in bank recapitalization, and the further development of non-bank credit markets are essential for raising the potential long-term growth path of the region's economies. The continuation of orderly capital flows will be threatened if financial markets perceive the present growth to be a temporary phenomenon brought on by the effect of inflationary measures on a low-activity base, rather than an improvement in long-term prospects.

Both Korea and Thailand have made significant progress in banking sector reform, but not as much in corporate-debt restructuring. In Indonesia, the reform process has barely started, and appears to be stalling. However, the countries suffering the least structural dislocation from the crisis—Singapore, Taiwan, Hong Kong, and the Philippines—are best situated to return to long-term strength.

WEFA's current forecast has growth returning to the entire region in 1999, with the exception of Indonesia. Despite its slight slowdown, China will grow around 7%. A de-valuation of the yuan early in 2000 is probable, but is unlikely to lead to a round of regional currency devaluations or disrupt the regional recovery.

Latin America: Weak and Unstable

The outlook for Latin America continues to depend on political actions rather than economic fundamentals. The only two major Latin American countries that will experience growth during 1999 will be Peru and Mexico. In 2000, we expect all the economies to grow, but it will not be a strong recovery. Chile and Mexico will have the strongest growth next year. However, a further increase in U.S. interest rates and a U.S. economic slowdown in 2000 could add to the region's weakness.

This recovery of growth during 2000 will depend on three conditions. **First**, commodity prices must continue to recover. **Second**, some major domestic political issues must be resolved. This is especially true in Brazil, Mexico, and Argentina. In Brazil, the current administration will have to gain domestic credibility to continue fiscal reforms. In Mexico, the year 2000 presidential elections could create uncertainty for foreign investors, leading to a flight of capital. In Argentina, the opposition Alliance, almost certain to triumph in the October elections, will need to demonstrate its commitment to economic liberalization. **Third**, an improved economic agreement among the Mercosur custom-union members is needed to reduce the unfair trade disadvantage Argentina now has with its strong currency.

Russia: Frail Economic Recovery

We expect the Russian economy to expand 1.5% in 1999 and 2.0% in 2000. GDP growth will continue to be stimulated by the ruble's undervaluation and relatively high world energy prices. At the same time, consumption and investment will remain depressed, thus preventing a growth surge. December-to-December inflation is likely to be around 40% in 1999 and 30% in 2000. Monetary and fiscal policies will stay relatively tight. The primary state budget, which excludes debt-servicing expenditures, is projected to post a 2% surplus in 1999 and about 3% in 2000.

A rise in political tensions constitutes the main risk for the Russian economy. The conflict in the Caucasus will exert pressure on the federal budget and may result in higher inflation. Also, Russia's monetary policy may be relaxed, thus accelerating inflation. Serious reforms are not expected until autumn of 2000.

Eastern Europe: Production Improving

The economic situation in the three major East European countries—the Czech Republic, Hungary, and Poland—improved in the second quarter of 1999 after generally poor performance at the end of 1998 and the beginning of 1999.

Of the three major East European countries, Hungary has the highest short-term growth potential. Its financial sector is the most developed, the country is friendly to foreign investment, and it has attracted, by far, the largest per-capita amount of foreign direct investment in the region. We expect the Hungarian economy to advance about 4% in 1999 and more than 5% in 2000. The Polish economy can also grow fast in the near future and especially in the long run. However, it seems to be less capable of adjusting to changes in foreign demand and may be dragged down by the inefficient mining sector and agriculture. Polish GDP will grow about 3% in 1999 and about 4% in 2000. The second-quarter recovery in the Czech Republic may not be sustainable. Several major deficiencies of the Czech economy remain, including underdevelopment of the financial sector and poor corporate governance. We forecast a 2% economic contraction for the Czech economy in 1999 and a moderate GDP increase of about 2.5% in 2000.

Middle East and Africa: Year of Transition

With improved oil prices in 1999, we expect the Gulf economies to grow by an annual average of more than 2% in 1999. The notable exception is Saudi Arabia where production cuts in excess of half a million barrels a day will force real GDP growth to register less than 1% in 1999. For most of the Gulf countries, we expect increased government spending on infrastructure, education, and healthcare, which will benefit the non-oil sector and provide added momentum to macroeconomic activity. Given the low CPI inflation in the region, the cash windfall will give a strong boost to consumption. Furthermore, the unexpected additional revenue will help most countries achieve lower-than-anticipated budget deficits, since most Gulf budgets in 1999 assume an estimated oil price of $11 a barrel, a figure that now looks very conservative given that the average price at the end of September was $22.86.

Israel and Jordan, both net-importers of oil, benefited from lower oil prices before June 1999, but real GDP growth was still low in both countries. In Israel, growth has been weakened by the Central Bank's high-interest rate, inflation-fighting policy. Rates only started to decline during the first quarter of 1999. If the rate cuts continue, real GDP growth will average around 3% in 1999 and around 4.5% in 2000. Jordan has been successful in negotiating a reduction in its foreign debt, but growth in 1999 will remain flat.

In Zimbabwe, ill-conceived macroeconomic and political policies, weak non-oil commodity prices and an uncertain political environment combined to push the economy into a recession in 1999.

In Morocco, another drought will constrain real GDP to only around 1.5% in 1999, compared to 6.3% in 1998. Tunisia, which is more resilient to the drought because of its relatively diversified economic base, will register a robust growth rate of 5.5% in 1999 compared to 5% in 1998.

Improved oil prices and a rebound in the tourism industry will push real GDP growth in Egypt to close to 6% in 1999 and 2000. Like other oil exporters, both Libya and Algeria will benefit from the recent increase in oil prices. Consumer inflation will continue to trend downward in most of North Africa due partly to declining prices of manufactured imports, and also to tight monetary policy.

For South Africa, the 1998 emerging market contagion effect led to a speculative run on its currency, the rand, pushing up interest rates and weakening domestic demand. However, interest rates have slowly fallen during the first half of 1999 and there is increasing internal pressure for the monetary authority to make further cuts. Weak domestic demand will be offset by an improvement to net exports driving real GDP growth to 1.2% in 1999.

In Nigeria, growth will average only slightly more than 2% in 1999 despite improvements in oil prices. In Cote d'Ivoire, low cocoa and coffee prices will constrain growth in 1999 and 2000.

Forecast Highlights:
The High Growth Industries

The industries that WEFA forecasts to have the most rapid growth over the next ten years, listed below, fall into the following general categories:

- High-tech industries, where continuing technological change and consumer and business acceptance will bring rapid growth, particularly in volume terms.

- Health services, medical instruments, and drugs, which will benefit from an aging population, advances in scientific research, and world-leading quality that will draw patients from around the globe.

- Air transportation, which will continue to grow modestly in its domestic passenger business, but more rapidly in international flights and in freight.

- Business, engineering, and management services, which will benefit from outsourcing and further expansion into foreign markets.

- In general, services rank higher in the sales ranking, with the exception of telecommunication services, where deregulation and technological change will put downward pressure on prices. Price increases will be considerably more modest for the goods-producing industries, which will continue to have limited pricing flexibility due to expanding global supply. The high-tech goods and services will also face weak pricing, and therefore rank lower in current-dollar sales than in real sales.

Top Sales Growth Industries

	Avg Annual % Change 1998-2008
Health Services	12.4
Electronic Components	10.1
Communication Equipment	7.8
Air Transportation	7.3
Business Services	7.2
Engineering and Management Services	6.8
Petroleum Refining	6.8
Insurance Services	6.3
Educational Services	6.2
Legal Services	6.2
Truck Transportation	6.1
Social Services	6.0

Top Real Sales Growth Industries

	Avg Annual % Change 1998-2008
Computers and Office Equipment	14.3
Electronic Components	10.0
Health Services	6.1
Communication Equipment	5.8
Communications, excl. Radio/TV	5.6
Communication Services	5.3
Business Services	3.8
Engineering and Management Services	3.4
Truck Transportation	3.2
Miscellaneous Manufacturing	3.2
Air Transportation	3.0
Search and Navigation Equipment	3.0

Part 1: Agriculture, Livestock, Mining, and Construction

Chapter 1: Agricultural Crops

Wheat

The United States typically accounts for 10% to 12% of global wheat production and harvested area. In terms of area planted to crops in the United States, wheat ranked number two in 1997 behind corn, and number three in 1998 and 1999 behind corn and soybeans. Wheat is grown in nearly every state, but most of the acreage and production originates in the Plains and Pacific Northwest. For the 1999/00 crop year (June 1999 to May 2000), North Dakota, Kansas, Oklahoma, and Texas account for an estimated 48% of U.S. wheat acreage and 41% of U.S. production. Kansas and North Dakota typically rank first and second, respectively, in terms of area and production.

Wheat is not a homogeneous crop, but is divided first into winter wheat and spring wheat; and then into six classes, each with unique flour-milling properties. Winter wheat is generally planted from August to November, remains dormant during the winter, and is harvested from late May to July. Spring wheat is planted in April and May and harvested in July and August. Spring wheat yields fewer bushels per acre than winter wheat, and is grown in northern regions where the winters are harsh. In 1998/99, winter wheat accounted for 67% of total wheat acreage and 73% of total production.

Acreage

Wheat acreage has ranged between 65.5 and 88.3 million acres over the 1975 and 1998 period. For much of the period, there was some type of annual acreage-retirement program in place that restricted plantings. Acreage planted is determined by agricultural policy, expected returns for wheat production relative to other crops, as well as weather prior to and during planting. In 1999, poor-price expectations led farmers to reduce wheat plantings to only 62.9 million acres. Grain prices climbed to record levels in the 1970s and early 1980s, and wheat acreage expanded. Less than 50 million acres were planted to wheat in 1970/71, but planted area and production reached a record 88.3 million acres and 2.79 billion bushels in 1981/82.

U.S. wheat exports collapsed in the mid-1980s, falling by nearly 50% between 1981/82 and 1985/86 as a result of a global recession, a strong U.S. dollar, and stiff export competition. Inventories grew substantially, and prices plummeted to below $2.50 per bushel. The United States made several policy changes aimed at reducing grain inventories. Price supports were lowered to make U.S. wheat more competitive on the world market, and the Conservation Reserve Program (CRP) came into existence as a long-term land-retirement program. These programs were effective, and in the late 1980s, exports also recovered. Acreage fell to 65.5 million acres in 1988/89, with 11 million acres of wheat-land retired under the CRP. Agricultural policy changes resulted in less stock holding by the government, and they made U.S. wheat more competitive in the world market.

In 1990/91 wheat acreage totaled 77.2 million acres, and between 1991/92 and 1995/96 fluctuated between 69.2 to 72.1 million acres. Wheat stocks generally declined, the result of the government's exit from the business of holding wheat inventories, poor yields in 1991/92 and 1995/96, and demand. Farm-level wheat prices recovered to between $3.00 and $4.00 per bushel by 1994/95. The next year brought lower acreage, a spring freeze that damaged winter wheat, and strong exports, including large shipments to China. With wheat inventories equaling only 60 days of use, prices set a new record, averaging $4.55 per bushel. High prices encouraged additional plantings in the United States and abroad, which, along with favorable weather, resulted in record or near-record spring wheat crops in the U.S., Argentina, Australia, Canada, and the European Union (E.U.). Countries that typically import wheat also experienced production increases, which lowered import requirements. Thus, high prices did their job by promoting increased production, which helped to partially rebuild wheat inventories.

Acreage in the United States climbed to 75.1 million in 1996, wheat supplies exceeded demand, and as a consequence inventories began to rise to levels capable of depressing prices. Since 1996, wheat prices have trended downward, wheat inventories have risen, and area planted has dropped to 65.9 million acres in 1998. With economic weakness in Southeast Asia and ample global supplies of wheat, inventories rose further in 1998/99, pushing prices below $2.90 per bushel. A poor-price outlook coupled with equally poor expected returns pushed wheat plantings down nearly 5% for the 1999/00 marketing year, the lowest level planted since 1973. As a result, year-end inventories are expected to begin to decline during the current marketing season.

Farm Policy

Prior to April 1996, government agricultural payments were linked directly to production, and expected returns for growing wheat were based on wheat prices and government programs. The wheat program insulated farmers' incomes by protecting them from low prices and yields. In order to participate in the program, farmers were often required to idle a portion of their land and meet other requirements, including conservation measures. Since the late 1980s, up to 23 million acres of wheat land were idled each year. Farmers had little flexibility in planting; because shifting acreage to alternative crops meant forfeiting government payments and reduced ability to receive future support.

Farm policy changed dramatically on April 4, 1996 when President Clinton signed the Federal Agriculture Improvement and Reform (FAIR) Act. The FAIR Act decoupled government support from production decisions. Farmers are now free to plant virtually any crop, and planting decisions do not influence government payments. Farmers will receive cash-transition payments to help them adjust to the new policy environment, and the level of payments is set to decline through fiscal 2002, when the FAIR Act expires. On average, eligible wheat farmers will initially receive payments of $20 per acre, with payments declining to $14 per acre by the end of the period. Some form of income support is likely, even after the FAIR Act expires. The implications of the FAIR Act are substantial. Farmers now have the ability to shift land to crops that command the highest returns, and government payments are no longer part of the planting decision.

The sole remaining supply management policy is the CRP. The CRP was aimed at reducing the grain surpluses of the 1980s by retiring farmland for a period of 10 to 15 years. Since its inception, the Reserve has been transformed to focus on retiring land that offers the most environmental benefits. Enrollment in the CRP is capped at 36.4 million acres, a limit that was reached in the early 1990s. Roughly 11 million of these acres were previously planted to wheat, and most of this land was located in the Plains. In September 1997, contracts on approximately 21 million acres of land enrolled in the Reserve expired. USDA accepted bids to re-enroll about 19 million acres of land. It was expected that some of the difference between what was released and enrolled in the CRP would return to wheat production in 1998, but due to poor returns, it did not. Because most CRP land is located in the Plains and was once wheat land, the level of the CRP has important implications for wheat area and, in the new era of planting flexibility, acreage of other crops. CRP enrollment in the Northern Plains has actually increased in 1998 over the past year. Nationally, CRP enrollment is expected to climb to another 2 million acres in the future.

Since the 1995/96 marketing year when farm prices peaked at $4.55 per bushel, prices have been adjusting downward. The FAIR Act enables farmers to use wheat crops for collateral to secure a non-recourse marketing loan. If market prices fall below the loan rate, farmers who have exercised the loan option may repay their loan at a lower rate, and those who are eligible but have not used the loan option may receive a marketing loan-deficiency payment (the difference between the loan rate and the repayment rate).

The use of the marketing loan program increased significantly during the 1998/99 season and will likely be used extensively in 1999/00 and 2000/01. The 1998/99 marketing loan rate was $2.59 per bushel, and market prices for wheat fell to the $1.50 level. As a consequence, loan-deficiency payments (LDPs) have ballooned.

In addition, in late 1998, Congress and the Clinton Administration passed and enacted an emergency bailout program for agriculture. Nearly $6.0 billion in emergency aid was provided to agriculture in total—$3.1 billion was based on poor-market prices and distributed based on the distribution of transition payments. The situation has deteriorated further in 1999, and it seems quite likely that an even larger aid package will materialize in late 1999.

Marketing Patterns

Wheat is either milled into flour for human consumption, used for seed, or fed to livestock. Food use is the most stable category of wheat use, accounting for roughly one-third of annual wheat consumption or disappearance. Flour-milling accounts for virtually all food use, with 45 pounds of flour produced from one bushel of wheat. Food use is relatively stable because flour is a high-value product, with large changes in wheat prices translating into relatively small changes in flour consumption. The key determinants of flour, and consequently wheat food, use are income and population growth, both of which are rising.

Seed use is a relatively small component of total wheat disappearance. Only about 5% of total disappearance is seed wheat. Its consumption fluctuates based on the number of wheat acres planted.

Feed use is a volatile category of wheat use, accounting for 2% to 20% of total disappearance. The amount of wheat fed to livestock depends on the demand for live-stock feed, the quality of the wheat crop, and the price of wheat relative to prices of other feed grains. The feed value of wheat is roughly 5% higher than that of corn, the primary feed grain. As wheat prices have plummeted, feed use of wheat has remained competitive with other feed grains and feeds.

International Trade

The United States is one of the five exporting countries that dominate world wheat trade. Historically, exports generally accounted for 50% of U.S. wheat disappearance, but this share has varied from 42% to 68% over the last 20 years. With ample global supplies and economic weakness in Asia, wheat exports, over the past three years, have accounted for 40% to 45% of disappearance. Primary trading partners include Egypt, Japan, South Korea, Pakistan, the Philippines, China, Mexico, and the EU. The Soviet Union was a major importer of wheat in the 1970s and 1980s, but purchases from its successor countries have since fallen sharply. China is now the major wildcard in the international wheat market, accounting for 11% of world trade in 1995/96, or 12.0 million metric tons (mmt). But in recent years, 1996/97, 1997/98, and 1998/99 China has accounted for less than 2.0% of world wheat trade.

The other major wheat exporters are the EU, Canada, Australia, and Argentina. The United States harvests its wheat earlier in the year than the EU and Canada, which opens a window of opportunity for U.S. exports before these competitors' wheat is available for shipment in late summer and early fall. Wheat from Australia and Argentina, on the other hand, is marketed on the world market in the late fall and early winter before the U.S. harvest. In the case of Argentina, wheat is aggressively marketed during the winter in order to free up storage and transportation resources for the corn and soybean crops, which are harvested in the spring.

The United States also imports wheat. Imports are a relatively small but growing component of U.S. wheat supplies. In the early 1980s, less than 3 million bushels of wheat were imported, but import shipments grew to nearly 110 million bushels in 1993/94. Most wheat imports in 1993/94 were from Canada, particularly durum and feed wheat, because U.S. prices were high relative to prices north of the Canadian border. Aggressive use of export subsidies by the United States pushed up domestic wheat prices and lowered international prices. Thus, Canadian wheat flowed south. Politicians from the Northern Plains states successfully lobbied for voluntary restraints on Canadian wheat imports. U.S. imports have since fallen, but at roughly 100 million bushels forecast for 1999/00, imports remain high by historical standards. The agreement that restrained Canadian shipments to the United States has since expired, leaving the door open for a resumption of imports from Canada and, perhaps, further trade disputes. In addition, the Canadian dollar has depreciated and weakness in the Asian market (which accounts for about 60% of Canada's wheat exports) have served to increase the attractiveness of the U.S. market.

U.S. Outlook

Above-trend yields pushed U.S. wheat production for 1998/99 an estimated 2.4% above the year-ago level despite a 6.4% decline in area planted. Yields are expected to be lower, but close to 1998's level. Planted acreage declined by 2.3 million acres in 1999/00 due to wheat's low price relative to alternative crops combined with the planting flexibility provisions of the FAIR Act. Collectively, lower yields and acreage is estimated to lead to a 9.3% drop in production for the 1999/00 marketing year. The price in 1999/00 is expected to be the "bottom" as expected supplies will decline and total use will grow, leading to a fall in inventories and price improvement. Then, further strength in planted acreage could come from rising wheat prices—albeit slowly.

Assuming normal weather, wheat production is expected to grow on the order of 2% per annum. Acreage and yields are expected to grow after 2000. Wheat acreage will get some additions and some subtractions from fluctuations in CRP acreage through the period. Wheat yields are expected to achieve average annual-growth rates of 0.8% to 0.9%, after being stagnant during the last 10 years. Higher growth rates are possible if current biotechnology research results in new varieties. Wheat is on the tail end of agriculture's biotechnology revolution, but new varieties are in the works that could result in double-digit yield gains. Future multilateral and bilateral trade agreements should raise U.S. export opportunities and spur additional wheat acreage and production. Farm-policy reforms that reduce internal-support prices will also affect U.S. export opportunities, wheat acreage, and production.

The Corn Belt and Lake States are expected to account for a smaller proportion of wheat acreage, as farmers there shift to corn and soybeans. Some acreage growth in the Southeast and Mississippi River Delta is expected because of growth in double-cropping practices. Higher wheat acreage is expected in the Plains, Mountain, and Pacific regions, mainly as a result of land expiring from the CRP. However, wheat acreage may decline in areas where alternative crops offer higher returns.

In the long term, food use is expected to continue to expand at a rate of about 1.5%–2.0% per year, as consumers, for health reasons, continue to show preference for grain-based products and as population ex-

pands. Feed use will likely be about 350 million bushels in 1999/00, although with low prices this could be higher. Then it is expected to trend down to a relatively flat pattern at 200–230 million bushels. Exports are expected to improve in the near term, rising to nearly 1.1 billion bushels as export opportunities improve due to potential imports by China, less area harvested in the EU and Brazil, limited exportable supplies in Canada, and improved economic activity in Asia. In the long term, export growth after 2000/01 is expected to be less than 2.0% per annum.

Wheat Supply and Use

Marketing Year	1996/97	1997/98	1998/99
Acreage & Yield			
Planted (Million Acres)	75.11	70.41	65.87
Harvested (Million Acres)	62.82	62.84	59.00
Yield (Bu/Acre)	36.31	39.50	43.20
Supply (Million Bushels)			
Beginning Stocks	376	444	723
Production	2,277	2,481	2,550
Imports	93	96	103
Total Supply	2,746	3,021	3,376
Disappearance (Million Bushels)			
Food & Industrial	892	914	905
Seed	102	93	84
Feed & Residual	307	251	400
Totals Domestic Use	1,301	1,258	1,389
Exports	1,002	1,040	1,042
Total Disappearance	2,303	2,298	2,431
Ending Stocks	444	723	945
Stocks/Use Ration (%)	19.3	31.4	38.9
Farm Level Price ($/Bu)	4.30	3.38	2.66

Rice

Rice production is relatively small in the United States as compared to other field crops. In 1998, rice-planted acreage was 3.5 million acres, accounting for about 1% of the total-planted area for major crops. In 1996, rice-planted acreage dropped to 2.8 million acres, and prices strengthened to $10/cwt. Rice prices have remained relatively robust and have led to higher plantings. Area planted in 1998 reached 3.35 million acres, but early wet weather in California and dry growing conditions in much of the South have adversely affected yields and production. Seeded area rose to 3.6 million acres in 1999, and prices are expected to weaken as inventories climb.

The U.S. rice-marketing year runs from August to July, with most of the crop planted in the spring and early summer and harvested in the summer and the early fall. Over 95% of U.S. rice production occurs in five states. Rice is produced mainly in the South, in the Delta region of the Mississippi, and along the gulf coast in Texas, Arkansas, Louisiana, and Mississippi. Rice is also produced in California.

Acreage and Domestic Supply

U.S. planted acreage for rice for the 1995/96 (August 1995 to July 1996) season was 3.1 million acres, with nearly 99% of that being harvested. This was only slightly below the record of 3.35 million acres, which was reached in the previous season. In the 1996/97 season, planted acreage dropped further, slipping to 2.8 million acres. This 10% decline from the previous year was primarily due to changes in farm-program provisions that separated program payments from the requirement to plant rice, resulting in greater planting flexibility. High prices for alternative field crops, therefore, contributed to this decline in rice acreage, and would have hurt more if rice prices had not remained relatively high.

The same factors that caused acreage to drop in 1996 led farmers to plant 3.35 million acres in 1998 and a record 3.6 million acres in 1999. Robust domestic use and exports helped to keep ending inventories from rising sharply in 1997/98. Prices remained relatively strong, providing the necessary incentive to push plantings higher in 1998/99. Area planted increased in all states except California, which produces mainly medium-grain rice, and Texas, which produces mostly long-grain rice and minimal amounts of medium-grain rice. Relatively strong prices in 1998 pushed acres planted in all states higher in 1999.

Changes to the rice-program provisions in the Federal Agriculture Improvement and Reform (FAIR) Act of 1996 were the most significant factors contributing to the fluctuations in planted acreage. The FAIR Act eliminated annual Acreage Reduction Programs (ARPs), target prices, and deficiency payments. In their place, production flexibility contracts and transition payments for participants were implemented. These payments are independent of planting decisions made by farmers, giving them complete freedom to choose what crops to grow. Returns to rice production are expected to decline in the next few years, which should lead some farmers to plant alternative and lower cost crops, such as soybeans or corn.

Despite the 7% increase in planted acreage in 1998/99, total domestic production rose only 2.8% due to hot, dry growing conditions that adversely affected yields in the South and wet weather that hurt the California yield. This year, yields are expected to improve by nearly 5% from last year, and coupled with acreage expansion, 1999/00 production is estimated to register a 12% growth over 1998/99's level.

Beginning stocks are also down in 1999/00, dropping to 22 million cwt. from 28 million cwt. the year before. This 21% decline is primarily due to low 1998/99 production, rather than robust disappearance. Domestic use is estimated to improve to 117 million cwt., and exports to drop 6% to 84 million cwt. The U.S. exports a high-quality rice and is one of the few countries that exports it in rough form rather than milled. Shipments to Latin America were particularly strong in 1997/98, but higher production levels in importing countries and competition from exporters are likely to reduce U.S. export opportunities.

The United States imported 9.8 million cwt. of rice in 1997/98, 200,000 cwt. less than in the previous year. In 1998/99, however, rice imports are expected to return to the 10 million cwt. level as high domestic-rice prices and a strong dollar attract rice to U.S. shores. Although imports account for only a small portion of the total U.S. rice supply, imports have been increasing steadily over the past 15 years, rising from 0.2 million cwt. in 1980/81 to 10 million cwt. in 1996/97. Most of the rice imported into the United States is jasmine rice from Thailand, while the rest is basmati rice from India and Pakistan.

Overall, total supplies of rice in 1999/00 are forecast to be 243 million cwt., up 7% from the previous year. This is also nearly 10 million cwt. higher than the peak year of 1994/95.

Farm Policy

Unlike in the past, producers with a program crop base receive transition payments under the FAIR Act regardless of what crops they plant. This means that planting decisions should be more responsive to expected profitability and market conditions. As a result, rice farmers may now plant alternative crops with less risk, such as corn and soybeans. Rice returns over total-cash expenses are dropped in 1998 from $133 per planted acre in 1997 to a low $40 level. 1999 returns are estimated to fall further. In the near term, rice returns are expected to remain weak.

In the past, rice producers have been foremost among major program crop producers in the consistency of program participation. Since 1986, participation has been between 93% and 98% each year, regardless of acreage-limitation requirements. In 1998, essentially 100% of rice acreage was enrolled in the program. Base acreage enrolled in the rice program has consistently been 4.1–4.2 million acres each year in this decade. Rice acreage set aside and idled under the Rice Program totaled 210,000 acres in 1995/96, or 5% of the total base acreage. From 1985 through 1995, total government payments to rice-program participants ranged from $400–$800 million annually. These payments were based on the difference between market-price and target-price levels. With the new provisions, government payments are much more consistent and well defined. Payments for fiscal year 1998 were $490 million.

In late 1998, an emergency-aid package was passed by Congress and approved by the Administration. Nearly $6 billion in total aid was provided to the agricultural sector. The 1998 aid package and poor price expectations in 1999 combined to push Federal outlays to the rice producers up to an estimated $800 million. This figure could rise further because Congress is likely to pass another aid package in 1999.

Marketing Patterns

Domestic demand for rice should increase at a 1.5% per-annum pace over the next few years. Since 1990/91, the domestic market, which has nearly doubled in the past 15 years, has been growing at about 3% annually. In 1997/98, total domestic use was a record 106.9 million cwt. In 1998/99, rice demand rose to an estimated 114 million cwt., and another 2.5% rise is forecast for 1999/00.

Rice Supply and Use

Marketing Year	1997/98	1998/99	1999/00
Acreage & Yield			
Planted (Million Acres)	3.13	3.35	3.60
Harvested (Million Acres)	3.10	3.32	3.56
Yield (Bu/Cwt)	58.96	56.69	59.35
Supply (Million Cwt)			
Beginning Stocks	27	28	22
Production	183	188	211
Imports	9	10	9
Total Supply	219	226	242
Disappearance (Million Cwt)			
Totals Domestic Use	107	114	117
Exports	85	90	84
Total Disappearance	192	204	201
Ending Stocks	28	22	41
Stocks/Use Ration (%)	14.4	10.8	20.5
Farm Level Price ($/Cwt)	9.64	8.51	7.29

Domestic-rice demand is composed of food use, brewer's use, seed, and residual. Out of the projected 107 million cwt. of domestic disappearance (consumption) in 1997/98, a record 83 million cwt. of rice was consumed as food. Food use has accounted for all of the growth in domestic demand, while brewer's use, seed, and residual categories have shown either no sustained growth or have experienced a decline. Food use is expected to rise to 88 million cwt. in 1998/99. Further growth is likely in 1999/00.

Over the past 15 years there has been a gradual change in culinary preferences towards grain-based foods in the United States, which accounts for a share of the substantial growth in domestic-rice food demand. Much of the expansion in rice's food use, however, is due to large increases in the Asian and Hispanic segments of the U.S. population over the past two decades. Per-capita consumption of rice by these two groups exceeds the U.S. average.

Per-capita consumption of rice has been growing steadily in the United States for the past decade. In 1984/85, 15.75 pounds per-capita was consumed; and in 1998/99 consumption was up to an estimated 27.3 pounds per capita. Almost all of this increase in per-capita consumption comes from food use, which has risen nearly 11 pounds per capita over that period, while brewer's use has remained steady at 4.1–4.2 pounds per capita each year.

Brewer's use of rice is projected to be 15.4 million cwt. in 1998/99; approximately the same as it has been the past three years. Peak brewer's use was in 1995/96, when 15.6 million cwt. was used. The reasons for this slight decline include lower per-capita beer consumption and the increased demand for light beers, which contain less rice than normal beers.

International Trade

About 45% of total U.S. annual rice demand is accounted for by exports, making U.S. rice producers susceptible to factors that influence the international market. With domestic-rice production forecast to increase in 1999/00, and the total supply of rice expected to rise 7%, supplies will be ample to meet rising domestic demand and export needs. U.S. exports of rice for 1999/00 will also be dependent on the price premium of U.S. rice as compared to foreign competitors' prices, especially those in Thailand, and other cheap food grains like wheat. Unlike many other rice-exporting countries, the United States services a large, high-valued domestic market that pushes the U.S. price above international levels. As the price premium rises, price-sensitive markets, such as Latin America and the Caribbean, switch to lower cost rice. In 1998/99, rice exports from the United States to-

taled 90 million cwt. In 1999/00, rice exports are forecast to drop 6% to about 84 million cwt.

Latin America, the Middle East, and Europe are expected to remain the most important export markets for U.S. rice in the upcoming years. Canada and South Africa are also slowly growing markets for U.S. rice. In addition, under agreements reached at the Uruguay Round of the General Agreement on Tariffs and Trade (GATT), Japan and South Korea have begun to open their markets to rice imports. Japan's minimum-access criteria will rise from 379,000 tons in 1995/96 to 758,000 tons in 2000/01. This is an increase of 76,000 tons annually for five years, pushing their imports from 4% of total domestic use in 1995/96 to 8% of total domestic use in 2000/01. In South Korea, 57,000 tons of rice was the minimum-import requirement in 1995/96, or 1% of total domestic use. By 2004, imports should be increased to 205,000 tons, or 4% of total domestic use.

The United States is expected to compete with Australia to supply medium-grain rice to these newly opened East Asian markets. There is a word of caution that needs to be stated here. First, improved import access will not necessarily translate into increased import volume by these countries in Asia. Import access refers to the amount that can be imported without tariffs. Secondly, the current weakness in the Asian market means that realized volume growth will be lower. Finally, the strength of the dollar vis-a-vis currencies in Asia, and in particular relative to the Thai baht, has sharply increased the price premium for U.S. rice.

The GATT agreement also maintains access to the European Union (EU), one of the largest markets for U.S. rice. The EU has agreed to convert its import levies into tariffs and reduce them by at least 15% for every commodity, with an average across all commodities of 36% over six years. This should lead to increased trade in the rice market. Additionally, the EU has agreed to bind the margin between the import price and its support price so that protection will not be increased in the future. Overall, U.S. rice producers should fare well under the Uruguay Round Agreement.

World Rice Markets

Global production reached near-record level in 1998/99 and consumption reached record high, with consumption slightly exceeding production and reducing world ending stocks to 50.4 million metric tons (mmt). Global consumption totaled 387 mmt, about 3 mmt more than production. The global stocks-to-use ratio for 1998/99 is forecast to be 13%, the lowest level in about 10 years and helping to support prices. While this level of stocks-to-use is on the low side of an acceptable range, it is not considered problematic.

World rice trade declined in 1998/99 to 24 mmt, dropping 10% from the record 27 mmt of the previous year. However, this trade volume is still relatively high, and only 1997/98 was higher. The slowdown in world-rice imports is partly a result of the Southeast Asian crisis and the depreciation of currencies in the region. Indonesia's 1999/00 import volume is expected to drop to 2.5 mmt this year, compared to last year's level of 3.7 mmt. In addition, large 1999/00 harvests by some of the region's major importers (including Indonesia) have reduced their reliance on rice imports. As a consequence, global consumption should rise, but global trade volume is expected to be stagnant at 24 million cwt. in 1999/00.

U.S. Rice Outlook

The 1997/98 marketing year for rice was a boon for U.S. rice exporters. Total rice exports rose nearly 8% to 84 million cwt. Weather disturbances crippled crops in Asia and Latin America and allowed U.S. producers to fill the void left by several major producing nations. Export momentum carried into the 1998/99 marketing year with exports rising to 90 million cwt, although many of the nations that had disappointing crops in 1997 returned to normal production levels. A strong dollar, good production in major importing regions, competition from other exporting countries, and a high premium for U.S. rice should retard U.S. export opportunities this year.

The exception may be China, where the 1998/99 rice crop was only 133 million metric tons due to heavy rains and flooding along the Yangtze River Valley. This caused a draw-down in China's stocks, and China could choose to rebuild some inventory this year by increasing import volumes. The Asian financial crisis hurts affordability of U.S. rice, but it is nonetheless expected to support relatively high U.S. exports as consumers in the region downgrade from wheat and meat consumption and return to their rice staple. U.S. exports are estimated to total 84 million cwt. in 1999/00, about 6% less than in 1998/99.

U.S. production for 1999 is estimated at 211 million cwt., up over 12% from last year. The higher production is coupled with lower exports, leaving 1999/00 carry-out at 41 million cwt, despite another year of strong domestic food use and exports. The farm-level price for 1999/00 is expected to plunge 14% to $7.29/cwt.

Higher carry-in for 2000 and lower prices will move approximately 300,000 acres out of rice production during the spring of 2000. WEFA expects Asia to continue to recover from its financial crisis. The financial recovery will mean that many consumers in that part of the world will once again be able to afford more expensive wheat grain, as well as meats, and will move away from rice as a principal component in their diet. U.S. rice exports, consequently, are expected to drop significantly during this time of Asian recovery. Following the Asian recovery, exports are expected to post consecutive yearly declines until 2006, and then remain relatively flat.

Domestic-food use should remain relatively strong, increasing at a rate of approximately 1.5% per year through most of the forecast period. Growth in domestic food use will be maintained as the Asian and Hispanic populations continue to expand within the United States. Planted area should remain flat through 2008, hovering at 3.0–3.2 million acres, while trend yield will provide for increased domestic demand, leaving stock levels in the 28 to 29 million-cwt. range.

Corn

Corn is the number-one feed grain in the United States and in the world. Over the last ten years, the United States has produced an average of 8.4 billion bushels per year, and in 1994 the United States produced a record 10.1 billion bushels of corn. Since annual acreage-reduction programs were eliminated in 1996, U.S. farmers have planted an average of 79 million acres of corn and produced an average of 9.4 billion bushels per year. As incomes increase around the world, the demand for meat products increases as well. Corn is one of the primary components of animal feed, and the number of animals has been steadily increasing in the United States and throughout the world.

With animal numbers and incomes increasing worldwide, it is not surprising that the second-largest segment of demand for U.S. corn is export markets. Export growth has been hampered by an economic downturn in Southeast Asia, including recession in Japan, and by disease outbreaks such as avian flu in Hong Kong, of hoof and mouth disease in Taiwan, meat shipments contaminated with the E. coli bacteria, and general food-safety concerns, all of which have hurt U.S. corn exports. In the long term, prospects for export growth to the Asian market are favorable. Growth in U.S. corn production and consumption has been relatively steady over the last 20 years, and it appears that continued growth in production will be necessary to meet the demand for corn in the future.

Acreage

Corn is grown throughout the United States, but most U.S. corn production occurs in a region bounded by Ohio to the east, Nebraska to the west, Missouri to the south, and Minnesota to the north. This region, known as the Corn Belt, produces approximately 80% of the corn grown in the United States. Iowa and Illinois are the top-producing states, typically accounting for more than a third of the U.S. corn crop.

Farmers in the United States have planted between 60 and 85 million acres of corn each year since 1950. In the past, government programs have influenced planted acres dramatically by requiring producers who participate in government programs to idle land. By idling land, the government was attempting to manage supplies and support prices. The precedent for idling acreage was set in the 1930s. Idling acreage was used extensively in the late-1950s, the 1960s, and sporadically during the 1970s. During the 1980s and early 1990s, government set-asides continued to exist, but were replaced with more commodity-specific programs. The 1985 farm bill included the establishment of the Conservation Reserve Program (CRP), which by 1996 had idled more than 34 million acres of farm land for conservation purposes. Presently about 33 million acres of land are enrolled in the CRP. The Federal Agriculture Improvement and Re-

form (FAIR) Act of 1996 eliminated acreage set-aside and acreage-reduction programs, and now the only way the government can idle acreage is through the CRP.

Under the FAIR Act, producers have the freedom to plant crops as demanded by the markets. Historically, shortfalls in planted acreage were caused by a combination of weather problems and government set-asides. In the future, annual corn plantings are not expected to fall below 78 million acres and could reach 83 million acres in some years.

Despite relatively small fluctuations in corn acreage, corn supplies have steadily increased since 1950. Increases are largely due to improved yield technologies and management techniques. Yields are expected to increase over the next decade by about 1%, or 1 to 1.5 bushels per acre, per year. Changes in weather patterns from year to year can cause yields to be either lower or higher than expected. Annual corn supplies have become more variable over the last decade. Some of this variability is a function of government programs and the rest is weather related. As the use of chemical fertilizers and pesticides has increased over the past three decades, crop yields, although increasing, have become more sensitive to weather patterns. Some crop scientists believe new genetically altered seeds will reduce some of this variability in corn yields in the future, even though they are not necessarily expected to improve yields. Genetically altered seeds can affect the output traits of the crop produced. High-oil and high-lysine content corn are examples. Similarly, genetically altered seeds can affect the input side too, by making the plant resistant to herbicides or toxic to certain pests.

Farm Policy

As mentioned in the previous section, government farm programs have influenced corn acreage dramatically by requiring producers who participate in government programs to idle land. Farmers who participated in corn programs would receive a deficiency payment when market prices fell below predetermined target prices. To control program cost, acreage set-asides were used to decrease supplies and increase market prices, which in turn would decrease deficiency payments. Between 1990 and 1995, acres set aside ranged between 4 and 8 million acres each year and deficiency payment levels ranged between 50 and 70 cents per bushel.

Since the implementation of the 1996 FAIR Act, producers have very few planting restrictions and no longer have to adhere to base-acreage requirements and acreage-reduction programs. Producers who have signed up for Production Flexibility Contracts under the new farm legislation will receive a transition payment that is decoupled from planting decisions. Corn producers will receive $16.5 billion in transition payments over the period from 1997 to 2002. Some form of government support for corn farmers is expected to continue after 2002, but it will likely be in the range of $1 billion to $2 billion per year.

Another part of the FAIR Act relates to what is called the marketing loan program and the marketing loan-deficiency payments. The FAIR Act allows farmers to use corn crops for collateral to secure a nonrecourse marketing loan at a specified rate, which is $1.89 per bushel for corn for the 1999/00 marketing year. If market prices fall below the loan rate, farmers who have exercised the loan option may repay their loan at a lower rate. Those producers who are eligible but have not used the loan option may receive a marketing loan-deficiency payment (the difference between the loan rate and the repayment rate times the number of bushels eligible). In both cases, the farmer, in effect, receives a higher amount for his crop than would have been earned in the marketplace. Corn prices have been under pressure and have been dropping since 1995/96. Increases in supplies have out-

paced demand growth resulting in burdensome and price-depressing inventories. Corn prices are estimated to have averaged about $1.96/bu for 1998/99, and at some locations in the U.S. dropped to $1.00 per bushel during the marketing year. As a result, the marketing loan program was used extensively in 1998/99, and should be used extensively again in the 1999/00 year.

Agricultural commodity prices have generally been trending downward since 1995/96. Market generated receipts have been adversely affected, and the farmers' ability to cash flow operations has been jeopardized due to the falling prices. In late 1998, Congress passed and the Administration approved an emergency-aid package for U.S. agriculture and injected almost $6 billion into the sector by early 1999. This amount was in addition to transition payments and Federal other payments to agriculture. Of the emergency-relief package, $3.1 billion was provided because prices deteriorated to low levels and were distributed based on the distribution of transition payments. Corn producers received about 46% of the $3.1 billion.

The situation in agriculture has not improved. Corn prices are expected to drop further during the 1999/2000 year. It appears Congress will approve another aid package to bail out agriculture. WEFA expects a financial-relief package of between $7 and $9 billion to be made available in 1999.

Marketing Patterns

Corn used in animal feed rations represents, on average, 75% of domestic corn use. Over the last decade, corn used as feed has averaged 4.8 billion bushels a year. The 1998/99 crop year is estimated to set a record feed use level of over 5.6 billion bushels of corn. (The crop year for corn starts September 1 and ends August 31.) Feed and residual use of corn is positively related to the number of cattle on feed, as well as the number of hogs and poultry. Variation in corn feeding represents adjustments made by livestock and poultry producers in response to relative prices and the availability of corn and competing feed grains or feed ingredients. Feed substitutes for corn include sorghum, barley, oats, and wheat. Nonetheless, as the demand for meat animals continues to increase in the future, animal numbers will increase and corn for feed will be in high demand. Over the next three years, feed use of corn is expected to grow by 100 to 200 million bushels a year, as the livestock sector expands. Feed use is expected to follow the cattle and swine cycles expanding and contracting as profitability in the livestock sector improves and falls, but exhibit growth of 50 to 100 million bushels per year towards the latter part of the next decade.

Although accounting for only 20% to 25% of domestic use, food, seed, and industrial (FSI) use has been steadily increasing over the years. In general, corn FSI demand is related to population growth and the general health of the economy. Use of corn in the industrial sector is particularly sensitive to corn prices. In 1995/96, corn prices increased by more than 43%, and the use of corn in starch and fuel dropped 20%. Since prices have declined from the $3.24 per bushel of 1995/96, industrial use has recovered. However, legislation and government policies play a critical role in the use of corn for ethanol, and indirectly in the use of corn sweeteners.

Demand for corn sweeteners is affected indirectly by U.S. sugar policies. Import fees, duties, and restrictive import quotas used to administer the current sugar program keep domestic refined-sugar prices at an artificially high level, making high-fructose corn syrup attractive to the soft-drink industry and other users. Use of corn sweeteners will likely continue to grow, but future growth is unlikely to match the very rapid growth of the early 1980s. Future adjustments in sugar policy could lead to some shifts in corn-sweetener use. The advent of new artificial sweeteners will likely reduce the demand for corn sweeteners.

Fuel alcohol use of corn depends largely on a mix of government incentives, technology, and prices of corn and substitute products. An income-tax credit of 54 cents per gallon of alcohol is allowed to blenders of alcohol and gasoline for use as a fuel, assuming a blend of 10% alcohol and 90% motor fuel. Use of corn for fuel has been growing rapidly in recent years. Such use is expected to exceed 500 million bushels per year over the next few years, representing between 4% and 6% of total corn use, up from less than 1% 14 years ago. Production of fuel alcohol from corn and other feed grains has become more efficient, reducing the need for large-government support and tax incentives. However, some government support to the ethanol industry, either direct or indirect, is a requirement for sustained growth in corn demand for industrial uses.

International Trade

The United States is the world's largest exporter of corn. Corn exports experienced their greatest growth in the 1970s; during which time U.S. exports more than tripled and reached a record high of 2.4 billion bushels during the 1979/80 crop year. While the retreat of the former Soviet Union (FSU) from the corn market has removed a large source of export volatility, China has appeared as a new source of export-growth potential. Income growth in China and other developing countries will offset the recent sharp drop in corn exports to the FSU. The contraction in the FSU livestock sector, combined with the problems in the economy in Russia, makes the chance that the FSU will rebound as a major importer of corn in the immediate future quite small.

Growth in U.S. corn exports will be indirectly and directly supported by Uruguay Round Agreement of GATT (the General Agreement on Tariffs and Trade) and the North American Free Trade Agreement (NAFTA). Both agreements are expected to directly boost U.S. agricultural exports through reducing trade barriers and indirectly raise exports through raising global income. NAFTA will have the most noticeable effect on U.S. corn exports. Corn exports to Mexico are expected to grow under NAFTA as corn tariffs decline and Mexican import quotas are lifted, and as Mexican meat consumption rises with stronger income growth. NAFTA included duty-free access for 2.5 million metric tons of U.S. corn in calendar year 1994, and that duty-free limit has increased by 3% each year. Mexico's 215% over-quota tariff for corn will be reduced by 24% in the first six years of NAFTA, then phased out completely in the following nine years. Future multilateral trade negotiations, including the WTO, are expected to support growth of U.S. corn exports.

The greatest uncertainty surrounding U.S. corn exports concerns China. During the 1994/95 crop year, China began to import corn for the first time since 1989/90, and in the long run China is expected to import more corn as its livestock sector expands. However, it is difficult to forecast the specific amount of corn that will be exported to China over the next few years, since it is largely dependent on Chinese-government policy and weather. China has not imported corn from the United States in the past three years. In years when China has a good crop, it will not import but could export. When crop production is poor, China may import and, perhaps, rebuild inventories, if the price is right.

Despite the uncertainty surrounding Chinese-corn imports, total U.S. corn exports are expected to increase by around 100 million bushels per year over the next few years. In the very near term, economic recovery in Southeast Asia, including Japan, and likely slow growth over the next two to three years, should help strengthen U.S. corn shipments to the region.

Japan and Taiwan receive more than 46% of U.S. corn exports. Exports to Taiwan are expected to fall by almost a million metric tons in the short term, due to the 1997 outbreak of hoof-and-mouth disease in Taiwan's hog sector. The time it will take and the extent to which Taiwan is able to rebuild its hog sector will determine when exports of corn to Taiwan will begin to increase, but we expect at least a three-year rebuilding period. The 1999/00 marketing year should see some improvement in U.S. shipments to Taiwan.

U.S. Corn Outlook

For the past three years, the corn market has been adjusting from the short supplies and high-price levels of 1995/96. The FAIR Act eliminated annual acreage reduction programs and farmers responded by increasing plantings. Farmers seeded 77.6 million acres of corn in the spring of 1999, a 3% decline from the year earlier. As the 1998/99 marketing year ends, WEFA estimates that carryover-corn stocks will rise to 1.7 billion bushels, the highest level since 1991/92. Yields are likely to be at trend level this year, however, since dry weather has affected yields in some southeastern and mid-Atlantic states. WEFA estimates that the 1999 corn crop will be 9.4 billion bushels. Total supplies will reach 11.0 billion bushels, about the same as in 1998/99.

Feed use for the year is projected to rise to 5.61 billion bushels and exports are expected to decline modestly to 1.9 billion bushels due to competition from Argentina, less cheaper soybean meal, and competition from feed wheat. Total use is estimated to rise only 50 million bushels, 0.6% growth over 1998/99. As a consequence, 1999 ending inventories are estimated to be 17.1% of total use or 1.6 billion bushels. The 1999/00 season average farm price is projected to fall 4.2% to $1.88/bu.

Farmers are expected to increase plantings in the spring of 2000 as corn prices improve relative to soybean prices. Acreage is expected to rise slightly to 78.2

million acres. Harvested acreage is estimated at 72.2 million and a trend yield of 132.6 bushels per acre result in an expected 9.6 billion bushel crop. Supply increases will again outpace demand growth for the year. Corn inventories are expected to rise marginally to 1.65 billion bushels and prices are estimated to improve to $2.00 per bushel for the 2000/01 marketing year.

Demand growth for corn will come from two key sources in the future. The first and most important source is the U.S.-livestock sector. Feed use is projected to expand based on higher levels of animal units. Feed use is forecast to rise from the 5.56 billion–bushel estimate of 1998/99 to 6.2 billion bushels in 2008/09, an average annual growth rate of about 1%. Exports are projected to improve from the 2.0 billion bushel estimate of 1998/99 to 2.5 billion bushels by 2008/09, about a 2.7% average annual increase. Growth in world incomes and population, changing preferences toward meat, and recovery in Asia in the next decade should pull corn exports to higher levels. Food and industrial use (including corn syrup and ethanol) of corn should expand at an average per annum rate of about 2.4% to 2.3 billion bushels in 2008/09.

Summary

Corn production will not be affected in years to come by government acreage set-aside programs, and producers are expected to respond to market forces and produce enough corn to meet growing domestic and export demand. Evidence of U.S. farmers' willingness to increase production in response to higher prices has been seen in the increases in planted corn and soybean acres during the 1996 and 1997 planting seasons. However, as prices declined or declined relative to other commodities, farmers appear equally willing to reduce plantings of all crops as well as specific crops in favor of another. Corn stocks are expected to fluctuate between 1.4 and 1.8 billion bushels over the next decade. Improvements in yield technologies and management techniques are expected to be the main source of production growth in the United States. Some land suitable for planting corn will be released from the CRP over the next decade, which will also increase corn production. The future role of biotechnology in corn production will be an important factor in future production levels of corn.

Corn Supply and Use

Marketing Year	1997/98	1998/99	1999/00
Acreage & Yield			
Planted (Million Acres)	79.54	80.18	77.61
Harvested (Million Acres)	72.70	72.59	70.98
Yield (Bu/Acre)	126.7	134.5	132.2
Supply (Million Bushels)			
Beginning Stocks	883	1308	1687
Production	9,207	9,761	9,380
Imports	9	20	11
Total Supply	10,099	11,089	11,087
Disappearance (Million Bushels)			
Food & Industrial	1,761	1,826	1,927
Seed	21	20	20
Feed & Residual	5,505	5,562	5,612
Totals Domestic Use	7,287	7,408	7,559
Exports	1,504	1,994	1,898
Total Disappearance	8,791	9,402	9,457
Ending Stocks	1,308	1,687	1,621
Stocks/Use Ration (%)	14.9	17.9	17.1
Farm Level Price ($/Bu)	2.43	1.96	1.88

Demand for U.S. corn will come primarily from animal feed demand worldwide. Animal numbers are expected to increase as the demand for meat increases with income growth. Food and industrial uses are forecast to grow at rates similar to population growth. However, the growth in industrial uses of corn, primarily ethanol, could exhibit some variability due to changes in government policies. Overall, the potential for corn's continued growth is favorable.

Soybeans

The market for the soybean complex (soybeans, soybean meal, and soybean oil) has undergone a number of changes in recent years.

A record-level soybean area of 74.1 million acres was planted in the spring of 1999. Soybean area is expanding farther north and west of the main production area, as growers react to relatively strong prices, high marketing-loan rate levels, and increasing demand in the United States and abroad. The sector will, however, face international competition in the expanding global market for oilseeds. In particular, policy changes will make South American crops more competitive with those produced in the United States.

Technological improvements in the sector have led to some controversy, especially concerning herbicide residue and genetically altered soybeans. Critics have fears about the risk of allergies and general food safety, but this is not expected to stop the marketing of genetically altered crops. Soybeans may be the first of a new generation of genetically altered agricultural products to reach consumers.

As the 1998/99 marketing year ends, U.S. soybean stocks continue to rise. Yields are expected to improve over the next few years. Improved yields, combined with the highest area planted since 1980/81, will lead to record U.S. production for the 1999/00 marketing year, which runs from the fourth quarter of 1999 to the third quarter of 2000. Market prices for soybeans will be under pressure in the U.S. market in the near term, as supplies exceed demand and stocks build.

Acreage

- Over half of U.S. soybean farms and production are located in the five Corn Belt states (Illinois, Iowa, Indiana, Ohio, and Missouri). Illinois and Iowa are by far the largest U.S. soybean producers, accounting for 35% (970 million bushels) of total U.S. production of 2.76 billion bushels in 1998.

- Soybean area has been expanding north and west into Wisconsin, Michigan, Minnesota, and the Dakotas. New high-yielding, short-season soybean varieties have displaced flax, oats, sunflowers, dry beans, alfalfa, and land that would normally be left fallow. Rotating soybeans with corn or spring wheat has positive agronomic attributes, a fact that has aided this northwestern expansion.

- In the South, the best land was historically devoted to the crops grown under the Federal government's former acreage-reduction and price and income-support programs. This meant that soybean acreage was generally on substandard soils, which contributed to slower yield growth in the South when compared to the mid-western region.

- Another factor that contributed to slower yield growth in the South is double cropping. Double-cropped fields are typically planted later than the optimal time of the year for soybeans, which leads to lower yields.

- Southern acreage will greatly depend on future world demand for soybean oil, soybean meal, and other oilseeds such as rapeseed and sunflower seed. Southern farmers' ability to improve yields and control currently high-production costs will also influence soybean acreage in that region.

U.S. planted acreage for soybeans has been growing since 1990 after falling through most of the 1980s. Soybean area reached 71.4 million acres at its peak in 1979, but with the implementation of government payments for corn, soybean acreage fell to approximately 58 million acres by 1990. The Federal Agriculture Improvement and Reform (FAIR) Act of 1996 eliminated annual acreage reduction and income support programs that prevented farmers from planting soybeans, even when they were demanded by the marketplace. With the planting restriction removed, farmers responded to relatively strong soybean prices and/or high marketing loan rates and increased planted acreage every year since 1996, reaching a record 74.1 million acres in 1999. Most of the decline in acreage between 1979 and 1990 occurred in the lower yielding, higher cost southern regions. According to the U.S. Department of Agriculture (USDA), of the 29 soybean-producing states, farmers in 27 states have expanded area devoted to soybeans since 1995. This reflects the planting freedom in place under the FAIR Act and market signals demanding more soybeans.

Despite declining soybean acreage before the implementation of the FAIR Act, yield improvements have allowed production to remain relatively stable since 1980. Average U.S. yields rose from approximately 32 bushels per acre in 1979, to a high of between 41 and 42 bushels per acre in 1994. In 1999, the national average-yield estimate is 37.6 bushels per acre, which has been adjusted downward due to dry weather in the southeast and Mid-Atlantic States.

In the near term, U.S. soybean producers need to adjust to rising inventories, a result of both excellent production levels and demand stagnating at about 2.6 billion bushels. Rising stock levels are pushing prices down by an estimated 15% during the 1999/00 marketing year from the price a year earlier and 43% from the 1996/97 high. In the medium and long term, when U.S. producers are expected to be faced with increased international demand and improved prices, soybean production should increase. Acreage needs to adjust down from its current record level in the near term, otherwise inventories will continue to rise in light of expected demand for soybeans. In the long term, acreage is expected to remain below the 1999 record. Farmers will, however, continue to plant 70 million acres or more of soybeans as long as the marketing loan rate for soybeans makes returns attractive relative to corn and cotton prices. Yield growth of about 1.0% per annum, coupled with fewer acres in production as compared to 1998, should enable some expansion in production.

Farm Policy

In the Unites States, there are no government support programs directed at soybeans except loan programs. In fact, outside of the European Union (EU), oilseed production is relatively unsupported worldwide, being relatively free of high tariffs, non-tariff barriers, and trade subsidies. Soybean area and production in the United States have been affected mostly by support programs for other crops, particularly corn, which have sometimes encouraged producers to plant other crops even when market prices favored soybean plantings.

In the past, multilateral trade negotiations, like NAFTA and the GATT (replaced by the WTO) had much impact on soybean production and trade, since soybeans had not been subject to significant trade support or restrictions in the past. Improved market access provided direct trade opportunities for soybeans, soybean oil, and soybean meal trade to increase as a result of the Uruguay Round. The main opportunities seem to be the East Asian developing countries and China, due to increasing income levels in those regions. Trade is expected to increase only marginally with Mexico, Eastern Europe, Korea, and Japan. Although medium- to long-term trade prospects are favorable due to the Uruguay Round Agreement, recession in Japan, economic turmoil in Southeast Asia, and potential devaluation of currencies in Latin America slowed U.S. export opportunities beginning in 1997. Economic recovery is underway in Asia and should help improve U.S. export volumes. However, the fact that global soybean prices have dropped below the U.S. marketing loan rate level, has changed the level of support afforded U.S. soybean producers. The Cairns Group, which includes Australia, Canada, Argentina, Brazil, and several developing countries have already raised the issue regarding soybean support. Soybean support will likely be an issue at the coming round of the WTO.

Another part of the FAIR Act relates to what is called the marketing loan program and the marketing loan-deficiency payments. The FAIR Act allows farmers to use soybean crops for collateral and secure a nonrecourse marketing loan at a specified rate, $5.26 per bushel of beans for the 1998/99 marketing year. If market prices fall below the loan rate, farmers who have exercised the loan option may repay their loan at a lower rate. Those producers who are eligible, but have not used the loan option, may receive a marketing loan deficiency payment (the difference between the loan rate and the repayment rate times the number of bushels eligible). In both cases, the farmer, in effect, receives a higher amount for his crop than would have been earned in the marketplace. The marketing loan program was used extensively during the 1998/99 year and will continue to be used extensively in the near future.

Technology

One of the more interesting developments in the soybean market in recent years was the introduction of Roundup Ready soybeans. These plants are genetically altered to protect them from the herbicide Roundup. Using the old technology, farmers were required to treat the soil before planting and react to weeds as they emerged. Roundup Ready soybeans give farmers the ability to spray their fields indiscriminately without damaging the crop.

There is concern from environmental groups that indiscriminate spraying of the crop will result in a residue on harvested soybeans, but resistance from the international community has been limited. In fact, Roundup Ready soybeans have already been reviewed and approved by regulatory bodies in Argentina, Mexico, Canada, Japan, the EU, and the United States. On the other hand, French and German farmers are not permitted to use the Roundup Ready technology. Despite this, soybeans are the first of a new generation of genetically altered products to reach consumers. Popular trade publications indicate that this new technology is being widely adopted by farmers. This technology is being applied to other crops as well, such as corn and canola.

Other research has focused on ways to genetically alter soybeans in order to increase the oil and protein content. Such a soybean could be used as a high-protein feed source for poultry or dairy feed. This technology is also likely to bring protests from environmental groups if it comes to market.

Another interesting development for soybeans is the biodiesel market, which is a potential new application despite the higher price of biodiesel relative to traditional diesel fuel. Common Agricultural Policy (CAP) reform limits on European oilseed acreage for food have spurred increasing interest in biodiesel in the European Union, since the reform allows additional limited production for industrial uses.

Marketing Patterns

Soybeans undergo a thorough selection process before being converted into edible products. They are first graded, screened, and cleaned. They are then dried to reduce their moisture content and to allow the hull to separate easily from the bean. Soybean hulls can be further processed into edible fiber for livestock feeding. The soybean meat is then rolled into a full, fat flake, and soybean oil is extracted from the flake. The result is a white flake containing about 52% protein.

Crude-soybean oil first undergoes a degumming process that separates crude lecithin from soy oil. The crude lecithin is further refined for use in both industrial and dietary products. The degummed oil is also further refined to produce salad oil, margarine oil, frying oil, and a number of other soy oils that can be derived through further processing.

Edible defatted flakes provide the basis for a variety of soy products. These flakes can be ground to specific granulations to produce soy grits or soy flour for use in baking. Sugars may be removed from the flakes to produce a soy concentrate containing about 70% protein on a dry basis.

Soy concentrate can be moisturized and processed through an extruder using high temperature and pressure to produce a textured soy-protein product with a fibrous, meat-like texture. Finally, the edible defatted flakes can be put through a series of protein precipitations to produce a soy-protein isolate with a protein level of about 90%.

- Soybean meal is the most valuable component obtained from processing the soybean, ranging from 50% to 75% of the soybean's value. It is by far the world's most important protein feed, representing around 60% of world protein meal.

- Edible soybean oil use in the United States has increased by about 3% per year over the last decade. This growth rate is on par with the consumption growth rate for all edible oils, but it lags behind the growth of canola and corn oil. Edible oil use could be revolutionized with the development of no-calorie "fat mimics" and engineered-fat substitutes.

International Trade

World soybean production has increased dramatically in the last thirty years. Five countries account for approximately 90% of the world's soybean production. The Unites States leads all producing countries, despite the fact that the 90% production share it enjoyed in 1970 has fallen to about 50% of world production today.

The other four, key producing countries are Brazil, Argentina, China, and India, in order of importance.

In 1997 and 1998, the United States accounts for about 50% to 60% of world-soybean exports. Brazil and Argentina combine to export another 30% to 35% of the world total for soybeans. In recent years, raw-soybean trade was stagnant due to declining food expenditures as a percentage of income in developed countries and the availability of inexpensive soybean meal from South America.

U.S. soybean exports are closely tied to U.S. production and consumption. Production outpaced consumption in the 1970s, increasing the availability of soybeans for export. In the 1980s, production remained relatively stable due to lower prices and high government support for grains and cotton. Consumption continued to grow in the 1980s, however, and soybean-export capacity suffered as a result.

Worldwide oilseed demand has been strong despite higher prices. China has imported substantial quantities of both soybeans and soybean meal, and the EU continues to import large quantities of soybeans. U.S. competitiveness in this market depends on a number of external factors, including domestic-trade policies in key importing/exporting countries, relative prices and yields, transportation and infrastructure costs, and exchange rates. Argentina and Brazil produce soybeans for processing into meal and oil primarily for the export market.

One of the most important recent policy developments affecting U.S. soybean exporters' competitiveness is the elimination of the Brazilian government's value-added tax on soybean exports. This tax was levied on exports of soybeans but not on the exports of its products. The tax put Brazilian soybeans at a price disadvantage on the international market and, as a result, it was often necessary for Brazilian soybean producers to sell directly to the domestic crushing industry. However, with the removal of the value-added tax, soybean products no longer enjoy such a large advantage over raw soybeans. With this in mind, Brazilian exporters are now poised to challenge U.S. exporters in the soybean market. Brazil and its neighbor, Argentina, had record soybean crops that competed well with U.S. soybeans in 1997/1998. Production in these two countries, though less than the 51.7 mmt of 1997/98, remains in the 47 to 49 mmt range. Jointly, Brazil and Argentina export

about 25% of their soybeans, 75% to 80% of their meal produces, and about 50% to 60% of their soybean-oil production. Like U.S. producers, producers in other countries are expected to react to falling prices and plant and produce less, but nonetheless, Brazil and Argentina are and will continue to be export-oriented producers and aggressive competitors in the global market. There is speculation that the Asian crisis that began with Thailand in mid-1997, and most recently led to a collapse of the Russian ruble, led to currency devaluations in Latin America, including Brazil. Devaluation improves the competitive position of Brazil vis-à-vis the United States.

A key advantage enjoyed by U.S. exporters is the country's efficient transportation and marketing systems, which reduce the cost of exporting as compared to other producers. However, cost differentials and competitiveness are always dependent on exchange rates.

U.S. Soybean Outlook

The luster is waning on soybeans' star. Since 1995/96, when supply shortages pushed the season price of soybeans to $6.72, the soybean sector has been the shining star of agriculture. Prices rose further in 1996 to $7.35 per bushel, as did area to 64 million acres. In 1997, farmers responded to their newfound planting freedom under the FAIR Act and planted area rose to 70.9 million acres, the highest level planted since 1982. During the spring of 1998, farmers seeded a record 72.4 million acres to soybeans. Record production of 2.76 billion bushels in 1998 helped push soybean stocks to about 400 million bushels by marketing year end. Farmers reacting to a $5.26 marketing loan rate planted more than 74 million acres in 1999. Supplies are exceeding demand, inventories are growing quickly, and prices are expected to plummet.

Crushings are expected to rise from 1998/99 levels, based on the U.S. economy's continued growth and relatively strong, offshore demand for oil and meal. However, export opportunities will be limited due to a still weak, but improving, Southeast Asian market and competition from Argentina and Brazil. In addition, a strong U.S. dollar will moderate some of the price decline expected for soybeans, some countries will import soybean meal and soybean oil instead of beans, and other oilseeds and oilseed products will compete for available markets. For the 1999/00 season, soybean exports are projected to rise slightly to 847 million bushels. Total use for the year is estimated to rise 85 million bushels from 1998/99 to about 2,650 million bushels. Available 1999/00 supplies will outweigh total use, and soybean-ending inventories are expected to rise substantially to 504 million bushels for a 19% stocks–to–use ratio. Soybean prices are expected to be under intense downward pressure this coming season. For the year, the average farm-level price is forecasted to drop nearly 15% to $4.33 per bushel. Marketing loan-deficiency payments will be quite important to farmers' income stream.

Although soybean market prices are expected to decline sharply relative to corn and cotton, the marketing loan rate will keep soybean returns at high levels. Subsequently, soybean plantings next spring are likely to decline only modestly and remain close to 74 million acres leading to large-production volumes and further aggravating an excess supply situation. Soybean prices will continue to be under pressure.

In the long term, WEFA projects a steady rise in crushings, as margins fluctuate around the $1.00 per bushel level. Crushings are projected to rise to 1.83 billion bushels by the end of the next ten years, compared to 1.77 billion bushels in 1998/99. Exports are expected to improve at a 1.5% annual rate and rise to 1.0 billion bushels in 2008/09. Low prices for soybeans and products should slow expansion plans in Brazil and Argentina and help support U.S. exports. Later, the further opening in markets that will come with implementation of the Uruguay Round commitments, the WTO, income growth, and increasing demand for protein meal and vegetable oils will favorably impact soybean exports.

Soybean prices are expected to be under significant downward pressure as inventories continue to rise to more than 700 million bushels.

WEFA assumes trend yield for soybeans over the 10-year forecast horizon. Productivity gains of 1.0% per annum are expected. Total use is projected to increase at an average rate of 1.1% to 1.3%. As a consequence, productivity gains will offset the advances in demand, and low prices will shift acreage to corn and cotton. In the long term, inventory levels must be reduced from the high levels if prices are to strengthen. This scenario leaves very little room for acreage to increase significantly.

Soybeans Supply and Use

Soybeans	1997/98	1998/99	1999/00
Acreage & Yield			
Planted (Million Acres)	70.01	72..38	74.14
Harvested (Million Acres)	69.08	70.78	73.26
Yield (Bu/Acre)	38.94	38.94	37.60
	——Million Bushels——		
Supply (Million Bushels)			
Beginning Stocks	132	200	395
Production	2,689	2,757	2,755
Imports	5	5	6
Total Supply	2,826	2,962	3,156
Disappearance			
Total Domestic Use	1,755	1,774	1,804
Exports	870	793	849
Total Disappearance	2,625	2,567	2,651
Ending Stocks	200	395	504
Stocks/Use Ration (%)	7.6	15.4	19.0

Cotton

The cotton sector has undergone significant changes in the last three decades, and the next five years appear to hold many changes as well. Some major issues cotton producers will continue to face include: the impact of the use of different methods of pest control on the total cost of production, impacts of the 1996 Federal Agriculture Improvement and Reform Act (FAIR Act), changing trends in domestic demand, and the impact of international trade agreements and global demand on exports.

Acreage

U.S. planted acreage for cotton grew from 10.6 million acres in 1989 to a peak of 16.9 million acres in 1995, a response to high 1994/95 price levels and no acreage-retirement program, only to drop back to 13.4 million acres by 1999. It is important to note that for the 1989/90 crop year, 3.5 million acres went unplanted due to the federal Acreage Reduction Program (ARP) policy. The level of area planted in 1998, on the other hand, is based on market signals since the Federal Agriculture Improvement and Reform (FAIR) Act of 1996 eliminated annual ARPs.

Major Cotton Producing Regions

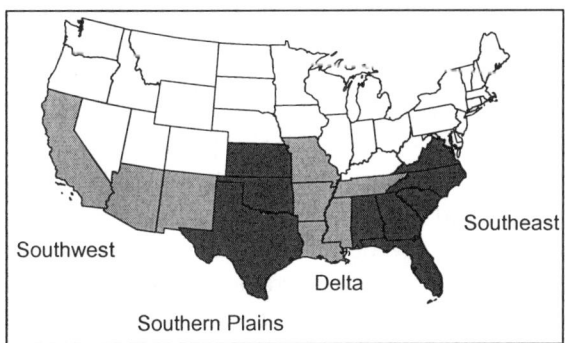

- The majority of the acreage gain in the 1990s came in the Southeast, where planted acreage grew from 0.85 million acres in 1989 to 3.46 million acres in 1995. In 1999, only 13.4 million acres were planted to cotton nationally, but 3.47 million acres were reported in the Southeast.

- While acreage in the Southwest did increase to 1.77 million acres in 1995 from 1.64 million acres in 1989, it fell to 1.2 million acres in 1999. Yields are traditionally above the national average in the Southwest, but declining cotton prices, pest problems, and the cost

of irrigation are forcing acreage out of cotton production in the region.

- The Delta also saw an increase in cotton planted acreage, from 2.99 million acres in 1989 to a peak of 4.9 million acres in 1995, before retrenching to 3.8 million acres in 1998.

- The Southern Plains region increased its cotton acreage from 5.10 million acres in 1989 to 6.82 million acres in 1995 before dropping back to 5.6 million acres in 1999.

This increase in acreage and yields boosted production from 12.2 million bales in 1989 to as high as 19.7 million bales in 1994. Production for 1997 totaled 18.8 million bales, but poor growing conditions in California and Texas in 1998 reduced yields and led to higher abandonment. As a result, 1998 production dropped to 13.9 million bales. Supplies of cotton increased more rapidly than demand. As supplies have outpaced demand, the seasonal average farm price has dropped steadily since the 1994/95 season.

U.S. domestic-mill use of raw cotton increased from 8.7 million bales in 1990 to 11.4 million bales in 1997, while U.S. exports dropped from 7.7 to 7.5 million bales over the same period. Developments in the technologies of textiles, such as wrinkle-resistant fabrics, and changes in fashion preferences to natural fibers have contributed to increased domestic demand. The increase in acreage planted in 1999 coupled with a recovery of cotton yield pushed the 1999 cotton crop estimate to 18.1 million bales, 30% greater than in 1998. The cotton market will be flush in 1999 and farm-level prices are estimated to move down 10% to 15%.

The shift of cotton production from the Southwest to the Southeast in the 1990s is in line with the downward shift in production costs in the Southeast during that time. Based on data from the USDA, total cash costs dropped from $359.36 per acre in 1990 to $326.35 in 1991. In 1991, chemical-control costs paralleled the downward shift in total-cash costs, dropping from $108.80 per acre in 1990 to $70.27 in 1991. This significant decrease in chemical-control costs can be partially attributed to the success of the Boll Weevil Eradication Program. Producers in the Southwest, on the other hand, are facing rising irrigation costs and new pest pressures. Technological change is also helping to shift cotton production back to the Delta and Southeast regions.

Technology

Recent developments in biotechnology could have a significant impact on chemical-control costs in the future. There are two major types of biotechnology impacting the cotton industry: Bt Cotton, in which the plant becomes toxic to pests; and Roundup Ready, in which the plant is resistant to the herbicide Roundup.

'Bt Cottonseed' has been genetically engineered to include the *Bacillus thuringiensis* gene, which delivers a natural-insecticidal protein that is toxic to the tobacco budworm, bollworm, and pink bollworm. The development of transgenic Bt cotton varieties has the potential to drastically reduce the amount of chemicals needed to control these pests. Roundup Ready and similar technologies are also promoted by manufacturers as having yield enhancing benefits and could increase the rate of growth in yields over time.

Biotechnology, whether it is for corn, cotton, or soybeans, seems to be readily accepted by the majority of producers. Although it is difficult to foresee the impact these products will have on consumer acceptance and pest resistance, the level of acreage planted with these new varieties is expected to increase in the future. However, this new technology also brings with it the risk of future litigation based on product performance. Resistance has developed in Brazil and Europe against accepting genetically modified organisms.

Farm Policy

Past farm policy legislation included supply-management programs, such as the acreage-reduction program, and price-support programs, such as target prices and defi-

ciency payments, which provided price safety nets and income support to producers. However, the 1996 Federal Agriculture Improvement and Reform (FAIR) Act has re-shaped the face of U.S. farm policy. Key provisions of the 1996 FAIR Act eliminated both the programs restricting planting and programs supporting prices and income.

Government support of the cotton sector has been extremely important over time. Direct price and income support averaged close to $840 million per year over the 1985–1989 period, and $870 million over the 1990-1995 period. Over the 1996–2002 fiscal years, the upland cotton sector is scheduled to receive $466 million to $675 million per year in transition payments. Emergency aid was provided in 1998 to agriculture and there is discussion in Washington D.C. that additional aid will be provided this year. Support is expected to be extended beyond 2002 and be maintained at $466 million per year. Under FAIR, price support is provided to participants through non-recourse loans.

Price and income support programs were replaced in FAIR with transition payments that are not tied to production of specific crops. This program will give producers more planting flexibility, and will encourage more market-based production decisions. However, it will also significantly increase price risk for producers, who will have to place more emphasis on risk management than they have in the past. Minimizing cash costs will be one of the simplest ways for producers to manage risk, and this may lead to a shift from cotton to other field and row crops with lower production costs, primarily corn and soybeans. This shift was actually evidenced in 1996 and 1997, in expected returns and cash outlays. The United States estimated average total cash cost for cotton producers was $355 per planted acre over the years 1996 to 1999, compared to $207 for corn and $127 for soybeans.

Marketing Patterns

Marketing cotton from farms to domestic-textile mills and foreign markets is a complex process. Cotton marketing begins when seed cotton is harvested and hauled from farms to local gins. At the gin, the lint, seed, and trash are separated, and the lint is compressed into bales. Most bales of lint are moved directly to a warehouse from the gin. The bales are weighed, sampled, and tagged and then placed in storage. Samples are sent to a USDA cotton classing office for quality determination. In some areas of the Cotton Belt, bales are shipped directly from farms to warehouses known as reconcentration points. The shipment of cotton from interior warehouses to re-concentration points is primarily in order to consolidate bales into larger lots of like qualities.

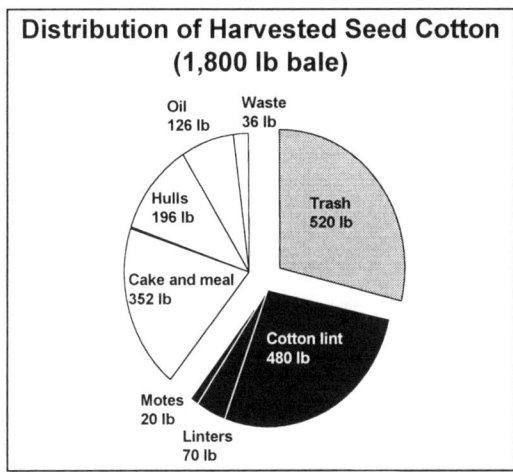

Distribution of Harvested Seed Cotton (1,800 lb bale)

Oil 126 lb
Waste 36 lb
Hulls 196 lb
Trash 520 lb
Cake and meal 352 lb
Cotton lint 480 lb
Motes 20 lb
Linters 70 lb

Domestic textile mills typically maintain only a 30- to 45-day supply of cotton. Bales are shipped from warehouses to mills in fairly even volumes throughout the year to replenish mill stocks. Exports are more seasonal, with January, February, and March being the heaviest export months. The United States is one of the two-largest cotton exporters in the world, exporting 7.4 million bales in 1997/98. Major markets included Taiwan, Japan, South Korea, Canada, and Mexico. China, potentially an important market for the United States, announced a policy aimed at reducing internal cotton stocks and has not imported as much in 1997/98 or 1998/99 as it did in 1996/97. Economic weakness in Southeast Asia adversely affected 1998/99 cotton exports too, which dropped to 4.2 million bales. 1998/99 exports were the lowest level in 13 years.

Aside from waste and tare (bagging and ties), the original cotton bale ends up in one of three major end-use categories: clothing, home furnishings, or industrial uses. Men's and boys' apparel is by far the largest individual market for cotton fiber, accounting for about 4.1 million bales of use in 1993.

International Trade

Many important developments in the cotton market are the result of agricultural and economic development policies of various governments around the world. The impacts of the Uruguay Round of the General Agreement on Tariffs and Trade (GATT) will be relatively small in the near to medium term, but could become significant early in the next century because of increased income growth and increased efficiencies in markets.

Much of the impact of GATT on the cotton sector will come through the phase-out of the Multi-Fiber Arrangement (MFA), which will open up textile markets after the turn of the century. The MFA is a system of bilateral trade agreements that has allowed signatories to place quotas on textile imports to prevent market disruption. The primary goal for its phase-out is the expansion of textile trade through liberalization of world trade and the reduction of trade barriers. The MFA has expired but quotas are to remain in place through 2005.

A major impact of the Uruguay Round should be an increase in demand for textiles and apparel due to increased efficiencies, lower prices, and the resulting expansion in income, particularly in the long run. In addition, the opening of textile and clothing markets will create trade opportunities for exporting countries, many of which are in the developing world. This liberalization will increase over time and become significant early in the next century.

As a result of these agreements and their effect on textile and apparel demand, some countries will reduce their production of cotton because of reduced domestic support. However, changes in the relative levels of cotton prices as compared to crops that compete for acreage, especially grains, are likely to have a larger impact on cotton production. Higher relative grain prices should lead to increased grain production and reduced cotton production, especially in the former Soviet Union and China. But, China remains a command economy and decisions to increase or limit imports can be political rather than economical.

Rising incomes will support demand increases for cotton and textiles in the future, resulting in expanding export markets for U.S. producers. However, U.S. exporters will also face increasing competition in these expanding markets. In general, the United States will benefit from an expanding world cotton market, but there will be considerable competition and shifting trade patterns.

■ Nations that are rapidly increasing mill capacity, including India and Turkey, are also implementing programs to increase domestic cotton production or investing in cotton growing regions in other countries.

This will limit the demand for cotton imports from other exporters.

- A recovery in mill demand in Russia will likely be at least partially met with trade from central Asian republics, but these republics' ability to increase cotton exports will be limited by their attempts to increase grain production.

- Declining planted-cotton area in Brazil is likely to lead to an increase in cotton imports by this country, a market easily accessible to Western Hemisphere exporters.

- Countries that are developing primary industries to take advantage of their relatively cheap labor will increase cotton imports as textile industries grow. This group includes many Asian and Latin American countries.

- However, newly industrialized countries, especially those in Asia (and prior to the economic slowdown that began in 1997), are expected to develop secondary and tertiary manufacturing (as the Asia area begins to recover). As competition in the labor pool increases with growth in industries further up the value–added chain, textile production may stagnate, as labor becomes more expensive.

- Export growth to the Asian region will be limited over the next year or two. Japan is emerging from its worst recession since World War II, and recovery is expected to be slow. Other importers such as Indonesia were also in recession and have been adversely affected by currency depreciation. As a result, many Asian countries cannot currently afford to import cotton, but will return to the market as their respective economies improve.

U.S. Cotton Outlook

Mother Nature wreaked havoc with the 1998 cotton crop. Severe weather has resulted in poor crops for the top two cotton states, Texas and California. Heavy rains in the early spring forced much of the California crop to be abandoned and severely limited yield potential for the crop that remained. The opposite is the case for Texas, where the worst drought in recent history has devastated the cotton crop. U.S. cotton prices were expected to rise, but actually dropped an average of 6% at the farm level.

Acreage seeded to cotton climbed to 14.6 million acres in the spring of 1999 and production is estimated to rise by more than 30% to 18.1 million bales—a result of higher yields, greater seeded area, and lower acreage abandonment compared to 1998.

Exports for the 1999/00 are estimated to improve. Several factors are contributing to the projected rise in exports. First, foreign production is down slightly and exportable supplies will be limited. Second, Asian country economies are beginning to recover from the financial crisis that gripped the region last year and should lead to demand for U.S. cotton exports. Third, China could rethink its policy to draw down cotton stocks. If prices drop sharply in 1999/00 as expected, China may find it attractive to purchase cotton in the global marketplace rather than use internal-cotton supplies. If China does decide to import, then export opportunities for the United States later in the marketing year and in the long term are likely.

Cotton Supply and Use

Cotton	1997/98	1998/99	1999/00
Acreage & Yield			
Planted (Million Acres)	13.90	13.39	14.60
Harvested (Million Acres)	13.41	10.60	13.55
Yield (Bu/Acre)	672.57	625.35	639.60
Supply (Million Bales)			
Beginning Stocks	4.0	3.9	3.6
Production	18.8	13.9	18.1
Imports	0.0	0.4	0.1
Total Supply	22.8	18.3	21.8
Disappearance (Million Bales)			
Total Domestic Use	11.4	10.5	11.2
Exports	7.5	4.2	6.1
Total Disappearance	18.9	14.6	17.3
Ending Stocks	3.9	3.6	4.5
Stocks/Use Ratio (%)	28.7	24.7	26.0
Season Average Farm Price (Cents/Lb)	65.20	61.61	52.40

A 1999 production level of 18.1 million bales coupled with a 3.6 million bale beginning stock level should outpace 1999 growth in domestic use and exports, forcing stocks higher and prices to begin lower. Once the supply shock from 1998 begins to subside, robust growth on the order of 1.5% to 2.0% per year in domestic-mill use is likely over the long term. WEFA estimates that it will take China one to two more years to draw down domestic cotton stocks and shift back towards the world market for cotton supplies. U.S.-cotton exports are forecast to rise in 1999 and then rise over the long term by 1.0% to 1.5% per year. Relatively flat acreage, combined with yields on an average trend that increases at a rate of 1.5% per year, should allow U.S. production to keep pace with increases in domestic mill use and export demand, allowing stock levels to stabilize between 3.5 and 4.0 million bales.

Cotton prices will ultimately dictate the amount of acreage dedicated to cotton, the amount of cotton used in the United States, and the volume exported. The FAIR Act has placed some downward pressure on cotton-acreage expectations. As producers respond to market forces, cotton acreage is not expected to climb above 14.5 million acres in the next five to ten years. Cotton has a relatively high cost of production and relatively high-cash outlays, so competition from corn and soybeans, which have lower costs of production and lower cash-flow requirements, will influence producers' planting decisions. In addition, market returns will be a key factor as well. Market returns are expected to decline in 1999 suggesting growers should switch to corn and possibly soybean production over the following year.

Summary

The U.S. cotton sector is poised for additional change over the next five years. The sector is adjusting to the FAIR Act of 1996, and producers must now manage risks differently than they have in the past as the Federal government retreats from intervening in agricultural markets. The agreement from the Uruguay Round of GATT offers opportunity for growth in world and U.S. cotton trade, but U.S. producers will face competition. Future multilateral-trade negotiations are expected to bring further reforms in the global-trading system and cotton should benefit additional improvements in market access. As growers attempt to manage risk, they are expected to do so by controlling costs and minimizing cash exposure. In addition, elimination of acreage-reduction programs will en-

able producers to respond to market prices and plant accordingly. Weather reduced the 1998 cotton crop and ending inventories declined about 300,000 bales, but cotton prices did not improve, but rather dropped 11%. A recovery in cotton yields, higher area seeded, and a more normal harvested-to-planted-area ratio are estimated to push 1999/00 supplies to nearly 22 million bales. On the other hand, demand is expected to be 17.3 million bales, about 2.8 million bales above the 1998/99 disappearance and still 1.5 million bales below 1997/98 use. Ending inventories should rise and the stocks to use ratio climb to 26%—cotton prices are forecast to remain under pressure. Minimizing cash exposure and the ability to plant more freely suggest that producers could shift easily to corn or soybean production in any given year.

Farm numbers will continue to decline, although cotton production in the Southeast and Delta will likely be maintained. Western producers are expected to face increasing costs of irrigation, while completion of boll weevil eradication in the Delta area is likely.

The biotechnology revolution also indicates change for the cotton sector. Bt cotton, Roundup Ready technology, and other new products are here and producers are responding favorably to this technology. How insecticide manufacturers respond with new product offerings, lower cost insecticides, and marketing strategies will affect how quickly biotechnology–based products are adopted. Costs of traditional chemical pest control regimens are dropping, posing some competition for biotechnology and genetically altered seed stocks. The next ten years will pose challenges to farmers, agribusiness, consumers, and governments. Those challenges will be met in different ways, but change is guaranteed.

Chapter 2: Livestock, Dairy, and Poultry

Livestock (Except Dairy and Poultry)

Red-meat (beef and pork) production in the United States represents the largest sector of the agriculture economy in terms of cash receipts received by farmers. Both the beef and pork sectors have seen significant structural changes over the past decade, and change is anticipated to continue in the future. Historical trends in consumption patterns and market conditions will play an important role in the future of the red-meat industry. Increasing incomes around the world, competition with poultry, and quality, health, and marketing considerations will largely dictate the path of beef and pork production in the future. Meat exports have shown robust growth since 1986. But, the Asian crisis, collapse of the Russian economy, and currency devaluations slowed the rates of increase in both 1997 and 1998. Stability in the financial markets and recovery in Asia, and growing world incomes should push meat exports upward after 2000.

Beef production has lost significant market share to the poultry industry. Relative-price competitiveness of broilers and health concerns related to red-meat consumption are the main causes in per-capita declines in beef consumption. The decline has tempered recently, mostly as a result of beef's cyclical nature. The cattle sector is beginning a slow rebuilding phase due to anemic profits by cow-calf operators in late 1997 and 1998. An extended period of cattle liquidation and liquidation of heifers has retarded expansion. Modest growth in the beef industry over the longer term can be expected, with exports continuing to gain output share, while domestic per-capita consumer demand declines. Concentration of the beef sector is likely to continue, but improvements in quality and marketing conditions will lag those of other meats.

The pork sector has undergone radical changes recently. U.S. per-capita pork consumption has continued to grow through a combination of large supplies and the industry being able to upgrade quality and consistency. Concentration and increased vertical integration have resulted in increased productivity and improved hog genetics. Production has exploded to record levels. Improvements are expected to continue, although environmental concerns of greater animal concentration will force the industry to absorb some higher costs. Per-capita consumption of pork is expected to flatten or increase only slightly over the next decade. Exporting will provide the greater growth opportunity for the U.S. pork industry in the coming years.

Demand Conditions

Over the past two decades, meat consumption in the United States has been shifting away from red meats in favor of poultry. Price competition, primarily from broilers, which experienced substantial industry restructuring and cost cutting, keeps eroding the market share of red meat and particularly beef. Negative health connotations associated with red meats contribute to the consumption erosion.

Per-Capita Meat and Poultry Consumption
Pounds Retail Weight

	1970	1980	1990	1998
Beef	84.4	76.5	67.6	68.1
% change		-9.4%	-11.6%	0.7%
Pork	55.2	57.0	49.2	52.5
% change		3.3%	-13.7%	6.7%
Broilers	40.1	46.6	60.9	72.6
% change		16.2%	30.7%	19.2%
Turkey	8.1	10.3	17.6	18.0
% change		27.2%	70.9%	2.2%
Total	187.8	190.4	195.3	211.2
% change		1.4%	2.6%	8.1%

Total red-meat consumption still exceeds poultry intake, although the gap continues to narrow. On a retail-weight basis, broiler consumption surpassed beef in the early 1990s. The pork sector, which has recently restructured, reduced costs, and increased quality, is expected to hold its ground and even increase slightly, avoiding further reductions in per-capita use. Vertical and horizontal consolidation is occurring in the hog sector. The established trends of broiler and red-meat consumption will play an important role in the future direction of the red-meat industry.

Beef and pork prices have risen relative to broiler prices, a trend that has contributed to the decline in red-meat consumption. Health concerns have also played an important role.

The poultry industry continues to be the most versatile and tightly run in the meat sector, thanks to well-established vertical coordination that can rapidly respond to market conditions. Chicken's short, biological cycle is key to this responsiveness. In addition, the poultry industry has also been more innovative than red meats in the introduction of new products. The steady growth in poultry per-capita consumption has been aided by the expanded variety of poultry products to the menus of fast food restaurants and the introduction of "poultry-specific" restaurant chains. Poultry has also made best use of the expansion of the "take out" habit and the need for convenience. Although total meat consumption will continue to grow slowly over the next decade, the persistent substitution of poultry for red meat is evidence of important changes in the way U.S. consumers make their food choices. As the hog production and processing sectors continue to consolidate, cost savings will be realized that could enable the hog sector to compete more effectively with both the beef and poultry industries.

International Markets

Whereas per-capita domestic red-meat consumption is on the decline, the opposite is true for beef and pork export demand. Temporary setbacks imposed by the Asian recession were offset by steadily growing demand from other regions. Red-meat exports have more than doubled this decade. However, U.S. meat export growth did slow to between 1% and 2% for 1998 and 1999. Stagnation and modest decline in U.S. meat exports is likely in 2000. A strong dollar, slow economic recovery in Asia, the stable-to-declining demand by Japan, and the absence of Russia from the commercial market result in the

poor 2000 forecast. The more open-world trading environment resulting from the Uruguay Round of the General Agreement on Tariffs and Trade (GATT), accompanied by several multilateral (NAFTA) and unilateral agreements earlier this decade, is fostering a greater presence of U.S. red meat in the world. Increased incomes around the globe have introduced consumers to red-meat products. The coming WTO and other multilateral trade talks are expected to continue to foster improved market access globally and promote trade.

Well-planned marketing campaigns in key markets have added to the U.S. industry's increased world-market share, including the marketing of high-valued prime cuts to Japan and Korea. The preference for marbled beef in Japan has additionally favored U.S. grain-fed versus Oceanic grass-fed beef. Japan is the primary importer of U.S. beef, receiving more than 50% of beef exports. Mexico and Canada also take large volumes. South Korea is buying less beef this year because of its economic crisis in 1997-1998. The strength of the dollar has affected competitiveness, although the value of beef exports (excluding variety meats) climbed in 1997 to almost $2.5 billion, up 3% from 1996, but fell back to $2.3 billion in 1998.

Adequate supplies of feed grains and oilseed meals give the United States a cost advantage over most other countries for producing grain-fed beef and pork. The U.S. share of world beef-export volume grew from 8% in 1992 to an estimated 14.5% in 1998. When values are considered, the share is larger, given the high-quality product the United States exports to many markets. The United States has become the number-two beef exporter after Australia, easily surpassing the European Union (EU). With GATT-mandated caps on export subsidies, EU exports of beef should decline. Disease outbreaks in the United States and general food-safety concerns have impaired the EU's beef-export capability.

Beef exports accounted for 8% of U.S. production in 1998, which was unchanged from 1997, up from 5% in 1990, and this share is expected to reach 15% over the next decade. Many countries, particularly those in Asia, face severe constraints to increasing domestic-meat output, and they will increasingly rely on lower cost imports. Improved transportation and refrigeration will also help to increase world meat trade. The developing world offers the best opportunities for significant import volumes of U.S. meats, since many developed countries (the notable exception being Japan) are close to saturation levels for meat consumption. Opportunities for more limited niche-markets exist in both the developed and developing world.

The United States has an opportunity to develop a beef-export market in Europe. Since 1989, the EU has banned such imports, alleging adverse health effects from the use of growth hormones. The World Trade Organization (WTO) earlier ruled that the ban violated the Sanitary and Phytosanitary (SPS) agreement of the Uruguay Round of GATT. The EU has still not removed the ban. In response, the United States and Canada imposed high tariffs on EU imports.

Australia is the world's largest beef exporter, and it exports a good portion of its output to Asia, particularly Japan and South Korea. Recession in Asia has hurt that market, so Australia and other exporters have been diverting beef shipments to the U.S. market. Beef imports, mostly low-valued product used for grinding, accounted for 10% of U.S. beef consumption in 1998 and 1999, and this share is expected to increase through 2000.

U.S. pork exports continue to gain strength due to increases in production, decreases in the domestic price of pork, and disease problems experienced in The Netherlands and Taiwan that effectively shut those countries out of export markets. However, Taiwan is expected to become a more active trader in 2000. These combined factors continue to more than offset the adverse effects of the strong dollar and the Asian recession. U.S. pork producers have been able to improve the consistency of their products, which also provides opportunities for export growth.

Pork exports topped $1 billion in 1997 and again in 1999, a record and a 3% increase over 1996. Japan is the largest market for U.S. pork accounting for 44% of U.S. pork exports in 1998. The increasing value of the yen relative to the dollar, Japan's improved economy, and the high quality of U.S. pork support modest export growth from last year's level. Increased exports to Canada and Mexico are evidence that NAFTA has had a positive effect on U.S. pork exports. Russia has essentially disappeared from the commercial pork market since its economy collapsed in early 1999.

Food Safety

Food safety is an emotionally charged area for meat production. The Federal government has a system of regulatory, inspection, and enforcement measures designed to insure the safety of red meats. Beginning in 1998, slaughter and processing plants were required to gradually adopt a system of process controls to prevent food-safety hazards. The new system is known as Hazard Analysis and Critical Control Points (HACCP). It replaces the old system of slaughter inspection that relied largely on sensory methods. HACCP is aimed more at invisible hazards, such as pathogenic microorganisms like E. coli and drug residues, and less at the animal diseases that were the key concern in the past.

Concentration in the packing industry and an industry trend toward a wider variety of products have led not only to vertical integration and greater control of some food-safety risks, but also to greater potential for the spread of contamination from others. In the last two to three years, there have been an unprecedented series of safety- and health-related events that have negatively affected livestock markets at least for short periods of time. For the last two years, record amounts of meat suspected of being contaminated with toxic strains of bacteria were recalled. Heightened public awareness of health issues will continue to put pressure on producers. One positive event in this area was the approval by the Food and Drug Administration (FDA) of red meat irradiation in late 1997, although its adoption by industry is expected to take time and may require the help of educational campaigns.

Food-safety issues will continue to play an important role in consumption patterns of red meat. Europe's struggle with BSE, bovine spongiform encephalopathy, and the contamination of food with E. coli (e.g., in Japan last year) will continue to haunt the red-meat industry in the future. Beef consumption was down 30% to 40% in the EU due to the BSE crisis. It is believed that the United States could win a significant share of the EU market with BSE-free beef if the EU comes around to accepting the WTO rulings.

Supply Conditions

Beef

In the United States, the beef-cattle industry is specialized into two main sectors. Cow-calf producers manage herds of beef cows that graze range lands or pastures and produce calves. Calves are sold at weaning or up to a year old. Calves can be grazed up to different ages based on forage availability and hay/grain cattle-price considerations. Some of these calves, known as feeder cattle, enter into feedlot operations until they reach slaughter weight. Feedlot operators feed cattle intensively with corn, other feed grains, and oilseed meals for up to five or six months before slaughter. Cattle going to slaughter are often referred to as slaughter or fed cattle. More than 75% of the cattle slaughtered in the United States come from feedlots, a proportion that has increased over the past three decades and is much higher than the share in any other cattle-producing country.

The cow-calf sector is made up of fewer than 900,000 operations. Although the beef-cow population is widely scattered across the United States, concentrations are found in the Southern Great Plains and Central regions. Measured by the population of beef cows, the top-five cow-calf states in 1997 were Texas, Missouri, Oklahoma, Tennessee, and Kentucky. Small operations remain more important in this sector than in the production of other types of livestock. Ranches with fewer than 100 cows account for more than 90% of cow-calf operations and half of the cow inventory. Farms with fewer than 100 cows are usually either supplementary enterprises on commercial crop farms or part-time farms or ranches used by major enterprises. Due to the prevalence of many small operations and the low-cash outlays typically required by cow-calf operations, the sector tends to react slowly and weakly to market signals.

Productivity increases in the cattle sector are expected to continue to lag those in poultry and pork. The ruminant nature of cows, adapted to converting roughage to meat in relatively harsh conditions, means that cow/calf operations are necessarily widespread and extensive. More intensive breeding programs are not cost-effective on a commercial basis. The longer biological cycle of cattle additionally places beef at a disadvantage relative to other major meats. Conversion rates from grain to meat lag those of poultry and hogs. Vertical coordination and contractual agreements typical in poultry and increasingly common in hog operations are not easily transferred to cattle. Many ranchers express opposition to contracts with feedlots and packers, and voice their concerns about concentration in the packing industry. As a result of all of these factors, beef is the meat that has adapted least to the fast pace of modern marketing. However, it is the only major species adapted to turning vast areas mostly unsuitable for other agricultural activities cost-effectively into meat.

Feedlot operations have become more concentrated over time. Out of 110,000 feedlots in the United States last year, the 2,000 largest lots (with over 1,000-head capacity) account for 85% of the nation's fed cattle marketed, and the 39 largest lots (each with over 50,000-head capacity) market 21% of all fed cattle. Ten years ago the over-50,000-head capacity yards accounted for about 16% of marketed cattle. Concentration in the packing sector has been more dramatic. In 1980, the top-four packing companies slaughtered 36% of the country's fed cattle. By 1997, the slaughter share of the top-four was 80%. Producer and feeder concern over packer concentration and captive supplies led to two recent U.S. Department of Agriculture (USDA) studies on the issue. Research to date suggests price impacts from packer concentration have been negative in general, but small. Continued monitoring of cattle-marketing practices can be expected.

The feedlot industry has been able to increase average dressed weights, conversion rates, and the quality of beef produced through better management and genetics over the past decade. Average dressed weight for total-cattle slaughter increased from 650 pounds in the mid-1980s, to over 700 pounds in the mid-1990s. Part of the increase in dressed weight is due to the decline in the number of dairy cows included in total slaughter, a trend that will continue. Producers are paying more attention to consumer demands for leaner and more consistent beef products, and some improvements along those lines have been made. However, the beef industry's biggest obstacle will be to continue to improve quality and consistency, either by forming strategic alliances among producers or moving toward some form of vertical integration similar to that found in the poultry and pork industries.

Pork

The 1990s have been a period of significant structural transformation for the hog industry. What some have called the "industrialization of the pork industry" began in North Carolina in the late 1980s. This process has been characterized by the appearance of very large operations, the rapid growth of contract production, a movement toward vertical coordination of production and processing, and an inflow of capital from outside investors. Some early enthusiasts speculated that the "industrial model" would replace the traditional industry, with 50 producers supplying all the hogs needed by the United States. However, recent events have been somewhat more complex than anticipated. In the traditional Midwestern hog-producing states, contract production and mega-integrators have not duplicated the early successes met in North Carolina for a number of reasons. Environmental concerns from both urban and rural sectors have become a factor in hog expansion.

In the Midwest, "medium-sized" producers, those with 250 sows or more, have adopted a variety of strategies to remain competitive with the mega-integrators from North Carolina. In Minnesota, the state school of veterinary medicine has included business training for its animal doctors, many of whom have gone on to organize production networks. In such networks, hog producers may build a shared-farrowing facility and own breeding stock in common, finishing their pigs at their respective locations. In Illinois, marketing networks are popular. Farmers pool their pigs into semi-truckloads, and negotiate improved prices in exchange for reliable supplies to packers. In Indiana, producers learned from a study by Purdue University that many of the technologies employed by the large integrators can be adopted, at least in part, by smaller operators. Artificial insemination, phased feeding, segregated early weaning, and other technologies can be applied by almost any size operation to reduce production costs and improve competitiveness.

Hog farms are becoming larger and more productive, increasing returns to scale and reducing costs. Capital-intensive technologies are substituting for both land and labor. Production has shifted regionally toward the South, and lately also toward the West, from traditional centers in the upper Midwest. According to the USDA, there were 139,000 hog farms in the United States in 1997, 11% less than the year before. Operations that marketed fewer than 1,000 hogs per year accounted for 126,000 (91%) of the farms and 29% of the hog count. This implies, then, that fewer than 13,000 farms accounted for 71% of all hogs. Operations with more than 5,000 hogs accounted for 35% of all hogs. The number of small operations has continued to decline, and dropped 12% from 1996 to 1997.

Greater size and concentration of animal numbers has not been without consequence. Forces both within and outside agriculture are determining the direction of structural changes in the hog industry. Externalities created by larger animal densities include concerns about the impact of animal waste and odors on water and air pollution. Retaining lagoons for hog waste have broken in a number of states, and the waste has contaminated surface water and water supplies. Nitrate seepage into well and other water supplies from feedlots is also a problem. Historically, operators were able to dispose of waste by spreading it on fields. With today's larger operations, the amount of waste can be too concentrated for the absorptive capacity of the small area of land used.

Areas with greater human densities are having the largest problems with these environmental issues, so corporate farms have tended to move to less densely populated areas in the South and West. Restrictions on new large farms have appeared in North Carolina and many other states.

More research on exact nutrient requirements for all ages and types of animals to avoid excessively "rich" runoffs, plus ongoing research to effectively suppress odors in lagoons, will help to further the development of environmentally friendly and efficient large-hog operations. Scientists and researchers indicate that the feeding of some nutrients, particularly protein and phosphorus, has been consistently in excess of requirements. However, these environmental improvements will likely require producers to incur added costs of production.

The Environmental Protection Agency (EPA) adopted a strategy in line with the current administration's Clean Water Action Plan announced in February 1998. The strategy essentially aims at promoting national standards and letting officials regulate large-animal operations much as they do industrial plants. EPA defined large-animal units as those with greater than 1,000 animal units. One animal unit is equivalent to one head of cattle, or 2.5 hogs, or 100 laying hens or broilers. The National Pork Producers Council (NPPC) participated in a National Environmental Dialogue on Pork Production with EPA, which concluded with a recommended comprehensive environmental framework for pork-production operations.

What, then, has been the result of the industry's transformation? Clearly, significant efficiencies have been achieved. The national average of pigs-saved-per-litter has increased nearly 12% in the last decade to 8.71 in 1997, with the most significant improvement made by large modern operations. According to the June 1999 *Hogs and Pigs* report, operations with more than 5,000 hogs averaged 9 pigs per litter. As smaller operations continue to disappear and technology advances, pigs per litter will continue to increase, albeit at a slower rate than the 2% rate experienced in 1996 and 1997. Reproductive efficiency has also improved with more intensive management of the breeding stock, since closer management of breeding and increased use of artificial insemination result in higher rates of conception. Sows require less "down time" between gestations, resulting in more farrowings per year.

Greater reproductive efficiency has resulted in greater productivity. From 1970 to 1998, the average amount of meat produced per breeding animal has increased 69% in the hog sector as compared to 26% in the cattle sector. Technological advances have also increased feed efficiency in the hog sector. Improved genetics and weaning and feeding practices have all reduced the amount of feed necessary to produce a pound of pork. Superior management provided by contract or voluntary networks has allowed producers to search for improved rations and to implement techniques such as split-sex feeding and phased feeding, where the ration is more specifically tailored to the individual hog.

The pork industry has also been successful in improving the quality and consistency of its product to please the consumer. Most packers offer a system of discounts and premiums to encourage the production of lean and consistent pork. Over the last several years, both the true and perceived quality of the pork product has improved in the domestic market. Together with an improved product, the pork industry has improved its marketing presence with advertising campaigns and the development of branded products.

U.S. Livestock Outlook

The U.S. livestock industry will depend increasingly on export demand in the future. Beef output, notwithstanding its cyclical nature, is projected to increase at moderate rates on average over the long term. Exports will tend to rise in the coming years, responding to growth in foreign income. Due to improved global economic performance, the Uruguay Round Agreement's improvements in market access, and likely further trade reforms, the United States is projected to be a net exporter of beef in the future. The Asian recession temporarily retarded beef-and-pork export growth to that part of the world, but rising demand in other markets is expected to support exports and lead to expansion.

The U.S. beef industry has lost a significant amount of market share in domestic-meat consumption since the 1970s, and this trend is likely to continue. Per-capita consumption of beef has leveled off recently, mostly as a result of cyclical supply increases. Rebuilding of the cattle herd will lead to lower production and higher prices in the near term.

Per-capita beef consumption is expected to fall sharply to close to 61 pounds by the end of the century on a retail-weight basis (from 68 pounds in 1998), and decline further to the high 50s by the end of the next ten years. Reduced beef supplies over the next several years, as cattle retention takes place, will result in stronger cattle prices.

The pork industry is poised to increase future production, largely spurred by structural changes in pork production and marketing. Lower prices in the short term will accelerate concentration, since the rising costs of environmental regulations are more affordable for large farms. Despite growing domestic demand, exports will be the pork industry's main source of growth. Taiwan's resolution of its hoof-and-mouth disease problems will increase its export opportunities next year, although low-hog prices have removed the incentives to expand rapidly. This will be somewhat dampened by the slow economic recovery in Asia and the strength of the dollar. The U.S. does appear to have some opportunities to make further inroads in Asia.

Per-capita pork consumption on a retail-weight basis is expected to increase this year to 53 pounds per year. The industry has increased productivity considerably since 1990. The cost of feed is projected to decline in the short term, helping to improve profits.

Poultry and Dairy

The broiler and dairy sectors are experiencing a period of record prices that have resulted from the inability of supplies to keep up with demand. Processors reduced chicken-expansion plans, adjusting for record red-meat output and lackluster profit margins over the past few years. Moreover, disease temporarily raised mortality in the hatchery supply flock.

The broiler sector is dynamic and innovative, rapidly adapting to market changes. Vertical integration has enabled producers to realize market efficiencies, react to changing consumer preferences, and deliver a product that is viewed as being low cost, healthy, convenient, and safe. Per-capita broiler consumption continues to rise, and is expected to grow at the expense of beef. Growth in world economies and trade has opened markets for U.S. poultry in Russia, China, Mexico, and elsewhere, despite short-term market concerns. In the future, a greater share of U.S. broiler meat will be exported, and diversification to avoid excessive reliance on Russia and China is anticipated.

In contrast to broilers, the turkey sector is experiencing contraction resulting from unprofitable returns over the last two years. Strong growth rates in the late 1980s and early 1990s have leveled off. Unlike broilers, much turkey is sold with little value added. Helping to depress turkey prices is the pressure from growing pork supplies.

The dairy industry is undergoing a period of restructuring. One of the more regulated agricultural sectors, it is moving towards being more responsive to market forces. Consolidation in the number of Federal Milk Marketing Orders and milk-pricing reform have been underway. Domestic dairy demand, composed of a vast array of products, is proving hard to predict, perhaps in part due to the deregulation process.

Milk prices are currently uncharacteristically strong. Milk-production increases have been limited by weather, but demand is robust, mostly from steady cheese takeoff. Per-capita demand and milk prices are expected to decline over the longer run. However, increased product diversification, focused on healthy lifestyles and convenience, could help offset per-capita declines in fluid milk and butter use. Due to continued increases in productivity, the number of dairy operations and dairy cow numbers will be on the decline. Dairy exports are not competitive in world markets. Commitments made in the Uruguay Round Agreement dictate that dairy export subsidies, although historically small, be reduced.

Demand Conditions

Poultry

Per-capita poultry consumption has doubled since 1970. The price of broilers and turkeys has fallen relative to beef and pork, making poultry very popular among cost-conscious consumers. The perception of poultry as a healthy alternative to beef and pork has also contributed to the increase in poultry consumption. Per-capita broiler consumption should continue to increase by 3.5% to 4% per year over the next few years and by 1% per year on average over the next decade. Turkey consumption is expected to rise at a more modest rate.

Convenience has played a role in the rise of poultry consumption. The amount of time spent in the preparation of food at home has declined, as higher incomes and the increased participation of women in the work force have led consumers to demand foods that are easier and faster to prepare. The poultry industry's ability to develop products for changing lifestyles has increased its popularity among consumers. Producers have increased the attractiveness of their products in the at-home market by introducing precut and prepackaged products that reduce the amount of time for at-home preparation. Greater variability in take-out preparations has also accommodated the need for convenience.

**Per-Capita Meat and Poultry Consumption
Pounds Retail Weight**

	1970	1980	1990	1998
Beef	84.4	76.5	67.6	68.1
% change		-9.4%	-11.6%	0.7%
Pork	55.2	57.0	49.2	52.5
% change		3.3%	-13.7%	6.7%
Broilers	40.1	46.6	60.9	72.6
% change		16.2%	30.7%	19.2%
Turkey	8.1	10.3	17.6	18.0
% change		27.2%	70.9%	2.2%
Total	187.8	190.4	195.3	211.2
% change		1.4%	2.6%	8.1%

Domestic per-capita turkey demand increased sharply in the early 1990s from about eight pounds in the mid-1970s to 18 pounds in 1995, and has essentially stagnated at that level. As in broiler production, gains in productivity and vertical integration led to cost and price reductions that resulted in increased turkey demand. Per-capita turkey demand stagnated, however, in the 1990s. Increased production, coupled with inadequate introduction and marketing of new products, resulted in unprofitable price levels starting in 1996. The marked seasonal-consumption pattern, combined with the large size of the typical turkey, has also hampered continued growth in the per-capita consumption of this bird. The industry has begun to market turkey parts like legs, breasts, turkey breast fillets, and ground turkey in an effort to expand demand.

Leading processors acknowledge that the sector is overproducing and "in crisis." The turkey industry has been less concentrated than the beef, pork, and broiler sectors over the last ten years, which has led to more price competition, overproduction, and unprofitable returns. To remedy the situation, output contraction began in 1997 and continued in 1998 and 1999. Improved profitability is expected to result in production increases in 2000. Future production advances are expected to be moderate over the coming years as the industry restructures.

Increased poultry exports are likely over the next decade. International trade agreements such as GATT and NAFTA have created new market potential for U.S. agricultural commodities. Despite this potential, the value of broiler exports declined in 1997 to $1.9 billion from 1996's $2.1 billion. Broiler-export values dropped further in 1998 to $1.7

billion. Prices fell from the high levels of 1996, which had been caused by high-grain prices, and more than offset the 6% rise in volume shipped. Chicken cuts and offals (mostly legs) to Russia and Hong Kong/China continue to be the major export types and destinations, although their dominance has lessened as other markets have gained share. China and Russia accounted for 54% of the volume and 50% of the value of U.S. chicken-meat shipments in 1998. The two countries accounted for 59% of the value of chicken-meat shipments in 1996. Mexico and Latvia are taking large volumes, as is Japan. Broiler exports represented 17% of U.S. production in 1998, up from only 6% in 1990. Export shares of output are expected to increase to 20% over the next decade.

Turkey exports have expanded considerably in the 1990s, with each year setting new records. Exports were more than ten times higher in 1997 than a decade earlier, reaching a record 600 million pounds for an export value of $289 million. In 1998, turkey exports dropped to about 400 million pounds and $202 million in value. Exports accounted for 8.5% of 1998 production compared to 11% of production for 1997. This compares favorably to only 1% in the mid-1980s. Turkey parts and offals make up most exports, with Mexico the largest buyer. Shipments so far in 1999 are below year ago. Reduced output, competition from other meats, and the strong dollar are the factors impacting sales to Asia and other markets. Weakness in the trade is hurting U.S. turkey producers.

Dairy

The consumption of dairy products in the United States has been closely tied to age, income, geographic location, and race. In the past, age more than any other factor had an impact on the demand for dairy products. During the baby boom years following World War II and extending through the 1960s, America's adolescent population grew at an average rate of about 3%. This growth in the adolescent population was accompanied by growth in fluid-milk demand, which fueled production growth in the dairy industry.

Beginning in the 1970s, the adolescent population began to decline for the first time in over 30 years. From 1970 to 1990, per-capita consumption of fluid milk declined from 240 pounds to 205 pounds, a 15% reduction. Not only has the consumption of fluid milk declined, but the type of fluid-milk products consumed has also changed. In general, consumers have switched from whole milk to low-fat milk.

New trends in both income growth and lifestyles came with the 1980s. Real per-capita income reached record levels, partly because of the increasing presence of two-income families. This demographic shift boosted incomes at the same time it reduced the time available for food preparation. As a result, there was increased reliance on partially and fully prepared food and more eating away from home. Both of these trends helped to fuel tremendous growth in per-capita consumption of cheese, especially pizza-type cheeses. Increased product diversification catering to healthy lifestyles, especially low-fat products, and convenience could help offset per-capita declines in fluid milk and butter use. Items such as yogurt and creamy non-fat spreads should see increased demand.

Foreign demand for U.S. dairy products has traditionally been modest, as U.S. prices were not competitive in a world trade market dominated by subsidized producers, predominantly from the EU. In addition, the United States has not historically been dependent on foreign markets for a significant portion of its commercial milk. International-trade agreements, notably GATT and NAFTA, have affected dairy trade. Under GATT, the level of subsidies on dairy exports must be reduced by the year 2000. NAFTA, which has been in effect since January 1994, set out separate bilateral agreements on cross-border agricultural trade between the United States and Mexico and Mexico and Canada. U.S.-Canada trade is still covered by the U.S.-Canada Free Trade Agreement. Under GATT and particularly NAFTA, U.S. dairy exports could show modest growth in the future.

Policy

The poultry sector received modest support from the Federal government in the past. This sector received assistance through the Export Enhancement Program (EEP), which provided export subsidies to combat unfair trade practices of other countries, and from market promotion programs. But, these funds were minimal and are to be phased down under the provisions of the Uruguay Round Agreement.

The dairy sector has been heavily regulated and supported in a number of ways. As mentioned earlier, U.S.

dairy products are not competitive in international markets, and as a consequence export subsidies for dairy products (mostly non-fat dry milk) are provided under the Dairy Export Incentive Program to get rid of surplus volumes. The milk price is supported by the Federal government through the markets for dairy products—if the fluid price of milk was expected to fall below the desired price level, the Federal government would enter the market and purchase butter, cheese, and powdered milk to prop up the fluid price. The government has not had to do this in recent years, as most supplies have cleared the market. The minimum-support price for fluid milk in 1999 is $9.90 per cwt., well below the current market price of over $13. The final component of dairy support is Federal Milk Marketing Orders. Marketing orders basically identify market areas in which producers deliver milk at specified prices.

In 1996, Congress passed the Federal Agriculture Improvement and Reform (FAIR) Act. The legislation will eliminate price supports for milk after 1999. The support price will be phased out to $9.9 per cwt. next year. Beginning in 2000, recourse loan rates for dairy products will be made available to promote price stability, at a milk equivalent value of $9.9 per cwt. FAIR also mandated a consolidation in the number of Milk Marketing Orders from 33 to 10–14. The USDA proposed 11. The reform process went through a preliminary USDA proposal and comment period in 1998 and again earlier this year. USDA is currently formulating a program to replace the market-order system. When complete, dairy compacts should be eliminated. Dairy compacts, notably the Northeast Dairy Compact, allow producers in member states to charge additional over-order milk prices, alleging public interest and presumably higher costs. Compacts have been criticized by many as perpetuating non-market clearing milk prices.

Export subsidies will be reduced for dairy products to levels required under the Uruguay Round Agreement of GATT.

Supply Conditions

Poultry

Following World War II, a number of firms known as integrators transformed the poultry industry. Integrators now contract with growers to raise broilers, providing them with baby chicks, feed, technical advice, and marketing. Growers are responsible for day-to-day care of the birds and the purchase and maintenance of the buildings and equipment required for raising them. Integrators pay growers on the basis of the pounds of broilers produced.

Many integrators use a tournament system of contracting, in which a grower's bonus compensation depends on his performance in comparison with other growers. This system is quite effective in an industry undergoing rapid technological change, because integrators do not have to continually recalibrate a system of incentives based on absolute levels of performance. Growers are continually motivated to improve performance. The sharing of responsibilities between integrators and growers allows integrators to concentrate efforts in genetic improvements, better health practices, and management innovations; and the benefits of these investments are shared with their networks of growers.

Technical and managerial change in the industry has resulted in increases in productivity. Broiler conversion rates were reduced from 2.85 pounds of feed per pound of live broiler in 1955 to under two pounds in the 1990s, a more than 30% increase in productivity. Conversion rates were reduced both through genetic selection and improved feeding processes and rations. Higher productivity resulted in a significant reduction in the real price of poultry to the consumer, contributing to the rise in per-capita consumption.

The consolidation and integration of the broiler industry led to geographic concentration in a few Southern states. Georgia, Arkansas, Alabama, North Carolina, and Mississippi produce almost 60% of U.S.-broiler meat. Through the adoption of an intensive system of vertically integrated production, the broiler industry gained a significant competitive advantage over the beef and pork sectors. Turkey production, on the other hand, is less concentrated in the South. North Carolina, Minnesota, Missouri, Virginia, and Arkansas are the leading turkey states accounting for about 55% of output.

Dairy

The dairy industry has been consolidating since the 1950s. The number of dairy farms declined from 2.8 million in 1955 to about 117,000 in 1997. Much of the consolidation was recent—the number of dairy farms was cut in half between 1980 and 1995—and more can

be expected in the future due to increased competition. More than 10,000 dairies exited the industry in the past three years, an 8% decline. Reduced government support, more stringent waste-management regulations, and new technologies all have contributed to the process.

A number of factors have led to dairy industry consolidation in the 1980s. Overall demand for milk declined in the early 1980s, although increased demand for cheese products reversed this trend in the mid-1980s. The general decline in milk prices that resulted from declining government-support prices forced many inefficient producers out of business. The need for increased investment in dairy equipment to remain competitive, including cooling tanks, improved milking-parlor equipment, and waste-management facilities, has also trimmed the industry of producers unwilling or unable to take on debt for such equipment.

The number of dairy farms has declined at a more rapid pace than has the number of dairy cows, meaning that herd size has increased. The average number of cows per farm in 1975 was 25, and by 1997 it had risen to almost 80. As less-efficient producers exited the dairy industry, and as genetics and management techniques improved, per-cow milk productivity greatly increased. The introduction of bovine somatotropin (BST), a natural hormone, which when combined with other inputs can improve productivity, has also supported the process. Between 1980 and 1998, production-per-cow increased by 43%. Larger herds and more productive cows support economies of scale in the dairy industry, and increased capitalization in modern equipment and waste-management facilities will continue to fuel consolidation in the dairy industry over the next decade.

Throughout the 1980s and 1990s, there was a considerable shift in dairy production from the Northeast and upper Midwest to the West and Southwest. Idaho is experiencing some of the sharpest expansions in milk output. The key factors causing this shift in production include a similar shift in U.S. population, and advantages in the cost of production, climate, and price. One of the most striking trends in the dairy industry has been the emergence of California as the leading dairy state. Former leaders Wisconsin and Minnesota, still produce more than 20% of the nation's milk supply, but California alone produces more than 17%.

Regulatory and Environmental Issues

The poultry and dairy sectors face similar regulatory and environmental issues. Food safety is an emotionally charged issue, and it is linked to environmental concerns. The Federal government has a system of regulatory, inspection, and enforcement measures designed to insure the safety of poultry and dairy products. Concentration and vertical integration in the industry have led to both greater control of some food-safety risks and greater potential for the spread of contamination. Beginning this year, poultry slaughter and processing plants were required to adopt a system of process controls to prevent food-safety hazards. The new system is known as Hazard Analysis and Critical Control Points (HACCP). It replaces the old system of slaughter inspection that relied largely on sensory methods. HACCP is aimed more at invisible hazards, such as pathogenic micro-organisms (notably Salmonella in poultry) and drug residues, and less at the animal diseases that were the major concern in the past.

In addition to food-safety issues, a major concern facing large-dairy operations and dairies is animal-waste management. Seepage of livestock waste into wells and surface waterways is a problem, and some smaller operations face problems from waste that is directly discharged into streams.

The FAIR Act of 1996 included provisions to begin to address livestock waste. Under the Environmental Quality Incentives Program (EQIP), livestock producers are eligible for educational, technical, and financial support (including cost sharing for adopting certain practices and incentive payments for animal-waste facilities) to address issues such as livestock-waste management.

The Environmental Protection Agency (EPA) has presented a strategy in line with the current administration's Clean Water Action Plan announced in February 1998. The strategy aims at promoting national standards and letting officials regulate large-animal operations much as they do industrial plants. EPA defined large-animal units as those with greater than 1,000-animal units. One animal unit is equivalent to one head of cattle, or 2.5 hogs, or 100 laying hens or broilers. The poultry industry entered a voluntary Poultry Industry Environmental Dialogue with EPA officials to deal with non-point source water quality. The dialogue is in response to the closing of some Maryland rivers last year due to outbreaks of a fish-eating microbe. Chicken manure was suspected as a cause of the outbreak. The dialogue is expected to lead to a set of recommendations for the poultry industry to follow in order to prevent water-quality problems.

U.S. Poultry and Dairy Outlook

The broiler sector is expected to continue to expand at robust rates. Although it is a mature industry, it should remain on the forefront of innovation, continuing to strive for new products, marketing alternatives, and cost-cutting manufacturing and delivery systems. The industry felt the pressure of record output of pork, compounded by disease problems, and high-feed costs as its production increases slowed to less than 3% in 1997 and 1998, the lowest rates of expansion since the early 1980s. The broiler industry has developed into a formidable complex unlikely to be deterred from its long-term objective of becoming the prime source of meat consumed at affordable prices. The industry's high level of integration allows it to perceive consumer preferences and respond quickly, as evidenced by the wide variety of product offerings. Per-capita consumption will expand for broilers by 3.5% to 4% per year in the near term and then at a slower rate in the long term. Higher broiler consumption will come at the expense of per-capita beef and veal consumption. Turkey expansion is expected to moderate over the next few years as the industry restructures and consolidates.

Productivity per dairy cow is anticipated to rise steadily in the range of 1% to 2% per year. Improved management, feeding, animal genetics, and technology (especially further adoption of BST) should keep productivity on an upward trend. Dairy-cow numbers are projected to decline at a rate of 1% per year. Farms will become fewer and larger. On net, U.S. milk production should expand at an average rate of close to 1% per annum. Per-capita milk consumption should level off to decline somewhat, with increases in cheese and other "convenience" products partially offsetting declines in fluid milk and butter. Production levels will increase a bit faster than demand, leading to higher dairy stocks and a downward trend in prices.

The export market will become increasingly important to U.S. poultry producers, and exports should grow at a rate averaging around 4% per year. Current uncertainties surrounding the strong dollar and the recession in Asia place some downside risk to this projection in the short term, but the long-term competitive advantage of U.S. poultry producers should keep exports rising. To meet these expected demands, broiler production is projected to expand at annual rates between 2% and 3%. Turkey output will rise at about a 1% to 2 % annual rate.

Chapter 3:   Mining

Metal Mining

As a result of the economic problems in Asia and elsewhere in the world, demand for primary metals was generally weak in 1998. So were metal mining shipments, which remained flat in real terms in comparison with 1997. For most of 1998, mining activity reflected lackluster demand and weaker prices for base metals. However, prices have increased during the first half of 1999, mostly in the nonferrous base metals area.

Prices are likely to continue to improve at a brisk pace over the next two years. Longer term, they will decelerate to a more sustainable average annual rate of about 2%. Mining activity is expected to increase by about 1% in real terms over the next ten years.

Market Overview

Metal mining includes establishments primarily engaged in mining, developing mines, or exploring for metallic minerals (ores). The ores are valued chiefly for the metals they contain, which are recovered for use as is or as constituents of alloys, chemicals, pigments, or other products. This major group also includes all ore dressing operations, whether performed at mills operated in conjunction with the mines served or at mills, such as custom mills, operated separately.

U.S. Metal Mining Industry Trends

	Value of Mined Production ($Mil)	Employment (000)	Capacity Utilization (percent)
1994	12,100	39	86
1995	14,000	41	87
1996	13,000	42	88
1997	13,100	41	91
1998	10,600	39	89

Source: U.S. Geological Survey, Mine Safety & Health Administration.

The U.S. economy grew rapidly in 1998. However, metal mining shipments plunged due to depressed prices. Volume remained unchanged from 1997. End-use market performance was robust including construction, industrial machinery and equipment, and durable goods in general. In contrast, the motor vehicle production, including trucks, buses, and trailers, increased only 0.4%. The GM strike during the summer of 1998 was mostly responsible for the flatness. The automobile sector is a major consumer of steel, along with aluminum, copper, lead, and zinc. Weakness in that sector kept both metal and metal mining output from rising in 1998.

Prices of Iron Ore and Major Metals

	1997	1998	% Chg.
PPI for Iron Ore (1982=100)	96.3	95.4	−1.0
Aluminum MW U.S. Market, ¢/LB	77.1	65.6	-14.9
Copper MW U.S. Prod Cath., ¢/LB	106.7	72.0	−27.3
Zinc MW NA SHG, ¢/LB	64.6	51.4	-20.3
PPI for Steel Mill Products (1982=100)	116.4	113.9	-2.1

Precious Metals: Gold

Low inflation in the United States and the strong dollar have been the significant reasons for the steady decline in the price of gold since the second half of 1996. From a high level of $400 per ounce at the beginning of 1996, gold prices have tumbled to $260 as of late August 1999. Investors have been lured away from gold, instead pouring their money into the stock market and other lucrative investments. In addition, the central banks of several European countries have sold large shares of their gold holdings to meet common-currency criteria of the European Union or simply to demonetize.

The plunge in gold prices has caused the metal mining industry to close or suspend operations at many gold mines, as well as revise or cancel plans for gold exploration. The continuation of a low-inflation environment, a strong dollar, and gold selling by central banks will maintain pressure on gold prices in the near term. Domestic gold-mine production over the last two years has lagged the record levels achieved in earlier years, but the United States still maintains its position as the world's second largest gold-producing nation after South Africa.

Base Metals

World mine production of copper increased by 4.4% in 1998. This is modest compared to rises of 7.4% and 7.9% in 1995 and 1996, respectively. Falling copper prices are to blame for the slowdown in production. In the United States, production declined 4.6%. Most of the added world production in 1998 came from mines located in Latin America, particularly Chile.

In the copper industry, a notable concentration of assets has taken place during the 1990s, from the mining stage through to the production of semi-manufactured goods. A sustained period of high prices has increased the funds available for exploration and encouraged the acquisition of smaller companies. The industry's concentration is most pronounced at the mining level. Although geographical dispersion is increasing, large corporations are dominating mining and taking share from small-scale enterprises.

Concentration has also increased in zinc mining in the 1990s, but not to the same extent as in copper since the production process is less capital intensive and the minimum efficient scale of output is lower. China overtook Canada as the largest producer of mined zinc in the world in 1997, and now accounts for two-thirds of non-Western production. Zinc production in the United States increased by 7.5% in 1998.

The United States is the largest consumer of zinc and zinc products, but domestic metal-production capacity accounts for less than one-fourth of the quantity consumed. Canada and Mexico are the leading importers of zinc to the United States because of their geographical proximity and low tariffs.

Iron Ore

The world's largest producers of iron ore are China, Brazil, Australia, the former Soviet Union, India, and the sixth-ranked United States. Although iron ore is produced by more than fifty countries, these six areas account for significantly more than two-thirds of global iron-ore production. The United States produced 62 million metric tons of iron ore in 1998, compared with 240 million metric tons produced in China. Reserves of crude ore in the United States are estimated at 10,000 million metric tons.

The U.S. iron-ore industry has seen significant growth between 1994 and 1997. However, revenues decreased from $1.94 billion in 1997 to $1.91 billion in 1998. Imports, however, have played an increasingly larger role, rising from approximately 13.2 million metric tons in 1991 to 18.5 million tons in 1998. Exports account for only 10% of domestic production. Virtually all exports are shipped to Canada. It is difficult for the United States to compete in the international iron-ore market because of the inland location of its mines and the high labor and energy costs required for transporting this raw material. Therefore, most of the domestically produced ore is consumed at home by basic oxygen furnaces (BOF) integrated steel mills.

From a demand perspective, the future of the iron-ore industry is heavily dependent on the growth of the BOF process. The U.S. steel industry is going through significant structural changes that have resulted in the BOF process playing a smaller role. In 1991, approximately 62% of the 88 million tons of steel melted in the United States were produced via the BOF process. The share in 1999 should decline to 54%. By 2001, it should fall below 50%.

Ironically, the rapid growth of steel's electric arc furnace process, which does not directly utilize iron ore as an input material, provides an opportunity for some growth in iron-ore consumption through the increased use of direct reduced iron (DRI). DRI uses iron ore as a raw material. Currently, five DRI projects are under consideration in the United States. If they all become operational, DRI capacity will increase from approximately 500 thousand tons per year to over four million tons. Therefore, the expansion of electric arc furnace capacity should provide a lift to iron-ore demand, but indirectly.

The combination of virtually stagnant BOF production and potentially strong DRI usage (from the planned additions to capacity) should lead to modest overall-demand increases for iron ore in the United States.

Over the forecast horizon, an average annual increase of 1.5% is likely.

Outlook

As a result of healthy economic growth in the United States in 1998, demand for primary metals was generally quite strong. However metal mining volume was flat. For most of 1998, mining activity reflected the strong import penetration and significantly weaker prices for base metals. However, prices have strengthened in 1999, particularly in the base nonferrous metals area. Prices are likely to continue to improve at a brisk pace over the next two years. Longer term, they will decelerate to a more sustainable average annual rate of about 2%. Mining activity is expected to increase by about 1% in real terms over the next ten years.

International Markets

During 1998, the mining industries of most countries suffered from weak prices. However, continued acceptance of foreign investment and privatization of formerly state-owned companies had a positive effect on production efficiencies. The Asian crisis led to a drop in metals demand in the region, but a turnaround has already begun, which will gather momentum in the near term.

Development of the Voisey's Bay nickel deposit in Newfoundland, Canada has been delayed. The site, which has an enormous reserve of nickel, faces many obstacles, both political and legal. Regulators remain to be convinced that the site is environmentally safe so that production can begin on schedule in late 2002. The panel reviewing the mine and mill development has asked for more information on issues such as waste management and the impact of the site on water supplies and people in the region. Inco, the world's largest nickel producer, is hoping that the environmental review process for the mine and mill will be completed soon and that it will have the environmental approvals and permits by 2001. However, this timetable remains at risk.

Trends in privatization of state-owned mining and processing enterprises are likely to continue in Europe, Asia, Africa, and Latin America. Governments will be more willing to take on private joint-venture partners in the future, even in countries where the national sentiment has been to maintain ownership of natural resources.

Regulations and Trade Issues

Legislation to reform the Mining Law of 1872 has been considered by the Congress and the administration for the past several years; however, no reform legislation was enacted in 1997. The Mining Law gives U.S. citizens and corporations the right to prospect for certain minerals on particular Federal lands and confers the right to file claims that permit the claimants to mine and sell minerals found. The Mining Law does not provide for a royalty payment to the Federal government for minerals that are mined. Under the Mining Law, claimants may also apply for a patent that transfers ownership of minerals and mineral lands to the claimant.

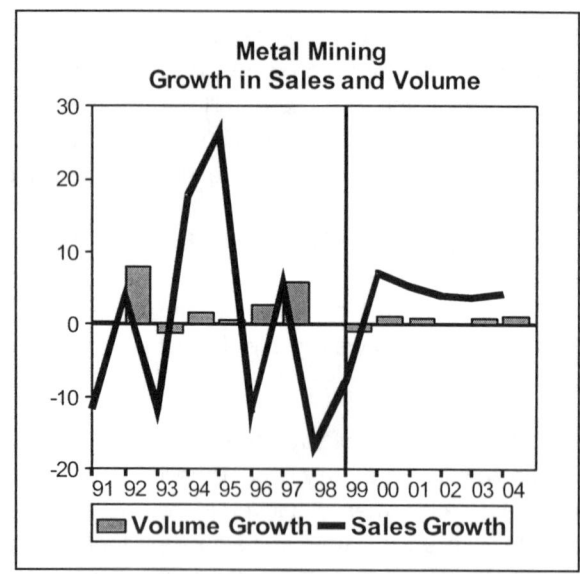

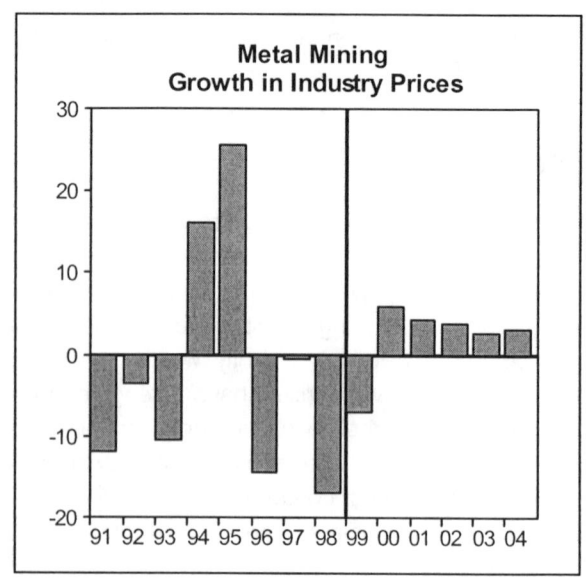

Metal Mining

SIC 10

		1992	1993	1994	1995	1996	1997	1998	1999	2000	2001	Compound Average 88-98	Annual Growth 98-08
Sales													
	Billions of $	10.69	9.45	11.13	14.11	12.37	13.06	10.86	10.01	10.72	11.29		
	% Ch	4.0	-11.6	17.8	26.7	-12.3	5.5	-16.8	-7.8	7.0	5.3	1.7	3.2
Volume													
	% Ch	7.8	-1.2	1.6	0.6	2.7	5.9	0.0	-0.8	1.1	1.0	4.2	1.1
Prices													
	% Ch	-3.5	-10.5	16.2	25.6	-14.4	-0.5	-16.9	-7.0	5.9	4.3	-2.4	2.0
Production Costs													
Avg. Hourly Earnings													
	$/hr	15.26	15.28	16.08	16.77	17.35	17.82	18.25	18.55	19.22	19.91		
	% Ch	2.6	0.2	5.2	4.3	3.5	2.8	2.4	1.7	3.6	3.6	3.3	3.3
Input Price Index													
	% Ch	0.4	-0.6	3.8	7.1	-2.0	0.5	-4.6	-0.9	2.9	2.9	1.0	2.3

Iron Ore

The U.S. iron ore industry's revenues fell 1.4% in 1998 to $1.91 billion, a significant change from the 8.5% average yearly growth rate from 1994 to 1997. The consumption of iron ore in the United States is largely dependent on the production of steel from basic oxygen furnaces (BOFs). While these furnaces primarily use iron ore as a metallurgical raw-material source, other materials such as direct reduced iron (DRI) and scrap steel can be used as substitutes; and relative prices of inputs drives material choices. Unlike BOFs, electric arc furnaces cannot use iron ore. Their main material source is scrap steel; however, in many cases, DRI or other comparable substitutes can also be used. The future growth of the U.S. steel sector will be concentrated in electric arc furnace production, which makes the growth potential of the U.S. iron ore industry limited at best.

Demand Conditions

The U.S. iron ore industry saw significant growth in the last seven years. Revenues increased from $1.5 billion in 1991 to over $1.9 billion in 1998. Demand grew even more rapidly, and imports took an increasing share of the market. In 1991, the United States imported approximately 13.2 million metric tons of iron ore. By 1998, imports had increased to 18.5 million tons. Canada provides well over half of U.S. imports of iron ore. The remainder comes form Brazil (27%), Venezuela (11%), and other countries, including Australia, Chile, and Peru.

The volume of iron ore exports is less than one-third that of imports. U.S. usable iron ore production amounted to 62 million metric tons in 1998, with exports accounting for only 10% of that output. Virtually all exports were shipped to Canada. It is difficult for the United States to compete in the international iron ore market because of the inland location of its mines and the high labor and energy costs required for transporting this raw material. Therefore, most domestically-produced ore is consumed in the United States.

From a demand perspective, the future of the iron ore industry is heavily dependent on the growth of the BOF steel-production process. The U.S. steel industry is going through significant structural change that has resulted in the reduced importance of the BOF process. In 1991, approximately 62% of the 88 million tons of steel melted in the United States were produced in BOFs. In 1998, BOFs produced only 55% of steel output. The share should fall to 53.8% in 1999.

U.S. steel-melting capacity has increased by about 16 million tons in the last five years. We estimate that it will increase by another 8 million tons during the next four. Almost every new steel-capacity project, however, involves the building or expansion of a mini mill or electric arc furnace. As a result, the BOF share of steel production is likely to fall below 50% by the year 2001. Steel output associated with the BOF process is expected to decline between 1998 and 2002, while production from electric arc furnaces will grow at a 5.9% average annual pace over the same period.

Ironically, the rapid growth of the electric arc furnace process, which does not directly utilize iron ore as an input material, provides an opportunity for some growth in iron ore consumption. Concerns about future steel-scrap shortages have caused the steel industry to boost its investment in iron-making technologies that produce alternative input materials for electric arc furnace steel production, such as direct reduced iron (DRI). Currently, five DRI projects are under consideration in the United States. If they all become operational, DRI capacity will increase from approximately 500 thousand tons per year to over 4 million tons. The process to manufacture DRI uses iron ore as its primary raw material. Therefore, the expansion of electric arc furnace capacity should provide a lift to iron ore demand, but only indirectly.

Since DRI is a substitute for steel scrap, the price differential between the two materials is a major determinant of the steel industry's usage mix. While there are some concerns over a steel scrap shortage in the United States, it is unlikely that a shortage will develop over the next five years. Sustained economic activity will provide the underlying impetus for sources of supply for steel scrap, as replacement demand for such items as motor vehicles and machinery should remainhealthy. As a result, WEFA expects steel-scrap prices to remain competitive with those of DRI.

The combination of virtually stagnant BOF production and potentially strong DRI usage from additions to capacity should lead to modest overall-demand increases for iron ore in the United States. Annual growth in real volume is likely to average only 0.9%.

Supply Conditions

At current consumption rates, U.S. iron ore reserves and imports are sufficient to meet demand easily over the next ten years. Because iron ore, like its substitutes steel scrap and DRI, is expected to post only relatively small price gains, it is unlikely that future boosts to its supply will come from greenfield operations. Instead, increases will come from the expansion of existing mines operated by low-cost producers. One complication lies in the fact that future, yet undiscovered, finds have a strong likelihood of being on Federal lands. Nearly 75% of U.S. metal mining takes place in the 12 western states in which 90% of Federal lands are located. Therefore, ore discovery and capacity expansion

are dependent upon access to federal land for exploration and mining, which has been restricted in recent years. Mining operations on these lands must also comply with natural resource development regulations specified by the U.S. Forest Service and by the Bureau of Land Management, and must strike a balance between environmental protection and economic use.

Although iron ore is produced in more than fifty countries, five countries produce more than two-thirds of the total world output. The United States is ranked sixth in world production, with 62 million metric tons in 1997, well behind China (260 million), Brazil (190 million), Australia (150 million), and Russia and India (70 million each). Reserves for crude ore in the United States are estimated at 16,000 million metric tons. This translates into 3,800 million metric tons of iron content. The risk that iron ore supplies to the U.S. steel industry will run short over the next ten years is quite low. The size of Canada's large iron ore reserves (4,600 million metric tons of iron content) and the freedom of trade that exists between the two countries make Canada a convenient pressure valve, should U.S. producers be unable to meet demand.

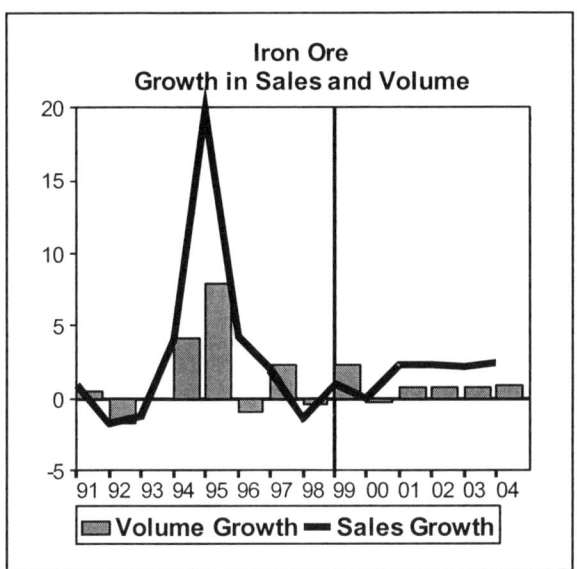

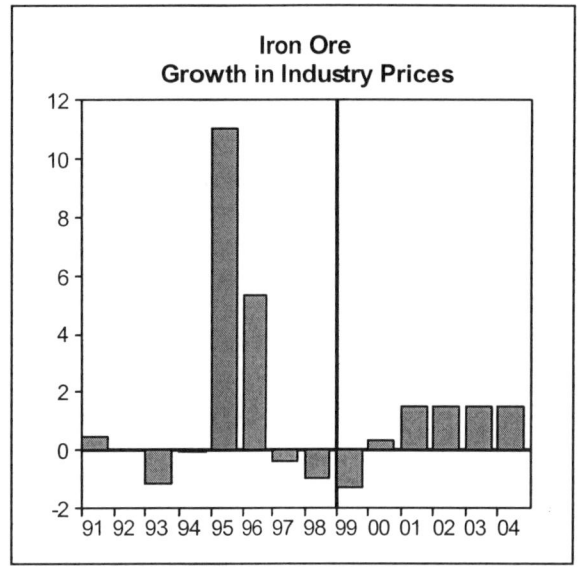

Iron Ore

SIC 101, 106

		1992	1993	1994	1995	1996	1997	1998	1999	2000	2001	Compound Average 88-98	Annual Growth 98-08
Sales													
	Billions of $	1.48	1.46	1.52	1.82	1.90	1.94	1.91	1.93	1.93	1.97		
	% Ch	-1.7	-1.2	4.1	19.8	4.3	2.0	-1.4	1.0	0.0	2.3	2.4	2.6
Volume													
	% Ch	-1.7	-0.1	4.1	7.9	-0.9	2.3	-0.4	2.3	-0.3	0.8	1.0	1.3
Prices													
	% Ch	0.0	-1.2	-0.1	11.0	5.3	-0.4	-0.9	-1.3	0.3	1.5	1.4	1.3
Production Costs													
Avg. Hourly Earnings													
	$/hr	16.50	16.63	17.87	18.49	18.70	18.85	19.91	20.52	21.06	21.65		
	% Ch	0.9	0.8	7.4	3.5	1.1	0.8	5.6	3.1	2.6	2.8	3.5	3.3
Input Price Index													
	% Ch	0.9	1.7	1.0	3.0	1.8	0.6	-2.3	-0.5	2.1	2.3	1.5	1.9

Coal Mining

Coal production should decline slightly in 1999 due to weak exports, sluggish non-utility demand, and excess inventories. Still, production will exceed 1.1 billion tons for the second year in a row. Growth in coal production going forward will be modest, reflecting the demands of the electric utility industry. By the year 2008, we expect coal production to reach 1170 million tons.

The coal industry is composed of establishments primarily engaged in producing and developing bituminous coal or lignite at surface mines, bituminous coal or lignite at underground mines, and anthracite. The industry includes underground mining, auger mining, strip mining, culm bank mining, and other surface mining, as well as coal preparation plants engaged in cleaning, crushing, screening, or sizing. It also includes establishments that perform primarily coal mining services for others on a contract or fee basis.

Demand Conditions

Domestic coal consumption reached 1019 million tons in 1998. Electric utilities accounted for 89.8% of domestic consumption in 1998. Coal accounted for 50.5% of net generation of electric power by utilities in the United States in 1998. Coal will remain the dominant fuel in electricity generation, but competition from natural gas will intensify.

Factors favoring increased use of coal in electric utilities include attractive delivered prices, abundant domestic supply, and a declining contribution from nuclear power over the next two decades. Factors that militate against coal use include the desire for less capital-intensive fuels by a restructuring electric utility industry, environmental problems associated with coal use, and strong competition from natural gas for electricity generation.

Other domestic coal users include the industrial sector (accounting for 6.7% of domestic consumption in 1998), coke plants employing metallurgical coal (2.8% of consumption), and residential and commercial uses (only about 0.6% of consumption). Consumption by both coke plants and residential/commercial users is expected to decline in the future. In the case of coke plants, stringent environmental considerations, greater coke-making efficiency, and alternative means of making steel will all tend to reduce future consumption. In the residential sector, environmental considerations and the availability of other heating sources suggest there will be no future growth in coal consumption.

Exports are a highly volatile market for U.S. coal. Major export markets include Canada, Japan, Western Europe, Brazil, and the Republic of Korea. Over the past 25 years, coal exports have varied between 53 and 112 million tons (mt). In 1996, the United States exported approximately 90 million tons. In 1997, coal exports fell 7.7% to 83.5 mt, as European and Asian sales weakened. In 1998, coal exports fell to 76.2 mt as the demand for metallurgical and steam coal faltered.

Supply Conditions

The United States possesses enormous amounts of coal. Proved recoverable reserves total 275,000 billion short tons. This generally results in a market condition of oversupply. Coal companies have been able to offset declining prices for most coals by demonstrating remarkable improvement in productivity.

Compared with the dismal 1970s, when mine productivity (measured as tons of coal produced per miner per hour, referred to as tpm) declined, productivity improved at an average rate of over 6% per year during the past decade. Productivity in surface mining operations increased by 6.6%. Underground mining productivity increased by 5.4%.

Productivity to the coal mining industry is extremely important for meeting the challenge of higher labor and material costs, additional costs borne by consumers associated with more stringent environmental requirements, and strong competition from other fuels, notably natural gas. There are a number of reasons why productivity has improved but the two most important reasons have been gains in mining technology and more-efficient work rules.

In underground mines, productivity has been improved by the expanded use of longwall techniques. Longwalls produce about 50% of underground coal in the United States. In longwall mining, a cutting machine is pulled back and forth across a panel of coal 450 to 750 feet wide and up to a mile long. A conveyor removes the broken coal. Since longwall mining is done under movable roof supports that are advanced as the bed is cut, the roof in the mined out area is allowed to collapse as mining advances. Longwall mining typically achieves recovery rates of about 80% to 90% of mineable coal, compared with 50% to 60% with traditional room and pillar methods.

In room and pillar methods, even in the "retreat" phase, when miners try to recover as much coal as possible, some pillars are left because of natural restraints, such as poor mine roof and floor conditions. However, expansion of the continuous mining techniques used in these methods improved productivity. A continuous mining machine cuts, drills, and loads coal in a single operation, and requires no blasting. By reducing the size of the crew required, from 10 miners to 6 for example, it improves labor productivity. In addition, the expanded use of "supersections" (the use of two or more continuous miners, where traditionally only one was used) has been a capital-intensive approach to expanding productivity.

In surface mines, productivity improved as surface production moved to the west, where major coal seams are thick relative to the amount of overburden that has to be removed and subsequently restored. In addition, the development of more efficient, large-scale equipment, such as gigantic draglines and extremely large haulage trucks, improved productivity. Future use of new mining technology depends in part on the ability of companies, faced with a sluggish market, to finance the large initial investment, and on the availability of mine sites with conditions suitable for employing the new technologies.

Changes in work rules have also contributed to productivity gains. Over the years, as employment in mining declined, the proportion of nonunion mines expanded. One result was that nonunion operations were sometimes able to take advantage of "alternate" work rules

that are more efficient than those provided for in the union contract. Examples include working fewer and longer shifts, cross training miners to do multiple jobs, and permitting supervisors to help out.

In 1987, coal production totaled 919 million tons. Production from mines, largely underground, located east of the Mississippi totaled 582 million tons. Production west of the Mississippi, largely from surface mining operations, totaled 337 million tons. The split between east and west was 63% versus 37%. As concerns about pollution and industry productivity mounted, the shift to low-sulfur, easier-to-mine western coal accelerated. In 1998, coal production totaled 1,118 million tons. Western production totaled 547.6 million tons or 49% of the total. Eastern mine output was reported at 560 million tons or 51% of output.

Coal imports, at 8.7 million tons in 1997, represented less than 1% of total U.S. consumption. This coal primarily comes from Colombia, Venezuela, Indonesia, and Canada. Most of the coal is used by eastern U.S. electric utilities capable of receiving coal by water. However, we have seen coal imports make inroads into the Texas utility market. Imports are expected to rise over the next decade, as a result of clean air legislation, which will promote the use of these lower sulfur coals especially after 2000. The strong price volatility of international coals, however, provides a disincentive to strong reliance by U.S. consumers on these sources.

Pricing

The delivered price of coal varies considerably around the United States, depending on transport costs, the energy content of the coal per unit weight, and its sulfur content. In 1998, the value of a ton of coal F.O.B. at the mine stood at $18. This represented a decline of 9.3% since 1993. The cost of a ton of coal at an electric utility averaged $28.58 per ton in 1993, but had fallen to $26.00 per ton by 1998, a decline of 9%.

The reasons for these price declines include the significant technology and labor productivity gains identified previously, strong competition from other fuels, and competitive pressures within the coal industry itself. Prices are expected to remain under pressure in the future, due primarily to the expiration of older, higher-than-market priced contracts, and their replacement with today's more competitively priced coal.

Environmental Issues

The coal industry must contend with some of the most difficult environmental issues in U.S. industry. Power plants built since 1978 are already strictly limited in the amount of sulfur dioxide they may emit. Consequently, they must install costly flue-gas desulfurization equipment (also called "scrubbers") or burn very low-sulfur coal. Additional sulfur emission controls, as stipulated in the Clean Air Act Amendments of 1990, are taking effect in two stages. Beginning in 1995, for the 110 power plants built before 1978, emissions are generally limited to 2.5 pounds of sulfur dioxide per million British thermal units (BTU) of energy consumed. The second stage, referred to as Phase II, taking effect in the year 2000, limits emissions for all power plants, old and new, to 1.2 pounds of sulfur dioxide per million BTU of energy consumed. Phase II—which virtually cuts in half the prevailing SO_2 standard during Phase I—will have a very real impact on coal markets. Low-sulfur areas should benefit, although competition will be keen—including a sharp rise in offshore imports. High-sulfur coal producers will come under enormous pressure to cut both prices and production. Producers will be jockeying to maintain some of their market until the post-2005 period when power companies may be more inclined to look favorably upon scrubbing.

The plant owners may choose how to achieve these emissions limits. They can retrofit scrubbers, switch to low-sulfur coal, blend low-sulfur coal with high-sulfur coal, co-fire with natural gas, repower with more efficient boilers, or close the plant. Companies that reduce emissions below the required limits can trade "emission credits" within their organization or sell the credits to other firms that can then continue to emit sulfur at levels above the limit. Utilities can also reduce their aggregate emissions below the limit and "bank" emissions credits so they can maintain emissions above the limit in a later year.

Use of these trading allowances or credits, is providing flexibility and cost minimization of compliance while improving air quality. For the majority of older plants, however, the preferred option for the mid-term appears to be switching to low-sulfur coal. Switching allows utilities to hedge between the future cost and availability of emission trading allowances and development of more efficient clean-coal technologies.

Industry Structure

There were 1,750 coal mines in operation in the United States in 1998, down from 2,475 in 1993. Coal mining employed 101,322 miners in 1993, but only 80,000 in 1998. The number of underground mines went from 1,196 in 1993 to 860 in 1998. The number of underground miners fell from 64,604 in 1993 to 51,000 in 1998. The number of surface mines fell from 1,279 in 1993 to 890 in 1998. Surface mines employed 36,718 miners in 1993 and only 29,000 in 1998.

On a national scale, the coal industry is relatively concentrated. The largest producer of U.S. coal, the Peabody Coal Co., accounts for 15% of the market. The top-10 producers accounted for slightly more than 51%. This reflects a very strong trend toward consolidation since the early 1990s, when it took the output of the top 20 producers to account for more than 50% of production.

Of even greater concern is the trend toward regional concentration of production. Many coal-producing regions in the country are dominated by one or two producers, giving them increasing market power within their geographic areas of competition.

International Trade

The United States has long been considered the "swing supplier" among international coal producers. Whereas the United States typically has had plentiful coal available, its delivered prices have historically been higher than other global suppliers have. As a result, significant demand for exports arises only when serious international shortfalls occur, most recently in 1995 and 1996.

Many international buyers felt that U.S. producers were slow to respond to the 1995–1996 supply shortages. This slowness in responding was due to several factors, some one-time phenomena, but others representing more long-term problems. Among the one-time concerns was the fact that 1995 was the beginning of Phase I of the Clean Air Act Amendments, and many producers who were uncertain about domestic requirements decided to remain out of the global market. Moreover, very few producers initially believed the shortfall would last more than a few months, which it did.

There were more structural concerns related to the 1995–1996 coal market that must be addressed as the international need for coal increases in the future. First, in sharp contrast to most world coal suppliers, the domestic market remains by far the most important to U.S. producers, so the interest level of U.S. companies in exporting is perceived by many potential importers as being quite low. Second, most international purchases occur on an annual basis, too short a commitment for most U.S. producers, who are more accustomed to longer contract duration.

U.S. exports of coal jumped from 71.4 million tons in 1994 to 88.5 million tons in 1995, and then edged up to 90.5 million tons the following year. However, over the next two years exports fell to 83.5 million units in 1997 and 77.2 million units in 1998.

Coal Outlook 1999–2008

The summer of 1999's blistering heat and the approach of Phase II would seemingly be prime ingredients for very active coal markets, but the reality is that procurement activity has been stuck in neutral for the first half of 1999. Much of the inactivity through the spring could be cast aside as the result of high inventories stemming from the mild winter, but coal observers differed on where the market is headed for the remainder of the year.

A case can be made that the market will not be moving for some time to come. There are higher-than-normal stockpiles in many areas and coal traders have been dumping coal at bargain prices. Many coal plants in the 12-state Ozone Transport Commission region are dispatching gas plants ahead of coal units. The huge bank of SO_2 emission allowances (EA) could forestall big buys of the compliance coals, a thought reinforced by the recent fall in these EA prices. Yet we do foresee a relatively strong uptick in market activity over the next few months. The high inventories will eventually be eroded and many new stockpiles must be built as many plants switch coal types to comply with Phase II requirements. Some of the quiet of the recent market can be explained by plants burning off the last vestiges of higher sulfur coals they will not be able to use in 2000. The availability of EAs and strong competition among low-sulfur coals will keep prices from rising dramatically, but we do expect some modest gains for low-sulfur

"compliance coals" over the next two years given the regulatory emphasis on using these coals with the arrival of Phase II.

The arrival of Phase II also signals a trend we have been forecasting for the last several years: the influx of foreign coals. The recent Southern Company purchase of 3.5 million tons-per-year from Drummond's Pribbenow operation in Colombia for Alabama Power's Barry plant gives further credence to our long-held projections that imports could reach as high as 20 million tons by 2005, from last year's 7 million ton level.

On the rail side, the logistical problems encountered by CSX and NS since their June 1, 1999 takeover of the Conrail system have been predictable (undertakings of this magnitude are never expected to run smoothly). Certainly the system-wide debacle associated with 1998's UP takeover of the SP has been avoided, and most problems should be resolved by year-end. At that point, longer term issues of service and rates will undoubtedly move to the forefront of coal buyers' concerns.

Coal Consumption

After increasing 1.6% in 1998 to 915 million tons, coal consumption by electric utilities should rise by a similar amount in 1999 due to the very hot summer weather. A return to more normal weather next year will allow utility-coal demand to rise by about 1% to 939 million tons. Longer term, utility-coal consumption is slated to expand by about 1% per year, on average, reaching 990 million tons by 2008.

Non-utility consumption declined slightly in 1998 as coking-coal demand faltered. There is little potential for residential, commercial, and industrial coal consumption as natural gas and fuel oil will be replacing coal-fired facilities. The demand for coking coal is also expected to drift down as the electric-furnace process for producing steel, which utilizes steel scrap exclusively, continues to gain market share. Non-utility domestic coal consumption is expected to fall to less than 100 million tons by 2008 versus 104 million tons in 1998.

All in all, domestic coal consumption went from 1019 million tons in 1998 to 1030 million tons in 1999, and is expected to rise to 1090 million tons by 2008.

MINING

Exports and Imports

It is clear that the global coal supply overhang has set the stage for numerous foreign coals to be bid into the United States at very competitive prices. High inventories have actually held down the need for low-sulfur imports through the first half of 1999, but volumes are expected to increase noticeably as we enter Phase II.

While we have already mentioned Alabama Power's contract for Colombian coal, Savannah Gas & Electric has recently signed for term coal from Venezuela and Tampa Electric has shown signs of increasing its burn from Indonesia. Imports are slated to rise to 10.6 million tons in 1999 up from 8.7 million tons in 1998. Coal imports may rise to 20 million tons by 2008.

Just when exports begin to look truly dismal, things get worse. Were it not for the higher Canadian take these last few years resulting from their nuclear outages, the U.S. export market would be almost non-existent. U.S. steam export shipments outside of Canada have plummeted more than 40%, and after four consecutive years of declines, total U.S. steam exports are now running some 36% behind 1998's pace. Indigenous production of coal continues to fall in Europe, but so do imports as a combination of cheap gas and environmental policies are working against further coal penetration. Historically, U.S. metallurgical coal shipments have been the steadying factor in the export picture, yet the bottom has dropped out of this market as well, owing to such factors as the Asian slowdown and stronger global competition. Exports of coal should slip to 74.6 million tons in 1999 down from 76.2 million tons in 1998. Longer term, coal exports may once again reach 100 million tons by 2008.

Coal Production

After increasing 2.6% in 1998 to 1118.1 million tons, coal production is slated to slip to 1114.9 million tons in 1999.

Production in **Appalachia** has been hit hard on a variety of fronts in 1999. Revised EIA data indicates fourth-quarter 1998 production was much less than originally

assumed, but that did not change the problem of huge stockpiles that led buyers to enter the spot market on a very selective basis during the first half of the year. The collapse of the export market has proven to be another negative, as has the decline in coal use in the 12-state OTC region during the ozone season. Finally, logistical difficulties associated with the CSX/NS takeover of the Conrail routes has delayed some coal getting to market, so production might actually have been slightly higher in the second quarter than is indicated in the DOE data. On the other hand, CSX reports coal shipments off in the first half of 1999 by 7.2% and NS also reports a drop by 2.6%, so the weak first-half numbers for Appalachia are clearly not an aberration.

The **Interior** region's production picked up quite a bit in the second quarter of 1999, but these are preliminary data subject to change. In some cases, this represents the final output from some mines that are being closed. We forecast a substantial decline in production for 1999 of over 6% compared to 1998, but an even bigger drop for the year 2000 (7.5%).

Western production has been booming in early 1999, in spite of the problems getting coal out of the Powder River Basin. Once again, we expect some revision of these numbers, but for 1999 overall we still project a better-than 4% improvement over 1998's dramatic increase of about 8.5%. Some of this increase is coming from new stockpile building by plants switching to PRB coal, so the flatter production output for 2000 is not surprising.

Data for the first four months of 1999 indicate the severity of the high-inventory problem that has plagued coal markets. Stocks have not reached these elevated levels since the summer of 1995, but the demand for electricity generated by the summer of 1999's intense heat should make a major contribution in trimming stockpiles.

Longer term, coal production is slated to slip by another 1.7% in 2000 to 1096 million tons. Thereafter we expect coal production to expand by about 1% per year, on average reaching about 1170 million tons by 2008.

3.14

U.S. Coal Overview – 1990 to 2008
(000 of Short Tons)

Year	Residential & Commercial	Coke Plant	Industrial & Other	Electric Utilities	Domestic Consumption	Coal Exports	Coal Production
1990	6724	38877	76330	773549	895480	105804	1029076
1991	6094	33854	75405	772268	887621	108969	995984
1992	6153	32366	74042	779860	892421	102516	997545
1993	6221	31323	74892	813508	925944	74519	945424
1994	6013	31740	75179	817270	930202	71359	1033504
1995	5824	33011	73055	829007	940897	88500	1032974
1996	6006	31706	70941	874681	983334	90473	1063856
1997	6463	30203	70599	900361	1007626	83545	1089932
1998	6463	28229	69246	914967	1018905	76200	1118100
2008	5500	25500	66000	991000	1088000	100000	1170000

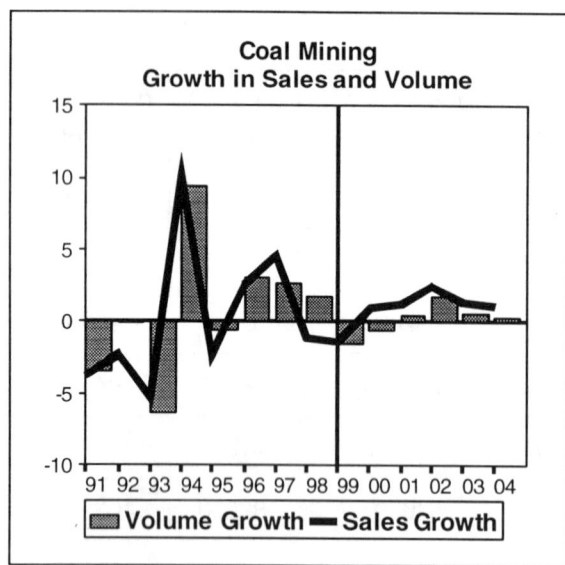

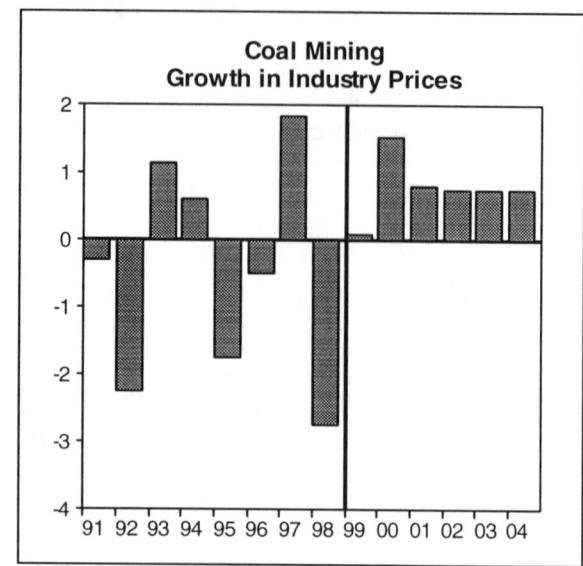

Coal Mining

SIC 12

		1992	1993	1994	1995	1996	1997	1998	1999	2000	2001	Compound Average 88-98	Annual Growth 98-08
Sales													
	Billions of $	26.68	25.28	27.84	27.19	27.88	29.14	28.82	28.43	28.69	29.03		
	% Ch	-2.3	-5.3	10.1	-2.3	2.5	4.5	-1.1	-1.4	0.9	1.2	1.2	1.5
Volume													
	% Ch	-0.1	-6.3	9.5	-0.6	3.0	2.7	1.7	-1.5	-0.6	0.4	1.4	0.6
Prices													
	% Ch	-2.3	1.1	0.6	-1.7	-0.5	1.8	-2.8	0.1	1.5	0.8	-0.2	0.9
Production Costs													
Avg. Hourly Earnings													
	$/hr	17.15	17.26	17.76	18.46	18.74	19.00	19.12	19.18	19.72	20.27		
	% Ch	0.5	0.6	2.9	3.9	1.5	1.4	0.6	0.3	2.8	2.8	1.8	2.9
Input Price Index													
	% Ch	-0.2	1.4	1.0	1.2	0.6	0.9	-1.4	0.5	2.3	2.3	1.0	2.2

Crude Petroleum

Crude oil prices collapsed to lows unseen in twelve years as oversupply plagued the world markets in 1998. Asian demand for oil fell substantially in 1997, and remained low throughout the year. Expectations of recovery were unmet, and a mild winter laid the groundwork for a price collapse in early 1998. Compounding the weak demand side was the behavior of producers who were unwilling to honor agreed production cuts until the spring of 1999.

Average crude prices in 1999 are expected to exceed the average level of 1998. The upward pressure on prices has come from a growing world economy, new production cuts under the Hague Pact, and stronger Asian oil demand in the fourth quarter.

Petroleum consumption is forecast to grow at an average rate of about 1% between 1998 and 2008. The transportation sector is likely to maintain the largest share of the projected petroleum-product demand. Demand for transportation services will expand during the decade on both an aggregate and per capita basis. Over the next ten years, U.S. crude oil production will continue its slow decline and the country will continue its trend toward increasing dependence on imported supplies.

In the long term, there are factors that exert upward price pressure and factors that will tend to hold prices down. On net, there will be modest upward movement of real crude prices over the next ten years.

Recent Events

Crude oil prices collapsed to lows unseen in twelve years as oversupply plagued the world markets in 1998. Asian demand for oil fell substantially in 1997, and remained low throughout the year. Expectations of recovery were unmet, and a mild winter laid the groundwork for a price collapse in early 1998.

Compounding the weak demand side was the behavior of producers. OPEC ministers meeting in late 1997 established a higher quota. Accommodating the return of Iraqi crude to world markets had created a Herculean task for the negotiators, and they were readily deluded by forecasts of improved economic performance. Their failure to address the mismatch between supplies and market demand nearly sealed the 1998 price collapse.

As oil markets failed to turn around in early 1998, leading oil producers from OPEC and non-OPEC countries signed the Riyadh Pact in March, agreeing to cut back 1.5 million barrels per day for the rest of the year.

Misleading data on consumption levels led producers to produce more than agreed. As prices tumbled during the second quarter, these same oil producers were forced to admit the consumption decline and agree to the Amsterdam Pact in June.

The second round of cuts raised the target cutback to 3.1 million barrels per day and was effective for one year. Although compliance steadily improved throughout the summer of 1998, prices remained in the doldrums. By November, there was speculation that OPEC may take further action at its ministerial conference. When the meeting yielded no new plans, crude prices spiraled to record lows.

Exacerbating the already tenuous supply/demand balance in crude oil markets was worldwide de-stocking. Economic weakness encouraged many countries to reduce holdings of crude oil. Countries in Asia, Russia, and Latin America destocked, effectively bringing more crude supplies into the world markets.

By year-end 1998, the U.S. refiners' average acquisition cost of crude oil was $12.49 per barrel, as compared to $19.11/bbl in year-end 1997 and $20.69/bbl in 1996.

These depressed price levels prompted another round of production limits, ratified in the Hague Pact near the end of March 1999. This agreement cut 2.1 million additional

World Oil Balance and Price
(Million Barrels per Day and Dollars/Barrel)

	97q1	97q2	97q3	97q4	98q1	98q2	98q3	98q4
World Consumption	74.35	72.28	73.45	75.41	75.22	72.66	73.34	74.80
Non-OPEC Production	42.87	42.45	42.57	43.50	43.47	42.90	42.22	42.29
OPEC Production	27.45	27.26	27.68	27.85	28.33	28.14	27.53	27.38
Quota	25.03	25.03	25.03	26.68	27.50	26.75	25.70	25.70
Overproduction-production	2.42	2.23	2.64	1.18	0.83	1.39	1.83	1.68
OPEC NGL	2.58	2.58	2.55	2.64	2.64	2.64	2.64	2.62
World Production	72.90	72.29	72.80	73.99	74.44	73.68	72.40	72.28
Inventory Change	1.45	-0.01	0.65	1.41	0.78	-1.02	0.95	2.52
Inventory (Days Cover)	75.56	78.69	78.20	76.90	76.91	81.54	81.82	80.46
U.S. Refiners' Price ($/bbl)	**21.70**	**18.36**	**18.10**	**18.29**	**14.01**	**12.70**	**12.25**	**11.54**

barrels per day from the production limits set in earlier agreements. Compliance has been high through the summer of 1999, and OPEC ministers insist that it will continue. However, there is always the possibility that more countries may cheat as prices rise. Even before the period of low oil prices, OPEC had not demonstrated that it practiced what it preaches. The past decade has shown that member countries manage their output levels at the expense of OPEC, as well as the world market.

In addition to the crude output cuts, refined product production has also been cut back in 1999, in response to poor product margins. In world markets, product prices have not moved up with crude prices. As a result, refining margins have either narrowed or turned negative, prompting refiners in Asia, Europe, and the United States to cut back refinery runs. Asia is already glutted with product stocks while Europe faces weak demand and a flood of Russian supplies.

World-oil markets are likely to benefit from stronger Asian markets in the second half of 1999. There are already signs of economic recovery in the region. First-quarter oil sales in South Korea were 10% higher than a year ago, and rising sales were also seen in India, Taiwan, and Thailand. So far, maintenance turnarounds and poor refinery margins have limited refinery runs. This should help run down product stocks during the third quarter. When seasonal demand returns in the fourth quarter, demand from Asian refiners is expected to increase by 1.5 million b/d.

With Phase 6 well under way, Iraq is looking to increase export capacity in the short-term. It could divert crude from its refineries, which would allow it to export more crude instead of smuggle products. To boost its sustainable export capacity beyond 2 million b/d, Iraq is planning to recommission a second pipeline of 400,000 b/d capacity to the Turkish port of Ceyhan, and using 300,000 b/d of capacity on a pipeline to the Syrian port of Banias.

Short-Term Crude Oil Outlook

Crude prices weakened in late summer 1999 due to planned and unplanned refinery shutdowns, which are backing up crude supplies. Motor gasoline demand over the summer is strong, but gasoline supply tightness may be averted due to adequate stocks and supplies worldwide. There is also a possibility for crude supplies to grow as more OPEC countries cheat and shut-in non-OPEC production returns to the market. The upside risks to this forecast include faster-than-expected stock draws and stronger-than-expected gasoline demand.

The start of the heating season will bring stronger distillate demand to the Northern Hemisphere. Weather and Asian oil demand will play a key role in determining the level of oil prices during the heating season. Average crude prices in 1999 are expected to exceed the average level of 1998. The upward pressure on prices has come from a growing world economy, new production cuts under the Hague Pact, and stronger Asian oil demand in the fourth quarter.

Inventories will return to normal in 2000, as OPEC adheres to the Hague Pact. Non-OPEC output supply is expected to be slow to recover, and higher economic growth in Asia should fuel a continued rebound in demand and prices. Over 2001–2003, crude prices should increase slowly as demand increases are met by a return of non-OPEC supplies.

Short-Term Crude Oil Outlook: Why Are Crude Prices Going to Increase?

The prospect for a sharp recovery in crude oil prices is dim because global fundamentals have to change before the market establishes an equilibrium that can be sustained for a long time. Several factors contributed to the collapse of prices. These include:

- Asian financial crisis

- Strengthening of U.S. dollar against major currencies

- Iraqi supplies

These extraordinary events are confounding a market that has been facing several major influences:

- Supply success

- Slow growth due to its loss of stationary markets to "domestic" fuels (gas, coal, lignite, hydro)

- Through paper trading and communications enhancements, an increasingly competitive market for sellers

As a result, crude oil prices are projected to recover to the level of the mid-1990s, but that level will not be reached until the end of the next decade. This outlook is based on three key assumptions.

First, the surplus of crude must be absorbed by spring 2000 so that a supply/demand equilibrium at a higher price level can be reached. Second, Asian oil-demand growth will resume at levels seen in the first half of this decade shortly after 2000. Finally, for a sustained recovery to take place, world-oil producers must implement strategies to keep production more in-line with consumption. This means that production and consumption levels must be maintained at equilibrium within a targeted price

range and any adjustment to production has to take place quickly.

Oil prices have failed to recover despite relentless efforts by world oil producers to shore up prices, because the system in place is ineffective. Non-OPEC oil producers bring as much oil as possible to the market. Most OPEC producers also bring as much supply as possible to the market. Both types of producers view themselves as price-takers, unable to individually influence the market. Only the major OPEC producers recognize their unique position in setting prices.

Through most of this decade, this behavior was not a problem because the market was able to absorb the oil, albeit with periods of price weakness. The collapse of Asian oil demand in 1997–1998 undermined demand growth, which resulted in oversupplied markets. When the financial crisis spread to Russia and Latin America in the summer of 1998, more crude supplies ended up in the markets.

To sustain price, this surplus of oil needed to be offset by production cuts. The question is: "who cuts?" At this point, the world turns to the major OPEC producers. However, after their disastrous drop in market share experienced in the mid-1980s, these producers have not been willing to support price alone. They insist upon participation from all members of OPEC and selected non-OPEC producers.

The willingness of the major OPEC producers also reflects the actions of the group. As demonstrated recently, they match their performance to the group's performance. The demonstrated success of this system is low. As non-OPEC producers rush to meet "new" demand, the small OPEC producers begin to cheat. As a result, the major OPEC producers produce to achieve the market share they designate as appropriate. Prices balance demand and supply. Therefore, world oil prices should be slow to recover as producers are expected to be only marginally successful at constraining production to demand growth.

The Long-Term Outlook for Crude Oil: Rising in Real Terms

The long-term outlook for crude oil is for the U.S. Refiners' Acquisition Price of Crude Oil (a good proxy for an average global price of crude) to rise steadily over the forecast, reaching $23.80 per barrel in 2010 ($18.62 in 1998$).

In real terms, crude prices reached unprecedented low levels in 1998. In nominal terms, they were close to twenty-year lows. Crude prices are expected to rise at a 4.2% rate in real terms between 2000 and 2005, and at a slower pace thereafter.

In real terms, we see four trading ranges for crude oil: low prices ($14-$17 per barrel), moderate prices ($17-$20 per barrel), moderately high prices ($20-$24) and high prices ($24 and above).

The moderate prices in the past decade resulted from steady world-demand growth that averaged approximately 1.5% per year, limited production from OPEC, and increasing supplies from non-OPEC producers. Advances in technology had reduced the cost to produce oil, allowing for a steady stream of supplies from non-OPEC countries. The overall picture, for most of the decade, was a delicate balance of:

- Demand growth, principally in Asia

- Non-OPEC supply growth at moderate-to-low prices due to technological advancement

- Sufficient demand to absorb the full output of minor OPEC producers

- Sufficient demand to absorb the "designated as appropriate" output of major OPEC producers

Late in the decade, the "picture" tilted. As the Asian financial crisis deepened and oil demand eroded, crude prices fell below the moderate-price range and oil producers' profits eroded. It was a setback for OPEC countries since their economies rely heavily on oil exports. In non-OPEC countries, the oil industry suffered a great deal as the loss of revenue shut down high-cost wells and slashed exploration and development budgets for oil companies. Consequently, non-OPEC and OPEC producers have been waging a battle against the oil glut to shore up oil prices. While consumers have benefited from the low prices in the last year, suppliers believe moderate prices are necessary to keep the oil industry healthy and growing.

Prices will recover to the moderate range again. World crude oil dynamics have been very evident lately. The

price of oil is established in the market place as the marginal "cost" of the last barrel. However, the "last barrel" is defined by the major OPEC producers, and its definition changes when supply and demand are out of balance:

- When demand is growing, the "last barrel" is defined by the major OPEC producers as the cost of the next barrel of non-OPEC production. OPEC restrains production to just allow that "new barrel" to meet "new demand."

- When supply exceeds demand, the "last barrel" is defined by the major OPEC producers as the number of barrels that total OPEC can produce that yields a designated market-clearing price. Under these circumstances, OPEC restrains production to meet that price.

As world oil demand grows, OPEC producers will increase output consistent with maintaining a designated share of the market. This allows non-OPEC producers to expand production, and identifies the market-clearing price for oil.

Over the coming decade, world oil demand growth is projected to rise along with the rate of world economic growth. The rate of world economic growth is the key driver for oil demand growth. WEFA's World Service calls for growth of approximately 5.0% per annum for developing countries and 2.2% per year for industrialized (OECD) countries in the medium term. While OECD demand for oil continues on its upward path at very moderate rates, the non-industrialized economies and newly industrialized economies are projected to experience significant oil demand growth.

While demand pressures are building, prices are not projected to escalate rapidly. First, oil demand growth is increasing, but not explosively. While transportation services and petrochemical feedstocks still require petroleum, economies worldwide are working to diversify their energy needs, actively seeking partners to develop their non-oil resources. Second, technology has maintained steady improvements in supplies from non-OPEC sources. Supply developments have exceeded all expectations, and over the near to mid term will play a large role in limiting price increases. That said, steady decreases in supplies from the OECD, the resource-poor countries of OPEC, and the fast plays of some non-OPEC sources contribute to the moderate upward escalation of real crude prices for the next ten to twenty years.

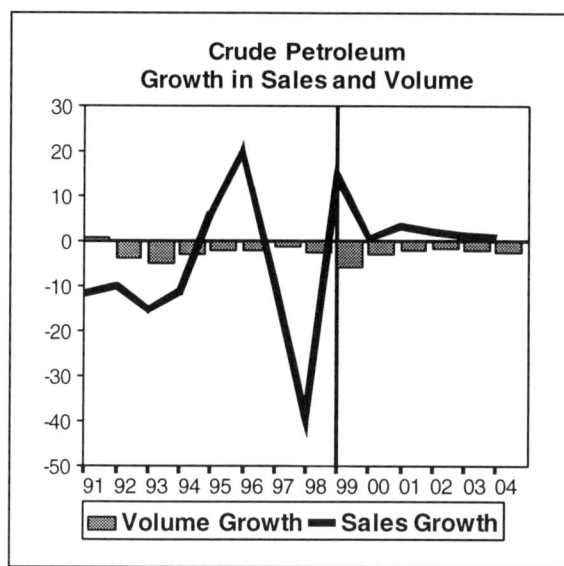

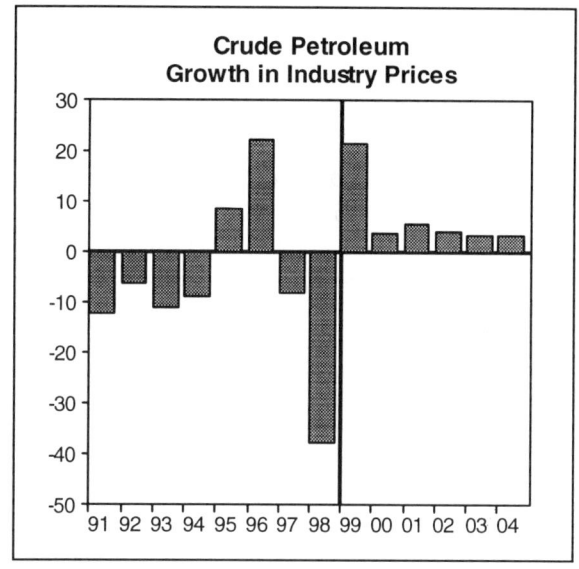

Crude Petroleum

SIC Part of 13

		1992	1993	1994	1995	1996	1997	1998	1999	2000	2001	Compound Average 88-98	Annual Growth 98-08
Sales													
	Billions of $	53.65	45.51	40.36	42.93	51.52	46.79	28.38	32.47	32.68	33.75		
	% Ch	-9.8	-15.2	-11.3	6.4	20.0	-9.2	-39.3	14.4	0.7	3.3	-5.2	2.8
Volume													
	% Ch	-3.6	-4.8	-2.8	-2.1	-1.9	-1.3	-2.6	-5.7	-2.9	-2.1	-2.8	-2.3
Prices													
	% Ch	-6.4	-11.0	-8.7	8.6	22.4	-8.0	-37.9	21.6	3.6	5.5	-2.5	5.3
Production Costs													
Avg. Hourly Earnings													
	$/hr	14.01	14.14	14.13	14.52	14.87	15.65	16.85	17.32	18.00	18.65		
	% Ch	3.5	0.9	-0.1	2.8	2.4	5.3	7.6	2.8	3.9	3.6	3.6	3.3
Input Price Index													
	% Ch	0.3	0.5	0.4	3.3	6.1	1.1	-3.7	0.5	2.9	3.0	2.1	2.9

Natural Gas

U.S. natural gas demand is expected to grow by about 2% per year. Environmental and economic advantages will cause natural gas to gain market share in almost all sectors of the energy industry. Efficient gas–fired, combined-cycle electric-generation units will force the retirement of old dual-fired steam units. Gas is also displacing oil in the residential and commercial sectors.

Over the next ten years, gas prices at the wellhead will increase at a faster pace than the rate of inflation from the price level reached in 1998. Gas prices were abnormally high in 1996 because of cold weather and a low level of gas storage at the beginning of the year; and in 1997, these high prices prompted additional drilling, but little incremental production was realized. In 1998, prices plunged with oil prices and supplies were plentiful. But, in 1999 they have rebounded and are expected to remain strong in 2000. The United States will continue to rely on Canadian imports to supplement its gas supply requirements.

The 1999 outlook for natural gas incorporates a major change in WEFA's assumptions about environmental regulations. This change reflects the Environmental Protection Agency's (EPA's) issuance of rules addressing the emissions of particulate matter (soot). The impact of these rules will be the equivalent to a "Marshall Plan" for electric-power generation. It will force the closure of 85 GW of coal-fired generation by 2010. The closure of these plants substantially raises our forecast of both natural gas demand and prices above last year's level.

U.S. Productive Capacity: Declining

Three years of warmer-than-normal weather and low oil prices have caused low natural gas prices, even though U.S. productive capacity has grown less than 1% per year during the last three years. High working gas-storage levels kept prices low through the early months of 1999. Low gas prices, coupled with low oil prices, have devastated producers, and in response to poor cash flows, the U.S. natural gas rig count declined 35% from December 1997 to February 1998. As a result of declining exploration and development activity, WEFA expects U.S. productive capacity to decline 2% further by the end of 1999. The decline in U.S. productive capacity is likely to cause substantial price increases in the second half of 1999 and in 2000.

In addition, Canadian supplies are growing slowly. Despite the addition of over one billion feet of additional pipeline capacity from western Canada, Canadian production has not changed significantly from the previous year, although exports to the United States are high. The addition of Canadian pipeline capacity has re-connected Canadian prices to the U.S. market.

The near-term outlook for natural gas prices will depend a great deal on the rate at which U.S. productive capacity declines, the rate of increase in Canadian supplies, the economic outlook, oil prices, and, of course, the weather. The forecast assumes a 2% decline in U.S. production, normal weather, and average increase in Canadian exports of 500 MMcfd for 1999.

Increased Canadian Supply

The most important changes in North American natural-gas supply and transportation logistics will be:

- The growth in export capacity from western Canada to the Midwest

- The construction of pipeline capacity to move natural gas from the Midwest to Northeast markets

- The growing importance of the Gulf as a supply source

The recent completion of the 700 MMcfd Northern Border expansion to ship western Canadian gas to the Midwest and the 1325 MMcfd planned expansion of Alliance from western Canada assure that the pricing of Canadian supplies will remain connected to the United States for the next several years. With compression, the Alliance pipeline will be able to expand to 2200 MMcfd. Further, additional expansions of Northern Border are possible.

Currently, demand in the Midwest market is approximately 11 Bcfd. The addition of over 3 Bcfd of capacity to the Midwest cannot be absorbed in the near term. Consequently, several pipeline projects are being proposed to move gas from the Midwest to the U.S. Northeast. The two major projects are Millennium (700 MMcfd) and Independence (1 Bcfd).

Long-Term Outlook

The table below summarizes the key assumptions driving the natural gas price outlook. The major uncertainties are the demand for natural gas for power generation and the impacts of technology and reserve depletion.

Key Assumptions of the Natural Gas Price Outlook

Gas Supply	Technological advancements continue at recent historic rates. Deepwater production in the Gulf of Mexico grows as a result of technology advances. Canadian supply grows and increases its share of the U.S. market.
Reserve Appreciation	Modest estimates.
Environmental Regulations	EPA's 2.5-micron particulate standard is partially implemented in 2008 with full implementation by 2015. Some plants are retired during the 2005–2007 period as owners decide to forgo investment in NO_x controls in light of the facilities economics under revised PM standards.
Nuclear Plants	Plants are not re-licensed and a significant number are retired early.
Coal Plants	Modest increases take place in the utilization of existing coal-fired plants. Regional capacity-utilization increases between 0.5% and 0.8% per year. The 2.5-micron rule forces the closure of 85 GW coal-fire plants by 2010.
Oil Prices	WTI recovers to over $18 per barrel by 2000 and $22 per barrel by 2005.

Power Demand for Natural Gas

Power generation will be the fastest growth market for natural gas demand. There are three primary forces driving the demand for natural gas in the power generation sector:

- Growth in electricity demand

- The retirement of nuclear plants

- The loss of coal-generating capacity due to environmental regulations

Incremental demand for electricity will be met through the increased utilization of existing coal-fired plants and the addition of new natural gas generation plants. A major question persists: how much can coal generation increase in the near future? As discussed below, there are opposing forces affecting coal generation.

Nuclear power plants will be shut due to operating problems and economic pressures as a result of de-regulation of the power industry. Our current outlook projects a decline of nuclear generating capacity of almost 17% by the year 2005 and approximately 53% by the year 2015.

Coal accounts for approximately 55% of total U.S. electricity generation. If all coal-fired generation were converted to efficient natural gas generation, the gas consumed from these plants would equal over 50% of current natural gas consumption. Clearly the future of coal-fired plants is extremely important to the outlook for natural gas demand.

Growth in coal generation can only occur during the next 7–8 years through increased utilization of existing facilities. Coal-capacity utilization is already high, 69% in 1998. Consequently, coal generation is only projected to grow by 0.3% per year from 2000–2005. Coal generation will actually decline from 2005 to 2015 as a result of the closure of a large number of plants.

Natural Gas Supply—Depletion versus Technology

On the supply side, the two major causes for the natural-gas price uncertainty are the characteristics of the recoverable resource base and the role of technology.

Over time, the depletion of low-cost reserves drives up cost. However, technology advances and increases in ultimately recoverable reserves offset the impact of depletion. The relative strength of these opposing forces will determine the level and prices of natural gas over time.

Developing estimates of oil and gas resources that can be produced economically is a complex process, which is typically characterized by initial uncertainty about the characteristics of the resource. Technologies to estimate the size and recoverability of resources involve considerable uncertainty. This uncertainty is typically addressed by making conservative estimates of the resource base.

As exploration and development activities take place, the uncertainty is reduced. This reduced uncertainty usually results in substantial upward revisions in the estimates of the ultimate recovery of reserves. Rather than new discoveries, this growth in what is ultimately recoverable from existing resources accounts for the current majority of both oil and gas reserves and supplies. The growth in the reserves that ultimately can be recovered is often called *reserves growth*. However, a more accurate term, used by the EIA, is *ultimate recovery appreciation (URA)*.

In addition, there are serious questions about the rate of change of technology advances. One side argues that the impact of technology changes will grow even stronger over time. The argument is that much of the advancement in exploration and technology advancement has taken place at the operating level. As more sophisticated information systems are developed, better strategic decisions will be made about where to allocate exploration and development expenditures. This will lower the cost of developing oil and gas reserves even further.

Others emphasize that the contribution of technology is overstated. They argue that the excesses of past periods allowed companies to draw down reserve inventories and take advantage of low-cost rigs and crews. They claim this factor, rather than technology, has kept costs low.

Prices

During the 1970s, natural gas wellhead prices were regulated at a level below market prices. This regulation created a severe shortage of natural gas. In response to the shortage, the Natural Gas Policy Act (NGPA) was passed in 1978. The NGPA created a complex scheme for gradually deregulating natural gas prices. Pipelines responded to the deregulation and the shortage by committing to long-term supply contracts at prices well above the level the market would support. The pipelines managed to keep prices high by using their monopolistic power to restrict supplies.

Under pressure from the courts and consumers, the Federal Energy Regulatory Agency (FERC) issued Order 436 in the fall of 1985 to be effective in the spring of 1986. Order 436 provided strong incentives for natural gas pipelines to offer "non-discriminatory transportation." Prior to Order 436, natural gas pipelines purchased most of the natural gas supply and bundled the sale of the gas with transportation. Order 436 allowed local distribution companies and large end-users, such as electric utilities, to purchase natural gas and transportation separately.

Order 436 allowed buyers direct access to producers and limited the pipelines' ability to restrict supplies. This direct access together with a sharp drop in oil prices caused the average wellhead price (in 1996 dollars) to fall 24.7% from $3.42 per million Btu (MMBtu) in 1985 to $2.57 per MMBtu in 1986. The general downward-price trend continued through the 1980s and into the mid-1990s. In 1995, average wellhead prices were 40% below their 1986 level.

During the last decade, natural gas supply and price behavior has been strongly affected by regulatory changes. The decade of 1985 to 1995 began with a surplus of gas reserves and productive capacity. Furthermore, there was an abundance of drilling rigs and support staff for exploration and production. It has been the contention of the supply bears that this starting point has had a great deal to do with the low prices of natural gas during the last decade.

WEFA believes that there is substantial merit in the supply bears' argument. Productive capacity, deliverability, and proved reserves have been in decline since 1985. During the last decade a disproportionate amount of production has come from the development of reserves. There is little statistical evidence on the ability of natural gas supply to respond to a full cycle of exploration and development. Consequently, there is a danger that price forecasts are too low because the gas market is about to encounter a change in the supply structure. Still, the following considerations lead WEFA to believe that well-head prices will not increase in real terms over the next ten years:

- Proved reserves have increased, and new reserve development is feasible in the $2.00 to $2.20 price range.

- The U.S. gas-directed rig count seems quite sensitive to price increases, so price hikes will be temporary.

- Proposed pipeline additions from Canada though the year 2000 could add 2 Bcfd of capacity.

- Up to 2 Bcfd of additions to supply are coming from the deepwater Gulf during the next five years.

Industry Structure

Hubs, Market Hubs, and Market Centers

A natural gas hub acts as a physical transfer point into which several pipelines flow and from which gas is redirected. Generally, such facilities are unidirectional, with little gas flowing back and forth. A market hub includes all the capability of a hub but also provides services for the buying, selling, and trading of natural gas. Both Henry Hub, Louisiana and the Katy Hubs, Texas are market hubs.

Market centers can exist without the physical infrastructure of a hub or a market hub. They act to arrange storage and transportation from a supply region. Union Hub, Ontario and Columbia Market Center in the Northeast are both market centers.

In recent years, the industry has developed these facilities to ease the transfer and distribution of natural gas. In an effort to reduce exposure to risk, futures markets have also developed at a number of hubs, including Henry Hub, Louisiana (NYMEX) and West Texas (NYMEX and KCBOT).

Although hubs and market centers have proliferated in recent years, they remain underutilized. Storage at these centers is often below 40% of capacity. Ostensibly, one of the key roles of hubs and market centers is to amelio-

rate price volatility. By releasing gas into the system, increases in demand can be met. However, judging by the consistent daily volatility of prices, hubs and market centers are not performing this task. This will continue to be an important factor to watch throughout the forecast period.

Storage

Natural gas demand is very seasonal because of weather-sensitive heating demand. Consequently, large amounts of gas are stored in depleted gas reservoirs. However, as a result of the deregulation of the gas industry, less gas is kept in storage. The use of high-deliverability storage or salt-cavern facilities has increased the speed with which gas can be brought from storage to the market. Moreover, such facilities are capable of handling increased cycling, which means that gas can be put into and taken out of storage in rapid bursts. This increased cycling allows for more efficient use of storage facilities and for better response to short-term changes in demand.

Pipeline Contracts

As a result of the changing regulatory environment and the construction of excess pipeline capacity, contracts between natural gas distribution companies and their pipeline-transportation providers have come under pressure. In a desire for greater flexibility and less cost, many gas shippers have decided to "turn back" or reduce their commitments when contracts expire.

By the end of 2001, half of the current gas-pipeline transportation-contract reservations will expire, and 90% will come due by 2010. Transportation providers are therefore facing significant uncertainty. In some regions, capacity exceeds demand as a result of increased energy efficiency and conservation efforts. Immediate concerns are greatest in the Southwest, Central, and Midwest regions because the majority of their contracts expire before 2001. In the Northeast, on the other hand, the greater portion of the contracts range from 20 to 30 years in commitment length.

These contract turnbacks may indicate a transitional period for the natural gas industry similar to the shift from long-term to spot and short-term contracts in the well-head market that occurred during the 1980s. However, pipelines in areas with excess capacity are likely to be under strong financial pressure. Transwestern Pipeline and El Paso have already been victims of excess capacity in the California market. Excess capacity to the Midwest may signal the advent of similar pressures for pipelines in this region.

Effect of Electricity Market Restructuring on Natural Gas Markets

Following the issuance of Order 888 in April 1996, more choices have been created for consumers and producers of electricity. Order 888 mandated electric utilities to give all generators equal access to transmission facilities, thereby increasing the competitiveness of the electric generation business. High-volume customers will be the first beneficiaries of the new regulations. It is possible that lower prices for electricity could lead to substitution of electricity for natural gas, specifically in the industrial sector. It is unlikely, however, that significant substitution will occur in the residential sector given the wide disparity in price and efficiency between gas and electricity.

Order 888 has created a more competitive wholesale market. However, initiatives are still underway at both the state and federal levels to increase retail competition. At the state level, the strongest initiatives are in areas where electricity costs are high, such as California and the Northeast. In expectation of deregulation of the retail market, a large number of gas-fired generation units are being proposed to take advantage of the current high cost of generation. This will force the retirement of older plants and increase the demand for natural gas in those areas.

Environmental Issues

Gases, including carbon dioxide, methane, and various nitrous oxides, the main sources of which are the combustion of fossil fuels, are suspected to contribute to an increase in global temperatures. Petroleum products have remained the largest single source of carbon emissions from energy use. The second-highest source of carbon emissions in the energy sector is coal. Natural gas, however, has remained the lowest contributor to carbon emissions of the three major sources. Moreover, average emissions per unit of input for gas are roughly half those for coal.

In terms of electricity generation, coal remains the leading contributor of greenhouse gases. Natural gas was, however, the most significant producer of methane emissions of the three major fossil fuels. This shouldn't be surprising given that natural gas is primarily composed of methane.

The largest source of nitrous-oxide emissions is energy use. Coal accounts for the vast majority of nitrous-oxide emissions from stationary sources, with fuel oil a distant second and natural gas emissions still lower. Nitrous-oxide emissions have remained relatively stable since at least 1988.

On the whole, natural gas continues to be the most environmentally benign of the three major fossil fuels.

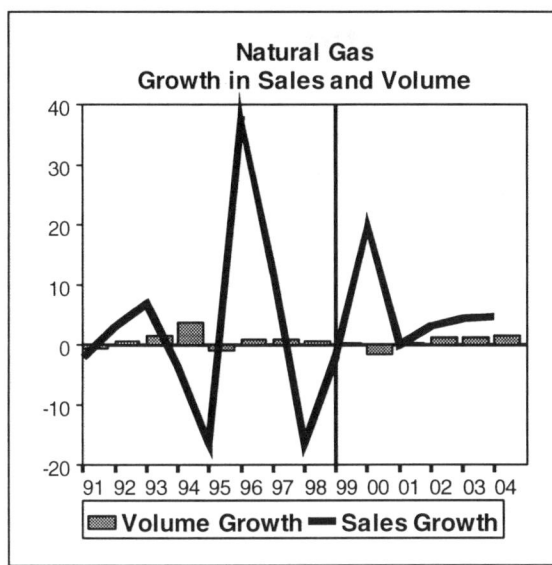

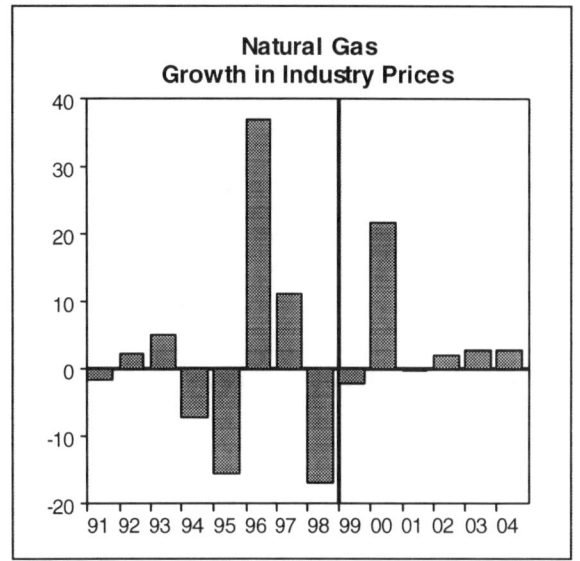

Natural Gas

SIC Part of 13

		1992	1993	1994	1995	1996	1997	1998	1999	2000	2001	Compound Average 88-98	Annual Growth 98-08
Sales													
	Billions of $	28.74	30.73	29.63	24.78	34.23	38.40	32.13	31.74	38.02	38.03		
	% Ch	3.0	6.9	-3.6	-16.4	38.2	12.2	-16.3	-1.2	19.8	0.0	2.1	4.7
Volume													
	% Ch	0.8	1.7	3.9	-1.0	1.0	1.0	0.8	1.0	-1.5	0.3	1.2	1.1
Prices													
	% Ch	2.1	5.2	-7.2	-15.5	36.9	11.0	-17.0	-2.2	21.6	-0.2	0.8	3.6
Production Costs													
Avg. Hourly Earnings													
	$/hr	14.01	14.14	14.13	14.52	14.87	15.65	16.85	17.27	17.82	18.35		
	% Ch	3.5	0.9	-0.1	2.8	2.4	5.3	7.6	2.5	3.2	3.0	3.6	3.2

Nonmetallic Mineral Mining and Quarrying

The nonmetallic minerals mining and quarrying industry includes minerals such as dimension and crushed stone, sand and gravel, clays, phosphate rock, potash, salt, soda ash, and boron. The largest sector of this industry by far is crushed and broken stone, comprised of limestone, granite, and others. Leading states in order of production are Pennsylvania, Texas, Ohio, Florida, Virginia, Missouri, Illinois, Georgia, North Carolina, Kentucky, and Tennessee. Together they account for slightly over 50% of output.

Demand Factors

The most important markets for crushed stone are construction and highway and road building, with the former being by far the largest. The surprising strength in housing in 1999 has certainly helped this industry, especially since nonresidential construction has held up at the same time. Over the next few years, there will be some payback for the current strength, however, as housing activity is likely to fall in 2000 and grow only slowly thereafter. Interest rates will be higher than recent levels, but will remain relatively low by historical standards, which will serve to limit the decline. But so many families have bought new houses during this expansion that little additional growth in existing home sales and the new-housing starts they often prompt seems possible.

Commercial and industrial construction is also unlikely to see much growth at this point in the economic cycle. The growth in commercial building over the last few years has included office building construction in outer-ring suburbs, made necessary by the strong economy and ongoing movement of businesses out of central cities. Industrial building has been limited, as most industries have expanded capacity using new equipment technologies rather than through plant expansion. There is no reason to expect this trend to be reversed.

The main source of strength in the next few years for demand for crushed stone and gravel will be highway and bridge construction funded by the Transportation Equity Act for the 21st Century (TEA–21). At $217 billion, TEA–21 is the largest public works measure ever authorized by Congress. The Act is scheduled as a six-year commitment through fiscal year 2003. Overall, the demand for crushed stone and gravel will grow at a slightly more rapid average annual growth pace over the next ten years, as compared to the last ten.

The United States is a major producer and consumer of fertilizer material. Reserves are key to the phosphate and potash business.

Demand for phosphate rock, 60% of which is sold to the agriculture industry for fertilizer, will depend on crop plantings. Worldwide consumption of these fertilizers has been increasing since the mid-1970s, but the rate of growth has slowed. Demand has eased somewhat in the United States and Europe as agricultural support programs have been reduced. The best prospects for phosphate fertilizers in the future are likely to be in the Middle East and Asia. The second largest segment of demand for phosphate rock is that for detergents. This market has been negatively affected by the belief that phosphates lead to increased water pollution.

The fate of potash demand also depends largely on agricultural output, as roughly 95% of output is used for fertilizer for such crops as soybeans, tobacco, potatoes, sugar beets, and corn.

Borax and other boron compounds are used as intermediate chemical supplies in a wide variety of industrial applications. Expect overall demand for these mineral products to vary with the health of overall industrial production, which is forecast to grow by 2.5% to 3.0% per year over the next ten years.

Soda ash is used in glass containers, chemicals, flat glass, and soaps and detergents. Use by the glass container industry has declined in recent years, as producers have turned more toward recycled glass as a raw material. However, during the same time, demand has been stimulated by growth in detergent use.

Looking at the overall demand for nonmetallic minerals, volume is forecast to decline in 1999, but increase 1.9% and 2.8% in 2000 and 2001, respectively. Public infrastructure construction should be the primary supporter of prices, which are forecast to average only 2.4% growth in 2000 and 2.5% in 2001.

Supply Conditions

In the past, most crushed and broken stone was mined from open quarries. Recently, however, the trend has moved toward underground mining. Underground mining reduces the cost of land for the producer, since it requires less surface space. Given the high cost of transporting crushed stone to its final destination, it is important for the quarrying process to be located near the product's market. The small size and large number of operators in the industry keep competition keen and pricing competitive. Moreover, large volumes and weights make for high transportation costs, which prevent imports from making significant inroads into the industry.

The United States has phosphate rock reserves in Florida, North Carolina, and in the West (Idaho, Montana, and Utah). Florida and North Carolina mines account for the bulk of phosphate-rock production, which in turn is processed into phosphatic fertilizer materials. Currently, U.S. producers are in a surplus phosphate rock situation— productive capacity exceeds demand by 4 to 6 million tons. The availability of rock reserves, the technology of the industry, and the availability of sulfur (sulfuric acid) enable the United States to compete in world markets. However, competitive forces are increasing. The United States exports phosphoric acid, super phosphoric acid, mono– and di–ammoniated phosphates, and phosphate rock. Morocco holds 50% of the world's phosphate rock reserves and is expanding its downstream processing capacity. Jordan, Senegal, and China are also adding to their productive capacity. In the future, it will be increasingly difficult for the United States to maintain its leadership position in the world phosphate market. U.S. production of phosphate rock declined 2.8%, to 44.6 million metric tons in 1998.

U.S. potash production is relatively modest and occurs in New Mexico, Utah, California, and Michigan. The United States relies on Canada as its primary source of potash, and Israel and Russia ship to the U.S. market as well. Due to limited production, the United States is essentially a non-exporting country.

Pricing Factors

Almost all businesses that depend on the construction industry encounter tremendous cyclicality in both demand and product pricing. Soft prices for nonmetallic minerals hurt producer margins during the 1990–1991 recession and immediately thereafter. Since then, however, prices have risen at a rate roughly in line with the all-industry average.

Prices for phosphate rock are expected to gain slightly relative to average for goods-producing industries in the longer term, however, due to the high cost of developing new supplies.

Trends Affecting the Outlook

Environmental concerns are growing in numerous industries in the United States and abroad, and crushed stone operators are not immune to such concerns. Many states now require operators in this industry to submit environmental impact reports before starting new facilities. These pressures will add to the cost of opening new supply facilities and for closing old ones.

Demand for soda ash is dominated by glass production. Glass containers represent about 27% of industry demand for soda ash with flat glass accounting for 14%. Recycled supply has cut into soda ash demand for glass container production, and this trend is likely to increase. The U.S. production of soda ash declined 3.7% to 10.3 million metric tons in 1998.

Risks to the Outlook

The largest sector of the nonmetallic minerals mining and quarrying industry is crushed stone, and the largest market for crushed stone is construction. Rising interest rates always pose a threat to construction spending, and that risk is all the more present now that the current economic recovery is in its seventh year. Consumer confidence also is very important to construction, and can change rapidly.

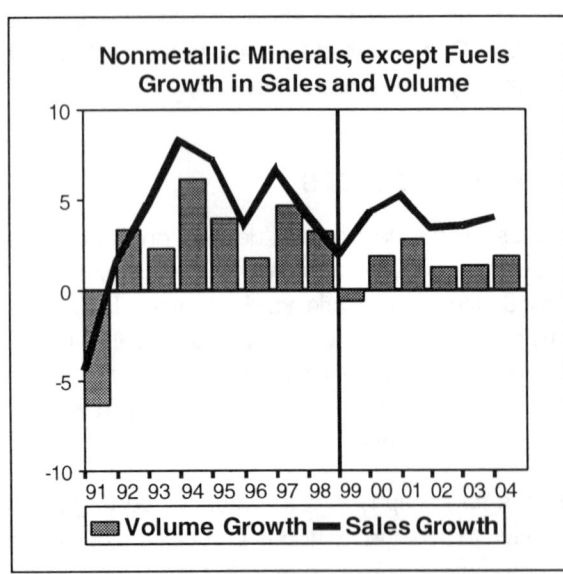

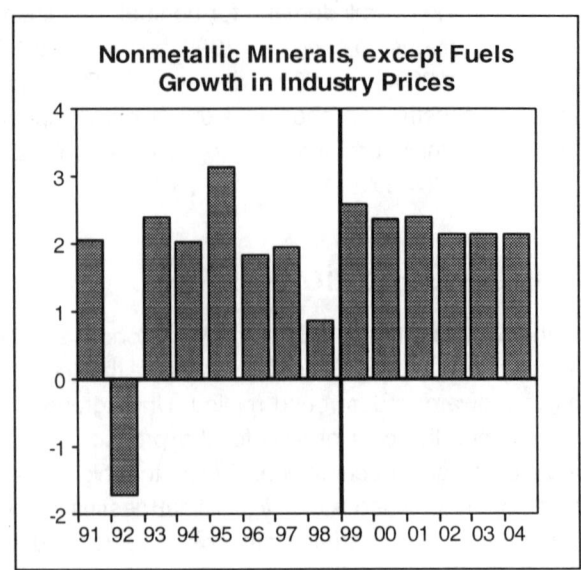

Nonmetallic Minerals, except Fuels

SIC 14

		1992	1993	1994	1995	1996	1997	1998	1999	2000	2001	Compound Average 88-98	Annual Growth 98-08
Sales													
	Billions of $	13.59	14.24	15.42	16.54	17.14	18.29	19.04	19.42	20.26	21.33		
	% Ch	1.6	4.8	8.3	7.2	3.7	6.7	4.1	2.0	4.3	5.3	3.4	3.8
Volume													
	% Ch	3.4	2.3	6.2	4.0	1.8	4.7	3.2	-0.6	1.9	2.8	1.9	1.5
Prices													
	% Ch	-1.7	2.4	2.0	3.1	1.8	1.9	0.9	2.6	2.4	2.4	1.5	2.3
Production Costs													
Avg. Hourly Earnings													
	$/hr	12.25	12.68	13.10	13.38	13.74	14.18	14.71	15.26	15.90	16.49		
	% Ch	2.7	3.5	3.3	2.1	2.7	3.2	3.8	3.7	4.2	3.7	3.0	3.7
Input Price Index													
	% Ch	0.8	1.8	0.8	3.1	2.1	1.2	-1.1	0.3	2.4	2.5	1.8	2.3

Chapter 4:   Construction

Residential Construction

After hitting a near-term lull during 1995, housing has experienced a remarkable resurgence. Since 1995, when total housing starts registered 1.36 million units, new-home construction has risen each year. Housing starts will peak in 1999 at 1.63 million units, 80% single-family. Residential investment, which includes renovations as well as new construction, climbed by nearly 22% during the 1996–1998 period in real terms.

Extremely low-mortgage rates (below 7%) and a booming economy have aided the tremendous surge in single-family home construction during 1998–1999. These factors increased affordability and incomes, driving new construction well ahead of any household formation measure. As a result of this buying spree, homeownership has risen to an all-time high of 66.5% during 1999. Recently, mortgage rates have moved up above 8%; this is expected to put a damper on construction activity in the months ahead.

Regional diversity has been another factor at work in the recent housing boom. As jobs shift from the Northeast and Midwest regions to the South and West, demand for housing followed. In particular the South region accounted for nearly half of all new-housing starts during the past three years. On an even more focused regional basis, the states of California, Florida, and Texas combined accounted for nearly one-quarter of new-housing construction since 1995.

Demand Conditions

The two primary drivers behind the demand for new-home construction are affordability, which includes home pricing, interest rates and buyer income, and demographic trends. Demographic factors are certainly key determinants in the long run, and the aging of the baby boom generation through the prime years for buying a first home helped to propel housing starts through the 1980s. The peak year for housing starts in the 1980s was 1986, at 1.81 million units.

Housing Starts
Millions of Units

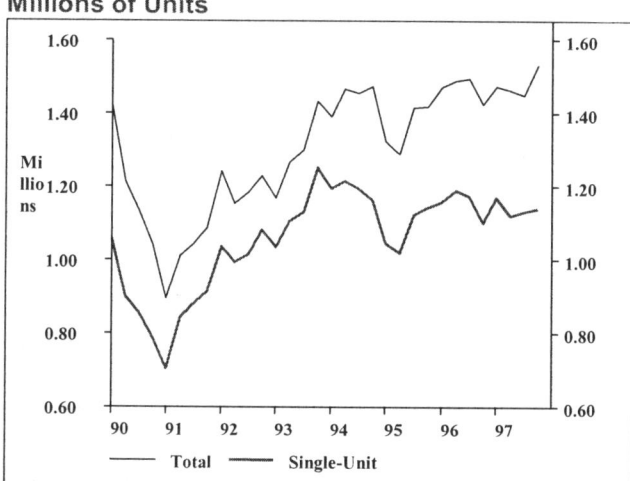

Single-unit housing starts stood at 852,000 units in 1980 and will peak in 1999 at an estimated 1.31 million units. The single-family market is benefiting from a robust job market, very low inflation, and favorable mortgage rates. Also aiding the surge in new construction is the record setting level of existing-home sales, which has led to robust trade-up buying of new homes. Multi-family housing starts increased from 440,000 in 1980 to 628,000 in 1986. However, in 1998 they totaled only 340,000.

Baby-boom demographics certainly played a role in these divergent trends: baby boomers were having families and benefiting from higher disposable income, and therefore preferred more roomy and costly single-family housing to apartments and condos. Tax laws also enforced the divergent trends—multi–unit housing was encouraged in the early 1980s by the investment tax credit, and the repeal of the credit later in the decade caused a major break in the market. A key affordability factor also helped single-unit housing—mortgage rates fell from an effective rate of 12.9% in 1980 to 10.3% in 1986, and then dropped to 6.9% by fourth-quarter 1998. During the next five years, effective mortgage rates are expected to hover in the range of 7% to 8%.

WEFA expects housing activity to decline after the sector's tremendous boom over the past three years. Total starts are forecast to reach 1.63 million units during 1999, and then fall back to an average of about 1.4 million units during the 2000-2004 period. Single-unit starts are projected to reach 1.3 million in 1999 and then range between 1.1 and 1.15 million during the next five years, accounting for about 80% of total starts.

Real disposable income growth is expected to peak in 1999 at about 3.5%, and slow down in the next five years to more sustainable rates. The combination of moderately higher mortgage rates and slowing income growth will result in lower affordability over the next five years.

From a regional perspective, residential construction activity will continue to be diverse. Those areas of the country that experience strong job growth are likely to see the largest increase in housing starts. WEFA forecasts that the South Atlantic, West South Central, and Pacific regions will have the highest rates of employment growth through the year 2008, and housing starts in these regions are expected to grow faster than the rest of the country. Slowest residential construction growth is expected in the East South Central and West North Central regions.

Upkeep and improvements as well as expenditures on maintenance and repairs for residential property are also classified under residential construction. While it is difficult to capture the full value of do-it-yourself projects, professional construction figures are readily available. In 1980, about $46 billion were spent for residential alterations and repairs in current-dollar terms. This spending was over $100 billion in 1990, and it reached nearly $131 billion in 1998.

The economic factors driving growth in renovations, upkeep, and alterations are similar to those behind housing starts. The need for baby boomers to increase living space to accommodate expanding families and the desire to upgrade homes as disposable incomes increase are the two main factors supporting residential alterations and repairs. The fact that Federal tax laws allow the interest on home-equity loans to be deductible has also stimulated residential renovations, since a large percentage of these loans are at least partially used for renovation work. In addition, the low-interest rates of the early 1990s encouraged many homeowners to refinance mortgages, often including an additional loan for home improvements. The forecast for spending on residential alterations and repairs is moderately bullish over the next five years, but the pace of activity is likely to decelerate,

given our expectation of slower income and job growth and moderately higher mortgage interest rates.

Material and Labor Costs

The building materials used for residential single-family structures are significantly different from those used in multi-unit housing, commercial structures, and public projects. Single-unit residential structures use a large amount of lumber and wood products, prepared paints, and plastic construction products. They may also use a significant amount of brick or stone, cement, or insulation materials. Unlike larger structures, very little steel is used. However, steel bracing is increasingly finding use as a substitute for lumber in homebuilding. Pumps, electrical equipment, and glass products that are used in quantity in multi-unit and commercial structures are used to a much smaller extent in construction of single residences.

Labor is the largest cost component in homebuilding. Over the last ten years, construction wages have averaged about 2.6% growth annually. Cement costs have also been stable over the past fifteen years. Lumber and wood products have been the most volatile cost element among residential building materials. Lumber prices have swung up and down over the period, but averaged a hefty gain of 5.5% per year, thanks to supply limits from environmental issues combined with strong demand. These increases are in fact the force behind the inroads made by steel bracing.

From a cost standpoint, WEFA expects few shocks in the residential-housing sector over the next five years.

- Labor costs are projected to continue to increase at only about 2.5% per year.

- Cement costs are expected to increase by roughly 2%-2.5%.

- Price advances for plastic construction products should average about 2% per year.

- Despite a robust domestic residential market, lumber prices tumbled in 1998, due primarily to the collapse of the Asian export market. However, lumber prices have surged since the beginning of 1999. They are expected to weaken in 2000 in response to lower housing starts before returning to a more normal trend-growth pattern.

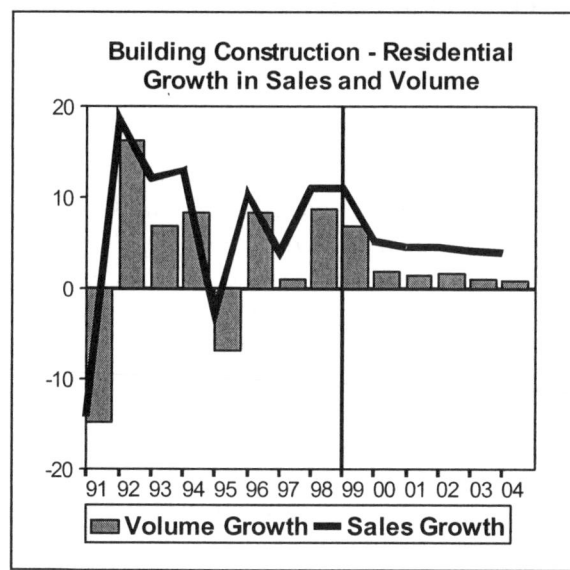

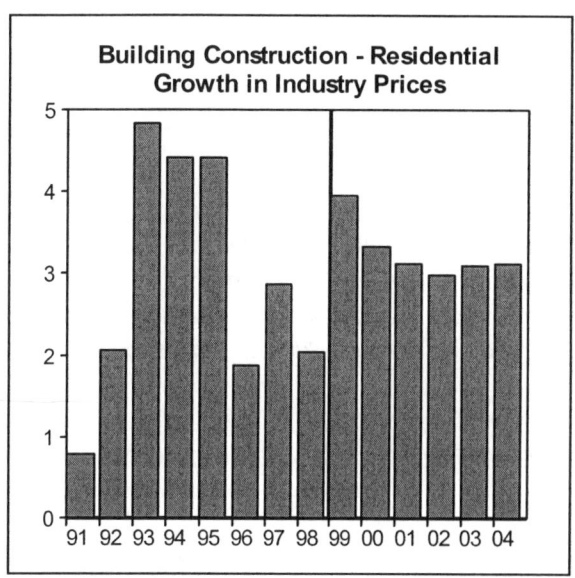

Building Construction - Private Residential
SIC Part of 15-17

		1992	1993	1994	1995	1996	1997	1998	1999	2000	2001	Compound Average 88-98	Annual Growth 98-08
Sales													
	Billions of $	148.6	166.5	188.2	183.1	202.2	210.1	233.2	258.9	272.5	285.0		
	% Ch	18.8	12.1	13.0	-2.7	10.4	3.9	11.0	11.0	5.3	4.6	4.1	5.4
Volume													
	% Ch	16.3	6.9	8.3	-6.8	8.3	1.1	8.8	6.8	1.9	1.4	1.0	2.0
Prices													
	% Ch	2.1	4.8	4.4	4.4	1.9	2.9	2.0	4.0	3.3	3.1	3.1	3.3
Production Costs													
Avg. Hourly Earnings													
	$/hr	12.54	12.68	12.92	13.29	13.51	14.18	14.84	15.13	15.47	15.75		
	% Ch	1.9	1.1	1.8	2.9	1.6	4.9	4.7	2.0	2.2	1.8	2.6	2.3
Input Price Index													
	% Ch	2.4	4.3	2.2	2.3	0.4	2.0	0.1	1.0	2.6	2.6	2.2	2.6

Nonresidential Construction

Following three years of double-digit growth in 1995 through 1997, the nonresidential construction market continued to expand in 1998 at a slower but still solid pace, with new construction put-in-place registering a gain of 8.5%. This expansion was well supported by the healthy economic performance in the United States. Four major sectors of the nonresidential construction market are expected to post strong increases in 1999 and beyond: transportation, technology, office buildings, and educational buildings.

Transportation Construction

During the next five years, the transportation construction market is going to receive a strong boost from the recently passed Transportation Equity Act for the 21st century (TEA–21). At $217 billion, TEA–21 is the largest public works measure ever authorized by Congress.

TEA–21 will unleash an average of $26.2 billion each year in transportation funds during the next five years, a 44% increase over its highly successful predecessor, the International Surface Transportation Efficiency Act (ISTEA). As a result, contractors can expect to enjoy the benefit of big-ticket highway programs.

Stiff competition and weak materials prices helped to knock down the Federal Highway Administration's bid–price index in 1998 and the first half of 1999. Over the next several years, we expect annual growth in that index to average close to 2.5%.

Despite the love of Americans for the automobile, railroads are poised for a comeback. Light-rail systems may be the latest rage across the United States—and a big winner of TEA–21 funding—but major metropolitan regions are also counting on new federal help to upgrade "heavy" commuter and high-speed rail lines.

One of transportation's hot markets is airport construction. Most major airports have some form of development underway. Grants from the Airport and Airway Trust Fund provide capital for some of these projects, but bonds still remain the most important revenue source.

Technology Construction

The technology market is another area projected to grow steadily over the next few years. Telephone vendors and carriers note that fewer than 30% of standard U.S. telephone lines are sufficient to carry the communication required by the latest modems on the market, which run with speeds up to 56 kilobits per second. New technologies like DSL and cable-Internet access are expected to explode over the next five years with access speed more than ten times faster than today's modems. Since much of the growth in sales and profitability experienced by the local telephone and cable companies during the last few years has been tied to Internet access, the infrastructure for this key new demand area will not be ignored.

Spending on technology infrastructure is also a high priority for companies outside the telecommunications services industry. Any company seeking a technological competitive advantage moving into the next century sees the need for technology structures investment. In addition, office buildings must have upgraded hardware, software, cabling, and high-electrical capacity in order to attract the best tenants.

Office Buildings

The national office market has enjoyed steadily improving conditions throughout much of the past five years. The office-vacancy rate has been more than cut in half, from close to 20% early in the decade to a 15-year low of 8.9% during the fourth quarter 1998. The good times may be ending as vacancy rates rose for the first time since 1991 during the first quarter of 1999.

The improvement in the office-building vacancy rate had been driven by robust office-space absorption created by the booming job market for business services. The national unemployment rate is the lowest in a generation. One of the most important sources of office demand, the financial services industry, has been on an astounding run of strong growth. The surge in the stock market had induced banks to hire aggressively in the last few years. However, the stock market cannot reasonably be expected to maintain their heady pace of growth forever.

There has been a clear acceleration in building activity recently, which is expected to continue into early next decade. The nation's office market will continue to enjoy strong conditions throughout 1999 before slowing in 2000 with the rest of the U.S. economy. While vacancy rates have hit bottom, they will remain low enough through 2000 to support strong rent growth. New-building activity will begin to weigh on office-space prices by 2000.

Government and Educational Buildings

Government building construction is expected to rebound sharply in the next few years, and the key areas of growth will be courthouses and education buildings. Building for the education sector has grown at a 3% annual rate over the last ten years, and it is projected to grow by 8% in 1999.

Due to demographic trends, the educational building push to date has been for elementary schools—districts are struggling to find the space to house children of the baby-boom generation. This same cohort will be moving on to secondary school in the years ahead, and high school enrollment is expected to grow by about 15% over the next ten years. WEFA expects this to stimulate additions and new building at the high school level. Furthermore, increased demand for more elaborate electrical and mechanical systems, especially those supporting computer systems and telecommunications, makes schools more expensive to build. In addition, the advent of vouchers and other school-choice plans has prompted further competition, and therefore more upgrades and enhancements to facilities in an effort to draw enrollment.

Industrial Construction

Industrial-construction activity has been declining since 1996. Industrial construction will decline again in 1999 and 2000 before a slight recovery in 2001. With a few exceptions, such as the large chemical producers and steel mini-mills, manufacturers have channeled their investment in the last few years into more efficient production machinery and high-tech gear at the expense of capacity expansion projects. This trend is likely to persist in the foreseeable future, but the rate of spending for equipment is likely to slow in the face of reduced business profits. The near- to medium-term outlook for industrial construction does not look promising, as the economy enters a lower growth phase. Slower domestic-demand growth and falling exports to Asia have combined to reduce capacity utilization rates for manufacturers, and with lower utilization comes reduced need to build more plants.

Most of the action in industrial construction is expected to be concentrated abroad, particularly in the Middle East and the richer developing countries of Asia and Latin America that are aggressively building their industrial infrastructure. The 1998 global financial crisis put a damper on construction projects in these regions. But WEFA expects this activity to resume its strong pace of growth once healthy economic growth returns.

Hotels and Recreational Facilities

Hotels, gaming centers, and sports facilities are additional markets of steady growth for the nonresidential construction industry. Convention centers and sports stadiums are viewed as great vehicles for urban renewal, particularly in mid-sized cities. If a city does not have a convention center or a sports team, it wants one; if it does, the city wants to expand it. Some cities are experiencing a resurgence of hotel activity, particularly in the business class niche, but as with office space, suburban projects are hotter.

However, WEFA expects a drop in those markets by 2000, with new amusement construction leading the downside trend. This industry is solid but volatile, and will simply be waiting for firmer footing to resume the fun and games.

Retail Space

One sector of the nonresidential-construction market that is not expected to see much growth is retail facilities. A decade of overbuilding has created a surplus of undifferentiated property. Regional malls have been subjected to the competition of big-box, get-it-all-in-one-place stores. Despite some strip-mall activity, tied mainly to newly developed suburban towns, the demand for additional retail space is forecast to be weak, but focused on big-box construction. The impact of the Internet also increases uncertainty in the conventional brick and mortar retail sector.

International Markets

The large American construction companies are increasingly chasing work overseas as competition intensifies in domestic markets with restrained public spending. Over the long run, construction growth in mature economies is expected to be modest.

Size is important in the multi-national construction market. The large companies with healthy balance sheets are able to make investments in power, water, and transportation projects. These companies also have the scale to provide a full range of skills for customers that is unmatched at smaller competitors. Also, these large groups are better positioned to set up cross-border takeovers, mergers, and joint ventures with foreign construction companies.

1997 was a stellar year in the international market. But, the Asian financial crisis put a damper on 1998. Recovery is now underway in many countries. WEFA is still optimistic about the tremendous growth potential of international markets in the longer term.

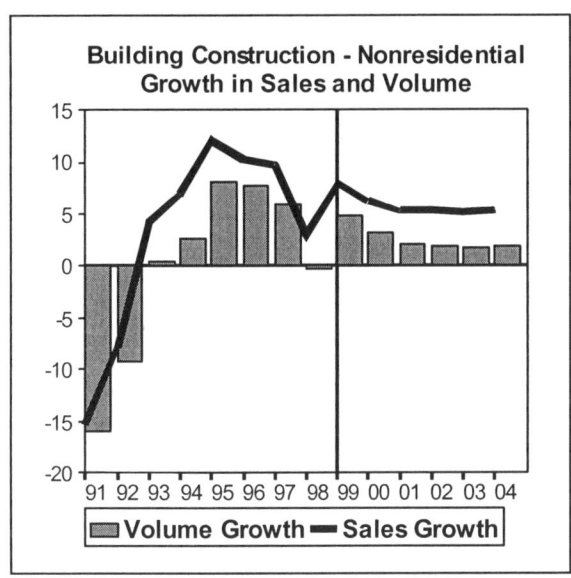

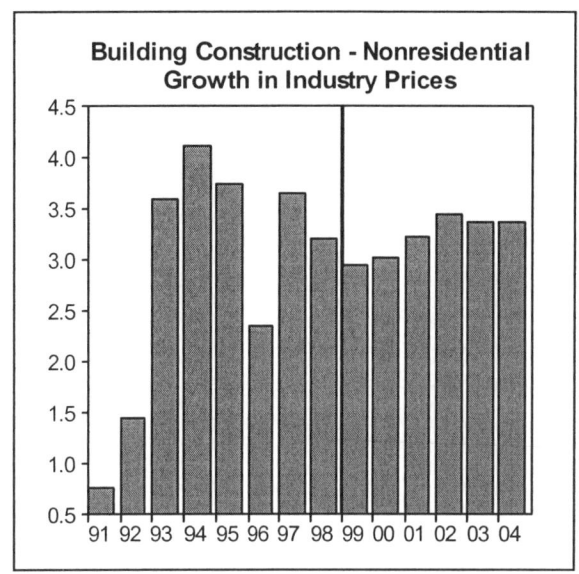

Building Construction - Private Nonresidential

SIC Part of 15-17

		1992	1993	1994	1995	1996	1997	1998	1999	2000	2001	Compound Average 88-98	Annual Growth 98-08
Sales													
	Billions of $	351.0	365.4	390.7	438.0	482.9	529.7	545.3	588.8	625.3	658.2		
	% Ch	-7.9	4.1	6.9	12.1	10.3	9.7	2.9	8.0	6.2	5.3	3.1	5.8
Volume													
	% Ch	-9.2	0.4	2.7	8.1	7.7	5.9	-0.3	4.9	3.1	2.0	0.1	2.3
Prices													
	% Ch	1.4	3.6	4.1	3.7	2.3	3.6	3.2	2.9	3.0	3.2	3.0	3.4
Production Costs													
Avg. Hourly Earnings													
	$/hr	14.30	14.55	14.99	15.30	15.79	16.23	16.90	17.50	18.00	18.44		
	% Ch	1.1	1.7	3.1	2.0	3.2	2.8	4.1	3.6	2.8	2.4	2.7	3.0
Input Price Index													
	% Ch	1.2	2.4	2.4	3.6	0.9	1.7	0.5	1.0	2.5	2.7	2.0	2.6

Part 2: Nondurable Goods Manufacturing

Chapter 5: Food and Kindred Products

Food and Kindred Products

With sales of $498 billion expected for 1999, the Food and Kindred products industry (SIC 20) comprises the largest manufacturing sector in the U.S. economy. The industry is composed of manufacturing firms that process and distribute intermediate and final goods, food, and beverage products. Specific industry classes include: meat packing and processing industries, dairy products industries, fruits and vegetables canning and processing industries, baked goods, sugar and confectionery processing industries, beverage industries that produce malt and distilled beverages, wine, and soft drinks, industries that produce cereal and breakfast foods, and those that produce convenience and snack foods. Recent demographic trends at the retail level towards poultry and fish products, foods that are lower in fat content, and prepared and ready-to-eat foods have made marked changes in the composition of production. For the industry as a whole, both volume demand and prices should continue rising at about 2% per year over the next ten years.

Consumer Markets

Several key trends have been responsible for changes in retail food and beverage markets. The United States has a large population, but one that is aging and more health conscious as it grows more slowly. Nevertheless, despite slow population growth, the secular increase in dual-wage earning families has expanded consumer incomes. However, smaller family size and a shift away from time-intensive activities have led to greater expenditure per capita on goods and services whose consumption requires less time. Hence, a more pronounced shift occurs away from foods prepared in the home and towards ready-to-eat and prepared foods outside of the home. Not only has change led towards an expansion of traditional restaurants, but it has also led to fairly dramatic changes in the types of food and beverages consumed. Indeed, higher incomes and greater consumer information about products and prices have expanded the demand for greater variety. Food and beverage manufacturers have found immensely more competition as the diversity of products has expanded through niche players and already established firms. The cola wars of the past have seemingly spawned the bottled water and juice wars of the present. Important income and demographic trends in the U.S. population have given rise to increased segmentation along price and quality dimensions.

Per-capita beef consumption in the United States has fallen by 25% since 1975, due largely to publicized concerns over heart disease and obesity. The trend leveled in the early 1990s but the movement away from red meat will continue, although perhaps at a slower pace, as health consciousness rises and the population ages. Pork consumption per capita, however, has remained stable or even gained a bit since 1970. Fish consumption per capita gained in the 1970s and in the early 1980s, only to level off since then. WEFA expects the uptrend in fish consumption per person to resume at a modest pace in the years ahead.

The big gainer in meat consumption has been poultry, where per-capita consumption has virtually doubled since 1975. Chicken and turkey are likely to continue taking market share from red meat, but at a slower rate.

Beverage demand has grown over the last decade, but not all sectors are gainers. Demand for soft drinks on a per-capita basis has risen quite sharply over the past few years with the economic expansion, but it is not likely to advance so rapidly in the period ahead. We expect upcoming soft-drink sales to rise more in line with the increase in population. Fruit beverages, at roughly 13% of total beverage volume, should experience solid gains and a rising share of the market as interest in health and nutrition increases. Bottled water is another category gaining increased market share. Beer consumption per capita, which had been declining through the mid-1990s, has increased lately, but only marginally. With the proliferation of microbreweries, the United States had more brewers in 1997 (1,250) than at any time since the end of Prohibition. However, microbreweries are at a consolidation and shakeout stage, somewhat similar to what has occurred among the large brewing companies over the past decade or so. This recent peak in the number of brewers will not advance much further; it is more likely to decline. Wine consumption per capita remains fairly stable.

The fourth-largest segment of the food and kindred products industry, after red meat, poultry, and beverages, is milk. Milk consumption per person in the United States has declined 20% since 1975, a decline almost as steep as that of red meat. Part of this decline is due to demographic changes and part is due to rising concerns about fat content in the diet. This health trend is observable in the details of consumption by type of milk: per-capita consumption of whole milk is currently 60% below its 1975 level, while that of low-fat and skim milk has almost doubled. The rising average age of the U.S. population and concerns about health suggest a continued, albeit slowing decline in milk consumption per capita.

Demand for processed foods that are easy to prepare continues strong. Margins on these products tend to be higher than for more raw foodstuffs, and U.S. companies are also looking to expand these product markets internationally. Overall food-volume demand should continue to grow at or slightly above 2% per year through the next 10 years. Prices will rise by a similar rate.

Industry Conditions and Trends

With sales of $498 billion expected for 1999, the food and beverage industries comprise the largest manufacturing sector in the U.S. economy. Although over 90% of U.S. output is shipped domestically, growth has been largely driven by exports. Indeed, the United States is second only to France in global shipments of food and beverages. With the U.S. population growing at slower rates, export markets will become increasingly important in value of future industry shipment. Unfortunately with a decline in world economic growth since late 1997, export markets for domestic producers have shrunk and a substantial amount of excess capacity has resulted. Capacity utilization for the industry, measured by the Federal Reserve Board of Governors, dipped to below 80% in 1999, well below the 85% peak of the mid-1990s. Consequently, capital expenditures for domestic capacity and R&D have been flat in nominal dollars. However with the increasing importance of foreign markets, U.S. firms in the industry have invested almost three times as much in foreign affiliates as they have in domestic capacity.

Most of the industries classified in the Food and Kindred sector tend to be concentrated. Cereal breakfast foods and cane sugar refining provide two highly concentrated examples in which the top-four companies make 85% of shipments. Indeed, roughly two-thirds of the industries classified in this sector have a four-firm concentration ratio (based on shipments) of 40% or greater.

Changing demographics and consumer tastes towards retail food and beverage products have dramatically changed the variety of products manufactured. Manufacturers have updated and extended product lines, whether through de novo production or acquisition. Private label products thrive despite strong branded product positions. Indeed the fortunes of manufacturers of national brands have varied with their focus on brand management. The soft-drink product lines of major national manufacturers have been extended to include juices and bottled water in a competitive effort to capture share in all market segments. Expect continued product extensions and shoring up of brand position by large manufacturers.

Price Factors

Longer term, prices for processed foods and feeds tend to rise in line with overall inflation, not in line with prices of the raw farm products that serve as the industry's primary inputs. Price surges in farm products due to supply shocks and crop problems are not passed on to consumers dollar for dollar. Consumers can often switch from one type of food that has increased sharply in price, to another where prices have not risen. As a result, processors will absorb some raw-input price increases in an attempt to remain competitive. Conversely, when input prices drop, food processors tend to retain the savings.

Outlook

Food processing companies have been devoting increasing energies toward the development and marketing of prepared foods, particularly items such as heat-and-serve products and multi-course meals. The demand for these options has expanded from dinner selections to items for both breakfast and lunch. This pattern is likely to continue as no reversal in the trend toward two-income, time-starved families is expected.

Interest in nutrition, a high priority for many Americans, has already played a role in reconfiguring the selection of edibles available to consumers. In general, WEFA expects health-related considerations to drive a gradual increase in market share for higher vitamin, fiber-rich, lower calorie, or otherwise nutritionally beneficial items. Yet a backlash against the health-oriented trend may simultaneously be emerging—at least in regards to a well-publicized, recent butterfat shortage. Consumers have not put their desire to indulge in high-fat foods such as ice cream in abeyance. Another question the food industry faces is whether consumers will embrace a newly approved fat substitute (actually made of real fat, but in molecules too large to digest), marketed in potato chips and other products under the trade name Olean.

The rising degree of consolidation in the supermarket industry will affect food product manufacturers. As retail distribution becomes increasingly dominated by a small number of ultra-large chains, smaller processors confront a greater challenge negotiating their way onto store shelves. An "echo" trend towards consolidation in the processing sector would not be a surprise. How- ever, small producers of niche foods—including natural foods and, especially, a widening range of ethnic foods—can probably maintain growth above the industry average.

Risks to the Forecast

Demand for food products overall tends to be fairly consistent with population growth, not responding in step with changes in income levels. In the long term, however, changing consumer needs will provide opportunities for new product offerings—for items geared toward ease of preparation and better nutrition—and the success of these offerings will come, to some extent, at the expense of traditional food products. Increasing restaurant traffic also represents a longer term threat to sales for the food-at-home market (though, of course, food product companies sell to restaurants, too). Eating out or buying ready-to-eat foods is more expensive than preparing meals, limiting the prospective decline in traditional food products. On the other hand, Americans spend a historically low percentage of their income on food.

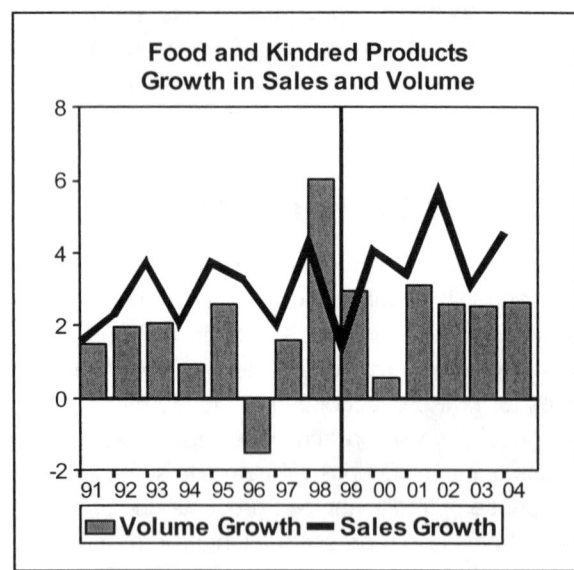

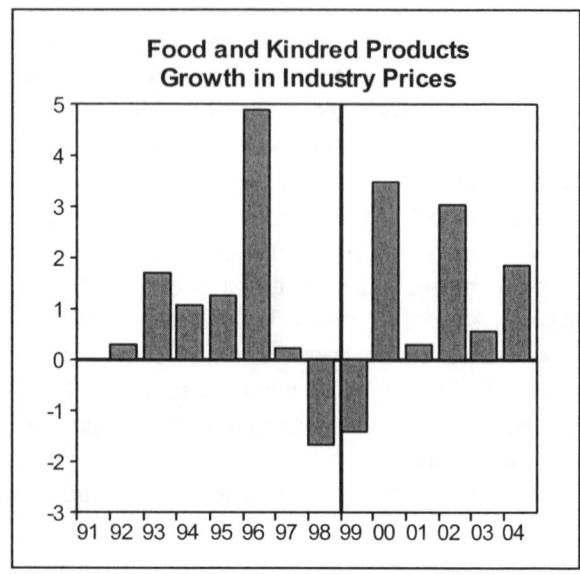

Food and Kindred Products

SIC 20

		1992	1993	1994	1995	1996	1997	1998	1999	2000	2001	Compound Average 88-98	Annual Growth 98-08
Sales													
	Billions of $	406.8	422.0	430.6	446.8	461.4	470.7	490.7	497.8	518.1	535.8		
	% Ch	2.3	3.7	2.1	3.7	3.3	2.0	4.3	1.4	4.1	3.4	3.3	4.3
Volume													
	% Ch	1.9	2.1	0.9	2.6	-1.5	1.6	6.0	2.9	0.5	3.1	1.7	2.3
Prices													
	% Ch	0.3	1.7	1.1	1.3	4.9	0.2	-1.7	-1.4	3.5	0.3	1.5	2.0
Production Costs													
Avg. Hourly Earnings													
	$/hr	11.94	12.24	12.47	12.73	13.05	13.37	13.70	13.97	14.49	15.01		
	% Ch	3.0	2.5	1.9	2.1	2.5	2.5	2.4	2.0	3.7	3.6	2.6	3.5
Input Price Index													
	% Ch	-0.6	2.4	-0.2	1.4	5.2	-0.6	-2.7	-1.8	3.0	-0.8	1.0	1.9

Chapter 6:   Tobacco

Tobacco

The U.S. cigarette industry remains in turmoil. Price increases, higher state taxes, expanding regulation, and declining consumption have forced the industry to significantly adjust their way of business. Furthermore, these issues are expected to continue over the foreseeable future.

Profits have been historically outstanding in the cigarette industry. However, the sector's operating performance and profitability will diminish significantly and become less stable. Legal battles, legal settlements, and other required payments are all impacting the bottom line. In contrast, cigar manufacturers are still seeing an increase in sales. However, the rate of growth is slowing.

Cigar smoking has increased steadily since 1993. Most of this growth is fad-related; but it has also been aided by the perception that cigars do not carry the same health risks as cigarettes. U.S. cigar makers, however, will have to contend with import penetration currently amounting to roughly two-thirds of cigar sales. This high level of imports has placed a few U.S. cigar manufacturers in a vulnerable position. Their long-term survival will be in jeopardy despite the domestic growth of cigar consumption.

Demand

The negative publicity associated with cigarette smoking has significantly altered U.S. demand. During the 1960s, approximately 42% of the population smoked. This share has fallen steadily to below 25%. In 1998, smokers consumed an estimated 470 billion cigarettes, 2.1% fewer than were consumed a year earlier. Additionally, consumption per person (16 years and older) declined 2.0%.

In foreign countries, per-capita cigarette consumption has historically been substantially higher than in the United States. This, along with the strong popularity and image of American cigarettes, has helped the U.S. tobacco-export market for years. However, the strong export market has turned soft lately. International demand for U.S.-blend cigarettes declined by more than 7% to 201 billion pieces in 1998. Exports to the European Union fell 3% and shipments to Asia declined 5%. Surprisingly, exports to Japan increased 5%.

The largest decline in foreign-cigarette sales last year occurred in Russia. Economic problems and the fall of the ruble led to a 40% decline in exports after a four-fold surge in 1996. From a value perspective, total 1998 U.S. cigarette exports actually increased by $137 million more than 1997, but they still remained $900 million below 1996's record $5.9 billion.

In contrast, the cigar market remains on the upswing. In 1997, the growth was 17%. In 1998, consumption increased 6% to 3.7 billion cigars. While this is still well below the 9 billion smoked in 1965, it implies that the current cigar fad is continuing. Another increase in cigar consumption is likely in 1999, and cigar bars and special-smoke shops will remain the focus of attention. Fads can change rapidly and cigars could easily fall out of fashion as fast as they entered. However, WEFA expects the cigar market will slow in growth rather than decline over the coming years. One upside to the cigar market is that its smokers have traded quantity for quality. They may smoke fewer in number than they did years ago, but they are more willing to pay extra for quality brands.

The consumption of pipe and roll-your-own cigarette tobacco has also fallen in 1998. Pipe smoking has not experienced the same popularity as cigars. It is possible that pipe smoking could come into vogue as did cigars, but such a trend has not yet materialized.

Overall, tobacco-manufacturers' sales volume eroded from 1991 through 1993, then surged in 1994 as demand picked up in response to the significant price cuts put in place for cigarettes in 1993 and 1994. Volume continued to grow during the 1995-1997 period, albeit at a more moderate pace, then took a dive in 1998. Sales in 1999 are expected to post another significant decline. Over the next few years, WEFA expects the downward trend to continue. Domestic demand will decline at a fairly consistent pace, but exports should also drop. The economic problems in Asia, which has one of the highest per-capita cigarette-consumption rates in the world, have not helped U.S.-cigarette exports. In Asia, domestic brands have been substituted for expensive U.S. products. This should slowly change as the Asian economies improve.

Pricing Environment

The rise of discount cigarette brands hurt industry pricing in the early 1990s. Prices received by manufacturers of tobacco products fell 5.5% in 1993 and 13.8% in 1994, in marked contrast to the industry's double-digit price hikes in the three prior years. In 1998, manufacturers increased wholesale cigarette prices five times. The final increase of 45 cents per pack in November 1998 was the largest. Total price increases in 1998 boosted the wholesale price by 49%, including federal excise tax. The wholesale prices of cigarettes, including federal tax, at the end of 1998 was $97.20 per 1000 cigarettes. In 1997, it was $65.45 per 1000. Cigarette prices jumped in response to the settlement between the state attorneys general and manufacturers.

Future cigarette price increases are likely to again exceed the average gains posted by the overall domestic-manufacturing industry. The ability to push through higher-than-average price increases reflects two forces: producers' desire to recoup litigation costs associated with the industry, and the rather low sensitivity of smokers to price increases.

Supply Conditions

By 1993, discount-cigarette brands had captured nearly one-third of U.S. sales volume. The two biggest firms, R.J. Reynolds and Philip Morris, did not sit idly watching their market ebb away—between the two of them, they managed to capture roughly 60% of the discount market. However, these product offerings were considerably less profitable than their name brands, so while the strategy may have saved some market share it didn't do much for profit margins.

The gradual return of market share for premium brands has been a hard-fought battle. Because image is such a

strong force in the cigarette market, a tremendous amount has been spent on advertising and other marketing campaigns. Coupons, special cigarette brand-name clothing catalogs, and trial-pack giveaways have all been featured for a number of years. We believe the industry will continue to seek a higher market share for its premium brands, despite a ban on giveaways and certain advertising channels. By the start of 2000, the discount-brand share will again fall below 25%. As a result, a more favorable profit outcome is to be expected.

Major Trends Affecting the Outlook

As the percentage of people who smoke in the United States declines, the domestic market will become even more difficult. However, the international market still presents a considerable opportunity. The problems in Asia and Russia will continue to have a significant impact on the foreign demand for U.S. cigarettes, but only in the short term. WEFA expects U.S. cigarettes to regain their popularity among foreign smokers, once these economies begin to improve and the dollar loses some of its strength. Internationally, U.S. cigarette manufacturers have a very strong competitive advantage with respect to marketing and manufacturing. This dominance is likely to grow in the long term, especially when many of the foreign-owned government monopolies in cigarette manufacturing eventually become privatized.

However, U.S. cigar makers have to contend with the opposite impact. The cigar-import penetration rate of close to 66% of sales has combined with the strong dollar to place the relatively few U.S. cigar manufacturers in a vulnerable position. Their long-term survival will be in jeopardy despite the domestic growth of cigar consumption.

Risks to the Forecast

The greatest risk to tobacco manufacturers continues to be the threat of new anti-smoking initiatives. Furthermore, new private legal battles are surfacing every day. The discovery that cigarette manufacturers have known the addictive properties of nicotine for many years also sheds light on the new judgments against the producers.

On November 16, 1998, the state attorneys general and cigarette manufacturers signed an agreement to reimburse states for the costs of treating smoking-related illnesses and to reduce underage smoking. Within a few days, 47 states and territories (there were four previous settlements) had signed on with the agreement. This does not require Congressional approval, unlike the 1997 agreement. The key elements of the pact are:

1) $206 billion to be paid to states over 25 years.

2) $1.5 billion over 10 years to support anti-smoking measures plus $250 million to fund research into reducing youth smoking.

3) Limitations on advertising.

4) Ban on cartoon characters in advertising.

5) Ban on "branded" merchandise.

6) Limitations on sporting-event sponsorship.

7) Disbanding to tobacco-trade organizations.

Another major threat to cigarette makers is the trend toward ever-rising taxation of tobacco products. It is popular among government officials needing extra tax revenue to add a few more cents to a pack of cigarettes, and such taxes are popular as a means to reduce teen smoking. Cigarette demand is relatively price inelastic, but there must be a threshold point when rising taxes will start to have a major impact on demand.

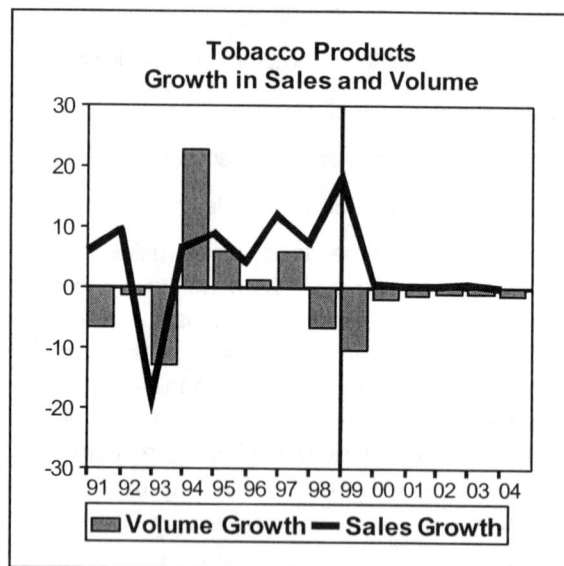

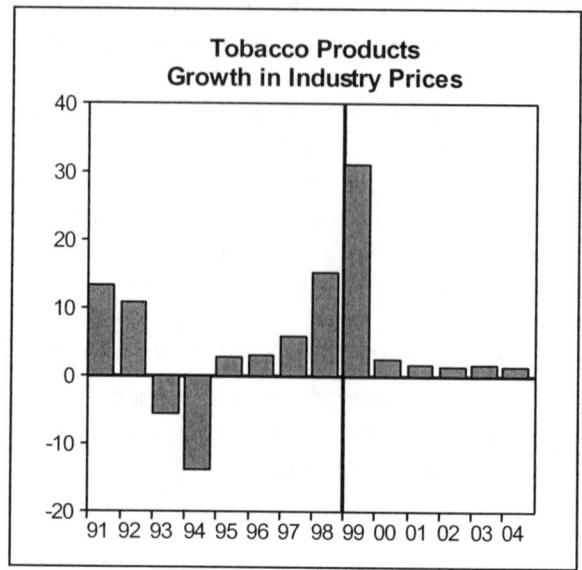

Tobacco Products

SIC 21

	1992	1993	1994	1995	1996	1997	1998	1999	2000	2001	Compound Average 88-98	Annual Growth 98-08
Sales												
Billions of $	34.82	28.47	30.37	33.08	34.49	38.69	41.57	49.12	49.43	49.54		
% Ch	9.5	-18.2	6.7	8.9	4.3	12.2	7.5	18.2	0.6	0.2	5.9	2.4
Volume												
% Ch	-1.3	-12.9	22.9	5.9	1.2	5.9	-6.5	-10.3	-1.7	-1.4	0.3	-2.0
Prices												
% Ch	10.9	-5.5	-13.8	2.9	3.0	5.9	15.3	31.2	2.4	1.6	5.5	4.4
Production Costs												
Avg. Hourly Earnings												
$/hr	16.99	16.97	19.12	19.53	19.45	19.39	18.74	18.86	19.38	19.96		
% Ch	0.9	-0.1	12.7	2.1	-0.4	-0.3	-3.3	0.7	2.8	3.0	2.4	2.7
Input Price Index												
% Ch	4.0	-1.6	-3.6	6.1	2.0	1.8	5.9	11.1	2.1	2.0	3.5	2.9

Chapter 7: Textile Mill Products

Broadwoven Fabrics and Other Textiles

Broadwoven fabrics basically consist of three categories: cotton fabrics, wool fabrics, and fabrics made of manmade fibers (polyester, etc.) and silk. Broadwoven fabrics are the largest single segment of the textile industry, accounting for about 60.0% of the $81.0 billion volume of textile mill product shipments. Finished output from these manufacturers in turn provides raw-material inputs for manufacturers of apparel, home furnishings, and other finished goods. Surging textile and apparel imports in recent years have resulted in substantial downsizing and consolidation within the industry. Volume demand for U.S. manufactures of broadwoven fabrics is expected to rise less than 1.0% in the next decade, along with about a 1.0% per annum gain for price.

Industry Demand

In 1998, the United States produced 16.8 billion square yards of broadwoven fabrics of all types—cotton, manmade fiber, and wool. This was down about 1.0% from the 17.0 billion yards woven in 1997; this sector's highest output since the early 1970s. Cotton broadwoven fabrics accounts for roughly 30.0% of the yardage, manmade fiber broadwoven about 69.0%, and wool fabrics not quite 1.0%.

Cotton fabrics are used as inputs for three general end-product categories: apparel, home furnishings, and industrial products. Within the apparel end-market segment, the largest demand is from the cotton outerwear market. Cotton outerwear is a mature industry, and has been hit hard by imports. A rise in outerwear imports usually also represents an indirect import of raw-cotton fabric, since most imported garments are cut and sewn from fabrics manufactured abroad. In recent years, imports have also been making some significant inroads in the home furnishings sector.

Second only to trade in its impact on demand for broadwoven cotton products is home construction, which drives the market for home furnishings. The demand for industrial products using fibers is concentrated in the auto market and construction activity on new highways and bridges. In 1997–1998, according to the American Textile Manufactures Institute, close to 5.1 billion square yards of cotton broadwoven fabrics were produced in the United States. This sector has been improving in recent years, from around the 4.5 billion square yards level that it had been stuck at for more than a decade. Denim fabric has come back to life in recent years, with production in

excess of a billion square yards for the last five years. Demand for denim has been a strong driver in the cotton broadwoven fabric sector.

In the manmade segment of broadwoven fabrics, imports and consumer preferences for natural fibers are key issues. Television and other media ad campaigns promoting cotton products have died down in recent years and manmade fiber consumption, up 10.5% versus 1995, has been making a comeback. The balance of these offsetting trends has kept manmade-fiber broadwoven fabric output fairly constant at about 11.5 million square yards since 1992.

Imports, both of finished products (apparel and home furnishings) and fabric, have done tremendous damage to the broadwoven fabric industry. In 1998, there was a record 25.9 billion square yards equivalent of textile and apparel manufactures imported into this country. This was 13.0% higher than the prior year and double the level at the start of the decade. The United States runs close to a $50.0 billion trade imbalance in textiles and apparel. This, too, has more than doubled in a 10-year span.

An important development was the recent accord with China, which will keep in place almost $20 million in tariff increases imposed on Chinese fabric imports at the end of 1996. This agreement also holds annual gains in textile and apparel exports to roughly 1.0%. In contrast to the substantial growth of imports in 1998, imports of textile products from China fell almost 10%, while apparel imports were off about 4%. This was a result of the Asian crisis and subsequent currency devaluation, which gave Indonesian, Malaysian, and Thailand textiles and apparel a competitive edge in world markets. Also, China was penalized for transshipping in 1997, which severely limited their quota for 1998.

High business-failure rates, strong unions, and large cyclical swings categorize most segments of the U.S. textile industry, including broadwovens. Another major issue for the industry is trade pacts, including the Multi-Fiber Arrangement (MFA) and NAFTA. With the phase-out of the MFA over the next 15 years and the GATT plan that will phase in completely by 2010, the industry faces a grave challenge to reshape itself so it can viably face international competition. Concerning NAFTA, many parts of the industry will suffer under the accord, finding it difficult to compete on an equal basis with lower wages. The trade pact will likely be positive, however, for the fabric portion of the industry since it requires full sourcing of fabrics from the United States in Mexican apparel production.

According to the American Textile Manufacturers Association, in 1998 the United States imported $7.5 billion of textiles and apparel from Mexico, an increase of almost 26.0% from the prior year. Exports grew also, +22.6%; but with only $4.5 billion exported to Mexico the trade deficit widened to $3.0 billion. This trade deficit with Mexico was almost all in apparel, a shortfall of $4.0 billion. U.S. fabric exports to Mexico amounted to $1.4 billion in 1997 compared to imports of only $353.6 million, a surplus of a billion dollars.

In dollar terms, industry shipments of broadwoven fabrics and other textiles peaked in 1997 at just over $51.0 billion. In 1998, shipments slipped almost 5.0% to $48.7 billion. WEFA expects more of the same in 1999, and some stabilization in 2000. Longer term, the outlook calls for expansion of 1.4%, with one-third of this gain coming from real growth and the rest from price appreciation. This represents a slight deterioration from the past ten years, when shipments rose 1.7% a year, with more inflation (+1.2%).

Supply Conditions

Surging textile and apparel imports in recent years have resulted in substantial downsizing and consolidation within the fabric industry. Both payroll expense and capital investment per establishment remain above the all-industry average, however, while shipments per establishment is below average. The result is lower profit

margins than the average U.S. manufacturing establishment. For the past three years, the net return on sales for the textile industry has averaged about 3.0% a year, compared to roughly 6.0% for all manufacturing.

The industry's high usage of capital equipment provides a barrier to entry, which protects long-time producers; but in times of sluggish profitability, the high cost of upgrading and modernizing a capital-intensive production process can hinder the industry's ability to remain competitive with foreign producers. The industry has spent between $2.5 and $3.0 billion on new plant and equipment in the last few years.

Pricing Environment

One of the problems affecting profit margins in this industry has been producers' difficulty in pushing through price increases. In the last two years, output prices for broadwoven fabrics have fallen. Over the next few years, we see little reason for this trend to change. The level of imports during this period will continue to play an important role in influencing domestic prices, and the Asian crisis and the strong dollar may well exacerbate already weak fabric pricing. The expected trend between output pricing and input prices translates to heightened profit pressures for the long haul.

Major Trends Affecting the Outlook

WEFA's outlook for the U.S. economy over the long term is for modest growth, in the area of 2.5% a year. U.S. housing starts, following an unexpected rise to about 1.6 million units in 1998 and 1999, are forecast to run at a trend rate in the low 1.4 million unit range for the long run. Personal consumption expenditures for apparel and shoes, discounted for inflation, have been outstanding in recent years, rising about 6.0% per annum since the recession low of 1991. Long-term apparel spending is expected to increase about 2.5% annually.

Major Risks to the Forecast

Raw-commodity prices for both cotton and wool play important roles in the health of the corresponding segments of the broadwoven fabrics industry. Bad weather or other supply problems can suddenly pose a threat to the stability of both the availability and cost of these important inputs. Pricing spreads between input costs and wholesale output prices in synthetic fibers can also be problematic. The outlook calls for relatively little materials disruption to occur, with input prices rising 1.2% a year for the next ten years, which is slightly lower than the last decade.

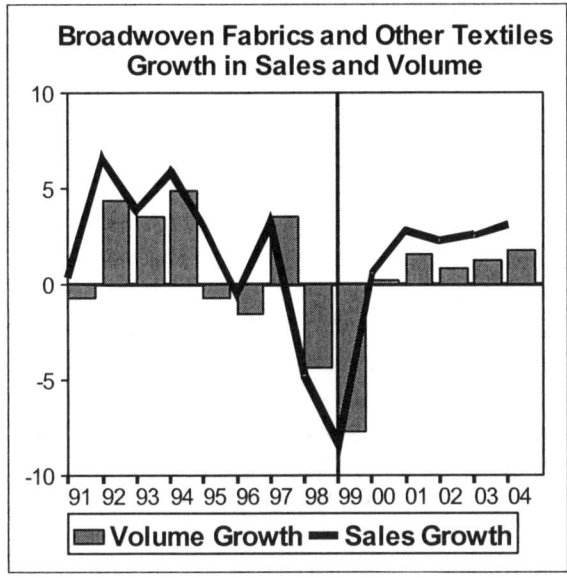

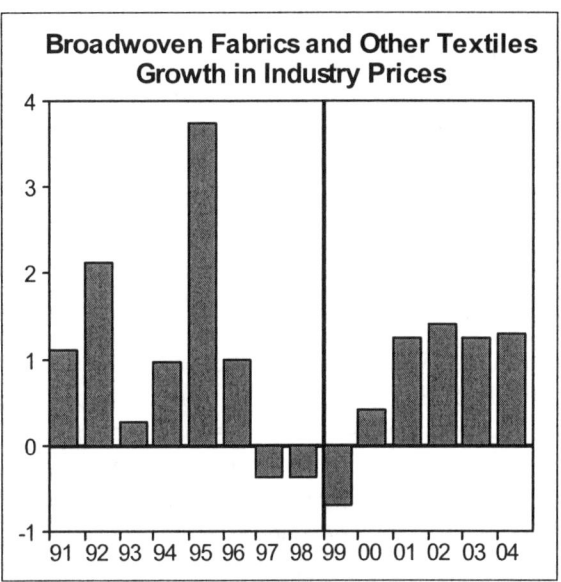

Broadwoven Fabrics and Other Textiles
SIC 221-4, 226, 228-9

		1992	1993	1994	1995	1996	1997	1998	1999	2000	2001	Compound Average 88-98	Annual Growth 98-08
Sales													
	Billions of $	43.97	45.66	48.36	49.81	49.55	51.14	48.71	44.64	44.91	46.17		
	% Ch	6.6	3.8	5.9	3.0	-0.5	3.2	-4.7	-8.4	0.6	2.8	1.7	1.4
Volume													
	% Ch	4.4	3.6	4.9	-0.7	-1.5	3.6	-4.4	-7.7	0.2	1.5	0.5	0.5
Prices													
	% Ch	2.1	0.3	1.0	3.7	1.0	-0.4	-0.4	-0.7	0.4	1.2	1.2	0.9
Production Costs													
Avg. Hourly Earnings													
	$/hr	8.96	9.26	9.50	9.79	10.06	10.43	10.79	11.02	11.28	11.56		
	% Ch	4.0	3.4	2.6	3.0	2.8	3.7	3.4	2.2	2.3	2.5	3.5	3.1
Input Price Index													
	% Ch	-2.0	0.8	3.7	6.7	0.5	-0.9	-1.9	-2.9	0.0	1.5	1.4	1.2

Knitting Mill Products

The knitting mill products industry ships roughly $20 billion worth of products at the manufacturer level, and represents about a quarter of the textile industry's overall shipments. Knitting mill products include women's hosiery (9%), hosiery other than women's (16%), knit outerwear (25%), knit underwear and nightwear (6%), weft (circular) knit mills (30%), and lace and warp knit mills (14%.). Surging textile and apparel imports in recent years have resulted in substantial downsizing and consolidation within the knit outerwear industry. Much of the final demand for this industry comes from apparel purchases. Overall, the knitting industry is expected to remain relatively flat in the next few years.

Industry Demand

Outerwear and weft, or circular, fabrics represent 55% of the output of this industry. Outerwear has performed better than weft fabrics recently due to changing trends in leisure and active wear. The T-shirt market has been one of the fastest growing in the textile industry, especially T-shirts with messages and logos imprinted on them. Weft, or circular, fabrics typically sell their output to manufacturers of outerwear, underwear, and other products in the apparel and home furnishings industries. In the latter, carpets and rugs are an important source of demand for knit mill products.

There are a few trends currently shaping the knit industry. In recent years, there has been a decided shift toward more casual and less formal dressing, especially in business, but also for personal. This has favored the use of knit construction, which is far less restrictive and comfortable compared to more traditional cotton and wool broadwoven fabrics. Athletic and logo apparel has been one of the growth engines for the knit sector. Unfortunately, this sector has been oversupplied and sales have slowed of late. This probably is only a temporary phenomenon and the athletic clothing sector, after a brief shake-out and adjustment phase, should return to long-term growth. The retail sector has been "over stored" for quite some time now. The long-term trend to consolidation and store closures reduces the need for inventory throughout the system. This translates to a somewhat lower demand for outerwear, and eventually fabric, down the pipeline.

Final demand for the bulk of this industry comes from apparel and home furnishings purchases, which in turn depend largely upon consumer income and confidence.

The apparel industry is a mature industry and one that has been hurt by imports. Net imports of apparel account for about 40% of consumer spending on apparel. Therefore, the knitting mill sector has not been able to capitalize on a robust economy and strong domestic demand. On a square yardage basis, apparel imports grew by 30% in the last two years, according to the American Textile Manufacturers Institute. The Asian crisis inundated the U.S. market, particularly in the last half of 1998, hurting the knitting industry. In real turns, shipments fell some 6% in 1998. In the long run, therefore, despite WEFA's forecast of 3% to 3.5% average annual growth in real disposable income, the volume of knitting mill product demand over the same period is expected to increase by slightly more than 1% per year.

Supply Conditions

The growth in textile and apparel imports in recent years has resulted in substantial downsizing and consolidation within the knit outerwear industry. The industry appears to have handled this downsizing rather well. Total payroll costs per establishment are on par with the all-industry average, while profitability is above the average—due largely to the industry's much lower capital investment cost per establishment. Weft knit fabric mills, on the other hand, have not suffered the decline in the number of manufacturing establishments that has occurred in the outerwear segment, but the industry has performed more poorly in terms of operating results. The weft industry (hosiery, underwear, lace, and similar products) has both payroll costs and capital equipment costs well above that of the average in manufacturing. Although sales per establishment are also above average, high costs mean that profit margins within the weft mill industry are below average. As a result, investment for either expansion or modernization will be difficult to finance.

Pricing Environment

One of the problems negatively affecting profit margins in this industry overall has been the difficulty the industry has had in pushing through price increases. Between 1990 and 1998, average output prices for all types of knitting mills rose by only about 1% per year. Over the next few years, we expect pricing to remain soft. The level of imports and their pricing play an important role during this period. Furthermore, input factor prices are expected to rise about 1.5% per year, with wages growing roughly 3.5% per annum. Consequently, net profit margins will remain under pressure for the duration of the outlook.

Major Trends Affecting the Outlook

WEFA's outlook for the U.S. economy over the next two to three years is for modest growth of approximately 2.5%. U.S. housing starts are expected to be essentially flat through this period. Apparel sales, discounted for inflation, are likely to be flat. All in all, the picture is one of a rather sluggish outlook for the macro-economic drivers of knitting mill products. Combining our expectation for 1.5% growth in volume and less than 1% expansion in price, overall sales in this industry should expand by about 2% per year on average, or about two full percentage points less per year than the last decade.

Major Risks to the Forecast

The crisis in Asia generated tremendous pressure worldwide in the textile and apparel markets. Asian producers, a key source for cheap clothing and fabric, will continue to try to export their way out of their recession. This will mean more clothing in the global market at distressed prices. Furthermore, China's growth is slowing, and the problems of Southeast Asia could spread. Should China devalue its currency, we may well see a flood of apparel in world markets.

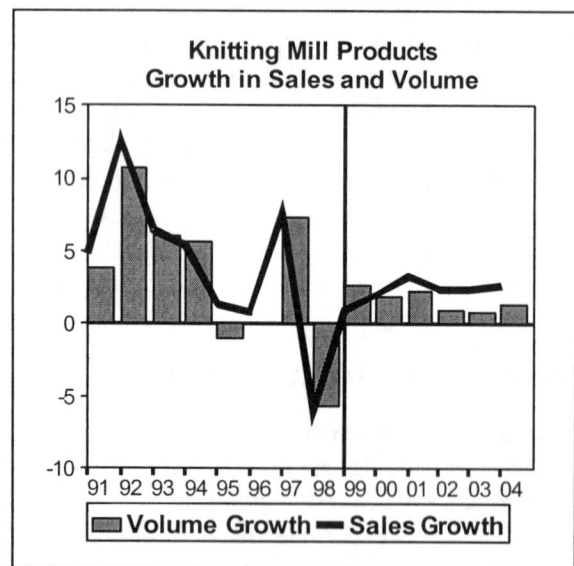

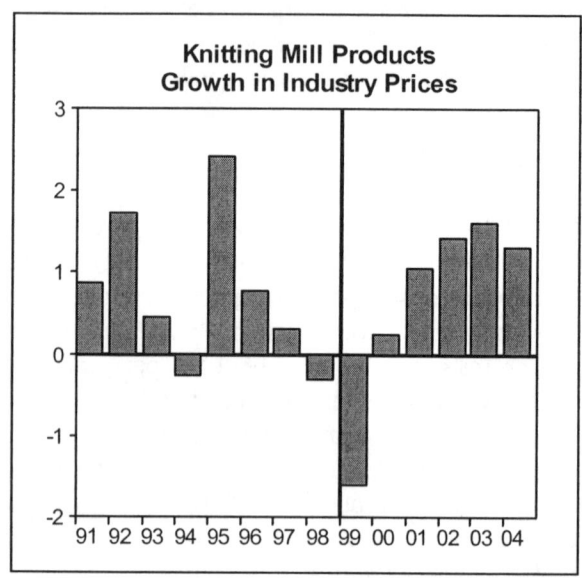

Knitting Mill Products

SIC 225

		1992	1993	1994	1995	1996	1997	1998	1999	2000	2001	Compound Average 88-98	Annual Growth 98-08
Sales													
	Billions of $	16.98	18.08	19.06	19.32	19.49	20.97	19.71	19.91	20.32	20.99		
	% Ch	12.6	6.5	5.4	1.4	0.8	7.6	-6.0	1.0	2.1	3.3	4.1	2.3
Volume													
	% Ch	10.7	6.0	5.7	-1.0	0.1	7.3	-5.7	2.7	1.8	2.2	3.1	1.5
Prices													
	% Ch	1.7	0.5	-0.3	2.4	0.8	0.3	-0.3	-1.6	0.2	1.0	1.0	0.8
Production Costs													
Avg. Hourly Earnings													
	$/hr	7.88	8.11	8.34	8.64	8.86	9.14	9.47	9.95	10.30	10.68		
	% Ch	3.2	2.9	2.9	3.5	2.6	3.1	3.7	5.0	3.6	3.7	3.5	3.5
Input Price Index													
	% Ch	0.9	0.7	1.3	4.8	1.2	0.1	-1.0	-1.2	0.5	1.5	1.4	1.3

Carpets and Rugs

The carpet and rug industry includes manufacturers of woven, tufted, and other carpets and rugs. It also includes aircraft and automobile floor coverings, except rubber and plastic. The manufacturers included in SIC 2273 shipped $12.5 billion in 1998, and the United States is the world leader in tufted carpet and rug consumption and production. Total revenues for the industry are expected to rise about 2.5% per year, long term, as volume demand rises by 1.7% annually and prices by 0.8%.

Demand

Carpets and rugs, although losing out somewhat to competing products, comprise the largest single segment of the U.S. floor coverings industry, roughly 71.0%. In recent years carpeting has lost share to other types of floor treatments—wood and wood laminate (10.5%), ceramic (7.0%), and vinyl (11.5%) tile. The carpet market is divided into two main categories: broadloom carpeting, which holds the lion's share of the volume (81.0%), and area rugs. Although relatively small, area rugs have been a fast growing segment. In the broadloom area, roughly 47.0% of the yardage is sold directly to consumers, mostly for use in renovating (around 75.0%) their current residence; about 24.0% goes directly into new-home construction. The remaining 29.0% is involved in commercial building—hotels, retail stores, hospitals, and offices. New construction generates only about 20.0% of all commercial activity, as renovation is the main driver in this area. Exports represent 8.0% of annual production, imports approximately 5.0%. A small, but very important niche is transportation carpeting, which is sold to the automotive and aircraft industries.

The industry is finally making some headway. The 1990-1991 recession really took its toll on the market, and for the longest time carpet industry sales languished around their low point of $10.5 billion. The last few years have been excellent, however, with revenues moving up into the $12.0 billion neighborhood. More importantly, most of the current growth is in real terms, with yardage expansion of 4.2% and 5.6% in 1997 and 1998, respectively.

Carpets and rugs are a major beneficiary of the spectacular economic climate. The economy has sustained a 3.5% to 4.0% real rate of growth in recent years. Inflation is benign. Stock prices have soared through the roof, taking consumer confidence with them.

Interest rates have been on a downtrend, with declining mortgage rates generating an excellent housing market. Housing starts exploded, jumping from 1.5 million in 1996–1997 to 1.6 million in 1998–1999. Existing home sales moved up to record levels and commercial building was also very strong. To top it all off, car and truck production is at an all-time high, which is good news for transportation carpet. The net result has been a retail boom, which produced a strong demand for replacement carpet, and a construction cycle, which has been conducive to commercial and residential carpet expansion.

Looking forward, the carpet and rug industry will follow the economic fundamentals that drive demand. Homebuilding, spending for renovation, and automobile production are the major sources of demand for carpets and rugs. Overall, however, consumer income and spending are the key variables to watch when analyzing market trends. Consumer spending affects both replacement and redecorating demand for the industry's products, as well as automotive demand. The most important influence on housing starts, and a key variable in auto sales, are interest rates.

Consumer disposable income, in real terms, is expected to grow at a fairly respectable pace over the next few years, in the 3.0% to 3.5% range between 1999 and 2001. On the other hand, the construction side of the equation will not be as robust in the future, with housing starts dropping down into the 1.4 million unit range, and commercial building rising about 1.5% per year. Thus, while the carpet market will do better in the next decade, growth will be tempered somewhat, lagging the recent performance. The forecast calls for carpet shipments to increase by 2.5% a year over the next ten years, a marked acceleration from the 2.0% growth in the 1988–1998 span. Price inflation in the carpet sector is expected to remain around the historical norm, about 1.0% per annum, implying stronger growth in yardage volume, 1.7% versus 1.0% in the last decade.

Supply

The United States is the world leader in tufted carpet and rug consumption and production. The trend toward size and consolidation in the industry is accelerating; in fact, merger mania went wild in the last couple of years. In an eighteen-month period, ending just prior to the start of 1999, approximately $2.5 billion in sales revenue changed hands in North America.

Shaw Industries, the largest carpet manufacturer in the United States, and the world as well, increased their sales from $2.6 to $3.5 billion through acquisition and internal expansion. The top four firms now control two-thirds of the industry, with 86% of the volume accounted for by the top ten. Nonetheless, the industry remains extremely competitive.

Shipment dollars per establishment in the carpet and rug industry is roughly 2.5 times those of the average manufacturing firm, as is the number of employees per establishment. The costs of material inputs to the industry, however, are quite high and these costs have offset the industry's advantages of lower-than-average hourly wages and capital investment cost per establishment. Steep input costs impede profitability and limit the industry's ability to react quickly to changing market conditions.

The situation has taken a dramatic turn for the better. The carpet industry currently consumes about 3.5 billion pounds of synthetic fiber—nylon, polyester, and olefin. Once the almost exclusive territory of the large chemical companies (Du Pont, Allied, and BASF), carpet-fiber production is being supplanted by small independent firms and the carpet companies themselves. Today, there are thirteen carpet mills and four independent producers, extruding (producing) about 1.4 billion pounds of fiber, mostly olefin. This has produced an oversupply, which coupled with declining raw feedstock costs, has caused input prices to fall to historical lows.

Pricing

The size of the players, ample productive capacity, limited growth potential, and competition from other products make price gains extremely hard to generate. Carpets historically have been a good buy for the consumer. Once the purview of the rich (oriental rugs, woven carpets), carpets and rugs are now among the most affordable of products.

A retailing revolution is occurring, which will ensure the bargain basement prices for some time to come. The retail scene is no longer dominated by department or specialty stores, but by mass retailers. Home Depot is the largest single store, with 15% of floor covering retail sales. Home Depot, coming from nowhere, is growing volume at the rate of 20.0% a year. Two other retail groups match Home Depot: Carpet Max and Carpet One. With 45% of the business in the hands of three discount operations, carpets and rug prices should remain in check, rising about 1.0% a year.

Key Trends Affecting the Outlook

Economic growth and job formation should be conducive to carpet activity; housing and new construction will not be a strong plus. Long term, we expect more consolidation at both the manufacturer and retail level. Raw material and selling prices should remain under pressure.

Major Risks to the Outlook

The major threats to the carpet industry appear to be under control at the moment. The carpet sector is extremely cyclical; it is tied to housing and is a deferrable, big-ticket purchase. Industry activity, therefore, typically over-swings in a business contraction. The United States has not only weathered the global crisis but also managed to come through with flying colors. The developing economies of the world appear to be back on track. Absent the international threat, and the probability of a U.S. recession in the next few years is very low. Short of a major downturn, rising interest rates always posed a problem for the carpet market. Even with rates moving up, hikes should be modest, on top of a low base.

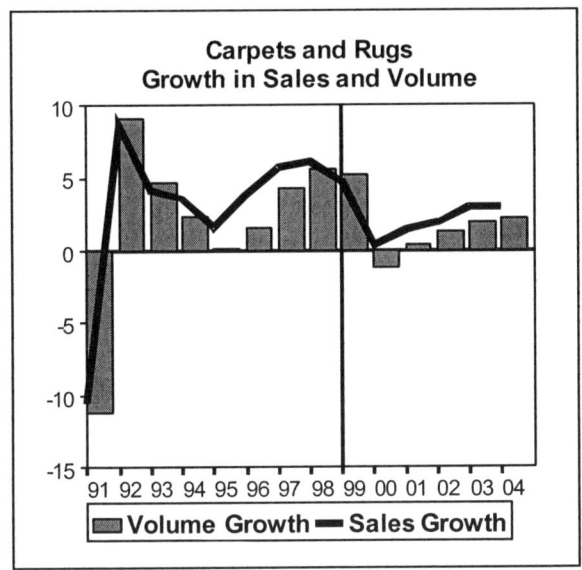

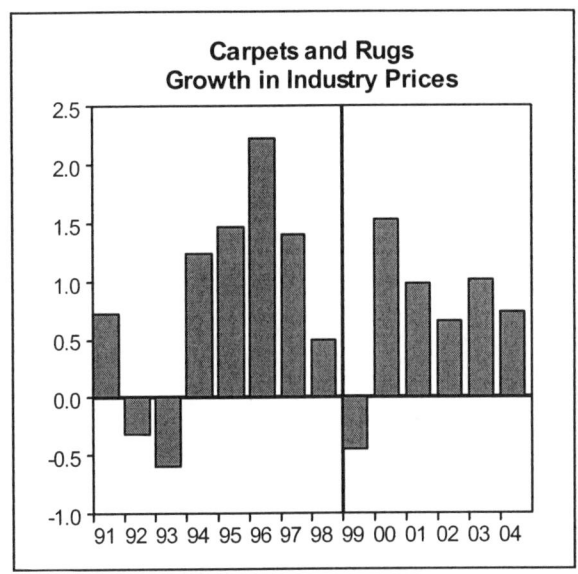

Carpets and Rugs

SIC 227

		1992	1993	1994	1995	1996	1997	1998	1999	2000	2001	Compound Average 88-98	Annual Growth 98-08
Sales													
	Billions of $	9.82	10.22	10.59	10.75	11.16	11.80	12.52	13.12	13.16	13.34		
	% Ch	8.7	4.1	3.6	1.6	3.8	5.7	6.1	4.8	0.3	1.4	2.0	2.5
Volume													
	% Ch	9.1	4.7	2.3	0.1	1.5	4.2	5.6	5.2	-1.2	0.4	1.0	1.7
Prices													
	% Ch	-0.3	-0.6	1.2	1.5	2.2	1.4	0.5	-0.4	1.5	1.0	1.0	0.8
Production Costs													
Avg. Hourly Earnings													
	$/hr	8.58	8.91	9.14	9.37	9.75	10.02	10.35	10.87	11.24	11.65		
	% Ch	2.4	3.8	2.6	2.6	4.0	2.8	3.4	4.9	3.5	3.6	3.0	3.6
Input Price Index													
	% Ch	0.6	0.5	1.3	5.6	1.4	0.1	-1.5	-1.6	0.5	1.4	1.4	1.2

Chapter 8:   Apparel

Apparel

The apparel industry includes the manufacture of men's, boys', women's, girls', children's, and infants' apparel and apparel accessories (excluding footwear). Apparel is made by cutting and sewing woven and knit textile fabrics or by knitting from yarn. Manufacturers' shipments totaled $80 billion in 1998. Most manufacturers produce more than one brand and, in many cases, private or store-brand labels as well. Roughly 40% of all apparel sold in the United States are manufactured abroad, and domestic apparel companies have increased their use of overseas contractors in order to compete with lower priced imports. WEFA's expectation for apparel industry sales over the next ten years is for no growth.

Demand

Employment peaked in the apparel industry in 1973 at roughly 1.4 million, and is currently close to trending down toward the 700,000 barrier. Two factors are largely responsible for this trend:

■ First is the flood of cheap imported apparel that has found its way into U.S. markets;

■ Second is the tremendous gain in productivity that the industry has achieved over the past 20 years.

Price pressure from this competition from low-wage countries has unfortunately overwhelmed the productivity-related cost savings for the industry, pressuring margins by preventing meaningful price increases.

What drives apparel sales? Clearly the economy and consumer spending trends matter. Consumer spending is expected to grow less than 2.5% per year over the next decade. In the 1980s, fashion tended to govern the market, but in recent years, particularly with business downsizing and job uncertainty prevailing, consumers are exercising both caution and a considerable degree of cost consciousness. Women's clothing designers have failed to introduce major trend-setting styles in the 1990s. Personal consumption expenditures for apparel and shoes, discounted for inflation, have been outstanding in recent years, rising about 6.0% per annum since the recession low of 1991. Long-term apparel spending is expected to increase about 2.5% annually.

Overall, consumers are shifting down their apparel purchases. They are spending less in total; they are buying less costly items; and they are deserting the department stores for discounters at a steady pace. Currently, every American spends about $933 a year on apparel, or about 4.0% of disposable personal income. In 1949, apparel spending was close to 10% of income.

Dollar shipments from domestic producers have done better in the last few years. After stagnating around $77 billion, dollar volume has grown by about 1.6% in the last two years, pushing shipments to $80 billion in 1998. Price inflation accounted for about 1.0% of this growth.

Of course it would be meaningless to talk about demand for apparel without mentioning the implications of foreign trade. Apparel imports account for approximately 40% of domestic consumption. Exports, on the other hand, are miniscule, due to high American wages in a labor-intensive industry. In 1998, apparel imports amounted to $53.7 billion, up 11.0% from the prior year, and more than twice the level at the start of the nineties. Conversely, exports of apparel amounted to $8.5 billion in 1998, only 1.0% better than 1997. Little consolation can be taken from the substantial expansion in U.S. exports over the past decade (from $2.5 billion in 1990), since the trade deficit in apparel is extremely large and widening. In 1990, the trade imbalance was a mere $23 billion; currently it is in excess of $45 billion. The growth in imports and the trade deficit is even greater in real terms because of lower import prices.

The WEFA outlook for the next decade expects the domestic apparel industry to stagnate. Overall dollar shipments grow less than 1.0%, as real volume remains flat, and prices rise approximately 0.8%. Wages within the apparel industry are likely to advance about 3.5% annually, putting a great deal of pressure on profit margins.

Supply Conditions

There is quite a bit of dispersion within the U.S. apparel-manufacturing sector; in fact, it is estimated that there are more than 20,000 firms in the industry. The industry is very cyclical, and it can be whipped around by the whims of fashion and consumer confidence. Apparel manufacturers have a capability, however, that many other manufacturers don't have — the ability to expand or contract output and costs rather easily. This is because the industry is very labor intensive and requires only modest amounts of capital equipment.

In addition to their internal flexibility, producers have increased their timely control over output and costs through the use of jobbers and contractors. Increasingly, these jobbers and contractors are foreign, due to cheaper labor costs abroad. As is the case with many labor-intensive industries, apparel manufacturing is very competitive and promotes low wages. Conditions within the industry also provide an environment where labor exploitation is not uncommon.

Important Industry Trends

Consolidation, an ongoing trend in apparel retailing, is leading to larger stores and smaller numbers of retailers in the U.S. marketplace. Larger stores are able to exert more bargaining leverage over prices and conditions of sale from manufacturers. Moreover, the squeeze on wages and jobs in all phases of the apparel industry, as in many other manufacturing industries, shows no sign of easing.

Another important trend is the development of international sourcing capabilities, which have a positive impact on profit margins. One area that shows particular promise over the next several years is sourcing in Mexico, due to its proximity to domestic markets and the NAFTA accord. Quite a brisk trade in apparel between the United States and Mexico has developed in recent years because of NAFTA. According to the American Textile Manufacturers Institute, United States apparel exported to Mexico amounted to $2.6 billion in 1998 up 16% from 1997. While not as impressive, U.S. apparel shipments to Canada totaled $700 million last year for a gain of 7.0%. On the other hand, Mexico has become our largest apparel importer. Mexican producers shipped $6.5 billion of textile and apparel merchandise into the United States in 1998, an impressive gain of almost 29% over the previous year's shipments. In effect, Mexico, and to a lesser extent Canada, buy an appreciable quantity of U.S. fabrics, and in return, ship finished apparel back into the United States

Within the material inputs segment of the apparel industry, which includes broadwoven fabrics and other textiles, high business-failure rates, strong unions, and large cyclical swings make the industry quite volatile. Intense competition from imports at the supplier level as well will continue to play a dominant role in the apparel industry's health and outlook.

Major Risks to the Forecast

Fashion trends are a constant risk for companies within the apparel industry—that is, the danger that shopping dollars will go to a competing brand or style rather than to your company's. However, the overall dollar amount spent is less sensitive to specific fashion trends.

The Asian economic crisis, which cheapened nearly all the region's exports, played havoc with apparel trade. In 1998, apparel imports from South Korea rose 44%, Malaysia was up 20%, Thailand +18%, and India +15%. Import growth would have been greater if it were not for quota limitations, or if the U.S. government had acceded to the requests of other countries for quota increases.

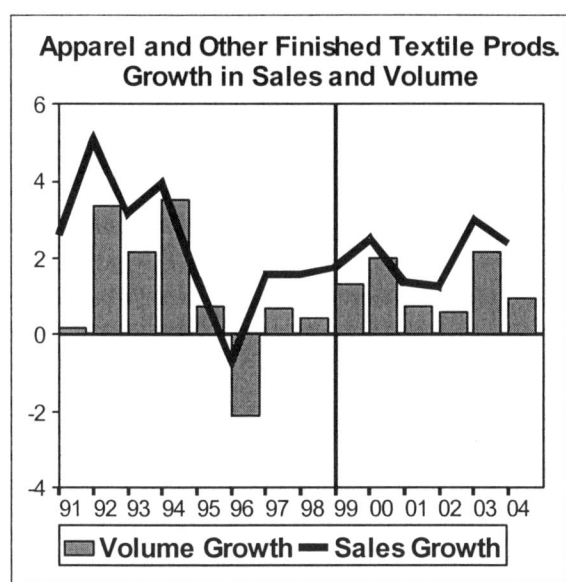

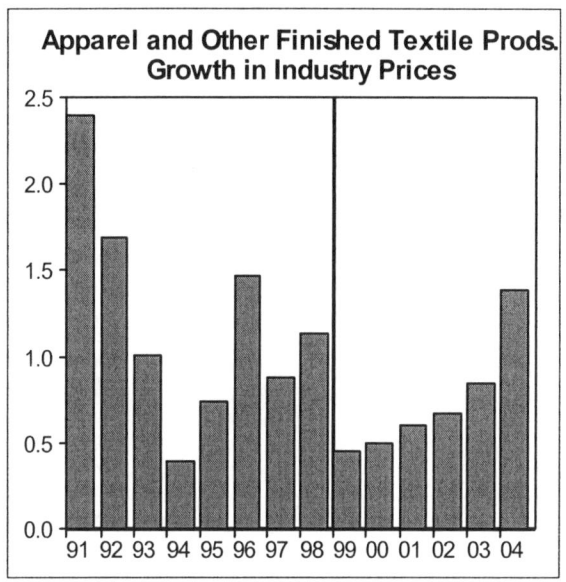

Apparel and Other Finished Textile Products
SIC 23

		1992	1993	1994	1995	1996	1997	1998	1999	2000	2001	Compound Average 88-98	Annual Growth 98-08
Sales													
	Billions of $	71.75	74.03	76.95	78.07	77.56	78.78	80.01	81.42	83.47	84.59		
	% Ch	5.1	3.2	3.9	1.5	-0.7	1.6	1.6	1.8	2.5	1.3	2.0	0.7
Volume													
	% Ch	3.3	2.1	3.5	0.7	-2.1	0.7	0.4	1.3	2.0	0.7	0.4	-0.1
Prices													
	% Ch	1.7	1.0	0.4	0.7	1.5	0.9	1.1	0.4	0.5	0.6	1.5	0.8
Production Costs													
Avg. Hourly Earnings													
	$/hr	6.95	7.09	7.34	7.65	7.96	8.25	8.52	8.82	9.16	9.51		
	% Ch	2.7	2.1	3.5	4.2	4.1	3.7	3.3	3.5	3.9	3.9	3.4	3.4
Input Price Index													
	% Ch	1.4	0.9	1.2	3.5	0.8	0.3	-0.4	-0.6	0.3	1.6	1.4	1.3

Chapter 9: Paper and Allied Products

Pulp Mills

The U.S. pulp industry suffered substantially in 1998. Economic problems in Asia caused U.S. pulp exports to decline by more than 13%. Exports normally account for over 70% of domestic production. Additionally, the demand for printing and writing papers declined in the United States, and inventories rose to uncomfortable levels. In response, bleached softwood kraft prices fell about 8% in the north and 14% in the south.

Since the beginning of 1999, there has been a moderate rise in Asian pulp demand, even though U.S. exports of wood pulp through mid-year were still down 10% from year-ago levels. This improvement in the Asian market, in combination with falling pulp inventories, producer downtime, and mill closures, has allowed some price increases to be implemented in 1999. Pulp prices are expected to continue to improve through 2001, as global demand picks up and operating rates increase.

Industry Structure

The companies in the U.S. pulp, paper, and lumber industries are quite integrated. More than 60 U.S. companies produce pulp of paper grade, but only about 20 of them sell pulp in the merchant market.

About 60% of U.S. consumption of paper-grade pulp is used to produce printing and writing paper. Other key markets include the production of tissue, fluff, and specialty papers. As a result of this customer distribution, U.S. demand for pulp is driven by, and closely linked to, U.S. paper production in general, especially that of the printing and writing grades.

Since the late 1980s, the link between traded pulp and the printing and writing grades has loosened, largely due to the increased integration of the companies in the forest products industry, as well as the strong growth in the use of recycled paper.

Pulp Market Cycles

Characterized by sharp inventory and price swings, the pulp market is highly cyclical. But, these cycles do not always coincide with overall economic cycles. In the last 20 years, there have been three sustained runs of pulp price increases followed by a price decline, but the latest cycle is without precedent. It peaked in October 1995 with a run-up to almost US$1000 per ton for NBSK (northern bleached softwood kraft), the sharpest rise on record. The collapse to US$500 per ton in March 1996 made earlier declines look mild.

A worrisome aspect of pulp markets is that price swings are getting shorter in duration. When demand falters, producers are reluctant to take downtime to correct for oversupply. Instead, they cut prices to move tonnage, adding to the instability of the market. For example, during the run-up in producers' inventories in the third and fourth quarters of 1996, producers failed to curtail production enough to keep stocks under control and continued to operate mills at greater than 90%, despite weak prices. Only when mills recognize the need to curtail pulp supplies, and manage to do so, will the pulp market become more stable.

Demand and Pricing Conditions

As of July 1999, benchmark NBSK was trading at $520/metric ton, close to 10% below its year-earlier level, in spite of a price increase during the second quarter. In contrast, at the start of the year, prices were running almost 20% below their year-earlier level.

Since the beginning of 1999, there has been a moderate rise in Asian pulp demand, even though U.S. exports of wood pulp through mid-year were still down 10% from year-ago levels. This improvement in the Asian market, in combination with falling pulp inventories, producer downtime, and mill closures, allowed pulp producers to hike their prices. Pulp prices are expected to continue to improve through 2001, as global demand picks up and capacity utilization rates increase further. As of this writing, U.S. operating rates are averaging around 90%. However, Canada, Sweden, and Finland have all significantly higher rates, which has helped to reduce the number of days' supply held by major producers.

International Market

The pulp market is global, with large volumes of pulp moving duty-free between net-producing regions and net-consuming regions. North America and the Nordic countries are the largest pulp-producing regions, although nontraditional supplying countries with fast-growing plantations—Brazil, Chile, Portugal, Spain, and Indonesia—are gaining in importance.

During the past decade, world shipments of chemical paper-grade pulp have grown at more than a 3.5% average annual rate. While shipments by North American and Nordic producers grew by almost 3% during that period, deliveries by nontraditional suppliers, led by Brazil and Portugal, grew at nearly twice that rate. As a result, the shares held by nontraditional suppliers increased dramatically at the expense of the North American and Nordic producers' shares. This trend is expected to continue, as substantial new capacity starts up in the developing regions of the world.

Western Europe (excluding Scandinavia) remains the largest destination for world chemical-paper-grade pulp shipments, accounting for about 40% of total shipments. The United States is the second-largest consuming market, while Japan still remains third.

Consumption by the emerging markets of the world—Latin America, Asia, and Africa—is growing quickly, however. As these countries progress further, their demand for consumer products will expand rapidly. The countries with the strongest long-term consumption growth are expected to be China, India, South Korea, and Indonesia.

Before being devastated by the recent economic downturn, Asia (including Japan) was expected to account for fully one-half of worldwide-tonnage growth in printing and writing papers and bleached pulp demand by the year 2000. However, this process has been somewhat delayed.

Increasing Global Capacity

Global capacity for pulp shows no signs of declining. However, overall capacity additions are likely to be modest over the next several years. Pulp producers are expected to add less than 1% to chemical paper-grade capacity by the end of 1999. Another 1.9% growth is expected by the end of 2000. A significant portion of the new capacity coming on-line will be in the Nordic countries, Latin America, Asia, and Africa, although the situation in Latin America and Asia has become somewhat uncertain due to the shocks recently suffered by their economies.

While the rest of the world is expanding rapidly, the expansion cycle in North America for paper-grade pulp is largely over, and little new capacity is likely to come on-line in the next few years. During the next eighteen months, total market-pulp capacity at North American mills is slated to rise by only 10,000 tons. In the United States, some capacity may even be withdrawn, as producers integrate pulp capacity to support new coated and uncoated free-sheet machines. Even if prices continue to improve, as WEFA forecasts, U.S. producers will be reluctant to invest in market pulp capacity, due to a shortage of southern pine pulpwood and the uncertainty surrounding proposed new environmental regulations.

Paper Mills

Demand for overall paper was up 2.2% in 1998. This was due largely to steady improvements in consumer confidence and spending over the course of the year. Catalog sales picked up nicely, and circulation was rising as catalogers increased their prospecting efforts. Print advertising also benefited from the strong economy.

In 1999, demand for paper products has been mixed. The domestic market remains healthy for certain grades and exports have begun to pick up, following the 1997-1998 Asia economic crisis, but the strength of the U.S. dollar continues to be a dampening influence on overseas demand while supporting imports.

While the importance of electronic communication is growing rapidly, this growth has not yet come at the expense of significant amounts of overall paper consumption. In fact, there is evidence that increased use of electronic communication has actually been a boon to consumption of uncoated free-sheet (UFS). In the long term, however, the increasing use of electronic media represents a significant threat to paper usage in this country.

Capacity growth is expected to be less aggressive in North America than in previous cycles, but capacity expansion overseas is projected to accelerate. The new foreign capacity hangs like a dark cloud over the paper market. Concerns are that if a significant number of projects come to fruition, the market could experience a glut of supply that would keep prices down in the long term. Developing countries that are currently producing at the low end of the paper chain are expected to break into the higher value markets within the next five to ten years. This could yield an interesting market situation for U.S. producers, who will be forced to either add greater value to the products they are currently producing or invest in new technologies to ensure they are low-cost producers if they are to avoid losing global share to foreign competitors.

Coated Paper Market Conditions

After experiencing nearly 3% growth in 1998, coated paper shipments softened in the first half of 1999. This was due to a number of factors, which included slower growth in the overall advertising environment, surging imports, and a work–off of customer inventories.

Industry shipments continue to be hurt by the strength of the U.S. dollar against the Canadian dollar. As a result, U.S. imports of coated papers increased in the first six months of 1999. According to the U.S. Dept. of Commerce, coated free-sheet imports rose 15% year-to-date through June. However, coated groundwood imports fell 3%. Imports have, in many cases, prevented U.S. producers from raising prices. In the short term, slower growth in the U.S. economy and continued strength in the dollar should keep a lid on prices.

Growth in the supply of coated papers throughout the world will continue to be robust in the next few years, with the bulk of the growth coming from outside of North America. While some of the proposed new capacity in

Asia is questionable, world coated-groundwood capacity is expected to increase by 3.5% in 1999 and another 2.8% in 2000. World coated free-sheet capacity should increase 5.3% in 1999 and 2.9% in 2000.

Coated Free–Sheet

In 1998, the U.S. coated free-sheet (CFS) market improved as the year progressed. However, because of import penetration prices fell over 5.0%, despite an increase in capacity utilization. Prices remained depressed through the year and into 1999.

The strength in consumer spending was a major force driving the demand side. Demand fundamentals are also on track through the first half of 1999. Overall, a 5.3% increase is estimated for 1999 and a 3.5% growth is projected for 2000.

In the United States, 1998 was a year of moderate expansion in capacity. American CFS capacity exceeded 1997 levels by an estimated 153,000 tons per year, or 2.9%. However, a marked slowdown in domestic capacity expansion is projected for 1999 and beyond. The opposite is happening overseas, where capacity is expected to grow much faster in the next few years than in the United States. Much of this new capacity is slated to come from Asia, but the fate and timing of several projects there remains uncertain in view of the economic turmoil in the region.

The continued increase in coated-paper imports in 1999 brought CFS prices down again. During the second half of 1999, there will be little support for a major market price increase. But, WEFA expects prices to begin firming up and rise at a modest pace through 2000.

Coated Groundwood Paper

Demand continued to grow for coated groundwood paper (CGW) in 1998. It reflected the effects of higher-than-expected consumer spending and inventory building by buyers.

However, during the first half of 1999, the market changed course. Demand fell approximately 5% from year-ago levels, as buyers began to de-stock, and prices dropped sharply, well over 10% from the same period in 1998.

Longer term, as long as the U.S. economy stays on course, CGW demand should post annual gains near 1%. This represents a slowdown in long-term growth rates, caused in part by substitution arising from attractive prices for CFS grades. Also contributing to this lower growth outlook will be increasing competition from high-quality, filled uncoated groundwood (UGW) papers. New high-quality supercalendered (SC) capacity in North America has already started to hurt demand for light-weight grades, as publishers switch to the more cost-effective SC paper.

Uncoated Paper Market Conditions

Uncoated Free–Sheet

The uncoated free-sheet (UFS) market dropped slightly over the course of 1998. Strong sales of ink-jet and laser prints were not enough to prevent a minor market adjustment. Imports are fast becoming a major cause for concern for U.S. UFS producers. Domestic demand has remained on the rise, but a sharp increase in imports displaced enough domestic tonnage to cause U.S. domestic shipments to drop in 1998.

Much of the import volume is coming from Canada, which is not surprising given the continuing slide of the Canadian dollar.

The outlook for UFS prices is mixed entering the fourth quarter of 1999. Cheaper imports are exerting considerable pressure on domestic prices. Even if demand remains on course, UFS pricing conditions are unlikely to improve much until the dollar loses some of its strength, imports become less competitive, and pulp prices continue to rebound.

Newsprint

On the demand side, the newspaper business remains positive. Newsprint usage by daily newspapers in the United States continues to run significantly above 1998 levels, although year-over-year growth rates have started to slow noticeably. The gains in newsprint consumption are resulting from rising ad lineage and higher page counts—both of which respond to the general business cycle—rather than from higher circulation. Considering the remarkable economic expansion in the United States in the 1990s—with incomes rising and consumers aggressively increasing purchases—it is rather surprising that circulation has not fared better.

In contrast to strong domestic demand, U.S. exports of newsprint have fallen sharply, and overseas paper continues to arrive in the United States, a direct consequence of the run-up in the value of the U.S. dollar. As is the case for many grades of paper, the influx of cheap newsprint imports and the drop in export demand are combining to erode the pricing power of newsprint producers in the United States. Further weakness will be introduced into the market by a new wave of machine startups overseas, which will at least temporarily push growth in worldwide capacity significantly above growth in demand.

In the near term, we expect domestic newsprint demand to remain healthy, as long as the economic expansion continues. We also forecast imports to remain strong and exports to stay relatively weak until the U.S. dollar reverses its course and business conditions gather more steam in Asia.

Environmental Considerations

Environmental issues and regulations have a profound effect on the paper industry. The impact points range from forestry practices and pulp production to product marketing and programs designed to convince customers to use greener buying patterns and recycle.

One long-term global issue is whether the world contains sufficient natural resources to support its fast-growing paper needs. While the resources appear to be sufficient, their harvesting and renewal will require huge investment. These resources will increasingly come from new pulp-supplying parts of the world.

A key environmental debate has centered on whether paper-industry feedstocks (i.e., pulp) should be elemental chlorine-free (ECF) or totally chlorine-free (TCF). Considerable progress has been made by the industry to clean up its effluent by using, for example, hydrogen peroxide rather than chlorine as a bleaching agent. The switch to environmentally friendly feedstock has required the investment of huge sums of money in capital equipment, research and development, and training of industry professionals. The costs associated with these projects have proven to be worthwhile, however— some of the mills that have been upgraded to include advanced pollution-abating technologies are now among the lowest cost facilities in the industry.

A continuing uncertainty for U.S. companies is how much money will be required to comply with new EPA regulations, such as the "Cluster Rule." Some companies estimate that they may have to spend between $400 million and $500 million to comply with the requirements.

Outlook

During the past decade, paper producers were rarely intimidated by the dawn of the electronic age and added new capacity quite liberally. As mentioned earlier, demand for certain grades, such as cut-size repographic, actually increased with the heightened use of computer desktop printers. Electronic media companies also contributed to the growth in magazines by their use of print advertising to market and sell digital media products. However, the threat of the paperless office is real and looming bigger on the horizon for paper demand, and the next decade promises to show an even greater transformation from paper to electronic media. Because of this threat and the growing danger of an oversupplied global paper market caused by the rapid expansion of overseas capacity, the number of new paper projects coming on stream in the United States has slowed compared to the last decade.

In the coming years, some traditional paper end-uses will be progressively replaced in the domestic market by digital media. Mail-order shopping will increasingly go through the Internet, rather than through printed catalogs. More data will be transferred electronically, rather than published and mailed to its user. More letters will be sent electronically, rather than printed and mailed. Banking services will expand on–line, to the detriment of the neighborhood branch and its paper usage.

Other segments of the domestic paper market will be endangered by emerging technologies. For example, the largest threat to the coated paper industry is not the initial electronic replacement of print media, but rather the impact on advertising from digital interactive media. Also, technology now allows a combination of computer, fax, and image technologies all in one machine, and paper-free fax transmissions.

The fastest growth in the paper market now and into the next century is outside the United States. As consumers in developing economies gain more purchasing power, there will be a great push to advertise and deliver consumer products. There will be a greater demand for magazines, books, and newspapers as higher income brings higher literacy.

Developing countries that are currently producing at the low end of the paper chain are expected to break into the higher value markets within the next five-to-ten years. This could yield an interesting market situation for U.S. producers, who will be forced to either add greater value to the products they are currently producing or invest in new technologies to ensure they are low-cost producers if they are to avoid losing global share to foreign competitors. The next few years will prove to be an exciting time for the paper industry as producers around the globe respond to new technologies and new competitors.

Paperboard Mills

The paperboard industry finished 1998 in slightly better condition as box demand improved. However, despite sharply lower exports, prices improved significantly. As consumer spending grows in 1999, paperboard should see further improvements in both demand and prices. Look for a similar scenario to occur in 2000.

Considerable growth in the paperboard market will also occur outside of the United States and Europe over the next decade. A number of grassroots projects and recycled mills in the developing regions of the world are expected to bring product to market within the next five to ten years. The economic problems in Asia and Latin America may slow this growth somewhat, but the long-run trend remains strongly positive. Until these projects are up and running, however, the North American and Western European paperboard industries will be called upon to meet worldwide demand. The need for high-end board products could be great news for the integrated producers in mature economies, including the United States. As various foreign sources of pulp and other crude-paper supplies spring to life around the globe, well-established producers may be required to refocus their attention on the value-added products that provide the greatest margins.

Containerboard Market Conditions

The containerboard industry finished 1998 in good condition as box demand remained strong. Total linerboard produced for domestic shipments in 1998 reached 20.8 million metric tons, an increase of 1.8% over the 1997 production level.

The industry has improved further in 1999. As a result, prices have turned upward for certain grades. Kraft linerboard prices, which averaged $370/ton in the first quarter, moved up to $400/ton in the second quarter. Despite the increase, linerboard prices were still running below their year-earlier level through mid-year.

Kraft linerboard exports through June were still down 19% from their year-ago levels, but improved economic conditions abroad should translate into accelerated exports over the next several months. We expect at least another round of price increases for this paperboard grade to take place before 1999 is over. The outlook for prices beyond 1999 is for further strengthening.

Boxboard Market Conditions

For the boxboard industry, 1998 was another year of record output. Prices improved for most major grades, except solid bleached sulfate (SBS). Producers of bleached and unbleached folding boxboard owed most of their increased production in 1998 to domestic de-

mand growth that was up 1.4%. But, the boxboard export market, unlike that for many other paper and paperboard grades, has not suffered much from the Asian flu. SBS board prices were unchanged in the second quarter of 1999 at $740/ton, a level that remained below 1998's second-quarter average. However, we expect them to increase in the near term, as the boxboard market gathers some momentum.

From 1993 to 1998, folding boxboard production increased by 478,000 tons. During that period, approximately, 290,000 more tons were produced for domestic markets and 188,000 tons for exports. Overall operating rates for boxboard grades averaged over 95.6% in 1998. However, this was actually below the 96.7% average between 1995 and 1997.

Industry Trends

Recycled Fiber Usage

There is a dramatic change taking place in the containerboard industry—a growing number of mills in the United States and other developed economies are producing board from 100% wastepaper. The principal wastepaper grades used are old corrugated containers (OCC) and new double-lined kraft (NDLK) cuttings. Traditionally, recycled liner was viewed as an inferior product, produced by smaller, older mills. New technology, however, now permits production of 100% recycled linerboard that is comparable with kraft linerboard in performance characteristics. U.S. recycled-linerboard production is approaching 20% of total linerboard output, up from only about 2% in the 1980s.

The heightened demand for recycled board has prompted many companies to refocus their expansion projects to include recycled mills. Mills that have come on-line recently and the ones still projected to come on-line are advocating more aggressive recycling programs. The paperboard industry must strive to increase recycling rates if it is to be ensured of a steady stream of feedstock for these efforts.

Mini-Mill Fever

Another new trend has been the rise of smaller "mini–mills" that use recycled fiber. These mills are typically about 250 to 450 tons per day (tpd) in size and are usually located near major urban areas, where wastepaper supplies are plentiful and transportation costs are low. These single-line, bare-bones facilities sometimes use steam from a nearby utility-power plant and hook into municipal treatment systems to keep capital costs at a minimum. Most mini-mill projects are sponsored by independent corrugated converters seeking more control over their raw material supply.

Outlook

U.S. containerboard demand is expected to continue to expand in 2000. The paperboard market is usually able to ride out periods of slow economic growth better than other sectors of the paper industry. This ability is derived from the fact that its key end-use markets rely more on consumers' purchases of necessity goods, such as food and clothing, than on purchases of more frivolous items.

WEFA projects economic growth will average in the 2.5% range over the next ten years. This level of growth will not provide paperboard producers in the United States the incentive to increase capacity rapidly. Nevertheless, moderate growth will ensure that demand for end-use products like beer and soda, soaps and detergents, drugs and cosmetics, cereal and breakfast foods, candy and cookies, and fruits and vegetables will grow modestly but steadily and, as a result, so will demand for paperboard.

Considerable growth in the paperboard market will occur outside of North America and Europe over the next decade. A number of grassroots projects and recycled mills from the developing regions of the world are expected to bring product to market within the next five to ten years, albeit at a slower pace than anticipated earlier due to the economic turmoil in Asia. Just as in other paper sectors, growing economies and expanding consumer demand will be the drivers behind these projects. More packaged foods and bottled and canned soft drinks will be penetrating the markets of developing countries. Sanitary paper products and toiletries will be another overseas growth area.

Until these projects are up and running, however, the North American and Western European paperboard industries will be called upon to meet worldwide demand. For those industries, this will mean continued growth in exports—as much as a 10% increase (year-over-year) at various times during the coming decade. The need for high-end board products could be great news for the integrated producers in mature economies. As various foreign sources of pulp and other crude-paper supplies spring to life around the globe, well-established producers may be required to refocus their attention on the value-added products that provide the greatest margins.

Converted Paper and Paperboard Products

Construction and related engineering and architectural services, medical services, and agriculture dominate the end-use markets for converted paper and paperboard products—accounting for more than one-third of total sales. The other markets are quite diverse and include various types of consumer durable and non-durable products. The construction market brings cyclical behavior to an otherwise stable industry. The nonresidential construction market is expected to register healthy increases in 2000 and beyond. This will result in an increase in demand from the construction industry for converted paper products through at least 2005.

Converted paper products will continue to compete for market share with plastic packaging, particularly with returnable, plastic shipping crates, which are gaining in popularity in some distribution channels. However, the relatively higher costs of some of those materials should help fiber-based products remain a contender in the packaging arena. Principal growth markets are expected to be shipping containers for food products, beverages and consumer goods, and point-of-purchase displays used for product promotion.

Corrugated Containers

Corrugated containers still dominate today's worldwide packaging industry. These containers, made by combining two grades of containerboard (linerboard and corrugating medium), are utilized for nearly 90% of industrial and consumer goods shipments. Seventy percent of the industry's output become corrugated boxes, while the remainder appears in the form of consumer packaging, printed displays, and cushioning material. Because corrugated containers serve so many markets, their shipments are considered an excellent barometer of economic trends.

While corrugated containers are highly efficient and cost effective, paperboard packaging is being subjected to severe competition from the plastics industry, particularly in the food sector. In Europe, plastic containers have already captured some market share from corrugated. The U.S. subsidiary of Taiwan's Formosa Plastics Group is now making plastic containers and bags at a new, large facility in Texas, and the company has plans for rapid growth through market penetration.

Industry Structure

The corrugated container industry is highly integrated with paper companies that also produce linerboard and corrugating medium. Vertically integrated firms typically operate between 10 and 40 corrugating medium plants with the ability to use one or more of the plants to produce linerboard. These integrated companies account for about 75% of total U.S. corrugated-box shipments. The remainder of the industry is comprised of independent box manufacturers.

Non-integrated producers generally operate sheet plants and depend on integrated producers for their raw materials. Consequently, independent producers are often at a competitive disadvantage, particularly when containerboard is in tight supply. In the past few years, a number of independents have financed small "mini-mills" to supply their box plants with 100% recycled linerboard and corrugating medium. These mills have substantially lower capital and operating costs than large kraft mills.

Changing Market Requirements

The warehousing and logistics industries, like many others, have been looking for ways to do more with less and do it faster. Many of the re-engineered methods of storing and moving product have led to demands for greater box strength and durability. Palletization and automated warehousing have eliminated much of the manual handling of individual corrugated cases in the distribution system and require stronger boxes to tolerate rougher handling. The trend toward stacking corrugated boxes to greater heights in warehouses has increased the demand for boxes with greater top-to-bottom compression strength. There is also a shift toward individual plastic packaging from rigid metal and glass containers, and this switch also requires stronger exterior packaging.

As a result of these changes, ring crush (compression strength) is replacing mullen as the most relevant performance requirement for corrugated board. Industry pressure for modifications of existing box specifications, from bursting strength to compression and edge crush, succeeded in early 1990. A number of producers are now marketing high-performance linerboard that offers higher strength and yield (surface area per ton) than traditional commodity linerboard.

High-quality printing directly onto corrugated boxes and displays is another trend driving quality changes in the corrugated market. One of the least expensive methods of printing—direct printing with either flexography or letterpress—is used on more than 80% of corrugated products. However, the rough surface of linerboard limits the quality of direct print. As a result, many mills have developed improved linerboard substrates, including mottled white and white-top boards. An alternative way to overcome many printing troubles is preprint linerboard. The use of this process is growing rapidly due to the increase in point-of-purchase retailing. North American preprint linerboard capacity is estimated to be about 550 million square feet on a total of close to 20 presses (including two in Canada).

Outlook

U.S. demand for corrugating products has kept pace with the U.S. economy in recent years. This has meant that shipments have increased steadily since 1994. In 1998, consumption increased 1.7%. Estimates for 1999 are for 3.4% growth, and for 2000 a 2.0% increase.

The United States is the lowest cost producer of corrugated containers in the world. This status will help the United States to retain approximately a 35% share of the total number of boxes produced globally over the next three to five years. U.S. exports of containerboard and corrugated boxes should increase to satisfy demand in Mexico, China, Latin America, and the expanding markets in Eastern Europe. In anticipation of greater trade with Mexico, several new box plants are being established on both sides of the border to serve Mexico's growing manufacturing base.

Converted products will continue to compete for market share with plastic packaging, particularly the returnable plastic shipping crate that is gaining popularity in some distribution channels. However, the higher cost of some of these competitive products should help fiber-based products remain a contender in the packaging arena. Principal growth markets are expected to be shipping containers for food products, beverages and consumer goods, and point-of-purchase displays used for product promotion.

Folding Paperboard Boxes

Packaging demand by the U.S. food and beverage industry is the driving force in sales of folding cartons. Folding cartons are the packaging protectors that manufacturers use to ship consumer non-durable goods through distribution channels. Folding cartons are also used to fabricate product displays. They are typically die-cut, printed, and shipped flat from folding carton plants to manufacturers. The end-user assembles and fills the cartons on high-speed production lines. The paperboard used for folding cartons must meet technical specifications for scoring, bending, and folding without cracking or breaking, for stiffness and resistance to bulge and surface slack, and for surface smoothness for printing, embossing, or laminating.

Clay-coated newsback (CCNB), solid bleached sulfate (SBS), and coated unbleached kraft (CUK) are the three major paperboard grades used to make folding cartons. Coatings such as kaolin clay, polyethylene, wax, and other special treatments are usually applied to the board to improve strength, moisture resistance, and printing-surface smoothness.

- SBS has traditionally been the highest quality grade used by the folding carton industry, preferred for its strength and appearance for packaging food products and consumer goods. This grade is also used for high-quality printing and embossing of packaging for cosmetics, toiletries, and tobacco products.

- CCNB is a recycled grade used most often for dry foods, soaps, and detergents, as well as for a wide variety of consumer goods. Markets that have traditionally used bleached board are losing some ground to high-quality recycled grades.

- Unbleached kraft board is used mostly for beverage carriers and multi-packs, but has also made gains in traditional folding cartons for both foods and nonfood products. The micro-brewery phenomenon and the thirst for specialty beverages, such as iced teas and fruit juices, provided the coated unbleached kraft sector with the highest growth rate of any boxboard grade during the past decade.

Folding-carton volume has suffered during the past decade, mainly as a result of competition from alternatives such as flexible packaging, rigid plastic containers, and E- and F-flute corrugated board. Although the manufacturers of many consumer goods switched to plastic packaging over the course of the last five years, there has been some consumer backlash against plastics due to environmental concerns. The folding-carton industry has continued to grow through new product introductions, especially those related to food. Food packaging accounts for approximately half of all folding-carton purchases.

Market Trends

The overall paperboard-box industry trend is expected to remain positive in both 1999 and 2000. However, there will be a shift in the market share among the three major boxboard grades. According to the Paperboard Packaging Council, recycled paperboard is now used in over 55% of all cartons manufactured, bleached paperboard is used in almost 30%, and unbleached kraft is used in less than 15%. Milk cartons and paper cups and plates (which are made exclusively from bleached paperboard) are not included in these totals.

The number of converting facilities has declined over the past several years. Less-efficient and less-profitable plants have been phased out, and merger activity has increased. The largest concentration of plants is in the Great Lakes, Northeast, and Mid-Atlantic regions. The Southeast, which also has a concentration of folding carton plants, has been the fastest-growing producing region during the past ten years, since integrated producers have chosen to move closer to their sources of raw materials.

Outlook

Domestic folding-carton shipments for specific end-use markets regularly shadow consumer-spending trends and real disposable-income levels. Look for moderate

increases in disposable-income growth through 2000. This will translate into continued moderate growth in spending on consumer products and food items. The small annual increases in volume of carton shipments, however, will not be a true indication of the industry's real growth potential. Improved technology has enabled folding carton makers to produce lower density, lighter weight, stronger cartons, while using less boxboard.

Exports have not been a major factor in the folding-carton industry because of the high cost of transportation compared with the value and bulk of folding cartons. It has been more economical to export large paperboard rolls, which can then be easily converted into folding cartons. The principal export markets for folding cartons are Canada and Mexico, which together account for about 80% of the industry's modest export volume.

Other Converted Products

Setup Paperboard Boxes

Setup boxes are custom-made for specific products that require good protection and high-quality appearance. Rigid boxes are used primarily to package high-value products, such as liquors, fine stationery, jewelry, toiletries and specialty foods, since traditional rigid boxes are more expensive to produce than folding cartons. Rigid boxes have also found new markets in computer software and video-game packaging.

In recent years, the industry has made a number of moves in an attempt to suspend the downward spiral that was occurring. Setup box producers have improved their cost-effectiveness and productivity, diversified their product mix, and entered new markets. Some makers have added folding cartons and paper/plastic combinations and lamination to their product lines. The industry has improved its competitive position through strategic restructuring, mergers, and acquisitions. Now the setup box industry has become a specialty market for the firms that have survived the industry's downsizing.

Annual variations in sales and shipments are largely attributable to U.S. economic trends and to changing disposable income and consumer spending levels. Rigid box shipments are expected to inch up in the near term, provided that the industry continues to adapt its packaging products for new classes of consumer goods. In some traditional markets, setup boxes will be challenged by folding cartons and plastics. Growth markets for the first decade of the new century are expected to include packaging for cosmetics, pharmaceuticals, confectionery, and electronics and software.

Paperboard Tubes, Cores, and Drums

Sonoco Products Co., Jefferson Smurfit, Caraustar Industries Inc., and Greif Brothers Corp. dominate the business of paperboard tubes, cores, and drums. Sonoco Products and Jefferson Smurfit are also major players in the consumer products sector—an area comprised mainly of composite cans for food products. Except for Greif Brothers, all of these manufacturers are vertically integrated producers who make nearly 100% of their own paperboard requirements.

Shipments of tubes and cores have shown slow growth at best. Consumer and industrial packaging and shipping are the largest markets for tubes. The paper industry, where cores are used for papermill roll cores, inner cores for towel and tissue products, and office supplies, is the single largest market for cores. The markets for solid-fiber drums account for about one-quarter of industry shipments and include the industrial, chemical, and construction sectors. Fiber drums have found a niche market in the hazardous-waste disposal industry. Growth in this sector should remain strong.

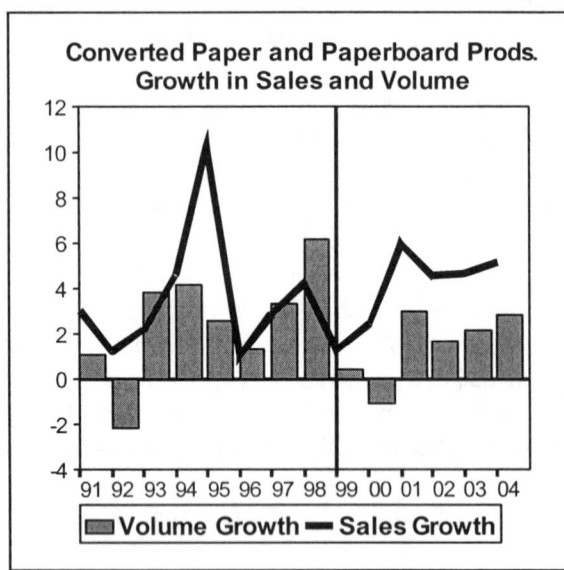

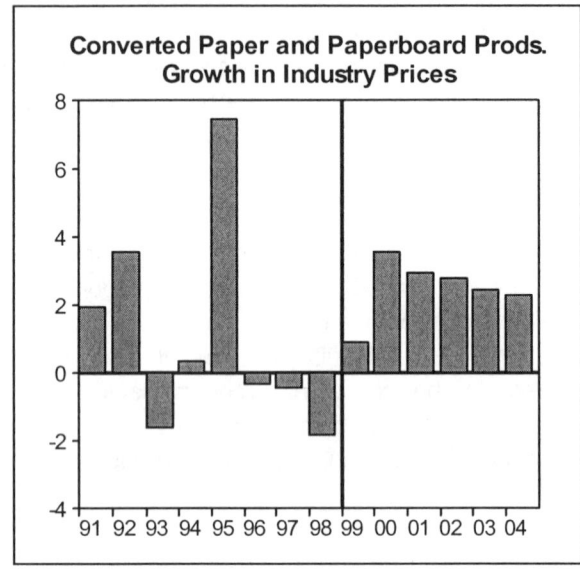

Converted Paper and Paperboard Products
SIC 265, 267

		1992	1993	1994	1995	1996	1997	1998	1999	2000	2001	Compound Average 88-98	Annual Growth 98-08
Sales													
	Billions of $	46.14	47.16	49.33	54.40	54.94	56.52	58.91	59.68	61.16	64.83		
	% Ch	1.3	2.2	4.6	10.3	1.0	2.9	4.2	1.3	2.5	6.0	4.0	4.5
Volume													
	% Ch	-2.2	3.8	4.2	2.6	1.3	3.4	6.2	0.4	-1.1	3.0	1.9	1.9
Prices													
	% Ch	3.5	-1.6	0.4	7.5	-0.3	-0.5	-1.8	0.9	3.6	2.9	2.1	2.6
Production Costs													
Avg. Hourly Earnings													
	$/hr	11.51	11.78	12.04	12.39	12.81	13.14	13.49	14.02	14.63	15.19		
	% Ch	3.3	2.3	2.1	2.9	3.4	2.6	2.7	3.9	4.3	3.8	2.9	4.0
Input Price Index													
	% Ch	-0.9	0.0	2.9	15.4	-4.6	-2.1	-0.3	-2.0	1.9	2.4	1.3	1.9

Chapter 10: Printing and Publishing

Printing and Publishing

The printing and publishing industry is made up primarily of commercial printers and newspaper, magazine, and book publishers. These four segments account for three-fourths of the publishing industry's total shipments. The remaining one-fourth consists of printers of business forms, greeting cards, and bookbinding and typesetting shops.

The largest—and fastest growing—segment of the industry is commercial printing. Despite the inroads made by computer-generated printing, growth in population and new businesses, plus a healthy trade balance, will allow commercial-printing shipments to advance faster than the industry's other components over the years just ahead. Newsstand circulation of magazines is soft, but profits have been up due to strong advertising expenditures. Adult hardcover books remain weak due to their high prices, but the educational market has posted stellar gains.

WEFA expects revenue in the printing and publishing industry to expand at a healthy 3.8% rate in 1999 and then slow to 2.6% in 2000. This reflects gains in prices of 2% to 3% per year.

Demand Factors

Commercial printing includes printers using both web and flat-sheet technologies. Terms describing these processes include offset printing, photo-offset printing, photolithography, and paleography. Two-thirds of the receipts of commercial printers come from work related to advertising, including ad posters, circulars, coupons, and labels, with most jobs being custom. The key to the outlook for this part of the industry is the overall health of U.S. businesses and the economy—for this is what drives advertising—as well as continued reliance on direct-mail advertising. Moreover, population growth and the addition of new businesses will keep demand for printing services rising at a rate somewhat above that of the average industry over the next few years, while a healthy trade balance will allow more comfortable pricing than faced by many manufacturers.

After a strong performance in 1997, magazine publishers posted another gain in 1998. This boost came with a hefty 4.9% rise in real personal consumption and increasing advertising expenditures. Though the magazine segment only commands about 5% of total-advertising expenditures, its growth has been among the highest in the industry. Magazines are expected to have another good year in 1999. One key reason for the positive forecast is the growing trend toward brand extensions, which is when a magazine produces goods for sale or licenses its name to a manufacturer. There remains a considerable amount of potential for magazine publishers in this area.

Real consumer disposable income, a key factor in book sales, is expected to grow fairly steadily over the next three to four years, experiencing average gains per year of around 3%. Consumers, however, will remain cost-conscious and thrifty. Despite a robust job market, uncertainty concerning jobs and incomes remains ingrained in consumer sentiment. WEFA's view is that weakness in adult hardcover-book sales is probably here to stay — at least through the remainder of the decade.

Looking at the printing and publishing industry as a whole, the next 10 years should bring annual-volume growth of 1.3%. This is greater than the paltry 0.4% per year rate achieved during the 10 years that ended in 1998, but significantly less than real consumer-spending growth overall. WEFA expects annual sales growth to average roughly 4.4% over the next 10 years. Included in this are projected annual price gains of 3.0%, a rate above the manufacturing average.

Supply Conditions

It is estimated that there are almost 40,000 commercial-printing establishments in the United States. These firms face demands for faster processes, quicker set-up times, better material-handling procedures, and enhanced and less expensive color reproduction in order to keep up with rapidly changing technology. The industry also faces a further shift into electronic publishing, and will need to compete in the labor force for increasing numbers of technologically proficient workers.

Healthy gains in revenues and profits were enjoyed in the newspaper industry in the last two years. A major factor was the decline in paper prices from the lofty levels reached in 1995. Newsprint prices plunged almost 20% from their 1995 levels during 1996-1997, and although they recovered some ground in 1998 they declined again in the first half of 1999. Paper prices are expected to increase during the forecast period, as the export market improves and a better balance is achieved between supply and demand.

The supply of magazine titles has ballooned over the last few years, even as newsstand sales have been declining. This additional supply, when coupled with less shelf space because of lower numbers of both convenience stores and corner newsstands, has significantly increased competitive pressures on magazine publishers.

With the exception of educational titles, book publishing is not highly concentrated. Interestingly, book publishing is one of the few traditional industries that experienced an increase in the number of companies operating over the 1982-1992 period, a time of significant consolidation for most manufacturing industries. It is estimated that there were approximately 2,000 companies involved in book publishing in 1982, and roughly 2,500 in 1992. The data does suggest, however, that there has been a small decline in the number of active companies during the years since 1992.

Pricing Factors

Prices for finished products shipped by the printing, publishing, and allied industries group of manufactures have consistently advanced faster than the overall wholesale price index in recent years. For the 10-year period ending in 1998, overall output prices advanced at an average pace of 3.7% per year. For the two years ending in 2001, prices for this industry are expected to rise close to 2.9% per annum, on average.

One factor that accounts for the healthy rate of price gains for the broad-industry composite is the trade situation. In many manufacturing industries in the United States, imports supply a large amount of domestic consumption, and this added supply prevents significant price increases. Imports of books, newspapers, and magazines, however, remain below exports, giving the United States a trade surplus, and the resulting strength of domestic manufacturers is reflected in their more robust pricing.

Major Trends Affecting the Outlook

Computer technology has eroded the market for commercial printing, as many jobs that used to require the typestyles, clarity, justified margins, and color provided by professional printing can now be produced on a personal computer. As technology evolves and competition intensifies, the growing use of information in non-print formats will also put pressure on the industry.

The type of magazines purchased has changed in recent years. Interest used to be in the glamorous and glossy, and now is centered more on computers and other technical titles, health, and home interest. In addition, as magazine prices have risen, the trend toward cost consciousness observed in so many consumer products in recent years is negatively impacting magazine sales at the newsstand as well.

Concerning the book trade, recent weakness in adult hardcover sales will likely continue due to high cover prices and the ongoing distraction of multimedia products. While some inroads are being made into the demand for books by such products, there is no imminent danger that book demand will collapse as the public switches en masse to computer-screen-generated reading material. The erosion will be slow, and books will continue to provide some advantages that multimedia information cannot yet—particularly portability. In both the magazine and book trades, WEFA expects consolidation to continue.

Major Risks in the Outlook

Risks in the printing, publishing, and allied industries include many of the risks other manufacturing industries face. The most important of these risks are sagging sales due to either recession or flagging consumer confidence. WEFA's forecast is for modest growth in consumer disposable income over the next three to four years. Print products by multi-media offerings remain a threat. Should some technological breakthrough occur that dramatically increases the portability and convenience of using these high–tech products, the expected gradual loss in market share suffered by the printing and publishing industry could become a larger one, and this loss could happen more rapidly.

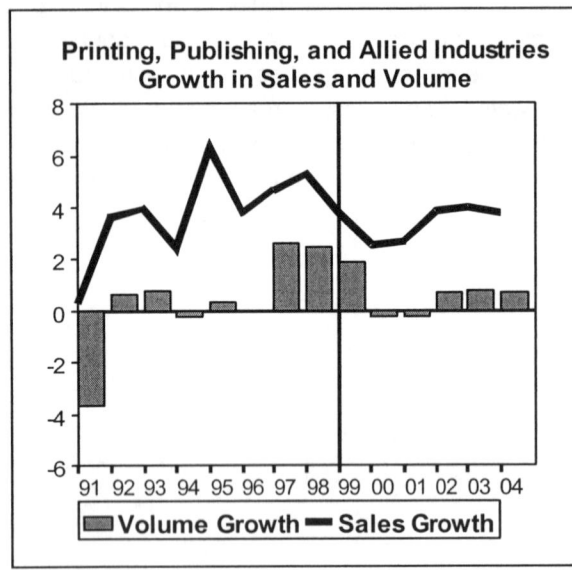

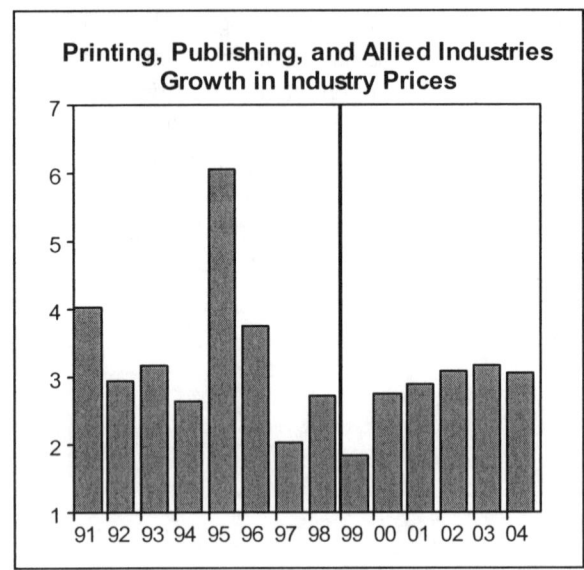

Printing, Publishing, and Allied Industries

SIC 27

		1992	1993	1994	1995	1996	1997	1998	1999	2000	2001	Compound Average 88-98	Annual Growth 98-08
Sales													
	Billions of $	166.0	172.5	176.7	187.9	195.1	204.2	214.9	223.1	228.8	234.9		
	% Ch	3.6	4.0	2.4	6.3	3.8	4.7	5.3	3.8	2.6	2.7	4.0	4.4
Volume													
	% Ch	0.6	0.8	-0.2	0.4	-0.0	2.6	2.5	1.9	-0.2	-0.2	0.3	1.3
Prices													
	% Ch	2.9	3.2	2.6	6.1	3.7	2.0	2.7	1.8	2.8	2.9	3.7	3.0
Production Costs													
Avg. Hourly Earnings													
	$/hr	11.74	11.93	12.14	12.33	12.65	13.05	13.44	13.82	14.23	14.69		
	% Ch	2.2	1.7	1.7	1.6	2.6	3.1	3.0	2.8	3.0	3.2	2.5	3.0
Input Price Index													
	% Ch	0.2	0.8	2.7	12.3	-2.7	-0.7	0.7	-0.3	2.3	2.7	1.9	2.4

Newspapers

In 1998, newspaper-advertising expenditures grew 6.3% to $43.9 billion. This represents over a 22% share of total-advertising dollars. Retail-ad spending was $20.3 billion, an increase of 5.7%. Classified expenditures grew to $17.9 billion, an increase of 6.6%, and national hit $5.7 billion for a gain of 7.7%. Nearly 60 million newspapers are sold daily, with an average readership of over two readers per copy. No other medium reaches so many people on a regular basis.

As larger proportions of the population become technologically proficient, greater shares of the information-delivery market will be electronic. The newspaper industry faces the choice of either accelerating its entry into these new media, and thereby transforming into and merging with other industries, or going through the consolidation and rationalization process that accompanies a declining market.

Trends in Demand

Newspapers are a major source of information for Americans. Today, almost 6 out of 10 (58.7%) adults read a newspaper every day. However, the percentage has fallen dramatically in the past few years. In 1970, for example, 77.6% of adults read a newspaper on a daily basis.

Americans have always maintained a strong relationship with the news. Furthermore, statistics show that as people grow older, and the more educated they become, the more likely it is that they will follow the news on a regular basis. With the population aging, and the job market forcing more and more people to obtain a college degree, the prospects for growth in demand for information from the public is strong. As a result, a lack of demand for news from Americans can not be used as a reason for the decline in newspaper circulation.

The main reason for the decline is the explosion of alternative sources of information available to the public. One culprit is the Internet, which has grown dramatically in recent years. In addition, there is now a glut of news stations on cable, providing increasingly time-constrained adults with a quicker source of information than reading a newspaper.

In response to these trends in consumer habits, the newspaper industry has taken steps to adapt to the changing times. Almost all North American daily newspapers have launched online services, including Web sites and partnerships with consumer online companies. Worldwide, there are more than 2,800 daily, weekly, and other newspapers online. The growth of newspapers on the Web has been extremely successful.

Newspaper sites are attractive to advertisers because online-newspaper readers are twice as likely to make purchases online as are the average Internet users. In addition, the Internet is a good way to stimulate the traditional sale of newspapers, since 82% of consumers who use the Web for news also read a newspaper regularly.

Supply Conditions

The number of daily morning and evening newspapers has fallen below 1,500. The number of weekly newspapers has also declined below 7,200. However in contrast, the number of Sunday newspapers has increased and now exceeds 900. The 20 largest newspaper companies dominate the industry, accounting for almost 75% of the consumption of newsprint.

Despite the decline in newspaper circulation, 1999 saw the industry continue to enjoy healthy gains in revenues and profits.

- A major factor in the improvement in profits has been the decline in raw-paper prices.

- Another source of profitability was the strong demand for advertising.

- Finally, the implementation of cost-cutting measures by the industry has been an additional factor.

In spite of the fact that paper prices have fallen sharply since the end of 1998, cost cutting is expected to remain a priority issue with newspaper publishers. This should provide a cushion against rising paper prices in the years ahead.

Environmental Issues

Close to 70% of all old newspapers in the United States are recycled. The newspaper-recycling rate has climbed steadily the last ten years when the newspaper and newsprint industries, with the help of communities, made recycling a priority. The average amount of recycled fiber in the newsprint used by U.S. newspapers and other newsprint consumers increased from 10% in 1989 to more than 28% today.

Key Risks to the Forecast

The key long-term risks in the newspaper industry are:

- The uncertainty about the degree to which the sector can adapt to continuous changes in technology, information gathering, and delivery.

- Market consolidation on an international basis.

As larger proportions of the population become technologically proficient, greater shares of the information delivery market will be electronic. The newspaper industry faces the choice of accelerating their entry into these new media, and thereby transforming into and merging with other industries, or going through the consolidation and rationalization process that accompanies a declining market.

Chapter 11: Chemicals and Allied Products

Chemicals and Allied Products

The chemicals and allied products industry is one of the world's most globalized industries. Production is becoming increasingly spread across a large number of countries and international trade is growing rapidly. The industry produces tens of thousands of products that can be broadly classified into three major groups: basic chemicals (organic and inorganic); chemical products to be used as intermediate materials in further manufacture, such as synthetic materials (plastic resins, fibers, and rubber) and dyes and pigments; and finished chemical products ready for consumption (drugs, cosmetics, soaps, and paints) or to be used as supplies in other industries, such as fertilizers, printing ink, and explosives. Together, the categories of basic chemicals and synthetic materials account for 50% to 55% of the U.S. chemicals and allied products industry's shipments. Petrochemicals, defined as carbon-derived products, comprise the vast majority of the organic chemicals and synthetic materials categories.

Following several years of solid growth, volume for the overall chemicals and allied products industry declined almost 1% in 1998, in response mainly to plunging exports to Asia. Over the next two years, growth will be moderate, as a rebound in Asia's economy will likely be offset by slower growth in the U.S. economy. While volume may surge in the fourth quarter of 1999 as consumers of bulk-commodity chemicals build up their material inventory as a precautionary measure against Y2K-related potential supply disruptions, the first half of 2000 could experience the opposite due to a de-stocking process.

WEFA's long-term growth forecast of about 2% for chemicals and allied products volume is virtually identical to the rate of increase achieved in the last ten years. One key long-term issue for the chemical industry is the cost of pollution abatement, which has doubled over the past decade and complicated the industry's ability to compete in the global marketplace. Environmental costs are expected to increase further in the years ahead.

Chemicals comprise a $1.6 trillion global industry that is characterized by large volumes of international trade. Virtually every country produces chemicals, but just a handful of industrialized nations account for the bulk of the world's total production. For example, the top-ten countries combined accounted for almost 70% of global chemical output in 1997—the United States, Japan, Germany, China, France, the U.K., Italy, South Korea, Belgium/Luxembourg, and Spain. With a 24% share of global output, the U.S. chemicals and allied products industry is the world's largest, followed by Japan (13%) and Germany (7.5%).

The chemicals and allied products industry also ranks among the largest and most internationally competitive industries in the United States. Chemicals are essential inputs to the production processes of the construction, manufacturing, service, mining, and agriculture industries. The chemical industry is the single largest purchaser of its own output, with about 25% of its production of basic chemicals used as captive products in the form of raw or intermediate materials. Chemicals range from basic commodities, such as ethylene and sulfuric acid, to the most sophisticated drugs and highly specialized high-tech composites used in aircraft and spacecraft. On a shipment value basis, the U.S. chemical industry accounts for roughly 3% of the nation's total gross output and 10% of its manufacturing sector.

Prices for many chemicals, particularly the commodity products, are set by global supply and demand. World trade reflects an intensely competitive struggle for markets. Traditionally, the U.S. chemical industry has enjoyed a positive balance of trade. It maintained its net export position in 1997, when the sector's trade surplus widened by an estimated 13% on export growth of 12.4% and import growth of 12.2%.

Canada represents the U.S. industry's largest single export market, followed by Japan and Mexico co-sharing the second spot. Chemical exports to Mexico have more than tripled in the past 10 years. On a regional basis, Asia/Pacific is the United States' largest export market with a 30% share, followed by Canada/Mexico and Western

Europe each with a 27% share, and Latin America/Caribbean (ex. Mexico) with almost a 12% share.

Despite its strong export position, the U.S. chemical industry exports much less of its production than many of its foreign competitors. Its exports represent only about 18% of its production, compared to 63% for Germany, 64% for the United Kingdom, and 52% for France. The key European exporters trade extensively among themselves, as well as with other parts of the world. After years of trailing Germany as the world's second-largest exporter of chemicals, the United States took the lead in 1997. Japan's chemical exports-to-output ratio of barely 15% is even lower than that of the United States. By nature, the Japanese chemical industry is not export-oriented and is geared primarily to supporting the needs of Japan's large-manufacturing sector.

In recent years, benefiting from very strong economic growth and an aggressive buildup of its petrochemical industry, the Asia-Pacific region has become a serious contender in the global chemical market, accounting for almost 10% of total world chemical exports. In the early 1980s, this region's share was less than 1%. The rapid increases in the export share of the newly industrialized Asian nations and other developing regions have come primarily at the expense of Western Europe. Since 1980, the U.S. share of global chemical exports has remained between 14% and 15%, while the combined shares of countries in the European Community fell from 63% to 57%. However, during the same time span, the U.S. share of world imports increased from 6% to almost 11%, suggesting some loss in competitiveness.

Oversupply is a global phenomenon for the petrochemical industry. In recent years, many countries have joined the United States' aggressive expansion push. There are a large number of petrochemical projects under various stages of construction or planning around the world. Even in Asia, which has been plagued by severe financial and economic woes, there are four new ethylene plants coming on stream in 1999—in Thailand, Taiwan, India, and Malaysia. Two more crackers will be added in Asia over the next two years, one in China in 2000 and the other in Singapore in 2001.

These crackers will probably be the last major projects completed from the flurry of new Asian petrochemical

plants that were planned in the early and mid-1990s. Until this new capacity is absorbed through a revival of regional and global demand, petrochemical producers will continue to grapple with an unfavorable worldwide supply/demand balance.

To stay ahead of the curve, every major chemical company in the United States continues to search for cost-cutting opportunities, even after years of achieving significant cost reductions. Driven by an increasing need for cost advantage and critical mass, the industry has embraced an aggressive consolidation strategy in the past year through deals of all varieties: outright acquisitions, mergers, spin-offs, rationalization, joint ventures, and loose business alliances. In Western Europe and Asia, restructuring is also underway. In South Korea, the government is pressuring the "chaebols" to reorganize and rationalize. The Japanese petrochemical industry is restructuring too, although deals of the magnitude of those seen in the United States, Western Europe, or even South Korea are unlikely to take place.

The chemical industry is one of the most capital- and energy-intensive industries in the United States, and one of the least labor-intensive. Ironically, with more than one million workers, it still ranks as one of the biggest employers in the domestic-manufacturing sector. Reflecting cost-cutting pressures, employment throughout the chemical industry has trended downward since 1980. In 1998, employment stabilized but the pressure to keep a lean labor force and enhance productivity has by no means let up. Most of the industry's labor force cutbacks have been shouldered by the basic chemicals and synthetic materials sectors. These sectors underwent two waves of restructuring during the last fifteen years that have resulted in a leaner and more competitive business. Drug manufacturing, on the other hand, has seen its head-count increase substantially during the 1980s and 1990s, reflecting strong profitability and volume growth.

Successful operation in the chemical industry, where technological and cost advantages are often the key to its members' survival, requires an enormous amount of capital, which makes entrance by newcomers rather difficult. The industry, therefore, tends to be dominated by a relatively small number of very large corporations, such as DuPont, Dow, Exxon, Johnson & Johnson,

Bristol-Myers Squibb, Merck, Abbott Laboratories, Monsanto, Arco, and Union Carbide (as of this writing, Dow Chemical is in the process of acquiring Union Carbide). The high level of capital is essential for building, maintaining, modernizing, and expanding the large plant facilities that are required to achieve the low-production costs that come with economies of scale. Significant funds are also required to support aggressive R&D programs and to meet the government's requirements on health, safety, and the environment.

The chemical industry uses energy not only as fuel and power for its operations, but also as a key raw material in its production process. Natural gas and oil derivatives account for more than 80% of its energy needs. Its overall energy usage amounts to about 7% of this country's total energy consumption. The industry has achieved significant energy efficiency gains during the past 20 years, and energy usage per unit of output has dropped by almost 40%. However, continued improvement in energy efficiency will be required for the industry to maintain its competitive position in the world market.

Complicating the U.S. chemical industry's ability to compete in a global marketplace is a constantly growing regulatory burden. The costs of pollution abatement alone, which represent only a portion of the industry's total regulatory costs, have doubled over the past ten years and are currently estimated at about $6 billion. Roughly 75% of this amount is borne by the industrial chemicals segment of the industry, which also faces the fiercest international competitive pressures. Environmental costs are likely to increase further.

Foreign chemical companies have been playing an increasingly important role in the domestic industry. Foreign direct investment in the U.S. chemical industry has more than tripled since 1987. In 1997, it totaled almost $89 billion, with European companies the dominant investors. In contrast, U.S. investment in foreign chemical industries was less than $74 billion.

Outlook

Following growth of 5.8% in 1997, total shipments of the U.S. chemicals and allied products industry grew by 0.6% in 1998. WEFA forecasts them to increase by about 1% in both 1999 and 2000. Prices are expected to remain largely unchanged in 1999, but they should trend slightly upward in 2000. Consequently, growth in volume and current dollar shipments are virtually identical in 1999, but in 2000, volume remains flat. Long-term growth of close to 2% is forecast on an average annual basis for volume.

Chemical prices increased by an average of about 3% per year during the past decade. Increases closer to 2% per year are more likely over the next ten years, as higher productivity, moderate production cost increases, and global competitive pressures put a damper on pricing, particularly for industrial chemicals.

WEFA expects the drug-manufacturing sector to continue to post growth above that of the overall chemical industry in terms of both sales and profits.

Industrial Chemicals

The industrial chemicals sector is comprised mostly of industrial organic and inorganic chemicals. Volume for this sector increased at an average annual rate of just 0.4% during the past ten years, while prices moved up at a 1.7% clip. Volume growth was held down by substantial declines in both 1996 and 1998; the former caused by inventory de-stocking and a slowdown in the U.S. economy and the latter due to the delayed impact of the 1997 Asian economic crisis. During the next few years, output growth will be back in-line with the industry's trend performance of about 2%, reflecting moderate increases in domestic demand. However, the industry will face lower price gains and a deteriorating balance of trade. Exports of industrial organic chemicals, long a major contributor to chemical-industry trade, are likely to come under pressure and so are prices, as capacity expansions in the United States and overseas result in global oversupply conditions. The mature industrial inorganic chemicals sector is expected to remain lackluster both in terms of overall demand and prices.

During the past two decades, the U.S. industrial-chemicals industry has developed costly programs to reduce the emission of the many types of materials that contribute to air, water, and land pollution. The pollution abatement costs associated with these programs have increased in proportion to the industry's sales, rising from about 1.9% of sales in 1984 to roughly 3% during the 1990s. Stringent environmental regulations at the federal, state, and local levels will remain a cost burden to the industry and will continue to adversely affect its competitiveness.

Industrial Organic Chemicals

Overview

Organic chemicals are defined as those chemicals that are compounds of carbon. Industrial organic chemicals account for about 60% of the industrial chemicals sector. They represent about 20% of total U.S. chemical-industry shipments, and rank second in importance to the pharmaceutical sector. On a trade basis, they account for almost 24% of all chemical exports and 34% of imports, far more than any other chemical group. They are the most energy- and capital-intensive chemical products, and perhaps those most subjected to environmental regulations by the U.S. government. The industrial organic-chemicals industry employs roughly 138,000 workers. Since 1990, head count has declined by about 1.6% per year, as the industry implements ongoing cost reduction programs aimed at increasing its competitiveness.

Industrial organic chemicals are obtained from many sources, including petroleum and natural gas, coal and coke by-products, fats and oils, and agricultural products. However, more than 80% of the industry's raw material requirements are derived from petroleum and natural gas products, leading to the designation of petrochemicals for most organic chemicals. The basic petrochemicals derived from petroleum and natural gas are primarily the building blocks such as olefins (ethylene, propylene, butadiene) and aromatics (benzene, xylenes) used to create thousands of downstream products. In terms of production, ethylene is by far the most important basic petrochemical, followed by propylene and benzene.

In subsequent processing, other chemicals are added to these organic building blocks to form various compounds with certain desired characteristics. The final output may be, for example: polyester fiber or nylon; PVC; anti–freeze; a pharmaceutical product; PET, the plastic resin used in making soda bottles; or the synthetic rubber used in the manufacture of tires. Other organic-product groups include cyclic intermediates, dyes, pigments, tar crudes, alcohols, plasticizers, leather-tanning agents, rubber processing chemicals, pesticides, and agricultural chemicals.

Most of the major petrochemical producers have a vertically integrated production process, which gives them better control of both raw materials and end-use markets. Industrial organic chemicals are classified for the most part as commodities, and producers face an intense struggle for markets. Cost competitiveness and technological advantage are often the determining factors of success.

Because organic chemicals are transformed into so many products with different properties and applications, their end-use markets are very diverse. They include consumer durable and non-durable goods, as well as capital equipment, construction, and various services. Demand for industrial organic chemicals is particularly sensitive to movements in the highly cyclical construction and automotive markets, two of the industry's largest single end-uses. The U.S. economy is the most important factor in determining the industry's profitability and performance. However, global economic conditions have taken on a more significant role in recent years, affecting virtually every facet of the industry, including trade, supply, and prices.

The organic chemicals trade balance, long a big contributor to chemical company fortunes, has turned negative since 1996, in part due to soft economic conditions in Europe, Canada, and Mexico in that year, the ongoing strength of the U.S. dollar, and the onset of the Asian-economic crisis in 1997. Another key factor is the massive petrochemical-capacity buildup in the Middle East and Asia that has cut into the U.S. trade balance. While the share of organic chemicals imports relative to total imports for the chemical industry has remained remarkably steady since 1990 at about 33%, the same cannot be said for organic chemicals exports whose share relative to total chemical exports has shrunk from 27% in 1990 to less than 24% in 1997.

The largest U.S. markets for organic-chemical exports are in Western Europe and Asia. But, while the former has been rather conservative in expanding its petrochemical capacity in recent years, the industrializing Asian countries, including China, have been aggressively building their own. South Korea now has the fifth-largest ethylene capacity in the world, and China is sixth. Based on announced projects, by the year 2001 Saudi Arabia will have the third-largest ethylene capacity in the world after the United States and Japan; China will be ranked fifth and South Korea sixth. A large portion of Saudi Arabia's petrochemical production is directed at the Asian market. Saudi Arabia has also targeted Europe, where it enjoys a strong production cost advantage over the European petrochemical producers. In the long run, the aggressive push by Asia and the Middle East to boost their petrochemical capacity and export share will not only hurt Europe's chemical trade, but the United States' as well.

Recent Market Conditions and Outlook

Despite gains in volumes, productivity, and prices, several major U.S. petrochemical companies posted sharp declines in their second-quarter 1999 earnings. Rising energy and feedstock costs were the main culprit, as these costs could not be passed along fast enough through higher selling prices.

For more than a year now, the U.S. petrochemical industry has been afflicted by poor market conditions. The Asian-economic crisis took a heavy toll on the industry in 1998, with second-half earnings registering more than 50% year-over-year declines. In 1999, first-quarter earnings showed some improvement, but results were still generally dismal on a year-over-year basis. For the remainder of 1999, we believe that the overall prospects for the industry are mixed.

U.S. petrochemical supply has tightened up since the beginning of 1999, mainly along the ethylene chain, due to production problems and scheduled maintenance turnarounds. Domestic producers have taken advantage of this temporary supply shortfall to implement price increases for ethylene and its main derivatives, including the commodity plastic resins. These hikes began taking place while the industry was enjoying near-record-low energy and feedstock costs early in the year. But, then, rapidly escalating crude-oil and natural-gas prices since March have pretty much wiped out the benefits of the price increases. Both oil and natural-gas prices have stabilized recently and another major run-up in the prices of those products is unlikely in the near term, a positive sign for the industry.

Another plus for the industry is the export market, which has been strengthening since the beginning of 1999. Although much of Latin America, as of this write-up, is still in recession, Asia's economy, including Japan's, has rebounded, and Western Europe is coming out of its lethargy.

There are increasing signs that the domestic market is slowing, particularly the interest-rate-sensitive sectors, such as residential construction. Interest rates are up and most likely will continue to rise, as the Fed enforces its preempting stance against inflation. Also, there is evidence that petrochemical downstream customers have been building inventory to protect themselves against further price increases, a move that is bound to have a corrective impact on both volume and prices in the months ahead.

Additionally, the tight-supply condition, which has characterized the U.S. petrochemical market since the beginning of 1999, has begun to dissipate. Production should gradually return to normal levels in the months ahead and, with some new capacity entering the market, supply should loosen up, making it harder for additional price increases to stick. Over the next two years, large amounts of new capacity for ethylene and its main derivatives are due on stream in the United States, raising once more the specter of a glut for those products.

There are a large number of petrochemical projects under various stages of construction or planning around the world, including the United States. Even in Asia, which has been plagued by severe financial and economic woes, there are four new ethylene plants coming on stream in 1999—in Thailand, Taiwan, India, and Malaysia. Two more crackers will be added in Asia over the next two years, one in China in 2000 and the other in Singapore in 2001.

These crackers will probably be the last major projects completed from the flurry of new Asian petrochemical plants that were planned in the early and mid-1990s. Asia/Pacific's buildup will raise its share of global ethylene production to equal that of North America, about 30% (Western Europe's share of the world's ethylene will be around 20%). Until this new capacity is absorbed through a revival of regional and global demand, petrochemical producers will grapple with an unfavorable worldwide supply/demand balance.

To stay ahead of the curve, every major petrochemical company continues to search for cost-cutting opportunities, even after years of achieving significant cost reductions. Driven by an increasing need for cost advantage and critical mass, the industry has embraced an aggressive consolidation strategy in the past couple of years through deals of all varieties: outright acquisitions, mergers, spin-offs, rationalization, joint ventures, and loose business alliances. Some of those deals in Europe and the United States include the mega-mergers of Amoco-BP, Exxon-Mobil, Total-Fina, and Lyondell-Arco, as well as Nova's purchase of Huntsman's polystyrene business, and OxyChem's polyvinyl chloride merger with Geon. They also include Oxy-

Chem's participation in the Equistar petrochemical venture formed in 1997 by Millenium-Lyondell, and more recently the announced merger of Dow Chemical and Union Carbide. This new company, which is keeping the Dow name, will create the world's second-largest chemical manufacturer. Together with Equistar and Exxon-Mobil, it will hold more than half of the U.S. polyethylene market.

In Asia, restructuring is also underway, particularly in Korea where the government is pressuring the chaebols to reorganize and rationalize. The biggest Korean deal announced so far is the proposed merger of Hyundai Petrochemical and Samsung General Chemicals. The Japanese petrochemical industry is restructuring too, although deals of the magnitude planned in Korea are unlikely to take place. Korea and Indonesia have seen the largest number of merger and acquisition deals involving western companies. However, those have mainly been buyouts of joint venture partners, not entire companies or petrochemical complexes.

U.S. production of organic chemicals decreased 1.1% in 1998, while prices dropped 5.2%. We forecast both production and prices to increase in 1999 on a quarter-to-quarter basis. On average, however, they will be flat for the year, dragged by significant year-over-year declines in the first half.

Industrial Inorganic Chemicals

Industrial inorganic chemicals constitute roughly 22% of the industrial-chemicals sector. They are produced from minerals other than hydrocarbons, as well as gases found in the atmosphere, and are used as inputs in the production of other chemicals and finished products. In terms of tonnage, eight of the top ten chemicals produced in the United States are inorganic. Nitrogen ranks first, followed by sulfuric acid, oxygen, lime, ammonia, chlorine, soda ash (sodium carbonate), and caustic soda (sodium hydroxide).

The industrial inorganic chemicals industry is mature. It is characterized by stagnant growth, over-capacity, and relatively low-capital expenditures for new plant and expansions. In spite of the industry's low level of capital spending for capacity additions, the value of its assets per employee is estimated to be four times higher than that for overall manufacturing, an indication of its capital intensity.

Company expansion is achieved mostly through mergers and acquisitions. Consolidations have taken place frequently in the last few years to permit better use of existing capacity and to tighten supply enough to support price increases. Industrial inorganic chemical companies have also tried to diversify into the production of more profitable and faster growing specialty and high-grade products. This trend should continue in the future.

Cost competitiveness is the key to survival in the industrial-inorganic chemicals business. As a result, companies have devoted much of their efforts to control or reduce input costs. The industry employs 117,000 workers. Since 1990, employment has declined by about 2.3% per year. Like their organic chemicals counterparts, producers of industrial inorganic chemicals have also been facing increasing costs for pollution abatement. This has added to their cost of production, and there is little hope that these costs will be recouped in the current pricing environment.

Shipments growth for inorganic chemicals has been less than 1% per year since 1990. With price increases averaging close to 1% per annum, growth in real output has been virtually flat. This lackluster performance will be maintained over the forecast period.

The trade balance for industrial inorganic chemicals turned negative during the 1994–1996 period, but it recovered modestly in 1997. Estimates for 1998 call for another negative performance. Trade in inorganic chemicals is largely influenced by the value of the U.S. dollar and growth in foreign-buyer economies. The major foreign buyers of U.S. industrial inorganic chemicals are: Japan, Canada, Mexico, and Western Europe. Most of these countries have experienced slower economic growth, or outright recessions in the case of Japan and Mexico, in the last few years. This, in conjunction with a strong dollar, may have been the culprit behind the deterioration in the trade balance. Exports should improve as these economies pick up steam over the forecast period.

There are four major categories of industrial inorganic chemicals: chloralkalis, which account for 10% of total industrial inorganic chemicals shipments; industrial gases, with a 13% share; inorganic pigments, with a 13% share; and inorganic chemicals, not elsewhere classified (n.e.c.), with the largest share of 64%. Over the past eight years, chloralkalis shipments growth has averaged about 1.8% per annum, industrial gases 3.4%, inorganic pigments 2.9%, and inorganic chemicals, n.e.c., 2.9%.

The chloralkali industry produces mainly chlorine, caustic soda, soda ash, sodium bicarbonate, potassium hydroxide, and potassium carbonate. Chlorine and caustic soda account for more than 80% of industry shipments, while soda ash represents 15%. Chlorine and caustic soda are manufactured as co-products through the electrolysis of brine.

■ Almost 50% of the chlorine produced is used to process organic chemicals, notably ethylene dichloride, the precursor of vinyl chloride and PVC. The remainder is used to make pulp and paper and other industrial products. In the last few years, PVC has benefited considerably from the residential construction boom in the United States. However, it has suffered a blow from the recent collapse of the Asian export market.

■ Caustic soda has a much broader use than chlorine, finding applications in many industries, including industrial chemicals, soaps and detergents, petroleum refining, textiles, and alumina (the raw material for producing aluminum). As mentioned earlier, caustic soda is a co-product of chlorine, but their markets do not always move together, which means that when one is in tight supply the other may be experiencing a glut. For this reason, their prices tend to move in opposite directions. Chlorine prices surged during 1996 and the first half of 1997, but turned down in 1998. In contrast, caustic soda prices were soft in 1996 and the early part of 1997, but have jumped in 1998.

■ Soda ash is mainly used to manufacture glass and glass containers. It is also a substitute for caustic soda in certain applications. Substitution tends to take place when caustic soda prices become prohibitive.

The chlorine industry has been adversely affected by environmental regulations in the past several years, particularly in applications such as chlorofluorocarbons (CFCs) and pulp bleaching. However, these setbacks have been partially offset by PVC's growing success in the housing market, increasingly becoming the material of choice for window frames, piping, soffits, and siding.

11.9

The industrial-gas industry markets gases in compressed liquid or solid form. Such gases include the basic industrial gases (nitrogen, oxygen, hydrogen, acetylene, and carbon dioxide) and about one hundred specialty gases that are used in a variety of electronics, aerospace, medical, and communications applications. Specialty gases account for a relatively small portion of industrial-gas production, but represent about one-third of the industry's revenues.

The two largest end-use markets for basic industrial gases are the chemicals and metals industries, in particular steel. Other markets include: electronics, oil recovery, fertilizers, refrigeration, petroleum refining, the space program, and beverages. Because of the diversity of their markets, industrial gases are largely dependent on total manufacturing performance. However, growth above that of manufacturing is occurring because of new applications in waste treatment, pulp bleaching, electronics, medical diagnostics, and communications. The industrial gas industry has gone through a period of consolidation in the past twenty years. Four major producers control an estimated 80% of the U.S. market. They are Air Liquide, Air Products, BOC, and Praxair. Industrial-gas prices have increased at an average annual rate of 2.3% during the 1990–1998 period.

The industrial-inorganic chemicals, n.e.c. category includes the basic bulk-inorganic chemicals, such as: sulfuric, hydrochloric, nitric, and phosphoric acids; aluminum, potassium, and sodium salts; calcium phosphates, hydrogen peroxide; and sulfur. This industry is very mature and offers no significant prospects of growth beyond that of its end-use markets. Some of its major markets are the fertilizer, metal, petroleum refining, mining, oil and gas production, housing, pulp and paper, and soap and detergent industries.

Inorganic pigments are also a very mature segment of the industrial inorganic chemicals business. It is a fragmented industry with many small players. Pigment growth is largely dependent on activity in the paint and coatings market, as well as the textiles and paper markets. Because of its strong tie to construction and automotive manufacturing, demand for pigments is very cyclical. The most important pigment in terms of volume and also the most widely used is titanium oxide, a white pigment. It ranks among the top-50, U.S.-produced chemicals, based on tonnage.

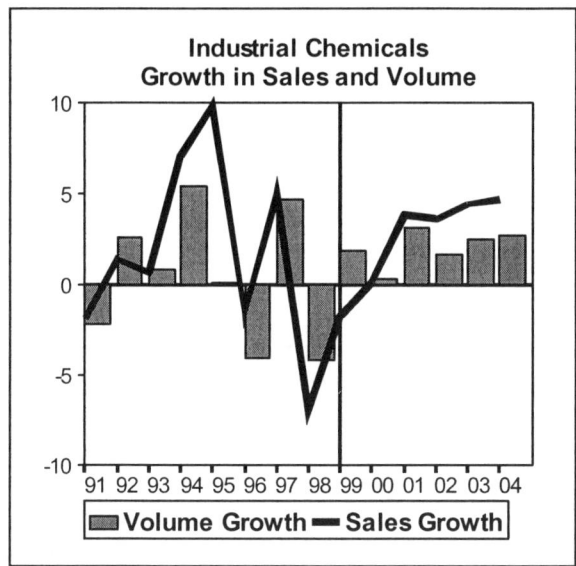

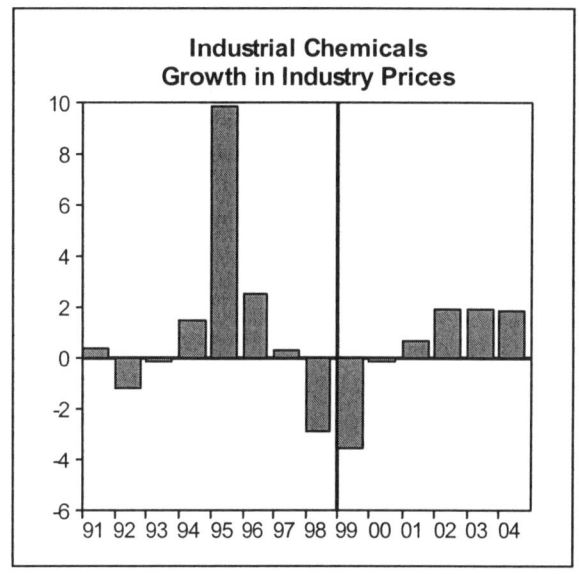

Industrial Chemicals

SIC 281, 286, 289

		1992	1993	1994	1995	1996	1997	1998	1999	2000	2001	Compound Average 88-98	Annual Growth 98-08
Sales													
	Billions of $	157.7	158.8	170.1	186.8	184.0	193.2	179.9	176.8	177.1	183.9		
	% Ch	1.4	0.7	7.1	9.9	-1.5	5.0	-6.9	-1.7	0.2	3.8	2.1	3.3
Volume													
	% Ch	2.6	0.9	5.5	0.1	-4.0	4.7	-4.2	1.9	0.4	3.2	0.4	2.3
Prices													
	% Ch	-1.2	-0.2	1.5	9.9	2.5	0.3	-2.9	-3.6	-0.2	0.6	1.7	1.0
Production Costs													
Avg. Hourly Earnings													
	$/hr	15.60	15.89	16.25	16.94	17.54	17.91	18.42	18.76	19.34	19.91		
	% Ch	4.3	1.9	2.3	4.2	3.5	2.1	2.8	1.9	3.1	2.9	3.1	2.8
Input Price Index													
	% Ch	-0.4	0.7	1.1	5.8	2.7	0.7	-3.4	-2.0	1.4	1.8	1.4	1.7

Plastic Materials

Plastics constitute the largest category of materials used in the United States. Plastic-resins production has grown at an average annual rate of about 3.7% since 1987, propelled by end-use market growth, new technology-driven applications, and plastics' displacement of traditional materials like glass, paper, wood, concrete, and leather in many uses. There are some 45 basic families of plastic resins, and each can be made with hundreds of variations, giving the industry almost unlimited possibilities in market applications.

The bulk of plastic-resins shipments is made up of high-volume, low-cost commodity products whose prices are determined by global supply and demand conditions and the cost of feedstocks. Plastic resins are used in the fabrication of plastic products, whose end-use markets span from packaging and construction to transportation, electronics, and toys.

In the past ten years, plastic-resins prices have risen at an average annual clip of 2.2%. This rate was almost one percentage point below the price gains achieved by their industrial organic chemicals inputs, resulting in a margin squeeze for resins producers and reflecting the intensity of competition that exists both in the United States and overseas.

The number of countries producing plastic resins has increased significantly in recent years, mainly among the newly industrialized and developing countries of Asia and the Middle East, giving birth to a large amount of new capacity that has eroded the U.S.' trade balance. This buildup of capacity will continue during the next ten years—albeit at a slower pace than predicted earlier because of Asia's economic problems — as those countries continue to develop their industrial infrastructure. The quest for larger market share in the U.S. market has also led domestic plastic-resins producers to considerably expand their capacity.

Products and Markets

Plastic resins are produced by processing petrochemical feedstocks and intermediate chemicals. Ethylene is the major feedstock, followed by propylene, benzene, xylene, toluene, butadiene, methane, and butylenes. Major intermediate chemicals include vinyl chloride, styrene, ethylene glycol, propylene glycol, and acrylonitrile.

The two major categories of plastics are thermoplastics and thermosets. Thermoplastics can be repeatedly softened or hardened by increasing or decreasing their temperature. Thermosets, on the other hand, cannot be resoftened by heat once they have been fully cured. Thermoplastics account for about 80% of U.S. plastic-resins sales and captive use. They are mostly low-cost, high-volume commodity products, which include polyethylene (PE), polypropylene (PP), polyvinyl chloride (PVC), polystyrene (PS), and bottle-grade polyethylene terephthalate (PET). Thermosets include: phenolic, unsaturated poly-

Estimated Market Distribution of Plastic Resins

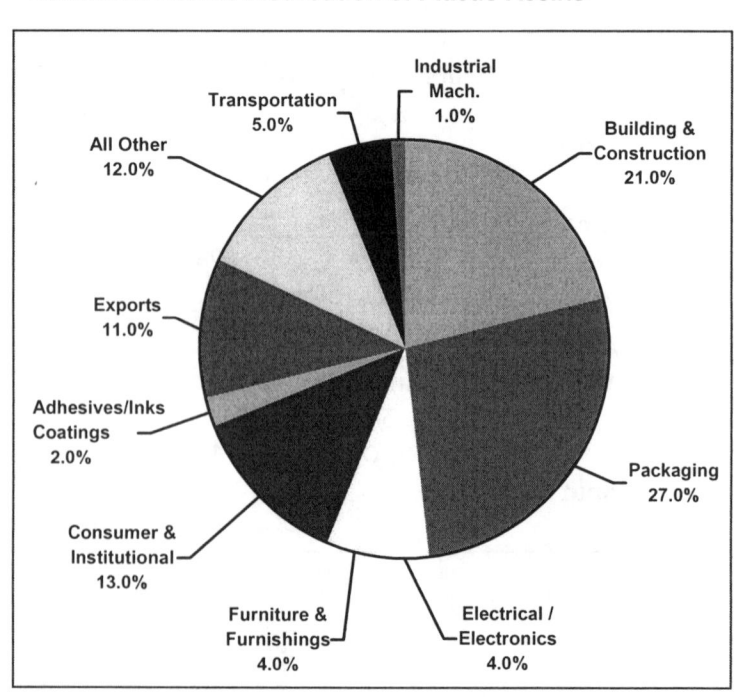

ester, urea and melamine, isocyanates, polyether and polyester polyols, and polyurethanes.

Plastic resins that are produced in small quantities but at a relatively high processing cost are referred to as engineering or high-performance resins. They represent about 8% to 10% of total plastic-resins shipments. These products are typically designed for specific applications that require high ratings for mechanical, thermal, electrical, and chemical properties. Fillers and reinforcements such as glass, carbon, and fibrous glass are often added to improve these properties. Research and development and marketing are the major cost factors in producing engineering resins, with feedstock the least important cost element. Historically, some of these resins have enjoyed double-digit growth rates, spurred by new applications in the aerospace, medical, and electronics industries.

Packaging is the largest single end-use market for the plastics industry, followed by building and construction and transportation equipment. Because of the plastics industry's market dependency on construction and the automotive industry, and durable goods in general, it is quite cyclical. Furthermore, additional shipments volatility is added by often-wide short-term inventory swings, caused either by buyers or producers, as witnessed in late 1994 and early 1995.

Plastic-material shipments were valued at over $40 billion in 1997. Exports represented roughly 25% to 30% of shipments, and imports about half those shares. Production gains in that year were estimated at 6% for thermoplastic resins and 5% for thermosetting resins. The largest gain was for polypropylene, which was up 11%. In 1998 domestic demand was up more than 7% for PP and 5% for PVC, the two best-selling commodity resins in that year. In the polyethylene area, domestic demand increased 3.8% for HDPE and 2.7% for LLDPE, but declined almost 1% for LDPE.

Growth in imports has surpassed growth in exports in the last several years. Since 1990, exports have increased at an average nominal rate close to 9% per year, while imports have surged at a 15% rate. The fast pace of imports reflects an acceleration in shipments in recent years from Canada, Mexico, Western Europe, and Japan, the largest importers of plastic resins into the United States. These countries took advantage of a booming U.S. plastics market and generally tight supply conditions

during the mid-1990s to boost their exports. Asia/Pacific ranks first as a foreign buyer of U.S. plastic resins, accounting for some 30% of total U.S. resins exports; Canada accounts for 24%, Western Europe 18%, Mexico 12%, and Japan 5%. Exports to Asia have been on a declining trend for the past few years as a result of the region's aggressive push to develop its own petrochemical industry. South Korea, Taiwan, Indonesia, and China have been the primary engines behind this push. However, their effort was interrupted in 1997 when economic conditions took a turn for the worse in Asia and regional demand for plastic resins fell sharply, driving U.S. exports down with a vengeance. Although the Asian market is expected to begin turning around in the next year or two, U.S. exports to the region will remain exposed. Some of the petrochemical projects that were on the table before the current economic crisis have been either put on hold or postponed indefinitely. In general, however, Asia's capacity buildup will resume once the region regains its economic momentum.

Plastic products account for about 20% of municipal waste in the United States. Recycling and disposal of these products have become growing environmental concerns, forcing the use of recycled plastic materials to increase in recent years. Domestic production of recycled material has been expanding rapidly in recent years. About 40% of this production is PET; 35% is high-density polyethylene (HDPE); and, roughly 10% is low-density polyethylene (LDPE/LLDPE). The remainder consists of small volumes of the other commodity resins. Recycled plastics are used in a wide variety of products, ranging from automotive bumpers to surfboards. WEFA expects the use of recyclate to increase by 7% to 8% per year over the next few years.

Recent Market Conditions and Outlook

Following production gains of close to 10% in 1994, the U.S. plastic-resins industry started 1995 on a high note. Despite running its plants flat out, it struggled to produce fast enough to satisfy the domestic market's voracious appetite. Prices jumped by 27% between mid-1994 and mid-1995. But, subsequently the market peaked. Consumption eased, throwing the supply-demand balance off kilter. Producer inventories snowballed, as buyers worked off the stocks they had built late in 1994 and early in 1995, when prices were surging. As a result, prices began a slide that lasted until the first quarter of 1996 and totaled 14%. The inventory depletion process for buyers of plastic resins ended in the early months of 1996, and the rebuilding of their stocks contributed to another rebound in domestic demand. At the same time, numerous upstream-plant problems during 1996 kept raw materials like ethylene, propylene, and styrene in short supply, which contributed to an increase in their prices. Skyrocketing energy costs added to this upward push. The combination of short materials supply, strong resins demand, and surging energy and feedstock costs led to another wave of plastic-resins price increases, which ended abruptly in the second half of 1997 at the onset of the Asian crisis. By the fall of that year, prices had begun to weaken, prompted by declining demand in Asia and an increasingly oversupplied global market.

The Asia crisis hit the global plastic-resins industry pretty hard in 1998. Plastic-resin consumption in Southeast Asia is estimated to have declined by as much as 50%, depending on the country. In the United States, resin exports took a nosedive as a result, and prices plunged in spite of a surge in domestic demand. Prices also declined sharply in Europe.

However, the U.S. plastic-resins industry has rebounded since the start of 1999. The continuation of healthy domestic demand combined with plant outages, a recovering Asian market, and signs of renewed life in the Western European economy have supported overall demand and prices.

Prices have been raised several times this year for polyethylene and PVC, reflecting particularly strong demand for those two resins. Price increases totaling more than 30% have been posted for both PE and PVC during the first eight months of the year. PE's packaging markets have generally benefited from robust domestic-consumption expenditures, while both PVC and PE have enjoyed the boom in residential construction. Further-

more, domestic supplies for most grades of PE and PVC have not been overly excessive in spite of recent additions to capacity by the industry, which has kept their overall demand/supply balance generally tight.

Prices for polypropylene and polystyrene were weak through the first quarter of 1999, but they have firmed since in response to renewed price initiatives by the industry. Demand for PS has been less spectacular than for PE and PVC, but like them it has enjoyed a fairly balanced market. In contrast, demand for PP has been quite strong, but it has been offset by an overload of supply.

Going forward, resin prices are likely to remain firm in the near term. However, frenzied pre-buying coupled with scheduled capacity additions, especially for PP and PE, and a return to production normalcy could result in both volume and price corrections toward the end of 1999 and the early part of 2000.

Over the next five to ten years, growth in overall U.S. demand for plastic resins will slow from historical rates of about 4% per year to around 3%. This will happen as the industry matures, exports increasingly come under pressure, and imports from Canada continue to grow under the freer trade conditions brought by the NAFTA agreement. On the positive side, the industry will be able to take advantage of expanding domestic markets and growing demand from Latin America and the Caribbean, where petrochemical production capability is still in its infancy stage. The United States will continue to be a world leader in engineering plastics, both in terms of R&D and commercialization of new product applications. This area will play a more strategic role in the long run as global competition intensifies in the commodity segment. Additionally, technology licensing, direct investment by U.S. firms in foreign countries, and alliances with domestic and foreign partners will have an increasingly larger role.

Drugs, Soaps, and Toiletries

The drug industry includes companies engaged in manufacturing or processing pharmaceutical products, medicinal chemicals, botanical preparations, and diagnostic products. The soaps and toiletries industry comprises manufacturers of soaps, detergents, surface-active agents, and cleaning and polishing preparations, as well as producers of personal-care products including cosmetics.

Sales of drugs, soaps, and toiletries combined have increased at an average annual rate of 7.1% in the last ten years, with volume growth of 3.6% and prices up 3.4%. Exports have increased at a faster pace than the domestic market but have remained relatively low as a percentage of total sales, at less than 10%. Imports have been gaining in importance as well, as their share of industry shipments almost doubled in the last six years, from 4% to 7%. As a group, drugs, soaps, and toiletries have typically enjoyed a positive balance of trade, although the drugs and pharmaceuticals sector's trade balance turned negative in 1997. Despite the recent increase in imports and the strength of the dollar, WEFA expects the United States to maintain its competitive advantage in this overall group during the next several years.

The drug industry is the fastest growing segment of the drugs, soaps, and toiletries group. With two-thirds of the group's sales and a consistently strong financial performance, it is also the largest and most profitable. Historically, shipments of drugs have increased at a 10% clip per annum, spurred by new product introduction and expanding overseas markets, compared with increases of 3% to 5% for shipments of soaps and toiletries. WEFA's forecast calls for drug sales to maintain their good historical performance over the next several years. Profitability in the drug-manufacturing business is also expected to remain the strongest in the chemical industry and among the best in the U.S.-manufacturing sector. Growth in shipments of soaps and toiletries, on the other hand, is expected to decelerate somewhat. The aging of the U.S. population will play a critical role in the outlook for not only the drug markets but also the soaps and toiletries business.

Drugs

The drug industry employs about 267,000 employees. It is by far the biggest employer among the major segments of the chemicals and allied products industry, and it is the only category that has increased head–count consistently over the past five years, with gains averaging over 2% per annum. Roughly 20% of its employees are full-time research and development (R&D) scientists and engineers, compared to 9% for the overall chemical industry and 4% for manufacturing in general.

Extensive research and development is required for continued growth in U.S. drug companies' sales, and a large fraction of the industry's funds are used for this purpose. R&D expenditures amounted to about 9% of industry sales during the 1980s, and 10% to 12% during the 1990s. In contrast, the R&D–to–sales ratio for the overall chemical industry has been relatively steady at 5% to 5.5% for the past ten years. The drug sector's commitment to invest in R&D has been the cornerstone

of its strong competitive advantage. This commitment has led to several new product discoveries in recent years that have contributed to the industry's remarkable performance. Among them are: early diagnosis products and home test kits, which can reduce cost and increase success in combating disease; nicotine patches; and drugs for prostate enlargement, cardiovascular disease, AIDS and cancer treatment, hypertension, depression and, more recently, male impotence.

Drug prices increased at a 5% average annual rate during the 1988–1998 period. However, during the 1994–1997 period, price gains slowed to an average rate of just 2.2% per annum before surging almost 11% in 1998. Notwithstanding 1998's rather unusual performance, drug inflation deceleration reflects a number of factors, some of which are:

■ Increasing public concern over health care costs;

- Combined purchasing by large hospital groups that gives hospitals more buying leverage;

- The need of the drug industry to develop and market lower cost medications to serve a growing aging population that lives on fixed incomes; and

- The growing trend toward replacing prescription drugs with less expensive over-the-counter and generic drugs.

The cost-containment push throughout the U.S. healthcare system, including numerous legislative proposals to control drug prices, has also kept the pressure on drug manufacturers to restrain price increases.

Drug industry shipments were estimated at close to $100 billion in 1997, representing roughly 25% of overall chemicals and allied products shipments in that year, up from 12% in 1980. Drug industry profits relative to overall chemical industry profits also increased considerably in the past fifteen years, from about 30% in the early 1980s to close to 50% in 1997. Volume and price increases above those realized by the overall chemical industry largely explain the relative gains in shipments and profits during that period, but cost reduction measures have also played a significant role in boosting drug companies' profitability.

Like many other industries, the U.S. drug industry has implemented aggressive cost reduction and management restructuring programs to increase its competitiveness over the last few years. It has gone through a series of mergers and acquisitions, which gave rise to increased foreign ownership in the domestic market. Today, 50 to 60 companies account for the bulk of drug sales in the United States. These companies include such world giants as Merck, Johnson & Johnson, Abbott Laboratories, Pfizer, SmithKline Beecham, Bristol-Myers Squibb, Rhone-Poulenc Rorer, and Bayer.

Drug exports and imports are both estimated at between $8 and $9 billion. Exports have been growing at an average annual rate of about 11% over the past several years, while imports have increased at almost double that rate. Western Europe is the largest recipient of U.S. drug exports, accounting for close to 50% of the total. Asia is in second place with a 20% share, and Canada is third with a 16% share.

Roughly 75% of drug imports originate from Western Europe; 13% are from Asia, with Japan being the biggest contributor to that share; and about 7% are shipped from Canada. The United States has run a trade deficit with Europe since 1991, but its overall balance of trade in drugs remained positive until 1996. In 1997, it went finally in the red, effectively ending the U.S.' global trade advantage in drugs.

Historically, senior citizens have consumed one-third of all prescription medication dispensed in the United States. With older people in the 50- to 75-year-old bracket expected to comprise 30% of the U.S. population in the next ten years, the drug industry will devote a considerable amount of its resources to making new medicines for the cure and treatment of diseases of the elderly. These include arthritis, Alzheimer's disease, and osteoporosis.

The trend to preventive disease treatment is growing rapidly, and with it the development of new bacterial and virus vaccines, as well as home diagnostic kits such as those developed for checking blood-cholesterol levels and diabetes. Also, with increasing consumer interest in natural products, drug companies are expected to accelerate plant research for potential drug applications and add more herbal ingredients to their products. Cancer treatment is a prime example of successful plant-derived pharmaceutical research by the industry, exemplified by products like Taxol.

Drug manufacturers are urging Congress not to establish a Medicare prescription drug benefit that would impose price controls on the industry. They warn that the development of new drugs for the elderly will depend on maintaining strong profits. Senior citizens who must buy drugs on their own pay substantially more than people enrolled in large health plans that negotiate bulk discounts.

Soaps, Detergents, and Other Cleaning Preparations

Shipments of the soaps, detergents, and other cleaning preparations industry are valued at roughly $30 billion. In the last five years, they have increased at an average annual rate of about 4%, while prices have gone up at a 1% clip. Over the next ten years, WEFA forecasts both shipments and prices for this industry to continue rising at their historical pace. Soaps and detergents account for better than 50% of total industry shipments, polishing and sanitation goods for almost 30%, and surface active agents for the remainder.

Industry exports are valued at roughly $2 billion, or 7% of total shipments, and imports are about $600 million. Although exports represent a relatively small portion of the market, they have increased at double-digit rates in recent years, reflecting good growth opportunities for the industry overseas.

A handful of companies account for the bulk of the industry's sales. They include Procter & Gamble (P&G), Johnson & Johnson (J&J), Dial Consumer Products, Colgate-Palmolive, Church and Dwight, Unilever, and The Clorox Company. P&G leads the group in laundry and automatic dishwasher detergent sales, with brand names like Tide, Cheer, and Cascade.

In the soaps and detergents category, detergents are by far the largest component. Household-laundry detergents are a major segment of the detergents market. Sales of soap consist largely of soap bars for personal use.

The U.S. laundry-detergent market is divided into liquid products, conventional powder, and super-concentrates. The latter, with built-in bleaching agents, constitutes the highest growth sector.

P&G, Unilever, Dial Consumer Products, and Colgate–Palmolive account for the bulk of soaps and detergents shipments in the United States. Mergers and acquisitions in the domestic market have slowed from the frantic pace of a few years ago, as the best opportunities have already been taken. However, producers are very active overseas, as competition in international markets heats up. For example, in the last few years, P&G has acquired several companies in Brazil and Peru, while Unilever has increased its presence in China and Israel.

New product introduction and R&D expenditures account for a large part of the cost of manufacturing detergents. In response to environmental concerns over the use of phosphates and trihalomethanes and the ban of these products in many states, detergent manufacturers have turned to zeolites, silicates, and citrates to achieve cleaning performance. In addition, manufacturers are moving to meet consumer and environmental demands for biodegradable products.

Personal soaps constitute a diversified market that reflects the changing needs of consumers. As a result, product innovation is a key success factor for companies in this business, which requires the support of high levels of R&D expenditures. Liquid hand soaps with anti-bacterial properties are an example of new consumer demand in recent years. Matching consumer preference with the right product characteristics has resulted in the market success of this type of soap, and sales have increased at a rapid clip. Of the four main producers of soaps in the United States, European-owned Unilever is the largest in terms of market share. This company claims an estimated one-third share of the domestic soap business with brands like Dove and Lever 2000.

The polishing and sanitation goods sector consists of polishes for furniture and metal, and for household, institutional, and industrial use. It also includes industrial disinfectants, dry-cleaning preparations, household bleaches, floor waxes, and solvents. The institutional and industrial (I&I) market accounts for two-thirds of polishing and sanitation products shipments. These markets are broken down further into various segments, which include janitorial, industrial, food service, and laundry applications. Janitorial applications make up the largest share of the I&I market, at about 40%.

Total shipments of polishing and sanitation goods are estimated at about $9 billion. The search for more convenience is the common tie that binds the demand preferences of the various end users of these goods. Convenience will remain the main driving factor of product sales over the forecast period, as buyers continue to demand multipurpose products that can achieve better cleaning with less time and effort.

Surface active agents, or surfactants, are used as wetting agents, emusifiers, and primary materials in the fabrication of soaps and detergents. Shipments are estimated at about $5 billion.

Surfactants are produced largely from petrochemical feedstock, mostly ethylene, but also from natural products such as vegetable oils and animal fats. Synthetic and natural surfactants are interchangeable in many applications, including laundry detergents. By and large, synthetic surfactants are commodities, while natural surfactants tend to be classified as specialty products. Production of surfactants is concentrated in industrial countries, as is the bulk of global consumption. However, specialty surfactants are increasingly produced by developing countries and newly industrialized countries, such as Malaysia and Thailand, due to the availability in those places of natural materials like coconut and palm kernel oils. Market growth for specialty surfactants has outpaced that for commodities in recent years. This trend is expected to continue in the future as more niche markets develop.

Linear alkyl benzene sulfonate currently holds about 50% of the commodity surfactant market. It has replaced ethoxylated alcohols as the most commonly used surfactant in the production of concentrated-powder detergents, and is rapidly increasing its use in liquid-detergents preparation.

Perfumes, Cosmetics, and Other Toilet Preparations

This industry consists of companies that manufacture a wide range of personal-care items, including hair-care products, skin-care products, fragrances, dentifrices and mouthwash/breath fresheners, deodorants and anti-perspirants, shaving creams, and other cosmetic products such as color cosmetics. Industry shipments are valued at more than $20 billion. Hair care, with an estimated 25% to 30% share of these shipments, is the largest business segment. It is followed by fragrances with a 20% to 25% share of the market, and skin care with about a 15% share. The other personal-care items make up the remainder.

During the 1990s, growth in the perfumes, cosmetics, and other toilet-preparations industry has averaged about 4% per year in nominal terms, and close to 3% in real terms. Exports represent close to 10% of industry shipments and are growing much faster than the domestic market. Imports are small, and account for less than 5% of sales. Demand tends to be very volatile, particularly for prestige products, as it is highly dependent on discretionary income and the spending habits of consumers.

Over the next five to ten years, WEFA forecasts industry shipments to continue to increase at their recent historical pace. The baby-boom generation, which by 2006 will be in the 50- to 75-year-old age group and account for nearly one-third of the U.S. population, will represent a considerable market for anti-aging products.

As a result, skin-care products are expected to offer the best growth opportunities for the industry. Other areas of strong growth include various domestic and foreign ethnic markets for makeup, skin care, and hair care.

In the past few years, manufacturers have had to contend with increasingly cost-conscious consumers, rising materials costs, and fewer outlets for their products, as consolidation occurred in the department stores and specialty drug store markets. This caused competition to heighten at a time when margins were weakening. To respond to these challenges, the industry restructured and consolidated. As a result, many small and mid-sized firms, including raw materials producers, were absorbed by the larger personal care companies. Today, the top-10 producers control two-thirds of the domestic market. Over the past four years, the industry has witnessed the public offering of two cosmetic giants: Revlon and Estee Lauder. Also, during that period, L'Oreal, another major manufacturer, bought Maybelline, the number-three U.S. mass-market cosmetics company, while Unilever acquired Helene Curtis.

Cosmetics are becoming high-tech products. In recent years, research and development expenditures and new product introductions have accounted for an increasing proportion of industry costs, as consumers have demanded more technically sophisticated and environmentally safe products. In 1996, Johnson & Johnson (J & J) introduced Renova, the first product approved by the FDA that claims to reduce wrinkles. This move to "cosmeceuticals", if successful, could tilt the competitive balance away from producers who do not have the same research facilities and regulatory approvals as J & J.

Hair-Care Products

Shampoos make up about 40% of all hair-care product shipments. Conditioners are estimated to account for about 20%; hair sprays 15%; and gels and mousses another 10%. Hair care is a mature industry, with little or no growth left in the overall domestic market. It is also a business where one product cannibalizes another. Typical examples of such a practice are the two-in-one and three-in-one formulations that offer the convenience of shampoo, conditioner, and more recently, shine enhancer in one bottle, displacing those products sold individually. Other examples include styling gels, which have been successful in recent years at picking up sales from hairsprays adversely affected by governmental regulations on VOCs (volatile-organic compounds).

Looking for offshore-market opportunities and securing a technological advantage over the competition have become important business strategies for U.S. hair-care products producers. Newly industrialized foreign markets in Asia and Latin America and other developing countries present attractive long-run opportunities, although the path to income growth in some of these countries has been seriously delayed by the 1997–1998 financial crises.

After several years of promoting the subjective results of hair-care products such as manageability, body, and luster, producers are now increasingly emphasizing the development and marketing of results through chemical performance. For example, the industry has developed a complex lipid that has been shown to replace the ceramide in hair, preventing loss of protein from cuticle damage. Other advances include those technologies that have crossed over from the skin-care industry, such as alpha hydroxy acids (AHAs) that are used for scalp conditioning, and naturally derived proteins used to provide moisture and sun protection. Sales of AHAs, which promise rejuvenated looking skin with improved color and texture, have surged since their introduction in the early 1990s.

Fragrances

The average annual-sales gain in the domestic fragrance market is normally only 3% to 4% in nominal terms. Competition is fierce in this slow growth environment, where it is very hard for smaller companies to survive. The men's market is growing at the higher end of that range, but still represents only about 20% of total industry sales.

Concern over profit margins has caused fragrance producers and retailers alike to rethink their strategies for the future, as cost-conscious consumers increasingly move away from prestige brands to mass market fragrances for value pricing. By promoting mass scents, retailers can also achieve higher margins because they do not have to go through the middlemen required for prestige merchandise. Ten dollars seems to be the magic upper limit for an acceptable fragrance price for consumers in the mass market. With this market traditionally yielding margins of 25% to 30% to retailers, fragrance manufacturers have started to make perfume

and cologne gift sets that will allow retailers that kind of margin and sell for under $10.

Spurred by the success of specialty outfits like Bath & Body Works, fragrance companies are increasingly broadening their market exposure through new and unique channels of distribution, such as the Banana Republic chain of clothing stores, the QVC network, and even the Internet.

The teen generation, which the industry views as a strong potential for its domestic sales, is the next frontier. Various products designed to appeal to this segment are in the offing. However, it is the adult category that comprises the lion's share of the market. Fortunately for the industry, product innovation for that segment is not as critical as it is for the teen population. Nevertheless, a certain degree of novelty is important, and mature, sophisticated, and comfort nuances have been introduced, as well as transparent fragrances that are lighter and do not wear heavily.

Skin-Care Products

Since the 50- to 75-year-old baby boomers are expected to represent close to 30% of the U.S. population in the next five to ten years, this segment will be responsible for fashioning a large portion of the domestic skin-care industry's product offerings. As these boomers battle the effects of time on their skin, they will constitute a vast market for anti-aging products. And, as their demands upon the personal-care industry increase, they will spur further research into slowing or even turning back the aging process.

Any products that deal with wrinkles, sun-damaged skin, and skin dryness, and are also biodegradable and multi-functional, are likely to be winners. An example of multifunctionality includes the use of sun protection agents, not only in sunscreens, but also in moisturizers and make-ups. Such applications will increase the frequency of wear of these sunscreen products from occasional to routine. Also headed for growth are the manufacturing ingredients that are gentle to older skin. They include: emollients, anti-irritants, conditioning agents, and natural extracts.

Overall, skin-care products are expected to offer the best growth opportunities for the personal-care industry through at least 2005, with annual sales gains on the order of 8 to 10%. In addition to the baby-boomer population, products designed specifically for darker skin will also contribute to strong growth, as the industry multiplies its efforts to cover the domestic-ethnic markets as well as foreign markets in Asia, Latin America, and Africa.

The desire for mildness is increasingly pushing surfactants out of non-cleansing formulations. Surfactants are irritating, and polymeric emulsifiers are used more and more to replace them in applications where emulsification is needed. Additional technological trends include water-based products, as consumers seek out the non–greasy feel. Environmentally improved, natural and clear products remain big favorites with consumers.

But, function is key, as these consumers will reject socially conscious products if they do not work.

As the demand from baby boomers plateaus, the younger generation will expect more advanced technologies from the skin-care industry. Research and development to improve the beneficial and even therapeutic properties of skin-care products will increase, slowly narrowing the gap with pharmaceuticals. As a result, a new regulatory category of "cosmeceuticals" or prescription cosmetics is likely to emerge.

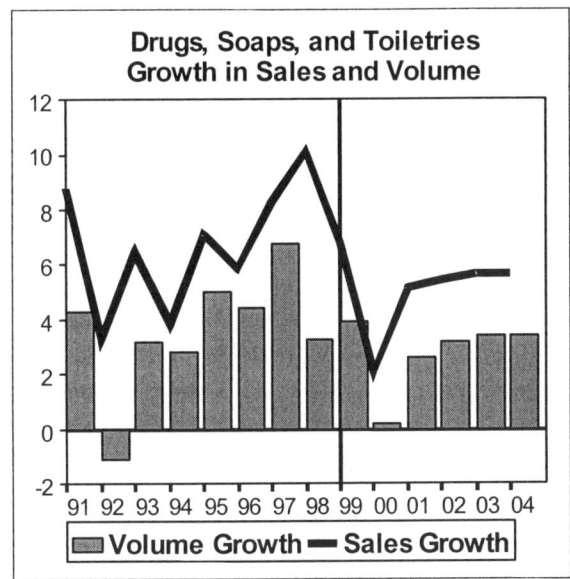

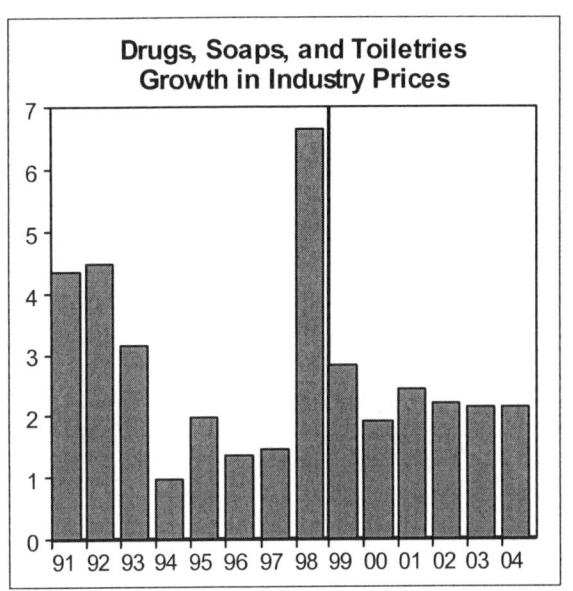

Drugs, Soaps, and Toiletries

SIC 283-284

		1992	1993	1994	1995	1996	1997	1998	1999	2000	2001	Compound Average 88-98	Annual Growth 98-08
Sales													
	Billions of $	110.5	117.7	122.2	130.8	138.5	150.0	165.1	176.4	180.1	189.3		
	% Ch	3.3	6.5	3.8	7.1	5.9	8.3	10.1	6.8	2.1	5.1	7.1	5.3
Volume													
	% Ch	-1.1	3.2	2.8	5.0	4.4	6.7	3.2	3.9	0.2	2.6	3.6	2.8
Prices													
	% Ch	4.5	3.1	1.0	2.0	1.4	1.5	6.6	2.8	1.9	2.4	3.4	2.4
Production Costs													
Avg. Hourly Earnings													
	$/hr	13.33	13.82	14.00	14.26	14.75	15.24	15.90	16.20	16.81	17.37		
	% Ch	3.1	3.7	1.3	1.9	3.4	3.4	4.3	1.9	3.8	3.3	3.2	3.2
Input Price Index													
	% Ch	1.1	1.5	1.6	4.6	1.5	0.8	0.5	0.1	1.8	2.1	2.0	2.1

Agricultural Chemicals

The key components of the agricultural chemical industry are fertilizer, plant protection (pesticides), and the relatively small animal-health sector. The outlook for the agricultural chemical industry is inherently tied to the future prospects of the U.S. agriculture sector, particularly for acreage planted. Agriculture legislation passed in 1996 eliminated annual Acreage Reduction Programs (ARP) and altered the way farmers receive price and income support. ARP idled an average of 21 million acres annually between 1990 and 1995. That land will now be available to plant and will require fertilizer and pesticides. As a result, agricultural chemical sales are likely to continue the expansion that began in 1993 for the next couple of years.

The fertilizer business is a commodity business—fertilizer is fertilizer, and it does not matter which company or which country is producing the product. Farmers typically satisfy their nitrogen needs first; and then, if funds are available, they purchase phosphatic and potassic fertilizer material. Of the three nutrients, nitrogen accounts for about 50% to 55% of total fertilizer sales and potash and phosphate the remainder. Potash usually accounts for a slightly larger share than phosphate. The United States is a net importer of nitrogen and potash. Canada is a major source for both. Mexico and Trinidad-Tobago are important sources of nitrogen. The United States is a net exporter of phosphate, but is facing increased competition from abroad. Consolidation in the fertilizer industry is continuing, a process that began in the 1980s.

Pesticides are used widely in agriculture production, with herbicides being the most widely used pesticide, followed by insecticides, fungicides, and other pesticides (growth regulators, rodenticides, etc.). Winter wheat receives the smallest amount of pesticides, 8 oz/acre, compared with more than 60 lbs/acre for potatoes. The continued increase in conservation-tillage practices indicates further growth in the herbicide market. Interesting technology issues are facing the pesticide industry. Corn, cotton, soybeans, and potatoes are now being produced from genetically altered seeds that make them resistant either to pests themselves, or to herbicides. Questions of consumer acceptance, pesticide residues, efficacy of protection with high pest pressures, and resistance should be considered. It is not clear that future pesticide use will decline with an increase of genetically altered seeds. Consolidation continues in the pesticide industry as well, and most companies operating in the United States are multinational. The United States should continue to be a net exporter of pesticide products.

Introduction

The U.S. agricultural chemical industry can be divided into three general subsectors: fertilizer, crop protection, and animal health. The animal-health industry is smaller than the other two and is often a subsidiary of a larger pharmaceutical company. Fertilizer tends to be a commodity with little brand-name recognition, and therefore foreign countries can and do compete effectively with U.S. producers, particularly for nitrogenous materials. The plant-protection industry, made up primarily of pesticides, does have branded products, and manufacturers may be able to extract price premiums from the market place. Technology within the crop-protection industry is changing significantly. Scientists have successfully engineered seed stock that makes plants toxic to certain pests (i.e., Bacillus thuringiensis, Bt technology) and/or resistant to pesticides (i.e., Round-up Ready technology). Many of the plant-protection companies operating in the United States are multinational firms.

Sales of agricultural chemicals expanded at double-digit rates in 1994 and 1995. The robust increase in sales was attributable to 8% to 9% price increases rather than significant volume increases. Nitrogen fertilizer prices, in particular, rose sharply in 1994 and 1995 due to supply shortages pushing aggregate fertilizer prices paid by farmers up about 25% over the two-year period. On the other hand, crop protection and animal-health product prices increased at an annual rate of 3.0%. Sales volume has moved sporadically in the 1990s and is tied to acreage planted, to which growers apply fertilizers and/or crop-protection applications, and animal numbers for the animal-health industry. Sales have been more anemic over the past three years, increasing 2.2% in 1996, 1% in 1997, and falling 4.7% in 1998. Estimates for 1999 indicate sales will be off again.

Fertilizer use is directly tied to the type of crop planted and level of plantings. Pesticide use is tied to the same factors as well, but weather, pest pressures, and the adoption of new crop-protection technology also affect usage. The animal-health segment can be segmented into vaccines (preventive treatments), feed additives and medicinals, pharmaceuticals, and nutritionals.

Prior to 1996, the Federal government administered acreage reduction programs (ARPs) in an effort to balance commodity supplies and demands. The Federal Agriculture Improvement and Reform (FAIR) Act of 1996 eliminated ARPs and deficiency payments and replaced them with production flexibility contracts and transition payments. Farmers idled, on average, 21 million acres annually between 1990 and 1995. The FAIR Act was enacted during a time of supply shortages and high prices. For the 1995/96 marketing season, farm-level prices jumped over 40% from the previous year to $3.24/bu and inventory dropped to about 400 million bushels or 5% of use. Similar price-strength and low-inventory levels were observed for wheat and soybeans.

Land that had been idled by ARP has been available to be planted since 1996. High prices brought acreage into production. Land planted to the principal crops rose to 334 million acres, compared to 323 million acres over the 1990 to 1995 period. Although farmers have had the opportunity to bring additional land into production, they have not.

Just as quickly as prices rise and inventories fall, the reverse can happen. Record yields, improved global production, and modest demand, in part attributed to a weakened Asian market from 1997-1999, have pushed U.S. crop inventories higher and prices lower. At the time this article is being written, cash-market corn prices have dropped to $1.63/bu and wheat is reported as low as $2.00/bu in some parts of the country. At these prices, farmers are reducing plantings and attempting to save costs where possible. Acreage planted to the principal crops dropped about 1% in 1999, the third successive year of decline under the FAIR Act. Efforts to reduce fertilizer and chemical usage, switch to lower cost inputs, and negotiate with suppliers for price reductions are all tactics farmers employed this year.

The animal-health industry is dependent on livestock-production cycles and the profitability of the livestock sector and the performance of the companion-pet (dogs/cats) market. The robust performance of the U.S. economy, increases in personal income, and growth in housing starts have favorably impacted the companion-pet segment. But, the livestock sector has had its good times and bad times. High feed costs in 1995 and 1996 adversely affected profitability of the livestock sector. Poor profitability in the cattle sector has kept beef production high as producers have slaughtered rather than retained animals. Large hog supplies, coupled with high beef and poultry production, have depressed prices and driven some independent producers from the industry. Hog prices averaged over $50/cwt in 1997, dropped to below $20/cwt in December 1998, and are currently hovering about $30/cwt. Broiler production seems immune from production cycles and wide swings in the cost of feed. Much of the production is produced under contract, which shifts risk to the contractor. As a consequence, broiler production continues to expand steadily.

The United States is a net exporter of crop protection and animal-health products and phosphate fertilizers, and a net importer of nitrogenous and potassic fertilizer materials.

Fertilizers

The Fertilizer Institute reports net fertilizer sales for U.S. producers surveyed equaled $11.1 billion in 1998, about 7% less than in 1997, and 3% less than in 1996. On a per-company-reporting basis, sales dropped 13% in 1998. The decline in sales is attributed to price movement. The average spot-market anhydrous ammonia price (FOB New Orleans, Barge) fell 30% in 1998, phosphate prices were unchanged, and muriate of potash prices rose 22%. The United States produces relatively modest amounts of potassic products.

There are three primary fertilizer nutrients: nitrogen, phosphate, and potash. In agriculture, nitrogen is typically viewed as the most essential of the three primary nutrients, and farmers purchase their nitrogen first. Then they satisfy their other nutrient needs with their remaining budget. For the 1997/1998 (July 1997–June 1998) fertilizer year, 12.3 million tons of nitrogen, 4.6 million tons of phosphate, and 5.3 million tons of potash were used by U.S. agriculture. Nitrogen typically accounts for between 50% and 55% of total U.S. agriculture demand. Phosphate and potash account for the remainder of nutrient demand, with potash use slightly larger than phosphate.

Corn is the major source of demand for nutrients by the agriculture sector, accounting for about 40% to 45% of nitrogen, phosphate, and potash use. Corn requires relatively large amounts of nutrient on a per-acre basis, and there were 80 million acres of corn planted in 1998 by U.S. farmers. Wheat accounts for 15% to 17% of the nitrogen and phosphate use, and 4% to 5% of potash. Soybeans, a legume that fixates nitrogen from the atmosphere, accounts for about 1% of nitrogen use, between 8% and 9% of the phosphate use, and 13% to 15% of potash use. The relative share of nutrient use of soybeans has been rising in recent years due to relatively more acreage planted to soybeans. However, the opposite is true for wheat, where share has been declining due to relatively fewer acres being planted.

There are a number of fertilizer materials that deliver nutrient at differing levels and costs to plants:

- Nitrogenous materials include anhydrous ammonia (82% nitrogen(N)), urea (46% N), ammonium sulfate (21% N), ammonium nitrate (33.5% N), nitrogen solutions (N content varies typically from 28% to 32% N), ammoniated phosphates (N content varies from 16% to 18% N most popular), and mixes.

- Phosphatic materials include normal (single) superphosphate (20% phosphate, or P2O5), triple superphosphate (46% P2O5), ammoniated phosphates (P2O5 content varies, with 46% and 52% P2O5 most popular), and mixes.

- Potassic products include muriate of potash or potassium chloride (61% potash, or K2O), potassium sulfate (50% K2O), and mixes.

Most of the nitrogen used by U.S. agriculture is delivered by anhydrous ammonia followed by nitrogen solutions. Muriate of potash is the primary source of K2O nutrient, and ammoniated phosphates, which deliver both N and P2O5, are the primary phosphate source.

Anhydrous ammonia is the basic feedstock for the manufacture of nitrogenous materials. Ammonia is made from the reaction of natural gas and nitrogen. Phosphatic materials are produced through a reaction of phosphate rock and sulfuric acid that results in phosphoric acid. The acid is further processed and reacted with phosphate rock and/or anhydrous ammonia to make end-product fertilizer materials. Potassium salts are mined.

Through the 1980s and the 1990s, consolidation has occurred in the U.S. fertilizer industry. The commodity nature of the business and foreign competition, particularly for nitrogen, and the industry's dependence on agriculture have all contributed to the decline in the number of U.S. producers. U.S. producers are able to satisfy the majority of nitrogen demand, but the United States is a net importer of nitrogen. Strong nitrogen prices in the mid- 1990s provided enough incentives for U.S. producers to invest in production facilities and expand nitrogen (anhydrous ammonia) capacity. Between 1998 and 2001 about 1.0 million metric tons of nitrogen capacity is expected to be added to the U.S. production capability, and another 14 million tons in other countries around the world. This additional capacity will keep pressure on nitrogenous material prices, and may result in investment plans to be scaled back globally.

The phosphate sector is able to meet U.S. needs and exports about 50% of production. No significant capacity expansion is likely in the United States over the decade. But, nearly 3.6 million tons of ammoniated phosphate capacity is projected to come on line abroad. Production from these new facilities will compete with the United States for export share.

The United States relies on potash imports, primarily from Canada, to meet domestic needs. Most world potash reserves have been identified and there is little expected with regard to growth in potash production capacity.

Outlook

The outlook for the U.S. fertilizer industry is dependent on the amount of acreage planted in the United States. Historically, the federal government exercised supply management practices to balance supplies and demands for agricultural commodities, primarily feed grains, food grains, and cotton. On average, between 1990 and 1995, 21 million acres were idled under annual Acreage Reduction Programs (ARP). Another 36 million acres were idled by the long-term Conservation Reserve Program (CRP). In April of 1996, President Clinton signed the Federal Agriculture Improvement and Reform (FAIR) Act. The FAIR Act eliminated the annual ARP and now provides farmers the opportunity to base planting decisions on market-price signals. The Act also continues the CRP, which currently has about 34 million acres enrolled. In the long term, the acreage enrolled in the CRP will rise to the maximum 36.4 million acre level.

Currently, the U.S. agricultural sector is faced with weak demand (in part due to the recent economic turmoil in Southeast Asia), robust 1998/1999 production levels and expected production for 1999/2000, high inventories, increased competition for available markets from both importing and exporting nations, and poor prices. Acreage planted for the 1998 season dropped on a year-over-year basis to 330 million, and further to 328 million in 1999, the lowest level planted under the FAIR Act, and the third year of decline since the Act was enacted. Acreage planted in 1996 equaled 334 million. The bottom line is that there will be ample acreage available to plant, but with commodity prices at their current level and expected to fall further during the 1999/2000 season, farmers are unlikely to increase total plantings next year. Farmers will not only evaluate their planting decisions carefully, they will also evaluate their input usage, perhaps reducing application rates, using generic products at lower cost, and changing from premium-priced inputs (i.e., seed) to other lower cost inputs. While there is a trade-off between land and fertilizer, future domestic demand for fertilizers is expected to have declined for the 1998/1999 season between 2% to 3%, followed by flat use in 1999/2000. After agriculture works excessive inventories down to manageable levels, economic vitality returns to Southeast Asia, and commodity prices begin to strengthen, acreage is expected to expand. This is not likely to occur until 2001.

There will be a number of other factors influencing demand for nutrients in the future, including tillage practices, crop rotations, and precision agriculture. Land in continuous corn or soybean crop production tends to receive more fertilizer than land rotated, although for some rotations a greater percentage of the area may be fertilized. The opposite tends to hold for cotton and wheat. Studies on precision agriculture indicate mixed results—some suggest higher nutrient use, but with more precise nutrient placement, while other studies suggest precision reduces fertilizer use. Based on changing production practices and acreage expansion after the turn of the century, per-annum growth in the demand or use of fertilizer nutrient in the 1.0% to 1.5% range after 2001/2002 is projected.

International Competition

The United States is a major producer and consumer of fertilizer material. Reserves are key to the phosphate and potash business.

The United States has phosphate rock reserves in Florida, North Carolina, and in the West (Idaho, Montana, and Utah). Florida and North Carolina mines account for the bulk of phosphate rock production, which in turn is processed into phosphatic fertilizer materials. Currently, U.S. producers are in a surplus phosphate rock situation— productive capacity exceeds demand by 4 to 6 million tons. The availability of rock reserves, the technology of the industry, and the availability of sulfur (sulfuric acid) enable the United States to compete in world markets. However, competitive forces are increasing. The United States exports phosphoric acid, super phosphoric acid, mono– and di–ammoniated phosphates, and phosphate rock. Morocco holds 50% of the world's phosphate rock reserves and is expanding its downstream processing capacity. Jordan, Senegal, and China are also adding to their productive capacity. In the future, it will be increasingly difficult for the United States to maintain its leadership position in the world-phosphate market.

U.S. potash production is relatively modest and occurs in New Mexico, Utah, California, and Michigan. The United States relies on Canada as its primary source of potash, and Israel and Russia ship to the U.S. market as well. Due to limited production, the United States is essentially a non-exporting country, although the 1998/1999 export statistics indicate a surge in exports to Central America. This is most likely due to transshipments to the United States from Canada and then on to Mexico and other Central American destinations. With some mines closed in Germany and Russia, continuation of transshipments is likely.

The cost of natural gas and the efficiency of the facilities converting natural gas to ammonia determine the competitive edge of U.S. nitrogen producers in global markets. U.S. production facilities are older and less efficient than new world-class facilities elsewhere. In 1998, U.S. ammonia facilities required between 33 and 34 million Btu (MMBTU) of natural gas per ton of ammonia produced, at an average gas cost of $2.10/btu. New facilities realize economies of scale and require only 26 to 28 MMBTU per ton of ammonia produced. In some developing countries that have natural gas reserves but no developed markets for natural gas, such as Mexico and Trinidad, the cost of gas is extremely low. Canadian gas prices are lower than those in the United States are as well. Thus, it is not surprising that these three countries are key nitrogen exporters to the United States. As a consequence, the United States will become increasingly dependent on imports as a source of nitrogen.

As was true for 1998, the 1999 year has been characterized with low gas prices. A mild winter, improved pipeline transmission, and ample reserves have all contributed to pressuring spot-market natural gas prices lower. On a calendar-year basis, about a 3% increase in natural gas costs is expected. But, if another mild winter occurs, the outlook for stronger gas prices could dissipate. U.S. anhydrous production costs are projected to be about 2% greater than in 1998. With ammonia prices 14% lower than in 1998, relatively stable gas costs have enabled U.S. producers to continue to operate, but margins for the industry are close to zero and are negative for some producers. Next year, U.S. natural-gas costs are expected to rise about 11%, which will be followed by another 4% increase in 2001.

Crop Protection

The U.S. crop-protection industry continues to consolidate. Three years ago, Ciba-Geigy and Sandoz, both Swiss companies, merged to form Novartis. Last year, American Home Products (American Cyanamid) and Monsanto flirted with a merger. DuPont and Monsanto also held talks. But, it is Rhone-Poulenc and AgrEvo which announced a merger this year. The merger is expected to be completed by the end of the year. In a poor economic environment, all companies that have business units that depend on the agriculture sector typically review their performance and may look for opportunities to invest and/or divest. Most crop-protection firms operating in the United States are multinational, and some are headquartered outside the United States.

As in fertilizers, the crop-protection industry is dependent on agriculture and acres planted. Pesticide use in any one year is also dependent on the occurrence of widespread pest infection or infestation, weather conditions that might increase or decrease the probability of pest infection or infestation (including over–wintering of pests), and whether there was an infestation or infection the year before. 1997 and 1998 were light pest-pressure years, although there was some concern expressed for potential pest pressure in California last year on cotton.

The pesticide industry may be further segmented into herbicide, insecticide, fungicide, and other chemical business lines. The global business is estimated to be in the range of $29 to $31 billion. Since 1998, the industry has been under significant price pressures. As products come off patent, generic products are making inroads. Secondly, as new biotechnology-based pest controls come on the market, they offer more competition to the traditional pest and disease controls. Third, commodity prices in the agriculture sector are currently correcting downward, causing farmers to re-evaluate their pest control strategies. Fourth, companies which have the biotechnology product, i.e. Round-up Ready technology, have reduced the price of the branded product, such as Round-up, forcing other competitors to reduce the price of their products. As a consequence, sales are likely to be off this year by about 5%.

Herbicides represent about half of the world crop protection business, insecticides 25%, fungicides 20%, and other chemicals (rodenticides, growth regulators, etc.) about 5%. The U.S. industry represents slightly less than one-third share of world sales, accounting for $8 to $9 billion in 1998. The composition of the United States market differs somewhat from the global business in that herbicides are more important, accounting for about 65% to 70% of the U.S. industry, followed by insecticides at 20%, fungicides at 7%, and the other chemicals category at 3%.

Pesticide use in the United States is measured by active ingredient (a.i.). The absolute level of a.i. applied peaked in 1982 at 572 million pounds and then dropped and fluctuated with acreage. In the 1990s, total active ingredient applied has been increasing, rising from 498 million pounds a.i. in 1990 to 565 million pounds a.i. in 1995. While there has been an increase in a.i. applied, the trend is toward low-volume products and away from high-volume products. Most of the increase has been in the fungicide and other pesticide market categories.

Pesticides were applied to virtually all fields of corn, soybeans, cotton, potatoes, and spring and durum wheat in 1998. Of the corn acreage planted in 1998, 96% was treated with herbicides (atrazine, a high-volume product, was the herbicide of choice) and 30% was treated with insecticide. Insecticides were applied to 71% of the cotton area, and 95% of the area received herbicide applications, compared to respective 1997 levels of 77% and 97%. Soybean area was treated predominately with herbicides (95%). Only about 47% of winter-wheat fields were treated with pesticides, compared to 60% in 1997. The corn crop tends to receive the highest level of herbicide and insecticide volume. Grains, cotton, and soybeans receive the majority of herbicide applications. Cotton and corn account for about 90% of the insecticide use.

Fruits, vegetables, and peanuts account for about 90% of the fungicide market. It is not surprising that the fungicide market continues to expand in the United States. A health-conscious population with growing incomes is demanding more fruits and vegetables. This high-valued product area of agriculture is delivering unblemished high-grade fruits and vegetables, and it has contributed to the growth in fungicide use. Potato acreage in 1997 was treated with insecticides (98%), fungicides (99%), and herbicides (95%). Fungicide use has grown significantly in recent years as pest and disease pressures have changed.

A 1995 U.S. Department of Agriculture survey indicated that soybean and corn area accounted for 58% of the herbicide used in the survey. The same survey indicated that 90% of the area surveyed received herbicide applications, but only 17% of the area received insecticides. For the fields in the survey and for the crop production year, the average amount of pesticide applied was 2.4 lbs/acre, but it ranged from a low for wheat area of 5 oz/acre to a high for potatoes of 60 lbs/acre. Farmers have been responding to growing concerns about pesticide use and acknowledging a greater need to monitor pest pressures in their fields. Nearly 80% of fields in the 1995 survey were scouted for pests, suggesting that growers do not treat fields indiscriminately.

Tillage practices also influence pesticide use. Those acres that were under no-till or minimum till practices received no post-plant cultivation. Those acres planted in narrow rows were treated most intensively with herbicides. Fields with wider rows and conventional tillage practices received less herbicide application.

Technology

Technological developments have a significant impact on the plant-protection industry. Some companies have invested heavily in biotechnology and have purchased seed companies. For example, DuPont completed the acquisition of Pioneer Hi-Bred International this year.

Technological developments in the pesticide area are evolving in two directions, both results of transgenic research.

- The first approach has the technology added to the seed, and the plant becomes toxic to the pest. *Bacillus thuringiensis*, Bt technology, is currently available for cotton, corn, potatoes, and sweet corn. Investments in research continue and second generation Bt products and products active on other pests, such as corn rootworm, are likely on the way.

- The other approach is to genetically alter the plant so that it becomes resistant to the pesticide. This technology is also currently available. For example, soybeans or corn acreage that is resistant to herbicides can be treated with a post-emergent herbicide without fear of damaging the crop. Pesticide residue issues have emerged, as have consumer issues. No official action has been taken in the United States to prevent the planting of crops with these characteristics.

The efficacy of genetically altered crops will likely be tested in many ways in the coming years. How these new crops will fair under varying weather conditions, pest pressures, and other stresses is unclear, but after three growing seasons, the acceptance by farmers is quite strong. Companies with patent rights think that their products will withstand the test of time. Others are not as certain, as evidenced by the cotton growers in Texas in 1996, who filed a lawsuit against the company that provides Bt cotton. The issue of resistance is also not clear. The pest population has shown an amazing ability to adapt to chemical controls over time. With the new technology, the chemistry of control is basically the same, and the difference is in how the control is delivered. One outcome of Bt technology is that the spectrum of pests that must be controlled is changing.

Outlook

The outlook for the pesticide industry is for contraction in the near term and mixed in the longer term. Sales in 1999 are likely to be off in the neighborhood of 5%. Low commodity prices are adversely affecting grower sentiment. Limited opportunities for area expansion is likely for 2000, although there could be an upswing in 2001. Undoubtedly, the elimination of the ARP suggests that more land could be planted.

In the long term, once surpluses are worked down and prices strengthen, land could be added to the production base; then this suggests expanded demand for pesticide products. However, the current economic environment of growing commodity inventories and declining prices will likely retard additional area being planted in the near term. This environment suggests that shifts between and among crops are more likely than additional lands coming into production. Generic products and alternative pest- and disease-control strategies will intensify price pressures for the pesticide industry.

Conservation tillage practices have been growing steadily since 1989, from about 25% of the area planted to field and row crops, to about 37% in 1998. No-till acreage has shown the greatest growth over this time period, increasing by more than threefold. This indicates likely growth for the herbicide market. Pest infections and infestations will also pull up demand for pesticide materials on an as-needed basis.

The issue of biotechnology is where the uncertainty about the future arises. Will consumers embrace genetically altered products? Will genetically altered products and technology be effective during times of high pest pressures and differing environments? Will growers continue to pay premium prices for licensing and technology fees to grow genetically altered crops? Will growers abide by the terms of agreements restricting areas planted, harvesting seed, and using only select products in the production process? Will manufacturers of traditional chemical controls reduce prices sufficiently to compete with genetically altered seeds? The answers to these questions and issues are not obvious. But, since their introduction, Round-up Ready and similar type technologies have gained market share. Also, countries are indicating that they will accept genetically altered commodities. Both indicate a trend toward greater use of biotech crop protection programs.

The United States is the world's largest producer of pesticides. Production facilities in the United States tend to be fairly efficient. Many firms have restructured to control costs and maintain a competitive advantage. This is an ongoing process. The outlook for global agriculture in the long run is favorable, and the United States should continue to be a net exporter of pesticide materials.

Environmental Issues

The use of chemicals in food production continues to be an emotionally charged issue. First, pesticide residues on food and fiber products raise questions as to the safety of food produced in the United States. Secondly, applications of fertilizers and pesticides do not remain where they are applied, and residual amounts do leech into ground and surface water. Until the mid-1980s, environmentalists and chemical manufacturers were in adversarial positions—one side arguing that people and the environment are at risk and the other side arguing that fertilizer and pesticide use was safe. Since then, there appears to have been a much more cooperative approach, in which industry is working with the public sector and consumers to address issues and concerns that arise from pesticide and fertilizer use.

Pesticides are regulated by the Environmental Protection Agency (EPA). The Food Quality Protection Act (FQPA) of 1996 included pesticide food-safety legislation that had broad-based support. The law amended the Federal Insecticide, Fungicide, and Rodenticide Act (FIFRA), which required registration of pesticides for use in the United States, labeling and other safeguards designed to protect the physical and human environment. The law also amended the Federal Food, Drug and Cosmetic Act, which regulates pesticide residue tolerance levels in food. The Department of Health and Human Services' Food and Drug Administration and the Department of Agriculture's Food Safety and Inspection Service carry out enforcement of food-tolerance levels.

The legislation eliminated what was known as the "Delaney Paradox," which distinguished between ready-to-eat processed food and raw agricultural commodities. It is possible for higher levels of cancer-causing pesticides to concentrate in processed food than in the raw commodity. If that higher concentration exceeded that of the raw commodity, the Delaney clause regulated zero tolerance. This had paradoxical effects: alternative pesticides could pose higher non-cancer risks; the EPA sometimes allowed the same pesticide in other foods based on negligible risk. The FQPA establishes that tolerances for pesticide residues in all food, raw and processed, will be set under the same provisions and the standards will apply to all risks (carcinogenic and non–carcinogenic). The EPA is also reviewing tolerance levels for pesticide residues.

FIFRA, as amended by the FQPA, requires the EPA to establish a periodic review of all pesticide registrations. In 1988, the EPA began the process of reviews on all pesticides registered before November 1984 and their associated tolerance levels. The review process was not mandated until the FQPA became law. The Act aims at establishing a 15-year review update cycle. A key element of the review process is that the EPA may call for a review at any time, and pesticide manufacturers must supply the data required. Other ways that pesticides and pesticide use are regulated include application and handling procedures, certification of applicators for some pesticides, and pesticide container disposal.

Water quality, like food safety, is an emotional issue. Fertilizer and pesticide run-off does end up in surface and ground water. However, given the non-point source nature of this pollution, it is difficult to regulate. The U.S. Department of Agriculture's Water-Quality Program is intended to reduce degradation of the country's water resources. The program, now in its eighth year, provides farmers with educational, technical, and financial assistance, and funds research projects designed to result in lower pesticide and fertilizer leeching into ground and surface water.

Animal Health

The global animal-health industry is about one-half the size of the crop-protection industry. The animal-health industry includes livestock species and companion pets. In order of importance, cattle accounts for nearly one-third of the world market, followed by swine and poultry.

The companion pet market is estimated to account for less than $4 billion in sales. The United States is a major market for animal-health products and accounts for about $4 to $5 billion of the world total.

The outlook for the animal-health segment is dependent on production cycles and profitability of the sector. Profitability for both cattle and hog sectors have eroded in recent years in the United States. Ample supplies of meat, heavier animals being slaughtered, changing structure within the hog sector, and food-safety concerns have all worked to keep a lid on livestock price improvement. As a consequence, 1999 sales are expected to be flat at best in the United States.

Poor profitability within the hog sector is driving small independent producers out of business. Large supplies of meat and the pricing situation are expected to force producers to reduce production. A larger share of hog production will be carried out under contract, reducing the risk of the farmer. The cattle sector is beginning to retain animals to expand the herd and will do so as long as low feed-grain prices keep the cow-calf operator profitable.

The outlook for the companion pet component is most favorable. The U.S. economy is growing at a robust rate of 4.1% in 1999. After 1999, the economy slows but grows at a 2% to 3% annual rate. Inflation is estimated to remain modest, thus eliminating the need for the Federal Reserve to raise interest rates further. The outlook is for housing starts to fall from the 1.6 million of 1999, and remain at a respectable 1.4 million level. All factors point to a positive outlook for the companion pet market.

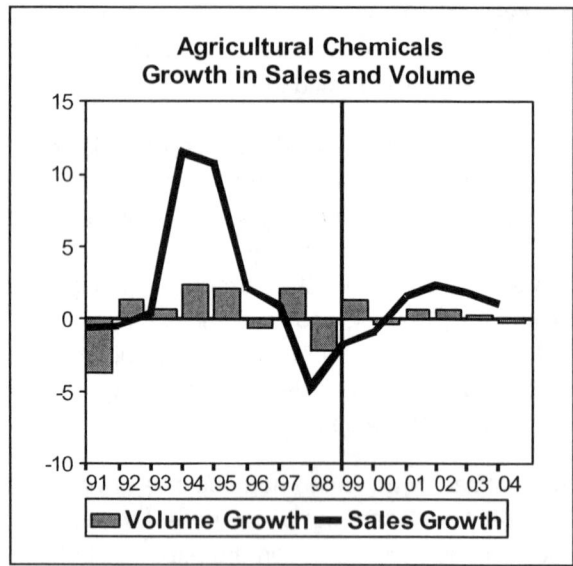

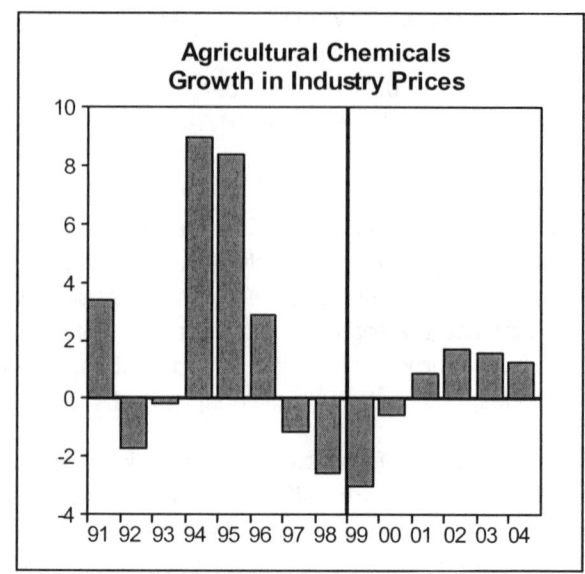

Agricultural Chemicals

SIC 287

	1992	1993	1994	1995	1996	1997	1998	1999	2000	2001	Compound Average 88-98	Annual Growth 98-08
Sales												
Billions of $	18.58	18.66	20.81	23.05	23.55	23.78	22.66	22.27	22.08	22.42		
% Ch	-0.4	0.5	11.5	10.7	2.2	1.0	-4.7	-1.7	-0.9	1.6	3.4	1.1
Volume												
% Ch	1.3	0.7	2.3	2.1	-0.7	2.1	-2.2	1.4	-0.3	0.7	1.5	0.3
Prices												
% Ch	-1.7	-0.2	9.0	8.4	2.9	-1.1	-2.6	-3.0	-0.5	0.9	1.9	0.8
Production Costs												
Avg. Hourly Earnings												
$/hr	14.82	15.09	15.34	15.73	16.17	16.61	17.11	17.69	18.15	18.57		
% Ch	4.3	1.8	1.6	2.6	2.8	2.7	3.0	3.4	2.6	2.3	3.3	2.7
Input Price Index												
% Ch	-0.7	1.6	2.2	3.9	3.9	1.2	-2.8	-1.8	1.8	2.1	1.5	1.8

Chapter 12: Petroleum Refining

Petroleum Refining

U.S. petroleum demand has continued strong during 1998 and 1999, and oil consumption outside the industrialized countries has rebounded. This strength, most notably from a recovering Asia, combined with a new round of OPEC production discipline, resulted in sharp rises in crude-oil prices in mid-1999.

Petroleum consumption is forecast to grow at an average rate of about 1% between 1997 and 2007. The transportation sector is likely to maintain the largest share of the projected petroleum-product demand. Demand for transportation services will expand during the decade on both an aggregate and per-capita basis.

The refining industry was squeezed by very tight margins during much of 1999, as refined-product prices have been slow to respond to the sharp surges in crude. WEFA expects the discount to remain wide through the winter. The discount will narrow, and margins improve, as crude prices edge off in the summer of 2000.

Growing demand for clean-burning fuels will enhance the market value and margins for light-end products, while residual products are projected to maintain at best their current value relative to crude oil. Motor gasoline and jet-fuel kerosene prices will be rising faster than the other product prices due to the growing demand for transportation and air travel.

The ongoing pressure on margins that will result from the cost of compliance with environmental regulations will be one factor prompting further consolidation to the U.S. petroleum-refining industry.

Petroleum Product Fundamentals

Distillate Fuel Oil

Distillate fuel oil, a No.2 oil, includes high-sulfur distillate (0.2% sulfur) and diesel (0.05% sulfur). High-sulfur distillate is a heating oil used for space heating, while diesel is a transportation fuel. Demand for the distillate fuel has held steady over the past two decades, averaging 3 million barrels per day.

Distillate fuel prices track a seasonal pattern, peaking in the winter and bottoming-out in the summer. This is largely due to the weather sensitivity of heating-oil demand. Commercial and residential consumers use distillate fuel oil for space heating, while utilities use it as a peaking fuel for electric generation. In the winter, when natural gas is scarce, utilities may also use distillate fuel to run their boilers.

Diesel fuel is primarily used in cars and trucks. Diesel prices tend to move closely with heating oil. However, demand for diesel is driven by economic growth, and fluctuations due to seasonal factors are relatively mild.

Diesel demand depends on macroeconomic conditions. For example, manufacturing requires the movement of raw materials, intermediate products, and finished goods. These materials are moved primarily by diesel-fueled rail and road transport. Because consumer demand peaks during the winter holidays, and the store shelf is the final stop on the production line, the demand for ton-miles typically displays strength from September through November.

Residual Fuel

Residual-fuel oil, a No. 6 fuel, is the residue from crude after distilling off the lighter components. Low-sulfur residual fuel (less than or equal to 1.0% sulfur) is generally used for space heating and power generation, while the high-sulfur grade (greater than 1.0% sulfur) is used for transportation. Residual-fuel oil is more hazardous to the environment than any other fuel oil. Thus, market shares for the product have been steadily declining since the 1970s.

Residual fuel is used by commercial and industrial consumers to heat apartment buildings and industrial facilities. Electric utilities use the fuel to run boilers. Demand from these sectors has been falling due to the displacement of residual fuel by natural gas. The latter has become a preferred fuel because of its cleaner-burning quality. Industrial demand has been falling more slowly than commercial demand since industrial facilities have longer life spans than apartment buildings.

High-sulfur residual fuel is used as a bunker fuel for ocean-going vessels. The lack of alternatives in the vessel-bunkering market has sustained demand for residual fuel. However, sales may be reduced slowly over time as larger vessels with more efficient engines come onto the market and ships more efficiently utilize their cargo capacity.

The declining demand from these sectors has led to the rapid growth of catalytic cracking. Due to surging worldwide gasoline demand, there is growing interest in upgrading refineries. More and more refiners are seeking to install coking units, which convert residual fuel into motor gasoline. The reduction in residual-fuel production may trigger opposition from bunker traders or force the bunker market to develop alternative sources.

Pricing Fundamentals

In their simplest terms, petroleum-product prices are comprised of two components: the value of the crude oil and the refinery margin. For light-fuel-oil products (gasoline, distillate/diesel fuel oil, jet fuel), there is a substantial premium related to the product specifications and complexity (type and capability) of the refining system serving broad local markets. For residual-fuel oil, this margin is generally a discount from crude, where the discount depends on the sulfur content of the final residual-fuel product. Product prices tend to move in tandem with crude prices, although unanticipated changes in petroleum product markets can affect crude prices. In addition, local market conditions, such as weather and storage capacities, can temporarily move petroleum-product prices above or below their technical relationship (defined by the supporting refinery system) to crude oil.

Petroleum products are priced according to their viscosity. The lighter the oil, the higher the refinery cost or the margin. Thus, prices are higher as the product moves from the bottom to the top of the barrel. On the low end, there is residual fuel. Residual-fuel oil is valued at less than crude because it is residue after the extraction of costlier, lighter-end products. As values for residual fuel rise with declining sulfur content, ratios for low-sulfur grades are closer to 1.00, since higher costs are attributed to the desulfurization process. Distillate fuel, motor gasoline, and jet fuel are priced at a premium to crude. Ratios of distillate fuel and motor gasoline are fairly close. Prices for these fuels tend to move within the same range, but they peak at different seasons of the year. Motor gasoline peaks in the spring or summer, while distillate fuel peaks during the winter.

Ratios of Petroleum Product Prices to Crude Oil Prices

	Petroleum Product	Ratios to crude
Lighter	Jet Fuel	1.20
	Motor Gasoline	1.18
	Distillate Fuel	1.17
	Crude Oil*	1.00
Heavier	Residual Fuel Oil (0.3% Sulfur)	0.93
	Residual Fuel Oil (1.0% Sulfur)	0.81
	Residual Fuel Oil (2.2% Sulfur)	0.75

*Crude oil = West Texas Intermediate

Recent Events

U.S. petroleum demand continued strong in 1999, buoyed by healthy economic growth and strong driving demand for gasoline in the peak seasons of spring and summer. Mild winters have made for weak demand for heating oil.

Stocks of crude steadily eroded through the third quarter of 1999, as the OPEC supply-constraint agreement was remarkably successful in the face of rising prices. Gasoline stocks also fell through the year, but stocks of distillate broke the trend and rose. Total world stocks of crude and refined products represented 1.1 fewer days of supply in August 1999 than they did a year earlier.

Crude oil prices bottomed out in early 1999 and rose sharply through the year, almost doubling between January and August. Gasoline spot prices followed a similar path, but distillate prices rose more modestly in the face of growing inventories.

Outlook for Petroleum Products

U.S. petroleum consumption is forecast to slow in growth in 2000 and 2001, as compared with 1999's increase. Between 2000 and 2005, growth in demand will average 1.1% per year. The transportation sector is likely to maintain the largest share of the projected petroleum-product demand. Demand for transportation services will expand during the decade on both an aggregate and per-capita basis, and both consumer and business demand will grow. The demand for travel will be only partially offset by improvements in capital efficiency. Consumers, for example, continue to choose performance, styling, and features over fuel efficiency in their vehicles, as evidenced by the increase to 50% in the share of the light-vehicle market taken by heavier, less fuel-efficient, light trucks.

Petroleum-product prices are forecast to track generally with crude prices, peaking in the fourth quarter of 1999 and edging off gradually during 2000, as OPEC's will to restrict supply erodes. Peaks in 2001 and later years will be reached during the summer driving season for gasoline and in late winter for residual fuel, and will show only modest growth as demand increases are met by returning non-OPEC supply.

Refining margins are projected to improve some over the forecast interval, but only for light-end products. Growing demand for clean-burning fuels will enhance their market value, while residual product margins will remain tight. Motor gasoline and jet-fuel kerosene prices will be rising faster than the other product prices, due to the growing demand for transportation and air travel.

There are two opposing forces working on the petroleum product markets: falling demand from the stationary markets (home heating and electric generation) and rising demand from the transportation sector. In the stationary market, oil use is declining as cleaner burning, natural gas becomes the more dominant fuel. More homes and apartment buildings are built with gas burners, while utilities are switching to gas-fired combined-cycle turbines. This decline is offset by growth in demand for gasoline in the transportation sector. With real GDP projected to grow at close to 2.5% per year for the next ten years on average, the transportation sector is expected to expand on both an aggregate and per-capita basis.

Petroleum-product markets are also influenced by environmental regulations and the restructuring of the refining industry. More stringent regulations are expected to raise oil prices as expenditures on upgrading refineries increase. To deal with higher costs, refineries have been restructuring downstream. The recent spate of mergers and acquisitions will help oil companies thrive in a more competitive environment.

Capacity

The total number of operable refineries has declined over the last five years, as many small refineries with capacities under 50,000 barrels per day were unable to survive the cost of the environmental requirements of the 1990 Clean Air Act Amendments (CAAA). The economics of refining are bearish, and as a result, refinery output should only increase very slowly. Net imports of refined products, on the other hand, will rise.

Mergers and Acquisitions

Downstream restructuring has shaken the U.S. refining industry. There have been many deals reached between refining companies in an effort to overcome poor downstream returns. U.S. refining margins have fallen by one-third over the last decade, while spending for upgrading plants to meet strict, environmental regulations has risen significantly. Consolidation seems to be the quickest way to improve profits, largely through economies of scale.

Environmental Regulations

The high cost of compliance with environmental regulations has hindered oil companies' efforts to cut costs. The negligent release of hazardous pollutants into the water is a crime under the Clean Water Act, and release of them into the air is a criminal violation of the Clean Air Act.

The Oil Pollution Act of 1992 requires various measures to reduce the likelihood of and damages from oil spills from tankers. It also requires tanker owners to have a substantial amount of liability insurance. These rules have driven some bunker-oil dealers out of business.

Clean Air Act Amendments of 1990

The Clean Air Act Amendments created a plethora of regulations that affect the composition and consumption of refined-petroleum products, as well as the refining process. Most of the regulations are to be promulgated by 2000. Some examples of these regulations are listed below to highlight the costs and constraints facing the industry over the near term. The industry has responded to the environmental challenge by changing processes, valuing input material differently, and changing marketing objectives. The impact of environmental protection on the industry has been substantial, and it will continue to have an effect at least through the end of the next decade.

- Stationary Source Emissions: Phase I, implemented in 1990, has raised the cost of producing heavy-fuel oil because of the requirement to upgrade refineries. In addition to refineries, power plants have also been affected since they emit sulfur dioxide (SO_2) and nitrous oxide (NO_x). The effects so far have been borne by only those plants with the largest sources of emissions. Phase II, to be implemented in 2000, will tighten emission limits imposed on large higher-emission plants.

- Oxygenated Gasoline Program (1990): Aimed at reducing carbon monoxide emissions. The CAAA winter oxygenated–gasoline requirement mandates that motor gasoline sold during at least four winter months in 39 areas of the country, where levels of carbon monoxide most seriously exceed Federal standards, must have a minimum-oxygen content of 2.7% by weight (2% in California). The program began November 1, 1992. The petroleum, ethanol, and petrochemical industries provided large volumes of oxygenates to specific, geographic areas.

- Reformulated Gasoline Program (1990): The requirement to meet specifications under this program has driven production costs up. One of the targeted emissions is nitrogen oxide. Beginning in January 1995, the nine areas with populations of more than 250,000 and with levels of ozone that most seriously exceed the Federal ozone standard, began using motor gasoline that meets emission and composition requirements. This reformulated gasoline must have a minimum-oxygen content of 2% by weight, not more than 1% benzene by volume, and no heavy metals. Nitrogen-oxide emissions may not exceed that of a 1990-summertime baseline gasoline, and there must be a 15% reduction in tailpipe emissions of volatile-organic compounds and toxic-air pollutants. Aromatics content (benzene, toluene, xylene) may not exceed 25%.

- Diesel Regulations: As of October 1, 1993, the sulfur content in diesel fuel must not exceed 0.05% by weight, and it must have a minimum-cetane index of 40. (The cetane index is a measure of ignition quality.)

U.S. refiners have had to re-examine their operations closely in light of the CAAA requirements. Large integrated companies with multiple-refining operations have committed considerable resources to plant additions and reconfigurations, product reformulation, and research and development in processing technologies. For smaller refineries, the required investments are even higher on a per-barrel basis. As a result, these facilities are unlikely to weather the continuing escalation in environmentally driven costs. Although the large, integrated companies are better positioned for this transition, they are not free from difficult decisions, including consolidation.

Increases in environmental costs come at a time of little growth in overall demand for petroleum products. While demand for higher-quality refined products is increasing, the quality of the refiners' crude-oil inputs is declining, forcing even more investment spending.

The new or tightened environmental regulations will make the major petroleum products less interchangeable between seasons, geographical areas, and uses. Refiners, shippers, storers, importers, and marketers will all be affected. Distribution costs, as well as production costs, will also increase.

Refining operations and capital investments will be affected by pending technological standards to reduce stationary-source emissions. Future regulatory changes will most likely force petroleum refiners to alter refinery configurations and invest heavily in downstream processes. In some instances, it may be more economical for certain refineries to close down partially or entirely, rather than upgrade facilities to meet the new standards.

Despite the resumption of refinery shutdowns in recent years, and the likelihood that these shutdowns will continue throughout the decade, total distillation capacity should remain relatively stable. Larger refineries will continue to make incremental additions to both crude distillation and downstream capacity. However, it is not expected that the incremental additions to capacity will keep pace with increases in petroleum demand.

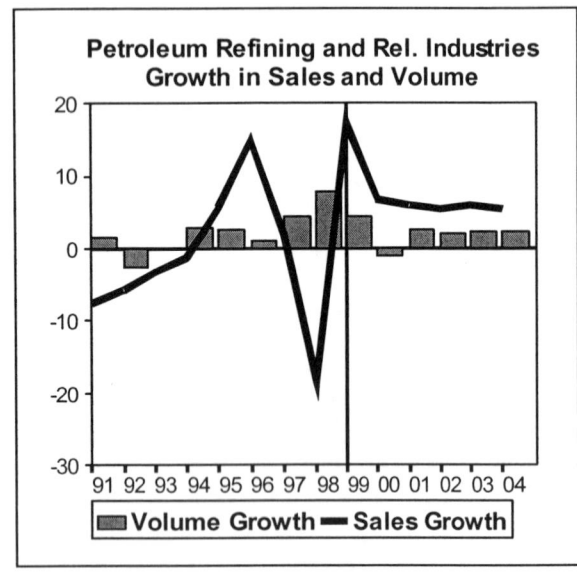

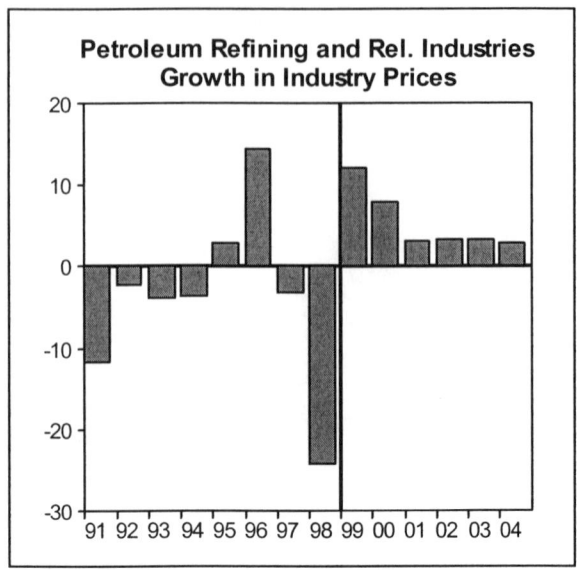

Petroleum Refining and Related Industries

SIC 29

		1992	1993	1994	1995	1996	1997	1998	1999	2000	2001	Compound Average 88-98	Annual Growth 98-08
Sales													
	Billions of $	150.1	145.1	143.3	151.6	174.0	177.4	144.7	169.6	181.0	191.9		
	% Ch	-5.8	-3.3	-1.3	5.8	14.8	2.0	-18.4	17.2	6.7	6.0	1.0	6.8
Volume													
	% Ch	-2.6	0.1	2.9	2.5	1.0	4.3	7.8	4.5	-1.1	2.7	1.4	2.2
Prices													
	% Ch	-2.2	-3.7	-3.6	3.0	14.4	-3.1	-24.1	12.1	7.9	3.2	-0.4	4.5
Production Costs													
Avg. Hourly Earnings													
	$/hr	17.90	18.53	19.06	19.36	19.32	20.19	20.90	21.40	22.07	22.74		
	% Ch	5.0	3.5	2.9	1.6	-0.2	4.5	3.5	2.4	3.1	3.0	3.4	3.2
Input Price Index													
	% Ch	-3.8	-7.0	-5.2	7.8	14.7	-4.3	-25.4	-7.0	1.2	2.1	-0.7	1.8

Part 3: Durable Goods Manufacturing

Chapter 13: Lumber and Wood Products

Lumber and Wood Products

U.S. softwood lumber demand continued at a record pace in 1998, growing 3.3% from the previous year and reaching 52.6 billion board feet (bbf), according to the Western Wood Products Association (WWPA). This high level of demand was driven by the highest single-family housing starts rates in 20 years. High consumption created the need for record lumber imports, as 18.7 bbf was imported, primarily from Canada. This amounted to approximately 36% of total U.S. lumber consumption last year. U.S. exports became a casualty of the Asian economic crisis, falling nearly 30% in 1998. Exports to Japan, a major market for U.S. lumber, dropped 53% compared to 1997. An early WWPA forecast for 1999 suggests that lumber demand will fall by 0.5 bbf as housing activity hits its peak and begins to decline in the second half of the year.

With the exception of a slight decline in April 1999, lumber prices have risen steadily since the low levels reached in November 1998. Potential lumber supply appears to be good as stable log prices and higher lumber prices have led to increased profitability for mills. Inventories in Canada are not tight, as is the case in the United States. A slight slowing in the housing market suggests that demand could dip at a time when supplies could increase. The implication is that prices will stabilize or even fall over the next several months. This is consistent with WEFA's forecast in which softwood lumber prices decline in the last quarter of 1999, before rising slightly early in 2000. On average for 1999, softwood lumber prices are forecast to be more than 8% higher than in 1998, but show only a marginal increase in 2000.

Near-Term Outlook

Figure 1

Softwood Lumber Price Index

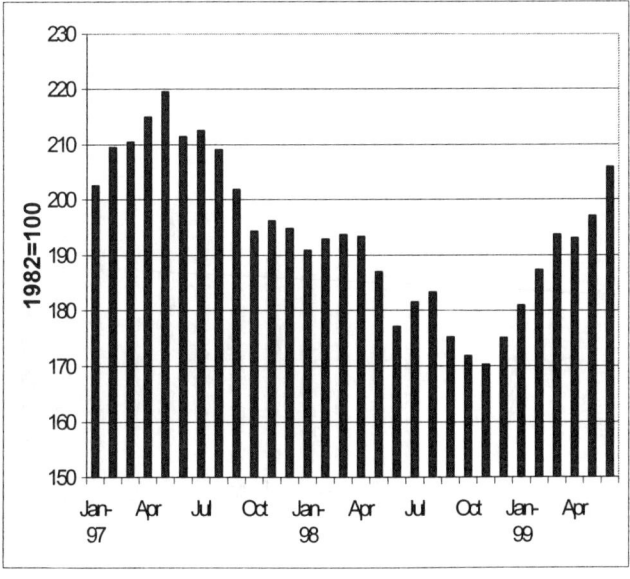

Domestic demand alone would not likely be sufficient to sustain the price increases we have seen during the first six months of 1999.

Strong domestic demand has certainly helped push lumber prices upward, but domestic demand alone would not likely be sufficient to sustain the price increases we have seen over the past seven to eight months. Domestic demand was strong in 1998, particularly because of housing construction, but prices tumbled throughout most of the year. Low exports, high inventories, and high output of lumber and competing materials forced prices lower to balance supply and demand. Indications are that demand may have peaked; therefore, other market activities must also have changed to support current prices, even as U.S. lumber production rose 4.6% and Canadian lumber output increased 3.6% in the first quarter of 1999 compared to the same quarter of 1998. Although declining, housing activity remains robust, particularly in the western United States. There has been a modest increase in the Asian export market and lower Canadian exports translate into a 0.4% decline in imports by the United States early in 1999.

Just-in-time buying has resulted in low inventories at both the buyer level and at mills.

However, the slight increase in Asian buying and decrease in Canadian exports are not likely sufficient to cause the run up in prices that has occurred over the past several months. According to *World Wood Review*, a more realistic cause of the lumber price strength is increased use of "just-in-time" buying this spring. This has occurred because buyers have expected lumber prices to ease back with expected slowdowns in construction activity. Such construction slowdowns did not occur until late July and just-in-time buying has resulted in low inventories at both the buyer level and at mills. The easing in housing construction in the second half of July led to a leveling off of prices, an indication that lumber supply and demand are in balance.

A slight slowing in the housing market suggests that demand could dip at a time when supplies could increase.

Another factor that contributed to higher lumber prices was limited transportation. In the South, produce began to compete for trucking in June, leading to a shortage of drivers. Railcars were also in short supply. In the Midwest and Northeast, the breakup of Conrail caused problems, as well. Whereas the transportation and inventory situation has led to price increases, these will likely be relatively short-run in nature. Potential lumber supply appears to be good as stable log prices and higher lumber prices have led to increased profitability for mills. Inventories in Canada are not tight, as is the case in the United States. A slight slowing in the housing market suggests that demand could dip at a time when supplies could increase. The implication is that prices will stabilize or even fall over the next several months. This is consistent with WEFA's forecast in which softwood lumber prices decline 5% in the last quarter of 1999 before rising slightly early in 2000. On average for 1999, softwood lumber prices are forecast to be more than 8% higher than in 1998, but show only a marginal increase in 2000.

Residential Construction

June 1999 showed the first year-over-year decline in actual housing starts since August 1997.

Recent signs of easing residential construction should not be construed as an immediate and dramatic drop in home building. In three of the last four years, housing starts peaked in the second quarter, and a similar pattern is expected this year. Summer heat usually leads to slower construction activity in the South and Southwest and this year the normal summer slowdown will likely be exacerbated by the 100 basis point rise in mortgage interest rates since the fall of 1998. This effect will be dampened by a backlog of orders for new homes that will keep construction crews busy for several months as indicated by increases in permits in June of this year, both relative to May and to June 1998. However, the fact remains that June showed the first year-over-year decline in actual housing starts since August 1997, also being lower than the May level.

WEFA forecasts housing starts for 1999 to be marginally higher than in 1998, reaching 1.63 million units.

Although not expected to remain at the high first-quarter-1999 rate of 1.77 million units, seasonally adjusted annual rate (SAAR), WEFA forecasts housing starts for 1999 to be marginally higher than in 1998, reaching 1.63 million units. However, WEFA forecasts the rate of housing starts to decline in each quarter of 1999. From the high of 1.77 million units in the first quarter, housing starts fell to an estimated 1.63 million units in the second quarter, with forecasts of 1.57 million units and 1.53 million units in the third and fourth quarters, respectively. The fourth-quarter forecast of 1.53 million units is still above the quarterly housing-start rates for 1997.

Figure 2
Housing Starts

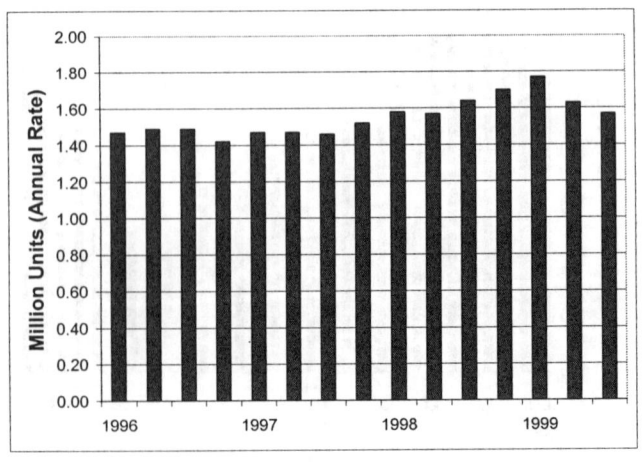

Because of the combination of declines in home construction and the increase in interest rates, the seasonal decline in lumber demand in the second half of 1999 could be greater than usual. Mortgage refinancing has been curtailed with higher interest rates, as well. This is typically a major source of financing for remodeling projects. On the other hand, existing-home sales have remained high, presumably as homebuyers attempt to beat further mortgage-rate increases. Remodeling activity stemming from purchases of existing homes usually occurs within six months of purchase, therefore remodeling activity could remain solid for the remainder of 1999, but is expected to fall in 2000 with declines in existing home sales later in the year.

Export Increases Unlikely to Offset Domestic Demand Declines

The Japanese mortgage-stimulus program has had its peak effects and the government's goal of 1.3 million units for 1999 is not likely to be met.

It is hoped that recovery in export markets, particularly Asian markets, and more specifically Japan, will help sustain the recovery in lumber markets that has developed in recent months. Total North American exports increased 1.5% in January through April compared to the comparable period in 1998. Even though U.S. exports to countries other than Canada increased 10% during that period, a 2.5% decline in Canadian overseas exports offset much of the U.S. increase. Even though large percentage gains have been made to markets such as Spain, Mexico, China, and South Korea, these markets are relatively small compared to Japan. Japan remains the key market for both Canada and the United States. However, the new government mortgage-subsidy program has provided only limited increases in lumber demand. Much of the increase in Japanese lumber requirements has been met through increased domestic production. Log imports have increased instead of lumber imports. Furthermore, the increase in Japanese housing starts seen this year is apparently leveling off. Housing starts fell to 1.24 million units in May, from 1.30 million units in March and 1.25 million units in April. Government-funded mortgages have reportedly fallen further in recent weeks suggesting that the stimulus program has had its peak effects and that the government's goal of 1.3 million units for 1999 is not likely to be met.

Wood-based housing starts actually increased 3.7% in the first five months of 1999, whereas total housing starts in Japan declined 3.8%.

Although housing starts may not get the boost that the Japanese government and North American lumber exporters had hoped, there is some good news in the data. Of the new-home construction in Japan, wood-based housing has increased from 44% in the January through May period of 1998 to nearly 48% in the comparable period this year. Wood-based housing starts actually increased 3.7% in the first five months of 1999, whereas total housing starts in Japan declined 3.8%. However, even with higher wood usage in home construction, lumber exports to that country fell 3% compared to year earlier levels. On the other hand, North American log exports rose 38%. Russian log exports to Japan are also on the rise because of the attractive exchange rates between the yen and ruble that make Russian logs inexpensive compared to North American logs.

Industry Mergers Reach Lumber Producers, Suppliers, Retailers

It is not anticipated that the lumber and panel industries will become highly concentrated, but there will definitely be fewer players at all levels.

Like many other industries, the forest products sector has seen its share of mergers in the past several years. This has occurred in North America as well as in other parts of the world as streamlining operations and cutting costs improve efficiency and competitiveness. However, until recent months, mergers and acquisitions among forest products firms have occurred primarily in paper manufacturing and building material retailing. It is not anticipated that the lumber and panel industries will become highly concentrated, but there will definitely be fewer players at all levels. Primary manufacturers will be fewer in number, but larger, reducing the number of choices that buyers have. Similarly, there will be fewer suppliers and buyers at the secondary level, causing uneasiness among dealers. Among the more notable mergers, acquisitions, and alliances are the Weyerhaeuser purchase of Macmillan Bloedel, the Louisiana-Pacific purchase of Le Groupe Forex, Boise Cascade's acquisition of Furman Lumber, and the alliance of Builder Marts of America with Ace Hardware LBM Division. This trend is likely to continue and changes to take place in the way lumber and panels are traded.

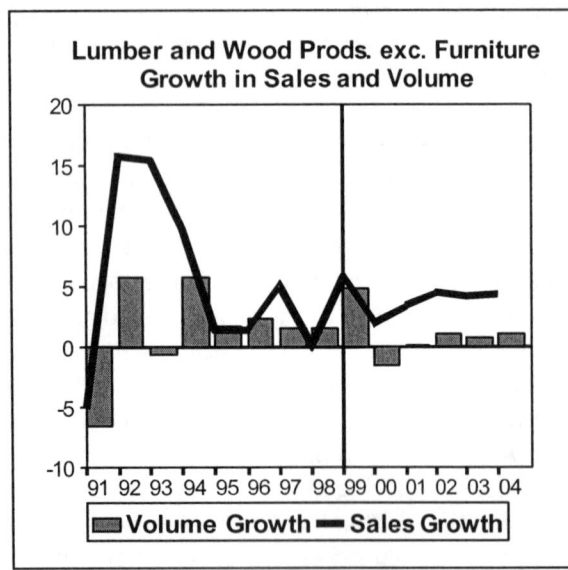

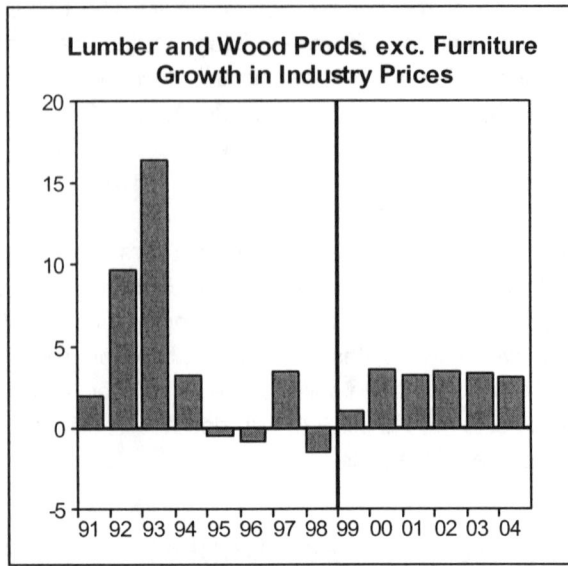

Lumber and Wood Products, except Furniture

SIC 24

		1992	1993	1994	1995	1996	1997	1998	1999	2000	2001	Compound Average 88-98	Annual Growth 98-08
Sales													
	Billions of $	81.5	94.2	103.4	104.9	106.3	111.7	111.9	118.3	120.7	124.9		
	% Ch	15.8	15.5	9.8	1.4	1.4	5.1	0.2	5.8	2.0	3.4	4.5	4.3
Volume													
	% Ch	5.8	-0.6	5.8	1.7	2.4	1.5	1.6	4.8	-1.5	0.2	0.6	1.2
Prices													
	% Ch	9.7	16.4	3.3	-0.4	-0.8	3.5	-1.5	1.0	3.6	3.2	3.9	3.1
Production Costs													
Avg. Hourly Earnings													
	$/hr	9.43	9.60	9.84	10.11	10.44	10.76	11.11	11.49	11.84	12.20		
	% Ch	2.2	1.8	2.5	2.8	3.2	3.1	3.2	3.4	3.1	3.1	2.6	3.3
Input Price Index													
	% Ch	4.8	9.1	2.6	1.4	-0.2	2.3	-1.7	0.2	2.2	2.6	2.6	2.4

Chapter 14: Furniture

Furniture

The furniture industry is comprised of producers of household furniture, public-building furniture, and office and store furniture and fixtures. Household furniture accounts for about 45% of all domestic-furniture manufacturers' sales. Ten years ago, that share was 50%. Wood and upholstered furniture makes up about three-fourths of U.S. household-furniture manufacturing, and most of the remainder is comprised of metal furniture and mattresses and bedsprings.

Shipments by the U.S. household-furniture manufacturing industry grew by more than 10% in 1998 and 7% in 1997. The surprising ongoing strength of home sales and residential construction has allowed household-furniture sales to accelerate last year, and a gain of 7% is expected for 1999 as a whole. Household-furniture output grew at an average annual rate of about 4.5% over the last ten years, with average annual growth of 2.3% in both volume and prices. WEFA forecasts a somewhat smaller increase in sales over the coming ten years, but more of the growth will come from volume and less from prices.

Shipments of office and public-building furniture averaged around 6% annual growth over the last decade. Public-building furniture will be influenced most over the next ten years by educational-building requirements, as the primary school-aged children of baby-boom parents stress the capacity of the nation's secondary school system. Office-building furniture and fixtures should see reasonable growth over the next ten years. Computer furniture, one of the sources of strength in office furniture over the past decade, will continue to grow but at a significantly slower pace.

Demand for Furniture

The demand for household furniture tracks with the sale of new homes and the patterns in remodeling and renovation.

New-housing starts surged to 1.62 million units in 1998, after totaling 1.48 million units in 1997. Consumer-income gains have been the support for this growth, at 2.8% in real terms in 1997, and accelerating to the 3.5% range last year thanks to a tight job market. However, WEFA expects housing activity to moderate in the near-to-medium term after the sector's tremendous boom over the past three years. Total starts are forecast to reach 1.63 million units during 1999, and then fall back to a range of 1.39 to 1.44 million units during the 2000–2004 period. Single-unit starts are projected to be 1.31 million and then range between 1.09 and 1.15 million during the next five years, accounting for about 80% of total starts.

From a regional perspective, residential construction activity will continue to be diverse. Those areas of the country that experience strong job growth are likely to see the largest increase in housing starts. WEFA forecasts that the South Atlantic, West South Central, and Pacific regions will have the highest rates of employment growth through the year 2008, and housing starts in these regions are expected to grow faster than the rest of the country. Slowest residential construction growth is expected in the East South Central and West North Central regions.

Upkeep and improvements as well as expenditures on maintenance and repairs for residential property are also classified under residential construction. While it is difficult to capture the full value of do-it-yourself projects, professional-construction figures are readily available. In 1980, about $46 billion were spent for residential alterations and repairs in current-dollar terms. This spending was over $100 billion in 1990, and it reached nearly $131 billion in 1998. The forecast for spending on residential alterations and repairs is moderately bullish for the next five years.

As a result, the outlook for household furniture over the next ten years is for relatively moderate growth. Compared to the 4.6% per-annum increase of the last ten years, growth should slow to the 3.5% range. In the long term, demand for household furniture will grow modestly, as slower growth in household formations slows the housing market. In real terms, sales of domestically produced furniture will average growth of about 2.5% per year during the 1998–2008 period. Price gains over that period will only be about 1% per year, reflecting an increase in import share and a more competitive market overall.

The national office market has enjoyed steadily improving conditions throughout much of the past five years. The office-vacancy rate has been cut more than half, from close to 20% early in the decade to a 15-year low of 8.9% during the fourth quarter of 1998. The improvement in the office-building vacancy rate has been driven by robust office-space absorption created by the booming job market for business services. One of the most important sources of office demand, the financial-services industry, has been on an astounding run of strong growth. The surge in the stock market induced banks to hire aggressively in the last few years. The nation's office market will continue to enjoy strong conditions throughout 1999 before slowing in 2000 with the rest of the U.S. economy. Computer furniture, one of the sources of strength in office furniture over the past decade, will continue to grow, but at a significantly slower pace.

Public-building furniture will be influenced most over the next ten years by educational-building requirements, as the primary school-aged children of baby-boom parents will stress the capacity of the nation's secondary school system. Over the next ten years, high-school enrollment will advance by about 15%, while that of elementary schools will grow by only 4%—virtually a reversal of the pattern observed over the last decade, and a switch that will create demand for school furniture.

Materials Prices Decline

Wood-furniture producers' profits were squeezed in 1997 by a rise in hardwood-lumber prices, which by year-end were up almost 7.5% from the year-earlier level. During the second half of 1998, however, hardwood-lumber prices began to weaken, a situation that has continued through mid-1999. Hardwood lumber is used in producing higher quality furniture. Softwood-lumber prices, on the other hand, have surged since 1998, averaging more than 20% higher than their year-ago level in July 1999. WEFA forecasts a near-term correction in softwood prices, followed by modest gains thereafter and a gradual improvement in hardwood prices over the forecast horizon.

Steel prices, which are more important to the public- and office-furniture markets, are forecasted to strengthen over the next decade, as steel imports, which skyrocketed in 1998 and exerted considerable downward pressure on domestic prices, decline and U.S.-steel producers increase their pricing power.

Furniture Industry Faces Continued Restructuring

Consumers' price sensitivity, along with increasing international competition, has made the furniture industry increasingly competitive. Several decades ago, the industry was dominated by many small retailers that were supplied in turn by many small manufacturers. However, in recent years retailers have consolidated, and the large furniture-store chains have pushed for lower prices and put pressure on producer profit margins.

While once there was a large number of local manufacturers, there are now large national manufacturers supplying retailers across the country and the world. The top-25 manufacturers produce almost half of U.S. furniture output.

International Trade

U.S. exports of furniture and household items grew by almost 15% in 1997 and 6% in 1998. The only year in the 1990s that exports did not increase was 1995. However, exports are less than one-fourth the size of imports in dollar terms. Import growth has exceeded export growth in every year since 1993, averaging almost 15% per annum over the 1992–1998 period versus 6% for exports.

The trade gap in furniture and household items stood at $626.5 million in 1998, up $254 million from the gap in 1990. Canada is the leading household-furniture importer into the United States, and the weak Canadian dollar has given Canadian exporters a significant price advantage.

Environmental Issues

The American Furniture Manufacturers Association (AFMA) has asked the Environmental Protection Agency not to adopt stricter clean air standards, saying they would particularly hurt smaller producers and further encourage imports. The AFMA said the proposal to reduce allowable ozone levels from 12 parts-per-million to between seven and nine, and to cover for the first time "fine" particulate matter of 2.5 microns and smaller, would cost upholstery and wood-furniture facilities between $50 million to $100 million per year. Two likely results of tighter standards are further consolidation in the U.S. furniture-producing industry and loss of market share to lower cost producers in Canada and Asia.

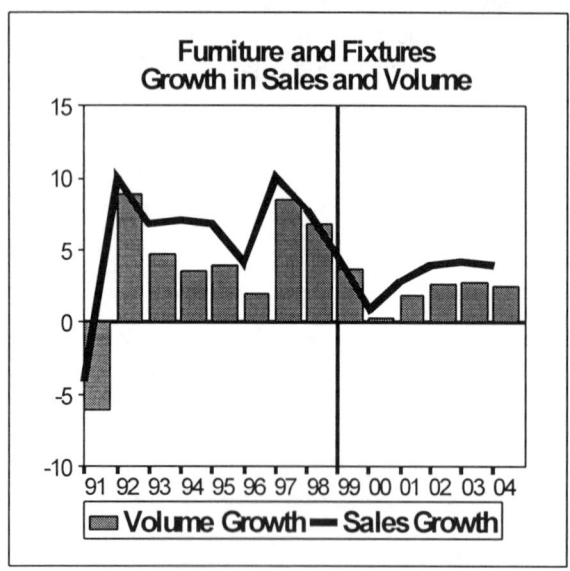

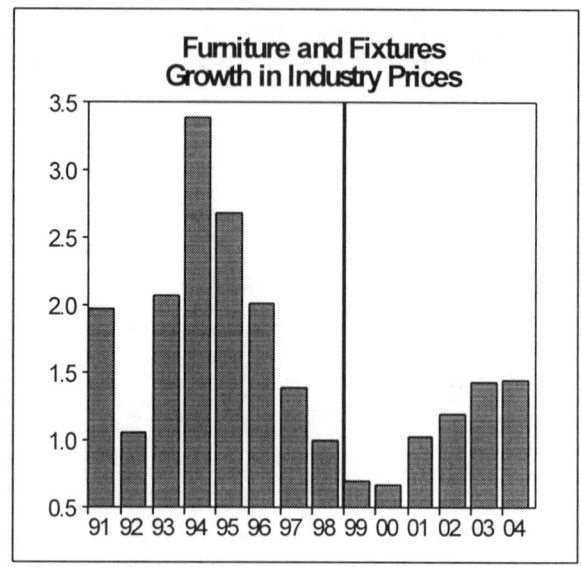

Furniture and Fixtures

SIC 25

		1992	1993	1994	1995	1996	1997	1998	1999	2000	2001	Compound Average 88-98	Annual Growth 98-08
Sales													
	Billions of $	43.81	46.79	50.08	53.46	55.67	61.28	66.09	69.03	69.67	71.66		
	% Ch	10.1	6.8	7.0	6.8	4.1	10.1	7.9	4.4	0.9	2.8	5.4	3.6
Volume													
	% Ch	8.9	4.7	3.5	4.0	2.0	8.5	6.8	3.7	0.2	1.8	3.1	2.3
Prices													
	% Ch	1.1	2.1	3.4	2.7	2.0	1.4	1.0	0.7	0.7	1.0	2.2	1.3
Production Costs													
Avg. Hourly Earnings													
	$/hr	9.04	9.30	9.57	9.84	10.16	10.56	10.91	11.26	11.60	11.96		
	% Ch	2.8	2.9	2.9	2.8	3.3	3.9	3.4	3.2	3.0	3.1	3.2	3.1
Input Price Index													
	% Ch	1.8	3.4	2.5	3.9	0.0	1.3	-0.4	-0.1	2.2	2.5	1.9	2.3

Chapter 15: Hydraulic Cement

Hydraulic Cement

The term cement will refer exclusively to hydraulic cement, which is cement that hardens when mixed with water. It is the overwhelmingly dominant category of cement manufactured in the United States. Portland cement is the predominant variety of hydraulic cement, accounting for more than 95% of the cement produced in the United States. In the short term, cement demand is subject to the cyclical nature of the U.S. economy in general, and the level of construction activity in particular.

The cement industry is regional in nature. Because the cost of shipping cement quickly overtakes its value, customers traditionally purchase cement from local sources. The vast majority of cement produced in the United States is shipped less than 300 miles. About 89% of U.S. cement is shipped to consumers by truck; barge and train shipments account for the rest of the cargo.

Cement manufacturing is a highly capital-intensive industry. The cost of a modern cement plant is $175 per ton of annual capacity, or about $150 million for an 850,000-ton-per-year plant. It is estimated that about three dollars of capital investment is needed to produce one dollar of annual sales. In 1998, approximately 85.5 million tons of Portland and masonry cement was produced, a 3.5% increase over 1997. The value of production, excluding Puerto Rico, was about $6.5 billion, and the dominant Portland cement component was used to make concrete worth at least $27 billion. California, Texas, Pennsylvania, Michigan, Missouri, and Alabama, in descending order, were the six largest cement-producing states, together accounting for 50% of total U.S. production. In terms of use, cement manufacturers sold about 70% of their portland cement output to ready-mixed concrete producers; 10% to producers of concrete products, such as block, pipe, and precast slabs; 10% to contractors (largely for roadpaving); 5% to building-material dealers; and 5% to miscellaneous users, including government and other contractors.

Demand Conditions

There is a very strong relationship between cement demand and the construction industry. Data collected by the Portland Cement Association show that 64% of total cement consumption is used in the construction of buildings. About half of that amount is used in residential projects, and the commercial sector consumes about another third. The remainder is used in public-construction projects. As a result of this diversification within the three main construction markets, as well as cement's use in both new construction and renovation work, the cement industry is somewhat less cyclical than sectors completely dependent on one component, as for example housing starts.

The cement industry, however, is highly seasonal. During the summer, always the most active time for construction, three times more cement is shipped than during the winter months on average. Nearly two-thirds of U.S. cement is consumed in the six months between May and October. The seasonal nature of the cement industry results in large swings in inventories at cement plants during the course of a typical year. Cement producers build up inventories during the winter and work them off with summer shipments.

Cement consumption has never been evenly distributed throughout the United States. For example, the Southeast has seen high growth in cement demand because its population is the fastest growing of the major U.S. regions. Florida continues to see rapid in-migration. Furthermore, resort and hotel construction in the Southeast has been surging.

The most dominant cement consumption areas in the country have been the South Atlantic, the West South Central, and the Pacific regions. WEFA expects those areas to continue to command the largest shares of cement demand in the United States.

Virtually all portland cement is utilized in making either concrete or mortars. As a result, cement competes with substitutes for concrete in the construction sector. There is a small but growing use in the United States of natural and synthetic pozzolanas as partial or complete substitutes for portland cement for some concrete applications.

The robust construction market in 1998 generated higher consumption levels for cement. In fact, total domestic-cement consumption reached a record 103.0 million tons last year. Demand growth was met through a combination of increased production (3.5%) and strong imports (24%). Passage of a major transportation-infrastructure spending bill in 1998 will support forecasts for higher consumption in 1999 and 2000. The first half of 1999 has already seen an 11% increase in shipments compared to year-ago figures. Therefore, the outlook for consumption growth looks healthy for the near future.

Supply

Cement companies in the United States range from small single-plant operations, which account for only tiny shares of U.S. production, to large corporations with many plants that produce as much as 13% of U.S. output. However, ownership of much of the domestic cement industry is in foreign hands. Foreign companies now own approximately 65% of U.S. cement capacity. Many of these were bought from U.S. ownership during the 1980s.

There are 116 portland cement-producing facilities in the country, with a total capacity of over 96 million metric tons. For years, domestic output was inadequate to meet demand, and imports filled the shortfall. The recent combination of only small-capacity growth and strong demand has boosted capacity utilization well into the 90% range. One new cement plant is expected to come online in 1999 and several other plants continue to be engaged in projects to upgrade their capacities. However, the United States remains dependent on imports. In 1994, the demand market share of imports was 10%. In 1997 it increased to 14%, and in 1998 a record 17% was reached.

In the period from 1994 to 1997, Canada accounted for 35% of cement and clinker imports; Spain, 11%; Venezuela, 10%; Greece, 8%; and other countries, 35%. Antidumping tariffs have been effective, and have reduced cement imports from Mexico and Japan, but other countries that do not fall under the agreement have simply filled the gap.

Perspective on Prices

Due to transportation costs, portland cement prices vary widely on a regional basis, by as much as $30/ton. Traditionally, some of the lowest prices are found in the Midwest. The highest are in Alaska, Hawaii, and Florida. During 1998, demand pressures have been strong enough to increases prices by 4.5%.

Employment Trends

Employment in the U.S.-cement industry has declined dramatically during the past couple of decades. Today, the cement industry employs approximately 17,900 workers, down more than 40% from the number of people who worked in the industry in 1975. The drop in employment is the result of efforts by the industry to increase efficiency by automating production and closing small kilns. The average kiln in use today produces twice the amount of cement that an average kiln produced twenty years ago.

Environmental Issues

Concern has been growing in recent years over the environmental impact of cement manufacturing, particularly the emissions of carbon dioxide and cement kiln dust (CKD). The Environmental Protection Agency has yet to release guidelines on CKD emissions, and it has not yet designated the material as hazardous waste.

A number of cement companies burn a proportion of solid- or liquid-waste materials in their kilns as a low-cost substitute for fossil fuels. Technically, cement kilns can be an effective and benign way of destroying such wastes. The viability of the practice and the type of wastes burned hinge on applicable current and future environmental regulations and their associated costs. The overall trend appears to be towards increased use of waste fuels, but some companies are abandoning the practice.

Although individual company reserves are subject to exhaustion, cement raw materials, especially limestone, are geologically widespread and abundant. Overall shortages are unlikely in the foreseeable future. Local shortages generally can be met through outside purchases, and both clinker and cement are widely traded on the world market.

Outlook

While residential construction is likely to slow in 2000 and grow only modestly thereafter, and nonresidential construction will also be modest, demand for cement will continue to rise at a healthy rate thanks to public construction. The latest Federal highway bill guarantees a substantial boost in building and rebuilding of highways, roads, streets, and bridges for the next three to four years.

Supply, on the other hand, has been already stretched to its limit in the summer of 1999. While some capacity-expansion projects are in the works, only moderate-capacity increases will be realized in the next twelve-to-eighteen months. As a result of the combination of these supply constraints with still-growing demand, cement prices are likely to continue to rise over the next two years, by about 3%. Furthermore, U.S. dependence on imports will remain strong.

Chapter 16: Primary Metals

Steel Works

Steel consumption was very strong in both 1997 and 1998. However, demand has slowed in 1999. Import pene-tration, particularly from Asia, has eased, but a significant recovery in prices is not expected until 2000. In the longer term, many steel-demand markets are still growing. Yet, their growth is decelerating from the strong gains of the past two years. WEFA estimates that overall steel shipments will be improved by 2.5% in 2000, while steel consumption will increase by 1.4%. The gap between shipments and consumption will be filled by an increase in domestic mill-market share. Beyond next year, we expect the industry to be back on a trend path, with consumption growth close to 3.5% and prices on the rise again.

Demand Outlook

The motor-vehicle sector represents approximately 30% of domestic steel consumption. The strong auto market during the first part of 1999 is expected to in-crease 1999-steel production by over .8 million tons. This increase combined with expectations of a healthy second half should result in a 6.2% decrease in steel shipments to the automotive industry this year. Next year, production of motor vehicles and parts is pro-jected to be more or less flat. This implies little or no growth in next year's steel shipments to the automo-tive sector. However, by 2001, WEFA anticipates steel shipments to this market to grow again. Flat-rolled steel will be the primary beneficiary of this turn-around, but cold-finished bars should also experience strong demand growth after next year.

Annual U.S. Steel Forecast

Million Tons	1994	1995	1996	1997	1998	1999	2000	2001
Total Shipments	95.1	97.5	100.9	105.9	102.1	103.1	105.5	110.2
% change, year ago	6.9	2.5	3.5	5.0	−3.5	0.9	2.3	4.5
Domestic Sales	91.4	90.4	95.8	99.8	96.6	98.3	100.5	105.1
% change, year ago	7.5	−1.1	6.0	4.2	−3.2	1.7	2.3	4.6
% of shipments	96.1	92.7	95.0	94.3	94.6	95.3	95.3	95.4
Exports	3.7	7.1	5.0	6.0	5.5	4.9	5.0	5.1
% change, year ago	−7.0	91.4	−29.7	20.0	-8.8	-11.7	2.4	2.4
% of shipments	3.9	7.3	5.0	5.7	5.4	4.7	4.7	4.6
Imports	30.1	24.4	29.2	31.2	41.5	33.1	32.7	32.7
% change, year ago	54.4	−18.9	19.5	6.8	33.1	−20.0	-1.4	0.0
market share, %	24.8	21.3	23.4	23.8	30.0	25.2	24.5	23.7
Apparent Consumption	121.5	114.8	125.0	131.0	138.1	131.4	133.2	137.8
% change, year ago	16.2	−5.5	8.9	4.8	5.4	-4.8	1.4	3.5

Historical Source: American Iron and Steel Institute; Forecast Source: WEFA

Traditional machinery, another major steel end-use market, is likely to continue to provide steady demand for steel products over the forecast period. Growth in that area is expected to average 1.5% to 2.5% on an annual basis. One notable exception is the steel-intensive machinery and equipment used by the oil and gas sector. Because crude-oil prices are still relatively weak, little near-term support is expected from the oil patch in terms of its purchases of new machinery and equipment. Drilling and exploration activity will remain weak over the next twelve months and will not grow significantly over the next ten years, meaning little demand for tubular steel products.

The construction sector will continue to boost steel demand. Public construction grew by an annual average of 4.2% between 1995 and 1997, and will continue to do well. WEFA forecasts another 6.5% increase this year and 3.5% further growth in 2000. One key to this outlook is the Transportation Equity Act for the 21st Century (TEA–21). At $217 billion, TEA–21 is the largest public-works measure ever authorized by Congress. The Act is scheduled as a six-year commitment through FY 2003, and some $175 billion will be invested in highways and $42 billion in mass transit over the period. While these projects will consume a wide range of building materials, steel will be one of the key supplies. Structural shapes (structurals), steel piling, reinforcing bars (rebars), plates, structural pipe and tubing and rails and accessories should all experience significant demand growth over the forecast horizon thanks to this bill.

Steel Shipments to the Construction Sector
Excellent growth to stay

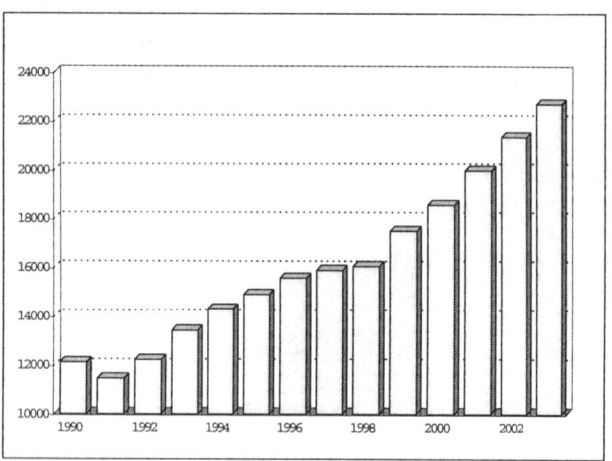

Steel Shipments to the Automotive Sector
No growth until 2000

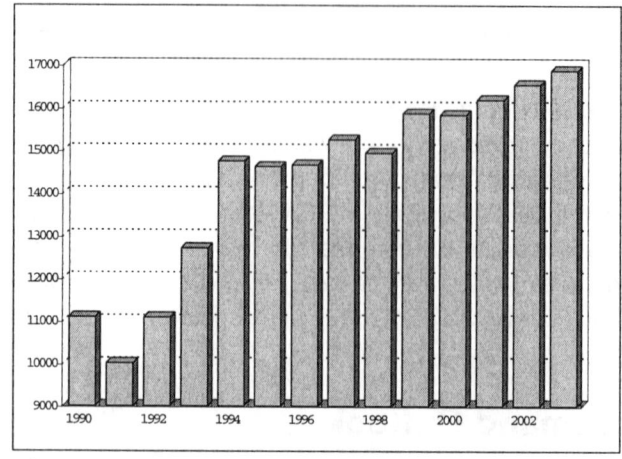

Overall steel end-use market activity will translate into roughly 145 million tons of annual domestic-steel consumption by the year 2003. With 1998 consumption pegged at 138 million tons, this represents an average annual growth rate of 1.0% over the next five years. It also means the United States will need another 10 million tons of steel by the year 2003. This increase is smaller than the 36 million tons added to consumption in the last five years, but is still a healthy rise.

In the first five months of 1999, total U.S. steel imports declined roughly 6% from year-ago levels. This drop in imports explains why WEFA expects 1999's steel shipments to improve slightly while total consumption drops by 4.8%.

U.S. Steel Demand
12 million additional tons by 2002

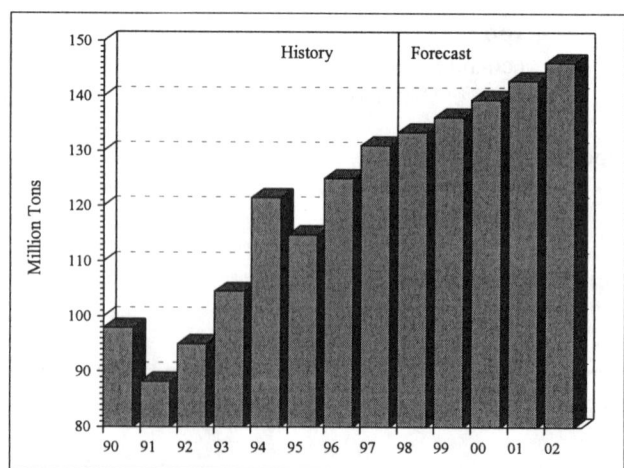

Most of the import decline in 1999 is coming from Japan and Russia. The weakness of the U.S. dollar has been a significant factor: The dollar fell 11% over the yen from the second quarter of 1998 to the second quarter of 1999, and has depreciated more than 14% relative to the South Korean won during the same period.

The economic improvements in Asia, even though they are slow, have also been an important factor in the decline in steel imports to the United States. The Korean economy is expected to improve by 5.4% in 1999, while the Japanese economy should increase by 0.8%. Small improvements in steel consumption in Asia have led those countries' mills to focus on their own markets. The share of steel imports in the U.S. market was 30% during 1998, a marked increase from the 1997 average of roughly 24%. Since we expect further softness in domestic demand during the second half of 1999, the import share should decline to 25.2%.

Trade conditions are likely to start improving further in 2000. WEFA expects the dollar to drop against the yen and the won. More importantly, the economies of Japan and South Korea should begin to move back into healthier growth rates. WEFA expects 1.1% growth in Japan and 5.6% in South Korea in 2000. For 2001, these economies should move further toward a more normal growth path, with real GDP up 2.0% in Japan and 5.7% in South Korea.

The recent wave of expansions by steelmakers has created new capacity in many product areas, including plate, structurals, and galvanized sheet. Although the pace is waning, still more expansions are planned. WEFA expects that about 8.2 million tons of additional steel capacity will come on stream in the United States over the next five years. These projects will focus on the industry trend toward higher margin, value-added products and away from lower value products. The list of steel companies planning expansions includes: Nucor, Ipsco Inc., Steel Dynamics, Inc., Chaparral Steel Corporation, North Star Steel Corporation, Citisteel USA Inc., and Tuscaloosa Steel Corporation. These producers plan to contribute new plate, structurals, and steel pipe to the market, in hopes of garnering market share with a lower cost product. The new, low-cost capacity will also be able to compete more effectively with imports.

The combined influence of a stabilized dollar, stronger economic growth in Asia, and U.S. mill capacity increases should lead to less import pressure in the United States, and steel imports should decline slowly through 2003. By the end of ten years, the import share should approach 18%—roughly the same as it was during 1993.

Price Outlook

Steel prices have firmed slightly in the third quarter of 1999. As foreign penetration weakens and demand slowly increases, price strength is likely to continue through year-end. Average 1999 hot-rolled sheet prices are projected at $270 per ton, down by more than 11% from 1999. Cold-rolled sheet has also strengthened this summer. However, we still expect them to be off by 7.7% on an annual average basis.

Steel products used in the construction industry have also seen improved prices. Rebar prices increased $20/ton since February 1999. However, rebar prices for the year should be below the 1998 annual average. Prices for structurals and plates have not done as well during the first half of 1999 and this year's annual average should be off 13.5% and 19.5%, respectively. The overall composite spot price for steel should average $348/ton in 1999, down 13.6% from 1998.

The strength of steel prices during the second half of 1999 should continue into 2000, and result in a composite steel spot price increase of about 6% for the year as a whole. Flat products should experience the brunt of this improvement. The major end-use markets for flat products, including transportation, appliances, and fabricated metals, are expected to continue to grow. Improvements in those markets will drive prices upward through most of the year.

The prices of steel products sold to the construction market are also projected to improve in 2000. The underlying strength of the construction industry should help support these prices. Tags for structurals and rebars are forecast to increase between 3% and 4% in 2000. Stainless-steel prices have experienced major declines in the last three years, and they are likely to improve slightly in 1999 by 1.5%. Per-capita consumption of stainless in the United States has been in catch-up mode with the penetration seen in other developed countries, and many new uses for stainless products are in the works in appliances and construction, as well as transportation and electronics. Overall, the longer term stainless market is favorable. In the near term, however, domestic-capacity growth and foreign competition will keep prices soft.

Between 2001 and 2003, domestic shipments and production should grow by over 3% annually while import penetration stabilizes around 23%. During that time, prices are expected to begin to grow again.

U.S. Steel, Spot Price Composite
1999 will be bearish

U.S. Steel Market: Annual Price Outlook

U.S.$/Ton	1994	1995	1996	1997	1998	1999	2000	2001
"Major–6" Average (1)	495	510	498	529	533	507	519	539
% Change	5.5	3.0	−2.3	6.3	0.8	−5.0	2.4	3.9
"Mini–10" Average (2)	395	421	391	391	399	359	369	388
% Change	9.1	6.6	−6.7	0.0	2.0	-9.9	2.7	5.1
Steel PPI (1982=100) (3)	113	120	116	116	114	106	109	114
% Change	4.4	6.3	−3.8	0.7	−2.1	−6.8	2.7	4.2
Spot Price Composite (4)	448	429	408	427	403	348	367	394
% Change	13.9	−4.2	−4.8	4.4	−5.5	−13.6	5.6	7.1
Integrated Spot Price (5)	481	453	426	449	420	359	382	412
% Change	15.8	−5.8	−5.3	5.6	−6.6	−14.5	6.5	7.8
Mini Mill Spot Prices (6)	352	357	360	358	353	316	324	341
% Change	6.0	1.2	0.7	−0.4	−1.5	−10.5	2.7	5.1
Scrap – No.1 Heavy Melt (7)	127	137	134	122	100	79	84	91
% Change	13.4	7.9	−2.1	−9.3	−17.7	−21.0	6.5	7.3

Mid–month, F.O.B. prices; Forecast Source: WEFA; Unless Otherwise Noted, Historical Source: Purchasing Magazine;
1– Avg. Value/Ton Steel Sold By Major–6 Steelmakers; Historical Source: Company Financial Reports;
2– Avg. Value/Ton Steel Shipped By Birmingham, Bayou, Chaparral, CMC, Florida, Laclede, New Jersey, Northwestern, NS Group, Nucor;
 Historical Sources: WEFA Survey; Independent Market Cross–Check;
3– Composite of all steel mill products; Historical Source: Bureau of Labor Statistics;
4– Composite of HR Sheet, CR Sheet, Galvanized Sheet, Plate, CF Bar, Structurals, Wire Rod and REBAR;
5– Composite of HR Sheet, CR Sheet, Galvanized Sheet and Plate;
6– Composite of CF Bar, Structurals, Wire Rod and REBAR;
7– Historical Source: American Metal Market.

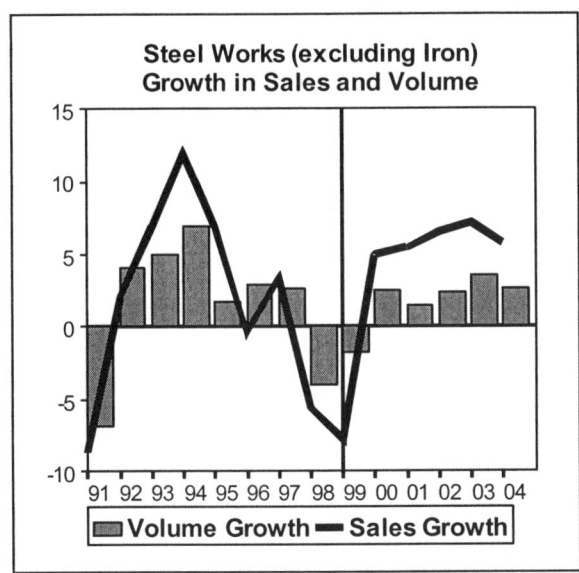

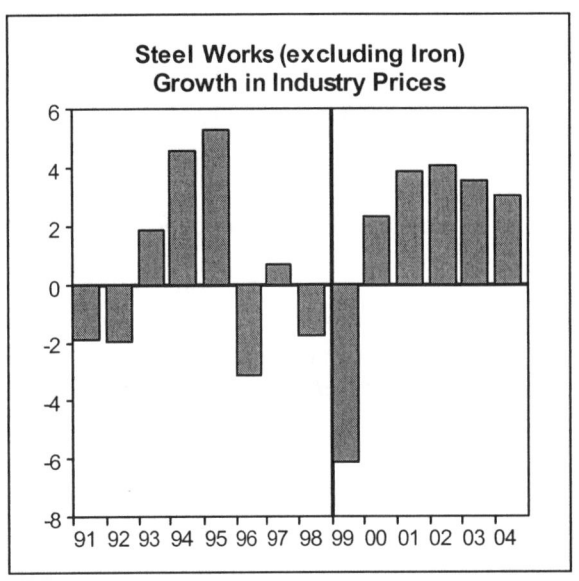

Steel Works (excluding Iron)

SIC 331, 332

		1992	1993	1994	1995	1996	1997	1998	1999	2000	2001	Compound Average 88-98	Annual Growth 98-08
Sales													
	Billions of $	58.48	62.51	69.98	74.87	74.59	77.05	72.75	67.08	70.38	74.23		
	% Ch	2.0	6.9	11.9	7.0	-0.4	3.3	-5.6	-7.8	4.9	5.5	1.3	3.8
Volume													
	% Ch	4.0	4.9	7.0	1.7	2.9	2.6	-3.9	-1.7	2.5	1.5	0.8	1.5
Prices													
	% Ch	-2.0	1.9	4.6	5.3	-3.2	0.7	-1.8	-6.1	2.3	3.9	0.5	2.3
Production Costs													
Avg. Hourly Earnings													
	$/hr	15.87	16.36	16.85	17.33	17.80	18.03	18.43	19.01	19.40	20.14		
	% Ch	3.3	3.1	3.0	2.9	2.7	1.3	2.2	3.2	2.0	3.8	2.8	3.5
Input Price Index													
	% Ch	-0.4	0.8	2.8	4.9	-0.6	0.8	-2.9	-1.9	2.2	2.7	0.9	2.1

Lead

Although lead consumption broadly follows trends in economic activity, lead is probably the least cyclical of all the major non-ferrous metals. A large and still growing proportion of lead is consumed by the replacement SLI (starting-lighting-ignition) battery market. This sector is most directly affected in the short term by seasonal-weather patterns and in the long term by trends in vehicle ownership and use.

In the United States, the transportation industry is the principal direct user of lead, accounting for 65% of lead consumption of batteries, fuel tanks, solder, seals, and bearings. Electrical, electronic, and communication uses (including batteries), ammunition, television glass, construction (including radiation shielding), and protective coatings combine for about 28% of consumption. The balance is used in ballast and weights, ceramics and crystal glass, tubes and containers, foil, wire, and specialized chemicals.

Lead prices dropped steadily throughout 1997 before stabilizing in 1998. Prices have remained steady in 1999. Nevertheless, a modest surplus of supply over demand is anticipated for the year, as world refined-lead demand is expected to reach 6.2 million tons compared with production of 6.3 million tons. As the surplus disappears, prices are forecast to strengthen, but the pace of increase is likely to be moderate on average.

Concentration among lead-consuming companies is less marked than among producers. However, the rising share of purchases taken by the battery sector, now accounting for over 85% of total lead consumption in the United States, together with supply-side changes in the lead industry, suggest that the market power of lead buyers is likely to grow. Battery manufacturers have also integrated backwards into secondary production.

U.S. Lead Industry Trends
(Thousands of short tons, unless otherwise noted)

Source: American Bureau of Metal Statistics

	1994	1995	1996	1997	1998
Mine Production	412	450	490	491	510
Refined Production	1,420	1,390	1,414	1,597	1,534
Refined Consumption	1,648	1,623	1,698	1,758	1,784
U.S. Product Price (¢/LB)	37.2	42.7	48.8	46.5	45.3

Demand

Western Europe, Japan, and the United States dominate lead consumption, although their share has been declining in recent years. Still, the seven leading industrialized countries account for over 60% of total Western consumption. The market share of developing countries, in particular that of the Asian newly-industrialized countries (NICs), has risen dramatically. Between 1987 and 1997 the proportion of consumption accounted for by Asian countries, excluding Japan, doubled to about 18%. It has since fallen to around 11% because of the Asian crisis, but it should pick up again as the region recovers from its severe downturn.

Trends for future lead consumption largely depend upon further developments in lead-acid battery usage. Two uses of lead-acid batteries have significant potential to expand lead consumption: electric vehicles and stationary (for uninterrupted power supplies, remote area power supplies, and telecommunications). Based upon regulatory, economic, and technical trends, the market for electric and possibly hybrid vehicles in Europe will be 200,000 vehicles in the year 2010, while that for the United States will be 160,000 and 100,000 for Japan. An Electric Vehicle battery can contain 600 pounds of lead, compared to an average of 20 pounds in a standard automotive lead-acid battery. In addition, it has a life expectancy of only two years. Although lead-acid batteries are technically advanced, they potentially face strong competition from nickel-hydride or lithium-ion alternatives.

Supply

The lead industry has a handful of large producers. The degree of concentration is similar to that of copper and zinc at the mining stage, but it is less concentrated at the refining stage, owing to the importance of secondary producers. U.S. mine production increased by about 4% in 1998 to 510,000 tons from 491,000 tons a year earlier. U.S. production remained third in the world behind China and Australia.

The recycling of lead is well developed compared to other metals. Secondary production involves the refining of scraps, residues, and wastes. World secondary output grew slightly in 1998 to a new high of 2.93m tons, representing almost 60% of total Western refined-production. Secondary output rose by 2.5% in the United States, due to easier availability of battery scrap, but by only 1% in Europe, where secondary raw materials were in short supply, largely because of lower battery-failure rates.

Over the long run, the growing share of batteries in total consumption and the intensification of environmental legislation (giving rise to enforced recycling) will ensure that the secondary sector increases in importance. This will, in turn, decrease primary mine production as smelters take more of their feed in the form of secondary materials. Consequently, the statistical distinction between the primary and secondary sectors, already hazy, will become even more uncertain.

Prices

The large share of secondary production in total refined-lead output means that refined-lead supply can be quite responsive to changes in prices, since secondary refineries can act as swing capacity during price upturns or downturns. This has tended to reduce the volatility of prices in recent years, at least when compared with other major metals, and on some measures, lead is now one of the least volatile.

The North American producer price published by *Metals Week* is based on the average list prices of a number of

U.S. and Canadian producers, weighted by their production levels for the previous year. Although this price normally shows a substantial premium over the London Metal Exchange (LME) price, the two markets often move in parallel. This is because many secondary producers base their quotations on the LME price.

Lead prices dropped steadily throughout 1997 before stabilizing toward the end of 1998. As with most commodities, the problems in Asia put a lid on lead's potential for growth in 1998. The market has improved since, as the resilient strength of the U.S. economy, along with a moderate recovery in the economies of the European Union and Asia, provided a lift to demand. Nevertheless, lead supply has continued to exceed demand globally, which has prevented prices from moving up. As the lead surplus disappears, prices are forecast to strengthen, but the pace of increase is likely to be moderate on average.

London Metal Exchange Cash Price

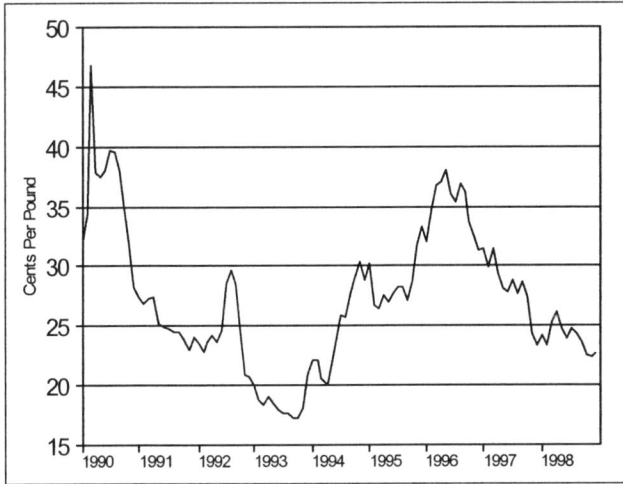

International Markets

The major developed countries dominate global lead consumption, accounting for two-thirds of the world total. However, their share has been declining for many years as consumption has risen more rapidly in developing countries, particularly in Asia.

The Western-world lead market moved into a 34,000-ton surplus in 1998 from a deficit of 6000 tons in 1997, according to the International Lead and Zinc Study Group (ILZSG). During 1998, Western-world lead consumption totaled 5.2 million tons for the third year running, with growth mainly coming from the United States, which offset the fall in Asian demand. In Indonesia and Thailand, consumption of refined lead has been halved since 1996. Western-world refined-lead production totaled 4.93 million tons, a decline of 0.8% from 1997, of which 59% was from the secondary sector. Mine output fell to its lowest level since 1992 at 2.19 million tons. The shortfall was filled by net exports from eastern countries and by releases from the U.S. strategic-defense stockpile. Global demand for lead remained largely unchanged at slightly over 6 million tons.

World lead consumption is expected to increase at an average annual rate of 1.7% from 1999 to 2008, with net mine capacity rising only 0.2% annually over the same period. Smelter utilization rates are forecast to rise from under 70% in 1998 to just under 85% in 2008.

Environmental Issues

The lead industry, long stereotyped as having a negative influence on the environment, has emerged as the only metals industry with "current noncompliance indicators" of zero percent for air, water, and solid-waste regulations among metal sectors covered in a new Environmental Protection Agency database put on the Internet. The agency defines the CSN indicator as "the most recent status for the facility with regard to whether more severe noncompliance has been detected." The database covers more than 650 facilities within the iron and steel, nonferrous metals, automobile assembly, pulp manufacturing, and petroleum refining sectors. By contrast to lead, indicators for air, water, and solid waste were listed as 17.4%, 13%, and 0% for aluminum; 4.3%, 4.8%, and 19% for copper; and 33.3%, 33.3%, and 0% for zinc.

Zinc

Among all the industrial metals, zinc is the fourth most-widely used after iron, aluminum, and copper. Most zinc is used for galvanizing and diecasting, making brass (as an alloying metal with copper), and in its chemical form in the production of paints and rubber. Galvanizing is the principal use of zinc, accounting for 54% of total U.S.-zinc consumption in 1998. Its share has grown rapidly in the last few years, largely at the expense of zinc diecasting.

Zinc mining is quite different from that of other non-ferrous metals. There is a high level of co-product and by-product metal production. These mines also produce lead as a co-product, and sometimes silver, copper, or gold as a by-product. Zinc mine output can therefore be strongly influenced by the prices and market developments for all of these metals.

The continued strength of the U.S. economy and the start of a rebound by Asian economies will push lagging zinc prices up moderately in 1999 and 2000. It is widely believed that zinc is undervalued and shows the best fundamentals out of all the base metals. However, there is little anticipation for a substantial price rise because higher prices would attract more material into the market, mainly from China.

Demand

The United States is the largest consumer of zinc and zinc products, accounting for about one-fifth of Western consumption. (The Western world is defined as the world minus China, the former Soviet Union, Eastern Europe, and other current or former communist nations, such as Cuba.) However, domestic-metal production capacity supports less than one-fourth of the quantity consumed. Canada and Mexico are the leading sources of zinc imports to the United States, because of geographical proximity and low tariffs. Under the North American Free Trade Agreement (NAFTA), which went into effect in 1994, tariffs on zinc and zinc–containing products from Canada and Mexico were either eliminated or lowered significantly. Canada is the second-largest zinc producer in the world after China, and Mexico is the sixth largest.

U.S. zinc consumption has been on a steady upward trend in the 1990s, averaging about 4% growth per year. Consumption has been following the two major zinc end–user industries: motor vehicles and construction. Zinc is used in the form of coatings (mainly for steel), diecastings, rubber, and brass in the automotive manufacturing process, totaling about 40 pounds of zinc used on average in a U.S.-manufactured car. Zinc's use in light vehicles continues to rise because of the corro-

sion protection, the added strength, and the durability offered by zinc-coated steel.

Zinc's Major Uses in the United States, 1998

Galvanizing	54%
Zinc Alloys	19%
Brass	13%
Other Uses	14%

An area of particular growth has been galvanized sheet, especially hot-dipped galvanized (HDG) strip. A new potential source of growth for zinc is in steel used in framing of residential construction in place of lumber framing. This use will likely be concentrated in galvanized steel, especially hot-dipped material.

The U.S. economy has continued to perform well in 1999, now in its ninth year of expansion. During the last couple of years, the U.S. zinc market has been able to deflect most of the consequences from the Asian crisis due to its strong dependency on domestic construction activity, which has remained buoyant. Zinc consumption by the U.S. construction industry is expected to remain strong in the near future, as well as the automobile sector, which is on pace for a record year in 1999.

Supply

Zinc mining is fairly concentrated in the United States, with more than half of it coming from Alaska. The biggest producer in Alaska is Cominco's Red Dog mine, the leading supplier of zinc in the United States. Cominco is a Canadian-based company, which has mines throughout North America.

In 1996, Red Dog embarked upon a project to increase production by 40% and signed a lease agreement with the Alaska Industrial Development and Export Authority. The first phase of the expansion project was completed in 1998. As a result, total U.S. zinc output rose by over 15% in 1998 from its year-ago level.

Total U.S. output is forecasted to continue to increase over the next couple of years, mainly due to increased output from Red Dog, as capacity expansions at the mine proceed.

Prices

A U.S. producer price (as published by *Metals Week*) is quoted for Special High-Grade (SHG) zinc. This is intended to be representative of U.S.-list prices for delivered metal, and traditionally carries a few cents per pound premium over the London Metal Exchange (LME) price. This premium reflects the cost of shipping metal from Europe to the United States and the different market conditions between the United States and Europe.

The U.S. producer price SHG averaged 51.4¢/lb in 1998, down over 20% from its 1997 average of 64.6¢/lb. This plunge was due to a drop in worldwide demand, mainly from Asia.

International Market

Large multinational companies have traditionally dominated zinc mining and smelting, and concentration has increased since the early 1990s. The six largest smelting companies located in Australia, Canada, and Europe, now account for as much as half of Western slab output. In the future, capacity in emerging economies, including China, India, Korea, and Taiwan, will increase, while structural change in the European and Japanese zinc industries continues.

London Metal Exchange SHG Cash Price

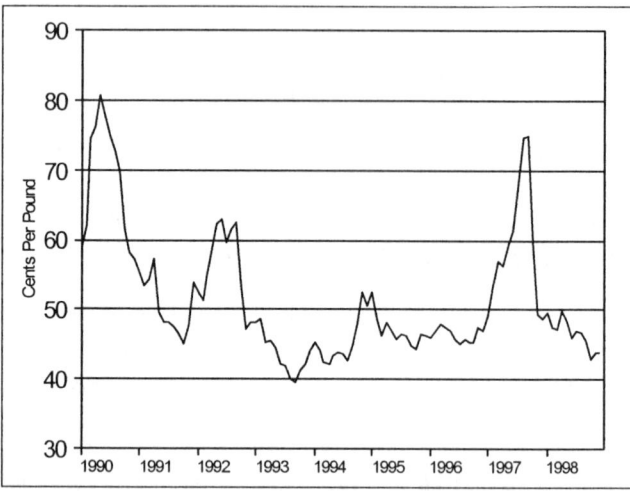

Cash-settlement prices on the London Metal Exchange averaged 46.5¢/lb in 1998; a decline of 22% compared with the 1997 average of 59.7 cents/lb. However, the 1997 average is a bit misleading due to a sudden upswing in prices, which peaked in August of that year because of a perceived shortage that never materialized. Prices plummeted in the fourth quarter as a major influx of zinc from China flooded the market, quickly squelching any fear of a shortage of zinc. Prices continued to decline in 1998, albeit at a more modest rate, as worldwide demand suffered from the Asian crisis.

The Western world remained in a zinc-metal deficit for the fourth year running in 1998, according to the International Lead and Zinc Study Group (ILZSG). Demand exceeded supply by 87,000 tons, following a shortage of 33,000 tons a year earlier. Western demand for refined zinc metal, at 6.43 million tons, was close to its 1997 level. Rises of 2.8% in Western Europe and 3.2% in the United States were offset by the fall in Asia demand. The most notable decline came from Japan, where demand dropped by 11% to 661,000 tons. Zinc demand fell by 8.2% in Korea, 27.4% in Indonesia, 23.8% in the Philippines, and 15.8% in Thailand. By contrast, demand increased by 5.8% in Taiwan. Worldwide, zinc consumption rose to 7.82 million tons.

Western refined-zinc production rose in 1998 by 2.4% to 5.7 million tons, the fourth successive year of growth. Global refined-zinc production increased to 7.9 million tons. Western mine output rebounded to 1996 levels in 1998 after falling in 1997, as a 1.7% increase took production to 5.58 million tons. U.S. output rose 15%, while

Australian production moved up 3.7%, European output remained the same, and Latin American production fell 4.4%.

Stocks in LME warehouses fell during the year by 175,000 tons to end 1998 at 317,000 tons. By contrast, producer stocks rose by 59,000 tons to 305,000 tons.

According to the ILZSG, consumption of zinc in 1999 is expected to rise by 3% worldwide to 7.99 million tons and by the same amount in the West to 6.57 million tons. Growth of 1.9% is forecast in Europe, 3.5% in the United States, and 2.8% in China. Demand is also expected to recover, albeit slowly, in Japan, South Korea, and other South East Asian countries. Significant rises in zinc-mine output of 5.1% to 7.87 million tons worldwide and 6.8% to 6.04 million tons in the West are predicted, mainly as a consequence of increases in Australia. Growth in refined-metal output is expected to continue in 1999 with increases of 2.1% globally to 8.09 million tons and 2.4% in the West to 5.87 million tons.

Other Industry Issues

Fate of the Penny

According to a study done by the General Accounting Office (GAO), the penny is no longer profitable because the cost of making it exceeds its value. The 98%-zinc penny uses approximately 35,000 tons of zinc, annually. However, some advocacy groups for the poor and charitable organizations strongly favor retention of the penny, as the poor and the elderly make more small cash purchases.

Substitution

There is no effective substitute for zinc in large-volume galvanizing, but in the coating of steel sheet and strip, high-aluminum-zinc alloys, such as Galvalume, have displaced high--zinc alloys. Aluminum, plastics, and magnesium are major competitors as diecasting materials. Plastic coatings, paint, and cadmium and aluminum alloy coatings are replacing zinc for corrosion protection, and aluminum alloys have been displacing brass in car radiators. Many elements are substitutes for zinc in chemical, electronic, and pigment uses.

Aluminum

1998 was marked by considerable declines in aluminum prices. At year-end, aluminum was trading around 56¢/lb on the London Metal Exchange (LME), 18% below its year-earlier level and a new four-year low. Ironically, the LME stockpiles, for most of the year, were down compared to their 1997 levels. Aluminum market conditions reflected the overall negative sentiment that had been pervading the whole base-metal sector and other basic materials since the onset of the Asian economic crisis.

In early 1999, prices continued their downward trend, reaching bottom in early March when they hit 52¢/lb—a new six-year low on the LME. Since then, however, prices have shot up 25% to around 65¢/lb on the LME, as of this writing. The sudden recovery of aluminum prices has been spurred by a number of factors: technical buying, a moderate rebound in demand in Asia and Europe, an improvement of sentiment in commodity markets and recent announcements of consolidation and minor cutbacks by producers.

The desire to manufacture lighter products in a range of industries will allow aluminum to remain a material of choice in the future. Consumption for the manufacture of motor vehicles and parts, for example, which has been a major driving force for aluminum demand worldwide, should see further growth in the next ten years. The U.S. and European aircraft industries have been benefiting from a surge in orders from airlines striving to replace aging fleets (although orders have been hurt lately by cancellations from Asia). This will boost aluminum requirements in the years ahead. Additional growth opportunities for aluminum will come from the can and packaging markets in emerging economies, as well as those economies' fast developing construction sectors.

WEFA forecasts that U.S. and global aluminum shipments will grow over the next ten years at an average annual rate of about 3.5% and 4.0%, respectively, in real-volume terms. Prices are likely to move up in line with increasing demand.

Global Industry Consolidation

The aluminum industry has moved aggressively to consolidate in an attempt to streamline operations and reduce costs in response to the depressed state the market has recently been in. During the summer of 1999, two mega-mergers were announced. First was the combination of Canada's Alcan Aluminum Ltd. with Alusuisse-Lonza (Algroup) in Switzerland and Pechiney in France. Then, shortly after, Alcoa won a hostile bid for Reynolds Metals, reaching an agreement to acquire the company for $4.4 billion in stock. If federal regulators approve the agreements, these two groups will control about one-quarter of the world's aluminum production.

Domestic Market

With production of 3.7 million tons in 1998 and almost a 20% share of the global market, the United States is the world's leading producer of aluminum, followed by Russia, China, and Canada. The largest agglomeration of aluminum capacity in the United States is in the Pacific Northwest (the states of Oregon, Montana, and Washington), which boasts 38% of the country's aluminum-production capacity. The Ohio Valley is another capacity center, accounting for 31% of the U.S. total.

Even though U.S. aluminum capacity is huge, it is not sufficient to satisfy this country's enormous appetite for aluminum. The United States is not only the world's largest aluminum producer, but also the largest consumer, with a 25% share of global-aluminum consumption. This high demand makes the United States the second-largest importer of aluminum. Most of the added metal comes from Canada, which supplies about 60% of U.S.-aluminum imports. The domestic demand for aluminum comes from two major consuming industries: transportation and containers/packaging.

- The transportation industry, especially the automotive component, leads aluminum consumption. In 1991, transportation made up only 17% of the aluminum market, and was the second-largest consumer of aluminum behind containers and packaging. However, this metal's unique properties (non-corrosive, lightweight, and strength), which make it an ideal substitute for steel in several automotive applications, contributed to a rapid increase in its use by the automotive industry. Today, the transportation share of U.S. aluminum consumption is almost one-third.

U.S. Aluminum Consumption by Industry

Transportation	32%
Containers & Packaging	26%
Building & Construction	16%
Electrical	8%
Consumer Durables	8%
Other	10%

- The containers and packaging sector is currently the second-largest end user of aluminum in the United States. This sector consumes almost a quarter of all the aluminum consumed in the United States. Aluminum cans control nearly 100% of the beverage can market, having displaced steel. However, the use of aluminum cans in beverage packing is facing a threat from cheaper plastic containers.

U.S. Aluminum Prices

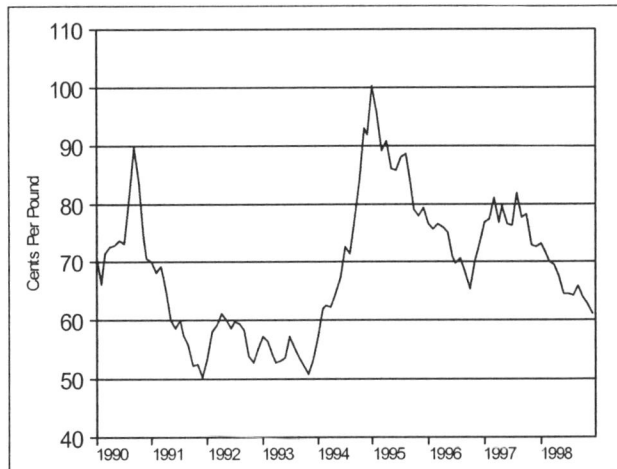

U.S. Service Center shipments of aluminum-mill products grew 5.4% in 1998 from the year before, according to the National Association of Aluminum Distributors (NAAD). With the U.S. economy remaining strong and few indications that the end is in sight for the consumer-led expansion, the NAAD predicts service-center shipments will increase again in 1999, totalling 2.405 billion pounds, up from the record 2.380 billion pounds shipped in 1998.

International Markets

Demand

The latest figures show world consumption of primary aluminum grew a scant 1.8% in 1998, after rising 5% the year before. In 1998, consumption increased around 5.1% in North America, but only 0.4% in Europe. By contrast, demand slipped 6.8% in Asia, which was wracked by economic problems. Global aluminum consumption has picked up in 1999, with consumption forecasted to increase around 3% for the year. But, as in 1998, regional-demand trends have remained widely divergent.

Since the successful launch of the Euro, the European economy has picked up some speed. In Asia, the economic recovery is already underway in several countries, sooner than many had expected. The Japanese economy is showing signs of renewed life. Business sentiment is shifting, and exports are picking up. Aluminum consumption is expected to continue to improve in the near-to-medium term in both the European community and Asia, as more favorable economic conditions set in.

In the long term, the outlook for global aluminum demand is optimistic. The transportation market offers considerable opportunities for new aluminum applications, which could help global consumption to grow by as much as 4% on average per year over the next decade. Increases in aluminum usage will be realized at the expense of steel and other materials.

Additional growth opportunities for aluminum will come from can-sheet growth in emerging markets, strong growth for all product lines in Europe, and a long-term rebound in the Asian construction market.

Production

World-aluminum production posted a record year in 1998, despite beaten-down prices. In 1999, production will remain on its course to another record due to the addition of new capacity worldwide, improvements in efficiency at existing smelters, and a lack of major production cuts.

Production would have been even higher in 1998 but for some involuntary losses of output. Drought affected hydroelectric supplies to smelters in Ghana and Indonesia, and operating problems were experienced in Venezuela and India.

As a result of the bullish long-term prospects for aluminum, the industry is expected to add capacity, in the form of both idled-smelters reactivation and new expansion projects.

The British Columbia (BC) region of Canada has become one of the major centers for new smelter projects. After reorganizing its power grid, BC has an estimated 1,400 megawatts of excess electricity. Rather than sell it to the United States, the BC government wants to turn the excess power into jobs for its citizens and has chosen to do so by offering very attractive power rates to aluminum companies. To take advantage of these attractive rates, Alcan, Alcoa, and Alumax all made announcements regarding new smelter capacity in BC.

Power cost is the main determinant in the location of new smelters, and the Middle East has begun to use its vast reserves of natural gas to attract the aluminum industry. The two largest smelters in the region are the 500,000-metric-ton Alba complex in Bahrain and the 380,000-metric-ton Dubai complex in the United Arab Emirates. Several other new projects are under serious consideration in the region. African production is on the rise as well. The Maputo smelter in Mozambique, for example, is expected to add another 250,000 metric tons of primary production to Africa around 2001.

Outlook

The desire to manufacture lighter products in a range of industries will allow aluminum to remain a material of choice. Consumption from motor vehicles and parts, which has been a major driving force for aluminum demand worldwide, should see further growth in the next ten years. The U.S. and European aircraft industries have been benefiting from a surge in orders from airlines striving to replace aging fleets (although orders have been hurt lately by cancellations from Asia). This will boost aluminum requirements in the years ahead. Additional growth opportunities for aluminum will come from the can and packaging markets in emerging economies, as well as those economies' fast developing construction sector.

WEFA forecasts that U.S. and global aluminum shipments will grow over the next ten years at an average annual rate of about 3.5% and 4.0%, respectively, in real-volume terms. Prices are likely to move up in line with increasing demand.

Copper

Notwithstanding a short-lived rally in April and in May, copper prices drifted lower for most of 1998 and the sell-off intensified towards the end of the year. The London Metal Exchange (LME) price finished the year at 65¢/lb. Shrinking order books in Asia, rising production, and speculative selling had caused inventories to pile up. Stockpiles in LME warehouses more than doubled in the second half of 1998, up to their highest level since January 1994. On the Comex Exchange, stockpiles were also very high by historical standards.

During the first quarter of 1999, copper prices kept sliding, while inventories continued to rise. In March, LME prices hit 61¢/lb, a level at which an estimated two-thirds of copper producers around the world were operating at a loss. Despite the gloomy picture, supply had surprisingly remained steady, without any significant cutback announcements by the industry.

Since March, however, copper prices have made a strong comeback, up over 25%. Short covering and hedge-fund buying, coupled with an improvement in demand in Asia and Europe and an apparent change in sentiment in major commodity markets have all contributed to the recent price run-up.

Longer term, world-copper demand looks to be strong for the coming decade, despite recent market conditions. However, copper supply, which has been the key behind the balance of the market for the last few years, will continue to dominate pricing. Without any major cutbacks in production, world supply is likely to outpace demand over the next two years.

Domestic Market

Demand

The seemingly never-ending strength of the U.S. economy has been a major factor underpinning copper demand growth for much of the decade, and domestic consumption of copper continues to exceed expectations. The construction market is still benefiting from solid fundamentals, demand from the high-tech equipment sector remains quite strong, and the motor vehicles market is enjoying record sales.

The construction market has been solid for the last few years due to low interest rates and sustained growth in personal income and corporate profits. The boom in construction activity has led to a surge in the demand for copper waterworks, a market that represents more than 40% of all copper demand in the United States.

Copper demand from the electric and electronic equipment industry (including the fast-growing computer market) has been growing at double-digit rates. It now accounts for almost a quarter of total domestic-copper consumption.

U.S. Copper Consumption by Industry

Building Construction	43%
Electric and Electronic	24%
Industrial Machinery and Equipment	12%
Transportation Equipment	12%
Consumer and General Products	9%

Supply

U.S. output of mined copper ranks second only to Chile, the king of the copper world. The United States produces about 20% of the world supply of mined copper, and ranks first in production of refined copper.

Domestic-mine production in 1998 was essentially unchanged at 1.9 million metric tons. The five main mining states (in descending order)—Arizona, Utah, New Mexico, Nevada, and Montana—accounted for 98% of domestic production. Refined production in 1998 was 2.5 million tons, essentially unchanged from 1997 as well. As the largest refined-copper-producing country in the world, the United States is also the largest importer.

Most imported copper comes to the United States from Canada, Mexico, and Chile.

U.S. Copper Prices

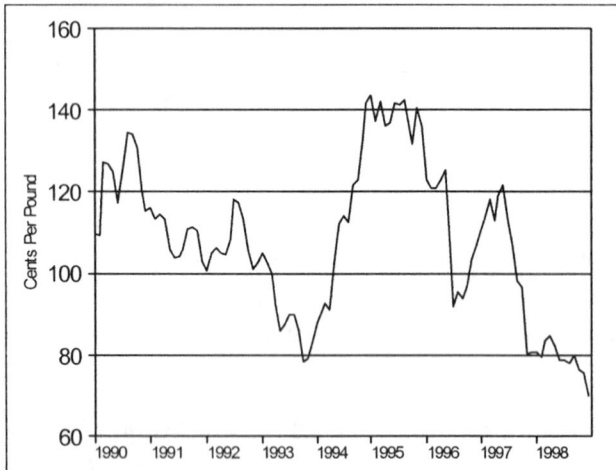

International Market

Demand

Worldwide-copper consumption has grown rapidly over this decade. Western world (the Western world is defined as the world minus China, the former Soviet Union, Eastern Europe, and other current or former communist nations, such as Cuba) copper consumption rose for the thirteenth successive year in 1998, but only by 1%. The economic and financial turmoil in Southeast Asia, which began in 1997, and the economic slump in Japan put a damper on copper demand.

However, the economic climate in Asia has brightened up since the beginning of 1999, with most of the Southeast Asian economies on their way up again. Industrial production has been rising at a healthy pace in those countries, and copper consumption has shown signs of moderate improvement. Nonetheless, the ultimate recovery of the region depends largely on Japan. The Japanese economy seems to have turned the corner as well, but growth prospects there are moderate.

Supply

Despite deteriorating copper prices, world refined copper production rose 2.8% in 1998, according to the International Copper Study Group (ICSG). This increase was fueled by a 4.6% rise in mine output.

Notwithstanding those production increases, depressed copper prices have taken their toll on many producers around the world. Producers on the high end of the cost curve have been forced to scale back production, especially the ones in North America. One example includes Canada's Highland Valley Copper, which shut down in May of 1999 despite serious efforts to reduce costs. When it closed, the mine's cash-production cost was still over copper prices.

On the other end of the spectrum, however, low-cost producers have shown no signs of production cutbacks. Copper production in Latin America is expected to continue to rise in both the near term and long term. Benefiting from economies of scale and new technology, costs in the region are generally lower, which provides great incentives to crank up the production.

As copper miners have continued to boost output, smelters have forged ahead with expansions and dumped metal into warehouses. Since March, of 1999, copper prices have made a strong comeback, up over 25%. Short covering and hedge-fund buying, coupled with an improvement in demand in Asia and Europe and an apparent change in sentiment in major commodity markets have all contributed to this price run-up. Given the recent price jump, producers will be even less likely to implement production cuts. In our view, the risk remains high that global demand will not be strong enough to bring this oversupplied market to a more balanced one in the months ahead. This raises once more the specter of another correction down the road.

The production of refined copper in the former Soviet Union has grown steadily since 1994. The increases recorded in Kazakhstan and Uzbekistan have been more impressive than those in Russia, where operations are restrained by feed and scrap shortages. Overall, it seems more than likely that total production in those countries will continue to increase, and in the absence of a marked upturn in local demand, a substantial volume of metal will continue to be exported. Exports from Russia have also received a boost from the devalued ruble.

Outlook

The copper market will once again record a surplus in 1999, as it did the year before. But, a revival in global demand and speculative interest will allow prices to continue to recover moderately from the beating they took the past couple of years.

Chapter 17: Fabricated Metal Products

Fabricated Metal Products

The fabricated metal products industry is made up of a large number of segments comprising companies that manufacture various types of metal products for both personal and industrial consumption. Over half of the broad industry's shipments, however, are produced by just seven industry categories. In order of shipment dollar size, they are: automobile stampings; sheet metal work; metal cans and shipping containers; non-automotive metal stampings; hardware not elsewhere classified (n.e.c.); fabricated structural metal; and fabricated plate work and boiler shops.

For the fabricated metal products industry overall, we expect modest volume growth of about 2% per year over the next decade with annual price increases of 2% to 3%. Considerable growth variation will exist between the industry's various segments, however, and import pressure will continue unabated for many products.

Recent History

The fabricated metal products industry is made up of a large number of segments comprising companies that manufacture various types of metal products for both personal and industrial consumption. Major sectors of the U.S. economy, such as housing and construction, automotive, and business investment have the greatest impact on the fortunes of the fabricated metal products industry.

Industry Output

The demand for fabricated metal products was hit hard during the last recession, with industry output falling by 3.3% in 1990 and 5.0% in 1991. As the U.S. economy staged its recovery, the fabricated metal products industry got back on track. Industry output expanded without interruption during the 1992–1998 period, propelled forward by expanding consumer and business spending, the recovery in construction activity and up until very recently, solid support from foreign trade.

Production of fabricated metal products expanded by over 4% per year, on average in 1992 and 1993. Growth then accelerated to 7.5% in 1994. The next three years, 1995–1997, saw industry output advance at over 3.5% per year on average. Last year, with ordnance production declining and the metal can and hardware, tools, and cutlery business limping along, production of fabricated metal products grew by only 2.2%. Production of metal cans used for food and beverages, paint and other products, and shipping containers, has grown by only 5.5% since the last recession.

The fabricated metal products industry as a whole grew by 32.5% during the 1992–1998 period. Beyond the economic and market fundamentals that drive the demand for metal cans, competition from plastics continues to intensify. Metal cans continue to lose market share versus other forms of packaging.

Hardware, tools, and cutlery output expanded by 32% from 1992–1998, with a very strong 10.7% increase in 1994. An expanding housing market and gains in consumer income and spending provided the support.

Production of fabricated structural metal products has benefited from the strong recovery in construction in recent years and the steady growth in business investment. Structural metal products includes fabricated structural metal products used in buildings, bridges, and ships, metal doors, sash, frames, molding and trim, fabricated plate work, sheet metal work, architectural and ornamental metal work, and prefabricated metal buildings and components. From 1992–1998 production of structural metal products grew by 28.5%. In 1998, production grew by 3.5%.

The output of fabricated metal fasteners, forgings, automotive and other stampings, and coatings grew by a whopping 50.5% from 1992–1998. This strong performance was triggered by robust activity in the motor vehicle, capital goods, and construction industries.

Over the past decade, ordnance production has declined at an average annual rate of 6.2%. The level of ordnance output was 47% lower in 1998 than it was a decade earlier in 1988. The downsizing of the military, particularly after the Gulf War, has seen the production of ordnance decline in eight of the last ten years.

Production of plumbing and heating products has benefited from the strong recovery in new home construction since the last recession. Additional support has come from growth in commercial building construction. The demand for automotive springs has expanded with light and commercial vehicle production. Production of valves and pipefittings has benefited from the strength in capital goods demand, but the recent slump in oil patch and process industry activity has taken a toll. Overall, production of plumbing and heating products, springs, valves, and pipefittings expanded 35% from 1992–1998. However, growth slowed from 6.3% in 1997 to just 1.6% in 1998.

Employment

Last year the fabricated metal products industry employed 1.5 million workers. Employment has increased steadily since the industry emerged from the last recession. The low point occurred in 1992 when the industry employed only 1.33 million workers. Producers of fabricated metal products have launched aggressive efforts to improve industry productivity and efficiency since the last recession. During the 1992–1998 period output-per-worker has grown by 20%.

Employment in the metal cans and shipping container industry averaged 36,600 last year. Employment in this industry has been in retreat for many years. Ten years ago in 1988 employment totaled 52,580.

The cutlery, hand tools, and hardware employed 126,200 workers in 1998. This represented a slight 0.5% increase over 1997. However, there has been a downward drift in the number of people employed in this industry over the past decade. In 1988, this industry employed 138,740 workers.

Employment among manufacturers of plumbing fixtures and heating equipment edged off by 0.9% in 1998. Since emerging from the last recession, employment in this industry has averaged 57,300, with a high of 58,040 in 1997 and a low of 56,000 in 1992. A decade ago in 1998 the industry employed 62,330.

Producers of fabricated structural metal products employed 391,850 workers at its low point following the last recession in 1992. With the strength in the construction

sector recovery, employment has grown without interruption over the past six years, reaching 463,730 workers in 1998.

The metal fasteners industry employed 106,470 workers in 1998. Strong gains in the construction, motor vehicle, and capital goods industries have forced the producers of screw machine products to expand their workforce. At the low point in 1992 the metal fasteners industry employed 90,290 workers.

Employment in the metal forgings and stampings industries bottomed out at 213,900 workers in 1991. The recoveries in light- and commercial-vehicle production, construction, capital goods demand, and consumer spending has triggered a steady expansion of the work force. Last year, employment in this industry totaled 257,240 workers.

The metal services industry, which includes plating and polishing, metal coating, and allied services employed nearly 144,000 workers last year versus 139,500 workers in 1997. Over the past two years, 1997 and 1998, employment has increased by nearly 9%. At the low point for employment in 1992 the metal services industry employed 115,230 workers.

Employment in the ordnance industry has fallen along with industry output, which has coincided with the downsizing of the military. In 1998 the ordnance industry employed 41,190 workers. A decade ago in 1998, employment totaled 77,250. Employment declined steadily through the decade.

Employment among producers of fabricated wire products, springs, valves, and pipe-fittings totaled 267,890 workers last year. The strength in construction and motor vehicle production has played no small role in pushing employment to current levels from a low of 225,100 workers in 1992. Employment increased for the first time in three years in 1993 and rose without interruption through 1998.

Outlook

The fabricated metal products industry is diverse, providing products to a broad range of both consumer and business users. This diversification in end-markets is both a blessing and a curse. Diversification helps to reduce the overall risk to the industry's growth, but it also makes the industry susceptible, so to speak, to everyone's problems. It also suffers from some very mature product lines, and from some that are losing share to competitive materials. WEFA forecasts growth in fabricated metal product volume of about 2% per year during the coming decade. We are anticipating above average growth in the capital goods market, particularly computers. However, the key construction, automotive and non–auto consumer-durable markets will be expanding at a slightly lower than average pace. Finally, we expect very limited growth from the metal container market where material substitution will continue.

Motor Vehicle Markets

The motor vehicle industry is enjoying another year of prosperity with both light-vehicle and commercial sales and production doing well. When all is said and done, motor vehicle industry output will increase by 6% this year. The year 2000 brings with it a modest adjustment in both light and commercial vehicle demand, and production slips by 1%. A pick-up in the replacement cycle and some fleet expansion will lift vehicle demand in 2000-2002 with production growing by 2% per year. Thereafter, light-vehicle demand is driven by growth in the number of households and replacement demand. The commercial-vehicle market responds to 3% growth in domestic manufacturing activity and increased NAFTA trade. This stimulates fleet expansion as well as replacement sales. Overall, we expect U.S. production of motor vehicles and parts to expand by 1.5% per year during the 2000–2008 period.

Construction Markets

Construction spending will certainly expand at a healthy clip again this year. New-home construction started 1999 off to a rocking good start thanks to very favorable fundamentals (income, employment, consumer confidence, and mortgage rates) and good weather. Housing starts will not remain at their lofty early-1999 level throughout the year, but should be able to finish the year in the 1.6-1.65 million units range versus 1.62 million units last year.

Nonresidential construction spending will increase modestly this year as gains in commercial and utility construction offset weakness in industrial projects. For public construction, 1999 started off strong due to very favorable weather. We are beginning to see TEA-21 projects take form and these will dominate public sector spending throughout the forecast period.

Next year will see construction spending growth slow to about 2%, a rate that should be maintained, give or take a few percentage points, through 2001. Thereafter, construction spending expands by 1.5%–2.0% per year on average. The market mix will change during this period. The residential building market, which has been the source of strength in construction, slows due to demographics and the absence of any pent-up demand for new homes after a period of very aggressive new construction. Housing starts averaged 1.6 million units in 1998–1999 but will slow to between 1.40–1.45 million units per year during the 2000–2004 period, and 1.4 million units per year through the rest of the forecast period. Nonresidential construction will show very little growth in 2000. Thereafter, some new industrial capacity will be needed, and there will be continued modest expansion in the commercial and utility markets. This will support average annual growth of about 1.5%–2.0% per year. Lastly, the growth in public construction spending is maintained at about 3.5%–4.0% per year during the 2000–2004 period as TEA-21 projects kick in. Public-project spending then tapers off after that.

Industrial Machinery Markets

Currently, domestic demand for traditional capital goods is mixed. Farm equipment, special and general industrial machinery, mining machinery, and material handling equipment are weak. Construction machinery and service industry machinery are doing well. The demand for computers and related equipment remains very strong.

Over the near term, the investment climate is not expected to actually turn negative, but limited growth in final demand, some pressure on profit margins, and the absence of a significant need to expand capacity suggest that the pace of investment will be moderating. The demand for computers and related equipment should remain strong through the end of this year. The absence of Y2K-related domestic spending programs in 2000 will dampen spending for computers and related equipment somewhat. However, the availability of new and more powerful products at lower prices will keep this market humming.

Longer term, domestic demand for traditional capital goods will be influenced by 3% growth in manufacturing activity and more modest rates of growth in construction, farming, and mining activity. In addition to pressure to expand productive capacity, competitive pressures will stimulate investment in new equipment that improves productivity and efficiency and replaces labor. Exports of traditional capital goods are depressed currently, but we expect overseas sales to lead the way on the growth front during the coming decade. Asian and Latin American demand will provide most of the lift to U.S. exports of traditional capital goods. Computers and related equipment will continue to reap the benefits of a steady stream of new and more powerful products at lower prices.

Production of traditional capital goods will show little, if any, increase this year. Longer term, our expectations for general economic conditions in the United States and overseas suggest a growth rate of 2.0%–2.5% per year on average. Production of computers will post another strong double-digit gain this year, probably in the 35%–40% range. Output growth then slows to 15%–20% in 2000 and should average 10%–15% per year thereafter.

Appliance Markets

The revival in new-home construction and growth in consumer income will allow appliance production to expand by 6% in 1999. With little support from the housing sector in the year 2000, and consumers already flush with new refrigerators, washers, dryers, and other appliances, household appliance demand will decline by about 1%. Longer term, housing starts will average about 1.41 million units per year, and real consumer disposable income is forecast to grow by roughly 2.5% per year. With this as a backdrop, WEFA expects appliance production to expand by close to 2% per year, on average, during the 2000–2008 period.

Aerospace Markets

The domestic commercial aircraft market is nearing the end of a significant buying cycle, driven by increasing

pressure to replace older units still in service, the introduction of new models designed to meet the needs of specific traffic corridors, and anticipated strong growth in a number of foreign markets. Deliveries of new aircrafts will peak this year and then drift off over the next few years. The Asian crisis has already dampened the order intake of both Boeing and Airbus and should show up in the delivery numbers in 2000–2001. Longer term, passenger and freight traffic worldwide will trigger another round of air transport purchases, which will begin to lift commercial air transport production in three or four years.

The defense portion of the aerospace industry has been in the doldrums in recent years, the victim of aggressive military downsizing. However, discussions about the next generation of military aircraft continue. WEFA expects defense-related aerospace to gain ground slowly and then accelerate through the middle of the next decade.

On balance, WEFA forecasts that production of aircraft and parts will increase 1% this year, following a 15.6% jump in 1998. Production then declines by 5% in 2000 and 3% in 2001, as the commercial transport cycle winds down. Longer term (2002–2008), we forecast production of aircraft and parts to expand by about 3% per year.

Containers

Metal cans have been hurt by trends in the food processing industry. The food market has turned toward convenience foods and easy-to-prepare offerings, especially microwave-ready food products, which are usually packaged in either paper or plastic. Metal cans will continue to face a serious challenge from new packaging developments in the future. We expect modest growth overall for this industry segment, with most of the gains going to aluminum cans.

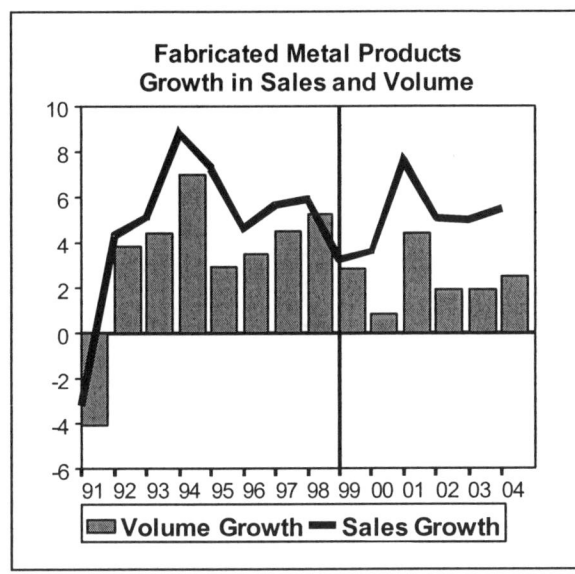

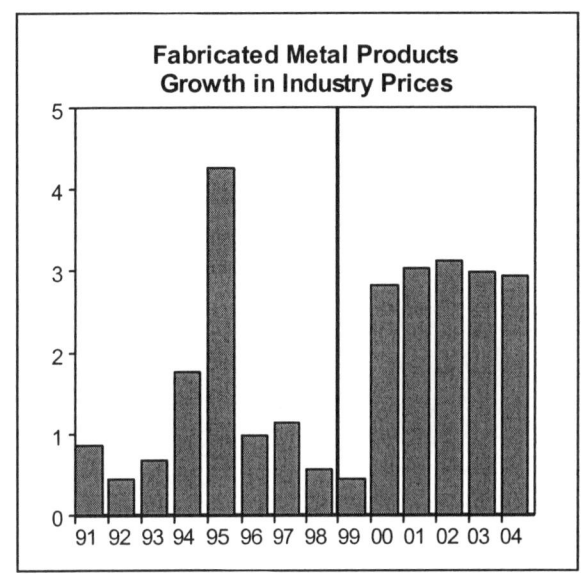

Fabricated Metal Products

SIC 34

		1992	1993	1994	1995	1996	1997	1998	1999	2000	2001	Compound Average 88-98	Annual Growth 98-08
Sales													
	Billions of $	166.5	175.1	190.6	204.5	213.9	226.1	239.5	247.3	256.3	275.9		
	% Ch	4.3	5.1	8.8	7.3	4.6	5.7	5.9	3.3	3.6	7.6	4.2	5.2
Volume													
	% Ch	3.9	4.5	7.0	3.0	3.5	4.5	5.3	2.8	0.8	4.4	2.4	2.3
Prices													
	% Ch	0.5	0.7	1.8	4.3	1.0	1.1	0.5	0.4	2.8	3.0	1.6	2.9
Production Costs													
Avg. Hourly Earnings													
	$/hr	11.37	11.62	11.86	12.08	12.46	12.76	13.05	13.44	13.90	14.35		
	% Ch	2.1	2.3	2.0	1.9	3.1	2.4	2.3	3.0	3.4	3.3	2.5	3.5
Input Price Index													
	% Ch	-0.5	1.1	3.1	5.7	-0.9	0.9	-1.5	-1.9	1.8	2.8	1.1	2.2

Chapter 18: Industrial and Electrical Machinery

Turbines and Generator Sets

Turbine and generator set sales slumped in 1996 and 1997, as the power industry cooled its heels in the face of looming deregulation and industrial market demand faltered. In 1998, utility purchases staged a comeback and the commercial market did well. This offset weakness in industrial sales and exports. During the coming decade, we expect a rebound in export demand and modest growth in the domestic utility, industrial, and commercial markets to support volume growth of close to 2% per year, on average. Equipment prices, which have gone nowhere in recent years, should strengthen in the 2.5% trend growth range as demand revives.

WEFA estimates that power industry generating capacity will grow at an average annual rate of less than 1% between now and the end of the next decade. Capacity at non-utility generators (NUGs) will remain stable, while utility capacity will grow by over 1% per year. Utilities will favor natural gas-fired equipment, at the expense of coal, petroleum, and nuclear power generating units.

Recent History

Investment in turbines and generator sets posted impressive gains coming out of the last recession, supported by utility, industrial, cogeneration, and commercial markets. Exports to Latin America, Mexico, Western Europe, and Asia provided additional support. From 1992 through 1995, industry shipments grew at an average annual rate of 4% per year, in real terms. The market suffered a reversal of fortune beginning in 1996 and shipments dropped 5.7% in that year and a whopping 13.7% in 1997.

During this period, U.S. electric utilities soft-pedaled investment in new generating capacity as they held their breath awaiting a deregulated environment. Cogeneration by independent power producers took a hit as a result of utility deregulation. Industrial demand for power generation also suffered as new industrial plant construction fell 1.7% in 1996 and 6.9% in 1997. The commercial and public-building market for power-generating equipment remained strong during these years. Exports continued to provide support during this period, but overseas sales were not enough to offset the softness in the domestic market.

Most recently, the domestic market has exhibited strength and the export market has been in the dumps. Shipments of turbines and turbine generator sets jumped 11.5% in 1998, largely as a result of utility-related equipment purchases and continued support from the commercial market. Public-building projects faltered in 1998. Export sales to Asia and parts of Latin America plunged, as those regions reeled from a financial and economic crisis.

Domestic Market

The electric power industry is about to be turned inside out again. Just about every ten years, the power industry is jolted by a shift in public policy.

In the late seventies, it was PURPA—the Public Utility Regulatory Policy Act—an administrative quagmire that resulted in artificial and contradictory regulations. Effectively, PURPA was repealed, but it led to the reintroduction of commercial and industrial cogeneration. Toward the end of the eighties, regulatory reform (commonly referred to as deregulation) was begun. In process for more than ten years now, it is slowly making the industry more competitive, with its largest impact to date on the power production industry.

The power production industry is quickly becoming much more efficient due to these policy shifts, but it faces a daunting new challenge. The new public policy agenda may be even more disruptive than earlier policy shifts, and very expensive to achieve.

Preoccupied with SO_2 (2000) and NO_X (2002), the industry is facing a major change in environmental compliance with the proposed limit on particulate matter (PM) emissions to 2.5 microns scheduled for 2008. The impact of the 2.5-micron standard for particulate matter will be large, tremendous—if fully implemented. Compliance will result in the replacement of large amounts of coal capacity, predominantly with more efficient gas combined-cycle units. Referred to as a "Marshall Plan" for the power generation sector of the economy, the latest environmental challenge will recreate the power industry in the United States.

Today, there is intense competition in the electric power generation industry. In the five years from 1993 through 1997, the system lambda in many regions dropped by 20% or more—an unprecedented change. This cutthroat cost competition is expected to continue through 2002, when the capital spending mandated by the NO_x rules kicks in.

To comply with the regulations on SO_2 and NO_x, power generators will have to make capital investments. Investment in Selective Catalytic Reduction will carry a total economic cost of approximately $6/mWh. However, once the investment is made, the plants' dispatch costs—their variable costs—will increase only 31 cents on average. The supply curve will hardly move at all.

Although meeting the new NO_x restrictions will be expensive, it is affordable. The increase in costs will not cause the economic shut-down of most current assets. While their earning potential will be seriously impaired—they may not be recovering any capital costs—they will keep running as long as they cover their operating costs and earn a positive margin. These plants generate cash flow, although they may not be covering what we used to call the "fixed charges component of rates."

Most utilities are working hard to run more efficiently than ever. Due to deregulation, wholesale competition is improving management and operating practices and plant engineers have become expert at de-bottlenecking. Independent power operators have also de-bottlenecked their plants. The result is an increasingly competitive environment, which is lowering the price of electric energy.

Consumers may be happy, but many traditional utilities are frustrated by their low margins. Many have found it "strategic" to sell generating assets, often with unanticipated results. For example, one southern utility sold a plant to an industrial customer as "scrap steel." However, the industrial customer did not scrap it. Instead, the plant was carefully moved and reconstructed at the industrial facility. It is now generating power for the industrial customer and excess generation is sold back to the utility.

Over the mid-term, power prices will increase by one-fifth as the industry adjusts to the new standards on particulates. An entirely new fleet of plants will be built—combined cycle gas turbines, with Selective Catalytic Reduction.

The only in-place coal plants that survive will be the largest and most efficient of the "flagship" plants. They will make huge investments in SCR and FGD whenever they believe they can cover the $12/mWh total economic cost required to achieve compliance. Once again, however, the increase in their dispatch costs will be much less—their variable costs will be only $1/mWh to $2/mWh higher.

Looking at the EPA timeline shows that SO_2 and NO_x compliance is a walk in the park compared to compliance with PM regulations. It is easy to argue that a 2.5-micron standard will not be implemented, but it is important to realize that every rule proposed by the EPA has been put in place. It is also likely that the full implementation will be delayed, and the analysis reported here assumes that implementation will be phased in over the period 2008 to 2012. The fact is that environmentalists and the EPA want scrubbed coal. That means FGD, and that means a wholesale shutdown of coal plants. Although the 2.5 micron rule will not bankrupt the industry, it is extremely expensive.

WEFA estimates that power industry generating capacity will grow by 13% between now and the year 2010, an increase of 93 GW's. Utilities will favor equipment fired by natural gas. The more stringent regulations of Phase II of the Clean Air Act, which come into force in the year 2000, will dampen utility enthusiasm to invest in coal-fired capacity. During this period, 1999–2010, gas-fired capacity will expand by almost 170 GW's, while coal, petroleum, and nuclear capacity declines. NUG capacity will remain stable at roughly 74 GW's. Natural gas-fired capacity, utility, and NUG, currently accounts for 21.5% of power generating industry capacity. By the year 2010, natural gas will account for about 38.5% of capacity.

The industrial market for power-generating equipment will drift over the near term, as capacity utilization rates remain in the very low 80% range due to recent aggressive expansion and the slump in Asian and some Latin American economies. However, with industrial sector output slated to grow by about 3% per year on average over the next decade, we can expect additional pressure to expand production facility power generating capacity. The long-term growth rate for industrial plant construction is about 1.5% per year, over the coming decade. The demand for industrial boilers will be a function of capacity expansion programs and efforts to improve the productivity and efficiency of industrial facilities through the use of state-of-the-art power generating equipment.

The commercial building market for power equipment continues to do well. However, growth in commercial construction will slow from nearly 6% this year to only 1.5% per year, on average, during the next ten years. An expanding economy should support modest growth in new commercial construction, including office buildings, hotels, and shopping malls. New construction, combined with efforts to upgrade power systems in older buildings, will provide the basis for commercial boiler demand. Public building construction is poised for a rebound over the near term, and growth during the coming decade is put at about 1.0%–1.5% per year, on average. With regard to the public-building market, which includes schools, hospitals, and other buildings, most growth will come from state and local governments, where real investment will grow by 2.5% per year on average.

Exports

Until the recent Asian crisis, the strongest component of turbine and generator set shipments was exports. Nominal exports grew at more than twice the 5% pace achieved by U.S. shipments during the past decade. Developing countries' infrastructure projects have been the main source of export growth. Strong economic growth in developing Asia, Mexico, Latin America, Eastern Europe, and Russia provided much of the lift to overseas sales during the past decade, with additional support coming from long-established markets, such as Canada and Western Europe.

Exports took a big tumble in 1998 as major infrastructure projects were cancelled. U.S. overseas sales of steam or other vapor generating boilers, super-heated

water boilers, and auxiliary plant and parts fell from $841 million in 1997 to $616 million in 1998, a decline of 27%. Exports of steam turbines and other vapor turbines and parts fell an equally impressive 23% from $823 million in 1997 to $631 million in 1998. Thus far in 1999, exports of steam turbines and boilers are still running 20%–25% below a year ago.

While exports are still reflecting the impact of the Asian economic crisis, we believe the longer-term outlook for U.S. exports of power equipment remains very bright.

Manufacturers have long cited Asia as the largest power market in the world. Orders for sets to equip Asian power plants showed considerable strength up until the recent troubles. The more developed markets of east Asia, in particular Korea, accounted for the largest share of orders. Steam turbines dominated developing Asia's orders, reflecting the construction of large solid-fuel-fired and nuclear projects. Japan, which has been in a long recession, was also a market for U.S. power-generating equipment. The demand for power-generating equipment in much of Asia plunged in 1998, and WEFA does not expect these markets to rebound for at least another year.

However, Asia as a whole remains a good long-term source of demand for generating capacity. This is particularly true in the lesser developed countries, such as China, India, Pakistan, Indonesia, Malaysia, the Philippines, Thailand, and Vietnam. Japan and South Korea are also expected to require some additional capacity in the years ahead. Eastern Europe may be an even more fertile market, since investment there in new capacity will be driven by not only power needs but also a real need to undo the environmental damage of past decades. Closer to home, both South America and Mexico have long felt the pressure to expand power generating capacity to meet electricity demand, and additional demand will come from expanding industrial and commercial sectors. Traditional markets of Canada and Western Europe will lend support to U.S. power-equipment exports on a smaller scale.

Outlook 1999–2008

After increasing 11.5% in 1998, volume growth in turbine and turbine generators will exceed 10% in 1999. Lackluster industrial and export demand will be offset by expanding utility purchases and a solid commercial/public-building market. Beyond this year, WEFA expects that a rebound in export demand, coupled with modest growth in the domestic utility, industrial and commercial markets, will support volume growth of 2.5% per year, on average. Equipment prices, which have gone nowhere in recent years, should strengthen into the 2.5% range as demand revives. Thus, shipments in nominal terms expand by roughly 4.5% per year.

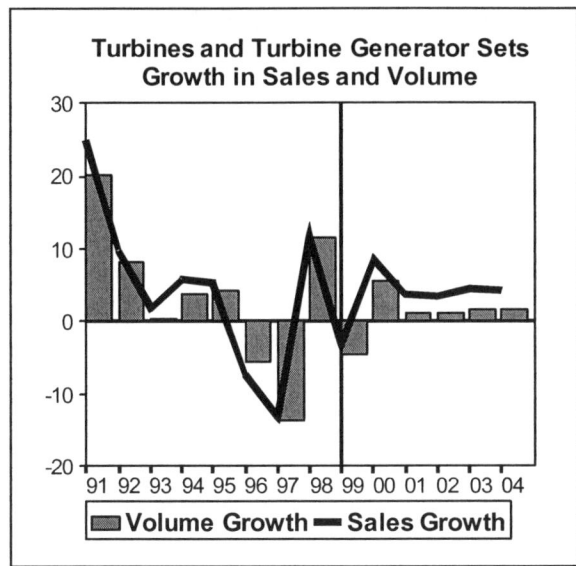

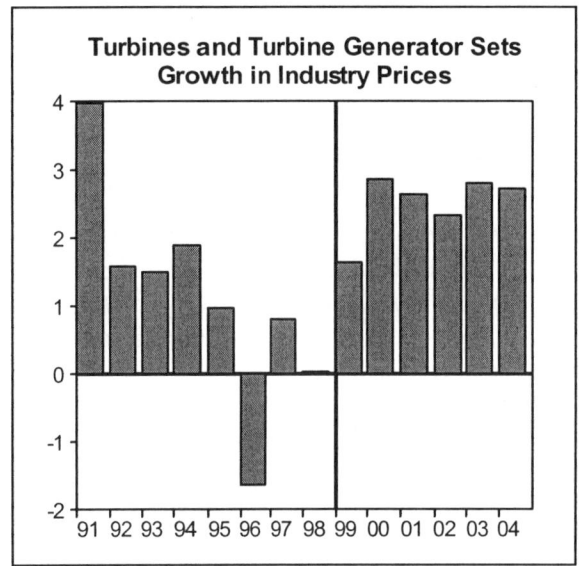

Turbines and Turbine Generator Sets

SIC 3511

		1992	1993	1994	1995	1996	1997	1998	1999	2000	2001	Compound Average 88-98	Annual Growth 98-08
Sales													
	Billions of $	5.89	6.00	6.35	6.68	6.20	5.39	6.01	5.82	6.32	6.55		
	% Ch	9.8	1.9	5.8	5.3	-7.3	-13.1	11.6	-3.1	8.5	3.7	5.2	4.3
Volume													
	% Ch	8.1	0.4	3.8	4.3	-5.7	-13.7	11.5	-4.7	5.5	1.1	2.7	1.6
Prices													
	% Ch	1.6	1.5	1.9	1.0	-1.6	0.8	0.0	1.6	2.9	2.6	2.5	2.7
Production Costs													
Avg. Hourly Earnings													
	$/hr	16.14	16.73	17.27	17.57	18.34	19.32	19.69	20.48	21.28	22.14		
	% Ch	3.0	3.6	3.2	1.7	4.4	5.4	1.9	4.0	3.9	4.1	3.5	3.9
Input Price Index													
	% Ch	0.5	1.3	2.1	3.6	0.7	0.7	-0.1	0.2	2.3	3.0	1.6	2.6

Internal Combustion Engines

Over the past two years, 1997–1998, shipments of internal combustion engines have grown close to 10% annually, in real terms. Weak exports and a slump in the farm-equipment market have dampened the growth in internal combustion engine sales this year. Longer term, modest growth in domestic demand and a stronger export market will allow shipments to expand at an annual rate of about 2.0% per year over the next ten years.

Key domestic equipment markets such as industrial power generation, transportation, construction, farm, lawn and garden, and marine will provide support. Exports will become more important in the years ahead as developing nations in Latin America, Asia, and Eastern Europe work to improve their infrastructure and industrial bases.

Recent History

The internal combustion engine market emerged slowly from the last recession, but has expanded steadily during the 1993–1998 period.

From 1993–1995, shipments expanded by over 10% per year, on average, in real terms.

- Industrial plant expansion, construction activity, a record rebound in commercial trucks, and gains in the marine market provided considerable support.

- Better financial conditions in the farm sector boosted demand for internal combustion engines used in agricultural equipment.

- The strength in new home construction bolstered demand for power mowers.

- Improving consumer incomes had a positive impact on outboard motor sales.

- Finally, favorable economic conditions in a number of key foreign markets and a weak dollar boosted U.S. exports of internal combustion engines.

In 1996, shipment growth slowed to 1.6% in real terms. Industrial plant construction was curtailed after a very strong 1995 and dampened demand for stationary power units. The transportation equipment market contracted after achieving very impressive gains during the three previous years. Power mower, garden tractor, and snow thrower shipments fell 12%, depressing demand for smaller engines.

Over the past two years, shipments expanded by 8.5% in 1997 and 10.5% in 1998, after adjustment for inflation. While the demand for stationary industry power units was sluggish during this period, other markets provided support. Sales of diesel engines to the makers of commercial trucks staged an impressive rebound. Furthermore, the construction, farm and garden, and marine markets continued to gain ground. Exports did well in 1997, but the Asian crisis took its toll in 1998.

Outlook 1999–2008

Shipments of internal combustion engines are expected to grow by another 5.5%-6.0% in 1999. The demand for construction machinery, medium and heavy trucks, and power-driven lawn and garden machinery remains strong, and this is having a very positive impact on internal combustion engine demand. This is being offset by a sharp drop in farm equipment production, nagging weakness in exports, and lackluster demand from the industrial sector.

Longer term, volume growth in internal combustion engines is put at about 2.0% per year, on average. With price increases expected to average close to 2.5% per year, current dollar shipments should grow by close to 5% per year.

Key domestic markets such as industrial power generation, construction, farm, transportation, lawn and garden, and marine will provide considerable support. Improvement in defense-related procurement is also anticipated. Exports will become more important in the years ahead, as developing nations in Latin America, Asia, and Eastern Europe work to improve their infrastructure and industrial bases.

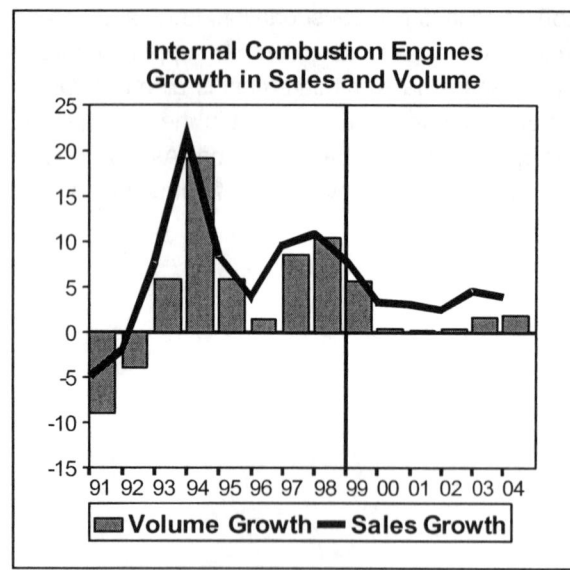

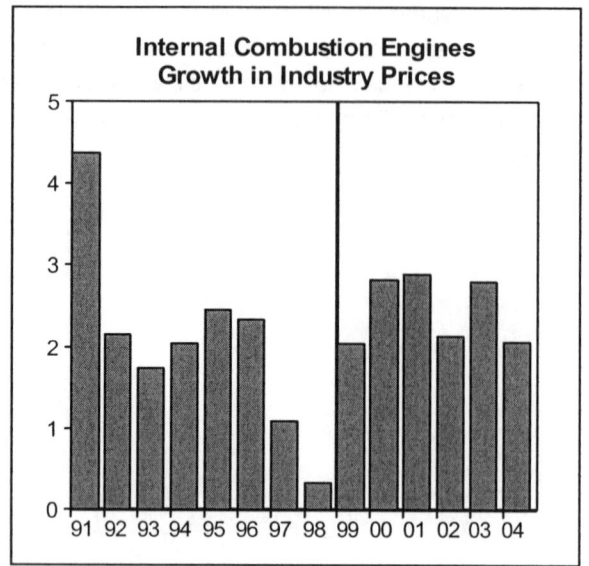

Internal Combustion Engines
SIC 3519

		1992	1993	1994	1995	1996	1997	1998	1999	2000	2001	Compound Average 88-98	Annual Growth 98-08
Sales													
	Billions of $	11.71	12.62	15.35	16.64	17.30	18.97	21.03	22.69	23.45	24.20		
	% Ch	-1.9	7.8	21.7	8.4	3.9	9.7	10.9	7.9	3.4	3.2	5.3	4.7
Volume													
	% Ch	-4.0	5.9	19.2	5.8	1.6	8.5	10.5	5.7	0.5	0.3	2.8	2.1
Prices													
	% Ch	2.2	1.7	2.0	2.5	2.3	1.1	0.3	2.0	2.8	2.9	2.5	2.6
Production Costs													
Avg. Hourly Earnings													
	$/hr	15.46	15.83	15.88	15.44	15.66	16.02	16.43	17.53	18.06	18.48		
	% Ch	2.2	2.4	0.3	-2.8	1.5	2.2	2.6	6.7	3.0	2.3	1.9	3.4
Input Price Index													
	% Ch	0.5	1.0	2.4	4.2	-0.1	0.2	-0.8	0.2	2.1	2.7	1.4	2.4

Farm and Garden Equipment

A divergence continues to exist between the farm and garden equipment industry. The lawn and garden sector is expected to continue to expand in the near term, based on the strength of the U.S. economy and robust housing starts. The farm equipment sector, however, which had expanded steadily since 1992, is expected to decline in 1999 and again in 2000. Farm-level commodity prices remain under pressure and farm income is declining from the record level of 1996, retarding sales of high-end tractors and combines. Incentive and promotional programs inflated 1998 sales, stealing some from 1999 sales, and, in the absence of such programs, shipments and sales are expected to register double-digit declines. An appreciation of the yen vis-à-vis the dollar helps farm equipment exports and retards higher levels of lawn and garden equipment imports from Japan.

In the long term, farm and garden equipment demand is expected to improve with much of the growth coming from the lawn and garden equipment segment. Most factors affecting sales are favorable over the next few years: income, housing starts, and real interest rates are forecast to be stable, supporting growth in sales. In the farm sector, area is projected to rise by 6 to 8 million acres in the long term. Farm income is expected to begin to recover, albeit slowly, in the next decade and improve as prices gradually strengthen. Government payments, which have been augmented by emergency aid in 1998 and likely again in 1999, are scheduled to decline through fiscal year 2002, after which the Federal sector is expected to continue transition payments to agriculture at the $4 billion level. A strong likelihood of supplemental payments exists for the near term.

Industry Overview

Between 1992 and 1998, the farm and garden equipment industry expanded steadily on the strength of a robust agricultural sector and an expanding economy. After two successive years of decline in 1991 and 1992, when sales dropped from $16.8 billion in 1990 to $14.8 billion in 1992, steady growth in the U.S. economy and improvement in the agricultural sector pushed sales to nearly $24 billion in 1998. The upward trend is estimated to come to a halt in 1999 as sales are estimated to decline to approximately $22.6 billion. The nearly 5% drop is attributed solely to the farm sector where low grain and oilseed prices and cash-flow difficulties have curtailed farmers' demand for new equipment. Through July 1999, year-to-date sales of two-wheel-drive tractors greater than 100 horsepower are lagging the comparable year-ago sales by about 40%, four-wheel-drive tractors are off 30%, and self-propelled combines are trailing year-ago figures by 50%. However, sales of tractors with less than 40 horsepower are running 20% ahead of last year's level. In total, this year's estimated drop in the value of sales is attributed to a drop of nearly 6% in volume, whereas price hikes of about 1% should offset some of the volume decline. This compares to the 1991 and 1992 decline in

sales that was solely attributed to a cumulative decline of 16% in volume. Prices between 1993 and 1996 rose at the rate of about 2% per annum. Since 1996, the rate of price increases has slowed to 1% per annum or less as a result of modest wage inflation, incentives, discounting, and promotional programs. Price hikes are expected to strengthen over the next two years as wages rise by more than 3% per annum.

The farm and garden machinery industry is dominated by the farm equipment sector, which includes commercial turf and ground-care equipment. Including replacement parts, farm machinery accounted for about 70% of the total value of shipments in 1997, and has accounted for between 62% to 70% of the total value of farm and garden equipment since 1991. The largest component of the farm equipment sector is the other farm equipment category, which includes wheel tractors and replacement parts, and accounts for nearly 45% of farm machinery shipments. Since 1991, this category has expanded by nearly 130%. This strong rate of growth is attributed to the reduced level of shipments in 1991 and the relatively robust economic health of the farm sector in the 1990s. That bubble is now bursting.

Harvesting equipment accounts for about 25% of farm equipment shipments, and planting, dairying, and haying machinery, each account for about 6% to 8% of shipments. In 1997, replacement parts accounted for about $989 million or 7% of farm machinery shipments. Sales of harvesting equipment are also soft.

There are two categories that make up the lawn and garden machinery sector. One category is comprised of consumer non-riding lawn, garden, and snow equipment, and the other is consumer riding lawn, garden, and snow equipment. Each segment accounts for about 50% of total lawn and garden equipment shipments, and each is growing.

Lawn and Garden Equipment

There are a number of factors that affect the lawn and garden segment of the farm and garden machinery industry. These factors include personal income, the number of single-family housing starts, and interest rates. Between 1991 and 1997, shipments of the lawn and garden segment rose from $4 billion to $6 billion, an average per annum increase of 8.4%.

The general economy was weak in the early 1990s, and housing starts had been in decline since 1987. From 1987 to 1991, housing starts suffered a cumulative drop of 45%, which contributed to the 1991 downturn in lawn and garden machinery shipments. Starts are expected to remain robust in 1999 at 1.6 million units, and then drop about 12% to 1.4 million units over the next two to three years. When compared to the early 1990s, 1.4 million units are nearly 40% better than the 1.01 million units of 1991. Single-family units are estimated to range between 1.1 to 1.15 million units over the next two to three years, nearly 0.5 million units greater than in 1991.

Overall, real personal disposable income and slightly higher, compared to 1999, but stable, real interest rates in 2000 and 2001 will be positive influences on lawn and garden equipment over the next few years. Housing starts, though expected to weaken after 1999, will not be in a free fall as they were in the late 1980s. The growth in the lawn and garden segment should continue in the near term, but at a slower rate than that of the mid-1990s—likely in the 4% to 5% range.

Farm Equipment

The farm equipment sector of the farm and garden machinery industry has been experiencing a strong resurgence since 1992. Farm equipment shipments had dropped 18% in the early 1990s, from $9.8 billion in 1990 to $7.2 billion in 1992. By 1997, shipments had grown to $14.0 billion (including parts for replacement units). Retail sales of tractors (greater than 40 horsepower) followed a similar pattern, falling from 66,300 units in 1990 to 52,800 units in 1992. Figures for 1998 indicate unit sales of tractors climbed to 76,000 units. However, tractor sales for January through July of 1999 are lagging last year's sales by 17%.

Obviously, the fate of the farm equipment industry depends on the economic well-being of the farm sector, and the U.S. farm sector has been relatively healthy in the 1990s. A number of factors specific to the farm sector impact the performance of the farm equipment industry, including interest rates on loans for equipment, farm debt, the farmer's ability to pay, asset value, liquidity, farm numbers, and farm size. The key is the cash farmers have available to spend. The 1991 and 1992 sales drops were due to declines in real net farm income. Farmers' income had fallen since 1987 before bottoming out in 1991 at $38 billion. Net farm income fluctuated, but increased from 1991's level rising to a record $53 billion in 1996. Since 1996, income in the sector has weakened and would be lower if the federal government had not provided aid to farmers.

The economic well-being of the farm sector may be measured by any of a number of factors: income, cash receipts, asset values (real estate and non-real estate), debt, and debt–to–asset ratios, to mention a few. Income by most measures peaked in 1996 when net-farm income reached $53 billion and net-cash income exceeded $56 billion. Although net-farm income fell in 1997 by nearly 7% to $50 billion, net-cash income actually rose to more than $60 billion. Income was supported by relatively high-commodity prices, direct government payments, and low energy prices and interest rates that kept production costs under control. Crop prices weakened significantly in 1998 and eroded crop cash receipts by more than $10 billion. Fortunately, loan deficiency payments and an emergency aid package supported net farm income at $46 billion, an 8% decline from 1997's level. Farm equipment manufacturers introduced incentive programs and discounted prices to shore up equipment sales, and it worked.

Value of Shipments of Farm Machinery and Lawn and Garden Equipment by Type of Equipment: 1991 to 1997
(Value in millions of dollars)

Product Description 1/	1997	1996	1995	1994	1993	1992	1991
Farm dairy machines, sprayers, dusters, elevators, and farm blowers..........	796.4	839.2	764.7	709.0	591.1	469.9	449.2
Planting, seeding, and fertilizing machinery.........	1,107.0	862.3	852.9	949.1	804.6	634.1	601.0
Harvesting machinery.......	3,248.7	2,966.8	2,666.8	2,201.4	2,036.9	1,863.7	2,158.0
Haying machinery........	792.5	670.3	729.4	748.6	622.5	558.2	659.1
Plows, harrows, rollers, pulverizers, cultivators, and weeders..........	695.3	542.0	512.5	480.4	404.4	380.8	441.1
Commercial turf and grounds care equipment..........	1,229.2	1,118.5	1,120.3	1,022.0	880.8	781.8	724.8
Other farm Equipment 2/	6,123.9	5,108.9	4,604.4	3,476.6	2,787.3	2,546.5	2,672.8
Total Farm Equipment	13,993.0	12,108.0	11,251.0	9,587.1	8,127.6	7,235.0	7,706.0
Consumer nonriding lawn, garden, and snow equipment.......	3,027.9	2,957.0	3,095.0	3,003.0	2,408.8	2,133.2	1,987.5
Consumer riding lawn, garden, and snow equipment.......	2,956.0	2,861.0	2,874.3	2,747.6	2,394.5	2,118.6	1,985.4
Total Lawn and Garden	5,983.9	5,818.0	5,969.3	5,750.6	4,803.3	4,251.8	3,972.9
Total Farm Equipment Lawn and Garden	19,976.9	17,926.0	17,220.3	15,337.7	12,930.9	11,486.8	11,678.9
Farm Equipment Share (%)	70.0	67.5	65.3	62.5	62.9	63.0	66.0
Lawn and Garden Share (%)	30.0	32.5	34.7	37.5	37.1	37.0	34.0

Source: U.S. Department of Commerce

1/ Each type of farm machinery, commercial turf and grounds care equipment, and lawn and garden equipment includes parts and attachments.

2/ Includes wheel tractors and replacement parts.

Net-farm income is expected to be about the same in 1999 as it was in 1998. However, commodity prices have weakened further and the attitude of farmers with regard to equipment purchases is poor. Cash flow is an issue at this time. Net-farm income is being maintained by the highest level of government payments since the mid-1980s, an estimated $22 billion compared to $12 billion in 1998.

Later this year, additional aid is likely to be forthcoming. In 2000, a presidential-election year, we will see high levels of government payments as well, more than $18 billion. Government and modest price improvement should keep net-farm income in the $40 to $45 billion range over the next two years. Government payments and the new farm policy are significant components to the farm-income picture. For the first half of the decade, farmers were eligible for price and income support program benefits if they participated in federal acreage-reduction programs. These acreage-reduction programs required that producers idle a share of their program crop base in return for price and income support.

On a calendar-year basis, support payments ranged from a low of $7.3 billion in 1995 and 1996 to $13.4 billion in 1993. Producers idled an average of 21 million acres in the annual acreage-reduction programs (ARP) and another 36 million in the long-term Conservation Reserve Program (CRP). Withholding acres from production adversely affects farm equipment demand, but a cash income stream, on the other hand, helps farm equipment sales.

In 1996, acreage reduction programs were eliminated as a major policy tool by which the U.S. Government controlled acreage. Approximately 16 million acres came into production in 1996, area planted rose to 334 million acres, as a direct consequence of the 1996 Farm Bill. WEFA is currently projecting that area planted to the principal crops totaled 328 million acres for 1999, and estimates about 325 million acres will be planted in 2000 and 2001. Poor crop returns have driven some land from production. The potential for additional negative area impact exists, but the magnitude is small at this time. The implications for the farm equipment sector suggest neutrality.

Agricultural policy changed significantly with the passage of the Federal Agriculture Improvement and Reform (FAIR) Act of 1996. This legislation eliminated annual acreage retirement programs and price and income support programs directly tied to production. The significance of this act is that the acres idled in annual programs are now free to be planted. Producers, for the most part, may plant based on market prices and not government programs. Producers who are eligible and enroll in the program will receive transition payments over the 1996–2002 period. Transition payments will range between $4.0 and $5.8 billion dollars over the period, and these payments are not tied to production behavior. The only requirement is that the land remains in agriculture. The FAIR Act continued the CRP, but the Administration has some discretion as to the level of acres enrolled. It appears that around 32 million acres will be enrolled in the CRP in the near term and 36 million in the medium term.

Another part of the FAIR Act relates to what is called the marketing loan program and the marketing loan deficiency payments. The FAIR Act allows farmers to use eligible crops for collateral to secure a non-recourse marketing loan at a specified rate, for example $5.26 per bushel for soybeans for the 1998/1999 marketing year. If market prices fall below the loan rate, farmers who have exercised the loan option may repay their loan at a lower rate. Producers who are eligible but have not used the loan option may receive a marketing loan deficiency payment (the difference between the loan rate and the repayment rate times the number of bushels eligible). In both cases, the farmer, in effect, receives a higher amount for his crop than would have been earned in the marketplace. The use of the marketing loan program should increase over the remainder of the current year and for the next two years, inflating direct government payments to farmers.

Interest rates for farm equipment loans follow general interest rate movements. Real rates were over 8% in the late 1980s and then declined to the 6% to 6.5% range in the first half of the 1990s. Real rates are expected to rise in 2000, compared to the average for 1999, but remain stable in 2001 and below the levels experienced in the early 1980s.

Tillage practices also influence the demand for farm equipment. Concerns over soil erosion and the introduction of highly erodable and environmentally fragile land into agricultural production in the 1970s and early 1980s mobilized environmentalists. Past farm legislation recognized the need for farmers to be stewards of the land, and producers were required to develop and implement conservation plans in order to continue to receive commodity program benefits. This spawned the adoption of reduced tillage, crop rotation, and residue management practices. Since 1989, the use of conservation tillage practices has expanded from about 25% of the area planted to field and row crops to about 36% in 1996. No-till acreage has shown the greatest growth over this time period, increasing by more than threefold.

The benefits of adopting reduced tillage practices are many, including fewer trips with tractors across fields, leading to reduced costs for fuel and oil, labor, and wear and tear on equipment, and reduced soil compaction. The adoption of reduced tillage practices will likely continue to grow as farmers strive to control, minimize, and reduce costs. Reduced tillage adversely affects the demand for farm equipment, especially tractors, by reducing the wear and tear on equipment. Equipment lasts longer and repairs are less frequent. Conservation tillage practices also require less horsepower than conventional tillage practices.

Other U.S. farm sector characteristics that are related to farm equipment demand are mixed. Farm numbers and land in farms continue to decline, but at differing rates. The average farm size decreased to 435 acres in 1998 compared to 436 acres in 1997. This compares to 447 in 1986. There are about 2.2 million farms in the United States. Asset values have climbed steadily in the 1990s, and land values jumped more than 4.4% in 1998 and another 1.8% in 1999. Asset values are growing at a more rapid rate than farm debt in recent years. As a consequence, debt-to-asset ratios are declining, indicating that farm sector debt is manageable and the sector is creditworthy, a factor that favorably impacts the farm equipment industry.

The farm equipment industry is very concentrated. Four to five companies produce the majority of tractors, combines, and other harvesting equipment, and baling and haying machinery in the United States. Further consolidation occurred in 1999 with the announced merger of New Holland and Case Corporation.

International Trade

The United States has shifted between being a net exporter and net importer in the overall farm and garden equipment industry. In 1993 and 1996, the industry was a net exporter of approximately $110 to $150 million of equipment. Over the 1990–1995 period, the value of imports exceeded that of exports by $20 million to $65 million in all years except 1993. The industry's status of net importer or net exporter has been swung by the volume of garden equipment imports. Japan is a major supplier of lawn and garden equipment to the United States.

Since 1990, the United States has been a consistent net exporter of farm equipment, exporting about $1 bil-

lion more than it imports. Key markets for U.S. farm equipment exports include: Canada (about 25% to 30% of the total), Mexico (typically 8% to 10%), Australia (6% to 7%), Germany (5%), France (3% to 5%), and the United Kingdom (3% to 5%). Canada, Germany, Japan, and the United Kingdom each account for 15% to 20% of U.S. farm equipment imports. Collectively, Italy, France, and Brazil account for between 14% and 18% of imports. The North American Free Trade Agreement (NAFTA) is likely to continue to expand equipment trade with Canada and Mexico. The Uruguay Round Agreement of GATT should also help expand world trade in farm equipment.

The Asian economic crisis and currency devaluation did not bode well for U.S. farm and garden equipment trade balances over the past two to three years. The Japanese yen has depreciated and is expected to remain within a range of 110 yen/dollar to 120 yen/dollar, as compared with the 1992–1996 average exchange rate of 109 yen/dollar and a 1998 rate of 130 yen/dollar. In essence, the depreciation of the yen reduced import prices of Japanese lawn and garden equipment by about 20% (all other factors constant) and increased prices of U.S. farm equipment to Japan by 20%. Recent improvement in the Japanese economy suggests that the yen will return close to the 1992–1996 average, making U.S. imports from Japan more expensive and exports to Japan cheaper. The U.S. dollar has also strengthened relative to the Canadian dollar, the German mark, the Italian lira, the French franc, the British pound, and the Brazilian real. The 1998 collapse of the Russian ruble and the Brazilian financial scare of 1999 increased the risk of other currencies being devaluated, but improvement in Asia and coordinated actions by developed countries seem to have stabilized currency markets.

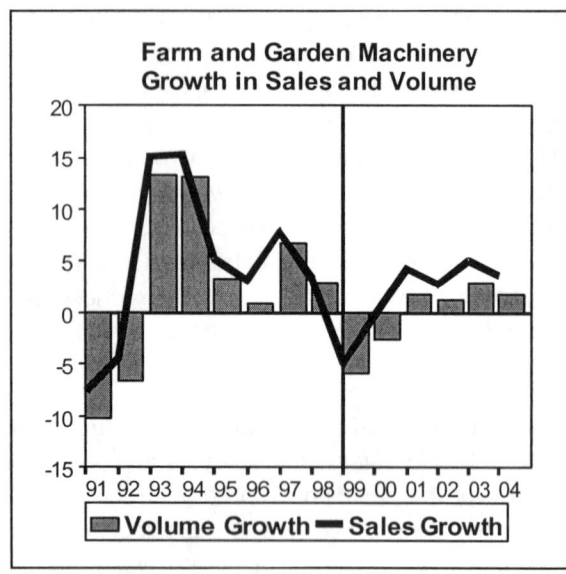

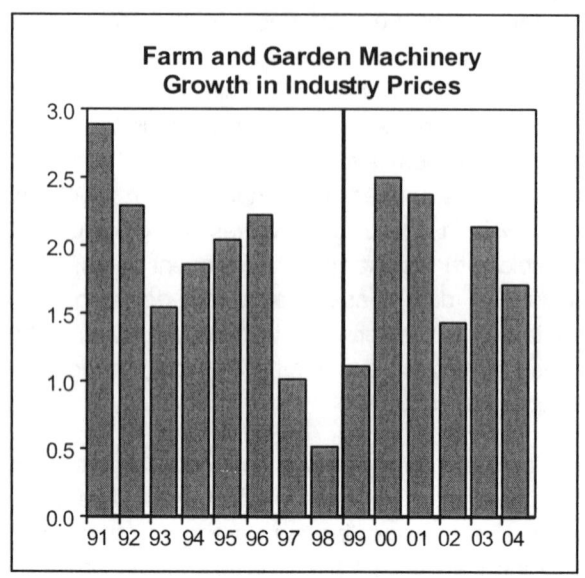

Farm and Garden Machinery

SIC 352

		1992	1993	1994	1995	1996	1997	1998	1999	2000	2001	Compound Average 88-98	Annual Growth 98-08
Sales													
	Billions of $	14.81	17.05	19.65	20.69	21.34	23.00	23.77	22.64	22.61	23.58		
	% Ch	-4.4	15.1	15.3	5.3	3.2	7.8	3.3	-4.8	-0.1	4.3	5.7	2.8
Volume													
	% Ch	-6.6	13.3	13.2	3.2	0.9	6.7	2.8	-5.8	-2.6	1.8	3.4	0.6
Prices													
	% Ch	2.3	1.5	1.9	2.0	2.2	1.0	0.5	1.1	2.5	2.4	2.2	2.1
Production Costs													
Avg. Hourly Earnings													
	$/hr	11.55	12.07	12.45	12.80	13.47	13.79	13.79	13.52	14.04	14.56		
	% Ch	2.2	4.5	3.2	2.7	5.3	2.4	0.0	-2.0	3.8	3.7	3.0	3.1
Input Price Index													
	% Ch	0.3	1.5	2.3	3.4	-0.1	0.2	-0.6	-0.1	2.1	2.7	1.3	2.4

Construction, Mining, and Material-Handling Equipment

Construction, mining, and material-handling equipment sales have performed well over the past decade, gaining an average of 3.5% per year, in real terms.

During the coming decade, domestic demand for such equipment will increase in response to the progress in the construction, surface and underground mining, oil and gas, industrial, and wholesale and retail trade sectors. Export markets are currently in the doldrums, but should gain considerable ground during the coming decade. Look for the growth in exports to be stronger than domestic demand.

Overview

Construction, mining, and material-handling equipment sales have expanded without interruption since emerging from the 1990–1991 recession. Equipment sales bottomed out at $27.2 billion in 1992 and grew at an average annual rate of 10.8% from 1993 through 1998. Growth dipped below double-digits only once during this period when it slipped to 7.9% in 1996. In 1999, shipments of construction, mining, and material-handling equipment rose 10.3% reaching $50.5 billion. With prices increasing roughly 2% per year, on average, real shipments of construction, mining, and material-handling equipment grew by 8.6% per year from 1993 through 1998.

Domestic spending for construction, mining, and material-handling equipment emerged from the last recession with a 23% increase in 1993 to $22.3 billion. Spending has risen without interruption since then, reaching almost $41.6 billion last year. During the period from 1993–1998, U.S. business investment in such machinery and equipment increased at an average annual rate of 15%.

On the foreign-trade front, imports have benefited from the strong demand for machinery and equipment in the U.S. market. Imports jumped 33% in 1993 to $6.1 billion and reached $12.6 billion last year. Exports were erratic in the early 1990s but posted very strong increases from 1994 through 1997, as key overseas economies gained ground and the United States asserted itself as the low-cost producer of the highest quality machinery and equipment. In 1993, exports were valued at $12.2 billion. Over the next four years, they rose 12.5% in 1994, 11.1% in 1995, 9.1% in 1996, and 17.9% in 1997. With the world financial crisis hurting a number of key foreign markets, oil prices sliding, and the dollar strong, exports rose by only 3.3% in 1998 to $20.2 billion. The United States has consistently had a trade surplus in construction, mining, and material-handling equipment. The surplus reached a peak in 1997 at $9.3 billion, but fell back to $7.6 billion last year.

Construction Machinery

Shipments of construction machinery hit bottom in 1992 at $13.1 billion, a whopping 18.6% below their 1990 level. As construction, logging, and surface-mining activity improved, shipments rose 17.5% in 1993. Strong domestic demand was joined by expanding export markets during the next four years (1994–1997), supporting average annual growth in construction machinery shipments of nearly 12%. Last year, the domestic market remained strong, but overseas sales softened as the world financial crisis spread and the dollar grew stronger. As a result, shipments of construction machinery increased by a more modest 6%, reaching $25.7 billion.

Domestic Market

Domestic spending for construction machinery bottomed out in 1991 at $7.55 billion and began to exhibit some signs of life in 1992, reaching $7.79 billion. Domestic demand began to hit its stride the following year rising 29.8% to $10.11 billion. Over the next four years (1994–1997), spending grew at an annual rate of over

18.5%. In 1998, U.S. spending for construction machinery increased 14.6% to $20.22 billion. Spending for construction tractors actually bottomed out in 1992 at $1.62 billion. This was followed by an 11.7% increase to $1.81 billion in 1993. Over the next four years (1994–1997), spending for construction tractors expanded at an average annual rate of about 9% reaching $2.46 billion in 1997. Spending rose another 9.8% in 1998 to $2.7 billion.

During the period from 1992-1998, real construction spending had grown at an average annual rate of 4%. This played no small role in the surge in domestic spending for construction machinery. Growth in logging and surface-mining activity also helped boost domestic demand for new machinery and equipment.

Housing starts were down to 1.01 million units in 1991, but registered impressive gains in subsequent years. Housing starts rose to 1.20 million units in 1992 and 1.29 million units in 1993. Over the next four years (1994–1997), starts averaged 1.44 million units, annually. Low-interest rates and a confident consumer propelled starts to 1.62 million units in 1998. Nonresidential construction bottomed out in 1992 at $169.2 billion ($92). The recovery was agonizingly slow over the following two years, barely 1.0% per year. However, the next three years saw increases of 4.7% in 1995, 5.1% in 1996, and 7.1% in 1997. With industrial construction under pressure, the nonresidential market took a breather in 1998 with spending holding at its 1997 level. Public construction increased 5.5% in 1992, fell 3.0% in 1993, and then flattened out in 1994. Public-projects spending then rose 4.1% in 1995, 2.4% in 1996, and 3.6% in 1997. Declines in public-building construction and highway and street projects resulted in a decline in public construction of 2.9% in 1998.

Logging has benefited from the rebound in housing activity and, up until recently, growth in exports. However, the performance of this market has been erratic, as has investment in new equipment. Emerging from the recession in 1992 with a 4.6% increase in output, the industry gave back 3.8% the following year. Over the next five years (1994–1998), logging activity grew by roughly 2.5% per year, on average. However, growth during this period saw increases that ranged from a high of 5% in 1997 to a low of 0.3% in 1998, when weak exports and strong imports from Canada depressed U.S. activity. Increased demand for low-sulfur western coal and the expansion

of output from surface coal mines had a positive impact on the construction machinery market. The output of coal mines west of the Mississippi River (most of which are surface-mining operations) began to grow at a healthy pace in 1993. During the 1993–1997 period, production of coal west of the Mississippi increased by 25%. Last year, western coal mine output grew by another 6.7%. From 1993–1997, the output from other surface mining operations expanded by 20%, with another 3% added on in 1998.

Construction Machinery Foreign Trade

Up until very recently, construction machinery producers were doing very well overseas. U.S. producers exported $3.23 billion worth of construction machinery and another $966 million worth of non-farm tractors in 1992, a total of $4.19 billion. By 1997, construction machinery exports exceeded $5.84 billion and non-farm tractor exports exceeded $1.33 billion. Total 1997 exports of construction machinery and non-farm tractors came close to $7.17 billion, an increase of 71% over the 1992–1997 period. The world financial crisis brought the export boom to a screeching halt, with construction machinery exports dropping 4% in 1998 to $5.61 billion and non-farm tractor exports slipping by 1.3% to $1.33.

Canada, which accounts for about 16% of U.S. exports, emerged slowly from the last recession but eventually hit its stride. Nonresidential structure investment in Canada emerged from a three-year slide (1991–1993) and grew at an annual average rate of over 4% from 1994–1998. The residential market in Canada has swung wildly throughout the 1990s. Residential spending declined 10% in 1990 and 14.1% in 1991. This was followed by a 6.9% increase in 1992, and a 4.2% decline in 1993. The following year brought a 3.5% increase followed by a 14.3% drop in 1995. The residential market then grew by 10.8% in 1996, 12.3% in 1997, and then slipped by 1.6% in 1998.

Latin America, excluding Mexico, accounts for about 25% of U.S. exports. Latin American economies expanded at an average annual rate of 3.3% from 1990–1997, but growth slowed to just 1.2% last year. With the exception of 1995, the performance of the Mexican market has been a positive one for producers of construction machinery. In recent years, Mexico has accounted for roughly 4% of U.S. exports. The Mexican economy grew at an average annual rate of 3.9% from 1990–1994, and then declined by 6.2% in 1995. The construction sector took a 23.5% hit in that year. Since then the Mexican economy has continued to gain ground, rising by 5.1% in 1996, 7.1% in 1997, and 4.8% in 1998. Construction in Mexico grew by 11.4% in 1996, 9.6% in 1997, and 5.5% in 1998.

Western Europe has long been a big market for U.S.-produced construction machinery and equipment, accounting for roughly 15% of exports. Economic growth in Western Europe has been sluggish throughout the decade of the 1990s, averaging about 2.1% from 1990–1997, although they did manage growth rates of 2.8% in 1997 and 2.7% in 1998. Eastern Europe, including the former Soviet Union and Turkey, account for only about 3% of U.S. exports.

Asia, including Japan, takes in 12%–15% of our exports of construction machinery and equipment. The Japanese economy was hitting on all cylinders in 1990 and 1991, but since then times have been tough. From 1993–1997, economic growth averaged 1.7% per year, helped along by a 5.2% spurt in 1996. Excluding 1996, growth averaged a paltry 1.0% per year. Things got worse in 1998 as the Japanese economy contracted by 2.9%. The Pacific Basin represented a fertile market with economic growth averaging 6% per year from 1990–1997. However, the region fell on hard times in 1998 with a decline in economic activity of 4.5%. China has grown as a market for U.S.-built machinery and equipment supported by very strong growth rates in the economy and large investments in infrastructure projects.

When oil prices were high, the Middle East was a big market for construction machinery. Oil prices faltered in 1997 and 1998, and with it the fortunes of the Middle East. Economic growth in that region went from 5.9% in 1996 to 2.8% in 1997 and –0.6% in 1998. Still, the Middle East has continued to account for 10% of U.S. exports in recent years. Rounding out the rest of the export markets are Africa 6%, Australia and New Zealand 3%, India and Pakistan 1%–2%,

Imports of both construction machinery and non-farm tractors benefited from the fertile U.S. market in recent years. In 1992, imports of construction machinery were valued at $1.7 billion. By 1997, sales of imported construction machinery reached $4.38 billion. Imports of non-farm tractors during this period rose from $421 million in 1992 to $705 million in 1997. Continued strength in U.S. construction activity and favorable exchange

rates supported strong increases in both construction machinery and non-farm tractor imports last year. Construction machinery imports jumped 25% to $5.48 billion in 1998, and non-farm tractor imports rose 15% to $814 million.

Mining and Oil-Field Machinery

Shipments of mining and oil-field machinery expanded throughout the 1990–1991 recession as exports of drilling and oil-field equipment continued to provide support, helped along by efforts to repair and rebuild Kuwaiti oilfields following the Gulf War. This more than offset weakness in the domestic market. Shipments of mining and oil-field machinery actually increased by 7.6% in 1990 and 4.2% in 1991. In 1992, shipments fell by 5%. In that year, exports rose modestly, but the domestic market faltered. In 1993, shipments of mining and oil-field machinery rose by 2.8%. Domestic demand increased but imports gained market share and U.S. exports retreated. Shipments declined by 2.6% in 1994 as exports flattened out and domestic demand drifted down. Over the next three years (1995–1997), shipments grew at an average annual rate of almost 15% supported by an expanding domestic market and strong growth in exports. Last year, despite the slump in oil prices, shipments of mining and oil-field machinery grew by another 16.5%, reaching $9.7 billion. Exports of drilling and oil-field equipment again provided most of the support.

Domestic Demand

U.S. spending on mining and oil-field machinery and equipment bottomed out at $1.18 billion in 1992. This represented a decline of 35% from the recent peak of $1.81 billion reached in 1989. Oil and gas exploration in the United States weakened considerably during this period as oil prices tumbled. Over the next five years (1993–1997), domestic spending staged an impressive comeback rising at an average annual rate of nearly 15% reaching $2.25 billion in 1997.

During this period oil and gas exploration activity expanded. The number of rotary rigs in operation stood at 721 in 1992 and then rose to 775 by 1994. Rig activity fell back in 1995 to an average of 723, but surged ahead the following year to 779 and then to 943 in 1997. The big gains throughout this period came in gas-well activity. The demand for underground mining and mineral processing equipment also improved during this period as metal, stone, and earth, and coal mining advanced prompting investment in new equipment. In 1997, mining industry capital spending increased by 24%.

In 1998, U.S. spending for mining and oil-field machinery and equipment rose by another 21% to $2.72 billion. The number of rotary rigs in use actually fell to an average of 827 as crude oil prices fell by over 30%. Domestic drilling and exploration-related capital expenditures by major U.S. corporations fell 13%. However, the demand for mining and mineral processing equipment remained very strong.

Mining and Oil-Field Machinery Foreign Trade

U.S. producers of mining and oil-field machinery depend heavily on the export market. During the period from 1990 through 1998, exports of mining and oil-field machinery have accounted for over 90% of total U.S. shipments.

U.S. exports of oil- and gas-field machinery and equipment stood at $3.14 billion in 1990, and rose without interruption to $4.39 billion in 1993. After a slight pause the following year, exports resumed their climb reaching $7.05 billion by 1997. In 1995, the number or rotary rigs in operation outside of the United States stood at 989. World rotary rigs in operation rose to 1,063 in 1996 and 1,184 in 1997. Last year, exports of oil- and gas-field machinery jumped by another 15.5% to $8.14 billion. This occurred despite the fact that the number of rotary rigs in operation fell by 14.4%. The United States has consistently run a trade surplus in oil-field machinery and equipment. In 1988, imports were valued at just $851 million, versus exports of $2.41 billion. This translates into a surplus of $1.56 billion. Last year imports were valued at $1.38 billion. The trade surplus for last year was $6.76 billion.

U.S. exports of mining machinery and equipment have shown very little growth in the past decade. Exports were valued at $525 million in 1988 and $528 million in 1998. During the past decade, exports ranged between a high of 738 million in 1995 and a low of 500 million in 1990. Most recently exports fell 26% in 1996, rose 3% in 1997, and then dropped 6% in 1998. Imports of mining machinery and equipment were even more erratic. In 1988, they were valued at $1.36 billion. The following year they fell to $493 million. During the period from 1990–1998, they ranged from a high of $778 million in 1995 to a low of 339 million in 1998. From 1988 through 1998, the United States has had a trade surplus in mining machinery and equipment in seven years and a deficit in four. Most recently, we ran deficits from 1995–1997 but reported a $189 million surplus in 1998.

Material-Handling Equipment

Material-handling equipment includes elevators and moving stairways, conveyors and conveying equipment, hoists, cranes, and monorails, and industrial trucks and tractors.

Shipments of material-handling equipment emerged very slowly from the 1990–1991 recession. Shipments had inched up by 0.7% in 1990 and then fallen 7.8% to $8.46 billion in 1991. Signs of life emerged during 1992, but shipments for the year as a whole were up only 1.5%. Over the next three years, shipments of material handling equipment staged an impressive recovery as domestic demand and exports expanded at a healthy clip. During the period from 1993–1995, shipments grew at an average annual rate of 13.5%. Growth then slowed to 2.3% in 1996, as domestic demand and export sales slowed. Shipments rose by 3.4% in 1997. Domestic demand and exports both accelerated, but imports gained share in the U.S. market. Last year, shipments of material-handling equipment jumped 14% on the strength of the U.S. market. Exports suffered as key overseas markets faltered.

Domestic Demand

In the United States, spending for material-handling equipment is driven by new construction of industrial plants, retail stores, warehouses, offices, and other commercial buildings. Spending programs designed to modernize and upgrade these facilities also have a profound impact on domestic spending for such equipment.

The slump in new-building construction in the early 1990s and the generally poor investment climate resulted in a sharp decline in spending for material-handling equipment by U.S. corporations. Such spending peaked in 1989 at $9.2 billion, and then fell 4.5% in 1990 and 14.5% in 1991. Signs of life emerged late in the following year, but spending for all of 1992 slipped by another 0.3% to $7.49 billion.

Domestic spending for material handling equipment has been on the rise since then, increasing 17.3% in 1993, 15.7% in 1994, and 17.2% in 1995. During these years, industrial construction staged an impressive comeback and commercial construction gathered momentum. In addition, with corporate profits posting impressive double-digit gains from 1993–1995, aggressive replacement and modernization spending programs were initiated.

Over the next two years, spending for material-handling equipment grew by only 3.6% in 1996 and 3.9% in 1997. New industrial construction faltered in those years and corporate-profit growth slowed to about 7% annually, down from 22% in 1995. With this as a backdrop, the domestic market was ready to move forward. Domestic demand roared back in 1998 with spending rising a whopping 24% to $15.9 billion.

Material-Handling Equipment Foreign Trade

In 1988, exports of material-handling equipment were valued at $1.54 billion. Exports rose without interruption over the next four years reaching $3.14 billion in 1992. Overseas sales slipped by 3% in 1993, and then posted increases of 18.3% in 1994, and 10.3% in 1995. After a subdued 1996 when exports rose by only 1.8%, they rebounded by 18.1% in 1997, reaching $4.78 billion. In 1998, a combination of weakness in key Asian and Latin American markets and the strong dollar resulted in a 3.3% decline in U.S. exports to $4.62 billion.

Canada and Mexico have long been the major markets for U.S.-produced material-handling equipment, accounting for almost a third of total exports. The rest of Latin America accounts for about 19% of the export market led by Venezuela, Brazil, and Argentina. Western Europe takes in about 20% of our exports. Rounding out the field of export markets: Asia, 13%; the Middle East, 4%; Australia and New Zealand, 3%-4%; Africa, 3%; Eastern Europe, the former Soviet Union, and Turkey, 3%; and India and Pakistan less than 1%.

The major foreign sources of imported material-handling equipment are Canada (22%), Japan (14%), Germany (10%), the United Kingdom (9%), Mexico (6%), China (4%), South Korea (3%), and Italy (3%). Imports totaled $1.92 billion back in 1988 and rose to $5.4 billion in 1998. During this period, the import share of domestic spending for material handling equipment rose from 22.1% in 1988 to 33.9% in 1998. Since the U.S. market emerged from the last recession in earnest in 1993, imports have expanded at an average annual rate of 17.7%.

Outlook for Construction, Mining, and Material-Handling Equipment

From 1998–2008, we expect shipments of construction, mining, and material-handling equipment to expand by 5.0% per year. This is a slower rate of growth than the 6.1% achieved in the previous decade. With equipment prices slated to increase by 3.0%, the real value of shipments will expand by 2.0% annually.

Domestic Demand Outlook

As 1999 unfolds, domestic spending for construction machinery, mining, and material-handling equipment remains fairly strong, but has begun to top out. There is little pent-up demand for equipment following five strong years of buying, and end-market activity is not strong enough to keep investment moving along at its recent fast pace.

Construction spending will certainly expand at a healthy clip again this year. New-home construction started 1999 off to a rocking good start thanks to very favorable fundamentals (income, employment, consumer confidence, mortgage rates) and good weather. Housing starts will not remain at their lofty early-1999 level throughout the year, but should be able to finish the year in the 1.6–1.65 million units range versus 1.62 million units last year.

Nonresidential construction spending will increase modestly this year as gains in commercial and utility construction offset weakness in industrial projects. For public construction, 1999 started off strong due to very favorable weather. We are beginning to see TEA-21 projects take form and these will dominate public-sector spending throughout the forecast period. Indications are now that we could see an increase in total construction spending of 6% this year, depending on how quickly TEA-21 projects build up a head of steam.

In 2000, construction spending will slow. Thereafter, it expands by 1.5%–2.0% per year, on average. The market mix will change during this period. The residential-building market, which has been the source of strength in construction, slows due to demographics and the absence of any pent-up demand for new homes after a period of very aggressive new construction. Housing starts averaged 1.6 million units in 1998–1999, but will slow to between 1.40–1.45 million units per year during the 2000–2004 period and 1.4 million units per year through the rest of the forecast period. Nonresidential construction will show very little growth in 2000. Thereafter, some new industrial capacity will be needed, and there will be continued modest expansion in the commercial and utility markets. This will support average annual growth of about 1.5%–2.0% per year. Lastly, the growth in public construction spending is maintained at about 3.5%–4.0% per year during the 2000–2004 period, as TEA-21 projects kick in. Public-projects spending tapers off after that.

Logging is off to a fast start this year due to the strength in the housing market. When all is said and done, look for an increase in logging activity of about 3% this year. This will be followed by a 1.5%–2.0% decline in the year 2000 as the housing boom subsides. Thereafter, new-home construction stabilizes, but the home repair and remodeling, material-handling, and export markets should be supportive. Overall, logging activity grows by about 0.5%–1.0% per year. The very modest expectations we have for U.S.-logging activity will be reflected in purchases of log skidders and other equipment used by the logging industry.

Surface-coal mining should grow modestly in 1999, as the market adjusts to the inventory buildup of 1998. Thereafter, look for surface-coal production to grow by 2.5% per year. The 1999–2000 period will see only very modest growth, 1.1%–1.5% per year, in non-coal surface mining. Mine output improves to 1.5%–2.0% per year from 2000–2004.

Underground-mining activity will grow very slowly during the coming decade. Domestic demand for coal from Eastern underground mines will be limited by environ-mental restrictions. Overseas demand for such coal will face stiff competition. The demand for iron ore will be limited as the scrap steel using electric furnace continues to gain market share. With this as a backdrop, look for very modest growth in spending for underground-mining machinery.

Oil and gas exploration in the United States should improve from current depressed levels as crude-oil prices rise. Following their sharp declines in 1997–1998, the refiners' acquisition cost of crude oil is slated to expand at a strong pace during the 1999–2001 period. Thereafter, we expect prices to rise moderately. Domestic spending for oil- and gas-well machinery and equipment should be the beneficiaries of rising crude-oil prices.

U.S. manufacturers will face some tough times over the near term, but the longer term future remains bright. During the coming decade, we expect output in the manufacturing sector to expand by almost 3% per year. In addition to prompting construction of new industrial plants, such activity will prompt manufacturers to continue to modernize and upgrade their material-handling equipment and systems. Modest growth in the wholesale and retail trade sector will provide additional support.

Export Outlook

Exports of construction, mining, and material-handling equipment will emerge very slowly from their current doldrums as key overseas markets eventually right themselves and the U.S. dollar depreciates slowly. Look for some signs of life in U.S. exports this year, a modest improvement in overseas sales in the year 2000, and a solid recovery during the 2001–2004 period. The Canadian, Mexican, Latin American, and Asian markets are expected to lead the way. Opportunities are also expected to emerge in Africa, Eastern Europe, and the Middle East. Western Europe and Japan will become less of a factor as economic growth trails.

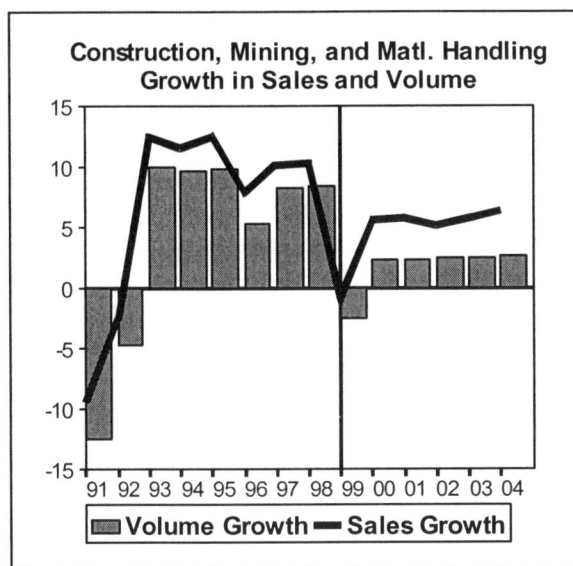

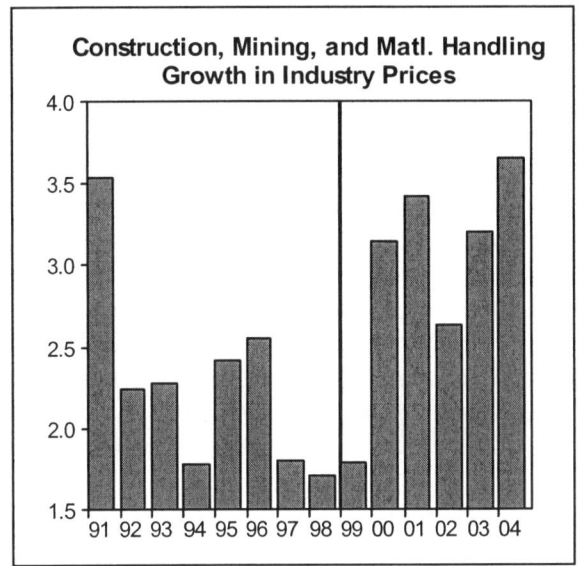

Construction, Mining, and Material-Handling Equipment

SIC 353

		1992	1993	1994	1995	1996	1997	1998	1999	2000	2001	Compound Average 88-98	Annual Growth 98-08
Sales													
	Billions of $	27.23	30.63	34.19	38.48	41.53	45.78	50.51	50.10	52.93	56.00		
	% Ch	-2.5	12.5	11.6	12.5	7.9	10.2	10.3	-0.8	5.6	5.8	6.1	5.2
Volume													
	% Ch	-4.7	10.0	9.7	9.9	5.3	8.3	8.5	-2.6	2.4	2.3	3.5	2.0
Prices													
	% Ch	2.2	2.3	1.8	2.4	2.6	1.8	1.7	1.8	3.1	3.4	2.5	3.2
Production Costs													
Avg. Hourly Earnings													
	$/hr	12.57	12.93	12.99	12.89	13.12	13.53	13.70	14.10	14.49	14.97		
	% Ch	1.9	2.9	0.4	-0.8	1.8	3.1	1.3	2.9	2.8	3.3	2.0	3.1
Input Price Index													
	% Ch	0.3	1.5	2.3	3.5	0.3	0.6	-0.3	0.0	2.3	2.8	1.5	2.5

Metalworking Machinery

Domestic demand for metalworking machinery is influenced by conditions in a number of key sectors of the U.S. economy. Activity and capital spending in the fabricated metal products, appliance, industrial machinery, motor vehicle, and aerospace industries drive the demand for machine tools and related accessories, which include special dies, die sets, jigs and fixtures, and industrial molds. The steel and aluminum industries call the tune for rolling mill machinery. Housing and construction and various assembly operations are critical to the power hand tool market. Finally, the demand for welding equipment is heavily influenced by the automotive, capital equipment, and construction sectors. Exports of metalworking machinery, primarily machine tools and related products, are tied to currency fluctuations and economic conditions in key markets such as Canada, Mexico, Europe, and Asia.

Recent History

Metalworking machinery came out of the 1990–1991 recession with an increase in shipments of 7.4%, 5.6% after adjusting for inflation. Business spending for such equipment rose nearly 4%. Exports jumped 12.3%, and imports tumbled by a similar percentage.

Over the next five years, metalworking machinery staged an impressive comeback as the equipment and fabricated and primary metals industries benefited from expanding demand for consumer goods and new housing, a strong revival in business investment, and considerable progress in foreign markets. Major retooling programs in the motor vehicle, aerospace industries, and off-highway markets, provided much of the support. Business investment in metalworking machinery grew by 62% during the 1993–1997 period. Healthy growth in key overseas economies and a favorable exchange rate also helped the metalworking industries directly, allowing exports to advance from $3.4 billion in 1992 to $6.5 billion by 1995, an increase of 91%. Shipments of metalworking machinery rose from $26.4 billion in 1992 to $41.2 billion in 1997, an average annual increase of 9.3%. Real shipment volume rose by 7% per annum during this five-year span.

In 1998, shipments of metalworking machinery grew by only 1.9% in nominal terms and 0.9% in volume terms. U.S. corporations increased their spending for new equipment by 3.7%, but exports faltered as the Asian flu spread. U.S. exports of metalworking machinery fell from $6.5 billion in 1997 to less than $6.3 billion last year.

Employment

In 1988, the producers of metalworking machinery employed 327,190 production and other workers. Employment rose to 336,080 in 1999 and then fell from 1990–1992, due to the recession, bottoming out at 302,830 in 1992. The strong growth in the demand for metalworking machinery in subsequent years pushed employment to 352,370 in 1998.

The machine tool industry reported employment of 66,010 workers in 1998. Employment grew to 67,120 workers the following year before the 1990–1991 recession took its toll. Employment hit bottom in 1993 at 52,170 workers. Over the next five years machine tool builders added to their payrolls every year with employment reaching 60,900 workers in 1998.

Employment in the tool and die industry stood at 145,530 production and other workers a decade ago in 1988. Employment fell during the recession and bottomed out at 138,160 workers in 1992. Expanding activity in the metalworking industries over the next six years pushed employment at tool and die makers to 168,330 workers in 1998.

Producers of machine tool accessories, such as cutting tools and precision measuring tools and accessories watched employment in their industry drop from 58,280 workers in 1989 to 48,360 workers in 1993. As activity in the metalworking industries improved over the next five years, employment rose, reaching 55,380 workers in 1998.

Employment among the makers of power-driven hand tools totaled 21,850 workers in 1998. The recession of the early 1990s had little effect on employment levels and, by 1992, employment had risen to 23,200 workers. Employment then gained ground until it reached 24,740 workers in 1995. Since then, employment has drifted down as companies invested in machinery and equipment to offset rising labor costs. Last year, there were just 20,990 people employed in the power-driven hand tool industry.

Foreign Trade

The United States has consistently run trade deficits in metalworking machinery since 1980. Between 1988 and 1998, imports of metalworking machinery, primarily from Japan, Western Europe, and Taiwan expanded from $3.68 billion to $8.81 billion, a growth rate of 14% per year on average. Imports, particularly of machine tools, have been a major factor in the U.S. market for metalworking machinery for some time. Aggressive marketing of simple low-priced stand-alone machines allowed the Japanese and Taiwanese to gain a foothold in the U.S. market many years ago. Manufacturers in Asia now offer a broad range of products, from very simple to very complex equipment. European producers have long been major producers of high-quality complex equipment.

Foreign manufacturers have been very aggressive in courting the U.S. market, and they have gained market share despite periodic unfavorable currency fluctuations. Imports accounted for 14.6% of the U.S. market in 1998. In subsequent years, the strong performance of the U.S. market resulted in import penetration rising to 19.8% in 1998. During the past decade, the metalworking trade deficit rose from $1.14 billion in 1988 to $2.54 billion in 1998.

Outlook

WEFA forecasts shipments of metalworking machinery to expand by about 2% this year, 1% after adjusting for inflation. Exports are soft, but domestic metalworking industry activity and capital spending are providing support. In the longer run, current dollar shipments expand by 6% per year, on average. With prices expanding by 3% per year, we expect volume growth of close to 3% annually as well.

We expect domestic demand for metalworking machinery to grow at a moderate pace during the 2000–2008 period, as metalworking industry activity expands by 2.0%–2.5% per year. Increased investment in metalworking machinery will be triggered by a combination of forces: pressures to expand capacity and introduce new products for both consumer and business markets; and the need to steadily improve productivity and efficiency.

Primary Metals Markets

1999 has been a tough year for the steel industry due to a surge in imports that began in 1998. Nonferrous metals output is also expected to be down this year. Overall, we expect the output of the primary metals industry to decline by about 2% this year. Over the next ten years, we expect the demand for primary metals to expand by 1.5%–2.0% per year, on average. Progress will be limited by the relatively modest growth we expect in the automotive and construction markets.

Fabricated Metal Markets

The output of fabricated metal products will expand by about 1% in 1999 with modest growth in all categories. Longer term, industry output expands by 2% per year through 2008. Structural metal products and plumbing and heating products should benefit from growth in construction. Fasteners and stampings will reflect activity in the automotive, aerospace, and capital goods markets. The capital goods market will expand in response to growth in both domestic and export demand. Motor vehicle production will expand by 1.5%–2.0% per year supported by fleet expansion pressures and replacement demand. Commercial air-transport production will reflect strong growth in Asian and Latin American passenger travel and growth in world air-freight traffic. We also expect some additional support from increased defense-aircraft spending.

Industrial Machinery Markets

Currently, domestic demand for traditional capital goods is mixed. Farm equipment, special and general industrial machinery, mining machinery, and material-handling equipment are weak. Construction machinery and service industry machinery are doing well. Over the near term, the investment climate is not expected to actually turn negative, but limited growth in final demand, some pressure on profit margins, and the absence of a significant need to expand capacity suggest that the pace of investment will be moderating. Longer term, domestic demand for traditional capital goods will be influenced by 3% growth in manufacturing activity and more modest rates of growth in construction, farming, and mining activity. In addition to pressure to expand productive capacity, competitive pressures will stimulate investment in new equipment that improves productivity and efficiency and replaces labor. Exports of traditional capital goods are depressed currently, but we expect overseas sales to lead the way on the growth front during the coming decade. Asian and Latin American demand will provide most of the lift to U.S. exports of traditional capital goods.

Production of traditional capital goods will show little, if any increase this year. Longer term, our expectations for general economic conditions in the United States and overseas suggest a growth rate of 2.0%–2.5% per year on average.

Appliance Markets

The revival in new-home construction and growth in consumer income will allow appliance production to expand by 8% in 1999. With little support from the housing sector in the year 2000, and consumers already flush with new refrigerators, washers, dryers, and other appliances, the growth in appliance production will slow to about 1%. Longer term, housing starts will average about 1.41 million units per year, and real consumer disposable income is forecast to grow by roughly 2.5% per year. With this as a backdrop, WEFA expects appliance production to expand by 2.5% per year on average during the 2000–2008 period.

Motor Vehicle Markets

The motor vehicle industry is enjoying another year of prosperity with both light vehicle and commercial sales and production doing well. When all is said and done motor vehicle industry output will increase by 6% this year. The year 2000 brings a modest adjustment in both light- and commercial-vehicle demand and production slips by 1%. A pick-up in the replacement cycle and some fleet expansion will lift vehicle demand in 2000–2002 with production growing by 2% per year. Thereafter, light-vehicle demand is driven by growth in the number of households and replacement demand. The commercial-vehicle market responds to 3% growth in domestic-manufacturing activity and increased

NAFTA trade. This stimulates fleet expansion as well as replacement sales.

Overall, we expect U.S. production of motor vehicles and parts to expand by 1.5% per year during the 2000–2008 period.

Aerospace Markets

The domestic commercial-aircraft market is nearing the end of a significant buying cycle, driven by increasing pressure to replace older units still in service, the introduction of new models designed to meet the needs of specific traffic corridors, and anticipated strong growth in a number of foreign markets. Deliveries of new aircraft will peak this year and then drift off over the next few years. The Asian crisis has already dampened the order intake of both Boeing and Airbus and should show up in the delivery numbers in 2000–2001. Longer term, passenger and freight traffic worldwide will trigger another round of air transport purchases that will begin to lift commercial air transport production in three or four years.

The defense portion of the aerospace industry has been in the doldrums in recent years, the victim of aggressive military downsizing. However, discussions about the next generation of military aircraft continue. WEFA expects defense-related aerospace to gain ground slowly and then accelerate through the middle of the next decade.

On balance, WEFA forecasts that production of aircraft and parts will increase 1% this year following a 15.6% jump in 1998. Production then declines by 5% in 2000 and 3% in 2001 as the commercial-transport cycle winds down. Longer term (2002–2008), we forecast production of aircraft and parts to expand by about 3% per year.

Export Markets

Exports of metalworking machinery declined 3.5% in 1998 and will remain in the doldrums this year. However, the long-term prospects for U.S. exports of metalworking machinery remain favorable.

WEFA expects real world economic growth to stabilize at 1.9% this year. Growth should improve to 2.6% next year and between 3.0% and 3.3% per year through 2008.

Canada and Mexico have been major export markets for the U.S. metalworking sector, largely because of auto industry production, expansion, and retooling. These projects have required investment in machine tools and power-driven hand tools used in the assembly process.

■ Canada represents the largest single market for U.S.–produced metalworking machinery. WEFA expects growth in Canadian real GDP to reach 2.8% in 1999 following a 3.0% increase in 1998. Growth will slow to 2% in 1999 and average 2.5% annually, or marginally higher, over the long term.

■ In recent years, Mexico has emerged as a major market for machine tools and other metalworking machinery. The Mexican economy is slated to expand by 3% this year following growth of 4.8% in 1998 and 7.1% in 1997. Thereafter, the Mexican economy should expand annually in the 5% range through the forecast period.

Other export markets also look promising, although we may have to wait longer for tangible results. Conditions in the rest of Latin America are expected to be good for U.S. exporters over the long term, although the picture currently is very mixed. Following an increase of 1.2% in 1998, the economies of Latin America lose ground with GDP declining by 2.3%. However, longer-term growth is put at 4%-5% per year. The Japanese economy has exhibited signs of life but has still a long way to go before it is out of the woods. Once the recovery really picks up steam, we believe the Japanese economy can maintain an annual growth rate in the 2.0% range. China, where economic growth is expected to remain close to 7%–8% per year, offers great opportunities for metalworking equipment. Opportunities will also abound in the rest of Asia once the recent turmoil is completely behind us. Economic growth in Western Europe will be modest, but the modernization of production facilities that will likely accompany European unification should stimulate investment in U.S. metalworking machinery. There is hope that the former Soviet Union and the rest of Eastern Europe will stage a general recovery during the coming decade. Within this group Russia still looks like the weak link, since its transition to a market economy has been slow and painful.

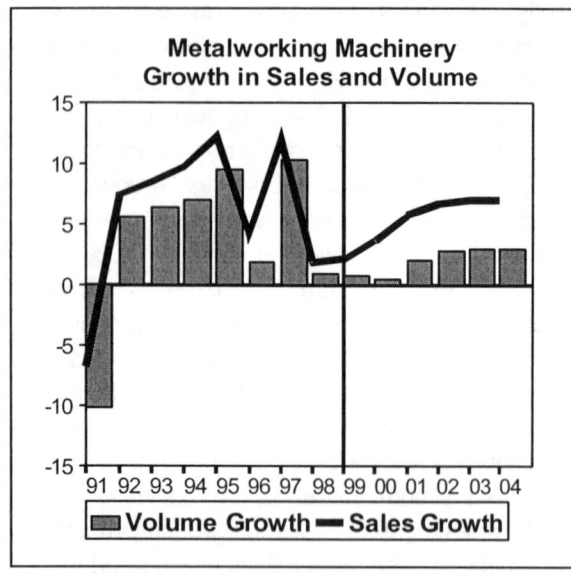

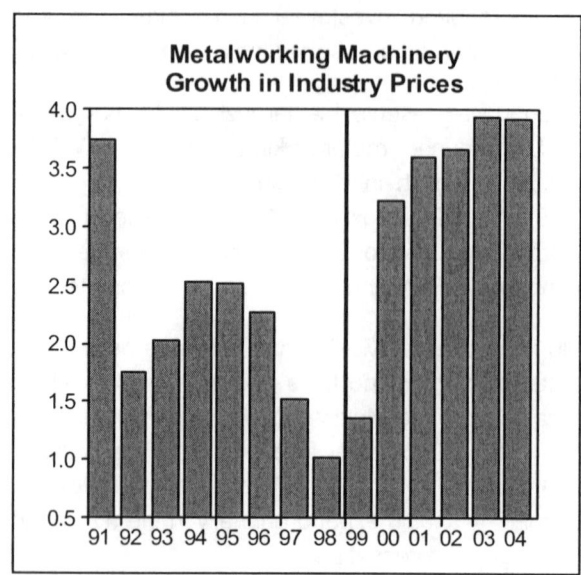

Metalworking Machinery
SIC 354

		1992	1993	1994	1995	1996	1997	1998	1999	2000	2001	Compound Average 88-98	Annual Growth 98-08
Sales													
	Billions of $	26.35	28.59	31.40	35.27	36.76	41.17	41.97	42.88	44.45	47.03		
	% Ch	7.4	8.5	9.8	12.3	4.2	12.0	1.9	2.2	3.7	5.8	5.7	5.9
Volume													
	% Ch	5.6	6.4	7.1	9.6	1.9	10.3	0.9	0.8	0.4	2.1	3.2	2.5
Prices													
	% Ch	1.8	2.0	2.5	2.5	2.3	1.5	1.0	1.4	3.2	3.6	2.5	3.3
Production Costs													
Avg. Hourly Earnings													
	$/hr	12.95	13.34	13.66	13.99	14.41	14.90	15.33	15.85	16.37	16.96		
	% Ch	2.8	3.1	2.4	2.4	3.0	3.4	2.9	3.3	3.3	3.6	2.9	3.7
Input Price Index													
	% Ch	0.3	1.4	2.5	4.3	-0.0	0.7	-0.5	-0.2	2.1	2.7	1.5	2.4

Special Industrial Machinery

Special industrial machinery includes equipment used by the food and beverage, semiconductor, paper, printing, textile, chemical, refining, rubber and plastic, and other industries that use unique machinery in production processes. During the ten years that ended in 1998, volume of special industrial machinery grew by 2.8% per year on average. Exports provided the support, as domestic business spending for special industrial machinery grew by only 2.6% per year in real terms. WEFA expects that activity in key domestic markets, coupled with favorable export prospects, will bring volume growth in special industrial machinery of about 2% per year on average during the 1998–2008 period.

Recent History

Production

Since emerging from the 1990/1991 recession special industrial machinery has experienced both feast and famine. The industry posted volume gains of 6.8% in 1993, 12.5% in 1994, and 18.8% in 1995. This strong surge in activity was triggered by healthy domestic spending for equipment in the semiconductor, food and beverage, paper, printing, and other so-called special industries. At the same time, export sales rose substantially. The table began to turn in 1996. Major domestic spending projects wound down, and with operating rates in the semiconductor, food and beverage, paper, printing, textile, apparel, and other industries running well below their 1994–1995 peaks, there was little incentive to aggressively expand capacity. Adding to the industry's troubles the Asian flu spread to a number of non-Asian countries and exports weakened. Volume rose 6.7% in 1996 but fell 3.5% in 1997 and 7.9% in 1998. Another decline of 4.5% is expected this year.

Employment

The producers of special industrial machinery employed 148,320 workers in 1992 as their industry began to emerge from the 1990/1991 recession. This was down from a pre-recession peak of 161,450 workers in 1989. Employment increased steadily since 1992, reaching 179,090 workers in 1998. However, employment growth was strongest from 1993-1996 when it increased by 20%. In the two years that followed, employment grew by only 0.5%.

Employment among producers of textile machinery has been on the decline almost without interruption since 1988. In that year, the industry employed 20,170 workers. By 1998, employment among producers of textile machinery had fallen to 14,250 workers.

Printing trade machinery industry employment went from a pre-recession high of 25,980 in 1989 to a low of 21,370 in 1993. Employment rose to 23,340 by 1995, but has been retreating ever since, dropping to 22,080 last year.

In the food products machinery, industry dipped slightly to 22,480 in 1991 at the height of the recession, and then roared back in the years that followed. As the demand for new equipment expanded, employment reached its peak in 1996 at 25,400. Employment slipped back to 25,300 in 1997 and 24,960 in 1998.

Employment among producers of other special industrial machinery bottomed out at 87,420 in 1991 and has been on the rise ever since. Employment jumped by 31% between 1991 and 1996, reaching 114,730 in that year. These were banner years for the electronic components industry and the makers of semiconductor manufacturing equipment aggressively expanded their workforce. Over the past two years employment growth has slowed with the number of people employed by makers of other special industrial machinery rising to 116,730 in 1997 and 117,810 in 1998.

Domestic Demand

After adjusting for inflation, domestic spending for special industrial machinery bottomed out during the last recession at $22.5 billion in 1992. As the economy roared back and key industries, such as semiconductors, pulp and paper, food and beverage, printing and publishing, and textiles and apparel turned the corner, capital spending programs in these industries became more aggressive. Expanding final demand, tightening operating rates, and competitive pressures, combined with improving profits, low-interest rates and attractive new equipment prices, triggered a surge in spending for new equipment. Business investment in special industrial machinery rose 10% in 1993, 4.5% in 1993, and a whopping 16.6% in 1995, which boosted spending to $30.18 billion ($92). Since then, business investment in special industrial machinery has basically treaded water with annual outlays of $30.54 billion in 1996, $30.68 billion in 1997, and $30.94 billion in 1998. This three-year lull reflects the huge spending spree in previous years and excess capacity in a number of industries, particularly semiconductors, textiles and apparel, and paper.

Foreign Trade

Exports of special industrial machinery posted impressive gains over the last decade and in the years following the 1990–1991 recession in particular. Expanding activity in key oversea markets such as Canada, Western Europe, and, in recent years, Mexico, Latin America, and Asia, provided much of the support. Favorable exchange rates didn't hurt. Overseas sales continued to perform well into 1997, but there were already signs that the bloom was off the rose. By 1998, exports faltered as the Asian flu took its toll.

- Exports of food products machinery totaled only $562 million in 1987, but had risen to over $1.1 billion by 1989 and continued to grow rapidly to over $2.2 billion in 1996. Exports slipped a bit to $2.15 billion in 1997, and then fell again to $1.97 billion last year.

- Paper and printing machinery exports totaled $1.28 billion in 1987 and rose almost without interruption to $3.26 billion by 1997. In 1998, exports fell 8% to $3 billion.

- Overseas sales of textile machinery totaled only $556 million in 1987. They broke the $1 billion mark in 1989 and reached almost $1.4 billion in 1997, rising 14% above their 1996 level. Last year, exports declined 5.7% to $1.3 billion.

- Exports of woodworking, glassmaking, and other miscellaneous types of special industrial machinery

grew from $1.14 billion in 1987 to $2.83 billion in 1997, posting an increase of 20% in that year. In 1998, exports inched ahead by 2% to $2.89 billion.

- Exports of other types of special industrial machinery also enjoyed good growth prior to last year but overseas sales faltered in 1998. Exports, including those of equipment used to produce semiconductors and other electrical components, dropped 14% last year.

Imports of special industrial machinery, primarily from Japan, Germany, and the rest of Western Europe, reflected the investment programs of key U.S. industries. Healthy demand in the United States and aggressive marketing by foreign producers supported strong import growth through 1995. Import performance since then has been mixed.

- Imports of food products machinery totaled $741 million in 1987, but rose to over $1.3 billion ten years later in 1997. Imports grew by only 2.5% last year exceeding $1.33 billion. In 1987, the United States had a trade deficit in food products machinery of $179 million. The United States moved into a surplus position in 1989, which we have maintained ever since. In 1998 our surplus in food products machinery trade was valued at over $640 million.

- Paper and printing machinery imports exceeded $2.2 billion in 1987 and totaled $3.26 billion by 1997. In 1998, imports increased 5.6% to $4.28 billion. The United States has consistently had a trade deficit in paper and printing machinery. In 1987 the deficit was valued at over $933 million. Last year, the deficit reached $1.23 billion.

- Sales of imported textile machinery totaled $1.38 billion in 1987. A decade later in 1997, imports reached $2.12 billion. Last year, imports increased by 12% to $2.37 billion. The deficit in textile machinery trade has grown from $824 million in 1987 to $1.07 billion in 1998.

- Imports of woodworking, glassmaking, and other miscellaneous types of special industrial machinery grew from $1.71 billion in 1987 to $4.63 billion in 1997, posting an increase of 90% in that year. In 1998, imports rose by another 5.7% to $4.9 billion. The United States had a trade deficit in woodworking, glassmaking, and other types of special industry machinery of $568 million in 1997. Last year, the deficit was valued at over $2 billion.

Outlook: 1998–2007

Currently the producers of special industrial machinery are still having a tough time. Domestic demand is running below a year ago in both current and constant dollars. Operating rates in key industries, such as pulp and paper, food and beverage, printing, textiles, and apparel remain low and we will not see any aggressive efforts to expand capacity over the near term. There are some signs of life in the semiconductor equipment business with manufacturers reporting strong first-quarter orders after a very weak 1998. Adding to the mix, export demand remains very weak in 1999 and is not expected to exhibit any real strength until we are well into 2000. When all is said and done, we do not expect to see a noticeable reversal of fortune in either domestic or export demand in 1999. As a result, production of special industrial machinery should fall 4.5% in 1999.

During the next decade, WEFA expects volume growth in special industrial machinery to average about 2% per year. The recovery will be sluggish over the near term, with production growth around 1.0% in 2000 and 2.0% in 2001. Thereafter, we expect solid domestic and export demand to support higher annual growth. Activity in the traditional markets for special industrial machinery, pulp and paper, food and beverage, printing and publishing, textiles and apparel etc., will be very sluggish in 2000, but should expand 2.5%–3.0% per year during the 2001–2008 period. This combined with pressure to improve productivity and efficiency and take advantage of new technologies will support relatively aggressive efforts to expand and modernize capacity. Overseas demand for traditional types of special industrial machinery will rebound during this period as established markets such as Canada, Western Europe, Mexico, Latin America, and Japan are joined by the rest of Asia and to a much lesser extent Eastern Europe and the former Soviet Union. However, the greatest potential lies in semiconductor manufacturing equipment. The United States is a dominant player in this market and worldwide demand for electronic components is forecast to expand at a very healthy clip during the next decade.

Semiconductor Equipment

Recent History

Global semiconductor sales went from $13.1 billion in 1980 to $50.5 billion in 1990. They reached $144.4 billion in 1995, and then fell back 8.6% the following year to $132 billion. In 1997, sales rose 4% to 137.2 billion, only to fall 8.4% in 1998 to $125.6 billion. The slump in sales in recent years took a toll on investment in the equipment used to produce semiconductors and related equipment.

In 1990, worldwide shipments of semiconductor equipment totaled $8.5 billion. By 1996, shipments were valued at $26.3 billion. Between 1990 and 1996, shipments grew at an average annual rate of 35%. The slump in semiconductor demand that emerged in 1996 took a toll on industry expansion. Orders for new equipment faltered in that year and shipments lost momentum. After increasing a whopping 64% in 1995, the growth in worldwide semiconductor equipment shipments slowed to 9.7% in 1996, 4.7% in 1997, and then dropped a whopping 20.9% in 1998 to $21.8 billion.

While all regions took a hit in 1998, the big losers were Korea and Japan with declines in shipments of 50.9% and 30.7%, respectively. North America experienced a 16.9% drop in shipments, followed by Taiwan at –14.1%; Europe, –5.7%; and the rest-of-world, –3.1%. The 1998 worldwide semiconductor capital equipment market was distributed as follows. North America, 34.7%; Japan, 21.5%; Taiwan, 15.0%; Europe, 13.2%; Korea, 5.9%; and rest-of-world, 9.6%.

By segment, the biggest declines in 1998 came in wafer manufacturing equipment (–62.4%) and wafer process equipment (–23.2%). Last year was a difficult one for silicon wafer manufacturers who wrestled with an oversupply of 200-mm wafers and delays in switching over to 300-mm wafers. Declines were also recorded in fabricating facility equipment (–17.5%), assembly and packaging (–17.1%), and testing equipment (–15.8%). The demand for mask/reticle equipment rose by 12% in 1998. Mask-making capacity was increased in 1998 due to increasingly complex chip designs and increased mask production times. By segment, the 1998 worldwide semiconductor capital equipment market was distributed as follows: wafer process, 65%; test, 20.1%; assembly and packaging, 7%; fabricating facility equipment, 4.1%; mask/reticle equipment, 3.2%; and wafer manufacturing, 0.6%.

Outlook

There are signs of life in the semiconductor equipment market after a very tough 1998. First-quarter 1999 orders for new equipment were $5.2 billion. This represented an increase of 37% from the fourth quarter and 88% from the low-point for orders, which occurred in the third quarter of 1998.

The long-term prospects for semiconductors and semiconductor equipment remain favorable. We are in the early stages of a recovery in semiconductor demand, which, coupled with the long-term trend towards technology, will trigger a new wave of investment by chipmakers. Worldwide business, personal, and government investment in computers and related equipment will only increase in the years ahead in response to a steady stream of new and more powerful products and declining prices. Internet use has been growing at a rapid pace in recent years and will continue to do so in the future. The demand for consumer electronics will continue to gain ground, which will have a positive impact on the semiconductor industry. Finally, the use of electronics in products such as automobiles, business equipment, and consumer goods will also increase. Recent estimates expect worldwide semiconductor sales to rise 9.5% this year to $137.5 billion and exceed $222 billion by 2002. This translates into an increase of about 15% per year, on average.

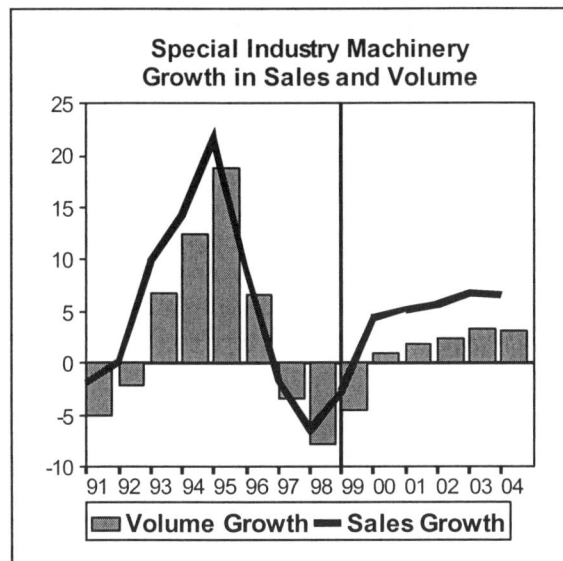

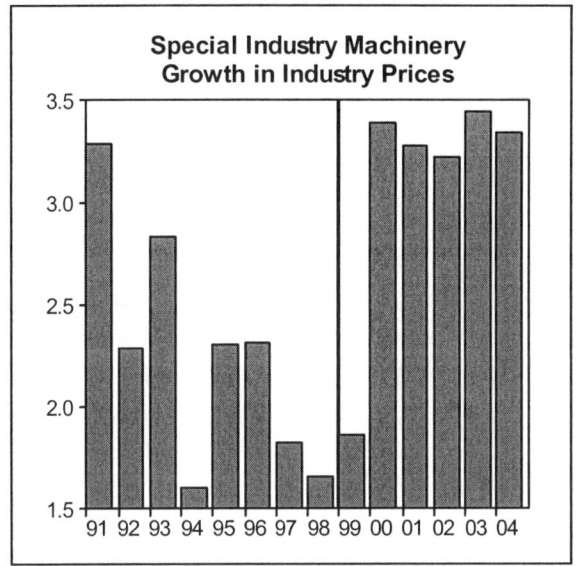

Special Industry Machinery

SIC 355

		1992	1993	1994	1995	1996	1997	1998	1999	2000	2001	Compound Average 88-98	Annual Growth 98-08
Sales													
	Billions of $	21.46	23.57	26.93	32.74	35.71	35.11	32.86	31.99	33.41	35.16		
	% Ch	0.2	9.8	14.3	21.6	9.1	-1.7	-6.4	-2.7	4.4	5.2	5.4	5.4
Volume													
	% Ch	-2.1	6.8	12.5	18.8	6.7	-3.5	-7.9	-4.5	1.0	1.9	2.8	2.1
Prices													
	% Ch	2.3	2.8	1.6	2.3	2.3	1.8	1.7	1.9	3.4	3.3	2.6	3.2
Production Costs													
Avg. Hourly Earnings													
	$/hr	12.70	13.15	13.49	13.64	14.06	14.68	15.08	15.55	16.10	16.72		
	% Ch	3.0	3.6	2.5	1.1	3.1	4.4	2.8	3.1	3.5	3.8	3.1	3.8
Input Price Index													
	% Ch	0.3	1.4	2.3	3.8	-0.0	0.4	-0.5	-0.0	2.2	2.8	1.4	2.5

General Industrial Machinery

The general industrial machinery industry includes the production of a variety of equipment and components that find their way into many segments of the U.S. economy. Industry volume expanded by 4% per year, on average, during the 1993–1998 period. We expect a modest 1.1% decline in volume this year as business investment in general industrial machinery and exports falter. Longer term, modest growth in domestic demand coupled with strong export potential will support volume growth of 2.5% per year through 2008.

Recent History

The general industrial machinery industry includes the production of a variety of equipment and components that find their way into many segments of the U.S. economy. Pumps and pumping equipment are utilized in the process industries, hydraulics, and construction. Ball and roller bearing production is tied largely to the automotive and capital goods markets. Air and gas compressors find their way into a multitude of industrial applications and are widely used at construction sites. Blowers and exhaust and ventilation fans are used in commercial buildings, industrial plants, and residential buildings. The demand for industrial patterns and process furnaces and ovens is heavily influenced by foundry activity, as well as other types of general manufacturing. General industrial sector activity also drives the demand for speed changers, industrial high-speed drives, gears, and mechanical power transmission equipment. Finally, the demand for non-food packaging machinery is influenced by manufacturing sector production levels and capital spending programs.

General industrial machinery did not emerge from the 1990–1991 recession until 1993 when real shipments rose 4.4% to $33.6 billion. Since then shipments increased by 5.2% in 1994, 5.0% in 1995, 2.8% in 1996, 5.2% in 1997, and a meager 1.5% in 1998. The rapid growth that was achieved during the period from 1993–1997 reflected strong gains in domestic capital spending and solid gains on the export front. The loss of momentum in 1998 was largely the result of weakness in export sales.

Domestic Demand

Business investment in general industrial machinery bottomed out at $17.72 billion in 1991. From 1992–1998, spending rose by 89.7%. In 1998, businesses spent $33.62 billion on general industrial machinery, 11% more than they did in 1997. After adjustment for inflation, spending for general industrial machinery totaled $30.21 billion last year, 66.4% more than they did back in 1991.

In addition to support from business capital investment, general industrial machinery has benefited from strong demand, particularly since the 1990–1991 recession, for light-motor vehicles, commercial trucks and trailers, farm and construction machinery, railroad equipment, and commercial aircraft. The strong expansion in construction and industrial activity since the last recession has also provided lift to various other components that fall under the banner of general industrial machinery.

Foreign Trade

U.S. exports of major types of general industrial machinery declined by 3.8% in 1998 to $13.3 billion, as the Asian flu took its toll on Asian and other economies. Exports of pumps for liquids declined 2.6% to $2.96 billion. Foreign sales of pumps (not for liquids), air or gas compressors and fans, ventilating hoods, centrifuges, and filtering apparatus dropped 8.1% to $6.36 billion. Overseas demand for ball or roller bearings edged off by only 0.9% to $982.9 million. Finally, exports of transmission shafts, bearing housings, shaft bearings, gears, gear boxes, ball screws, and clutches showed improvement, rising 4.3% to $2.99 billion.

U.S. imports of major types of general industrial machinery jumped 9.6% in 1998, as key domestic markets continued to do very well. Imports of pumps for liquids increased 7.8% to $2.42 billion. Sales of foreign-made pumps (not for liquids), air or gas compressors and fans, ventilating hoods, centrifuges, and filtering apparatus jumped 11.2% to $5.4 billion. U.S. demand for imported ball or roller bearings advanced by 4.8% to $1.57 million. Finally, imports of transmission shafts, bearing housings, shaft bearings, gears, gear boxes, ball screws, and clutches rose by 10.2% to $4.0 billion.

In these major types of general industrial machinery, the United States went from having a trade surplus of $1.59 billion in 1997 to a trade deficit of almost $100 million in 1998.

Employment

The general industrial machinery industry employed 236,380 workers in 1992, down from a pre-recession level of 247,250 workers. Employment didn't really improve until 1994 when it rose to 242,180 workers. Since that time the number of people employed by makers of general industrial machinery has increased every year, reaching 269,050 workers in 1998. Strong domestic demand and, up until 1998, growing exports provided the incentive to the producers of general industrial machinery to expand their workforce.

The pump and pumping equipment industry employed 27,030 workers in 1988. Employment hit 31,600 by 1990. The 1990–1991 recession had very little impact on employment in this industry. However, by 1995 employment had fallen to 29,470 workers. In recent years employment has expanded once again reaching 31,600 workers in 1998.

Producers of ball and roller bearings employed 43,040 people in 1989, prior to the last recession. Employment dropped steadily to 37,310 by 1993. Things began to look up after that with employment rising to 41,390 by 1998.

The air and gas compressor industry employed 22,920 workers in 1988. Five years later in 1993, employment reached 24,990 workers. In 1998, with construction sector activity humming, the air and gas compressor industry employed 26,310 workers.

Producers of blowers and fans employed 30,750 workers in 1988. Five years later in 1993, employment had risen to only 31,960 workers. The strong construction markets in subsequent years has triggered a rebound in industry activity pushing employment to 36,640 workers.

Manufacturers of speed changers, drives, gears, and other power transmission equipment employed 33,620 workers in 1998. Five years later in 1993 employment totaled only 34,480 workers. Strong demand for mechanical power transmission equipment has triggered an increase in employment since 1993. In 1998, the industry employed 40,110 workers.

Outlook 1999–2008

The demand for general industrial machinery has slowed in 1999. Business capital outlays for general industrial machinery is running below a year ago. Furthermore, exports are still reflecting the weakness in key Asian and Latin American markets and the strong U.S. dollar. Support is coming from the various components that fall under the banner of general industrial machinery. Production of capital equipment and commercial aircraft is expanding further. Light vehicle, medium and heavy truck, freight car, construction equipment, and commercial aircraft production are all running ahead of their 1998 pace. The one exception in all this is farm equipment, which is in the midst of a major correction. Residential construction has proved stronger than anticipated, and commercial and utility construction has more than held its own. This has more than offset weakness in industrial plant construction. Public construction has started to heat up as TEA-21 funded projects are now underway. When all is said and done, we expect shipments of general industrial machinery, in real terms, to slip by 1.1% in 1999.

Longer term, 2000–2008, we expect volume growth in general industrial machinery of 2.5% per year through 2008. Domestic and overseas demand for construction, mining, and material-handling equipment and farm machinery is put at about 2% per year on average. Production of motor vehicles and parts, including light and commercial vehicles, is slated to expand by 1.0%–1.5% per year. The current buying cycle in commercial aircraft will begin to wind down in 2000–2001, but we should see the early stages of another cycle begin around the middle of the next decade. This cycle will be driven by the capacity needs of specific traffic corridors and anticipated strong growth in the Asian and Latin American markets. We expect defense-related aerospace to gain ground in the years ahead and begin to accelerate through the middle of the next decade. Finally, rail equipment production will peak in 1999 and then retreat over the next two years. Thereafter, growth in traffic and replacement demand will support modest year-to-year increases in production.

Process industry output is likely to grow by roughly 2% per year on average through 2008. Oil and gas extraction will show little or no growth during the forecast period. Construction activity is likely to drift for a while, following a long period of strong expansion, and then show somewhat stronger growth. WEFA expects construction-sector volume to grow at a strong pace in 1999, with residential up 6.8%, public up 6.5%, and nonresidential up 4.9%. Longer term, 1998–2008, construction activity expands by roughly 2.5% per year. Residential and nonresidential construction is expected to grow 2% and 2.3% per year, respectively. Public construction grows 3% per year from now through

2004, and then slows to about 2% annually thereafter.

Exports of general industrial machinery will still feel the impact of the Asian crisis and the strong dollar in 1999. Longer term, the export market looks very promising. WEFA expects real world economic growth to average above 3% per year over the long term. Canada remains the largest single market for U.S.-produced general industrial machinery, and Canadian economic growth is likely to range between 2.5%–3.0% per year. Mexico will remain a fertile market. WEFA projects real growth in the Mexican economy of 4.5%–5.0% per year through 2008. Conditions in the rest of Latin America will improve, with GDP growth forecast at 4.0%–4.5% annually. The Japanese economy will limp along in the near term, but should eventually be able to establish a growth pace of 2% per year. China offers great opportunities, with annual economic growth expected to remain close to 7.0%–8.0% into the next decade. Opportunities will also eventually return at a fast pace in the rest of Asia. Finally, while economic growth in Western Europe will be modest, Eastern Europe is likely to stage a recovery during the coming decade.

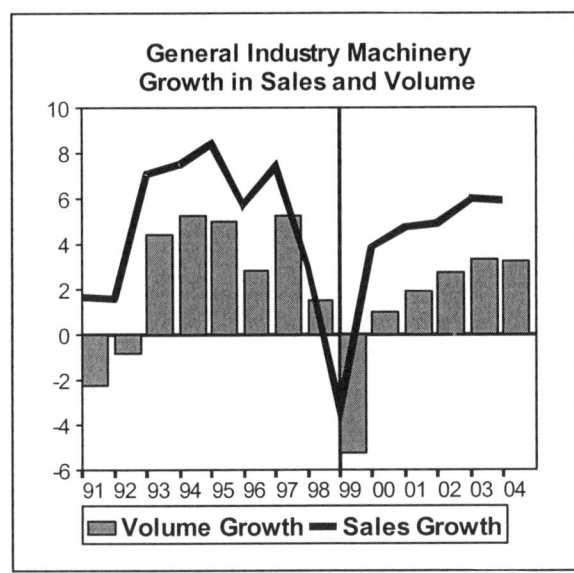

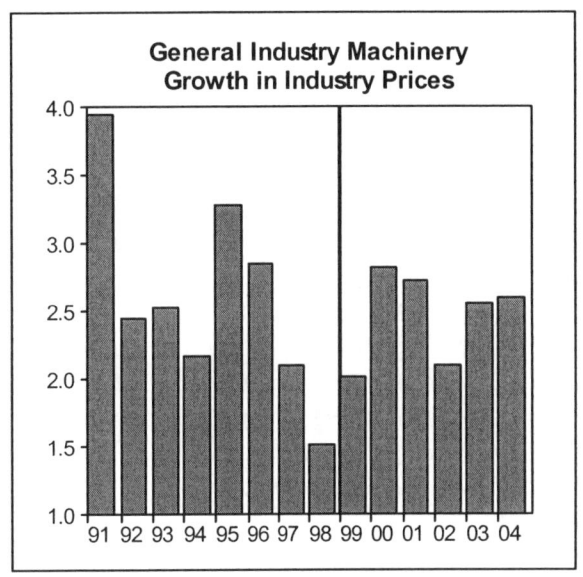

General Industry Machinery

SIC 356

		1992	1993	1994	1995	1996	1997	1998	1999	2000	2001	Compound Average 88-98	Annual Growth 98-08
Sales													
	Billions of $	31.41	33.63	36.16	39.21	41.47	44.56	45.92	44.39	46.12	48.30		
	% Ch	1.6	7.1	7.5	8.4	5.8	7.4	3.0	-3.3	3.9	4.7	5.4	4.7
Volume													
	% Ch	-0.8	4.4	5.2	5.0	2.8	5.2	1.5	-5.2	1.0	2.0	2.2	2.1
Prices													
	% Ch	2.4	2.5	2.2	3.3	2.8	2.1	1.5	2.0	2.8	2.7	3.1	2.6
Production Costs													
Avg. Hourly Earnings													
	$/hr	12.08	12.45	12.76	12.95	13.35	13.77	14.05	14.30	14.78	15.36		
	% Ch	2.9	3.1	2.5	1.5	3.1	3.1	2.0	1.7	3.4	3.9	2.9	3.7
Input Price Index													
	% Ch	0.4	1.4	2.3	4.0	-0.1	0.3	-0.5	-0.1	2.1	2.7	1.4	2.4

Refrigeration, Heating, and Service Industry Machinery

The demand for refrigeration, air conditioning, and heating equipment is tied to both consumer and business spending patterns. New-home building, additions and alterations, and replacement buying are the driving factors in the unitary air conditioner and residential heating market. Capital investment calls the tune in the commercial and industrial refrigeration and heating markets. Exports, particularly to Canada and Mexico, but increasingly also to the rest of Latin America and to Asia, round out the major markets for refrigeration, air conditioning, and heating equipment. Service industry machinery includes commercial laundry and dry cleaning equipment, vending machines, and equipment used by gas and service stations, restaurants, car washes, and commercial cleaning services. WEFA expects volume in refrigeration, air conditioning and heating equipment, and service industry machinery to grow by 4% in 1999 and about 3% per year over the next ten years.

Recent History

The demand for refrigeration, air conditioning, and heating equipment is tied to both consumer and business spending patterns. New-home building, additions and alterations, and replacement buying are the driving factors in the unitary air conditioner and residential heating market. Historically, replacement demand has accounted for about 50% of unitary air conditioner sales. Capital investment calls the tune in the commercial and industrial refrigeration and heating markets. Exports, particularly to Canada and Mexico, but increasingly also to the rest of Latin America and to Asia, round out the major markets for refrigeration, air conditioning, and heating equipment. Service industry machinery includes commercial laundry and dry cleaning equipment, vending machines, and equipment used by gas and service stations, restaurants, car washes, and commercial cleaning services.

The slump in home building, consumer spending, and business investment during the early 1990s triggered a drop in the sales volume of refrigeration, air conditioning, heating equipment, and service industry machinery of 7.7% in 1990 and 5.2% in 1991.

During the period from 1992 through 1998, real shipments rebounded by over 40%, culminating with a 5.3% increase last year.

- During this period housing starts rose by 60%, from 1.01 million units in 1991 to 1.62 million units in 1998. Nonresidential construction, including commercial and office building and industrial construction also staged an impressive comeback.

- The transportation market provided considerable support. Solid demand for meat, dairy, and food products, coupled with a strong replacement cycle, triggered a surge in demand for refrigeration units used in commercial trucks and truck trailers.

- The strength in new home construction and concern about drinking-water quality bolstered demand for household water filters and softeners and water purification equipment.

- Corporate downsizing and restructuring resulted in increased outsourcing of tasks that were previously handled in-house. This boosted activity and investment among business services firms, such as commercial cleaning services.

- Restaurant patronage increased at a solid pace as consumer income grew and consumer confidence reached record levels. This stimulated investment in commercial cooking, food warming, and dishwashing equipment.

- Gas and service stations benefited from favorable economic fundamentals that triggered steady growth in motor-fuel consumption and vehicle miles driven.

- Gains in personal income and the trend to more two-wage-earner households had a positive impact on consumer spending on services, which grew by 3% per year, in real terms.

Business investment in refrigeration, air conditioning, heating equipment, and service industry machinery grew by 35%, in real terms, during the 1992–1998 period. In addition, major export markets performed well, allowing export sales to gain ground through 1997. The Asian financial crisis, which spread to other countries in the world, including many in Latin America, began to take a toll on export sales during 1997, but hit hardest in 1998.

Employment

The number of workers engaged in the manufacture of refrigeration, air conditioning, and heating equipment hit a pre-recession peak of 132,230 in 1989. Over the next two years, employment fell 17,200 to 115,030 in 1991. Among producers of service industry machinery and equipment, employment peaked at 56,780 in 1989 and bottomed out at 54,450 in 1991.

The strong demand for new machinery and equipment in subsequent years required an almost equally robust expansion in employment. Among producers of refrigeration and heating equipment employment rose without interruption for five years reaching 142,760 workers in 1996. Over the following two years, employment retreated to 140,100 workers in 1997 and 137,570 workers in 1998, as companies increased their use of equipment and technology at the expense of labor. Among producers of service industry machinery, employment grew to 62,540 workers in 1995, faltered over the next two years to 61,550 workers in 1997, and then rose again to 62,450 workers in 1998.

Long-Term Outlook 1999–2008

WEFA expects volume in refrigeration, air conditioning and heating equipment, and service industry machinery to grow by 4% in 1999 and about 3% per year over the next ten years. Equipment prices, which have grown in the 1.5% range in recent years, will accelerate into the 2.5%–3.0% growth range in the years ahead. After a strong performance in 1999 domestic demand will grow modestly, with limited support from the residential, industrial, and commercial construction markets. Exports are still being hampered by the slump in Asian markets, which account for roughly 25% of overseas sales. However, over the long-term, exports are expected to in-

crease in importance, with Latin America holding out the most promise.

The U.S. market for refrigeration, air conditioning, and heating equipment will expand modestly through the next decade. Exports, particularly to Mexico, the other Latin American countries, and Asia will exhibit considerable strength.

- After a banner year in 1998 of 1.62 million units, housing starts will reach 1.63 million units in 1999. During the period from 2000–2008, housing starts average 1.41 million units per year.

- Consumer income growth reached 3.2% in 1998 and will range between 3.5%–4.0% in 1999 and 2000. Longer term income growth averages 2.5% per year.

- Growth in commercial construction is put at 7% in 1999, but it slows to about 1.0%-1.5% per year, on average, over the long pull. Industrial construction will decline by 7% in 1999, and then expand by 1.5% per year thereafter through 2008.

- Above-average economic growth in the warmer climate regions of the United States, such as California, the South, and the Southwest will have a favorable influence on air conditioning equipment used in residences, schools, office buildings, stores, and other buildings.

- The demand for refrigerated trucks and trailers is currently very strong. Over the long term, steady growth in the demand for fresh and frozen food items will allow the demand for this type of equipment to remain healthy.

- Foreign trade in food products requiring refrigeration will continue to support investment in refrigerated containers.

- Exports of refrigeration, air conditioning, and heating equipment will continue to increase in importance. The prospects for the Canadian economy are generally favorable, with growth of roughly 3% per year likely. Developing warm-weather regions, such as Latin America, Africa, and India, where new housing, industrial, and commercial construction projects will be expanding at a healthy clip, should also be sources of demand growth. Additional support will come as the economic recovery in Asia continues. Signs of economic prosperity and demand for this type of equipment are also expected to emerge in Eastern Europe.

The long–term outlook for service industry machinery is promising. WEFA's view of the overall economic climate suggests a continued focus on corporate cost-containment, and assumes that the two-wage-earner household remains the norm. This alone ensures that business and personal service sector activity will expand at a decent clip. In fact, real consumer spending on services is slated to expand by 2.5%–3.0% per year, on average, during the coming decade. Business services spending growth is put at 3.5%–4.0% per year. An aging population and expanding incomes will have a positive impact on restaurant patronage and related equipment. Additionally, WEFA anticipates stable markets for new-home construction and additions and alterations during this period, which, in conjunction with health concerns, will have a positive impact on the demand for water filters, softeners, and purification equipment.

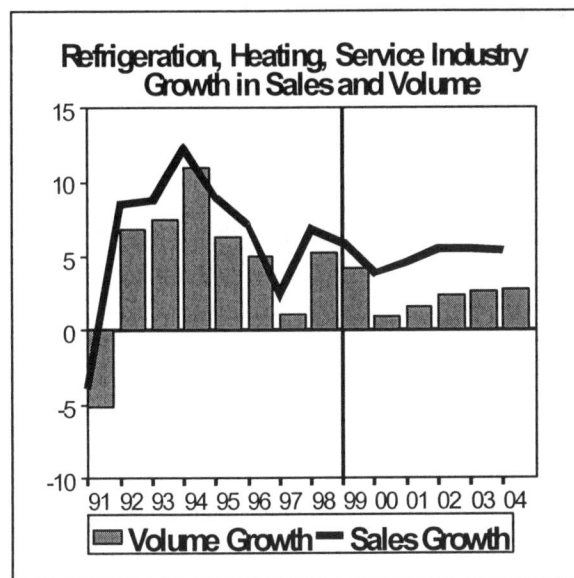

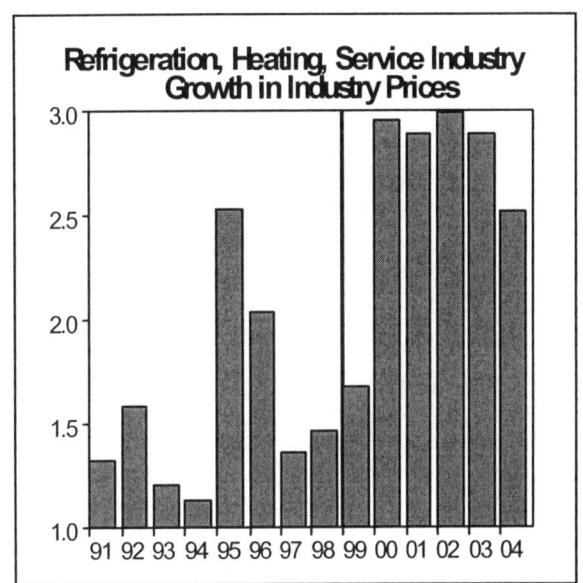

Refrigeration, Heating, and Service Industry Equipment
SIC 358

		1992	1993	1994	1995	1996	1997	1998	1999	2000	2001	Compound Average 88-98	Annual Growth 98-08
Sales													
	Billions of $	27.54	29.94	33.61	36.61	39.22	40.19	42.94	45.47	47.24	49.42		
	% Ch	0.5	8.7	12.3	8.9	7.1	2.5	6.8	5.9	3.9	4.6	5.3	5.7
Volume													
	% Ch	6.8	7.4	11.0	6.2	5.0	1.1	5.3	4.2	0.9	1.7	3.2	2.8
Prices													
	% Ch	1.6	1.2	1.1	2.5	2.0	1.4	1.5	1.7	3.0	2.9	2.0	2.8
Production Costs													
Avg. Hourly Earnings	$/hr	11.29	11.50	11.62	11.98	12.30	12.81	13.00	13.39	13.78	14.21		
	% Ch	1.4	1.9	1.0	3.1	2.7	4.1	1.5	3.0	2.9	3.1	2.2	3.3
Input Price Index	% Ch	0.2	1.3	2.4	4.3	-0.4	0.4	-0.8	-0.3	2.1	2.6	1.3	2.4

Industrial Machinery NEC

This catch-all category includes carburetors, pistons, piston rings and valves, amusement park machinery and equipment, and a whole host of miscellaneous machinery and equipment. Machine shop activity is also included in Industrial Machinery NEC. Machine shops are heavily influenced by activity and capital spending in the industrial machinery, motor vehicle, aerospace, and mobile off-highway equipment industries.

Recent History

During the last recession, real shipments of industrial machinery not elsewhere classified (NEC) held up fairly well, inching up by 0.3% in 1990 and declining by less than 2% in 1991. Employment stalled during 1990 and then fell by nearly 4% in 1991 to 308,050 workers.

Since emerging from the 1990–1991 recession, the demand for industrial machinery NEC has grown dramatically. Business investment in new equipment and the motor-vehicle industry and off-highway equipment markets, in particular, have done very well during the 1992–1998 period. The commercial-aircraft market has provided support since 1996. During the seven years from 1992–1998, the industrial machinery NEC industry recorded average-volume growth of nearly 8.5% per year. Double-digit gains were reported in 1994, +13.7%; 1995, +14.2%; and 1997, +10.1%.

Employment actually declined by 5% in 1992 to 293,280 workers. However, solid gains in key industry segments, particularly the recent rebound in commercial aircraft, brought the number of workers in the industrial machinery NEC industry to 381,920 by the end of 1998.

Forecast 1999–2008

Over the next two years, the Industrial Machinery NEC category will be influenced by conflicting developments. Business investment will expand at a slower pace in 1999 than it did in 1998, and will moderate further in 2000. 1999 will see gains in light- and commercial-vehicle production and commercial aircraft and construction machinery assembly, but farm-equipment production will drop sharply. In 2000, we expect a loss of momentum in light-vehicle production and declines in the commercial vehicle, construction, farm, and aircraft markets. Given our outlook for business investment, and the transportation and off-highway equipment markets, machine shop activity will be slowing over the near term. During this period, we would expect major retooling projects to wind down and metalworking industry activity to proceed moderately. In addition to developments on the domestic front, exports will remain anemic in 1999 and will provide very little support in 2000. Our current forecast has real shipments of industrial machinery NEC moving up by 1.9% in 1999 and 1.8% in 2000.

As the next decade begins to unfold, a replacement cycle in light and commercial vehicles emerges and growth in the mobile off-highway equipment and commercial-aircraft markets resume. This will bolster production of carburetors, pistons, piston rings, and valves. These markets will also have a positive impact on machine shop activity. Additional support will come as the auto industry continues to alter its product lines. Modest growth in business investment and a relatively healthy export market should also bolster demand for miscellaneous industrial machinery. On balance, real shipments are slated to expand by about 3.0% per year during the 2001–2008 period, reflecting our expectations for the general economy, motor vehicle and aerospace industry activity, business investment, and foreign trade prospects.

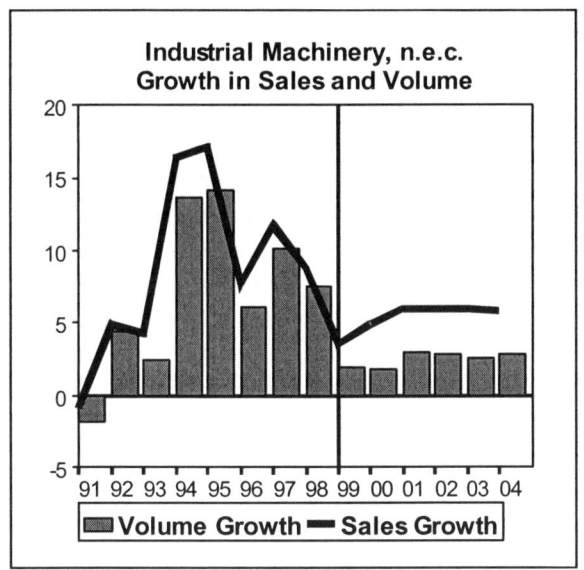

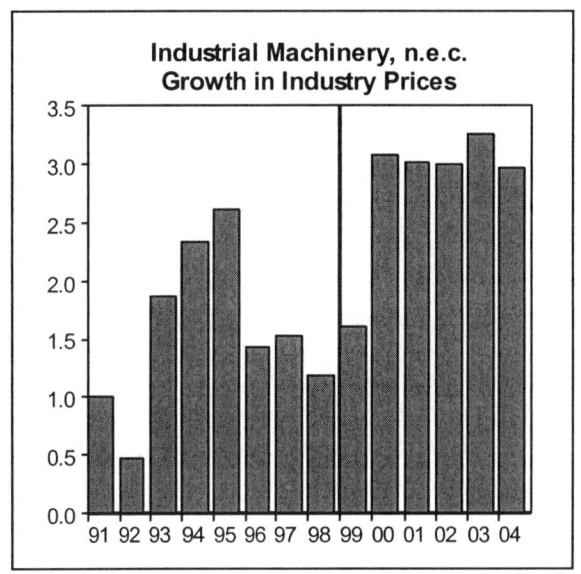

Industrial Machinery, n.e.c.

SIC 359

		1992	1993	1994	1995	1996	1997	1998	1999	2000	2001	Compound Average 88-98	Annual Growth 98-08
Sales													
	Billions of $	25.46	26.56	30.91	36.20	38.96	43.54	47.37	49.04	51.46	54.55		
	% Ch	4.9	4.3	16.4	17.1	7.6	11.7	8.8	3.5	4.9	6.0	7.9	5.6
Volume													
	% Ch	4.4	2.4	13.7	14.2	6.1	10.1	7.6	1.9	1.8	2.9	5.8	2.7
Prices													
	% Ch	0.5	1.9	2.3	2.6	1.4	1.5	1.2	1.6	3.1	3.0	2.0	2.8
Production Costs													
Avg. Hourly Earnings													
	$/hr	11.93	12.16	12.42	12.81	13.14	13.66	14.07	14.41	14.81	15.23		
	% Ch	1.0	2.0	2.1	3.1	2.6	4.0	3.1	2.4	2.8	2.8	2.5	2.9
Input Price Index													
	% Ch	0.6	1.2	2.8	4.7	0.1	1.1	-0.1	-0.0	2.2	2.8	1.6	2.4

Home Appliance Manufacturers

Household appliances include both major appliances such as stoves and refrigerators, and smaller items like vacuum cleaners and hot plates. The industry is subdivided into cooking equipment, refrigerators and freezers, laundry equipment, electric housewares (generally small electrical items such as blenders and can openers), vacuum cleaners, and other appliances, which includes water heaters, sewing machines, and garbage disposal units. The category does not include electronic and entertainment equipment such as televisions and computers.

In the last ten years, domestic sales of household appliances increased at an average annual rate of 3.9%. Over the same period, prices advanced by less than 1% per year, while input costs rose by about 2%, which put a damper on the industry's margins. Through 2008, sales will continue to increase at a rate close to 4% per year on average, but price increases will be more in line with input costs.

Demand

Fluctuations in the demand for appliances are closely related to fluctuations in housing demand. Appliance shipments therefore jumped in the early 1990s after the end of the recession. In fact, the rise in appliance shipments was faster than the modest housing recovery would have justified. This was caused by several factors, which include: the continued increase in sales of existing homes, which have been trending upward since the early 1980s; a rash of home-improvement projects in conjunction with refinancing that resulted from low mortgage rates; and pent-up demand caused by the recession. In 1995, appliance shipments declined about 4.5%, in both volume and dollar terms, in response to higher interest rates and their negative impact on the economy and the housing market in particular.

Since 1995, household appliance shipments have been on a roll, spurred by the booming housing market. For the period 1996–1998, volume grew at an annual average rate of more than 5%. The revival in new-home construction and growth in consumer income will allow appliance shipments to expand by 6% in 1999. With little support from the housing sector in 2000, and consumers already flush with new refrigerators, washers, dryers, and other appliances, household appliance demand will decline by about 1%. Longer term, housing starts will average about 1.41 million units per year, and real consumer disposable income is forecast to grow by roughly 2.5% per year. With this as a backdrop, WEFA expects appliance shipments to expand by close to 2% per year, on average, during the 2000–2008 period.

Major appliances dominate the industry's shipment value. Each of the main types of appliances accounts for roughly 15% to 20% of total shipments, with refrigerators and electric housewares on the higher end of that range and cooking appliances at the lower end. For the past several years, shipments have grown faster in the "other appliances" category for the overall industry, while shipments of electric housewares and fans have hardly grown at all. This is the result of technological change, which has allowed the price of these appliances to fall, as electromechanical controls are replaced by electronic controls, and foreign competition, which is greater in this area than in the traditional "white goods" such as refrigerators and laundry machines. Shipments of the "white goods" categories have grown at about the same rate as that of the overall industry over this period.

Shipments Are Not Dominated by One Type of Appliance

Refrigerators & Freezers	20%
Electric Housewares	21%
Laundry	16%
Cooking	15%
Other Appliances	18%

Supply and Industry Structure

Major household-appliance manufacturing is dominated by five large manufacturers. Each manufacturer may have several name brands, the result of past mergers and the desire to provide a broad spectrum of products. Major manufacturers are generally older, established companies, and there are few new entries into this industry. Several, such as GE and Amana, are divisions of large diversified manufacturing corporations.

Because it follows housing, home-appliance manufacturing is quite cyclical. Shipments typically drop at double-digit rates from year-ago levels during recessions, as demand declines in both the new-housing and the replacement markets. The 1990–1991 recession brought a combined drop of 11% in household-appliance volume.

Foreign Trade Issues

U.S. manufacturers specialize in certain portions of this industry. The United States tends to manufacture and export the so-called "white goods," which include refrigerators, freezers, and laundry machines. Imports are concentrated in electronic-type appliances, such as microwave ovens and smaller appliances. In aggregate, the value of imports and the value of exports are generally very close, so that overall the United States runs an approximate trade balance.

NAFTA presents a major trade challenge to U.S. appliance manufacturers. While "white goods" have traditionally seen little trade across borders due to differences in country electricity systems and housing construction conventions, they can clearly be as easily manufactured in Mexico as in the United States or Canada. With the proximity of Mexico to U.S. markets, the major manufacturers will almost certainly move some production there to take advantage of lower costs, resulting in lost production in the United States. On the other hand, high-end appliances (those that are larger and have more features) will continue to be produced in the United States, and NAFTA will likely result in a significant increase in the export market for these goods in the long run. On the whole, however, the United States is likely to see its trade position in this industry erode over time because of NAFTA.

Pricing

Appliance prices, like the prices of many goods, have risen very slowly over the past few years. Between 1988 and 1998, prices of household appliances rose an average of only 0.8% per year, while input costs increased an average of 1.3% per year. Appliance manufacturers responded by implementing cost cutting programs while maintaining shipment levels. Employment in the industry has thus grown more slowly than production, and wage increases have been generally kept under control.

Environmental Issues

Aside from normal environmental issues faced by all manufacturing firms, appliance manufacturers must deal with two special concerns:

- *Energy Use.* Both consumers and government regulators desire more efficient appliances. Over the past 20 years, the manufacturers have made important strides in improving the energy use of some appliances (notably refrigerators). U.S. manufacturers are world leaders in this area.

- *Refrigerants.* Until recently, chlorofluorocarbons (CFCs) were considered the ideal substance for refrigerants. Unfortunately, these substances contribute to the depletion of the ozone in the Earth's upper atmosphere. In 1990, the United States and many other countries signed the Montreal Protocol, which required countries to phase out the use of CFCs. The industry responded by developing refrigerators using hydrochlorofluorocarbons (HCFCs), but these are due to be phased out by 2030. The industry continues to sponsor research to find new non-chlorine refrigerants that meet the standards of the protocol. The new technology will likely add to costs, however, in an environment where consumers are clearly unwilling to pay more for appliances.

Outlook

The aging of the population and slow growth in the number of households will help to keep growth in the household-appliance industry at moderate levels. Production volume will rise at an annual average of about 1.5% to 2% per year, as the industry continues to experience severe competition from both imports and other consumer spending opportunities. Export growth will not remain as strong as in the past 10 years. Imports, however, will grow rapidly, as U.S. manufacturers take advantage of lower production costs in Mexico and as the heavily imported small electronic appliances grow more rapidly than the market overall.

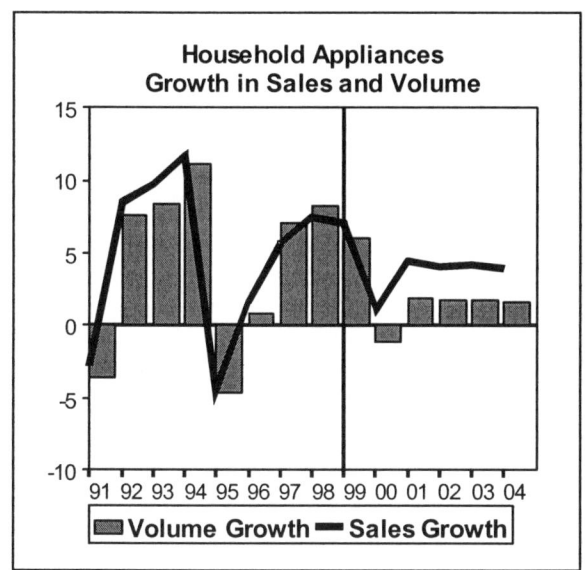

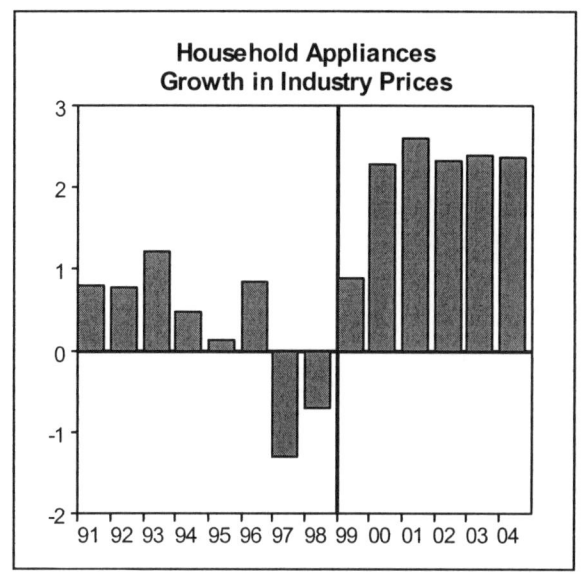

Household Appliances

SIC 363

		1992	1993	1994	1995	1996	1997	1998	1999	2000	2001	Compound Average 88-98	Annual Growth 98-08
Sales													
	Billions of $	18.61	20.42	22.81	21.78	22.15	23.41	25.16	26.92	27.22	28.45		
	% Ch	8.5	9.7	11.7	-4.5	1.7	5.7	7.5	7.0	1.1	4.5	3.9	4.2
Volume													
	% Ch	7.6	8.4	11.2	-4.6	0.8	7.1	8.2	6.1	-1.1	1.8	3.2	1.8
Prices													
	% Ch	0.8	1.2	0.5	0.1	0.9	-1.3	-0.7	0.9	2.3	2.6	0.7	2.3
Production Costs													
Avg. Hourly Earnings													
	$/hr	10.51	10.47	10.86	11.49	12.01	12.18	12.43	12.79	13.06	13.39		
	% Ch	1.2	-0.4	3.7	5.8	4.5	1.4	2.1	2.9	2.1	2.5	2.1	2.8
Input Price Index													
	% Ch	0.1	1.4	2.3	4.6	-0.3	0.3	-0.6	-0.7	1.9	2.5	1.3	2.2

Chapter 19: Computers and Electronic Equipment

Computers and Office Machines

The technology-driven computer and office machine industry has grown at a sprint since 1992, posting average sales growth of 11.6% per year. Volumes have exhibited frantic growth, due in great part to the large price declines that have become a steadfast feature of this industry. Volume growth last year of 63.3% far outstripped sales growth of 16.8%.

Shipments of new technology products remained quite brisk in 1999, as the move to ensure the hardware and software compatibility with the millennium induced many businesses and individuals to accelerate plans for purchases of compatible products. WEFA holds high expectations for both volume and shipments of computers and office machines over the next ten years.

Market Segments

The fastest growing subset of U.S. computer and office equipment in 1998 was the communication interfaces segment—fax modems, PCMCIA cards, and Ethernet cards. The industry's attention is focused on Internet access. This focus is driven by businesses and individuals alike. The Internet, used in this analysis to refer to both the text and graphics portions, has reached 147 million users worldwide in 1998. That figure from the Computer Industry Almanac is up from 61 million users in 1996, and is forecasted to grow exponentially. Sales of communication interfaces jumped by 9.8% in 1998. Performance was contained by the global effects of the Asian financial crisis last year. These 1998 results followed average increases of over 30% in the previous two years.

The central processing units (CPUs) and memory segment led the computer equipment sector in dollar value with production of nearly $68 billion in 1998. Consumers and computer manufacturers upgraded to chips with the increased performance required to keep up with new operating systems and software. U.S. producers' sales of CPUs targeted for personal computers and workstations added 4.8% in 1998. That pace marked an easing from the nearly 10% average in the two preceding years. The pace is likely to ease further in the next few years. Price drops will outweigh volume growth for desktop PCs; however, portable PCs—including laptop, notebook, and palmtop varieties—will be a stable support to CPU growth over the next several years. An emerging segment—Internet appliances or stripped-down PCs—has entered the market and is expected to nearly double in size on average each year. Through the long term, workstations and portable computers will be growth engines for the CPU and memory market.

The introduction of new chip technologies by Intel Corporation underlies the upward trend of the CPU and memory sector. Pentium III chips have been released at speeds of up to 600 megahertz. Multimedia chips, such as Intel's MMX technology, are in demand. Multimedia activities are improved by video compression and decompression, image manipulation, and encryption functions. Multimedia activities cut a wide swath of applications, including use in many software suites, advanced business media, communications, and Internet capabilities.

Not all segments of the computer industry were fortunate in 1998. Sales of storage products—add-on memory, disk drives, and mass storage drives—fell by 2.1% in 1998, due in large part to dropping prices.

The advent of new technology inevitably pushes out the old. Two product groups that are highly vulnerable to this phenomenon are large mainframes and minicomputers. The Achilles heel for these products is the server. Current technology enables servers to be lower priced, almost as powerful, and to run visual operating systems, which are more intuitive for many users. These features compare favorably against mainframes and minicomputers. Growth in the market for mainframes and minicomputers is shrinking.

Other types of U.S. office equipment experienced a better sales increase of 7.7% in 1998, compared to the performance of the generalized computer equipment sector. This compares favorably with the average of about 4.0% growth seen in the prior two years. Color copiers—the largest segment next to monochrome copiers—jumped by 26.6% in 1998. By comparison, although with sales almost twice as large, monochrome copiers gained only 2.7%. Businesses again took advantage of diminished price tags of color copiers. Prices have eased for the past two years, after many years outside a feasible range for many companies. Color copier prices should continue to abate.

The largest share of U.S. computer and office machine exports went to European Union (EU–15) countries in 1997. Asia and neighbors, Canada and Mexico, also took substantial shares. Asia was the largest regional source of imports, by far.

Outlook

Several factors combine to support ongoing growth in computers and office machines. Technical innovation and stiff global competition are prime grounds for continued lower prices in the market. Prices fell by close to 28% in the U.S. market for computers and office equipment in 1998. This followed nearly the same degree of decline in 1996 and 1997, and is expected to be repeated in 1999. Secondly, demand for business equipment remains on a fast track. Business investment in information processing equipment has posted distinguished growth since 1992. Real investment grew by 30% in 1998. In 1999, it is estimated to have captured nearly 25% growth, due in part to preparations for the Year 2000.

As a result, the pace of dollar spending on information processing equipment in the United States over the next five years will be trimmed to an average of around 10%. Trends toward telecommuting and toward home businesses will support continued growth. The proliferation of computer equipment necessary to set up off-worksite operations will fuel investment. Demand for scanners, printers, fax machines, copiers, and calculators, among other products, will be affected.

Business Investment —
Information Processing Equipment
($ Billions)

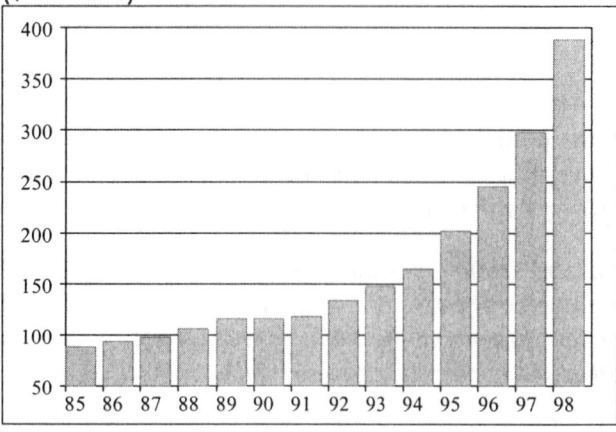

A third factor supporting a positive outlook for computers and office machines is the widening of the "information superhighway". Mass embracing of the Internet is well documented. The number of people worldwide who access the Internet from home or business at least once per week is expected to top 300 million by 2000. Online commerce is booming, as well. Sources put the number of Americans involved in online investing (buying or selling) at more than 4 million. Broader financial services, including loans and mortgages, other business to business sales, entertainment event ticket sales, books and music vending, sales of computer hardware and software, online automobile purchases, and online auctions are other online transactions occurring in dramatically increasing volumes. With estimates that upwards of one-third of American households access the Internet, and forecasts for this figure to soar, connectivity equipment will be a rapid growth sector.

Multimedia will retain its importance through the outlook. This functionality complements the Internet revolution: Music is sampled on the Internet and the increasingly popular gaming industry has users clamoring for higher definition action and speed. Meanwhile, video-conferencing is gaining more acceptance as a business application.

The largest area of growth potential may be the television and telephone market. In the next several years, it will become more difficult to distinguish television sets from computers. In fact, some experts question whether PC sales will overtake television sales in 2000. The low cost of computers and the popularity of the Internet argue for this hypothesis. Digital technology will infiltrate electronics into the long term, with HDTV as just one example. Plans to make digital television transmission (HDTV) the standard by 2006 have opened the door to a large market for computer monitor and computer hardware manufacturers. Digital-display telephones may become standard, as we move into the new millennium.

PC/TV/communication convergence is on the forecast horizon. Digital HDTV, picture telephony, satellite communications, and digital data transmission will stimulate demand for the next generation of PCs and peripherals. Picture-quality printing will also expand the reach of PCs into the multibillion-dollar photography market, while cable modems and dedicated phone lines compete for real-time applications.

Computer Equipment

The depressed Asian situation contributed to a bit slower growth in the U.S. computer equipment industry in 1998, compared with the rate to which the industry has become accustomed. In the preceding years, U.S. sales growth stayed in the double-digit range or close thereto. Acceleration was in the outlook in 1999, as companies ready themselves for 2000 and spent more on new equipment. Post-1999, spending for computers should grow between 6% and 7% per year for the next few years.

Computer costs have been declining for more than a decade. Even as a succession of more powerful products hit the market, prices continue to dive. The sub-$1,000 personal computer (PC) segment is dominating growth among personal computers. Then the "Nearly free PC" appeared. Internet service providers subsidize the purchase of PCs to consumers with certain agreements regarding the consumer's Internet service plan.

Computer Equipment Prices
(% Change, Annual Average Rate)

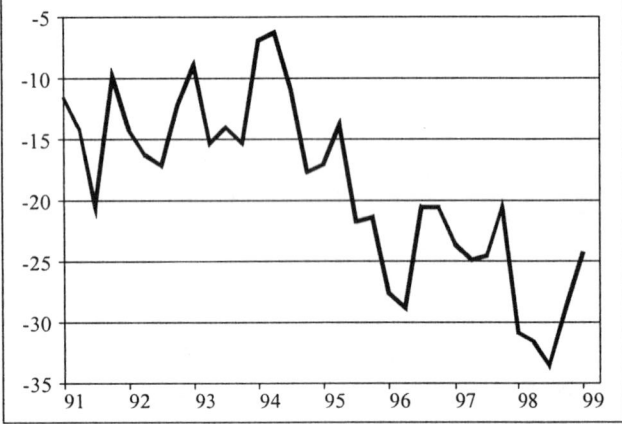

An equally steady stream of faster, more capable computer systems and software has accompanied the steady drop in computer prices. Worldwide, the PC industry grew by about 15% last year. Compaq remained the top seller. Workstations worldwide grew in shipment volume, but sales lapsed. New Pentium III chips are now available in speeds up to 600 megahertz. Portable computers— laptop, notebook, and palmtop varieties—are leading the charge in the race. The top-selling handheld device in 1998 was 3Com's PalmPilot.

By some estimates, there are now more than 129 million computers in use in the United States, and 364 million in the world in total. In the face of rapid technological obso-

lescence, many users will upgrade their system every three years. This fact creates a huge replacement market that will sustain PC sales.

PCs In Use — 1998

Rank	Country	PCs In Use, Millions
1.	United States	129.0
2.	Japan	32.80
3.	Germany	21.10
4.	United Kingdom	18.25
5.	France	15.35
6.	Canada	11.75
7.	Italy	10.55
8.	China	8.26
9.	Australia	7.68
10.	South Korea	6.65

Source: Computer Industry Almanac

The date protocol of many older models of hardware and older versions of software were not compatible with the turn of the millennium. As companies readied themselves for the Year 2000, many opted to accelerate the purchase of new equipment instead of investing resources to retrofit the old.

Domestic Consumption

Real business investment in information processing equipment has kept up a brisk pace—between 21% and 22% growth in each of the previous three years. Personal and public sector spending on computer equipment also carried a strong pace. Growth is expected to slow in 2000 as the Y2K bubble deflates and customers absorb the huge influx of new equipment they have purchased. Long-term momentum in the industry is guaranteed.

The surge in business spending for computers and related equipment was triggered by a combination of low-interest rates, lower prices, corporate profits, Y2K preparations, pressure to improve productivity, and advances in information technology. The climate of declining prices and technological improvement also influenced consumer spending for computers and related equipment.

Another double-digit price drop is in store for the computer industry this year. Computer prices will decline further, but we assume that declines will moderate somewhat throughout the forecast horizon. Several factors will continue to motivate computer purchases:

- One sure bet is that computer and software companies will continue to introduce new, more powerful products that will continue to energize the market.

- The consumer market will continue to embrace the sub-$1,000 PC market. As PC prices sink lower, computer and components makers will be forced into a new realm of price ceilings.

- Government revenues will be closely held, but pressure to enhance public sector productivity and efficiency will intensify. The result may boost public sector spending on information technology (IT) goods and computer equipment in particular.

- The education system increasingly incorporates computers into the curriculum to promote student computer literacy. Such reforms stimulate public sector and personal outlays for new equipment.

- More and more information is made available on the Internet every day. The number of Internet viewers worldwide was pegged at 147 million in 1998, up appreciably from 61 million in 1996. That number is expected to continue to grow furiously, as the Internet becomes an increasing sales media, business tool, focus of education, and entertainment medium.

- Corporate profits and consumer income growth will soften, but these sources of demand will remain in the market.

The factors that have driven the domestic market for computers over the past few years will continue to have a positive tilt and stimulate spending for new equipment. Domestic spending for computers should grow by between 6% and 7% per year for the next few years. Long-term growth is assured.

International Trade

The United States first recorded a trade deficit in computers and office machines—$2.9 billion—in 1992. Since then, the deficit has grown dramatically. The U.S. deficit in computers and office machines reached $20.9 billion in 1997. Imports of personal computers, for example, have been gaining in volume each year. These units are absorbed by U.S. domestic demand, but may also displace domestic production. Japan, Singapore, Taiwan, and South Korea continue to be primary overseas sources. Additional developing Asian countries are gaining share, as well. U.S. subsidiaries based abroad will increase significantly among providers.

**Volume of Imports — Personal Computers
(% Change, Year Ago)**

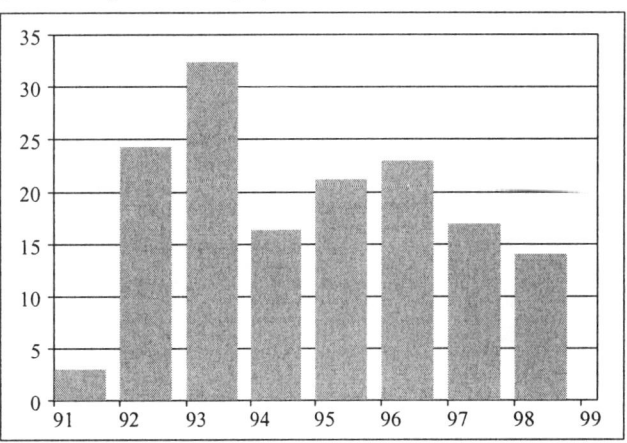

Major export markets for U.S. manufactured computer equipment include Canada, Japan, Western Europe, Asia, Mexico, and other Latin American countries.

Exports look to improve in 1999, along with economic recovery in Asia. Canada, Mexico, and Latin America, may provide sources for continued improvement in exports. The Internet bandwagon in Europe and Asia promises increased PC demand and export opportunity.

Imports will gain ground faster. Increasing amounts of U.S. production are moving abroad in order to gain comparative cost advantages. International Business Machines Corporation's (IBM) transfer of manufacturing to Acer Electronics of Taiwan is one example. This move may slow domestic production of PCs beginning in 2000 and 2001.

Storage Devices

Slow world demand combined with excess supply to produce sizable revenue declines in global sales of storage devices in 1998. Prices languished; sales of storage products in the United States slipped by 2.1%. However, shipment volumes exhibited strength in some segments. Price degradation explains the gap between dollar sales and shipments. Mass storage and optical disk drives, including CD-ROMs, were the bright spot. This segment grew by more than 40% last year. Domestic production is fading, however, as Singapore, Malaysia, and other Asian nations take a comparative advantage in storage production.

Optical Drives

The United States was once a leader in the manufacture of optical storage devices, but has since been displaced by Asian producers. Worldwide production by companies with U.S. ownership has a higher share, however.

Since their introduction to the computer market in the early 1990s, CD-ROM drives have not skipped a beat. Readable CD-ROM drives have accounted for the bulk of all optical storage device shipments, but writable drives are proliferating. As prices of writable drives fall, the read-only CD-ROM will fade. Newer, read-writable CD-ROMs (CD–RW) require newer multiread drives to read them.

DVD-ROM provides a jump in storage density; the capacity of a DVD-ROM is 750% that of a CD-ROM. This product is a growth source for the optical device segment. DVD-ROM can handle digital audio and video, and can play Digital Video Disk (DVD) movies. It is expected to become the next CD-ROM and primary digital movie medium, taking share from Video CDs, analog Laser-Discs, and eventually VHS tape. The outlook sees Original Equipment Manufacturers (OEMs) shifting into installations of this storage technology.

Removable Disks

Removable storage devices have provided another support for storage device shipments. Iomega Corporation's Zip drive takes credit for spurring demand for removable data storage devices. These devices let a user store up to 250 megabytes of information on a removable 3.5 inch disk. The Iomega Jaz drive can store up to 2 gigabytes and operates at speeds approaching many hard drives. The Zip and Jaz drives are primarily used for backup storage, but have everyday applications for various profes-

sions from finance to computer-aided design. Other storage devices—rigid disk cartridge drives and removable small optical drives—are also gaining in this sector. Portable optical drives designed to work with handheld electronic devices are being introduced. Uses include portable applications like digital cameras and personal digital assistants.

Rigid Disks

Rigid disk storage devices slackened last year; U.S. sales showed about a 28% drop. This performance echoes drops in each of the previous two years. Substitution of optical and removable drives is squeezing these shipments. Also, U.S. production has been vulnerable to migration abroad. Singapore is the world's largest producer of rigid disk drives, manufacturing approximately 40% of the world total. In 1998, the Singapore industry shed workers and output there fell by 2%, on a local currency basis. The outlook for U.S. shipments of rigid disk drives is for a gradual decline in sales, as this segment succumbs to the greater storage industry trend toward offshore production, and is supplanted in part by other storage media.

Mainframes and other large computers effectively use RAID (Refundant array of inexpensive drives—a group of standard rigid disk drives that work together as one drive. RAIDs are more economical than a single-disk drive with large hard disks.

Computer manufacturers continue to ship more units in response to burgeoning demand. This generation of PCs is shipped with a greater number and complexity of software packages—each of which can demand 100 megabytes of storage space. In addition, users are continuously upgrading both operating systems and software, which generates demand for greater storage capacity and a different mix of devices. The portable computer segment of personal computers will be the growth leader, fueling demand for portable storage options.

Computer equipment shipments leading up to 2000 should be particularly brisk, which will in turn drive the storage devices market.

Communication Equipment

Communication equipment roared out of the 1990–1991 recession with an increase in shipments of 12.6% to $42.8 billion. This was followed by a much more modest 5.7% increase in 1993. Over the next five years, 1994–1998, shipments of communication equipment really hit their stride with an average annual increase of nearly 14%. Strong support from domestic and overseas markets pushed shipments of communication equipment to $85.7 billion by 1998.

Over the next ten years, positive economic and market fundamentals in the United States, competition within the telecommunications industry, and ongoing efforts to upgrade and modernize voice and data communication systems will bolster domestic sales. U.S. exports will expand steadily, supported by solid economic growth overseas, the efforts of developed nations to follow the U.S. lead in voice and data communication, and developing nation investment programs aimed at establishing a modern communications infrastructure.

Background

Communication equipment can be divided into two major categories: telephone and telegraph apparatus, and radio and television broadcasting and communication equipment. Telephone and telegraph apparatus includes switching and transmission equipment, telephones, and fax machines. Radio and television broadcasting and communication equipment includes fixed and mobile radio systems, cellular radio telephones, radio transmitters, transceivers, receivers, fiber-optics equipment, satellite communication systems, television equipment, and studio audio and video equipment.

Communication equipment roared out of the 1990–1991 recession with an increase in shipments of 12.6% to $42.8 billion. This was followed by a much more modest 5.7% increase in 1993. Over the next five years, 1994-1998, shipments of communication equipment really hit their stride with an average annual increase of nearly 14%. Strong support from domestic and overseas markets pushed shipments of communication equipment to $85.7 billion by 1998.

Domestic Demand

Domestic spending for communication equipment grew at an average annual rate of 11% during the 1992–1998 period, with an increase in 1998 of 15%. This surge in spending occurred during a period of very little inflation in communication equipment, with prices rising only about 0.8% per year on average.

Business investment in communication equipment expanded by 14% per year, on average, from 1992–1998, with a 17% increase in 1998. Corporate America has made great strides in its efforts to expand and upgrade voice and data communication systems in order to improve operating efficiency and reduce costs. The explosion in spending for computers, the increased use of local and wide area networks, and very strong growth in business activity on the Internet have played no small role in all of this, and preparation for Year 2000 compliance has also likely caused extra spending. Growth in corporate profits and the rebound in new-office construction have bolstered spending for telephone network and on-premises equipment, such as phones, fax machines, voice mail systems, and modems. Finally, the use of commercial satellite communication has expanded dramatically during the past decade.

The communication industry itself has been taking advantage of new technology, strong demand for a widening array of services and deregulation, and is spending freely. Both local and long-distance telecommunications companies have been investing heavily in an effort to meet the current demands of their customers and in order to position themselves for the future. Broadcast and cable television companies have also been investing aggressively.

The progress in new-home construction since the last recession has had a positive impact on the demand for phone transmission systems and switches purchased by public- and private-service providers and private-branch exchanges. Second or third lines have been added in millions of households to link home computers to the Internet. In addition, the demand for telephones, including portables and cellular phones, paging systems, modems, and satellite TV dishes has gained ground, as consumer income expanded and the prices of new equipment became more attractive.

Department of Defense outlay for communication equipment averaged $4.6 billion annually from 1990–1992. However, spending retreated during the past six years as a result of major budget cuts. Shipments of military communication equipment exceeded $4.7 billion in 1992, but fell to less than $3 billion in 1998. On the other hand, non-defense federal, state, and local government purchases of communication equipment have been expanding, driven by a pressing need to upgrade communication systems, improved economic conditions that boosted government receipts, technological advances, and attractive equipment and systems prices.

Foreign Trade

Ten years ago, in 1988, exports of telecommunication equipment were valued at $6.3 billion. In 1998, exports were put at almost $25 billion. From 1989–1993 exports increased at an average annual rate of 22%. Over the past five years, 1994–1998 export growth "slowed" to only 17%. Western Europe, Canada, Japan, Mexico, and, in recent years, China are the major export markets for communication equipment. The economic slump in Japan, much of the rest of Asia, and parts of Latin America did take a toll on exports last year. After increasing by 18% in 1997 exports slowed to a crawl in 1998 increasing by only 4%.

Imports of telecommunication equipment, primarily from Japan, China, other Asian countries, and Canada, grew from $9.4 billion in 1988 to $17.1 billion in 1997. From 1989–1993, imports increased at an average annual rate of 4%. Over the past five years, 1994–1998, imports have expanded at an average annual rate of 10%. Foreign manufacturers have a commanding presence in the line and cordless phone, fax machine, and paging systems markets.

The United States had a trade surplus in telecommunication equipment of $9.2 billion in 1998. The last deficit year for the United States was 1990, when imports exceeded exports by $353 million. The United States is still in a deficit position in the customer premises equipment market (telephones, fax machines, etc.) but it is more than offset by a strong surplus in network, transmission, radio communication, broadcasting, and other communication equipment.

Employment

The communication equipment industry employed about 281,560 workers in 1998. The recent low point in employment came in 1992 when the industry employed 238,530 workers. The producers of telephone and telegraph apparatus employed 125,860 workers in 1997. Employment in this industry has been on the rise since 1995. The producers of other communication equipment industry employed 155,700 workers in 1998. Since 1992 employment has increased by almost 21%.

Forecast

It looks like 1999 will be another banner year for producers of communication equipment with shipments increasing 18.6% to $101.6 billion.

Over the next two years, WEFA is projecting growth in shipments of communication equipment of about 9% in 2000 and 6% in 2001. The demand for communication equipment slows over that period due to the absence of support from Y2K-related spending, a more modest pace of investment spending, a slowdown in residential construction following two very strong years, and a more subdued pace of consumer spending. Export sales, on the other hand, should be improving as key foreign markets continue to gain ground.

In the long term, industry sales will be favorably influenced by general economic conditions, growth in consumer income and corporate profits, and steady markets for new housing and commercial building. The pressure on U.S. businesses to improve productivity and efficiency, along with public-sector efforts to further improve voice and data communications systems, will lend additional support. The use of computers, LAN and WAN networks, the Internet, portable phones, fax machines, paging systems, voice mail, satellite communication systems, and related products will remain healthy in the coming decade, as consumers, businesses, and the public sector continue to embrace new technologies.

Commercial use of GPS (Global Positioning System) navigation systems has been rising and will continue to provide support during the forecast period. Over-the-road truckers, railroads, and the shipping industry have already turned to satellite communication systems that are used to pinpoint the location of equipment. This allows equipment owners to better monitor equipment utilization and more efficiently schedule traffic flows.

Stiff competition in the telecommunication industry will result in an interlocking of the various communication industries, including telephone services, cable television, and even information services. The goal is to put together packages of local and long-distance phone, data, and video services. To accomplish this end, it will be necessary for those industries to maintain a high level of capital investment.

The Defense Department and commercial aircraft markets will also provide some support. The big reductions in defense spending are behind us, and we are entering a period where spending will be rising not falling as the DOD looks to modernize ground, air, and naval forces. Spending for state-of-the-art communication equipment will be a big part of this effort.

Commercial-aircraft production is headed down for a few years after posting some very impressive gains during the 1997–1999 period. Longer term, 2002–2008,

we will see another commercial-transport buying cycle triggered by strong growth in passenger and cargo traffic and efforts to replace the older planes currently in service.

Growth in air traffic worldwide will certainly boost investment in air-traffic control and communication systems throughout the next decade. This will have a positive impact on the communication equipment industry. There is considerable concern about the quality of air-traffic control and communication systems in developing regions of the world, which are expected to experience the most dramatic gains in traffic. We also expect aggressive efforts to modernize these systems in traffic lanes that are currently well traveled and experiencing congestion.

Growth in communication-equipment exports will remain strong over the next decade. We anticipate steady growth from our traditional export markets, primarily developed countries, as they continue their efforts to expand and upgrade communication systems and adopt emerging technologies. However, the real support in the coming decade will be from China, Southeast Asia, India, Mexico, Latin America, Eastern Europe, and the former Soviet Union. These areas of the world have the greatest need to expand and upgrade existing communication capabilities or, in some cases, to establish a modern communication infrastructure from scratch.

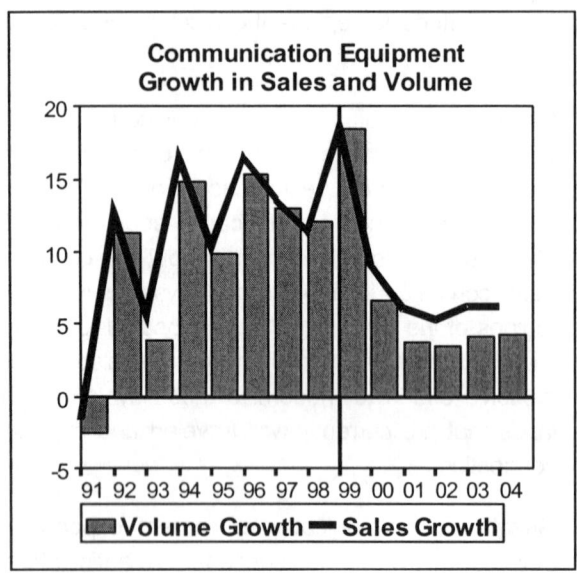

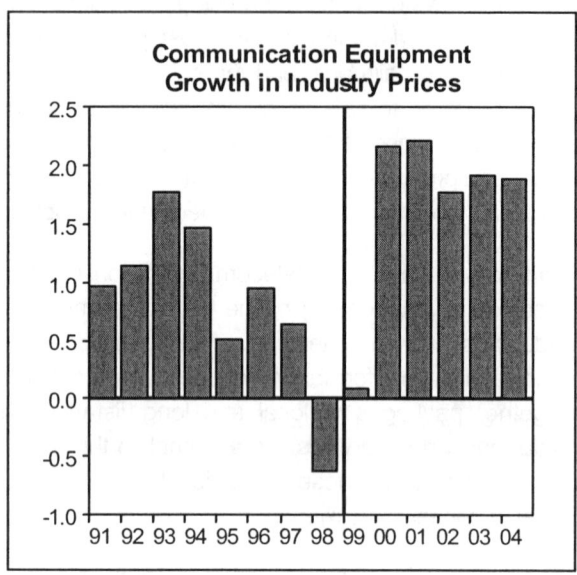

Communication Equipment

SIC 366

		1992	1993	1994	1995	1996	1997	1998	1999	2000	2001	Compound Average 88-98	Annual Growth 98-08
Sales													
	Billions of $	42.8	45.2	52.7	58.1	67.7	76.9	85.7	101.6	110.7	117.4		
	% Ch	12.6	5.7	16.5	10.4	16.5	13.6	11.4	18.6	8.9	6.0	9.1	7.8
Volume													
	% Ch	11.4	3.8	14.8	9.8	15.4	12.9	12.1	18.4	6.7	3.7	8.0	5.8
Prices													
	% Ch	1.1	1.8	1.5	0.5	0.9	0.6	-0.6	0.1	2.2	2.2	1.0	1.8
Production Costs													
Avg. Hourly Earnings													
	$/hr	11.47	11.75	12.25	12.03	12.87	13.87	14.02	14.36	14.86	15.32		
	% Ch	0.2	2.4	4.3	-1.8	7.0	7.8	1.1	2.4	3.5	3.1	2.6	3.0
Input Price Index													
	% Ch	-0.3	0.7	1.0	1.4	-1.9	-1.7	-1.3	-0.1	1.4	1.7	0.0	1.7

Electronic Components

Total sales by the U.S. electronic component industry rose to $154 billion in 1998, more than double the sales level of 1990. The 7.3% growth in sales in 1998 was slow compared with the pace of the previous year. The slackening of Asian demand, as a result of 1998's financial crisis there, hemmed in growth. Ramifications of the crisis—inexpensive imports and lackluster demand from other world regions—were felt throughout the global electronic components industry in 1998.

Single-digit growth is expected to persist in the U.S. industry this year, but momentum is gaining. In the long term, expect growth in the U.S. industry to plateau or gradually slow, as the industry matures and faces greater competition from sources in the rest of the world. Electronic components worldwide will flourish as they become part of a greater number of business and consumer products.

Electronic components are the fundamental building blocks for a broad range of electronic products. The term, electronic components, refers to a wide array of products—printed circuit boards, semiconductors and related devices, electron tubes and parts, capacitors, resistors, coils, transformers, connectors, and others. Components are integral to electronic products in many industries, but the largest sources of direct demand are the computer, telecommunications, instrumentation, medical equipment, and transportation markets.

Market Overview

Growth in the overall electronic components market dipped in 1998, as much of the world recoiled from the effects of the Asian crisis. The plunge in the value of the Asian currencies made for inexpensive imports into markets like the United States. Despite the negative impacts on demand and prices in 1998, U.S. electronic components managed to increase sales by 7.3%, a performance that many other industries might envy. The U.S. market had regained speed in 1997 after a pause in double-digit growth in 1996. Over-supply and price declines of semiconductors and other electronic products explain the 1996 slowdown. Over-capacity in some components manufacturing persists from the past two to three years. The overstock is still leveling prices. The U.S. electronic components market should experience a sales jump of 9.5% in 1999, but prices are expected to be off by nearly 2.0%.

Inventories have become difficult to gauge, which can exacerbate any industry cycle. The growing importance

of contract assembly and distribution functions is at issue. Contract manufacturers have become middlemen for an increasing number of computer equipment manufacturers, and are taking a greater role in stocking components. Distributors, too, are often forced to hold inventory at greater levels. Nonetheless, the total U.S. components industry is expected to turn in an improved performance in 1999, compared with 1998. Strong growth should extend into the beginning years of the next decade.

Electronic Components, Value of Inventory ($ Billions)

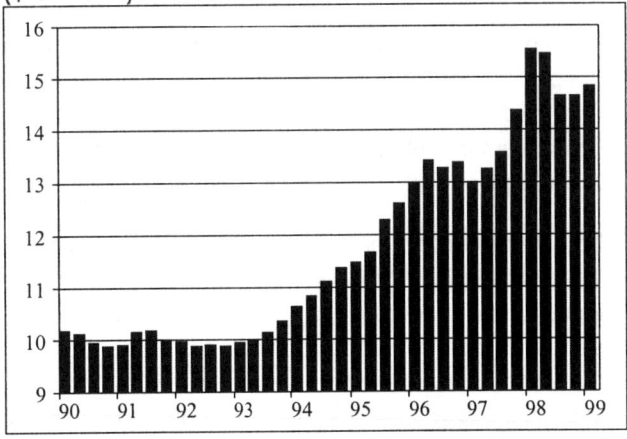

Component prices are taking longer than expected to firm. Prices lost more than 4% in the United States in 1997, 3% in 1998, and are forecast to remain weak in 1999. Dropping prices for PCs and other electronic technology flow upstream to contain component prices. Price competition from imports is another source of downward pressure. By 2000, demand should be better aligned with production levels, absorbing much of the over-capacity. Despite a better short-term balance between supply and demand, U.S. prices are likely to see little improvement.

The outlook for key end-use markets in the United States remains favorable. Persevering economic growth has translated into significant investment in efficiency–boosting equipment, and this progress looks to continue. Demand for computer equipment will continue its excited pace through 1999, and slow, but remain at double-digit rates, in 2000 and beyond. Moreover, the personal computer (PC) is a megaproduct in terms of growth and also as the centerpiece of productivity enhancement in the workplace. The PC is thriving in its consumer-entertainment and education roles, as well. In these roles, the PC is increasingly becoming a family focal point.

The U.S. trade deficit in electronic components averaged $2.8 billion from 1991 through 1997. The prospect in the near term is for a widening in the trade balance for the U.S. electronic components industry. The economic recovery in Japan and other large-scale Asian electronic component producers is beginning to weaken the U.S. dollar, but imports from those locations are still relatively inexpensive. For as long as this situation lingers, price–competitive imports can swing the U.S. trade balance in electronic components to the negative.

Developing economies are a highlight of the long-term industry outlook. Many developing countries have adopted plans to dramatically upgrade telecommunications and other technological infrastructures. Electronic component manufacturers will be the main beneficiaries of these plans during the next few years.

Long-term outlook for the U.S. electronic components industry includes a gradual movement to a more mature industry and moderating growth rates. Industry participants will face consistent demand for higher performance products. The increased complexity of miniaturized, high-performance systems places a premium on sophistication, compatibility, and functionality among components. For U.S. companies, the biggest challenge is how to benefit from productivity and technological advantages to maintain the leading role in the industry, when faced with intense international competition. Globally, the electronic components industry will thrive with burgeoning demand from developing countries and from technological improvements and upgrades in others.

International Competition

Growth in Europe is currently picking up. The improving exchange-rate situation will help to support the European electronic components industry. Spin-offs of state-owned enterprises and deregulation of the telecommunications industry across Europe are boosting demand for communication products, which are rich in electronic components.

The short-term outlook projects a continued economic recovery in Asia. The Japanese electronic component industry slumped along with the country's economy in 1997 and 1998. The bright spot was the export market. Planned reforms to the telecommunication sector were put on hold, as the country focused attention on its financial services sector. More deregulation is likely in the long term. Deregulation will bring a more competitive market environment and growth opportunities for the Japanese electronic component industry.

The slowdown in economic growth in Asia and the Pacific Basin intensified in 1998 as the financial crisis spread through the region. Previous to 1996, the countries of the Asia/Pacific region had registered economic-growth rates in excess of 7.0% for an extended succession of years. This region will remain a prime source for both supply of and demand for electronic components in the long run. Low production costs give the Asia/Pacific region a comparative advantage in the production of less-sophisticated products and increasingly higher tech products, rendering the region the major world supplier. Asia and the Pacific Basin are also large consumers of technically advanced products—target markets for U.S. electronic component manufacturing.

Trade Issues

The deadline for implementation of the World Trade Organization (WTO) Information Technology Agreement (ITA) tariff reduction mechanism is approaching. WTO countries agreed to the ITA in December 1996. The ITA provides for the removal of customs and other trade barriers among WTO member countries on a multitude of electronic component and other information technology products by the year 2000. For some developing countries and for some sensitive products, this deadline may be extended.

By 1999, the ITA had 48 participants. The group is a mix of both developed and developing countries and is a diverse geographical representation. The ITA countries account for more than 90% of world trade in IT products. With this majority, the ITA should level the playing field in the industry, and may promote the competitiveness of the U.S. electronic component industry in markets outside North America.

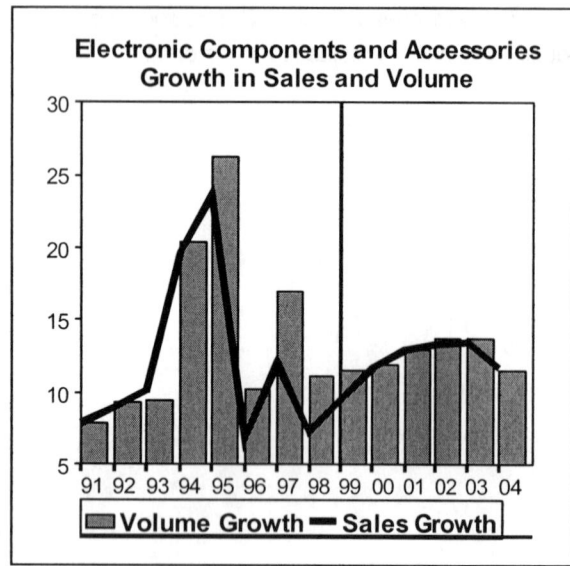

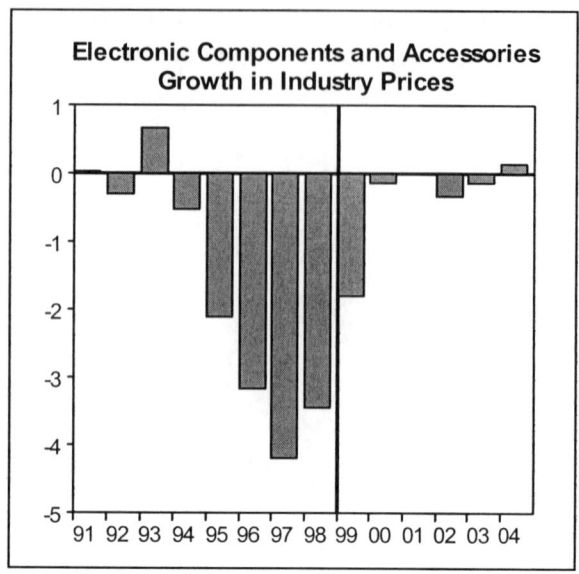

Electronic Components and Accessories

SIC 367

		1992	1993	1994	1995	1996	1997	1998	1999	2000	2001	Compound Average 88-98	Annual Growth 98-08
Sales													
	Billions of $	73.5	81.0	97.0	119.8	127.9	143.3	153.7	168.4	188.1	212.4		
	% Ch	9.0	10.2	19.7	23.6	6.7	12.1	7.3	9.5	11.7	12.9	10.3	10.1
Volume													
	% Ch	9.3	9.4	20.3	26.3	10.2	17.0	11.1	11.5	11.9	12.9	11.7	10.0
Prices													
	% Ch	-0.3	0.7	-0.5	-2.1	-3.2	-4.2	-3.4	-1.8	-0.1	0.0	-1.2	0.1
Production Costs													
Avg. Hourly Earnings													
	$/hr	10.89	11.20	11.28	11.49	12.02	12.52	13.26	13.82	14.51	15.20		
	% Ch	4.3	2.9	0.6	1.9	4.7	4.1	5.9	4.2	5.0	4.8	3.7	4.5
Input Price Index													
	% Ch	-0.1	0.6	1.6	3.8	-1.1	-0.3	-1.3	-0.3	1.6	2.0	0.7	1.9

Printed Circuit Boards

Under the cloud of the Asian debt crisis, the U.S. printed circuit board (PCB) industry showed an anemic 0.4% growth in 1998. Preparations for the Year 2000, the gradual economic recovery abroad, and currency stabilization in Asia combined to produce a more optimistic year in 1999. Growth in U.S. PCB production should methodically regain its former momentum to average approximately 7.0% growth per year in the short run.

Printed circuit boards (PCBs) provide the physical structure for mounting electronic components and the electrical interconnection between these components. Industry professionals often refer to printed wiring boards (PWBs) as the bare circuit board, but in this analysis we will use the term PCB to refer to the bare board. Printed circuit boards are used in a wide variety of telecommunications, automotive, aerospace, and specialty electronics applications.

PCBs are usually classified into two major categories — rigid boards and flexible boards—depending on the base material used.

PCB manufacturing has historically been an entrepreneurial business in the United States. Companies range in size from family-owned enterprises with under $1 million in sales to public companies, which generate $300 million in revenue. PCB manufacturers serve every facet of the electronics industry. Boards for industrial and environmental controls, for computer central processing units (CPUs), and for storage devices are examples. While the large companies dominate the business, small companies can be competitive by focusing on niche-customer markets.

Year 2000 readiness loomed large in 1999 for many small- and medium-sized U.S. companies that still needed to replace computers and other electronic equipment before year-end. This concern boosted demand for printed circuit boards throughout the year.

The U.S. Market

The U.S. PCB industry saw nearly 15.0% sales growth in the boom year 1995. An inventory correction and other factors tamed the pace to the high, single-digit range in 1996. Write-offs for plant start-ups and business consolidations detracted from 1996 earnings or resulted in losses in 1996 at many U.S. PCB makers. Domestic PCB production registered a good performance in 1997, but continued to fall short of consumption. 1998 results were marred by the South-East Asian financial crisis. Through its adverse impact on trade flows and prices, the Asian crisis squashed U.S. PCB production to only 0.4% growth in 1998. Slow global consumption of electronic components in 1998 also contributed. Rigid board shipments accounted for approximately 85% of total printed circuit boards, while flexible boards took about 15%.

1999 begins a return to a brighter outlook for U.S printed circuit board production. Growth at an average pace of 7.0% per year should prevail beyond this year. Global PCB shipments may see approximately 5.0% growth in 1999 and 7.0% in 2000.

At least one trend has remained a constant in U.S. PCB manufacturing over the past quarter century—original equipment manufacturers (OEMs) outsourcing PCB production. Outsourcing has been a critical business strategy. In the race to remain viable, OEMs increasingly focus on core-business competencies and enlist vendors for key intermediate goods. From an original equipment manufacturer's perspective, printed circuit boards are one such intermediate good. Merchant market producers have ample technological sophistication and usually can produce PCBs at lower prices than an OEM could in house. As a result, the share of OEMs that produce their own boards (captive production) dropped from 60% in 1979 to about 5% in 1998. Likewise, the percent of PCBs produced by independent manufacturers had grown to

95% by 1998. In that year alone, captive production dropped by more than one-quarter.

U.S. Rigid PCB Market in 1998

	Output, Billion Units	Growth Rate, %
Non–captive Prod	22.5	3.6
Captive Prod	1.3	-26.1
Total Prod	23.7	1.4
OEM Purchase	24.5	4.2
Consumption	25.3	5.6
Exports	1.3	3.4
Imports	3.5	12.9

Source: Electronic Outlook Corporation

Since all outsourcing growth opportunities have essentially been exhausted, the continued growth of the U.S. PCB market will rely on expansion of the scope and pace of the global electronics industry and on increased global competitiveness in capturing that business.

Computers and telecommunications are the largest end-users of total printed circuit boards in the United States. At nearly 50% of U.S. consumption, computer equipment is the largest end-market for PCBs. This industry saw a boost from preparations for the millennium, when all computer systems' dating mechanisms had to be compliant with a four-digit date year. For older equipment, this was often problematic; thus many business and individual users opted to accelerate replacement of equipment to occur before January 1, 2000.

The second largest demand market—communication hardware—will be the faster growing throughout the outlook, however. Deregulation and burgeoning international markets are good prospects for the communication industry. Wireless communications will particularly fuel demand for boards produced with microvia technology. A projected pickup in military search and navigation equipment and industrial instruments and controls should also contribute to PCB sales. As these markets are not the traditional targets of offshore PCB manufacturers,

new resurgence in these segments may bode well for U.S. domestic-PCB makers.

In addition to growth in existing demand markets, a new customer has entered the scene for U.S. PCB fabricators—the electronics manufacturing services industry (EMSI). Electronics manufacturing services (EMS) companies are contract assemblers of printed circuit boards. Electronics manufacturing services are taking over many of the traditional assembly functions formerly performed in house by OEMs. All manner and size of PCB manufacturers now sell to EMS providers. EMSI growth should be on the order of 20–30%, while PCB manufacturers will grow at a more subdued 5–10%. The growth differential between PCB fabrication and assembly will continue until assembly outsourcing is complete. The willingness of EMS participants to source within the United States bodes well for the domestic-PCB industry. Long-term supply contracts and customer partnerships will be a key tool for PCB makers.

There is an increasing degree of crossover functionality between PCB makers and the electronic manufacturing service industry. With the fast growth seen in EMS, some independent PCB manufacturers are beginning to add assembly operations. To a larger degree, contract assemblers are beginning to make their own boards.

International Markets

In most of the world, the PCB market in 1998 was flat with depressed currencies and prices, which offset any unit growth. When Asian currencies collapsed in value, the export market was one of the few bright spots from the perspective of Asian-PCB producers. A marketing rush on the United States resulted, and imports soared. The U.S. trade deficit in glass-based printed circuit boards, which make up a significant portion of total rigid circuit boards, rose to $361 million in 1998 on the back of both inexpensive imports and reduced export opportunities. This deficit is 4.0% greater than that reported in 1997. Notable exceptions to the global PCB doldrums of 1998 are build-up board technology in Japan and substantial expansion in Taiwan. As Asian currencies strengthen again, hope is renewed that the U.S. trade balance for PCBs will improve.

In 1998, Japan was the second largest world PCB producer, next to the United States. Production of multi–layer boards (MLBs) in Japan will be brisk in 1999. The MLB market is a growth hotspot in the global PCB market. In Japan, boards with five-to-nine layers are expected to jump particularly. Demand for cellular phones and personal computers (PCs) are major drivers of the Japanese-PCB industry.

Like other Asian countries, South Korea experienced depreciation of its currency against the U.S. dollar last year. Due to the depreciating Won, Korean PCB makers did not need to lower prices, and were able to see handsome growth in its exports of PCBs.

Taiwan has developed into a leader in electronics and PCBs in Asia, trailing only Japan in terms of quality and level of sophistication. Taiwan has a current competitive advantage: the country is self-sufficient with respect to material inputs. Taiwanese producers thereby gain a competitive edge over other Asian countries that must import PCB materials. Future plans of producers in Taiwan and Hong Kong include a focus on more detailed circuitry.

PCB production is beginning to trickle into mainland China. Three large Taiwanese manufacturers have recently opted to expand their operations in mainland China. Still in its infancy today, long-term prospects for the mainland Chinese electronics and printed circuit board industries are remarkable. The size of the domestic market, growth in domestic demand, and appeal to foreign investors will combine in the long term as the right recipe for the development of this Chinese industry. Mainland China will see a slow but steady climb from a manufacturing center for low-end consumer electronic goods to a producer of low-to-medium level products.

Mexico and Vietnam are emerging sites of printed circuit board production. Mexico is the world's largest producer of color televisions, which have PCB content. Location of PCB manufacturing in Mexico will displace some PCB imports to the color TV sector.

Industry Structure

OEMs have divested PCB businesses in favor of focusing on their core businesses—the design and marketing of computer products. The company now called Viasystems Incorporated was created when the investment firm Hicks, Muse, Tate & First Incorporated purchased Lucent Technologies' PCB business. That deal left International Business Machines Corporation (IBM) as the last major captive PCB maker. IBM sold its Austin, Texas PCB manufacturing facility to Multek Incorporated in 1997, however.

Mergers and acquisitions continue to change the landscape of the PCB market. Viasystems acquired Kalex, the PCB manufacturing division of Termbray Industries International Holdings Limited. This was the company's eighth major acquisition since its inception in 1996. In another example this year, Innovex Incorporated has purchased ADFlex Solutions Incorporated. That combined company will be the largest, flexible-circuit manufacturer in the United States, as well as in North America. This and other recent acquisitions have shrunk the pool of suppliers, and have left the industry more concentrated.

A shift in OEM priorities also has a presence in the PCB industry. OEMs formerly required PCB production in geographic proximity to their own facilities, but now prefer to deal with only a limited number of strong suppliers. PCB suppliers to OEMs will ideally offer a complete array of products and interconnect services, and do so globally. As the electronics industry spans the globe according to regional comparative advantages, this recommendation on the part of OEMs becomes more natural. To get to this ideal and to compete in the global marketplace, acquisition has been the route most often taken.

Price and technology may give an edge to large PCB manufacturers. However, due to the entrepreneurial character of the industry, small players still offer niche functions, including prototype services, design and testing, and industry-specific focuses. International competitive pressure will push more consolidation of the industry in the future.

Semiconductors and Related Devices

It took the semiconductor industry more than two years to break from the slump that began in 1996. During that period, capacity exceeded product demand and hammered prices. By comparison, the industry saw uninterrupted growth in the preceding ten years.

A recovery toward normal market conditions is just beginning to surface in 1999. The slow global economic recovery is taking the semiconductor industry along with it this year. Personal computers (PCs) and network communications equipment sales are strong and will drive the rebound in the semiconductor industry. New products will continue to expand semiconductor usage. A gradual return to the industry's traditional robust growth should follow.

Market Overview

The global semiconductor industry rang in another sorry year in 1998. That year's 8.4% decline marked the third successive year of poor results. Persistent excess capacity and a slow worldwide economic recovery will conspire to tame the industry's recovery. The 9.5% advance forecast for 1999 will be welcome by producers, but barely enough to cover the losses of 1998. Following that, the outlook forecast for 2000 and 2001 is optimistic, but growth will not duplicate the grand levels of past industry recoveries.

History

Through 1995, the global semiconductor industry saw ten years of uninterrupted prosperity. For more than a decade, the semiconductor industry grew by an average of 15% a year. An 8.8% decline in sales and plummeting prices in 1996 meant the first bad year for the industry since 1985. 1997 and 1998 lost even more ground. Excess manufacturing capacity and falling personal computer prices conspired to pull down semiconductor prices. Strong unit shipments helped to support the 1997 semiconductor market. In 1998, it was an inventory correction that combined with fundamentally weak global demand to kick support from the industry. Unit growth fell to a low of 5.0% in mid–1998. The value of total shipments of semiconductors in 1998 came in beneath the $144 billion delivered in 1995. The U.S. industry fared somewhat better last year. Revenues declined by only 0.4% according to an Electronic Outlook Corporation survey of 45 U.S.–based corporations. Asia's economic problems also intervened. The weaker Japanese Yen, South Korean Won, and other South-East Asian currencies diminished Asian demand for finished electronics goods and made imports relatively inexpensive.

Demand has firmed since last year. The three-month moving average of global semiconductor shipments finally crossed into the positive in March 1999. According to the Semiconductor Industry Association, worldwide semiconductor sales rose to $11.3 billion in May 1999, up nearly 12.0% from one year earlier. This performance was possible with support from the beginning stages of economic rebound in Asia.

As of March 1999, the three-month average growth rates in the major semiconductor product areas worldwide are ahead of their twelve-month counterparts. This indicates that market momentum is accelerating. The worldwide semiconductor market is recovering from its longest-lived downturn.

General Outlook

Growth this year in the worldwide semiconductor industry is expected to see a jump close to the double–digit range. The downturn of the past two years has created opportunity for a spurt of fast growth. Equipment demand is strong—both for computers and telecommunications. Early 1999 semiconductor orders are rising on a year–over–year basis, but comparison is based on the anemic performance of early 1998. Microprocessors, and some memory products too, will start on an accelerating pattern of growth this year.

Lingering supply-side bulges for some products, including DRAM (Dynamic random–access memory), will extend downward price pressure in the short term, however. The greatest amount of support for semiconductor growth this year will come from strong PC sales and sales of other devices used for Internet connectivity. Economic recovery in Asia is occurring, but methodically. The United States looks to be on par with the global market in 1999 with 9.8% growth, compared to worldwide shipment growth of 9.5%. On the whole, 1999 could be the first year of a cyclical upturn.

The global semiconductor industry is forecast to reach $156 billion in 2000. This assumes a reasonable semiconductor share in the cost of equipment production. By 2001, all regions — the Americas, West Europe, Japan, and "Rest of World" — will see satisfactory growth in semiconductors. The near-term growth of the Japanese semiconductor industry and the "Rest of World" industry will be buoyed by the appreciation of the Yen, in the case of Japan, and several Southeast Asian countries, in the case of the "Rest of World" category. If a sudden currency devaluation should occur in chip–producing countries, the orders that were previously booked at then high prices could turn out to be considerably less valuable in dollar terms. This constitutes a risk to the forecast.

Longer term, semiconductor activity will converge with the growth rate of electronic equipment, because of inherent limits to the semiconductor share of total equipment cost. There is increasingly little mobility to displace costs of passive components, assembly expenses, or other business expenses.

Grounds for optimism lie in the ever–increasing demand for newer, faster, and more powerful chips to enable leading technology. More versatile microprocessors, digital signal processors, systems–on–a–chip, advanced communications devices, new networking devices, and new consumer electronic appliances, like digital cameras, digital video disks (DVD), and hand–held computer equipment, are drivers of the new growth cycle. National Semiconductor recently unveiled the first in its family of processors termed "PC–on–a–chip". This first chip is targeted for TV set–top boxes and integrates digital video functions and major PC functions onto a single chip. The torrid pace of Internet usage is also driving demand.

Memory

The memory segment includes many sectors — DRAM, EDO RAM (Extended Data Out random access memory), VRAM (Video random access memory), SRAM (Static random access memory), SDRAM (Synchronous DRAM), ROM (read only memory), EPROM (Erasable, Programmable, read only memory), and flash memory.

Memory chips retain information for logic chips to use. For example, software applications in use and contents of documents currently open are stored on memory chips. DRAM is the type used most in computers, and comprises between 15% and 30% of the total semiconductors market. By far, DRAM is the most significant from the perspective of total worldwide revenue. However, EDO RAM is most often the RAM choice for Intel Corporation's prevalent Pentium–class PCs. Others vying for market share are VRAM, RAM optimized for video adapters, and SRAM, which is usually faster than DRAM but more expensive. SDRAM is designed to keep up with the speeds of fast processors. Compared to logic chips, memory chips require denser transistor layout and slightly more complex transistor structure.

Non–volatile memory, such as flash and EPROM, holds information in the absence of power supply. EPROM typically stores a computer's BIOS (basic input/output system) information, which is the fundamental layer of functions between a computer's operating system and its hardware. Flash memory is gaining ground in portable devices, including personal digital assistants (PDAs), consumer electronics — digital cameras and audio recorders — and test equipment. Flash memory is a good match for these applications for which its smaller capacity is adequate.

Over the past few years, reduced trade barriers, global fabricator expansions, new vendors, and over–capacity have significantly boosted competitiveness in the memory industry. The overall semiconductor industry at first benefited from the successful DRAM segment, then semiconductors suffered from the impacts of plunging DRAM prices in 1996–1997. Of all semiconductor products, DRAM saw the largest revenue drop last year. Heightened competition in the memory market persists, and prices and margins have continued to decline into 1999. The supply–demand gap has been closing, but aggressive facility expansion by Taiwanese manufacturers will assure there will not be a DRAM shortage. April 1999 saw prices rise for the overall memory segment, even amidst well–publicized DRAM price declines.

Some of the progress in the memory market is deceiving: a significant percentage is due to international monetary markets instead of fundamental progress in electronics. For example, South Korea and Japan are the number one and two DRAM-producing countries. Their currencies are appreciating now after the crisis of the past two years. When sales are measured in U.S. dollar terms, growth is in part a function of the fluctuating exchange rates and not a strengthening semiconductor market.

As supply and demand finally come into balance, 1999 through 2001 looks promising for an approach to historical DRAM 20–30% growth rates. Within DRAM, migration to higher capacity chips is taking place. This phenomenon will partially offset the general DRAM price decreases. With strong demand from DRAM end–markets, this product may again be in short supply by 2001.

Microprocessors

Microprocessors or logic chips compute problems, make decisions, or complete other actions. Compared to the memory chip, logic chips require more levels of metal wiring or interconnect. The current standard for a high performance chip is the Intel Corporation Pentium II chip.

Intel Corporation has dominated the microprocessor segment throughout most of the history of personal computers. The first processor in an International Business Machines Corporation (IBM) PC was Intel's 8088. That processor operated at 4.7 megahertz (MHz) and could handle eight bits of data at once. By comparison, the 80486, often called the 486, can operate at 133 MHz and handle 32 bits of data. Intel's microprocessors currently power the majority of the world's PCs. The most recent microprocessor from Intel is the Pentium III chip, offered at speeds of up to 600 MHz and able to handle 64 bits. Other Intel processors of the same family include the Pentium MMX, Pentium Pro, Celeron, and Xeon. Offerings from Advanced Micro Devices Incorporated (AMD) and other competitors are increasingly gaining market share against Intel, however.

The sub–$1,000 segment of the personal computer market is currently dominating growth, but is squeezing microprocessor prices. This important PC market has been particularly susceptible to AMD market share gains. In January 1999, according to PC Data, the AMD–K6 family of desktop PC processors outsold all Intel–based desktop PCs in the U.S. retail market for the first time.

Greater performance requirements will force microprocessors ahead of DRAMs as the largest semiconductor segment over the next ten years, however. High performance requirements push most users to upgrade their computer equipment in less than three years, fueling demand for microprocessors. The explosion of interest in Internet access and the increasing complexity of servers that host this function ensure that the server segment will also grow as a microprocessors consumer in the long term.

Demand Situation

PC manufacturers continue to call for new and faster microprocessors, DRAMs, and other semiconductor products. Through 1999, the computer equipment market experienced extremely fast growth, as some businesses and consumers accelerated purchases of new computers to replace old technology in anticipation of the Year 2000. January 1, 2000 was the date by which computer-dating systems must be reprogrammed for the new millennium year. Post–1999, PCs are expected to proceed with steady growth, which bodes well for semiconductor devices.

- Faster speed and higher performance will continue to be required of PCs, as they assume the role of core equipment for the multimedia era. The arenas of computer–aided design and database development, along with hungry Internet users will clamor for more video, audio, and graphics sophistication in applications.

- The explosion in Internet usage and of mass electronic commerce will underscore long-run semiconductor growth.

- Telecommunications is a surging consumer of memory. As wireless communication continues to expand, a drop in price and increased usage will follow. This will particularly push demand for flash memory.

- Another formidable buyer of semiconductor devices will be the portable-computing sector. As PDAs and personal electronics goods for entertainment, featuring digital cameras, grow in popularity, semiconductor development will be stimulated.

- Demand will be geographically spotty in the short term. Asia is strengthening, but European demand is somewhat fragile.

- Longer term, automotive electronics, personal computers, consumer electronics, and communications equipment will drive the semiconductor industry.

Such demands will be enabled by an evolution of semiconductor technology. For example, early in 1999, IBM announced technology for creating complete electronic systems, including logic and memory, on a single chip. In addition, semiconductors are being included in more products, advancing well beyond their initial inroads in automobiles, consumer electronics, and household appliances. Network PCs, digital video disk (DVD) systems, mobile telephones, PDAs, TV set–top boxes, and other emerging applications will add to demand for semiconductors in the future.

Abroad, developing economies represent a large potential market for semiconductor devices. Attendant to the development process, investments will be made in communication and information infrastructures. Both areas are rich in semiconductor content. This potential is truly an opportunity of large dimensions. The bastions of the semiconductor market as a whole will continue to be the tremendous growth in its end–markets and rapid technological change.

Supply and Investment

As a result of the integration of the world semiconductor markets, business success requires a strategy of global vision and investment on a global scale. Semiconductor companies are one of the topmost cutting edge industries in the United States. As such, semiconductor companies in the United States and the rest of the world are well aware of the importance of investment in capacity additions in anticipation of future growth opportunities. Although the industry may be overbuilt in some sectors, all capacity is not the same. Most production facilities are highly specialized and geared to build very specific products. Some facilities currently in operation in the United States are not able to produce the complex chips that are expected to dominate future demand. Although spending for DRAM capacity may have been excessive in recent years, the same cannot be said for capital outlays on cutting–edge logic products — microprocessors, multimedia chips, digital signal processors, and ASICs (Application specific integrated circuits).

During 1999, new 0.18 micron chip manufacturing technology will begin to be used. This will enable the manufacture of its 600 MHz and faster chips. Currently, a 0.25 micron process is in use for chips as fast as 450 MHz.

Capacity in such low sub-micron ranges will have a better likelihood of being in short supply. Large micron ranges capacity, for example in the 0.8 micron and greater range, is likely to be in excess supply.

Capacity expansion and product mix management become keys to remaining competitive in the global semiconductor industry. To maximize their flexibility to react to changing market conditions, semiconductor makers often choose to make additions or upgrades, purchase existing facilities, and/or build new constructions. The southeastern United States and Europe are two of the geographies that are actively wooing semiconductor manufacturers. U.S. manufacturers often find offshore locations that have comparative advantages – lower labor, raw materials, or other costs. National Semiconductor plans to exit the personal computer microprocessor business, however, by selling its loss–making Cyrix unit to Taiwanese manufacturer Via Technologies.

In the long run, supply is expected to play catch–up with voracious demand. Without the overbuilt situation, and in the face of a gradually depreciating dollar, the industry can expect a greater degree of price stability in 1999 and during the next few years. There may actually be a medium–term problem with shortages of memory if players do not plan new capacity additions now. The problem becomes complex when one considers that Asian producers may have difficulty accessing financing for large–scale projects in the wake of the financial market crisis there. New fabrication facilities typically carry a price tag of several hundred million dollars each.

Global Market

The semiconductor industry is soundly a global industry. Calculated at fluctuating foreign exchange rates, worldwide shipments showed a three-month-moving-average growth rate in April 1999, compared with the prior year. When calculated at fixed exchange rates, that growth slipped to 3.6%. The difference is the bonus attributable to the appreciation of the Asian currencies, notably the South Korean Won and the Taiwanese Dollar. In 1998 the European semiconductor industry was the only market to post positive growth in shipments, and correspondingly Europe is the market not to report significant resurgence in 1999 to date. Japan is the strongest this year, sporting growth of 10.7% in April 1999. But this industry is digging its way out of a deep hole.

Global Semiconductor Sales

	Sales, $ Billions	Growth Rate, %
1980	13.1	27.2
1985	22.1	16.8
1990	50.5	1.6
1995	144.4	41.7
1997	137.2	4.0
1998 F	125.6	-8.4
1999 F	137.5	9.5
2000 F	156.0	13.4
2001 F	183.3	17.5
2002 F	222.6	21.5

Source: Electronic Outlook Corporation, World Semiconductor Trade Statistics

The Americas market looks to consume nearly one–third of worldwide semiconductors. The Asia-Pacific region, defined here as Singapore, Korea, China, Taiwan, and India, looks to be the second largest consumer, followed by Europe and Japan. Over the short term, these rankings look to solidify.

Semiconductor Equipment

The organization, Semiconductor Equipment and Materials International (SEMI), reports that North American semiconductor equipment orders are again on the rise. This is heartening news after the trough experienced over the past three years by semiconductor equipment makers. July 1999 showed a book–to–bill ratio of 1.11. This encapsulates the relationship between the dollar amount of orders received and the dollar amount of equipment shipped, on a three month moving average basis.

The book–to–bill ratio of July 1999 means $111 worth of orders was received for each $100 worth of products shipped. The gain in orders relative to shipments signals that the bottom of the trough for the semiconductor industry has likely been reached. This coincides with April 1999 data that world semiconductor orders were growing smartly at 26.8% on a three-month moving average basis. Integrated circuit makers, especially in Korea and Taiwan, are beginning to place equipment orders, and more are forecasted as company revenues improve.

Passive Components

Volume growth of passive components weakened in 1998 in the United States and in Europe and contracted abruptly in Asia. Component prices sagged as a result of the demand situation, sharp currency devaluations, excess production capacity, and a host of other factors.

Some of the same factors again faced the industry in 1999. Lingering impacts from the Asian crisis and risk to economic growth in Europe supported continued buyer-market conditions. The worldwide electronics industry gradually strengthened in 1999, helped by preparations for the Year 2000. Growth at a modest, healthy pace should follow for the next few years. The rising importance of contract subassembly manufacturers and the increasing migration of passive component production to low-cost sites are trends that will underscore the future of the U.S. passive components industry.

Broad Passive Components Market

The term passive components refers to connectors, capacitors, resistors, relays, switches, coils, transformers, and piezoelectric devices. In the current landscape of price degradation, the United States is increasingly squeezed by lower cost producers offshore, and domestic original equipment manufacturers (OEMs) are increasingly contracting out subassembly.

The Electronic Outlook Corporation estimates U.S. passive-component production at $12.9 billion in 1998, a small dip from 1997. U.S. passive-component grew 10.2% in 1997. Prices dropped sharply in 1998 on inventory correction, weak OEM demand worldwide, and lower currencies against the U.S. dollar, particularly in Asia. Like semiconductor manufacturing, 1998 saw sharp price attrition in passive components—double-digit declines in some products—which hit revenues and bottom lines.

Passive components will have a role in the ramp-up to the Year 2000, as well. Stepped-up demand for computer equipment will fuel passive components upstream, while OEMs, contract manufacturers, and distributors will boost demand with their plans to hold greater inventories of components.

Prices

Component prices in general terms took a steep drop in 1997, and have remained in the doldrums since then.

The currency devaluations of 1998 have lingering effects on the U.S. passive components. Prices are generally ex-pected to remain suppressed in the near term. Supply is adequate, and imports are priced very competitively. Japan, Taiwan, and Mexico were the top sources of imports of passive components into the United States in 1997. The Asian countries of China, Singapore, South Korea, and Malaysia made up the four next largest. The strong U.S. dollar exchange rate against the currencies of these importers made imports attractively low priced, although moderate depreciation of the dollar is in the forecast.

In addition, OEM demand worldwide was weak. With gradual recovery progressing for many countries, future prospects are favorable. Meanwhile, raw-material prices are deflated and efficiencies of scale are prompting consolidation and further expansion into global markets. These factors reinforce the downward pressure on component prices. Additional price-cutting is allowed by a pause in research and development and capital equipment investment.

Contract subassembly manufacturing continues to grow in importance as an option for OEMs. The large purchase volumes of contract manufacturers and distributors command lower piece prices, which also produce a squeeze on pricing and profits.

This pricing climate existed in 1998 and looks to moderate only slightly in 1999. Low pricing is a boon to buyers, but will prompt producers to accelerate migration of manufacturing from the United States to offshore locations. Mexico is among the top alternatives. The increasing shift to offshore assembly marks a major trend for U.S. passive components.

Value of U.S. Passive Components Production (% Change, Year Ago)

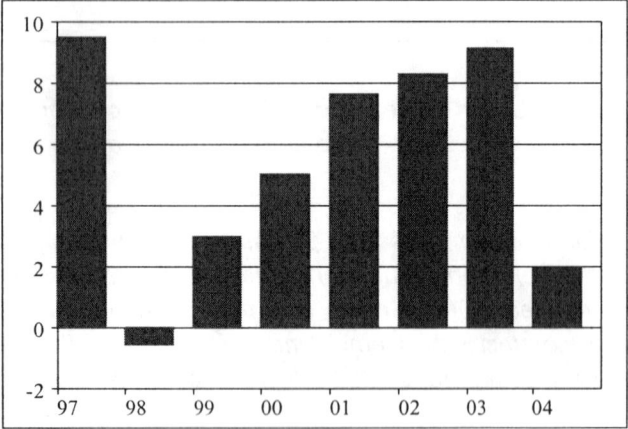

Source: Electronic Outlook Corporation

Inventory Management

Changes in inventory management are also ongoing in the passive components industry. There is evidence that OEMs have shifted their inventories to below historical trends. Downstream, finished-goods distributors are forced to hold more inventory, and upstream, contract subassembly increasingly fills the void. Trade data demonstrate the significance of equipment contract subassembly: passive-component exports have soared, while subassembly imports have grown substantially. The U.S. passive-component industry will be adversely affected by the increasing share of subassembly manufacturing that is permanently migrating overseas to low labor-cost sites.

Passive-component sales saw a short-term boost from preparations for the Year 2000 computer problem. OEMs and subassembly manufacturers held more inventory of components to prevent a would-be production glitch if passive-component suppliers are unable to deliver in early 2000. In many cases, consumers and businesses prepared for Y2K by accelerating purchases of new computer equipment and other electronics before the millennium.

Compared to the United States, Year 2000 preparations were not as complete in some other countries vital to the world passive-component supply chain. Most OEMs were aware of this status and took preventative measures to build inventories and contingency plans in case key supplies were disrupted. The timing of this process coincided with worldwide supplies entering a tighter phase and demand entering an expansionary mode. The result has been a likely three- to six-month inventory cycle with implications for orders, lead times, and prices. One complication is that December 31, 1999 played an artificial role of synchronizing the players: most buyers simultaneously increased inventories in 1999Q4 and reduced them in 2000Q1. The total number of players acting "in unison" has mobilized additional demand, but also agitated short-term conditions.

Communications equipment will replace computer equipment as the engine of growth for passive-component demand through the next few years. The outlook for U.S. passive components will strengthen over time.

Connectors

Connectors create the electrical junctions or interconnections in virtually all electronic products. They comprise the second-largest U.S. passive-component market behind printed circuit boards (PCBs).

Inventory-driven cyclicality was behind the mid-1990s heyday for the U.S. connectors industry. The industry has been sensitive to the flood of telecommunications-related activity and the relentless personal computer (PC) boom. Total U.S. production of connectors is estimated at close to $7.0 billion in 1998, a 1.8% drop over 1997. However, lower prices prevailed last year, especially because a strong U.S. dollar made foreign imports inexpensive.

U.S. Connectors Market in 1998

	Output, Billion Units	Growth Rate, %
Non-captive Prod	113.4	6.1
Captive Prod	3.1	-2.4
Total Prod	116.5	5.9
OEM Purchases	113.7	6.0
OEM Consumption	116.9	7.5
Exports	22.4	2.6
Imports	23.1	2.4

Source: Electronic Outlook Corporation

The major U.S. end-markets for connectors in 1998 were computer equipment (47%), communications (26%), electrical equipment (11%), industrial electronics/instruments (8%), military electronics (2%), and consumer electronics (2%). Connector end-markets are expected to sustain average to better-than-average growth. PCs and communications will remain driving forces, with Y2K accelerating computer demand in 1999. Communications products are expected to see explosive growth from worldwide telecommunication deregulation, privatization, and the wireless communications boom. PCs, among computer equipment, are expected to flourish. Government spending may also stimulate military electronics. Industrial/instrumentation will trail among connector end-markets in the short term.

Inventories at OEMs are low, but are high at distributors and contract manufacturers. The U.S. connectors industry will be less susceptible than other types of passive components to the inventory cycle, and the near-term cycle is expected to be relatively mild.

U.S. domestic connector producers are facing increasing competitive pressures not only from foreign manufacturers, but also the offshore operations of U.S.-owned corporations. To stay competitive, companies attempt to contain costs by designing more cost-effective products and by leveraging global resources. One result is the transfer of production, including contract subassembly, to Mexico, China, and other low-cost regions. Migration is ongoing and is accelerating, and the still strong U.S. dollar can only hasten the process. Companies are exploring alternative materials. The squeeze on profit margins produced by suppressed component prices places greater importance on such cost-saving research efforts.

Another issue confronting the connectors industry is the OEMs search for one-stop shopping. OEMs seek the minimum number of suppliers possible. In response, the connectors industry is moving to broader-based product lines. To accomplish this goal, affiliations, mergers, and acquisitions are becoming more frequent.

Capacitors

Capacitors are used for filtering, tuning, coupling, isolating, and storing electrical energy. Primary end-markets for capacitors last year were computer equipment (39%), communications (23%), consumer electronics (23%), instruments (6%), and business/retail/education (5%).

Capacitors experienced their heyday in the mid-1990s as well. OEM demand was strong. Prices shot up in response to tight supply conditions. Several end-markets grew rapidly—PCs, telecommunications, and local area networks (LANs).

However, in 1996 new capacitor orders crashed. World OEM demand was weak due to overstocked inventories. North America and Western Europe posted negative growth, and significantly lower capacitor prices prevailed. Supply and demand gradually returned to balance in 1997. 1998 saw overall domestic passive-component demand from Asia drop by double-digit rates, due to the financial crisis there. U.S. passive-component production fell correspondingly: output of U.S. capacitors in dollar terms fell by 3.2% in 1998.

U.S. production of capacitors this year is estimated to grow by 1.9% to $3.0 billion. This implies firming prices, but another slip in unit demand. Beginning in 2000, unit demand looks to accelerate.

U.S. Capacitors Market in 1998

	Output Billion Units	Growth rate, %
Non–captive Prod	25.2	-13.9
Captive Prod	0.5	2.4
Total Prod	25.7	-13.6
OEM Purchases	33.2	-3.1
OEM Consumption	46.2	10.4
Exports	34.5	22.0
Imports	42.9	26.1

Source: Electronic Outlook Corporation

Consolidation of the capacitor industry is expected to continue, as the business environment favors larger players. Fewer, but bigger companies will be seen in the next decade. Global diversification will also continue. Full-spectrum global companies will increasingly dominate the marketplace: the capacitor industry will be more concentrated and more competitive, with moderate and sustainable growth rates expected in the longer term.

Resistors

Overall, the U.S. resistor industry is mature, and profit margins are slim. Unexpectedly strong growth in the mid-1990s collapsed in 1996. Average to better-than-average growth reappeared in 1997, because OEM production was greater in 1997 than expected, and inventories at OEMs were generally in line. However, 1998 saw a 5.2% drop in U.S. resistor production to $1.2 billion. Slack worldwide demand and inventory adjustment were responsible.

U.S. Resistors Market in 1998

	Output, Billion Units	Growth rate, %
Non–captive Prod	5.5	-8.8
Captive Prod	2.0	29.0
Total Prod	7.5	-1.0
OEM Purchases	60.7	8.0
OEM Consumption	68.5	10.6
Exports	6.8	9.7
Imports	62.1	10.0

Source: Electronic Outlook Corporation

As expected for the broad passive-component market, 1999 should see a slow recovery, as inventories are built in preparation for the millennium, and as Asia and other global markets revive. Consumer electronics will bolster resistors. The computer and communications sectors will also remain vital to the growth of the industry. Industrial/instrument production is likely to return to a more traditional pace and remain a helpful source of resistor demand. While a gradually improving marketplace is developing abroad, subdued optimism is in the U.S. resistors picture over the next few years.

Relays and Switches

Relays

The U.S. relay market is primarily dependent on machinery, industrial electronics, and factory automation. Relays scored high growth on the back of good-manufacturing prospects in the mid-1990s, but fell victim to the 1996 inventory cycle and weakness in cellular communications and consumer and automotive markets. The industrial electronics sector turned in a better-than-average performance in 1997, which boosted relays. The all-important communications market will also figure prominently into the future of the industry, as communication equipment will be the frontrunner of electronics industry growth in the near term.

The U.S. relay market in 1998 is estimated to be off by 4.1% at $913 million. 1998 saw some inventory correction again, as well as slower equipment growth outside the United States. 1999 looks to see a repeat of some of the same factors, but positive prospects return in 2000 and beyond. The long-term tendency away from electromechanical relays in electronics will continue, with solid-state relays (SSRs) increasing market penetration. Computer and communication-equipment demand will sustain relay producers in the near term. Consumer and automotive electronics are the main future-growth opportunities.

Switches

Communication, computer equipment, consumer electronics, and instrumentation are the largest switch users. Switches historically lag the electronics industry as a whole. U.S. switch production reflected the robust domestic electronics industry of the mid-1990s, and then also its weakness in 1996. 1997 growth exceeded expectations, but last year a combination of slipping prices and unit production caused a fallback to an $887 million production level. This constituted a drop of 6.5% from 1997.

1999 looks to eke out positive growth, with a small amount of pricing stability and very modest gains in production. Market conditions will favor switch producers whose products target telecommunications. Long-term prospects for the industry point to strengthening annual growth in line with historical averages. Solid state and software functions are still influencing the switch market. Keyboards and optical and other non-contacting functions are also gradually replacing mechanical functions. While standard switch functions stagnate, use in sensor applications will expand, and the trend toward miniaturization and surface mounting will accelerate.

Chapter 20: Transportation Equipment

Motor Vehicles and Parts

Automotive manufacturing is one of the cornerstones of the United States industrial base. Motor vehicles and parts are comprised of five major product areas: automobiles (cars), light-duty trucks, medium- and heavy-duty trucks, truck trailers, and motor vehicle parts. In 1998, shipments amounted to almost $358 billion, with automobiles and light-duty trucks accounting for 63% of shipments, parts around 32%, and trucks, trailers, and some miscellaneous activity the remaining 5%.

The automotive industry directly employs over 990,000 workers, accounting for roughly 5% of U.S. manufacturing employment. The industry forms an important cog of the country's manufacturing base, consuming in a typical year 15% of the steel, 25% of the aluminum, and 75% of all the natural rubber purchased by U.S. industries. According to the Department of Commerce, every dollar of production of automobiles generates on average $2.50 of activity in the U.S. economy.

The motor vehicle sector has undergone a dramatic transformation. This once-moribund sector has taken on the characteristics of a growth industry with near-record sales and production, mergers and combinations of global proportions, rock-solid financial performance, and new and exciting technology. The 1994–1999 span ranks as the best six years on record for the U.S. automobile sector, with almost 92.0 million cars and light trucks sold. To top it all off, by the time 1999 is finished, car and light-truck sales should total more than 16.0 million units, finally matching the peak established in 1986. In addition, there was a peak 527,000 medium- and heavy-duty trucks and 279,000 complete trailers sold in 1998.

The light-truck phenomena is no longer a craze. The popularity of minivans, sport utilities and pickup trucks is the single most-important feature in the industry's spectacular growth this decade. Once a small niche relegated to light commercial usage, light trucks now share close to fifty-fifty billing with passenger cars. Furthermore, the cutting edge of design is spawning a new generation of vehicles—car-truck hybrids, cars that perform like trucks, trucks that drive like cars—blurring the normal lines of distinction in the market and giving the consumer tremendous value and use.

The face of the industry has been irrevocably altered. The distinction between domestic vs. import, Detroit vs. foreign was forever shattered with the Chrysler, Daimler-Benz merger. Daimler-Chrysler, a combination of international auto giants, creates the world's fifth-largest automotive assembler. The resulting powerhouse has little redundancies, an almost seamless product line from entry-level cars all the way to luxury cars and sport utilities and medium- and heavy-duty trucks in every region of the globe. The Asian currency crisis has given birth to other international combinations with implications for the U.S. market. Nissan, in order to stay afloat, has merged with Renault. The Korean automotive sector has experience a serious bloodletting with Hyundai acquiring Kia, and other manufacturers either merging or shuttering their assembly plants. Not to be left out in the cold, Ford acquired the luxury car operations of Swedish manufacturer Volvo, to go with Jaguar and Aston-Martin. General Motors has assumed total control of Saab cars. Longer run, some industry analysts have gone as far as saying that there will only be six mammoth firms dominating auto assembly in the future.

The trend to foreign producers establishing plants in North America has intensified. Toyota, Honda, Nissan, BMW, and Mercedes-Benz are all either putting up new green-field facilities or enlarging existing operations. The parts supply base continues to consolidate—both in the United States and throughout the word. The ongoing trend to modularity, supplying complete parts systems (i.e. entire interiors) to increase productivity, has caused many more takeovers in the auto parts sector. Concerns over the energy and environment are generating the next technological wave. Electric, hybrid (gas/electric), fuel cell-powered cars will constitute the next major change to alter the face of this once-staid industry.

Between 1988 and 1999, the total value of shipments for motor vehicles and parts grew 4.9% per year, with 3.1% in real growth and a 1.7% per-annum rate of price increase.

WEFA expects that the real value of shipments will average about 2% per year between 1998 and 2008.

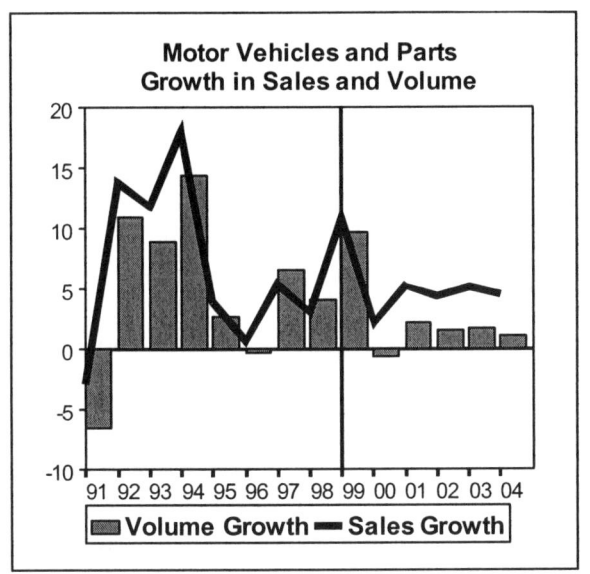

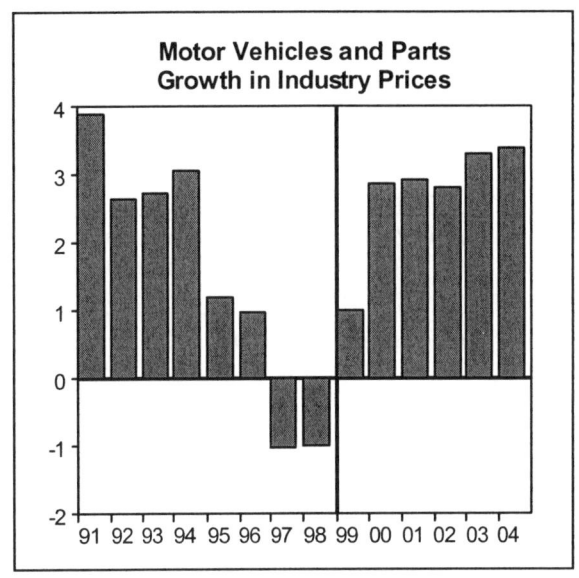

Motor Vehicles and Parts

SIC 371

		1992	1993	1994	1995	1996	1997	1998	1999	2000	2001	Compound Average 88-98	Annual Growth 98-08
Sales													
	Billions of $	238.8	267.1	315.0	327.2	329.5	347.3	357.9	396.6	405.3	426.6		
	% Ch	13.9	11.8	18.0	3.9	0.7	5.4	3.0	10.8	2.2	5.3	4.9	5.1
Volume													
	% Ch	10.9	8.9	14.5	2.6	-0.3	6.5	4.0	9.7	-0.7	2.3	3.1	2.1
Prices													
	% Ch	2.6	2.7	3.0	1.2	1.0	-1.0	-1.0	1.0	2.9	2.9	1.7	3.0
Production Costs													
Avg. Hourly Earnings													
	$/hr	15.44	16.09	17.01	17.34	17.74	18.06	17.92	18.01	18.60	19.31		
	% Ch	1.6	4.2	5.7	2.0	2.3	1.8	-0.8	0.5	3.3	3.8	2.5	3.5
Input Price Index													
	% Ch	0.8	1.6	2.3	2.8	0.4	0.0	-0.6	0.4	2.0	2.4	1.4	2.3

Light Vehicles

The last five years have been outstanding for the U.S. light-vehicle sector. Since 1994, there have been approximately 15.0 million cars and light trucks sold in the United States per annum. This is very close to the long run potential for the market. The industry has been on a sustained pace that will exceed the peak sales period of the mid-1980s. Furthermore, the North America Free Trade Agreement (NAFTA) has turned North America into an automotive powerhouse. Because of NAFTA, automotive production should be viewed from the perspective of the Continent as a whole. With the current wave of plant relocation and expansion, there will be 91 plants in North America, of which 64 are in the United States, 14 in Canada, and 13 in Mexico. The United States accounts for 75.0% of North American output, Canada 16.0%, and Mexico 9.0%. Each year, there is a tremendous volume of vehicles shipped between the three countries, generating economies of scale and cost rationalization.

North American light-vehicle production has been running at record levels, with car and light-truck assembly at a peak 15.6 million units in 1997 and 1998. The passenger-car sector, which has been on a long term decline, accounted for only 51.0% of output, or 8.0 million units. Light trucks, the hot number of the nineties, has posted seven consecutive record years. In 1998, light-truck output totaled 7.6 million units compared to 4.5 million units at the start of the decade. Currently, light trucks account for 49.0% of North American light-vehicle production compared to 37.0% in 1990.

The accelerated trend by the Japanese and Europeans to expand North American output at the expense of operations at home will be conducive to growth throughout the next ten years. By 2005, output is expected to approximate 18.0 million units. Mexico will assume a greater role by then, accounting for 12.5% of light-vehicle production, Canada 17.5%, and the United States only 70.0%. Cars in the next century will be lucky to hold their own, with energy and environmental concerns helping this beleaguered sector to maintain its slim majority over light trucks.

The merger between Chrysler and Daimler-Benz has created a true super-class global colossus. More mergers will come in the future; no company appears untouchable. The crisis in Asia has opened up opportunities for the strong players. The Nissan-Renault marriage is the latest industry megadeal.

Consumer Affordability

The health of the U.S. light-vehicle market is largely a function of improving consumer affordability. In the second half of the decade, the industry has not only increased the absolute level of promotional dollars per vehicle, but has sought new and creative methods to give the consumer a bargain. The market has resorted to a multi-faceted approach to combat sticker shock. First and foremost, the old stand–by, a heavy dose of incentives! The grand experiment to wean the consumer off incentives has failed. Rebates, a feature of the late eighties, have resurfaced with a vengeance in the late nineties. Aggressive lease deals are very prevalent in the marketplace. A sharp pencil has been used when calculating the prices on new models. The operating buzzword in the industry is zero-price inflation. The only way to raise prices on new models each year is to add new features or increase per-

formance. Many manufacturers are entering the sub-prime loan market in order to insure ample loan availability. Interest rates on auto loans from captive finance companies (Ford Credit, Chrysler Credit, GMAC) are at an all-time low, with zero financing on select models. In 1994, it took almost twenty-five-and-a-half weeks worth of family earnings to purchase a new vehicle. Currently, it takes less than 23.0 weeks, or the best affordability level since 1985.

The marketing aggression by the industry has been the trump card, capitalizing on an almost idyllic economy. A high level of economic growth, tight labor market, roaring stock market, soaring consumer confidence, and almost no inflation are the perfect environment for a rock-solid auto market. Add an ample supply of good bargains and exciting new models, and the end result is a red-hot auto market.

The underlying factors point to a continuation of this trend:

- Economy—Real Gross Domestic Product has managed to exceed all expectations in recent years, averaging close to a 4% increase. The WEFA long-term forecast expects expansion to moderate but still remain robust, around 2.5%.

- New Car Prices—If the new car and truck prices are adjusted for comparable equipment, auto price inflation in the closing years of the 1990s has been for all intents and purposes zero. WEFA anticipates that, from this point onward, all announced sticker increases on new model introductions will approximate zero.

- Incentives—A heavy dose of incentives has been applied in recent years. The high-water mark of the nineties was 1997-1998, when total promotional dollars per vehicle averaged between $3,300 and $3,500, or roughly 15.0% of the base price. In some months, incentives were as high as 17.0% of the sticker. The red-hot economy allows manufactures to cut back on bargains, dropping incentives down into the 12.0%–13.0% range, which is probably more realistic for the long run.

- Leases—Lease activity has maxed out. Penetration has more than doubled since 1993, peaking at 35.0% in 1998. WEFA believes the equilibrium share for leases will be in the 30.0%–32.0% range.

- Auto Loan Rates—New auto loans have been and will remain very subdued. Since 1996, commercial bank rates remained very modest, around 9.0%. Captive finance companies have been charging around 6.0%, or an all-time low. Zero-percent financing deals have become commonplace.

The Fleet and the Replacement Cycle

According to the latest R.L. Polk ownership survey, there are approximately 205.0 million cars and trucks on the road at this time. This translates to 2.00 vehicles per household. In recent years, the overall number of vehicles in use has grown about 2.0% a year, about twice as fast as the rate of household formation. The average age of the fleet is roughly 8.5 years for both cars and trucks,

or the highest level since the Korean War. Replacement demand has risen in the second half of the nineties. The scrappage rate (vehicles not registered versus total registrations) did, however, decline in 1998, averaging 5.7% compared to 6.2% in the prior year. In absolute volume terms, replacement demand in 1998 fell somewhat, from 12.5 million in 1997 to 11.7 million. This is actually a very positive factor, indicating that the robust level of sales in the current cycle is being generated by first-time buyers and household fleet expansion, rather than cars and trucks wearing out. Thus the pool of replacement demand, instead of being depleted, is actually expanding, hence a safety net for future sales.

The fundamentals of ownership and replacement driving the market for the long run include:

- Age of Fleet—New sales have been decent in this past cycle, averaging 15.0 million units per annum. Over the next few years, the average age of the fleet will shift downward, but not drastically. This will put pressure on sales in the short run, but should not pose a major problem. As we move through the next century, the fleet will drift upward in age, and this will add impetus to sales after the year 2000. Age, however, is no longer a critical factor, either up or down, in the purchase decision.

- Vehicle Ownership—The forecast expects that household penetration should move up minimally over time, hitting 2.1 million by 2005. Fleet growth generates about 3.5 million new units per year in new sales during the next ten years.

- Replacement Cycle—The trend to higher vehicle quality, longer vehicle life, and hence a much lower level of scrappage has been evident for some time now. In the sixties, scrappage rates averaged close to 8.0% a year. By the seventies, they had fallen to 7.0%, and in the eighties were down to 6.0%. We expect the scrappage rate to remain just under 5.5%. Therefore, the replacement component of new car and truck demand should rise close to 12.5 million units by 2005.

Outlook

U.S. light-vehicle sales in the closing years of the nineties have exceeded all expectations. Reflecting a spectacular fourth quarter, volume in 1998 totaled 15.6 million cars and light trucks. Expectations were that this outstanding showing could not be repeated, no less exceeded. By the time 1999 is complete, the sales tally should be around 16.0 million units.

Two factors will cause activity to drop out of the clouds. The economy will downshift in 2000 because of the problems associated with the Y2K computer phenomenon and remain on a more modest long-term plateau in the next decade, +2.5% versus +4.0% at the end of the nineties. The auto market's trend fundamentals of ownership and replacement point to a sustainable sales level of 15.5 million, not 16.0 million. After a brief slow down in 2000, with sales dropping down to about 15.2 million units, volume moves back to 15.5 million units and then drifts upward, getting back close to 16.0 million in 2008.

The car market has not quite reached bottom yet. We expect car sales to fall from around 8.1 million units in 1998 to a low point of 7.7 million in 2000, or the worst volume level since 1963. The light-truck sector has continued to grow, but at a high price. It has taken a tremendous amount of incentives, rebates, and lease deals to keep truck sales moving ahead. By shifting an appreciable amount of capacity from car assembly into trucks, the industry has made the growth of the truck segment a self-fulfilling prophecy. Our expectations are that light trucks will peak out just under 8.0 million units in 1999. At this level, trucks would account for about 49.0% of the light-vehicle market. In WEFA's assessment, concerns over energy conservation and the environment will stop light trucks short of the 50.0% magic barrier. Moves are underway to apply the same tailpipe emission standards and similar mileage restrictions across car and truck sectors. This would raise the price and limit the size of some of the most popular vans and sport utilities and slow the truck juggernaut.

Production does better than sales, as another wave of transplant capacity is installed. In 1998, transplant capacity in North America increased by 180,000 units. In 1999 it jumps another 540,000. Another increment of 200,000 comes on stream by 2001, raising total North American built to 4.3 million cars and trucks for the transplants. Production in North America should rise to 16.5 million units by 2000, and hit 18.0 million in 2005.

Cyclicality

The automotive sector is a true "cyclical." Vehicles represent one of the largest single expenditures in the con-

sumer's household budget, second only to housing. Since they have an extended life span, purchases of cars and trucks are readily postponed at the onset of any business contraction. In addition, the volatility of the market is exacerbated by competitive practices, particularly the use of incentives, leases, and fleet sales to rental companies.

For the long haul, WEFA continues to project a very sanguine climate—sustained modest growth and low inflation: real economic growth in the area of 2.5% and annual inflation running between 2.0% and 2.5%. This means that, as long as the economy stays on course, there is no reason to believe that the light-vehicle market cannot sustain a trend level of sales and maintain this almost indefinitely.

While there is no justification for arbitrarily imposing a cycle on sales, has the industry become less cyclical? Unfortunately, WEFA Automotive believes the answer is no. The industry has gotten a lot smarter and more productive. Most of the excess capacity is gone from North America. However, the more benign cyclical prospects for the market are a reflection of the stable economic performance. Should the economy take a nosedive, the industry is as vulnerable as it ever was. In fact, leases, a high level of incentives, just-in-time inventory, extended product life, and global over-capacity, all have the potential to destabilize the marketplace in a recession. In the final analysis, there are no typical recessions. Based on historical performance, however, the industry could contract anywhere from 20% to 25% with a sales drop of 3.0 to 4.0 million units.

Retailing Trends

The automobile industry has been making giant strides in an effort to revolutionize its oft-maligned approaches to selling cars and trucks. Once the sole sphere of influence of independent and franchised dealers, the market is now evolving, employing a myriad of new marketing approaches.

Initially, one price shopping (a la Saturn) appeared on the scene. Leases were added to the repertoire of straight consumer incentives and low-rate financing. Leases have become a key marketing tool employed by the automobile industry to promote sales. According to CNW Marketing and WEFA, leases have risen from roughly 7.0% of all consumer car and light-truck purchases in the 1984–1986 period to approximately a third.

Mega-dealers, such as AutoMax and Auto Nation, initially entered the used-car market. While some of these giant retailers are currently experiencing financial difficulties, customers like their modern sales approach and no-haggle pricing. These new outlets are giving traditional dealerships stiff competition in both the used- and, in the long run, new-car channel. The advent of the mega-dealers has accelerated the consolidation trend in dealerships. In 1970, there were 31,000 franchised dealerships in the United States. By 1990, the number had fallen below 25,000, and currently there are about 22,000. Over the next few years, we expect to see another 2,500 to 3,000 dealers. Manufacturers, in an attempt to control distribution, are employing various techniques to buy back dealerships and consolidate franchises in various locations; a move that has not been welcomed by the dealers in a good many locations.

The industry has finally found the worldwide web. Initially employed to provide browsers with vehicle profiles and ratings, consumers can now locate the best price, obtain financing, and even purchase a car or truck on the web. While the large super-dealers have made the most of the internet, all participants in the marketplace—retailers, manufacturers, banks—are getting involved with the web. It has been estimated that around 25% of all consumers consult the internet before entering the showroom to buy a new or used vehicle.

Labor Issues

A few years ago, the U.S. automotive industry entered a period of heightened labor conflict, with strikes or some sort of labor conflict in every year, not just periods of major contract renegotiations. Highlighting the recent outbreaks:

- In 1996, the United Auto Workers (UAW), as well as the Canadian Auto Workers (CAW) renegotiated their contracts with the Big Three. Chrysler and Ford managed to get through the process quietly, while GM could not. GM suffered three work stoppages: one local strike early in the year, one general strike with the UAW, and another with the CAW.

- In July 1997, a walkout at a Chrysler engine plant in Warren, MI idled the profitable truck lines of Grand Cherokee, Ram full-size pickup, and Dakota compact pickup for nearly over a month. The issue, to no surprise, was the continuing trend of outsourcing, which entails suppliers (mostly non-union) taking on more responsibility and more assembly of parts and components.

- In 1998 a local dispute between General Motors and the UAW centering around GM's Flint, Michigan operations erupted in a summer-long, 54-day strike, which eventually shuttered most of GM's facilities. By the time the dust had settled and the plants were up and running, GM had lost about 500,000 units of output, $2.6 billion, and suffered irreparable damage to the start-up of key new models.

The issues are not new. The companies feeling the heat of a mature market and global competition need to constantly reduce cost and improve productivity. The successes of the industry in recent years are readily apparent—rock-solid profits and balance sheets and an enhanced productivity report card that rivals any nation in the world. Efforts continue, with more pressure to outsource and move to modular assembly.

The union for its part needs to protect jobs, demonstrate political clout, and stem the tide of dwindling membership. In 1979, the high-water mark for UAW enrollment was attained at 1.5 million workers. In 1998, after a 10.0% gain, membership was only 846,000. Furthermore, the union could take little consolation from the increase, as enrollment in the automobile industry actually declined, supplanted by gains in healthcare and other fields.

To add fuel to the fire, record sales and earnings make it difficult for the union to offer give backs. The situation could come to a painful head, as the national contract comes up for renewal. The list of union demands is exhaustive:

- Guaranteed jobs and income, improved profit sharing, shorter workweek, reduction in overtime.

- Removal of all financial caps on job security programs. First shot at jobs made available by attrition.

- Reduction in the number of allowable layoffs for slow business. Currently management can idle workers for as much as 36 weeks for slow sales.

- Commitment by the company to modernize and grow the business; no more plant closures. Employee participation in product development and decisions, especially restructuring. Jobs lost to restructuring to be supplanted by increased in-sourcing.

- Outsourcing—the OEMs have been using independent, largely nonunion parts suppliers more and more. The UAW wants the assemblers to assist in their organizing efforts with their outside parts manufacturers. No outsourcing without mutual consent, and the right to strike over outsourcing. No work moved from UAW to non-UAW suppliers.

- The issue of GM's Delphi and Ford's Visteon parts divestitures. These new firms are at the top of the parts supply chain and the UAW will want to negotiate a separate contract with them.

- Modularity would result in the loss of assembly plant jobs. The union wants a hand in the job security of these workers and the unionization of the modular supplier.

- Flexible work rules—the manufacturers want more of a say in adjusting shifts and overtime in order to improve efficiency.

- The need to improve safety.

- Negotiations with the new Daimler-Chrysler entity, and its Alabama assembly plant.

- The union probably is looking for a four- instead of the normal three-year pact.

Who the union targets, or whether there will be contentious negotiations or a strike, remains to be seen. The manufacturers are certainly in the strongest position they've been in for a long while and the UAW has increased its strike fund. However, neither side really wants a strike.

Globalization

The global automotive market attained a high-water mark in 1997. Worldwide output hit a peak in that year at 58.0 million vehicles. This was the fourth straight year of growth, with vehicle assembly rising close to 9.0% over 1996, and some 15.0% higher than the start of the decade. Unfortunately, the currency crisis in Asia brought this to a crashing halt at the end of that year. With 1998, the automotive industries of both Asia and South America (i.e. Brazil) had entered a recession. In 1998, global automotive output declined more than 4.0%. However, this apparent minor decrease masks the disruption caused by the crisis in the world's emerging markets. Production in South America fell 18.0%, while assembly in Asia dropped around 12.5%. The big producing regions maintained the sanity in the global marketplace, as output was essentially flat in North America and Europe.

While the risk of a global economic meltdown remains, the probability gets less and less. WEFA believes the crisis has bottomed in Asia, and while recovery has begun, progress will be slow and erratic. In this climate, auto output continues to suffer, and activity drops another 4.0%, or just above 53.0 million cars and trucks. With the exception of North America (+5.0%), the other regions of the world contract: South America (-21.5%), Asia (-9.5%), and even Europe (-5.0%).

By 2001, the global auto market gets back on track, and resumes growth. The trend toward globalization was not derailed by this crisis, only slowed. Even as the markets contracted, the stronger manufacturers were going ahead with their expansion plans, albeit at a slower pace in some regions. Weaker players (the Koreans and Nissan) sought the shelter of mergers and plant divestiture. The global crisis has cost the auto industry five years. If the recovery proceeds as we expect, the auto industry in 2005 would be in the same relative state and similar size as originally estimated for 2000, if the Asian crisis had not occurred. In addition, the crisis has generated about 7.0 million units more of excess capacity. The global auto industry by its very nature normally has a good deal of unused plant capacity; currently there is about 25.0 million units in assembly capacity sitting idle, and the industry has an operating rate of only 66.0% globally.

Foreign Trade

The international trade in motor vehicles and parts is a critical issue for U.S. foreign-trade policy. The growth in U.S. exports of motor vehicles and parts, although considerable, has had little impact on the auto trade deficit. Auto exports have risen from $46.8 billion in 1992 to $71.3 billion in 1998. Despite trade initiatives and industry attempts, the U.S. trade imbalance in motor vehicles and parts is growing by leaps and bounds. In 1998, the U.S. trade deficit in motor vehicle and parts was $77.5 billion, compared to $52.0 billion in 1990. Over 90.0% of this shortfall are made up of vehicles, and only 10.0% are parts. One critical and contentious issue has been the motor vehicle and parts trade deficit with Japan, which in 1998 stood at $33.0 billion.

While light-vehicle imports from Japan have dropped significantly, and as Japanese producers expand their productive capacity in North America, the 1.3 million light vehicles imported from Japan by the United States in 1998 still dwarf the 53,500 American vehicles sold in Japan last year (because of the recession in Japan, U.S. exports decreased 36.0% in 1998).

Trade friction was the inevitable result, and in 1995 a trade war between Japan and the United States erupted. That year, the two countries signed the U.S.–Japan Automotive Framework Agreement. This agreement was designed to increase sales of U.S.-produced vehicles and parts to Japanese consumers and producers both here and in Japan. The treaty's progress has been slow and disappointing, but Japan's commitment to producing more vehicles and sourcing more parts in North America and its reluctance to greatly expand its exports to the United States have kept the situation from going critical.

On most other fronts, the U.S. world-trade picture has become quite favorable. Almost 80.0% of all cars and trucks sold in Canada are produced in the United States, while 80.0% of Canadian output is sold here. With the North American Free Trade Agreement (NAFTA), Mexico has been included, increasing prospects for further growth and rationalization in North America. The Asian currency crisis hit Brazil, and while the prospects for South America remain excellent, North-to-South auto trade has taken a turn for the worse.

North America is increasingly viewed as a good place to locate assembly plants, not only to serve North America, but also as a base for exports to other parts of the world. By 2001, there will be close to a million more units in transplant (foreign badged vehicles assembled in North America) capacity operating in North America—spearheaded by world class producers, such as Toyota, Honda, Daimler-Chrysler, and BMW.

In 1998, there were 365,000 new cars and light trucks exported outside of North America. This was off a third from the prior year. The Asian and Latin American markets were closed by the Asian flu. It will take another year or so to get foreign trade back on track, but the long-term potential for North American exports to the rest of the world remains healthy, about a 5.0% per annum rate of growth.

Energy and the Environment

From an environmental perspective, the automotive industry took a giant step toward the new century one year before the millennium. In 1999, the Environmental Protection Agency (EPA), from the mandate under the Clean Air Act, seized the initiative from the California Air Resource Board (CARB) by proposing a phase in approach to standard emissions reduction for both cars and trucks, Tier 2 Vehicle Pollution Rollback. Starting in 2004, passenger cars and light trucks will have to limit nitrogen oxide (NOx, a smog-producing agent) to 3.1 grams per mile. In layman's terms, this means that cars will burn 77% cleaner than today, and light trucks would become 95% less polluting. On the truck side, there will be a three-step, phase-in period: 2004, 2007, and 2009, when the biggest of the sport utilities must comply.

While a court ruling threatens the EPA's proposal, it appears to be a viable solution to all parties. The cost of compliance would be about $100 per car, $200 to $300 per light truck; for the consumer, two cents (five cents according to the oil refining industry) more for a gallon of gasoline, and the refiners about five cents more to produce a gallon of gasoline. Summarizing the new guidelines for Tier 2:

- Cars & trucks will have the same emissions rules.

- Assemblers can earn credits for making clean vehicles in 2001–2003.

- Requires a nation-wide low-sulfur gasoline by 2004.

- Permits cleaned–up diesels.

- Challenges the industry to develop better pollution equipment.

While much of the rhetoric and anger from environmentalists, legislators, and the industry is subsiding, compliance dates are rapidly approaching. CARB has postponed and loosened its standards, but as it stands now, 4.0% of the new vehicles sold in California have to be Zero emission Vehicles (ZEV). Electric vehicles fit the bill, but they are costly and under-powered, and appear doomed to extinction. Hybrid (gasoline/electric-powered cars) are now entering the U.S. market (Toyota's Prius). They offer a compromise between cost and performance, but don't qualify as zero emission. Fuel-cell technology (similar to a battery) holds the promise for the future, but probably will not be commercially cost effective until after 2005.

Even though never ratified, the Kyoto treaty still hangs over the industry's head. In an effort to push the industry to more fuel-efficient vehicles, 31 senators have proposed applying the same Corporate Average Fuel Standards (CAFE) for cars (27.5 miles per gallon) to light trucks (20.7 mpg). Since the 1993 model year, Ford has met the truck CAFE standard only three times, GM only twice, and the former Chrysler Corp. only once. If it were not from credits earned in the past or borrowed from the future, huge fines could have been levied against the industry. Exceeding the CAFE by one mile per gallon for a fleet of 300,000 vehicles would cost a manufacturer a fine of $16.5 million. The House has voted down a similar measure, but the specter remains over light truck sales.

Medium and Heavy Trucks

The medium- and heavy-truck market includes vehicles over 10,000 pounds in Gross Vehicle Weight, or GVW, which includes the weight of both the truck itself and its recommended maximum contents. The market is segmented into size classes, defined by GVW and designated by a GVW or Class number from 3 to 8. The small commercial truck market (GVWs 3 and 4) ranges in weight from 10,001 pounds to 16,000 pounds. It includes large pickup trucks and low cab–over–engine trucks used primarily by contractors, small retailers and wholesalers, and the service industries. The midrange market covers GVWs 5 through 7, which consist of trucks and school bus chassis within the GVW range of 16,001 pounds to 33,000 pounds. Midrange market trucks are used primarily for the distribution of a wide variety of products by manufacturers, wholesalers, retailers, and trucking companies. The heavy-duty or GVW8 market covers trucks with a GVW rating of 33,001 pounds and over. The heavy-duty market includes over-the-road tractors and equipment that is used in heavy industrial applications such as construction, mining, and logging.

Small Commercial Trucks (GVWs 3–4)

Recent Developments

The small commercial truck market is divided into two types of equipment: conventional trucks produced primarily by Chrysler and Ford; and low cab-over-engine, which includes trucks produced by General Motors and vehicles imported by Isuzu, Mitsubishi Fuso, and other Japanese truck manufacturers.

Since emerging from the 1990–1991 recession, the small commercial truck market has posted impressive sales gains. Solid economic and market fundamentals have played a big role, but truck producers have also broadened their product lines in GVW's 3 and 4. In 1991, U.S. retail sales of GVW 3 and 4 trucks totaled 45,085 units. By 1998, sales had risen to 145,855 units.

Between 1991 and 1998, sales of trucks rated in GVW 3 went from 21,256 units in 1991 to 52,804 units in 1997. Sales of GVW 4 trucks rose from 23,829 units in 1991 to 56,526 units in 1997. Last year saw the sea change in the small commercial truck market. Ford, which had long dominated GVW 4, broadened its product line with a product (F-350) in GVW 3. As a result, GVW 3 sales swelled to 102,497 units, and GVW 4 sales fell back to 43,358 units.

In GVW 3, the U.S. market was divided up as follows in 1998: Ford, 49.9%; Chrysler, 35.8%; GM, 4.9%; Isuzu, 6.5%; Mitsubishi Fuso, 2.2%; and Nissan Diesel, 0.1%.

GVW 4 sales are split out as follows: Ford, 45.3%; GM, 21.6%; Isuzu, 16.1%; Freightliner, 10.5%; Mitsubishi Fuso, 3.0%; Nissan Diesel, 2.8%; and Hino, 0.6%.

Small Commercial Truck Outlook

The small commercial truck market continues to be driven by favorable economic and market conditions, low interest rates, and the positive reception of new products such as Ford's F350 and F450.

The consumer-oriented sectors of the economy drive small commercial truck sales. As the second half of 1999 progresses, consumer confidence remains at a lofty level, unemployment is low, income is expanding, and consumers are spending freely. In point of fact, consumers are spending well ahead of their income stream, adding to their debt load and dipping into savings. Such aggressive spending by the consumer has an important positive impact on a whole host of end-markets for small commercial trucks.

Small retailers (food and apparel stores, furniture and appliance stores, hardware stores, etc.) and distributors are continuing to experience solid gains in sales and earnings. Consumer spending on furniture and household goods, other durables, clothing and shoes, and food and beverages will post another impressive increase this year. Small retailers, wholesalers, and distributors will reap the benefit of this aggressive spending spree. The service sector (including tow-truck operators, lawn and garden care companies, and repair and cleaning services) is also experiencing sales and earnings gains, as rising consumer incomes allow individuals to pay someone else to take care of certain tasks and chores.

New-home construction and the repair and remodeling business have continued to do very well in 1999. The strength in this market has had a very favorable impact on construction and electrical contractors, and trades people. Employment among special trades contractors and automotive and repair services continues to expand. Special trades employment should expand 4%–5% this year, largely due to the strength in new-home construction and home remodeling. Consumer spending on new structures and additions and alterations will increase at a near double-digit pace for all of 1999. Employment at automotive repair and other repair services appears headed for a 3.0%–3.5% increase, as 1999 turns out to be a banner year for driving, and therefore, tow-truck operators and related service providers.

Small truck sales are also still reaping the benefits of expanding activity and earnings in the business services sector. Economic growth and the trend to "outsourcing" all but core-business activities are still having a positive influence on commercial electrical and construction contractors, cleaning services, etc. Finally, small businesses performed well over the past year and appear to remain fairly confident about the near-term outlook. Small businesses announced very aggressive 1999 capital-spending programs and there is no evidence yet that they are now thinking dramatically different about their planned outlays. Small businesses and individual owner-operators provide the foundation for the small commercial truck market.

Most of the sectors that are key to small commercial trucks are doing very well in the current economic climate, and should continue to experience growth over the remainder of this year. However, WEFA still expects a less favorable economic environment to emerge and this will eventually dampen small commercial truck sales.

As we indicated above, it is the consumer-related sectors of the economy that really drive the small-truck market. The consumer has been spending at a frenetic pace expanding their debt loads and driving down savings. The stock of consumer durable goods has been well upgraded and there is certainly little, if any, pent-up demand left in the system. We believe consumers will soon reach the point where they take stock of their financial situation and begin to bring their spending more in line with in-

come growth and devote some of their financial resources to improving their balance sheets. With this as a backdrop, we expect consumer spending on furniture and household goods, other durables, clothing and shoes, and food and beverages to increase by only 2.0%–3.0% in the year 2000.

New-home construction is expected to slow due to slightly higher mortgage rates and the strength of the market over the past two years. The home repair and remodeling market also faces more modest growth for the very same reasons. Spending on new homes, additions, and household repair is slated to expand by roughly 2.5% next year. As the support from the consumer wanes, small businesses that are consumer-oriented, and individuals, such as independent contractors, can expect more modest progress on the sales and earnings front. As far as the services sector goes, there is no reason to assume that consumers will cut back their lawn and gardening services in such an environment, but the number of new customers added by individual companies is sure to slow. Lastly, the year 2000 promises slower growth in U.S. economic activity and some pressure on profit margins. As was the case with consumer services, business services firms will not suffer net losses of clients, but the growth in their sales will certainly moderate.

When all is said and done, there will be enough of a loss of forward momentum in end-market activity and growth in traffic to cause a very modest correction in small commercial truck sales. The year 2000 brings on a period of adjustment in the small commercial truck market, which is followed by renewed growth beginning in the year 2001 and continuing through the end of the forecast period.

Activity in small truck buying markets is dominated by wholesale and retail trade, the service sector, and the residential and home repair and remodeling segments of construction. These markets have performed exceptionally well in recent years and this has helped propel small commercial truck sales to their very lofty 1997 and 1998 levels. Activity in key small-truck markets grew by 6.1% in 1997, and 4.1% in 1998. We expect small-truck end-market activity to expand by 3.5% in 1999. As key end-markets begin to experience more subdued gains in sales and activity, we believe they will tone down their equipment acquisition programs. Given our expectations for consumer spending and construction, the growth in small- truck, end-market activity slows to less than 2% in the year 2000 and then ranges between 2.0%–2.5% per year during the 2001–2008 period.

Small-truck traffic is driven by consumer goods, such as furniture, appliances, household goods, and apparel, with some support from construction and business supplies and food products. We estimate that small-truck tonnage grew by 4.2% in 1998 following an increase of 4.7% in 1997. Indications are now that traffic will grow by about 3.5% in 1999 and 2% in the year 2000. With traffic growth slowing, the incentive to expand fleets will subside over the next two years. Beyond 2000, look for small-truck traffic to expand by 2.0%–2.5% per year, on average.

U.S. retail sales of small commercial trucks (GVW's 3-4) should finish 1999 at 181,200 units, an increase of 24%. Sales of conventional trucks appear headed for a 25.4% increase to 153,900 units. The low cab-over-engine segments should see sales rise 17.7% to 27,300 units.

We expect a modest correction in small commercial truck sales next year as end-market activity and traffic growth slow. GVW 3-4 sales are pegged at 177,600 units next year, a decline of about 2%. Conventional sales will slip to 127,000 units while low cab-over-engine truck sales drift off to 25,600 units.

Sales pick up beginning in 2001, as signs of life emerge in economic and market activity. Sales continue to gain ground thereafter. By the year 2008, we forecast small commercial truck sales to reach 220,000 units, broken out as follows: conventional trucks 189,000 units and low cab-over-engine trucks 31,000 units.

We expect additional competition in the conventional truck segment. Chrysler had been the dominant player, but fell to second place as Ford entered the market. GM has its new CK pickup waiting in the wings, and some of these units will carry a GVW rating in excess of 10,000 pounds. We expect GVW 3 CK pickup production to be fully ramped up by the end of 1999. We may also see more sales in GVW 3 than we are projecting if the trend among GVW 2 truck buyers to trade up to larger-sized vehicles accelerates.

Mid-Range Market (GVWs 5–7)
Recent Developments

The midrange market took a big hit in the 1990–1991 recession, with sales bottoming out at 98,344 units in 1991. They had peaked at 164,900 units in 1989. Since then, the market has recovered nicely with U.S. sales reaching 141,062 units in 1997 and 171,406 units in 1998.

GVW 5 has seen the most change in recent years. Sales never exceeded 10,000 units until Ford entered the market with its F-550 last year. As a result sales in GVW 5 jumped from 9,262 units to 25,185 units. With Ford now the dominant player, the market in 1998 was split up as follows: Ford, 74.9%; Isuzu, 6.3%; Nissan Diesel, 5.7%; Freightliner, 4.4%; Navistar, 3.6%; Mitsubishi Fuso, 3.4%; Hino, 1.2%; and GM, 0.3%.

Sales of GVW 6 trucks and buses peaked back in 1988 at 53,599 units. Changes in the school-bus market caused a wholesale graduation out of GVW 6 buses and up to GVW 7. As a result GVW 6 sales of trucks and buses fell to a low of 18,111 units in 1997. Ford moved aggressively into the market last year pushing total GVW 6 sales up to 31,556 units. With Ford now the dominant player, the market in 1998 was split up as follows: Ford, 33.9%; Freightliner, 30.6%; GM, 16%; Navistar, 7.6%; Nissan Diesel, 2.8%; Mack, 2.7%; Mitsubishi Fuso, 2.6%; Isuzu, 2.0%; and Hino, 1.9%.

Sales of trucks and buses bottomed out in 1991 at 72,598 units and then expanded to 106,724 units by 1995. Sales dipped to 103,528 units in 1995, and then rose to 114,665 units by 1998. Navistar remains the dominant player in GVW 7 selling both trucks and school-bus chassis. Navistar accounted for 53.4% of all U.S. GVW 7 sales last year. The rest of the market was divided as follows: General Motors, 17.3%; Freightliner, 15.4%; Ford, 9.5%; and other domestic producers and imports, 4.4%.

Mid-Range Market Outlook

The mid-range market continues on track for another banner year. Strong growth in end-market activity and mid-range truck traffic in 1998 and continued growth in 1999 are prompting truck buyers to press ahead with equipment acquisition plans. Canadian sales have not been as strong, but are still well ahead of their 1998 pace. Reported production and factory sales have reflected the strength in the mid-range market. The momentum in the economy and the order board suggest that the mid-range market will continue to exhibit strength throughout the year.

We still believe that the mid-range market will lose some of its luster next year, as a slower pace of economic and end-market growth emerges. We expect some signs of slowing late in 1999, but any real "softness" in the mid-range market will not show up until next year. At that point there will not be enough underlying momentum in either end-market activity or mid-range truck traffic to keep fleet expansion programs proceeding at their recent fast pace. Furthermore, we believe replacement pressures will be easing. In addition to slower growth in end-market activity and traffic, we expect to see diesel-fuel prices rising over the near term, which will put some pressure on motor-carrier profit margins. The factors influencing mid-range vehicle sales turn up once again in the year 2001, setting the stage for long-term expansion.

The mid-range market is dominated by wholesalers and retailers, and the local power needs of the trucking industry. Major trucking companies have gained long-haul traffic at the expense of the railroads, particularly in recent years. This additional volume has flowed through and put pressure on trucking companies to expand and upgrade their local power, as well as their line-haul fleets. Activity in the major markets for mid-range trucks grew by 3.5% last year, following an increase of 5.5% in 1997. Growth in mid-range end-market activity should slow to about 2.9% in 1999 and 1.5% in 2000. Thereafter, growth in end-market activity continues to hover in the 2% range per year.

Mid-range truck traffic, which is composed largely of local and short-haul tonnage, but also some long-haul tonnage, rose by 5.0% in 1998, following a 5.6% increase in 1997. Traffic growth is slated to slow to about 4.0% this year and 1.9% in 2000, based on our most recent expectations for production of materials, intermediate goods and final products, and import volumes. Thereafter, we expect traffic growth to improve to 2.5%–3.0% per year through 2008.

Fundamentals suggest that the demand for mid-range trucks will be slowing over the near term. We have taken in a huge amount of new equipment during the current cycle and the factors that would support continued aggressive investment will be losing some of their favorable tilt going forward.

Slower growth in mid-range truck traffic and end-market activity will translate into an easing of the pressures to expand fleets. Replacement demand should also be tapering off as 1999 draws to a close and the year 2000 unfolds. The mid-range truck fleet has been getting younger following a number of strong sales years, including 1999. During the period from 1994–1998, U.S. fleets added 575,000 new GVW 5-7 trucks. If we are right about 1999, the figure for new trucks added to the U.S. fleet for the 1994–1999 period will be on the order of 750,000. Furthermore, the pattern of past sales indicates that "normal" replacement demand should be leveling off or actually declining slightly over the near term. With this as a backdrop, we expect mid-range truck owners to adopt a more restrained approach toward equipment acquisition.

However, at this point in 1999, truck makers are still sitting on a hefty order board and truck buyers appear to still have a healthy appetite for new equipment. The major buyers of mid-range trucks have continued to do very well for themselves in 1999, following good years in 1997 and 1998. It is this past and current performance strength that continues to drive the 1999 surge in truck sales and production.

We are still projecting an adjustment in mid-range truck demand next year as end-market activity and mid-range truck traffic moderates and fuel costs rise. The market will lose some momentum late in 1999, and this will set the stage for lower sales and production levels in 2000. As better economic and market conditions emerge beyond the year 2000, sales and production will improve.

Mid-Range U.S. Retail Sales

U.S. retail sales of GVW 5-7 trucks and buses are now expected to advance by 19% in 1999 to 204,000 units. The mid-range market should start to slow down as 1999 draws to a close, but the true impact of slower traffic growth and end-market activity will not be felt until the year 2000. U.S. retail sales are now slated to fall back by about 7.3% next year to 189,000 units. Sales remain sluggish as 2001 unfolds, but eventually respond to the improvement we expect in the economy and key end-markets. However, for the year as a whole, we expect mid-range market sales to total just 188,100 units. Beyond the year 2000, sales rise to 205,100 units in 2004 and 225,000 units by 2008.

School Buses

U.S. school-bus sales hit a low of 28,564 units back in 1992. From 1993–1997, sales totaled 178,174 units, reaching 37,068 units in 1997. We believe 1998 sales exceeded 38,000 units.

The market for school-bus chassis is a mature one driven forward by growth in school-age population and replacement demand. School buses are owned by a large number of school districts and private carriers. Last year, the top 100 school districts in the United States had a total fleet of 58,962 school buses. Contractors provided 34.5% of these buses, or 20,325 units. The top 50 private carriers have a fleet of 75,000 school buses.

The school age population is expected to expand by almost 2 million students between now and 2008. Such growth should stimulate some fleet expansion. Regional shifts in population should stimulate some school bus fleet expansion. As long as we continue to see growth in the U.S. economy, school-bus sales will expand modestly. We expect U.S. school-bus chassis sales to reach 40,500 units by 2004, and flirt with 42,000 units by 2008.

Class A Motor Homes

The Class A motor-home business came out of the last recession with a vengeance. Wholesale deliveries bottomed out at 23,500 units in 1991, and then rose to 27,300 units in 1992, 31,900 units in 1993, and 37,300 units in 1994. Deliveries then faltered to 33,000 units in 1995, but resumed their upward march thereafter, reaching 36,500 units in 1996 and 37,600 units in 1997. Class A motor homes had their best year since 1984 last year, as deliveries totaled 42,900 units, an increase of 14.9%.

Motor-home sales continue to do well due to very favorable demographic and economic factors. The number of people in the prime-buying cohort for motor homes (over 55 and under 65) has been expanding for a number of years and grew by over 4% in 1998. Not only are there more people available to buy motor homes, but more of them have the money to do so. Consumer incomes continue to expand at a healthy clip, and the impact of the wealth factor arising from stock market gains has been an added plus. Low fuel prices have also had a very positive impact on motor-home sales, but fuel prices have begun to move upward recently. In past years, the high price of fuel has seriously depressed motor-home sales. Finally, interest rates have been very attractive.

The fundamentals that drive the Class A motor home market suggest that demand will remain strong during the forecast period. Demographics (people over 55 and under 65) will remain supportive. Between now and 2008, the number of people between the ages of 55-65 will expand by nearly 10 million. Obviously only a few of these will be buyers of Class A motor homes. Growth in consumer disposable income is put at over 2.5% per year. Interest rates will be less supportive over the near term, but will not become onerous. We expect fuel prices to continue to gain ground, but not rise to the level where they restrict motor-home sales.

Consumer confidence currently remains high. We do expect some erosion of confidence over the near term as employment and income growth moderate, but the major buyers of Class A motor homes will not be affected much by this development. On balance, the climate for purchasing motor homes will turn less favorable in the next few years than it has been recently but conditions will remain favorable enough to keep sales at very lofty levels.

On balance, the positives will continue to more than outweigh the negatives and this will prop up the market for Class A motor homes in 1999. The Class A motor-home market will once again post impressive numbers in 1999. All in all, we now expect 1999 deliveries to reach 49,000 units. Thereafter, we expect wholesale deliveries to retreat to 47,000 units in the year 2000 and 45,000 units in 2001. By the year 2008, we expect Class A motor-home sales to reach 52,500 units.

GVW 5-7 Factory Sales and Production

U.S. and Canadian (Can/Am) mid-range truck and bus factory sales reached 166,100 units in 1998, an increase of 9.9%. Strong demand in the U.S. and Canadian markets and a buildup in inventories offset a decline in exports. Mexican assembly of GVW 5-7 trucks and buses rose from 14,000 units in 1997 to 24,400 units in 1998. North American factory sales/production of GVW 5-7 trucks and buses came in at 190,100 units in 1998, up from 165,200 units in 1997.

Can/Am factory sales continue to do well in 1999, due to robust retail demand, and will post a very healthy increase for the year as a whole. Factory sales data from Ward's put five-month GVW 5-7 Can/Am factory sales at 79,017 units, an increase of 36.8%. Mexican mid-range assembly was running well ahead of last year due to strong increases in the production of trucks destined for the U.S. market. Additional support has come from modest improvement in GVW 6-7 truck sales within Mexico. We now expect Can/Am GVW 5-7 factory sales to advance to 184,100 units this year. Mexican assembly is slated to rise to 36,300 units. North American factory sales/production totals 220,400 units this year, an increase of 15.9%.

The U.S. and Canadian midrange markets will not do as well in 2000 as they did in 1999. At best we expect Can/Am exports to barely hold their own. The Mexican market will begin to exhibit signs of life as growth in that country's economy stages a comeback. Our current forecast has Mexican sales of GVW 6-7 trucks increasing to 7,100 units in the year 2000, up from 5,200 units this year. Can/Am factory sales fall to 163,400 units in 2000, due to declining demand, inventory adjustment, and shifts in production to Mexican facilities. Mexican assembly rises to 36,300 units due to increased Mexican demand and export activity. Overall, North American factory sales/assembly come in at 198,200 units.

North American factory sales/assembly will begin to improve in 2001 and will continue to gain ground throughout the forecast period. We now expect Can/Am factory sales and Mexican assembly to reach about 250,000 units by 2004 and 275,000 units by 2008.

Heavy Duty Market (GVW 8)

Recent Developments

Heavy trucks roared out of the last recession with U.S. retail sales going from 98,730 units in 1991 to 201,303 units in 1995. Sales fell back to 170,009 units in 1996 and then advanced to 178,551 units in 1997. Sales of heavy trucks in the United States surged ahead to a record 209,483 units in 1998.

Freightliner has been the dominant player in the heavy-duty (GVW 8) market since 1992, and the company has steadily increased share from 1990–1996. In 1997, Freightliner accounted for over 28.2% of U.S. sales, down slightly from 29.4% in 1996. Last year, Freightliner boosted market share to 30.7%. During 1997, Freightliner acquired the heavy truck business of Ford, which had accounted for roughly 9% of the U.S. market. This entity, now known as Sterling Trucks, accounted for 2.4% of the U.S. market in 1998. PACCAR (Kenworth and Peterbilt) was second in size with 20.8% of sales. Navis-

tar came third in heavy duties with a market share of over 18.4%. Fourth place belonged to Mack Truck, which boosted its share in 1998 to 12.8%. Rounding out the major producers was Volvo–GM Heavy Truck, with 11.5% of sales in 1998. Approximately 2% of the U.S. market goes to Western Star, a Canadian manufacturer, and a number of smaller specialty truck producers.

Heavy Truck Market Outlook

It is all but impossible for 1999 not to be another record year for the heavy-truck market. Retail sales and production through the first half of the year were running far ahead of their 1998 pace, and there is enough business already on the books to keep truck plants humming throughout the balance of the year.

The economy, end-market activity, and heavy-truck traffic will slow in the year 2000 as consumer spending for durable and non-durable goods, residential construction, and business investment expand at a slower pace than in 1999. In addition, expanding worldwide demand for crude oil and OPEC cutbacks will put upward pressure on petroleum product prices. Rising diesel-fuel costs will put some pressure on motor carrier profit margins. With this as a backdrop, the pressure and incentive to continue to aggressively expand and upgrade fleets will ease.

The U.S. heavy-truck fleet has been both expanded and upgraded dramatically during the past five years (1994-1998). U.S. fleets purchased 945,000 heavy trucks in these years. When you include the 255,000 units we expect this year, the 1994–1999 sales total will reach 1.2 million. We estimate that the U.S. fleet of heavy trucks numbers about 1.8 million. Thus as the year 2000 unfolds, two-thirds of the fleet will be only six years or younger. There is little reason to believe that there is still a large amount of pent-up replacement out there to provide additional lift to the market and the "normal" replacement demand level should only be about 190,000-200,000 units. In addition, slower growth in end-market activity and traffic implies that there is less reason to expand the fleet at the robust pace we have witnessed in recent years.

The factors that drive heavy-truck demand in the United States do not go from very positive in 1999 to negative in the year 2000. What we envision is enough of a loss of support from the "economic" factors that drive the market to cause a decline in demand from record levels. We do not envision the kind of deterioration in either end-market activity or traffic or enough of a rise in fuel prices to knock demand down to recessionary levels. In our view of the world, end-market activity and traffic continue to gain ground and motor carriers continue to experience gains in revenues and earnings. Furthermore, the enormous competitive pressures within the freight transportation industry continue to compel motor carriers to invest pretty aggressively in new equipment.

The economic and market fundamentals that drive the demand for new equipment do improve as the year 2000 progresses, and continue to gain ground through 2001 and beyond. This sets the stage for somewhat stronger fleet expansion and joins forces with expanding replacement demand. "Normal" replacement demand will be the driving force during the near term, as the units brought into the fleet during the 1994–1999 period provide the replacement pool during the 2000–2004 period. Better economic conditions, including expanding traffic and end-market activity, rising profits, and attractive interest rates allow the necessary replacement of older units to proceed. The demand for new equipment remains subdued as 2001 unfolds, but picks up momentum during the second half of the year, setting the stage for a better 2002. Thereafter, growth in traffic and a rise in replacement demand allow the market to stage a comeback and then expand through the end of the forecast period.

Activity in the major markets that purchase heavy trucks (trucking companies, retailers, merchant wholesalers, manufacturers, and construction) expanded by 6.5% in 1997 and 5% in 1998. The trucking industry provided the lion's share of the support. We expect the growth rate in end-market activity to slow to 4.4% in 1999 and 2.0% in the year 2000. Conditions begin to improve in 2001 with end-market growth of 2.7%. Thereafter, we expect market expansion of about 2.5% per year through 2008.

Heavy-truck tonnage growth was estimated at 6.0% in 1998, following an increase of 6.9% in 1997. Heavy-truck tonnage is based largely on our estimates for long-haul (over 500 miles) and intermediate-haul (100–500 miles) traffic. There is a lesser contribution from off-road, short-haul, and local traffic. Tonnage growth is slated to slow to 4.6% this year and 2.5% in the year 2000. As the economy strengthens traffic growth then accelerates to 3.6% in 2001, and roughly 3% per year thereafter.

Summarizing the Forecast

U.S. retail sales should reach 250,000–255,000 units for 1999. We still expect signs of a slowing in demand to emerge late in 1999 leading to a decline in sales to 225,000 units in 2000. Sales are slow to recover late in 2001, but end the year at 210,000 units. Thereafter, we see US retail demand reaching 234,000 units in 2004 and 257,000 units by 2008.

Canadian retail sales go from 29,100 units in 1998 to 31,000 units this year. Sales fall back to 28,500 units in 2000. Sales will then advance to 33,500 units in 2004 and 37,000 units in 2008. Mexican heavy-duty sales reached 13,250 units last year and should edge up to 13,790 units this year and 19,500 units in 2000. Mexican sales rise to 44,500 units by 2004 and 55,000 units by 2008.

North American factory sales of heavy trucks totaled 278,000 units in 1998. They will rise to 320,000 units this year and then fall back to 280,000 units in 2000. Thereafter, look for factory sales to reach 325,000 units by 2004 and 370,000 units by 2008.

Truck Trailers

The demand for commercial trailers is driven largely by manufacturing activity, which involves the multiple moves of raw materials, intermediate goods, and finished products. Merchandise imports and construction activity also have an impact on the market. The major buyers of truck trailers include trucking companies and private fleets that are owned by manufacturers, retailers, merchant wholesalers, and distributors. The farm, mining, and logging sectors are major players in the market. U.S. trailer manufacturers have increased their focus on Canada, Mexico, and the rest of Latin America in recent years, and will continue to do so in the years ahead. Exports account for 10%–15% of total shipments. Imports, primarily from Canada and Mexico, account for 15%–20% of the domestic market.

Van trailers account for about three-quarters of all shipments. Van trailers are generally used to carry general merchandise, food products, household goods such as furniture and appliances, and other manufactured goods. Platform trailers, low–bed heavy haulers, and dump trailers are closely linked to construction industry activity. Tank trailers are used to transport liquid chemicals, petroleum products, and food products. The top-10 trailer manufacturers accounted for 70% of the industry's output in 1998.

Recent Developments

The truck trailer business took a beating during the 1990–1991 recession, as shipments dropped 32.5% to 122,361 units in 1991. Since then the demand for truck trailers has surged ahead with complete trailer shipments reaching 234,287 units in 1994 and a new record of 279,144 units in 1995. Sales fell back to 202,102 units in 1996 and then advanced to 233,483 units in 1997. Final figures for 1998 are not yet available, but preliminary data suggest shipments in the vicinity of 280,000 units. To put this performance in some perspective, prior to 1994, shipments had exceeded the 200,000 units mark only three times since WWII. Between 1994–1998, shipments of complete trailers exceeded the 200,000 mark each and every year and averaged 246,000 units

Wabash National was the nation's leading trailer manufacturer in 1998 with 18.4% of the market, based on registration data. Wabash was also number one in 1997 with 15.4% of the market. The rest of the 1998 U.S. market for truck trailers was divided as follows: Great Dane, 13.1%; Utility Trailers, 8.2%; Trailmobile, 7.3%; Hyundai, 5.5%; Stoughton Trailers, 4.6%; Strick Trailers, 4.3%; Pines Trailers, 4.0%; Lufkin Trailers, 2.4%; and Dorsey Trailers, 2.2%.

Truck Trailer Outlook

It looks like 1999 is on track to become another record year for complete trailer shipments, by beating out the next best two years, 1995 and 1998, by just a bit. There is still plenty of forward momentum in the economy and key trailer-buying end-markets, and we still expect shipments of complete trailers to exceed 280,000 units this year. If we are right about 1999, it will mark the sixth consecutive 200,000-unit-plus year for shipments.

End-Market

The major truck trailer buying markets include trucking companies, wholesale and retail trade, manufacturers, construction, mining and logging, and agriculture. Historically, end-market activity has been a good gauge of the strength or weakness in trailer demand. Periods of accelerating growth or sustained strong growth in end–market activity have triggered periods of healthy investment in new equipment. Conversely, periods of decelerating or declining growth in end-market activity have been accompanied by lackluster-to-weak equipment acquisition programs. We are currently seeing very strong performances in the trucking and construction industries. Manufacturing and retail and wholesale trade remain supportive, but are having less of a positive influence than either trucking companies or construction. Going forward, we expect to lose support in the year 2000 from all major trailer markets. Longer term, most trailer markets will do reasonably well as the U.S. economy expands by 2.0%–2.5% per year and U.S. industrial output grows by 2.5%–3.0% per year.

Historically, end-market activity has been a good gauge of the strength or weakness in commercial trailer demand. Periods of accelerating growth or sustained strong growth in end-market activity have triggered periods of healthy investment in new equipment. Conversely, periods of decelerating or declining growth in end-market activity have been accompanied by tamer equipment acquisition programs.

Trailer market activity, which is weighted to reflect the importance of each buying market, grew by 7.7% in 1997 and 6.3% in 1998. We expect a loss of momentum going forward, with growth slowing to 4.6% in 1999 and 2.1% in the year 2000. Thereafter, we expect end-market activity to expand by 2.8% per year from 2001–2004 and 2.5% per year from 2005-2008.

Trailer Traffic

We estimate that trailer tonnage grew by 4.6% in 1998, following a 6.1% increase in 1997. Since emerging from the last recession (1992–1998), trailer tonnage has expanded by 35%. This strong growth in trailer traffic played no small role in the dramatic increase in truck trailer shipments in recent years. Historically, the performance of trailer tonnage has been a good indicator of the strength or weakness in trailer demand. Periods of accelerating growth or sustained strong growth in traffic have been accompanied by healthy investment in new equipment. Conversely, periods of decelerating or declining traffic growth have triggered periods of cautious investment in new equipment.

Over the next two years, trailer-tonnage growth is put at 3.3% in 1999 and 1.8% in 2000. This represents a significant slowdown in the rate of expansion in traffic and will eventually trigger a more conservative pace of fleet expansion. Beyond the year 2000, we expect trailer tonnage to accelerate. We are anticipating a moderate pick-up in domestic economic activity, a slower rate of import penetration, and signs of life on the export front. Trailer traffic stages a comeback in 2001 and then continues to gain ground thereafter. Our current forecast

has trailer tonnage growing by 2.5%–3.0% per year during the 2001–2008 period.

Truck Trailer Forecast

We expect an adjustment, not a correction, in trailer demand next year. The economy, end-market activity, and trailer tonnage will continue to expand in the year 2000, but growth will be considerably slower than we have experienced in recent years. In addition, fuel costs will be on the rise, which will put some pressure on motor-carrier profit margins. With this as a backdrop, the pressure and incentive to continue to aggressively expand and upgrade fleets will subside. The trailer fleet has been both expanded and upgraded dramatically during the past five years. Fleet operators responded to the growth in traffic, low-interest rates, strong financial performance, competitive pressures, shipper demands for high-quality/low-cost/problem-free service, and the availability of new state-of-the-art equipment, by investing aggressively in new van and other trailers.

U.S. trailer builders shipped over 1.2 million complete trailers from 1994–1998. When you add in the 280,000 units we expect this year, the 1994–1999 shipments total 1.5 million units. Van trailer shipments totaled almost 925,000 units during this period. This total rises to 1.15 million units when you add in our estimate of nearly 225,000 vans shipped in 1999. The trend to larger sized vans, 53 footers becoming the industry-standard when adding new units to a fleet and replacing 48 footers, implies an even more dramatic infusion of new carrying capacity.

With fleet expansion pressures subsiding as traffic growth moderates, pent-up replacement demand all but satisfied, "normal" replacement demand stabilizing, complete trailer shipments drop to 250,000-255,000 units in the year 2000.

The economic and market fundamentals that drive the demand for new equipment begin to improve late next year and continue to gain ground through 2008. This sets the stage for stronger fleet expansion and more aggressive equipment replacement programs. The units brought into the fleet during the early stages of the current buying cycle should be coming up for replacement during the 2001–2004 period. Better economic conditions, rising profits, and attractive interest rates allow the necessary replacement of older units to proceed. At the same time, expanding traffic will require new additions to the fleet.

The demand for new equipment remains sluggish as 2001 unfolds, but picks up momentum during the second half of the year, setting the stage for a better 2002. Thereafter, growth in traffic and a rise in replacement demand allow the market to stage a true comeback.

We expect complete trailer shipments of 240,000 units in 2001, rising to 275,000 units by 2004 and 300,000-310,000 units by 2008.

Motor Vehicle Parts

The automotive parts industry in this country is made up of over 5,000 firms, employing more than 710,000 workers and a value of shipments in excess of $125 billion. There are two main sectors to the parts industry: original equipment parts (OEM), which are used in the manufacture of new cars and trucks, and the replacement market. For many years the largest parts supply operations were divisions of the major original equipment manufacturers (OEMs), i.e., General Motors and Ford. Both firms have spun off these internal operations, establishing them as separate companies. GM's Delphi divestiture, with $26.4 billion in global revenues, remains this industry's volume leader, but Ford's Visteon spin-off ($17.8 billion) has fallen to third place, behind Robert Bosch ($18.4 billion).

In the past, automobile assemblers (OEMs) considered a high degree of vertical integration desirable for quality control and low cost, hence the existence of large internal parts divisions. As the auto market matured, competition in the United States intensified. Smaller, non-union, independent suppliers placed the bigger, unionized OEM divisions at a cost disadvantage. The growth of the global automotive industry and onset of global parts sourcing only heightened competitive pressures.

First Ford divested its parts division, now known as Visteon, then GM (Delphi). While these mammoth suppliers still do a great deal of business and maintain financial ties with their former parent companies, their mandate is to develop a diversified customer base both in the United States and abroad. This is creating unique opportunities and threats for the independent parts supplier. On one hand, there is the potential for greater business with GM and Ford; on the other, the competition with other assemblers has increased, from both the new domestic operations and from parts suppliers throughout the world.

With outsourcing and competition, and the demands of modularization, i.e. component manufacturers becoming responsible for the development, design, manufacture, and sometimes installation of entire component systems, parts suppliers must get bigger. For example, instead of having separate suppliers responsible for brake pads, brake drums, and brake shoes, one producer will furnish all of these components or a complete brake system. A single supplier is now often responsible for the entire vehicle interior, as opposed to the old way of separate suppliers for seats, carpeting, and upholstery. This results in larger firms dominating the supply chain, generating a wave of mergers and acquisitions throughout the industry. In 1998, six different parts firms increased their revenue base by roughly $1.0 to $2.0 billion each by absorbing other companies. In 1998, the top-100 parts suppliers generated global sales totaling $298 billion, a gain of 9.0%. Seven of the top-ten global firms were located in North America. The sales boom in the United States and wave of assembly plant expansion in North America have enabled the parts industry in North America to grow twice as fast as the global average.

All of the major vehicle manufacturers are committed to outsourcing and modularization. General Motors has announced an ambitious expansion and modernization strategy, all geared around new modular assembly and parts suppliers who are able to support this plan. The main goal is to raise productivity and reduce labor content. This move to modularity and outsourcing is a source of friction between the manufacturers and the United Automobile Workers (UAW). The UAW wants to protect as many existing union jobs as possible. Thus, it is seeking to limit the extent to which the OEMs can reduce the employment level of the new plants relative to their existing operations. It also wants to relocate laid off employees at other facilities. The UAW is also seeking the manufacturer's aid and support in unionization drives at non-union parts suppliers and transplant facilities. Labor strife can only be avoided through a heavy dose of cooperation between management and the UAW. This partnership is always essential but will be especially critical in 1999, as the UAW is renegotiating its annual contract.

Even though the average age of cars and trucks on the road is at its highest level in over 40 years, the replacement market–parts and service–has come under pressure. Vehicles are easier to maintain, experiencing far less problems and breakdowns each year; parts last longer. The auto replacement market is around $150 billion a year at retail, and has been that way for the last few years. Even so, major manufacturers, i.e. Ford and Dana, have made significant acquisitions of after-market firms, in an effort to get closer to the consumer.

The OEMs maintain constant pressure on parts suppliers to cut costs and have now moved to worldwide sourcing of parts. In 1998, U.S. parts imports exceeded $54.0 billion, up from $32.0 billion in 1990. On the other hand, the United States exported $47.0 billion, up even more, from $23.0 billion in 1990. However, the global crisis dampened the growth of U.S. exports in 1998 (even with 1998) and the expense of imports (up around 7.0%).

Aircraft and Parts

During the 1988–1998 period, aircraft and parts industry shipments rose at a compound annual rate of 2.5%. However, this is certainly not a stagnant industry, despite showing little point-to-point growth during the last ten years. This performance is the direct result of violent swings in the two major industry segments, commercial aircraft and defense. During this period the aircraft and parts industry experienced a full cycle (first up, then down, then up again) in commercial-transport demand. Equally important, the industry weathered the dramatic downsizing of the Defense Department and restrained spending by NASA and other government agencies.

The most recent buying cycle in the commercial-aircraft market is coming to an end. This year will be the peak for commercial-transport deliveries in the current cycle. Capacity additions were greater than traffic growth in 1998 and the same will hold true this year. Orders for new aircraft have fallen below their year-ago level, and we expect deliveries to decline over the next two years. The defense portion of the aerospace industry is emerging from a very deep hole, due to the pressures to modernize aircraft and missile resources. The most recent budget includes increases in funding.

The WEFA forecast calls for aircraft and parts shipments to increase by 7% in 1999 to $147 billion. Shipments decline by 7% in 2000 and 4% in 2001, due to weakness in the commercial air-transport market. For the rest of the ten-year period, shipments should grow by about 5%–6% per year supported by another round of commercial-transport buying and increases in military outlays.

Recent History

The aircraft, missiles, and parts industry has experienced some wild swings over the past decade or so. These swings have been triggered by economic conditions, specific market factors, world events, and politics.

Industry shipments rose from $102 billion in 1986 to $133 billion in 1991, an increase of 30%, or about 6% per year on average. Over the next four years, shipments fell 25% to $100 billion in 1995, as the civilian aircraft market dried up and the reductions in military outlays accelerated. The aircraft and parts industry reported sales of almost $101 billion in 1996. This represented an increase of only 0.9% above the 1995 level. However, with a rebound in commercial aircraft sales in full swing, shipments surged ahead by 20% in 1997 to $121billion. Last-year sales rose another 14% to $137.7 billion.

While aerospace industry shipments have remained strong, orders have lost their forward momentum. At their most recent low point, the aerospace industry reported orders valued at $88.4 billion in 1993. Orders then rose to $129.2 billion in 1996. In 1997 and 1998 orders flattened out at about $124 billion per year. Thus far in 1999, orders have been roughly stable with their 1998 pace. Shipments, on the other hand, are running about 10% ahead of last year. As a result, the order backlog in the aerospace industry has fallen by 10% over the past year.

Business Investment

The commercial aircraft market has experienced more than its share of ups and downs in the last decade or so. U.S. business investment in new aircraft totaled $9.7 billion in 1997 and then rose to $10.4 billion the following year. In 1989, spending dropped 20% to $8.3 billion. This was followed by four strong years that saw spending of $11.8 billion in 1990, $13.0 billion in 1991, $13.2 billion in 1992, and $13.1 billion in 1993. In 1994, business outlays for new aircraft dropped 32% to less than $8.9 billion. The last four years have been good ones with spending averaging $13.2 billion per year in 1995 and 1996, rising to $17.9 billion in 1997, and then jumping 64% to $29.5 billion in 1998. During the first half of this year, business outlays were running 18% below the same period in 1998 and 7% behind the spending pace achieved during the second half of last year.

Government Spending

Government spending for aircraft, missiles, and parts includes outlays for new equipment and spending for spare and replacement parts. In 1987, government spending for aircraft and parts totaled $49.2 billion. With the exception of the Gulf War-related blip in 1990–1991, spending has fallen steadily ever since as the "downsizing" of the military proceeded. By 1996, government spending for aircraft missiles and parts totaled just $25.5 billion. Spending then fell another 17% in 1997 to $21.1 billion and held at roughly that level last year. Things have brightened in 1999. Through the first half of this year, government spending for aircraft missiles and parts is running nearly 17% ahead of last year's pace.

Government spending on new aircraft totaled $17.6 billion in 1987. Spending fell almost without interruption throughout the next decade, reaching slightly under $6 billion in 1997. In 1998, spending slipped to $5.7 billion. However, the year was characterized by a very weak first half and a strong comeback during the second half of the year. In fact, second-half outlays for new equipment were 40% higher than they were in the first half. This year has started off on a positive note. Through the first half of 1999, government investment in new aircraft was running 38% ahead of its depressed year-ago level.

Government spending for spare and replacement parts totaled $18.2 billion in 1987 and bottomed out at $8.9 billion in 1995. Since then spending increased 2% in 1996 to $9 billion, 6% in 1997 to $9.6 billion, and about 5% in 1998 to $10.1 billion. Through the first half of this year, spare and replacement-part spending was running about 2% behind last year's pace.

Investment in new missiles totaled $8.7 billion in 1987, $7.9 billion in 1988, and $8.9 billion in 1989. From 1990–1992, spending averaged $10.7 billion per year largely as a result of the Gulf War. Spending for new missiles declined steadily during the 1993–1998 period, reaching a paltry $3 billion last year. New missile procurement has been on the rise this year, with outlays running a whopping 44% ahead of their 1998 pace.

Missile spare and replacement-part spending grew from $4.8 billion in 1987 to $5.5 billion in 1991. Outlays then fell without interruption to $2.4 billion in 1998. We have seen a pick-up this year, as spending for spare and replacement parts is running 17% ahead of last year's pace.

Foreign Trade

Foreign trade has long been a bright spot for the aircraft and parts industry. The United States continues to maintain a significant trade surplus in aircraft and parts, due to two key factors: Boeing's strength in the world commercial-transport market; and strong demand overseas for military aerospace products. However, competition from Airbus in recent months has intensified, and the recent order flow suggests that our trade advantage in commercial transports will be narrowing over the near term.

During the last decade, exports of civilian aircraft, engines, and parts grew from $16.2 billion in 1987 to $41.4 billion in 1997, an average annual increase of 15.5%. Last year, exports jumped another 29% to $53.5 billion. Thus far in 1999, U.S. exports are running 29% ahead of their 1998 pace. Imports also grew, from $6.6 billion in 1987 to $16.6 billion in 1997, and jumped another 31% to $21.8 billion last year. This year, imports of aircraft and parts are running about 12% ahead of last year's pace.

Exports of complete civilian aircraft totaled $7.7 billion in 1987 and hit a peak of $24.5 billion in 1992. With the commercial-aircraft market in a slump, foreign sales drifted off to a low of $12.9 billion in 1995. With another commercial transport cycle underway, exports of complete aircraft rose 21.8% in 1996, 50.6% to $23.6 billion in 1997, and 34.9% last year to $31.8 billion. Thus far in 1999, exports of complete civilian aircraft are running better than 35% ahead of their 1998 pace. Historically, the vast majority of the commercial planes used to be produced by Boeing and McDonnell Douglas. However, Airbus has made significant inroads into the world and U.S. markets in recent years. Imports of complete aircraft were valued at only $2.1 billion in 1987. They hit $3.8 billion in 1992, and then drifted off to $3.6 billion in 1995. As the commercial transport market headed up again, and the foreign consortium Airbus made inroads in the U.S. market, imports rose to $3.9 billion in 1996, $4.5 billion in 1997, and $7.0 billion in 1998. Imports of complete aircraft are currently running 24% ahead of last year. The trade surplus in complete aircraft has grown over the last decade from $5.6 billion in 1987 to $19 billion in 1997 and $24.8 billion in 1998. Thus far this year, the trade surplus in complete aircraft is running 40% ahead of a year ago.

Exports of civilian aircraft engines were valued at $3.8 billion in 1987, $7.8 billion in 1997, and almost $10 billion last year. Thus far this year, exports are running better than 20% ahead of their 1998 pace. During the past decade, engine sales mirrored the good and bad years for the commercial aircraft market. Imports of engines were valued at only $2.2 billion in 1987, but rose to $7.6 billion in 1997 and $9.4 billion in 1998. This year's imports of aircraft engines are running between 5%–6% ahead of a year ago.

The civilian aircraft parts business is influenced by the utilization and age of the commercial fleet, as well as by demand for new planes. Both exports and imports were hurt by the slump in the economy in 1990–1991, and by the weakness in commercial transport production during the 1992–1995 period. U.S. exports of aircraft parts were valued at $4.8 billion in 1987 and reached $10 billion in 1997. Part exports rose another 18% last year to $11.8 billion. Thus far this year, part exports are running better than 20% ahead of a year ago. Imports of aircraft parts went from $2.2 billion in 1987 to $4.5 billion in 1997 and $5.4 billion last year. Imports of civilian aircraft parts are currently running about 10% ahead of their 1998 pace.

In 1987, U.S. exports of military aircraft were valued at $5.5 billion. Exports rose almost without interruption for nearly a decade, reaching $14.8 billion in 1996. Overseas sales fell back by 9% the following year to $13.5 billion, but surged ahead by over 10% last year. Thus far this year, U.S. exports of military aircraft are running almost 11% ahead of their 1998 pace. We import very few military aircraft. Throughout the late 1980s and until 1996, imports averaged less than $750 million per year. In 1997 imports jumped to $1.1 billion and then rose another 11% last year. Thus far in 1999, imports of military aircraft are running about equal with last year's pace.

Employment and Earnings

Employment in the aerospace industry follows the swings in the two volatile sectors, commercial transport and defense. Aircraft and parts industry employment stood at 712,000 back in 1990, but had slumped to 450,500 by 1995. Among airframe manufacturers, employment went from a high of 382,000 in 1989 to a low of 243,000 in 1996. For producers of engines and parts,

employment crested in 1987 at 158,000 and bottomed out in 1996 at 94,700. In the area of guided missiles and space equipment, employment peaked in 1988 at 208,000, and fell to just over 90,000 in 1996.

Triggered by the start of the current rebound in the commercial-transport market, there were considerable improvements in industry employment. For the aircraft and parts industry as a whole, employment rose to 500,000 in 1997 and 523,650 in 1998. Among airframe producers, employment jumped by 20,000 in 1997 to 263,000, and rose to 269,790 by the middle of 1998. Engine and part producers increased employment from 94,700 in 1996 to almost 100,000 in 1997 and 103,350 in 1998. There has been some improvement in employment in guided missiles and space equipment. Employment went from 90,390 in 1996 to 90,380 in 1997 and then up to 91,700 in 1998.

Average hourly earnings in the aircraft and parts industry stood at $13.55 in 1988. A decade later that figure had risen to $19.17 per hour, an increase of 4% per year, on average. Among producers of aircraft, average annual earnings rose from $14.18 in 1988 to $21.08, an increase of almost 5% per year. In the aircraft engine and parts business, average hourly earnings went from $13.80 in 1988 to $18.94 in 1998 an increase of about 3% per year. In guided missiles, space vehicles, and parts segment of the industry average annual earnings totaled $13.13 in 1998. Over the next decade earnings rose 5% per year, on average, to $19.96 in 1998.

Forecast 1999–2008

The WEFA forecast calls for aircraft and parts shipments to increase by 7% this year to $147 billion. However, the stage has been set for a modest correction during the next two years. The Asian crisis disrupted the order flow to Boeing and competition from Airbus has intensified. U.S. spending on military aircraft, missiles, and parts should gain ground based on the latest Defense Department budget numbers and following operations in the Balkans. The general aviation market should do well again this year, but growth will slow over the near term, as profits come under pressure and fuel costs rise. Over the next two years, we expect sales of aircraft and parts to slip by 7% in 2000 to $136.5 billion and then decline by 3.6% in 2001 to $131.6. After adjusting for inflation, this translates into volume declines of 10% in 2000 and 7% in 2001.

Longer term, 2001–2008, look for a recovery in the commercial-aircraft business, as world revenue passenger miles and cargo traffic continue to expand. This will require additional capacity to be added to the passenger and cargo fleets. Additional support comes from pressures to replace the older airplanes currently in service. Military spending for aircraft, missiles, and parts should begin to improve, as the United States looks to meet new challenges throughout the world. General aviation will continue to expand as corporate profits increase and the trend towards personal-use aircraft continues among upper-income individuals. Shipments should grow by 5%–6% per year, on average, and exceed $180 billion by 2008.

Commercial Transports

The demand for commercial transports is largely a function of expansion pressures, which rise and fall with traffic trends; changes in the traffic mix, which may signal that a change in the type of equipment is needed; and aircraft replacement, which is a function of the aging of the existing fleet. Pressures to reduce noise pollution and improvements in aircraft technology are also important. In the past ten years, the commercial transport market has gone through a number of cycles. The commercial transport business became a two-horse race when Boeing took over the commercial-transport business of McDonnell Douglas in 1997. Boeing/MD remains the leader followed by the European consortium Airbus, which has become a major threat.

Deliveries by U.S. airframe manufacturers bottomed out in 1984 at 185 units and began to improve thereafter, rising to 357 by 1987. The market hit its stride over the next five years, with deliveries averaging 500 units per year. Deliveries peaked in 1991 at 589 units and then edged off to 567 units in 1992. For the 1988–1992 period, Airbus Industries reported deliveries of 581 new aircraft, 163 units in 1991 and 157 units in 1992. New orders for aircraft actually peaked back in 1989, but swollen backlogs kept airframe manufacturers' production going for another three years.

The airline industry took a hit during the 1990–1991 recession. World airline traffic experienced a significant loss of momentum at the same time that deliveries of new commercial transports were peaking. The combination of sluggish traffic and a huge influx of capacity drove down load factors and severely weakened airline finances. U.S. scheduled airlines reported operating losses of $6.1 billion from 1990–1992. Foreign airlines did not fare any better. Reflecting the sharp fall off in orders that began in 1990, U.S. airframe manufacturers reported deliveries of 408 units in 1993, 309 units in 1994, 256 units in 1995, and 269 in 1996. Airbus industries saw its deliveries slip to 138 units in 1993, 123 units in 1994, 124 units in 1995, and 125 units in 1996.

The seeds of the next upswing in commercial aircraft were planted as we emerged from the 1990–1991 recession. From 1993–1998, the airline industry did well, reflecting the strength in the U.S. and most world economies and restrained fuel costs. World revenue passenger miles and cargo traffic expanded at a healthy clip during most of this period. Airline profits staged a dramatic comeback. From 1993–1998, U.S. scheduled airlines posted operating profits of $34 billion, $9.3 billion in 1998 alone. Beginning in 1998, the Asia economic crisis did take a toll on traffic related to that region and airlines with a heavy Asian exposure. Overall traffic volumes in Asia fell by almost 8% in 1998. Southeast Asia traffic dropped by 20%.

For U.S. scheduled airlines, traffic turned the corner in 1992, as passenger miles increased 6.8%. Over the next five years, 1993–1997, passenger traffic expanded by nearly 5.5% per year, on average. In 1998, however, passenger-traffic growth slowed to only 2.3%. Domestic-passenger miles increased 4% in 1992 and then expanded by 5.6% per year, on average, from 1993–1997. Last year, growth slowed to 2.5%. International-passenger miles grew by 13% in 1992 and 4.5% per year, on average, from 1993–1997. In 1998, international-passenger miles edged upward by only 1.8%. Cargo ton-miles also turned the corner in 1992, expanding by 8.8%. Over the next five years, 1993–1997, cargo traffic expanded at an average annual rate of 12%. Traffic growth stalled, however, in 1998.

The revival in airline fortunes coming out of the last recession triggered a surge in new orders for commercial aircraft. The U.S. airframe business reported net new orders for 421 new aircraft in 1995, up from 79 in 1994 and only 31 in 1993. In 1996, orders jumped to 595 new aircraft. In 1997, orders fell back to 501. Last year, Boeing reported net new orders for 601 aircraft. Airbus reported orders for 106 in 1995, 336 in 1996, and 438 in 1997. In 1998, Airbus reported net new orders for 529 new aircraft.

With orders on the rise and the order backlog swelling once again, aircraft deliveries began to accelerate. Boeing delivered 374 commercial transports in 1997, up from 269 the previous year. In 1998, Boeing delivered 559 new aircraft. Airbus reported deliveries of 182 new aircraft in 1997 versus 125 in 1996. In 1998, Airbus deliveries rose to 229 units.

At the end of last year, the order backlog for commercial aircraft stood at 3,095 units, up from 2,753 units a year earlier. U.S. customers accounted for 1,704 planes or 55% of the total. Foreign customers accounted for the remaining 1,391 planes or 45% of the total. Boeing with a backlog of 1,786 planes and almost 50% of the planes on order, continued to dominate the market. For Boeing, 61.5% of its customers were domestic, the remaining 38.5% foreign. Airbus with a backlog of 1,309 planes accounted for 42% of the planes on order. Airbus has made inroads into the U.S. market, accounting for 35.5% of the planes on order and destined for U.S. customers. Airbus Industries backlog was split 46% U.S. customers and 54% foreign. Airbus has made significant inroads in the U.S. market this year. Through July, Boeing had announced orders for only 121 new aircraft. Airbus Industries reported orders for 240 new planes during the same period. On the delivery side, Boeing had delivered 349 planes versus 167 for Airbus.

Outlook

This year will represent the peak in the current buying cycle for commercial aircraft. Orders in 1998 were far stronger than anticipated, especially in light of the economic and financial troubles that plagued much of Asia and parts of Latin America. Delivery dates were stretched out, some orders were cancelled, and others that had been expected were never placed. However, economic conditions in most of the rest of the world remained supportive. In contrast, aircraft orders in 1999 are running well behind both their 1997 and 1998 pace. As a result, orders this year will probably fall to between 600–700 units. We expect further erosion in orders next year and into 2001, as airlines digest the new capacity that has been taken into the fleet in recent years. The real surge in commercial-transport deliveries began in 1997 when 556 new planes were delivered. Capacity growth exceeded traffic in 1998 when Boeing and Airbus combined delivered 788 new planes. We expect new plane deliveries to total 890 units this year, with Boeing at 620 units and Airbus at 270. Thus, 1999 will

be another year where capacity growth exceeds traffic growth.

The longer term prospects for commercial transport demand remains favorable. Passenger-traffic growth worldwide is put at about 5% per year. Look for above-average traffic growth in Latin America and Asia. The vast majority of the aircraft delivered beyond the year 2000 will be for passenger service. However, strong growth is also expected in world cargo traffic, about 6% per year, which will require the expansion of the freighter fleet. Most of the additions to the cargo fleet will be largely filled by used passenger aircraft conversions. This implies that there will be a healthy market for used passenger aircraft, which will only help convince the airlines to purchase new planes. In addition to expansion pressures related to growth in passenger and cargo traffic, the demand for new planes will be supported by mounting pressures to replace older units in the fleet with new aircraft that have been configured for use in specific traffic corridors and that meet the latest noise pollution regulations.

Commercial-jet transport deliveries are slated to fall back to 720 units in 2000 (480 for Boeing and 240 for Airbus). In 2001, deliveries drop to 600 units, with Boeing at 375 units and Airbus at 225 units. Longer term, we are projecting average annual demand for new aircraft at between 600–700 units per year. If Airbus Industries is correct about stronger demand for planes in the 400- to 500-seat or larger category, unit deliveries will average closer to 600 units per year. If Boeing is correct and the market leans more to single-aisle and intermediate-size commercial transports and increases its dependence on regional jets, deliveries should average closer to 700 units per year.

Defense: Better Days Ahead

The Reagan Administration boosted production of tactical aircraft in the late 1970s to counter a modernization push by the Soviet Union and a perceived military threat in Europe. Production remained at high levels well into the following decade. Between 1987 and 1998, defense-related spending for new aircraft and missiles and spare and replacement parts fell from $49.2 billion to $21.1 billion.

The pressure has been building to replace older aircraft and take advantage of emerging technologies. There are major concerns about the readiness of our defense aircraft due to spare parts shortages, and missile defense has become an issue once again due to the renewed proliferation of nuclear weapons, sales of advanced guidance technology to foreign countries, and increased terrorist activity. Spending programs will be designed to modernize the existing fleet of strategic and fighter aircraft. The initial stages of the programs that will yield the next generation of fighter aircraft are also underway. Greater expenditures are expected for cruise and other missiles, which are viewed as the ideal vehicle to strike against terrorists without any risk to personnel.

Spending has turned up this year and, based on the most recent Department of Defense budget numbers, we believe we have entered a period of more robust spending for military aircraft, missiles, and spare and replacement parts. It is our belief that DOD aircraft and missile modernization spending could grow by 5%–6% per year, on average, through the middle of the next decade.

Department of Defense efforts to modernize aviation forces include the Joint Strike Force (JSF), which is a family of aircraft designed to serve different functions. This is DOD's largest acquisition program. The JSF is designed to replace the F-16 in the Air Force, F/A-18c in the Navy, and F/A-18D and AV-8B for the Marines. The F-22 represents the replacement for the F-15C/D in the air-superiority role and provides air-to-ground capability as well. The Navy's F/A-18E/F should provide greater survivability and payload over earlier F/A-18 models. Longer term, the Navy indicates that it will transition from F/A-18E/F to the JSF.

Modernization of ground forces includes upgrades of the Apache longbow helicopter and the Comanche helicopter. Marine Corps modernization programs include the V-22 tilt-rotor aircraft, and upgrades of utility and attack helicopters and the AV-8B. By the end of fiscal year 2003, procurement of 120 C-17 aircraft will be completed. Additional acquisitions are also planned.

These planes are viewed as necessary to increase our ability to project military power throughout the world. The KC-135 tanker and C-5 transport are set to have major avionics upgrades and other improvements.

The most recent budget includes funding for the Patriot PAC-3 and Navy Area, THAAD and Navy Theater Wide missile defense systems that are designed to defeat shorter-range missiles. To counter theater-range missiles funding is included for an Airborne Laser system. Funding for the National Missile defense program totals $10.5 billion for fiscal years 1999–2005.

All the news about defense-related spending for aircraft and missiles is not good however. On July 22, the House of Representatives omitted funding for the F-22 jet fighter citing concern about cost overruns in the $70 billion F-22 program and a desire to evaluate other alternatives. Politics, no doubt, also played a role. Congress in the past has complained that the Pentagon has too many new aircraft under development—the F-22, the Navy F/A-18E/F, and the JSF, which is a multiservice aircraft. In response, the Pentagon scaled back the F-22 program from its original 750 planes to 339 planes.

It is our belief that funding for the F-22 will eventually be restored when the House and Senate meet to hammer out the differences between their views of defense spending. The Senate has approved the Air Force request for $1.8 billion to pay for the first six F-22's.

The F-22 is far superior to any other fighter/bomber, including a greater range than our current longest range fighter, the F-15C; enhanced technology, which makes it easier on pilots to deal with a greater range and number of targets; and lower support costs. One alternative to proceeding with the F-22 would be upgrading the F-15, which would be very costly and would not result in a plane with F-22 capabilities. A second alternative would be to depend on the Eurofighter, a politically difficult choice to sell on the home front.

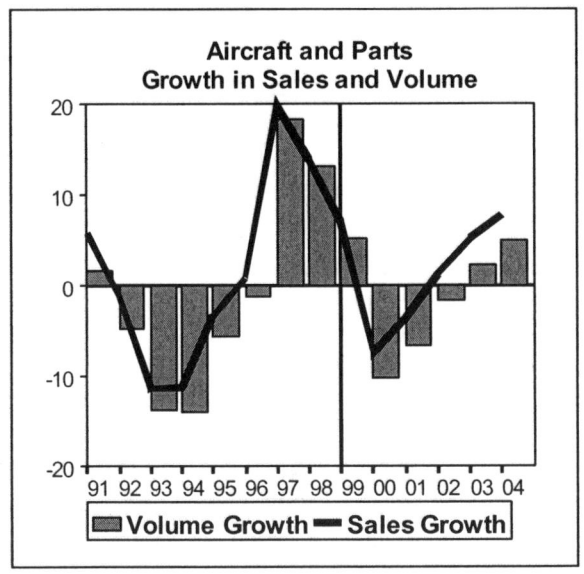

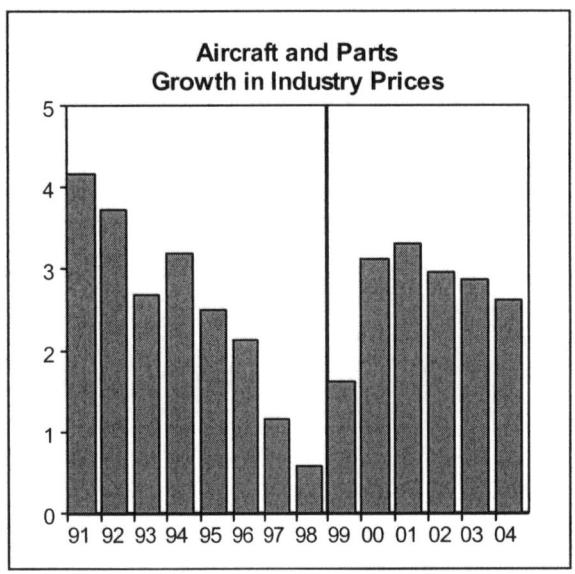

Aircraft and Parts

SIC 372

		1992	1993	1994	1995	1996	1997	1998	1999	2000	2001	Compound Average 88-98	Annual Growth 98-08
Sales													
	Billions of $	131.4	116.5	103.4	100.0	100.9	120.9	137.7	147.4	136.5	131.6		
	% Ch	-1.1	-11.3	-11.2	-3.3	0.9	19.9	13.9	7.1	-7.4	-3.6	2.5	3.3
Volume													
	% Ch	-4.7	-13.7	-14.0	-5.7	-1.2	18.4	13.2	5.3	-10.2	-6.7	-0.7	0.6
Prices													
	% Ch	3.7	2.7	3.2	2.5	2.1	1.2	0.6	1.6	3.1	3.3	3.2	2.7
Production Costs													
Avg. Hourly Earnings													
	$/hr	16.68	17.43	18.24	18.43	18.99	19.37	19.66	19.98	20.49	21.13		
	% Ch	6.4	4.5	4.6	1.0	3.0	2.0	1.5	1.6	2.6	3.1	3.7	2.7
Input Price Index													
	% Ch	2.2	1.6	2.3	3.1	1.0	1.0	0.3	1.1	2.5	2.9	2.1	2.5

Boat and Ship Building and Repair

The boat and ship building and repair industry consists of establishments primarily engaged in building and repairing pleasure craft, commercial boats and ships, and military vessels.

This industry was in distress for most of this decade. In 1997, fewer than 160,000 people were employed in the boat and shipbuilding and repair industry. At its most recent peak in 1988-1989, employment approached 196,000. With defense on the rise, and with modest support likely from the commercial marine and pleasure boat segments, WEFA expects this industry to continue to gain ground throughout the forecast period.

Recent History

The U.S. boat and ship building and repair industry was in distress for much of the past decade. The commercial and recreational segments of the business had their share of ups and downs during the decade, and the sharp reduction in defense purchases of ships and boats had a major impact on industry performance.

Business Investment

Business investment in ships and boats faltered during the 1990–1991 recession and has performed erratically since then. There have been some gains in waterborne commerce since the 1990–1991 recession, but the recent weakness in coal and grain exports has hurt. Business spending on ships and boats bottomed at $1.3 billion in 1992. Spending rose to $2.2 billion in 1993, dropped to $1.5 billion in 1994, and then rose to $1.8 billion in 1995. Over the next two years, 1996 and 1997, business spending for ships and boats averaged $2.4 billion per year as increased world trade and an aging fleet prompted an increase in investment. Despite the increase in spending levels in 1996 and 1997, the pressures to replace older vessels in operation remained intense. At the end of 1997, 69% of U.S. flag vessels had been in service for over 15 years, 19% had been in service for 21–25 years, and 21% for more than 25 years. Last year, business spending for ships and boats jumped to almost $3.5 billion.

Defense Spending

Department of Defense (DOD) spending on new ships and boats averaged over $10 billion a year from 1989 to 1992. In 1993, spending fell to $8.65 billion. Over the next four years DOD spending has been in a free fall, dropping to $6.1 billion in 1997. Last year saw a slight increase in outlays to $6.4 billion. DOD spending for spare and replacement parts for its ships and boats grew from $980 million in 1987 to $2.25 billion in 1993. Since then, spending has fallen steadily, reaching $650 million last year.

Consumer Spending

The recreational boat business was hurt during the 1990–1991 recession, but tumbled further as a result of the 10% excise tax that was placed on luxury items in 1991. Between 1989 and 1992, spending fell by 22%. This tax was removed in 1993, but by then the damage had been done.

Last year, consumers spent approximately $15 billion on pleasure boats and related products. Spending for power boats, sail boats, jet skis, wave runners, and other products have been on the rise since 1993. During the period from 1993–1998, consumer outlay for pleasure boats and related products grew by 136%. Strong growth in consumer-disposable income, a lengthy recovery in Florida and the rest of the Southeast, and a long-awaited recovery in California have propelled consumer spending for pleasure boats forward. Florida and California are both major pleasure and recreational boating states.

Foreign Trade

Since 1990, U.S. exports of ships and boats have exceeded imports every year with the exception of 1996. In 1990, exports were valued at $1.3 billion and rose to $1.4 billion by 1992. Exports then fell to $976 million in

1993. Over the next three years, exports averaged $1.1 billion annually and then accelerated to $1.4 billion in 1997, and $1.7 billion in 1998.

From 1990 through 1992, imports of ships and boats averaged about $300 million per year. In 1993, imports surged to $967 million. This was followed by imports of $809 million in 1994 and $816 million in 1995. In 1996, imports swelled to $1.1 billion and then fell back to $875 million in 1997. Last year, imports of ships and boats rose to $1.1 billion.

Employment

The ship and boat building and repair business employed 166,000 workers in 1998. This represented the highest employment level since 1992 when it employed almost 170,000. During the five years from 1993–1997, employment was stagnant at about 159,000. The peak employment years for ship and boat building and repair were 1988 and 1989, when employment averaged 194,000 per year.

The shipbuilding and repair business employed 106,000 workers in 1998. The surge in business spending on new commercial vessels boosted employment by nearly 5% following six straight years of declines. Employment had peaked at 131,140 back in 1991 and then plummeted to 101,560 by 1997.

The boat building and repair business employed 60,200 workers in 1998, an increase of 6% over the prior year. Employment has been on the rise since 1993, which followed four consecutive years of declining employment. In 1988, employment peaked at 71,610 and then fell to 45,230 by 1992.

Outlook

The long-term prospects for ship and boat building and repair remain positive. Consumer and business spending for boats and ships should continue to gain ground. However, the big change will be renewed strength in DOD outlays for naval vessels.

The demand for commercial vessels should remain supportive. Growth in waterway traffic will be modest, but the pressure to replace the older units in the fleet remains intense. Despite the recent increase in commercial vessel spending, we estimate that more than a third of U.S. flag vessels have been in service for over 20 years. In addition, there is an interest in the barge business to go after more NAFTA-related trade. Success in this endeavor could stimulate additional investment in barges and towboats.

Spending for pleasure boats has been expanding at a very brisk clip in recent years, but is likely to slow over the near term, given our expectations for national and regional income growth. However, long-term income growth at the national level will be supportive, and California and Florida will be near the top of the list for income growth over the next ten years. Furthermore, as the baby-boomers retire in large numbers they will finally have the time to enjoy such pursuits as recreational boating.

DOD spending for new naval vessels is expected to rise during the forecast period. Modernization programs include procurement of the DDG-51 destroyer, LPD-17 amphibious transport dock ship, T-ADC(X) logistics support ship, and New Attack Submarine (NSSN). The tenth Nimitz-class carrier (CVN-&&) is completely funded in fiscal year 2001. The budget restores the ability to build eight to ten ships a year over the next five years. Finally, the new highway bill TEA-21 includes $220 million for ferry boats.

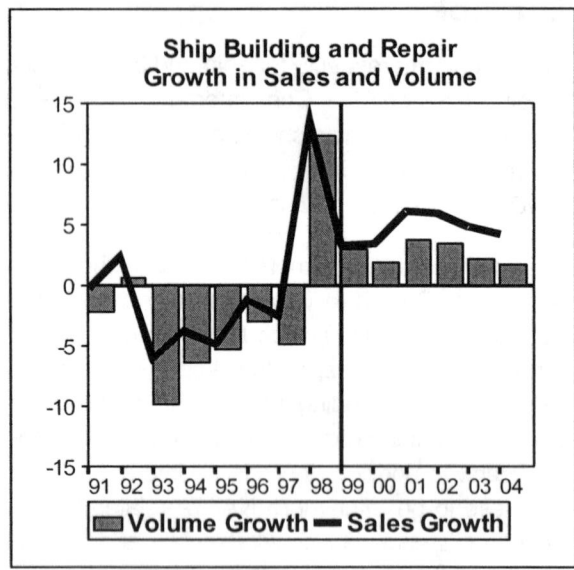

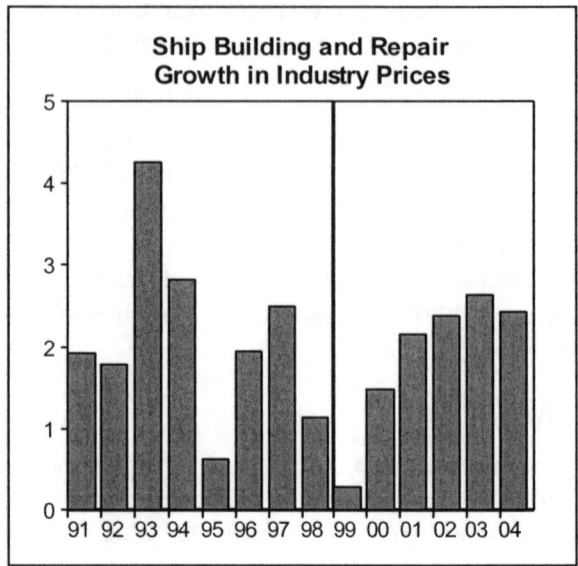

Ship Building and Repair
SIC 3731

		1992	1993	1994	1995	1996	1997	1998	1999	2000	2001	Compound Average 88-98	Annual Growth 98-08
Sales													
	Billions of $	12.82	12.04	11.60	11.04	10.91	10.64	12.09	12.49	12.92	13.71		
	% Ch	2.4	-6.1	-3.7	-4.8	-1.2	-2.5	13.6	3.3	3.4	6.1	1.1	4.4
Volume													
	% Ch	0.6	-9.9	-6.4	-5.4	-3.0	-4.9	12.3	3.0	1.9	3.8	-1.3	2.2
Prices													
	% Ch	1.8	4.3	2.8	0.6	1.9	2.5	1.1	0.3	1.5	2.2	2.5	2.2
Production Costs													
Avg. Hourly Earnings													
	$/hr	12.91	13.44	13.84	14.10	14.33	14.58	14.65	14.97	15.14	15.65		
	% Ch	5.4	4.1	3.0	1.8	1.6	1.8	0.5	2.2	1.2	3.3	2.4	3.2
Input Price Index													
	% Ch	0.3	1.5	2.7	4.1	-0.2	0.7	-0.4	-0.1	2.1	2.7	1.5	2.4

Railroad Equipment

WEFA expects new freight-car deliveries to exceed 75,000 cars in 1999. Beyond this year, the demand for new equipment falls back to 50,000 cars after back-to-back, 75,000-car years range. Longer term, there should, however, be some additional fleet expansion, particularly over the next few years in covered hoppers, flat cars, tank cars, aluminum coal cars, and mill gons. In addition, new car demand will benefit from pressure to replace older equipment. New car deliveries should average 50,000 units per year during the 2001–2008 period.

Recent History

The performance of the freight-car industry during the past five years (1994–1998) is nothing short of amazing. During the period from 1982 through 1993, deliveries of new freight cars ranged from a low of 5,772 units in 1983, the darkest hour for the business, to a high of 35,239 units in 1993. New car deliveries averaged 20,176 units per year from 1982–1993, and 28,319 units from 1988–1993. During much of this period, many in the industry looked upon a 40,000-unit year as the best that we could possibly hope for, and a long-shot at that. For our part, we continued to beat the age-of-the-fleet drum pointing out that replacement pressures were mounting as the fleet continued to age, and that we would see years that exceeded 40,000 units as long as the underlying economy lived up to expectations.

In 1994, freight car deliveries surged past the 40,000-unit mark very early in the fourth quarter and didn't stop until they reached 53,281 units. This represented the best year for the industry since 44,825 new cars were delivered back in 1981. Since then, freight car demand has continued at a very healthy pace with deliveries reaching 60,853 units in 1995, slipping to 57,877 units in 1996 and 50,396 units in 1997, and then exploding to 75,685 units last year. Our current estimate for 1999 deliveries is 75,600 units. This brings the 1994–1999 delivery total to 373,000 new cars. The revival of the freight car industry was triggered by growth in traffic and a need to expand the fleets of selected freight car types, the advancing age of the fleet, shipper demands for high-quality/low-cost/ problem-free service, rail-service disasters (UPSP), truck competition, and technological innovation.

Factors Influencing Freight-Car Demand

Rail Traffic

Rail traffic may not have roared out of the last recession, but it did gain enough ground to act as a prime driver in the revitalization of the freight-car market. Between 1992 and 1998, rail commodity loadings rose by 1.2% per year, on average. However, with average car-carrying capacity on the rise, tonnage growth was more impressive, about 1.8% per year. Although growth in percentage terms was not spectacular it was consistent, only stopping for a breather in 1996. Intermodal-traffic growth was much more spectacular, nearly 6% per year. Here too, traffic grew every year but one—1995. Class I Railroad loadings by type of equipment (box cars, covered hoppers, refrigerators, gondolas, open-top hoppers, flats, and other), which includes commodity and intermodal loadings, increased by 2.8% per year during the 1992–1998 period. Class I railroad revenue ton-miles grew 4.6% per year from 1992–1998.

Most recently, U.S. railroad-commodity traffic grew by 2% last year to 18.1 million carloadings. Intermodal loadings expanded by 0.9% as trailer traffic fell 2.9%, offsetting a 3.3% gain in container loadings. Class I Railroad loadings by type of equipment grew by 3.1% in 1998, following a 1.7% rise in 1997. U.S. rail traffic, measured by revenue ton-miles, grew by a very modest 1.8% last year to a record 1,376 billion. This followed a slight decline (-0.6%) in ton-miles in 1997.

Rail mergers such as the BNSF, UPSP, CSX–Conrail, and NS–Conrail are assumed to eventually stimulate rail long-haul traffic. However, in the near-term, these ventures are doing little to lure back shippers or trucking companies. Rail alliances such as that between Canadian National, Illinois Central, Kansas City Southern, and Transportacion Ferroviaria Mexicana should also have a positive impact on rail traffic. Improved rail service will eventually lead to increased use of rail transport by trucking companies. We are not, however, expecting the rush to rail-truck joint ventures that we witnessed a few years ago. Shippers and truckers have been burned over the past two years and it will take hard evidence that service has improved to get shippers and truckers back on board.

We expect rail tonnage to grow by 1.0%–1.5% this year and 1.0% in the year 2000, as industrial-sector activity moderates. Longer term, expect tonnage growth of about 2% per year from 2002–2004 and 2.0%–2.5% from 2005–2008. The stronger growth rate during the latter part of the forecast period assumes some improvement in rail service. Support during the next decade will come from rail staples such as coal, grain, chemicals, motor vehicles, forest products, steel, and intermodal.

Intermodal traffic should expand by 2.6% this year and 2.8% in the year 2000. Longer term, we expect intermodal traffic to expand by 5.0% per year, on average. Support will come largely from healthy volume increases in merchandise imports and exports. We also expect continued expansion of domestic-container traffic, including tank and refrigerated containers. Container traffic is slated to expand by 5.5% per year during the coming decade. Intermodal-trailer traffic will benefit from increased domestic-manufacturing activity, NAFTA trade, and greater utilization of rail services by major trucking firms and private carriers. However, we will see some erosion as domestic containerization continues to gain ground. Average annual growth in trailers loaded is forecast to average 2.0%–2.5% per year.

Rail ton-miles are slated to expand by about 1% this year and 1.4% in 2000. The annual growth rate beyond the year 2000 is put at 3.0%. The WEFA forecast assumes that railroads will be successful in their efforts to improve service, which is expected to result in continued progress on the long-haul traffic front. East–West intermodal operations will be upgraded and expanded and we will see additional expansion of North–South traffic as NAFTA trade accelerates.

Fleet Expansion

Fleet expansion has played a major role in the explosion in freight car that we have been witness to since 1994, accounting for roughly half of the new cars delivered. This represented a dramatic reversal of fortune for the freight-car fleet. The railroads steadily reduced the size of their fleet for more than a decade. At the end of the last great buying cycle in 1982, the freight-car fleet stood at 1.588 million cars with an aggregate capacity of 129.54 million tons. The fleet fell without interruption to 1.173 million cars with an aggregate capacity of 106.33 million tons a decade later. This represented a loss of 415,000 cars, or 23.21 million tons of capacity, all of it coming out of the railroad fleet.

During 1994, this trend began to reverse itself as traffic expanded and the railroads found improving car utilization a daunting task. While railroads have continued to rationalize their rolling stock, leasing companies, shippers, utilities, and the rail-owned TTX have been adding capacity. The fleet stabilized at 1.173 million cars in 1993–1994, and then began to expand. At the beginning of this year, the fleet stood at 1.316 million cars with a capacity of 127.8 million tons.

We will see only modest unit expansion in the fleet during the 1999–2008 period. However, the trend to larger sized cars will ensure that the carrying capacity of the fleet grows faster than the number of units in the fleet. Fleet expansion will also be dampened if the railroad industry is at least somewhat successful in improving service and efficiency.

According to our calculations, freight-car utilization peaked in 1994, a year of very strong growth in rail traffic. Our definition of car utilization is simply loadings/fleet. This calculation yields a "gross trips-per-year" figure that measures how many times each car in the fleet has to be utilized to carry a certain level of traffic. Obviously, there are some cars that are more heavily utilized because of the particular service they are in or commodity they carry (coal cars, for example). On the other side of the coin there are cars that have extremely low-utilization rates (tank cars and plastic pellet cars, for example) because they are used as storage facilities or require special handling because of the commodity carried. There are also cars that during a given year may be out of service for repair or rebuilding for a period of time and are utilized very little. Finally, there are older/smaller cars that are way down in the food chain. These cars of last resort spend much more of their time sitting than moving. Since 1994, car utilization has drifted reflecting overall traffic performance and the traffic mix, and rail service problems. According to our estimates, car utilization in 1998 was about 7% lower than in 1994. We are assuming that the rail industry's hefty investments in new equipment and in infrastructure will eventually begin to pay dividends. This will allow car utilization to improve very modestly during the coming decade.

Modal Competition: Size Matters

Both the trucking and railroad industries have been aggressively investing in new equipment. How much of an impact this surge in new equipment spending will have on the modal split between the two modes is anybody's guess at this point in time. Clearly, trucking has gained share at the expense of the railroads in recent years. The railroads are looking to stop the loss of share and regain some traffic where they can.

Productivity and service gains are one way of making a mode more attractive to a shipper. Thus, the focus of spending by both the railroads and truckers has been on expanding and upgrading capacity and infrastructure. The move to larger sized equipment is part of all this and it is here that the railroads and truckers butt heads.

The railroads look at any effort to increase truck-weight limits as a real threat. The railroads were successful in stopping these efforts the last time out thanks to a very successful advertising and lobbying program from CRASH and the Coalition Against Bigger Trucks. Given the fact that the railroads have been losing ground in recent years vis-à-vis trucks, new talk of raising gross-truck weights from 80,000 pounds to 97,000 pounds and the greater allowance of longer combination vehicles, like doubles and triples, go over like a lead balloon with the railroads. Utah Republican Merrill Cook and Minnesota Democrat Collin Peterson recently introduced legislation, which would give states the flexibility to allow 97,000-pound trucks on their roads. The nationwide weight limit has been frozen at 80,000 pounds since 1991. Over a dozen states do allow vehicles above 80,000 pounds under "grandfathered" rights. The trucking industry and shippers, particularly those in the agriculture, steel, paper, building materials, chemicals, and processed foods industries, have already lined up in support of the bill. On the other side of the fence, the Association of American Railroads and a number of public-safety advocate groups who are against any legislation that brings about heavier or longer trucks, have already voiced their opposition. In addition to the ability to raise truck weights by over 21%, this legislation would include the following:

- States would not be allowed to change existing vehicle configurations to allow longer trailers or new vehicle combinations (LCVS).

- Heavier vehicles would be limited to Interstate Highways.

- Heavier loads would require an additional axle on trailers to distribute the cargo weight.

There is some irony in the railroad industry's efforts to limit truck weight and size. For some time, railroads have been increasing the size of the equipment they use in an effort to improve productivity and efficiency. Currently, railroads offer incentives for using grain-carrying covered-hopper cars with a net weight of 286,000 pounds. These cars offer 11% more carrying capacity then the equipment that had been the standard with a net weight of 263,000 pounds.

The rail industry fears that raising truck weight limits and allowing greater use of longer combination vehicles put their intermodal operations, which account for about 25% of their business, in jeopardy. According to the railroads, the loss of even a small amount of intermodal traffic will hurt revenue and limit the railroad industry's ability to invest in new equipment and infrastructure and continue to improve service. Simply put, raising the gross-truck weight and promoting greater use of LCV's puts the railroad industry on a slippery slope to greater losses in modal share. On the other side of the aisle, shippers who use outside carriers, shippers operating private truck fleets, and trucking companies are very outspoken in their support for raising gross-truck weights and increasing LCV use.

The Age of the Fleet

In a highly competitive environment, the pressure to upgrade the rail-car fleet intensifies. The availability of new state-of-the-art equipment that delivers on promises of improvements in efficiency and productivity is an added incentive to scrap older units and replace them with new ones. The advanced age of the fleet has had a very positive impact on new car demand, and will continue to do so. It remains our belief that replacement pressures will remain strong in the years ahead. As fleet expansion pressures ease, replacement demand will become an even more important factor in the outlook for freight cars.

The most recent data on fleet age was published in January of this year. According to the UMLER File, the average age of the fleet stood at 17.3 years, versus 17.6 years a year earlier. Obviously the strong delivery level in 1998 continued to push down the average age of the fleet. The average age of railroad-owned cars slipped from 20.0 years in 1998 to 19.8 years in 1999. The average age of the private-owned fleet experienced a similar change going from 15.3 years in 1998 to 15.1 years in 1999.

While the average age is finally trending downward, it remains high by historical standards. At the end of the last great buying cycle in freight cars, the average of the fleet had dropped to about 14 years. More important from our point of view, at the beginning of this year 24.9% of the cars in service were over 25 years old. This actually represents a slight increase from the 24.3% of the fleet at the beginning of 1998. In January of 1983, only 12.7% of the fleet had been in service for more than 25 years. We view cars that are over 25 years old as being in the "replacement pool". These older/smaller cars do not fit the bill in today's highly competitive, freight-transportation climate. Another 17.5%–18.0% of the cars in the U.S. fleet are 21–25 years old and many of these will enter the "replacement pool" during the forecast period. We view these cars as prime candidates for replacement during the forecast period.

Replacement pressures should also be building in the Canadian and Mexican freight-car fleets. From 1998 to 1999, the average age of the Canadian fleet rose from 20 years to 20.3 years. Over 31.5% of the Canadian fleet has been in service for more than 25 years. The Mexican fleet also aged a bit as the average age edged up from 23.3 years in 1998 to 23.4 years in 1999. Over 29% of the cars in the Mexican fleet are over 25 years old.

Forecast Update: 1999–2008

As 1999 draws to a close, there is still enough business on the books to make this year about as good a year as 1998. Last year, car-builders delivered 75,685 new cars, the best year since 86,030 new cars were delivered way back in 1980.

At this point in the game, we believe most freight car-builders and component suppliers are asking themselves the question "When will it end?" Things have been so good for so long that we have to wonder whether or not the next major correction is just around the bend. Certainly, there were fears that the Asian flu would spread and damage the U.S. economy. However, while U.S. exports took it on the chin, the domestic economy continued to roll merrily along. And now as we approach the summer of 1999, it looks like the worst of the world economic crisis is behind us. Most recently, new orders have softened averaging just 8,754 units per quarter, versus 21,746 units per quarter in 1998 and 22,000 per quarter in 1997.

When all is said, economic and market fundamentals will not be strong enough to keep freight-car demand at its very lofty 1998–1999 level. With traffic growing very modestly in 1999 and 2000, the pressure to expand rail fleets will be easing. Replacement pressures, however, will be intense as large segments of the rail fleet remain aged and obsolete relative to shipper requirements. There are still plenty of freight cars in service that shippers do not want to see rolling up to their loading docks. Beyond the impact of age, competition from the trucking industry remains intense and will continue to stimulate investment in new freight cars. The split of Conrail, the CP-IC-KCS merger/marketing agreement, the UPSP's efforts to rebuild confidence with shippers, and efforts by other major railroads to improve efficiency and deliver better service will continue to act as a powerful incentive to invest in new equipment. Finally, the availability of new state-of-the art equipment (greater carrying capacity, efficiencies in loading and unloading, advanced truck design) will also stimulate new car demand.

First-half 1999 orders were a sign that the freight-car market had lost some of its forward momentum. We do not believe there will be enough deterioration in the factors that drive equipment investment to trigger the kind of sustained weakness in orders, and ultimately production and deliveries that were experienced in the early 1990s. In our long-term outlook, the traffic pool continues to expand and competitive pressures remain a powerful incentive to continue to upgrade and modernize rail equipment fleets. We do expect order rates to pick up during the second half of this year after a lull in order activity among leasing companies, which pro-

vided so much lift to the market over the past two years. Orders in the second half of 1999 should be stronger than in the first, but they will still pale in comparison to the quarterly average for new orders, roughly 22,000 per quarter, achieved in 1997 and 1998.

Simply put, economic and market conditions in the year 2000 will not be favorable enough to keep freight-car deliveries at their very lofty 1998–1999 levels. However, they will remain favorable enough to keep freight car deliveries north of the 50,000-unit mark.

Longer term (2001–2008), fleet expansion, in unit terms, slows to a crawl as the trend to larger capacity cars continues and the rails are moderately successful in their quest to improve service and efficiency. Replacement demand emerges as the driving force behind new car orders. Freight-car deliveries total 51,500 units in 2001. Replacement demand triggered by a resumption of stronger traffic growth will provide lift to the market thereafter. New car deliveries reach 54,200 units in 2002, 57,400 units in 2003, and 59,500 units in 2004. Longer term deliveries average 50,000 units per year.

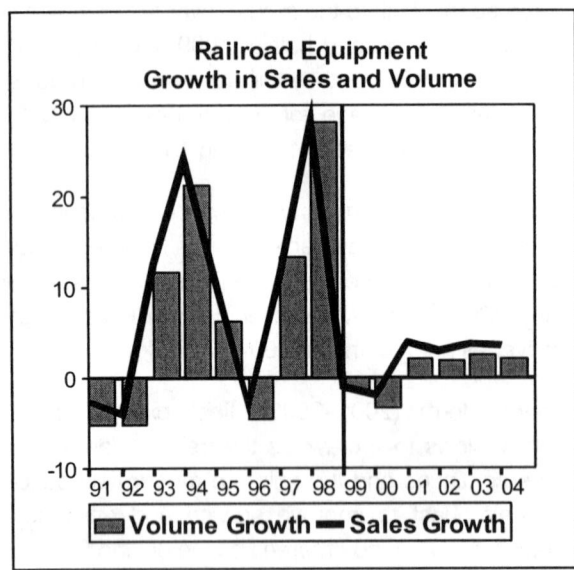

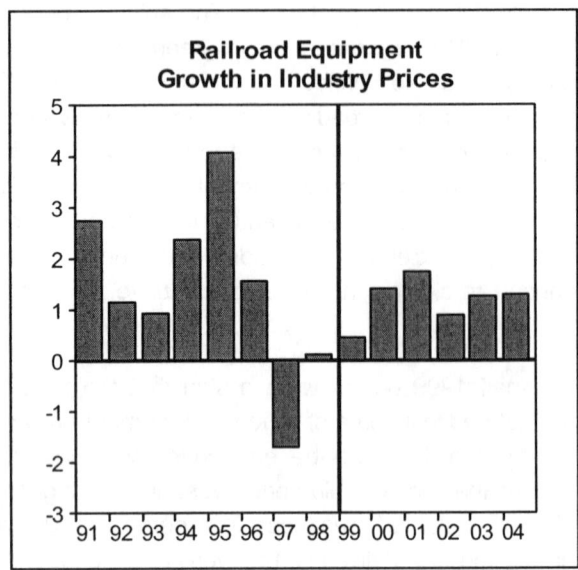

Railroad Equipment

SIC 374

		1992	1993	1994	1995	1996	1997	1998	1999	2000	2001	Compound Average 88-98	Annual Growth 98-08
Sales													
	Billions of $	4.71	5.31	6.59	7.28	7.07	7.87	10.10	10.00	9.81	10.20		
	% Ch	-4.0	12.6	24.2	10.5	-3.0	11.3	28.3	-1.0	-1.9	3.9	11.5	2.7
Volume													
	% Ch	-5.1	11.6	21.3	6.2	-4.5	13.3	28.1	-1.4	-3.2	2.2	9.2	0.9
Prices													
	% Ch	1.2	0.9	2.4	4.1	1.5	-1.7	0.1	0.5	1.4	1.7	2.1	1.8
Production Costs													
Avg. Hourly Earnings													
	$/hr	14.33	14.89	15.59	15.07	16.31	16.81	16.90	16.27	16.66	17.09		
	% Ch	2.2	3.9	4.7	-3.3	8.2	3.1	0.5	-3.7	2.4	2.5	3.4	2.3
Input Price Index													
	% Ch	0.3	1.2	2.3	3.6	-0.4	-0.3	-0.3	-0.3	2.1	2.9	1.4	2.5

Chapter 21: Instruments and Related Products

Instruments and Related Products

The instrument industry includes a number of very diverse segments — search and navigation equipment, measuring and controlling devices, medical instruments and supplies, ophthalmic goods, and photographic goods. Each one of these categories marches to the beat of a different drummer, and reflects specific segments of the U.S. economy.

The instrument and related products industry emerged slowly from the 1990–1991 recession with shipments increasing by only 4% in total between 1992–1994. Improving economic and market conditions in the United States and solid gains in overseas markets supported growth in shipments of 4.5% per year in 1995 and 1996, and 7.8% in 1997. In 1998, shipments rose by only 3.6%, as export sales and business spending for photocopying and related equipment faltered. The instrument industry appears headed for an increase in shipments of 2.3% in 1999. Longer term, 2000–2008, shipments should increase by 5.5% per year.

Overview

The instrument industry includes a number of very diverse segments—search and navigation equipment, measuring and controlling devices, medical instruments and supplies, ophthalmic goods, and photographic goods. Each one of these categories marches to the beat of a different drummer, and reflects specific segments of the U.S. economy.

The instruments and related products industry emerged slowly from the 1990–1991 recession with shipments increasing by only 4% in total between 1992–1994. Improving economic and market conditions in the United States and solid gains in overseas markets supported growth in shipments of 4.5% per year in 1995 and 1996, and 7.8% in 1997. In 1998, shipments rose by only 3.6%, as export sales and business spending for photocopying and related equipment faltered. The instrument industry employed 867,580 workers in 1998. Employment has risen almost 3% since 1995. As recently as 1990, the industry employed over 1 million.

U.S. exports of instruments and related products increased without interruption from $5.2 billion in 1988 to $16.1 billion in 1997. This represents an average annual increase of over 20%. The slump in economic activity in Japan, other Asian markets, and parts of Latin America took a toll last year and exports declined by 2%. Imports have increased without interruption over the past decade. Imports totaled $3.4 billion back in 1988 and rose to $9.6 billion in 1998. During the period from 1989–1993, imports of instruments grew by almost 69%. Over the past five years, 1994–1998, import increased by 67%. The United States has maintained a trade surplus in instruments. In 1988 the surplus stood at $1.8 billion. It rose to $4.8 billion in 1993 and $6.2 billion in 1998.

Forecast 1999-2008

The instrument industry appears headed for an increase in shipments of 2.3% in 1999. Longer term, 2000–2008, shipments should increase by 5.5% per year.

Measuring and Controlling Devices

The demand for automatic controls that regulate residential and commercial environments, industrial processes, and appliances is driven by activity in the housing, construction, manufacturing, and consumer durable markets. Shipments rose from $33.3 billion in 1991 to $50.2 billion in 1997, an increase of over 50%. Last year, a decline in industrial plant construction and weaker exports resulted in a decline in shipments of 2.7% to $48.8 billion.

Employment in this industry peaked at 330,370 back in 1989 and declined steadily to 283,260 in 1994. Employment grew from 1995–1998 reaching 304,210 last year.

- New-home construction will be relatively stable at about 1.4-1.45 million units per year during the next ten years.

- Nonresidential construction will reflect modest expansion of industrial, commercial, and electric utility capacity. Look for the strongest growth to occur in the Southwest, Southeast, Pacific, and mountain regions of the United States.

- Manufacturing activity and capital spending will proceed at an annual rate approaching 3% per year, in constant-dollar terms, in response to domestic and overseas demand. We expect the demand for industrial process controls and instruments to receive an added push as the pressure on manufacturers to improve productivity and efficiency remains intense.

- Consumer spending on appliances will expand by about 2% per year, and this will govern the growth in domestic demand for appliance controls.

- Measuring and controlling devices that find their way into defense and space equipment will begin to improve as defense-related procurement stages a comeback.

- Finally, United States exports of measuring and controlling devices should do well during the forecast period as industrial, commercial, and consumer markets, particularly in developing countries, expand at a healthy pace.

Medical Instruments and Ophthalmic Goods

Shipments of medical instruments increased 6.5% last year to $54.2 billion. This followed increases of 7% in 1997 and 9% in 1996. Ten years ago in 1988, shipments were valued at $25.8 billion. From 1988 through 1998, shipments more than doubled. The strong increase in sales, particularly in recent years, reflected the increased use of high-technology equipment in medical treatment. The medical instruments and supplies industry employed 279,100 workers in 1998, up from 269,000 five years ago and 231,000 a decade ago.

Shipments of ophthalmic goods increased 8% in 1998 to $5.5 billion. This followed increases of 21% in 1997, and 7% in 1996. Ten years ago in 1988, shipments were valued at $3.3 billion. From 1988 through 1998,

shipments grew by 66%. The ophthalmic goods industry employed 34,940 workers in 1998. Last year was the first time in seven years that employment increased in this industry, and the increase in 1998 was less than one-half of one percent.

Our forecast calls for shipments of medical instruments and ophthalmic goods to increase by 6.0%–6.5% per year, on average, during the coming decade.

The medical instruments and ophthalmic goods industry is being influenced by a number of factors. Technology is allowing for the development of highly sophisticated diagnostic instruments, which usually carry a hefty price tag. Discussions on how to control medical costs continue, and the debate at the federal, state, and local government levels is never-ending. WEFA expects the growth in prices for medical equipment to pick-up during the coming decade. During the period from 1978–1988, medical care inflation for consumers grew by 8.7% per year. In the following decade the cost had moderated to less than 6% per year, and down to about 2.5% in recent years. WEFA's current forecast is for medical care inflation of 5%–6% per year, on average from 1999-2003, and 6.0%–6.5% from 2004–2008. At the same time, the pressure to apply new technologies to medicine is not abating. On a more basic level, the population is aging and requiring more medical care.

The net result of all these factors is that the demand for medical instruments and ophthalmic goods in the United States will remain strong. Overseas demand will provide additional support. Asian markets have begun to recover. Furthermore, we are optimistic about Africa, Latin America, and Eastern Europe. Improving economic conditions in developing countries will lead to efforts to improve the quality of medical care in these regions.

Photographic Goods

Photographic goods include cameras for commercial and consumer use, photocopying machines, and a whole host of products that are used to develop and process film. Shipments grew by 1.5% per year, on average, during the past ten years, but were erratic during the decade as consumer and business purchases ebbed and flowed. From 1989–1993 photographic goods shipments increased by about 2% per year. Over the past five years from 1994–1998, shipments grew by less than 1% per year. In 1998, shipments slipped 0.3%

to $23.5 billion, following increases of 5% in 1997 and 3% in 1996.

The photographic goods industry employed 81,100 workers in 1998, down from 85,650 in 1997. In 1995 and 1996 employment held steady at roughly 85,000 workers. In 1988 the industry employed over 109,000 workers.

Shipments of photographic equipment are slated to expand by about 5% per year during the next ten years.

Consumer photography is influenced by consumer confidence and income growth. Spending on vacation and recreational activities has been gaining ground in recent years, and this has had a positive impact on the equipment and supplies market. Expected nominal growth in consumer disposable income of 5% per year over the next ten years will provide support to this segment of the market. Furthermore, an aging population with more leisure time and disposable income will also lift sales.

The demand for photographic equipment and related products by the business sector has benefited from generally favorable economic conditions and healthy corporate profits. The real estate, advertising, financial services, and entertainment industries heavily influence spending for equipment and supplies. Corporate profit growth will benefit from expanding final sales, relatively low (albeit rising) interest rates, and a corporate culture that promotes efforts to reign in and even reduce operating costs. Profits over the next ten years will be more than adequate to keep the commercial segment of the photographic goods market expanding at a decent pace.

Japanese producers have long been important in the U.S. photographic equipment market, and this is unlikely to change. Imports from Japan and the rest of Asia have accounted for over 70% of sales of imported equipment and supplies in the United States in recent years. Export markets will provide support to domestic producers, but competition from European and Japanese producers in their home markets will remain intense.

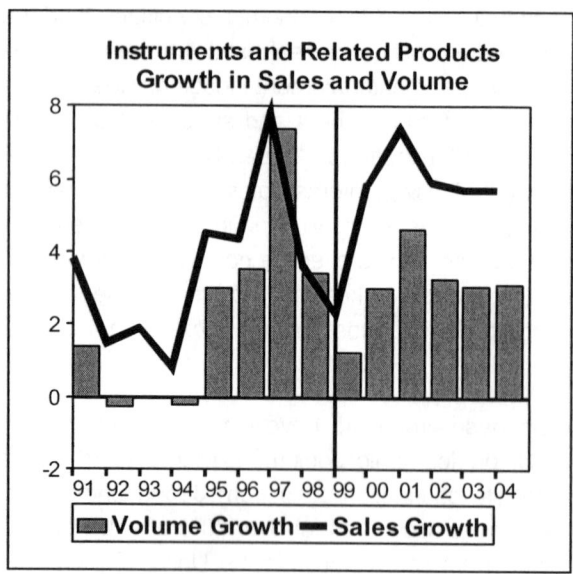

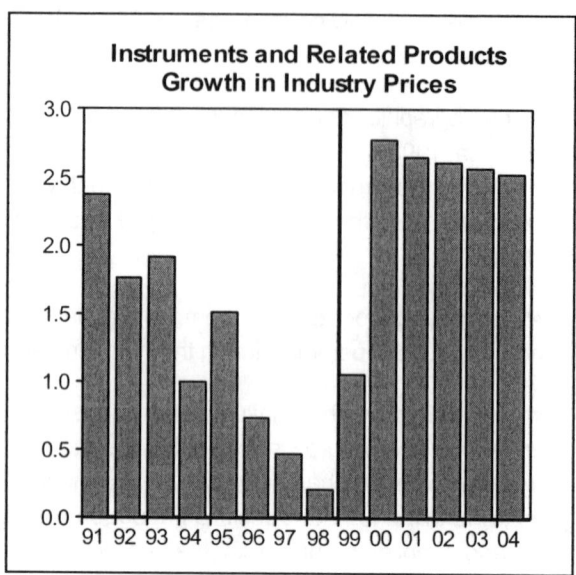

Instruments and Related Products

SIC 38

		1992	1993	1994	1995	1996	1997	1998	1999	2000	2001	Compound Average 88-98	Annual Growth 98-08
Sales													
	Billions of $	134.8	137.4	138.5	144.8	151.1	162.9	168.8	172.7	182.8	196.3		
	% Ch	1.5	1.9	0.8	4.5	4.4	7.8	3.6	2.3	5.9	7.4	3.8	5.4
Volume													
	% Ch	-0.3	-0.0	-0.2	3.0	3.5	7.4	3.4	1.2	3.0	4.6	2.1	2.9
Prices													
	% Ch	1.8	1.9	1.0	1.5	0.7	0.5	0.2	1.1	2.8	2.6	1.7	2.4
Production Costs													
Avg. Hourly Earnings													
	$/hr	12.37	12.72	12.93	13.10	13.52	13.88	14.20	14.56	15.11	15.68		
	% Ch	1.9	2.8	1.7	1.3	3.2	2.7	2.3	2.5	3.8	3.8	2.5	3.7
Input Price Index													
	% Ch	0.2	0.9	1.5	3.2	-0.7	-0.4	-0.8	-0.1	1.8	2.2	0.8	2.1

Search and Navigation Equipment

The search and navigation equipment industry has been on a roller-coaster ride over the past decade, reflecting the swings in activity in key markets. From 1992–1996, shipments declined in four out of five years. Shipments increased 9% in 1997 and 11% in 1998. In 1992, shipments were valued at $35.1 billion. Due to the ups and downs of this industry, shipments in 1998 had risen to only $36.9 billion. Longer term, we expect shipments to expand by 5% per year supported by the defense, commercial jet transport, air transport, and global positioning markets.

Recent History

In the late 1980s and early 1990s shipments of search and navigation equipment were riding high. Defense spending was at very lofty levels, NASA outlays were rising, and signs of life were emerging in the commercial aircraft market. From 1987 through 1991, shipments averaged $37.5 billion per year and totaled $38.7 billion in 1991. Over the next five years, shipments fell sharply to $30.4 billion in 1996. The industry turned the corner in 1997 with shipments rising 9% to $33.2 billion and then increasing 11% in 1998 to $36.9 billion.

The Defense Department and NASA represent the largest domestic markets for search and navigation equipment. As a result, search and navigation equipment lost considerable ground with the end of the Cold War and the downsizing of the defense budget.

During the past decade, the commercial aircraft market went from boom to bust and back to boom again. The buying cycle that was beginning a decade ago lasted through the early 1990s, and then slumped in the mid-1990s. Commercial-aircraft production picked up again in 1997, and posted a healthy increase in 1998.

Both the light- and commercial-vehicle markets have done very well in recent years. Both are also increasing their use of satellite tracking devices.

In 1988, producers of search and navigation equipment employed almost 316,000 workers. Employment fell steadily to just under 161,000 workers in 1995. This decline was partly a function of the fall off in defense-related business, but also a result of industry efforts to improve productivity and efficiency and reduce labor costs. Since 1995, employment in the industry has hovered around 161,000.

Outlook 1999–2008

Over the near term, we expect shipments of search and navigation equipment to increase 3.9% in 1999 and 5.6% in 2000. Longer term, growth is pegged at 5% per year, on average. Based on the most recent Department of Defense budget numbers, we believe we have entered a period of more robust spending to upgrade and modernize land, air, and naval forces. The demand for commercial aircraft worldwide will remain strong, as will investment to improve air travel operations and safety. Finally, use of satellite-positioning systems will increase as well.

Department of Defense efforts to modernize aviation forces include the Joint Strike Force (JSF), which is a family of aircraft designed to serve different functions. This is DOD's largest acquisition program. The JSF is designed to replace the F-16 in the Air Force, F/A-18c in the Navy, and F/A-18D and AV-8B for the Marines. The F-22 represents the replacement for the F-15C/D in the air superiority role and provides air-to-ground capability as well. It has come under pressure from the House, but is expected to go forward. The Navy's F/A-18E/F should provide greater survivability and payload over earlier F/A-18 models. Longer term, the Navy indicates that it will transition from the F/A-18E/F to the JSF.

The most recent budget includes funding for the Patriot PAC-3 and Navy Area, THAAD and Navy Theater Wide missile defense systems that are designed to defeat shorter-range missiles. To counter theater-range missiles funding is included for an Airborne Laser system. Funding for the National Missile defense program totals $10.5 billion for fiscal years 1999–2005.

Modernization of ground forces includes upgrades of the Apache longbow helicopter and the Comanche helicopter. Marine Corps. modernization programs include the V-22 tilt-rotor aircraft, and upgrades of utility and attack helicopters and the AV-8B. By the end of fiscal year 2003 procurement of 120 C-17 aircraft will be completed. Additional acquisitions are also planned. These planes are viewed as necessary to increase our ability to project military power throughout the world. The KC-135 tanker and C-5 transport are set to have major avionics upgrades and other improvements. Ground force modernization also includes upgrades of the Army's Abrams tank and Bradley Fighting Vehicle.

DOD spending for new naval vessels is expected to rise during the forecast period. Modernization programs include procurement of the DDG-51 destroyer, LPD-17 amphibious transport dock ship, T-ADC(X) logistics support ship, and New Attack Submarine (NSSN). The tenth Nimitz-class carrier (CVN-&&) is completely funded in fiscal year 2001. The budget restores the ability to build eight to ten ships a year over the next five years.

Commercial aircraft is another major market for search and navigation equipment. This customer market posted very impressive production levels in the period between 1990 and 1992, and then fell into a slump that has only recently ended. Commercial aircraft production surged ahead over the past two years and will continue to gain ground this year. The demand for navigation equipment utilized by the air transport industry should also be gaining ground. Commercial jet transport deliveries are slated to fall back to 720 units in 2000 (480 for Boeing and 240 for Airbus). In 2001, deliveries drop to 600 units with Boeing at 375 units and Airbus at 225 units. Longer term, we are projecting average annual demand for new air

craft at between 600–700 units per year. If Airbus Industries is correct about stronger demand for planes in the 400- to 500-seat or larger category, unit deliveries will average closer to 600 units per year. If Boeing is correct and the market leans more to single-aisle and intermediate-size commercial transports and increases its dependence on regional jets, deliveries should average closer to 700 units per year.

In addition to a recovery in the commercial air transport market, strong growth in air traffic worldwide will certainly require expansion of air traffic control systems throughout the next decade. There is also considerable concern about the quality of air traffic control systems in developing regions of the world, where the most dramatic gains in traffic will occur during the next ten years. Finally, WEFA also expects aggressive efforts to modernize traffic control systems in traffic lanes that are currently well traveled and experiencing congestion and safety problems that will only worsen over time.

Commercial and personal use of Global Positioning System (GPS) navigation systems has been rising and will continue to provide support during the forecast period. In addition to continued growth in domestic markets, the next decade will see an expansion of GPS throughout the world. Over-the-road truckers, railroads, and the shipping industry have already turned to satellite navigation and tracking systems that can pinpoint the location of equipment. This allows equipment owners to better monitor equipment utilization and more efficiently schedule traffic flows. Owners and lessors are using tracking devices to reduce theft of high-priced construction machinery and other mobile off-highway equipment. Hospitals have begun to use positioning systems as a way of keeping track of patients, particularly infants, within their facilities. There also has been an increase in the use of GPS navigation systems in passenger cars and light trucks.

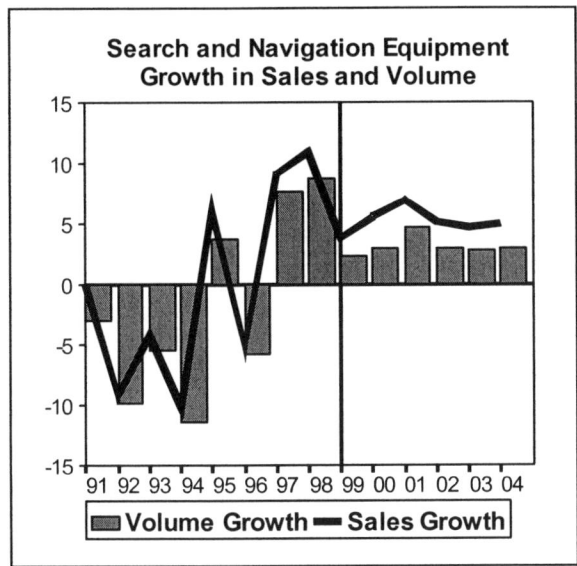

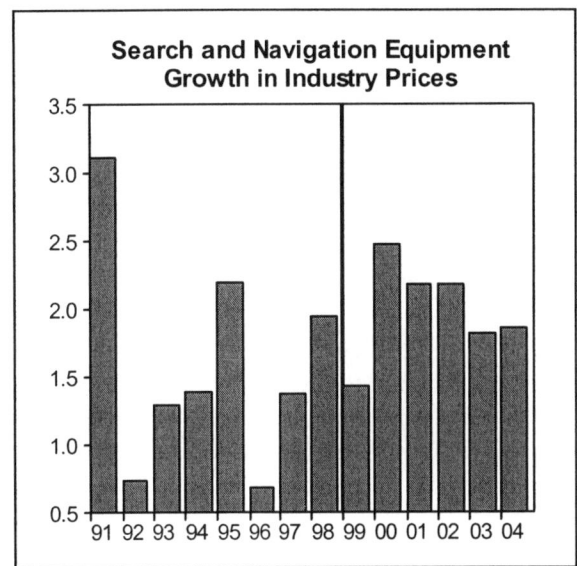

Search and Navigation Equipment

SIC 381

		1992	1993	1994	1995	1996	1997	1998	1999	2000	2001	Compound Average 88-98	Annual Growth 98-08
Sales													
	Billions of $	35.13	33.66	30.24	32.08	30.44	33.24	36.87	38.30	40.45	43.28		
	% Ch	-9.2	-4.2	-10.2	6.1	-5.1	9.2	10.9	3.9	5.6	7.0	-0.1	5.2
Volume													
	% Ch	-9.8	-5.4	-11.4	3.8	-5.8	7.7	8.8	2.4	3.1	4.7	-2.1	3.0
Prices													
	% Ch	0.7	1.3	1.4	2.2	0.7	1.4	1.9	1.4	2.5	2.2	2.1	2.1
Production Costs													
Avg. Hourly Earnings													
	$/hr	15.54	16.12	16.60	16.39	16.67	16.82	17.32	17.71	18.34	18.98		
	% Ch	2.7	3.8	3.0	-1.3	1.7	0.9	3.0	2.2	3.6	3.5	2.6	3.4
Input Price Index													
	% Ch	-0.2	0.8	1.1	1.7	-1.3	-0.9	-1.0	-0.0	1.6	2.0	0.3	2.0

Chapter 22: Miscellaneous Manufacturing

Miscellaneous Manufacturing

Miscellaneous manufacturing industries include two large industries and four small craft-related sectors. The second largest category is dolls, toys, games, and athletic and sporting equipment, with about 30% of total shipments. Fine jewelry and silverware accounts for 13% of the total, but much of the value of the sales involves the cost of precious metals and gemstones, rather than the industry's value added.

The largest category is other miscellaneous manufacturing, which includes a variety of small products including brooms and brushes, signs, burial caskets, and other small products. Signs and advertising specialties are the largest sub-industries in the other miscellaneous categories.

Many of the items in these industries are specialty consumer items, and are extremely dependent on consumer spending and income levels. Industries such as jewelry and toys have wide-cycle swings.

Miscellaneous Manufacturing Industries by Share of Total Shipments, 1996

Dolls, Toys, and Games	30.3%
Fine Jewelry	13.1%
Pens and Pencils	9.0%
Costume Jewelry	4.9%
Musical Instruments	2.3%
Other Miscellaneous	40.4%

Jewelry, Silverware, and Plated Ware

The jewelry, silverware, and plated-ware industries are mostly supported by the precious metals and gemstones market. Therefore, their shipment figures can be misleading. Large swings in precious metal and gemstone prices can grossly change industry-shipment values, while production levels remain flat. Shipments grew rapidly in the late 1980s, but fell by about 9% during the 1990–1991 recession, and didn't regain their 1989 level until 1994. Since 1993, growth in dollar terms has averaged under 3%. The business cycles in this sector can be extremely large, because it is highly dependent on income levels. Prices of raw materials will also affect the industry's cycle.

Musical Instruments

Shipments of musical instruments totaled just over $1.1 billion in 1996. Exports account for about 25% of shipments, and imports provide an additional $900 million to domestic supply. The United States, thus, has a trade deficit in these items. Consumer spending on musical instruments currently totals about $2 billion per year. Spending on musical instruments is at a significantly slower pace than income levels. Additionally, it is highly cyclical. The slower growth expected in consumer spending and economic growth over the next few years is expected to be a dampening influence on musical instrument sales.

Pens, Pencils, and Other Artists' Materials

Shipments of pens, pencils, and other artists' materials grew quite rapidly in the late 1980s and then stalled from 1991 to 1993. A pick-up to double-digit growth in 1994 was followed by only 1.4% growth in 1995. However, the over-10% growth was seen again in 1996. Domestic manufacturers shipped over $4 billion in 1996. Exports account for about 15% of total shipments, while imports supply about 17% of domestic sales.

Miscellaneous Manufacturing Industries: Brooms and Brushes, Signs and Advertising, Burial Caskets, Linoleum and Other Hard Surface Floor Coverings, and Others

Signs and advertising dominate this category of miscellaneous manufacturing, accounting for about one-third of the sales of the category overall. Other industries include a wide variety of consumer products and some service-industry products, such as beauty shop and barber supplies. As a whole, these industries are very volatile, with recent annual rates of growth in shipments ranging from more than 25% (in 1987) to 0.7% (in 1992). The sum total of shipments from the industries in this category totaled $19.6 billion in 1996, a 7.7% increase over 1995.

Forecast

Most miscellaneous manufacturing items are highly dependent on income levels and employment. As a result, the sector has seen large peaks and valleys. Continued growth in consumer income should support further growth in this sector in 2000 and 2001, albeit at a more moderate pace than in recent years. But, look for increasing import penetration, especially in musical instruments and fine jewelry. On average, prices should grow at about the same rate as those of other manufactured items over the next 10 years.

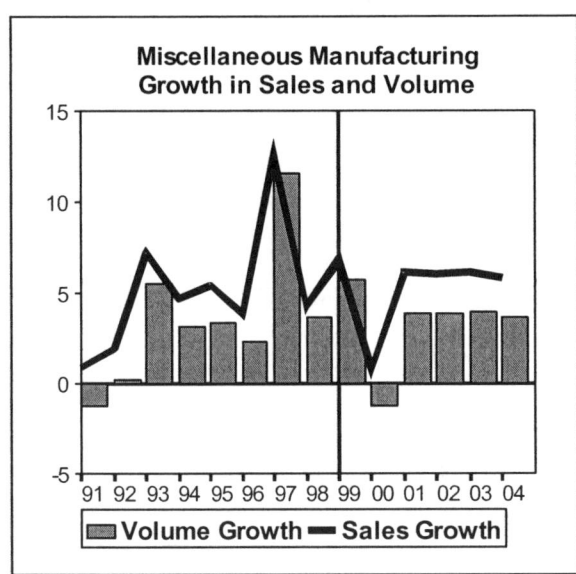

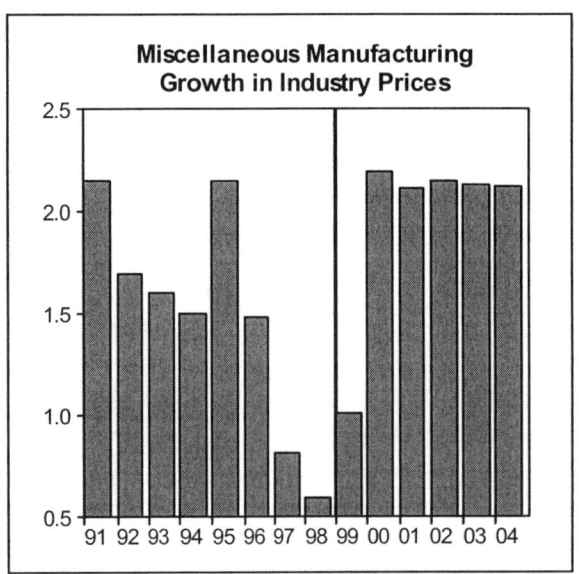

Miscellaneous Manufacturing

SIC 39

		1992	1993	1994	1995	1996	1997	1998	1999	2000	2001	Compound Average 88-98	Annual Growth 98-08
Sales													
	Billions of $	39.46	42.31	44.31	46.72	48.53	54.61	56.96	60.86	61.41	65.16		
	% Ch	2.0	7.2	4.7	5.4	3.9	12.5	4.3	6.8	0.9	6.1	4.9	5.3
Volume													
	% Ch	0.2	5.5	3.2	3.3	2.3	11.5	3.7	5.8	-1.3	3.9	3.0	3.2
Prices													
	% Ch	1.7	1.6	1.5	2.1	1.5	0.8	0.6	1.0	2.2	2.1	1.9	2.1
Production Costs													
Avg. Hourly Earnings													
	$/hr	9.15	9.39	9.67	10.05	10.38	10.59	10.87	11.26	11.65	12.05		
	% Ch	3.4	2.6	3.0	3.9	3.3	2.0	2.7	3.6	3.4	3.5	3.1	3.4
Input Price Index													
	% Ch	0.7	1.6	2.4	5.2	0.1	1.0	-0.5	-0.1	1.7	2.2	1.6	2.1

Costume Jewelry

The costume jewelry industry is made up of establishments engaged in the manufacturing of jewelry composed of anything except precious metal, precious and semi-precious gemstones, goldplate, and gold-filled materials. Both the manufacture and retail sales of costume jewelry are important, because the activity of each affects the other.

The industry is in a state of decline in the United States, and domestic employment has been falling due to low-domestic demand and strong foreign competition.

Jewelry Demand

Consumer spending on jewelry and watches has grown between 4% and 7% each year since 1991 in current dollar terms. Since 1995, prices have been declining, so real spending has risen more rapidly, by 9.3% in 1996 and 8.0% in 1997. However, much of this demand is being met by imports. Domestic producers face strong competition from less expensive, more fashion-trendy, foreign-made necklaces, pins, earrings, and other novelty items. Export demand is, in general, more healthy than the domestic market. Demand for U.S.-made costume jewelry in Japan, for example, is high because of the high quality, good design, and low prices.

American jewelry manufacturers can also look forward to continued success in Mexico. Exports of American costume jewelry to Mexico have increased at a faster pace than total jewelry exports, making Mexico one of the United States' major markets for jewelry exports. The elimination of tariffs on costume jewelry trade that came with the North American Free Trade Agreement (NAFTA) has contributed to U.S. producers' success south of the border. The U.S. Department of Commerce points to the jewelry industry as a major beneficiary of Mexico's increasing demand and rising standard of living.

Panama is another good market for U.S.-manufactured costume jewelry, primarily because the level of its own domestic production is very small. In Panama, American-produced jewelry tends to sell at higher prices than Asian goods because of its high quality. Relatively free trade also exists between the United States and Panama.

Supply

The demand for imported, less-expensive costume jewelry has affected the American suppliers' job market. In addition to demand competition, high-labor costs have propelled some U.S. firms to consider producing their goods overseas.

Jewelry imports have been on the rise for twenty years. In 1998, approximately 50% of the jewelry sold in the United States was imported. In general, the competition comes from countries with much lower wages than the United States. Price competition from foreign producers resulted in weak sales for American jewelers and increased business for foreign companies.

Shipments of inexpensive, manmade gemstones from China and Russia have been on the upswing, not only causing a slip in the prices of many moderately priced synthetics and high-priced naturals, but also negatively impacting American-jewelry makers. Highly and moderately priced natural and synthetic gemstones face competition in both pricing and appearance. The Asian-produced hydro-thermal amethyst, for example, is very popular among consumers because of its uniformity in color and size—not to mention its affordability. Although many of these less-expensive manmade pieces are clearly being marketed as "cheap synthetics," there is the possibility of these stones being mixed in with the supply of naturals and sold at prices higher than their true value.

Industry Structure

Facing the prospect of continuing sales losses, some costume jewelry manufacturers have revamped their business strategy. One example is The Monet Group, based in New York. When Monet's ornamental pieces began losing their appeal among consumers, the company decided to change not only its designs, but also its marketing approach. The turnaround, however, did not occur without some downsizing and cost cutting. As a result, The Monet Group is one jewelry-design firm that remains successful in a declining industry.

The U.S. costume jewelry industry continues to experience an imbalance in merchandise trade, with higher imports than exports. Taxes on imports remain low, while in many countries U.S. goods face high-trade barriers. Although some American jewelers have lobbied for a quota on imports, others have looked toward technology and marketing improvements to increase sales overseas.

Conclusion

American costume jewelry manufacturers produce high-quality pieces, but not necessarily at a price low

enough to prevent domestic consumers from demanding less-expensive imports. However, demand for American jewelry overseas is increasing, and American manufacturers see an opportunity to gain success in the export business, especially in countries like Mexico where NAFTA's elimination of tariffs on exported goods is in effect. Employment, however, may continue to decline, as lack of sales growth forces manufacturers to downsize, or, in extreme cases, close shop. Some American-jewelry firms, however, are finding success as they venture into manufacturing agreements with overseas firms. Other companies are forecasting growth as a result of improved technology and stronger marketing techniques.

U.S. Employment, Costume Jewelry *(thousands of workers)*

1992	1993	1994	1995	1996	1997	1998
18.67	18.15	17.48	15.22	13.89	13.28	12.28

Dolls, Toys, and Games

The industry designated as dolls, toys, and games (SIC 394) consists of established manufacturers of games and both mechanical and non-mechanical toys, including children's vehicles, dolls, and stuffed toys. The industry shipped about $14.7 billion of manufactured toys in 1996 and is driven by family income, the state of the economy, and young demographics. Primarily, the population of doll, toy, and game users can be broken into three key segments. The outlook for these specific demographics is key to the forecast for total toys and for the mix of product demand by age group.

Industry Demand

There are currently 19.4 million children under five years of age. The size of this segment of the toy-consuming population is expected to grow by 5% over the next ten years. The 10-to-14-year-old population is currently nearly identical in size to that of the under-five group. A similarly modest rate of growth of 3.5% is expected during the next decade. The third of the three key segments, the 5-to-9-year-old segment of the population, currently records 20 million persons. This group is predicted to decline slightly over the upcoming decade.

Since the source of demand for these entertainment and leisure products is such a young cross-section of the population, this industry is particularly susceptible to swings in preferences and fads. In actuality, parents control the "purse strings", at least for the under-10 age group, but parents cannot always withstand pressure and high emotions from a child. Stuffed toys, Furbies, and Teletubbies were highly sought in 1998. This year, the collectable card game known as Pokemon has been en vogue. Star Wars-related products are also highly sought, following the release of another in the series of Star Wars movies.

Consumer income and spending patterns in aggregate are also important to this industry. In real terms, consumer spending should average 2.9% gains per year through the next five years, with spending in 1999 estimated to grow by more than 5%. The rate of increase in the demand for toys looks to duplicate the average real growth rate of personal-consumption expenditures in the short term.

Shipments of toys, dolls, and games grew quite strongly in the latter half of the 1980s. In 1987–1988, annual growth averaged 14% in current dollar terms. Sales con-

tinued their upswing through the recession in the early 1990s, by averaging just 2%–4% during that period. Recent spikes were seen in 1993 and 1995, when growth of 10.8% and 8.4%, respectively, was recorded.

Domestic shipments of toys, dolls, and games are also quite sensitive to dollar exchange rates, since imports are significant and often lower priced.

Pricing Trends and Outlook

Along with much of the manufacturing sector, pressure from customers to contain costs has allowed the greater toy industry only very modest pricing gains since 1989. Sources of downward price pressure on toys, games, and dolls come from more than one direction. Budget-conscious parents and other retail customers are one source. Foreign manufacturers are another, as they present intense competition to domestic toy makers. Retailers themselves are a third source of pressure, pushing prices at toy manufacturers down. Consolidation in the retail-trade industry and the influx of superstores have upped the buying power of retailers, giving more clout to their demands for low pricing.

WEFA projects that this industry will continue to find it difficult to raise prices. An increasing number of dolls, toys, and game product lines faces import competition from Asia. These will feel price weakness most acutely.

Supply Conditions

Toy-manufacturing establishments are smaller than the average manufacturing facility. There may be approximately 800 establishments in operation in the United States. Industry shipments per establishment tend to run 45% below those of the average U.S. manufacturer, but costs per establishment are lower. The combination suggests that toy manufacturers are more profitable than the average. This is accomplished by using less capital equipment and by paying relatively lower wages. The net effect has the toy manufacturing industry managing rather well, despite modest volume growth, sluggish product pricing, and import competition.

The toy industry is a mature industry. The domestic industry outlook is one of modest growth for the next few years, but international markets may hold more robust opportunities. To answer this challenge, domestic manufacturers are attempting to expand. Merger and acquisition are the means of choice, rather than Greenfield expansion. This strategy allows U.S.-toy makers to buy into existing locations, products, and distribution pipelines.

Major Trends Affecting Outlook

Comparatively, the doll, toy, and game industry is not a highly cyclical industry. Instead, it has a different, somewhat-chaotic character: Constant turmoil in the industry is driven by the ever-changing inclinations of the 7- and 8-year-old population. The result is something of a free-for-all. Important trends that will affect the industry in the near future are the following:

- Retail margins will continue to shrink, as customers remain cost-conscious.

- Retail cost cutting may result in more intense competition for shelf space. This climate punishes marginal and low-volume products.

- As the use of computers expands and penetrates increasingly younger age groups, greater and greater interest will be shown for multimedia products.

- The share of licensed dolls, toys, and games, which have TV and movie ties-in will increase, due to the advertising advantages of such products.

- Production will continue to move overseas to take advantage of cheaper labor.

- The merger and acquisition trend will continue. Due to the maturity of the market, this is one way to achieve a cost advantage.

- Exports will rise as foreign markets offer good demand potential.

- Established brands and classic products will be revitalized periodically, given the success of such classics as Barbie, Monopoly, erector sets, and yo-yos.

Games on multimedia platforms—including Sony PlayStation, Nintendo 64, and Sega Genesis and Dreamcast—are popular with the older age groups discussed. Such video games have also transcended these age groups to appeal to teenagers and young adults. Additional mechanical games of other types have undergone the same trend.

Risks to the Outlook

The toy industry is a fickle industry. Periodic boom-bust cycles are always a threat to the kind of orderly market participants like to expect. Many products in this field have a short-life cycle, and it is difficult to determine in advance which ones will succumb early. This frustrates production planning and inventory management, in turn, heightening the importance of information technology tools and information transfer from customers to manufacturers and retailers. Finally, the toy industry has but one major-selling season: the winter holiday season encompassing Christmas, Hanukkah, and others. The holiday season accounts for between 50% and 60% of the industry's annual sales. The risk that an externality can upset this crucial selling season is keen. Buying in this market is based on emotion and driven by the confidence of the consumer public in their economic situation. These crucial factors are always subject to change.

Part 4: Transportation, Communications, and Utilities

Chapter 23: Transportation

Railroad Transportation

The nation's railroads account for roughly 25% of U.S. intercity freight tonnage. The two major competing modes—truck and water—account for 49% and 12%, respectively. On a ton-mile basis, which reflects both tonnage and distance, these three modes stack up as follows: rail 39%, truck 31%, and water 13%. Over the last ten years, railroads have lost some of their share of intercity tonnage due to service problems and increased truck competition. Up until the recent service problems associated with the UPSP merger and the split-up of Conrail, railroads had gained ground in long-haul movements of various commodities.

Background

Traffic

Railroads accounted for almost 25% of intercity tonnage in 1998. The railroad share of this measure of the traffic pool has slowly eroded by about three percentage points over the past decade. Last year, railroad traffic was hurt by lackluster grain, chemical, metallic ore, lumber and building material, food and kindred product, scrap metal movements, and a decline in intermodal trailer loadings. In addition, shippers continued to lean toward truckers as a result of the 1997–1998 Union Pacific-Southern Pacific (UPSP) service meltdown.

Over the past ten years, railroads have lost a portion of their share of intercity tonnage due to service problems and increased truck competition. Railroads have gained ground in long-haul movements of various commodities, however, allowing their share of intercity ton-miles to grow. Railroad ton-miles grew by nearly 4% per year on average during the past ten years, and growth over the past five years has averaged 4.5%, largely as a result of surging traffic from 1994–1996. Ton-miles actually declined slightly in 1997, and then rose by less than 2% in 1998.

The railroads report traffic by separating commodity from intermodal traffic, a split that was implemented in their reporting in 1988. Commodity traffic includes the number of freight cars loaded (carloadings) with coal, grain, chemicals, paper, lumber, metals, and other commodities. Rail commodity carloadings are influenced by U.S. production and import levels of individual commodities, modal competition, and the steady increases in the carrying capacity of freight cars. A major revision to U.S. rail statistics in 1996 excluded the traffic of the Grand Trunk Western and SOO Railroads from U.S. rail traffic and reported them as Canadian traffic.

These changes in reporting make historical comparisons of commodity traffic particularly difficult. While carloadings are a key reported statistic for railroads, data are also reported sometimes by the weight of the freight (tonnage) or the combination of weight and distance carried (ton-miles).

U.S. railroads reported 18.1 million carloads of commodity traffic in 1998. Coal was king among rail commodities, accounting for 38.9% of total carloadings in 1998. Strong growth in coal production coming out of the Powder River Basin in Wyoming and Montana has allowed rail-coal traffic to gain considerable ground, since Powder River Basin coal is basically rail-captive. Rounding out the top-ten rail commodities were chemicals and related products, 8.8%; motor vehicles and parts, 6.7%; grain, 6.6%; metallic ores, 5.2%; crushed stone, sand, and gravel, 5%; metals, 3.9%; pulp and paper, 3%; waste and scrap, 3.1%; and grain mill products, 2.8%.

Commodity carloads by major U.S. railroads stood at 17.55 million in 1988 and fell to a low of 16.83 million in 1992. Commodity loadings jumped to 18.29 million by 1995, as the U.S. economy surged ahead. Since then, commodity traffic drifted down by 0.5% in 1996, and then increased by 0.9% in 1997, and 2.0% in 1998. Loadings of major rail commodities performed in 1998 as follows: coal ,+3.5%; chemicals, −1.4%; motor vehicles and parts, +15.3%; grain, −1.1%; metallic ores, −4.2%; crushed stone, sand, and gravel, 9.7%; and metals and products, +4.9%.

Intermodal traffic measures the number of trailers and containers that are loaded on designated intermodal freight cars. These units travel the long stretch of their journey stacked on rail cars and are transported for short hauls on either end by truck. Manufacturing and foreign trade are the driving forces of this traffic, but the intensity of truck competition is very important, and intermodal service is most cost effective in the heavily traveled east–west, north–south lanes.

The most striking development in intermodal traffic was the introduction in the early 1980s of articulated double-stack equipment. These were usually five connected platforms, each with the capacity to handle two containers stacked one on top of the other. Using this equipment, intermodal service had been moderately successful in pulling long-haul traffic off the highways. However, the rail-service problems of 1997–1998 did take a toll on shipper and trucking company use of rail intermodal services. Over the past two years, shippers and truckers have increased their complaints about quality and delivery times. In most cases, truckers can still deliver a trailer or container load point-to-point faster than a combination of rail and truck. The more time-sensitive the load, the more likely it will go by truck alone, rather than intermodally with a rail long-haul.

U.S. railroads reported intermodal loadings of 5.78 million units in 1988, comprised of 3.48 million trailers and 2.30 million containers. Trailer loadings, which are sensitive to domestic manufacturing, fell to 3.20 million units by 1991. Container traffic, on the other hand, grew steadily throughout this period as railroads aggressively marketed double-stack service. By 1991, the number of containers loaded had grown to 3.04 million. As the economy emerged from recession and foreign trade picked up steam, rail intermodal traffic began to gather momentum rising 6% in 1992 to 6.63 million. Trailer and container traffic grew 2% and 10%, respectively.

The following two years, 1993 and 1994, saw a dramatic surge in both trailer and container traffic. Economic fundamentals proved to be very favorable, as domestic manufacturing and foreign trade volumes surged ahead. At the same time, equipment and driver shortages plagued major trucking companies, and they directed as much traffic as they could onto the rails. This was also the period when rail–truck joint ventures proliferated. Railroads reported increases in trailer loadings of 6% in 1993 and 8% in 1994. Container loadings were even stronger, rising by 9% in 1993 and a whopping 19% in 1994.

Payback began in 1995, as economic growth slowed a bit and the equipment shortage eased considerably. Trucking companies began to take delivery of large numbers of trucks and trailers in 1994, which continued throughout 1996. Improvements in driver pay and working conditions may not have resulted in people lining up to become truck drivers, but retention rates did improve somewhat. Rail-intermodal loadings fell back by nearly 2.5% in 1995, and managed a modest 2.6% increase in 1996. Trailer loadings were especially hard hit, declining 7% in 1995 and 5% in 1996. Growth in container traffic slowed to a crawl, growing by only 1.6% in 1995. However, growth in foreign-trade volume of 7.5%, improvements in service, and aggressive marketing allowed container traffic to expand by 8.9% in 1996. 1997 brought a rebound in trailer traffic of 4.6% and another strong 8% increase in container traffic. Last year's weakness in U.S. exports, and shipper disgust with rail service dampened intermodal traffic. Container traffic increased by just 3.4%, while trailer loadings dropped by 2.9%.

Employment and Earnings

Class I Railroads employed 298,000 workers back in 1988. The railroad industry went through a period of aggressive "downsizing" during much of the past decade in an effort to improve productivity and efficiency. Employment declined without interruption to 226,400 workers in 1997. The industry may have gone too far as service problems plagued the railroads during the 1997–1998 period. In response, the railroad industry increased its workforce to 230,700 workers last year.

Average hourly earnings in the railroad industry stood at $15.00 in 1988. Hourly earnings hit a peak in 1997 at $18.10 when severe service problems increased rail-worker overtime. Average hourly earnings fell back to $17.95 in 1998. Between 1988 and 1998 the average hourly earnings for railroad-industry workers rose by 2% per year, on average.

Rail/Truck Competition

Railroads and trucks do not compete in every market. There is limited competition in the area of bulk commodities such as grain, coal, and chemicals. The competition to rail in bulk commodities comes primarily from barge lines.

Rail/truck competition is largely defined by length of haul. The average-truckload delivery nationwide is about 350 miles, and trucks dominate the market up to about 750 miles. Railroads compete very successfully over 750 miles, especially when delivery times are not a critical factor. Trucks remain the faster mode of transportation, with a cross-country trip taking as little as four days. The conventional wisdom is that it will be very difficult for the railroads to pull freight away from trucks for trips under 750 miles.

The trucking industry remains one of the largest customers of the rail industry. WEFA's discussions with trucking company sources indicate that truckers would be very happy to utilize the rails even more than they already do for long-haul transport, but the lack of service makes that very difficult.

The UPSP service meltdown turned shippers and trucking companies away from railroad service. Shippers have indicated that they are willing to pay the higher cost of truck service because they know their products will arrive where they are supposed to and when they are supposed to. Truckers are reluctant to put their faith in railroads until there is evidence of real improvements in service. The recent Norfolk Southern/CSX division of Conrail has done little to ensure truckers and shippers that things are running smoothly over the rails. The NS/CSX Conrail split-up is not the meltdown that we experienced with the UPSP, but there have been more problems than expected and we are not out of the woods yet.

Rail Traffic Forecast 1999–2008

Rail mergers such as the BNSF, UPSP, CSX-Conrail, and NS-Conrail are assumed to eventually stimulate rail long-haul traffic. However, in the near term, these ventures are doing little to lure back shippers or trucking companies. Rail alliances such as that between Canadian National, Illinois Central, Kansas City Southern, and Transportacion Ferroviaria Mexicana should also have a positive impact on rail traffic. Improved rail serv-

ice will eventually lead to increased use of rail transport by trucking companies. We are not, however, expecting the rush to rail-truck joint ventures that we witnessed a few years ago. Shippers and truckers have been burned over the past two years, and it will take hard evidence that service has improved to get shippers and truckers back on board.

We expect rail tonnage to grow by 1.0%–1.5% this year, and 1.0% in the year 2000, as industrial sector activity moderates. Longer term, expect tonnage growth of about 2% per year from 2002–2004, and 2.0%–2.5% from 2005–2008. The stronger growth rate during the latter part of the forecast period assumes some improvement in rail service. Support during the next decade will come from rail staples such as coal, grain, chemicals, motor vehicles, forest products, steel, and intermodal.

Intermodal traffic should expand by 2.6% in 1999 and 2.8% in the year 2000. Longer term we expect intermodal traffic to expand by 5.0% per year, on average. Support will come largely from healthy volume increases in merchandise imports and exports. We also expect continued expansion of domestic container traffic, including tank and refrigerated containers. Container traffic is slated to expand by 5.5% per year during the coming decade. Intermodal trailer traffic will benefit from increased domestic manufacturing activity, NAFTA trade, and greater utilization of rail services by major trucking firms and private carriers. However, we will see some erosion as domestic containerization continues to gain ground. Average annual growth in trailers loaded is forecast to average 2.0%–2.5% per year.

Rail ton-miles are slated to expand by about 1% this year and 1.4% in 2000. The annual growth rate beyond the year 2000 is put at 3.0%. The WEFA forecast assumes that railroads will be successful in their efforts to improve service, which is expected to result in continued progress on the long-haul traffic front. East-West intermodal operations will be upgraded and expanded, and we will see additional expansion of North-South traffic as NAFTA trade accelerates.

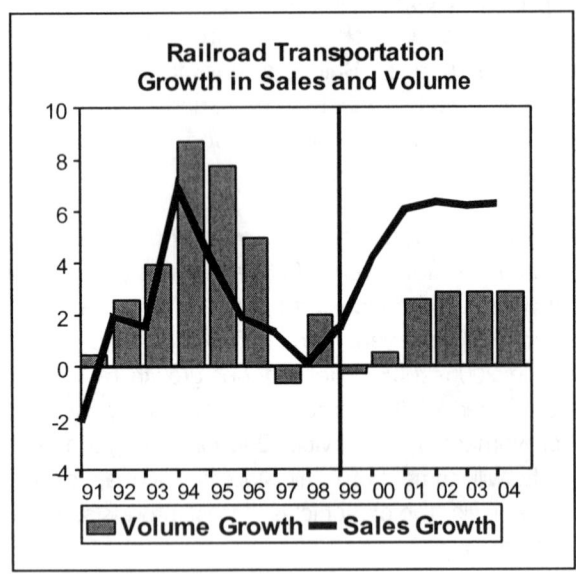

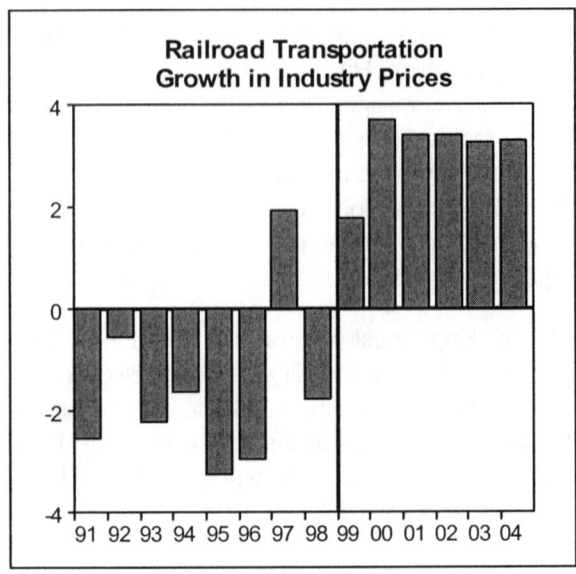

Railroad Transportation

SIC 40

		1992	1993	1994	1995	1996	1997	1998	1999	2000	2001	Compound Average 88-98	Annual Growth 98-08
Sales													
	Billions of $	33.03	33.55	35.87	37.39	38.09	38.59	38.64	39.23	40.89	43.36		
	% Ch	1.9	1.6	6.9	4.2	1.9	1.3	0.1	1.5	4.2	6.1	1.8	5.5
Volume													
	% Ch	2.5	3.9	8.7	7.7	5.0	-0.6	2.0	-0.3	0.5	2.6	3.3	2.4
Prices													
	% Ch	-0.6	-2.2	-1.6	-3.3	-3.0	1.9	-1.8	1.8	3.7	3.4	-1.4	3.0
Production Costs													
Avg. Hourly Earnings													
	$/hr	16.66	16.93	16.76	17.47	17.71	18.10	17.95	17.99	18.48	19.09		
	% Ch	6.3	1.6	-1.0	4.3	1.4	2.2	-0.8	0.2	2.7	3.3	1.8	2.8
Input Price Index													
	% Ch	0.7	1.1	1.4	2.5	2.5	1.5	-1.5	1.1	2.8	3.0	1.7	2.9

Truck Transportation

Trucking is composed of two major segments, private and for-hire carriers. Motor-carrier traffic is influenced primarily by manufacturing activity and the multiple moves that occur as a result of transporting raw materials, intermediate goods, and finished products. Construction activity and the demand for imported goods also have their impact on truck traffic. Although air freight has made significant inroads into trucking's transportation share in recent years, trucks still account for 70% of small-package shipments. Trucks account for over 49% of intercity tonnage and 30% of intercity ton-miles. Over the last ten years, intercity truck tonnage has grown by 6% per year on average. Competition from rail in the long-haul market should intensify once the railroads can improve service. In recent years, severe rail-service problems have helped trucking gain a bigger share of the traffic pie.

Overview

Traffic

The mix of commodities carried varies between trucks, railroads, and barges. Raw building materials like crushed stone, sand, and gravel, which usually are moved over very short distances, generally account for over 25% of truck tonnage. Stone, clay, and glass manufactured products account for over 13% of truck tonnage. Farm products and foods and kindred products each represent between 11% and 12% of truck volumes. Other key commodities include lumber and wood products and petroleum products, which account for 8% each; chemicals and products at 5%; metals and fabricated metal products at 4%; and waste and scrap and paper and printed matter, which each account for between 2% and 3%. Machinery and electrical equipment, motor vehicles, rubber and plastic products, and textiles and apparel each account for about 1% of truck tonnage. Miscellaneous manufactured goods account for another 2%. Coal, which is the dominant rail commodity at 40% of tonnage, accounts for less than 2% of total truck tonnage. A very strong construction market in recent years has increased the importance of building materials to motor-carrier traffic.

In 1998, rail tonnage was dominated by coal (45%), farm products (8%), chemicals (8%), nonmetallic minerals (7%), and intermodal (5%). Food and kindred products and metallic ores each account for about 5% of rail tonnage. Lumber and wood products, petroleum products, stone, clay, and glass products, primary metal products, motor vehicles and parts, and waste and scrap, each account for between 2% and 4% of total-rail tonnage.

Coal is also the dominant internal waterway commodity at 27.9% of total tonnage in 1998. Petroleum and products accounted for 24.6%. Food and farm products accounted for 13.4% of total tonnage. Chemicals made up 7.7% of internal waterway tonnage, and metals 5.2%. Finally, crude materials, such as forest products, pulp and waste paper, metallic ores and scrap, non-metallic minerals, and manufactured goods accounted for 21% of internal waterway tonnage in 1998.

Truck/rail competition is largely defined by length of haul. The average truckload delivery nationwide is about 350 miles, and trucks dominate the market up to about 750 miles. Railroads compete successfully over 750 miles, especially when delivery times are not a critical factor. Trucks remain the faster mode of transportation, with a cross-country trip taking as little as four days. The conventional wisdom is that it will be very difficult for the railroads to pull freight away from trucks for trips under 750 miles. The trucking industry remains one of the better customers of the rail industry. WEFA's discussions with trucking company sources indicate that truckers would be very happy to utilize the rails even more than they already do for long-haul transport, but the lack of service makes that very difficult.

Private Carriers

Private fleets are owned and operated by businesses whose main purpose is not transportation. Many retailers, major food chains, building materials suppliers, and manufacturers own and operate their own fleets. We estimate that intercity truck tonnage is split roughly 57%

on private carriers and 43% on for-hire carriers. On a ton-mile basis, the mix tends to be closer to 70/30, because private carriers have more short-to-moderate haul loads while for-hire carriers are dominant in longer hauls. In the case of for-hire carriers, the average miles per shipment exceed 400 miles. For all private-truck movements (inter-city and intra-city movements), the average miles per shipment are barely over 50 miles.

Private fleets dominate the movement of food and kindred products, lumber and wood products, and building and paving materials. They handle roughly 30% of all chemicals, paper products, fabricated metal products, and other manufactured goods. In recent years, many private fleet owners, wanting to focus exclusively on their core businesses, have put their transportation needs in the hands of logistics companies. These companies handle all scheduling, hiring, and firing, and equipment acquisition. During the last ten years, we estimate that private-carrier, inter-city tonnage grew by about 5% per year.

For-Hire Carriers

For-hire carriers are trucking companies that transport the freight of others. The for-hire segment includes truckload (TL) and less-than-truckload (L-T-L) carriers of general freight, as well as specialized carriers. Trucking-company inter-city tonnage expanded by about 7% per year on average over the past ten years.

■ Truckload refers to hauls with loads that fill a truck, usually in excess of 10,000 pounds. Major general freight truckload carriers include J.B. Hunt, Werner Enterprises, and M.S. Carriers.

■ Less-than-truckload refers to shipments of a quantity of freight less than required for the application of a truckload rate. This is usually below 10,000 pounds and generally involves the use of terminal facilities to break and consolidate shipments. Yellow Freight, Roadway Express, and Consolidated Freightways are major L-T-L carriers. United Parcel Service, the small package delivery company, would also fall into the L-T-L category.

■ Specialized carriers are trucking companies franchised to carry products which, because of size, shape, weight, or other inherent characteristics, require special equipment for loading, transporting,

or unloading. Tank truck carriers hauling petroleum products and liquid chemicals, motor vehicle transporters, refrigerated commodities carriers, and moving companies fall into this category.

Trucking companies' financial performance is heavily influenced by swings in economic activity and fuel costs. The loss of momentum in the economy that emerged in 1989 and the recession in 1990–1991 resulted in a marked deterioration in trucking company profits. As the pool of available freight dried up, trucking companies turned to rate discounting to attract freight and keep their equipment moving. This severely depressed carrier profits.

Adding insult to injury during this period was a sharp increase in diesel-fuel prices. Fuel can account for 15% of a truckload carrier's operating costs. For L-T-L carriers, who carry the added cost of services at terminals where loads are broken up and consolidated, fuel represents about 8%–10% of operating costs. Retail diesel-fuel prices had been in the $0.90–$0.96 per–gallon range from 1986 to 1988, before moving up to $1.01 in 1989. The Gulf crisis pushed prices up to $1.21 in 1990, and they averaged $1.15 in 1991. Not surprisingly, the number of intercity trucking company failures rose by 36% in 1990, and another 15% in 1991.

Since the economy emerged from the last recession, trucking companies have done much better on the financial front. Traffic growth has been very strong. The American Trucking Associations (ATA) tonnage index, which measures the traffic of major truckload and less-than-truckload carriers, grew by 8.5% per year on average during the 1992–1997 period. Fuel prices have generally been under control throughout this period, actually dropping sharply in 1998. Freight rates did come under some pressure late in 1995 and into early 1996, as growth in the economy slowed down. However, the recent performance of the economy, combined with persisting rail-service problems, has allowed trucking companies to increase freight rates. Competition between major national and regional carriers remains intense, but trucking industry finances are generally in pretty good shape. Most major trucking companies reported very strong revenues and profits in 1998.

Employment

Employment in the trucking and warehousing industry stood at 1.24 million back in 1988. Ten years later in very strong growth in motor-carrier traffic has played no small role in the 2.5%–3.0% increase in employment over the past decade. Average hourly earnings in trucking and warehousing stood at $11.14 back in 1988. Since then, hourly earnings have increased by 2.5% per year, on average.

Attracting and retaining high-quality long-haul truck drivers has long been a problem for motor carriers. Working conditions generally leave much to be desired, characterized by long hours and much time spent away from home; and drivers' salaries are not at the top of the blue-collar list. During exit interviews, drivers usually cite working conditions, rather than the pay scale, as their reason for leaving. Shortages of drivers usually become a major problem during periods of strong economic growth. That is when drivers are needed the most, but also when they have more job opportunities in other fields, such as construction, to lure them away. This is particularly true in fast-growing regions of the United States, such as the Southeast and Southwest. In order to make the job more attractive, there have been efforts to raise driver pay, increase the creature comforts within the truck cab, smooth out the ride by using better suspension equipment, and reduce the number of hours on the road and days away from home.

Truck Traffic Forecast

Private and for-hire carriers have been aggressively upgrading and expanding their fleets with state-of-the-art equipment since we emerged from the last recession. During the period from 1994–1998, U.S. fleets added 575,000 new GVW 5-7 trucks. If we are right about 1999, the figure for new trucks added to the U.S. fleet for the 1994–1999 period will be on the order of 750,000. The U.S. heavy-truck fleet has been both expanded and upgraded dramatically during the past seven years (1992–1998). U.S. fleets purchased over 1.2 million heavy trucks in these years. When you include the 255,000 units we expect this year, the 1994 to 1999 sales total will flirt with 1.5 million. We estimate that U.S. fleet of heavy trucks numbers about 1.8 million. Thus, as the year 2000 unfolds, two-thirds of the fleet will be only six years or younger.

Shippers are demanding service that is high-quality, low-cost, and problem-free, and the trucking firms that can deliver are the ones that will win share. The long-term outlook concerning for-hire carriers is generally constructive. However, we expect consolidations and other changes in the cast of characters in both the L-T-L and truckload segments of the for-hire carrier industry as intramodal competition intensifies. Among private fleets, we believe the trend of outsourcing to logistics firms will continue, but at a slower pace than in the recent past. It makes sense in many cases for companies to focus on their core business and leave the transportation portion of the business to someone else. However, each company is different, and private fleets will remain a very large portion of the transportation industry.

We expect motor-carrier tonnage to expand at an average annual rate of 2% during the 1998–2008 period. Ton-mile growth will be only marginally faster, as increased use of rail intermodal in East-West and North-South corridors limits the growth in average length of haul among motor carriers. For-hire carrier tonnage will grow at a faster pace than private carrier tonnage. Motor-carrier tonnage will reflect growth in manufacturing activity of roughly 3% per year, 3.5% growth in non-oil merchandise imports, and an increase in NAFTA-related trade. Despite increased competition from railroads and barge lines, motor carriers will continue to reap the lion's share of the benefit from NAFTA trade. Trucks account for more than 85% of the goods moved from the United States to Canada and 65% of the goods moved from Canada to the United States. Roughly 90% of U.S. exports to Mexico are moved by truck, compared to 80% of the goods shipped from Mexico to the United States.

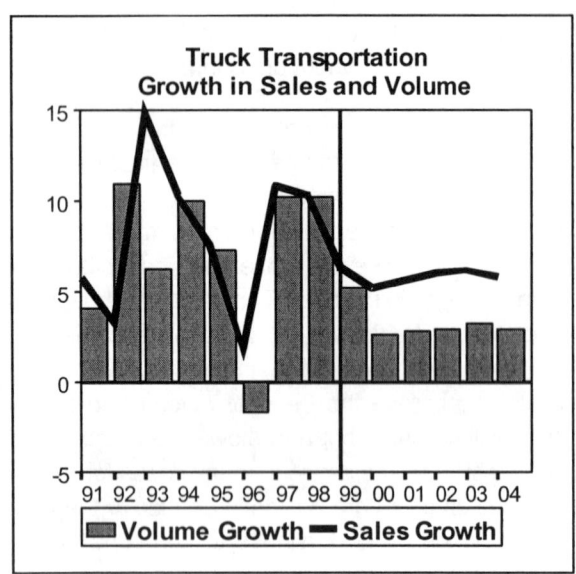

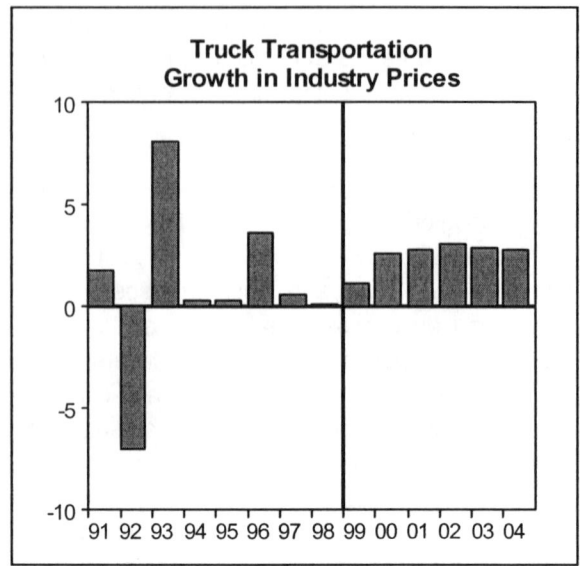

Truck Transportation

SIC 42

		1992	1993	1994	1995	1996	1997	1998	1999	2000	2001	Compound Average 88-98	Annual Growth 98-08
Sales													
	Billions of $	141.3	162.3	179.1	192.7	196.4	217.6	240.1	255.4	268.7	284.0		
	% Ch	3.3	14.9	10.3	7.6	1.9	10.8	10.3	6.3	5.2	5.7	6.8	6.1
Volume													
	% Ch	11.0	6.3	10.0	7.4	-1.6	10.2	10.2	5.2	2.6	2.8	5.5	3.2
Prices													
	% Ch	-7.0	8.1	0.2	0.3	3.6	0.5	0.1	1.1	2.6	2.8	1.2	2.8
Production Costs													
Avg. Hourly Earnings													
	$/hr	12.06	12.26	12.50	12.72	12.95	13.22	13.62	13.96	14.43	14.93		
	% Ch	2.0	1.6	2.0	1.8	1.8	2.1	3.0	2.5	3.4	3.5	2.2	3.1
Input Price Index													
	% Ch	-2.1	4.2	0.8	1.8	3.7	0.9	-2.0	0.6	2.7	2.9	1.8	2.7

Water Transportation

Internal waterways provide efficient low-cost transportation for bulk commodities, and one-eighth of the tonnage for domestically transported goods moves via these waterways. The Internal Waterway System consists of more than 25,000 miles of navigable channels, including the Inland Waterway System and the Intracoastal Waterway System. The Inland Waterway System consists of the Mississippi River and its major tributaries: the Arkansas River, the Illinois Waterway, the Missouri River, the Ohio River, and the Tennessee River. Other major rivers comprising this waterway system are the Black Warrior River and the Columbia–Snake River System. The Intracoastal Waterway System includes the Atlantic Intracoastal Waterway and the Gulf Intracoastal Waterway, and provides sheltered navigation routes along the Atlantic and Gulf of Mexico coastlines. The Great Lakes make up about 12% of water-transport tonnage.

Recent Performance

Waterborne tonnage has been declining as a share of total intercity freight transportation. In 1987, domestic waterborne traffic accounted for 16.4% of total intercity tonnage. In 1998, waterborne tonnage represented only 12.5% of the total.

Domestic U.S.-waterborne traffic has been relatively stable for the past decade. In 1988, traffic totaled 1,111.8 million tons. In 1997, traffic totaled 1,112.5 million tons. During the period from 1988–1997 traffic averaged 1,098.3 million tons. The high point during the decade occurred in 1990, when traffic hit 1,122.3 million tons. The low point came in 1993 when traffic sank to 1,068.2 million tons. Last year, domestic U.S.-waterborne traffic edged off by 1.0% to 1,100.9 million tons.

Domestic traffic is broken down into three main categories: Lakewise, Coastwise, and Internal. Internal is the largest category accounting for between 55%-60% of total domestic U.S.-waterborne traffic. The difference between these three categories and the total is accounted for by local and intraterritorial traffic.

Lakewise

Lakewise refers to traffic between the United States ports on the Great Lakes System. The major commodities hauled are iron ore, limestone, and coal, which account for over 90% of total Lakewise tonnage. Manufactured goods and cement each account for 3%. Lakewise traffic totaled 109.7 million tons back in 1988. The 1990–1991 recession drove Lakewise traffic down to 103.4 million tons in 1991. As the U.S. and Canadian

economies improved, Lakewise traffic grew by 3.9% in 1992, 2.3% in 1993, and 4.5% in 1994. Traffic growth slowed to 1.1% in 1995, and then slipped by 1% in 1996. The following year brought a 7% increase in traffic as the U.S. and Canadian economies grew by 4%. Lakewise traffic then slipped by just under 0.5% in 1998.

Coastwise

Coastwise refers to traffic receiving a carriage over the ocean or the Gulf of Mexico. Traffic between Great Lakes ports and seacoast ports, when having a carriage over the ocean, is also termed Coastwise. Petroleum and petroleum products are far and away the dominant Coastwise commodity, accounting for more than 70%-75% of total tonnage. The remaining 25%-30% is divided between chemicals 6%, soil, sand, gravel, rock, and stone and other crude materials 7%, manufactured goods 5%, coal 5%, and food and farm products 3%. Coastwise traffic has been on a downward trend during the past decade. Coastwise traffic totaled 325.2 million tons in 1998 and fell by 16.5% to 271.7 million tons by 1993. Traffic then rose 2% in 1994 to 277.0 million tons in 1995. However, over the next two years, traffic averaged 267.0 million tons annually and then slipped another 1.5% to 263.1 million tons in 1997. Last year Coastwise traffic declined another 2.5% to 256.5 million tons.

Internal

Internal refers to vessel movements that take place solely on inland waterways. An inland waterway is one geographically located within the boundaries of the contiguous 48 states or within the boundaries of the State of Alaska. Internal traffic accounts for between 55%–60% of total domestic U.S. waterborne traffic.

A decade ago in 1988, internal traffic totaled 588.1 million tons. Traffic peaked at 622.6 million tons in 1990 and then fell 3.6% to 600.4 million tons in 1991. Traffic staged a comeback the following year increasing by 3.5% to 621.0 million tons. This was then followed by a 2.2% decline in tonnage in 1993. Over the next four years internal traffic grew by 3.8%, reaching 630.6 million tons. Last year, internal traffic declined 0.6%, largely as a result of weakness in chemicals.

■ Coal is the dominant internal waterway commodity, accounting for almost 29% of the total during the 1988–1998 period. Coal traffic totaled 161.7 million tons in 1988 and rose to 166.8 million tons in 1989. The period from 1990–1992 were the banner years for internal coal movements as traffic averaged 186.7 million tons per year and accounted for over 30% of internal waterway traffic. During the period from 1993–1997 traffic averaged 177.2 million tons, peaking at 182.2 million tons in 1994. Coal traffic declined 0.5% last year to 175.1 million tons from 176.0 million tons in 1997. Coal accounted for 27.9% of internal waterway traffic last year.

■ In 1988, 160.4 million tons of petroleum and products were transported over internal waterways. In that year, petroleum accounted for 27.3% of internal waterway traffic. The peak year occurred in 1990 when petroleum traffic totaled 166.6 million tons, accounting for only 26.8% of the total. This was followed by a 6.6% decline in 1991. Over the next three years, traffic grew by 3.3%, reaching 160.8 million tons in 1994. Two years of declines brought traffic down 5.6% to 151.8 million tons by 1996. Petroleum traffic rose 2.4% in 1997, only to decline 1% in 1998 to 154.0 million tons.

■ Internal waterway movements of crude materials, such as forest products, pulp and waste paper, metallic ores and scrap, nonmetallic minerals, and manufactured goods totaled 111.8 million tons in 1988, accounting for 19% of total traffic. Crude material and manufactured goods traffic reached 132.0 million tons last year, an increase of 1.3% over 1997, and good for 21.1% of total internal waterway tonnage.

■ In 1988, 85.8 million tons of food and farm products were transported via internal waterways. Food and farm products accounted for 14.6% of total traffic that year. During the next decade, 1989–1998, food and farm product traffic ebbed and flowed rising to 95.8 million tons in 1992, falling back to 83.5 million tons in 1994, and then jumping to 94 million tons in 1995. In 1992, the peak year for tonnage, food and farm products accounted for 15.4% of total internal waterway traffic. Since then food and farm product tonnage has been declining, reaching 83.9 million tons last year. Traffic in 1998 declined 1.6% from 1997 and accounted for 13.4% of the total.

■ Chemicals moved via internal waterways totaled 52.9 million tons in 1988, accounting for 9% of total traffic. They declined over the next three years, reaching 45.6 million tons in 1991. This was followed by four years of growth, which saw chemical traffic rise to 53.3 million tons in 1995. Traffic slipped by 2.3% the following year, and then increased 2.8% in 1997 to 53.6 million tons. Last year, chemical movements via internal waterways fell 9.8% to 48.3 million tons and accounted for only 4.4% of total traffic.

■ In 1988, metal and products traffic totaled 15.5 million tons, or 2.6% of the total. In subsequent years, metals traffic increased to 19.8 million tons by 1990 and then fell off to 17.7 million tons by 1992. From 1993–1998 internal waterway movements of metal and products rose 84% reaching 32.6 million tons last year. In 1998, metal and products traffic accounted for 5.2% of total internal waterway tonnage.

Waterborne Commerce on Selected Waterways

The Mississippi River (including domestic coastwise tonnage) has remained the dominant waterway in the United States. In 1988, the Mississippi accounted for 26.9% of all domestic-waterborne commerce of the United States. Last year, the Mississippi accounted for 29.6% of total traffic. The Ohio River ranks second handling 21.9% of traffic in 1998, up from 17.3% in 1988. The Gulf Intracoastal Waterway handled 116.1 million tons of domestic-waterborne traffic last year, good for 10.5% of the total or about the same share as in 1988. The Tennessee River accounted for about 5%

of domestic waterborne traffic, while the Illinois Waterway was responsible for about 4%.

Industry Structure

The barge transportation industry has long been highly concentrated. Until early 1998, three carriers controlled 50% of the covered-hopper barge fleet, and eight firms controlled 78% of these barges. Open-hopper and tank barge ownership was also highly concentrated. There has been a trend toward concentration as grain firms and other shippers shed their water-transportation assets. In early 1998, two major barge lines joined forces under the American Commercial Lines name. This new entity has set its sights on NAFTA trade in bulk commodities.

Equipment Profile

Dry Cargo Barges

In 1997, the latest year for which we have data, there were 29,006 non-self-propelled dry-cargo barges operating or available for operation. These barges had a carrying capacity of 43.7 million tons. The Mississippi River System and the Gulf, Intracoastal Waterway accounted for 25, 648 units; Atlantic, Gulf, and Pacific coasts, 3,127 units; and the Great Lakes System, 231 units. In 1990, there were 27,170 non-self-propelled dry cargo barges operating or available for operation. The average carrying capacity of a non-self-propelled dry-cargo barge increased by 7% from 1990 to 1997. The number of self-propelled dry cargo barges was reported at 2,905 units in 1997 versus 2,678 units in 1990. These barges had a carrying capacity of 6.7 million tons. The average carrying capacity of a self-propelled dry-cargo barge fell 14% from 1990 to 1997. These units were distributed as follows: Mississippi River System and the Gulf Intracoastal Waterway, 1,435 units; Atlantic, Gulf, and Pacific Coasts, 1,249; and Great Lakes System, 221 units.

Tanker Barges

Since 1990, the number of non-self-propelled tanker barges has been relatively consistent. In 1990, there were 4,003 units and in 1997 the number stood at 3,971 units. These units had a carrying capacity of 11.3 million tons. The average carrying capacity of these barges has risen nearly 6% since 1990. These units were distributed as follows: Mississippi River System and the

Gulf Intracoastal Waterway, 3,286 units; Atlantic, Gulf, and Pacific coasts, 635 units; and Great Lakes System, 50 units. There were only 147 self-propelled tanker units in operation or available in 1997; 139 of them were in service on the coasts.

Towboats

There were 5,173 towboats in operation in 1997. These units were distributed as follows: Mississippi River System and the Gulf Intracoastal Waterway, 3,284 units; Atlantic, Gulf, and Pacific coasts, 1,679 units; and Great Lakes System, 210 units. The average horsepower of these units has risen nearly 8% since 1990.

Employment and Earnings

Water transport employed 13,600 workers in 1998. Employment peaked at 15,320 workers in 1990 and hit a low of 12,870 workers in 1994. In recent years, the number of people employed in water transport has been on the rise reaching 14,650 last year. Average hourly earnings totaled $14.69 in 1988. Over the past decade, earnings have increased by 3.5% per year reaching $20.03 in 1998.

Outlook 1999-2008

We are headed for another decline in waterborne-commerce volume in 1999, but the performance by major commodity groups will vary. Through May, internal domestic-waterborne tonnage, which accounts for over 55% of total traffic, was 6% below a year ago. Coal and coke tonnage was also down about 6%. Petroleum and chemicals tonnage was running ahead of last year's pace. Waterborne shipments of food and farm products were well ahead of a year ago. River movements of crude materials, such as forest products, pulp and waste paper, metallic ores and scrap, nonmetallic minerals, and manufactured goods were down over 35%. When all is said and done, we expect total domestic-waterborne commerce to slip by about 2% in 1999. Coal shipments will benefit from a very severe summer this year and some Y2K-related inventory building at electric utilities. Water movements of crude materials and manufactured goods are expected to improve as well from their very depressed recent levels, as the economy and selected markets continue to gain ground.

In the longer run, rates must cover investments in new barges and towboats. A sizable portion of the barge fleet is going to reach retirement age during the next five to ten years, but rates are currently inadequate to justify new investments. Demand for barge shipments is also expected to grow in the long run, as coal, chemicals, metals, materials, and food and farm product markets expand modestly. Increased trade with Canada, Mexico and Latin America will provide additional support. We expect tonnage to expand by less than 1% per year on average over the coming decade.

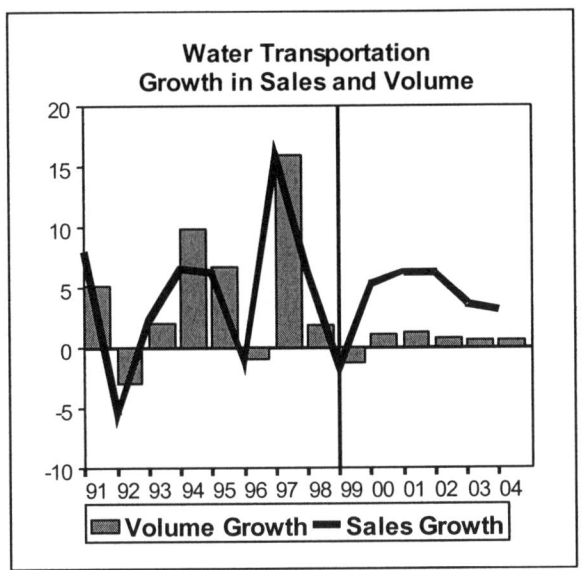

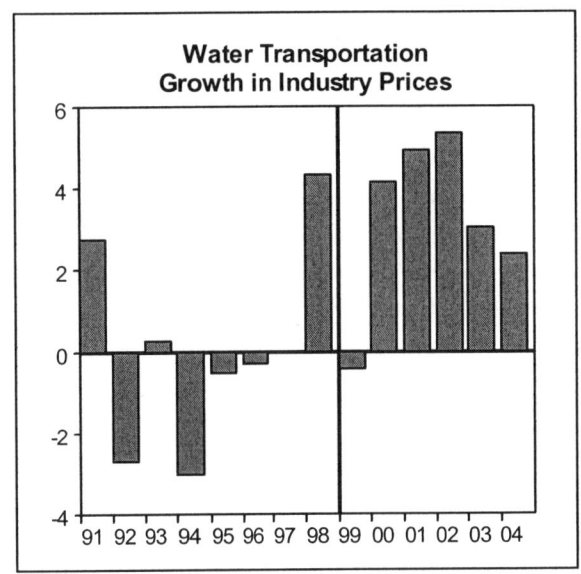

Water Transportation

SIC 44

		1992	1993	1994	1995	1996	1997	1998	1999	2000	2001	Compound Average 88-98	Annual Growth 98-08
Sales													
	Billions of $	29.72	30.43	32.45	34.46	34.07	39.47	41.96	41.29	43.50	46.25		
	% Ch	-5.5	2.4	6.6	6.2	-1.1	15.8	6.3	-1.6	5.4	6.3	5.2	3.7
Volume													
	% Ch	-2.9	2.1	9.9	6.8	-0.9	15.9	1.9	-1.2	1.1	1.3	5.0	0.7
Prices													
	% Ch	-2.7	0.3	-3.0	-0.5	-0.3	0.0	4.3	-0.4	4.2	4.9	0.2	3.0
Production Costs													
Avg. Hourly Earnings													
	$/hr	16.66	17.14	17.77	18.26	17.90	19.68	20.53	20.54	21.29	21.99		
	% Ch	0.3	2.9	3.7	2.8	-2.0	9.9	4.3	0.0	3.6	3.3	3.4	3.0
Input Price Index													
	% Ch	0.7	1.6	0.1	2.7	1.4	1.4	1.0	1.0	2.8	2.9	1.8	2.6

Air Transportation

During the past decade, 1989-1998, U.S. airline passenger miles (RPMs) grew by an average annual rate of 4.6%. International RPMs on U.S. carriers grew by 7.5% over the same period, while domestic activity grew by 3.8% and air cargo ton-miles grew by 88%. Domestic traffic increased by 42%, but international ton-miles more than doubled. During the 1990–1992 period, U.S. airlines reported operating losses of $6.1 billion. U.S. airlines have done very well on the profit front in recent years. In 1998, operating profits totaled $9.3 billion, up from $8.6 billion in 1997, $6.2 billion in 1996, and $5.9 billion in 1995. Operating profits in 1993 and 1994 totaled $1.4 billion and $2.7 billion, respectively.

Over the long term, passenger miles are slated to expand by roughly 4% per year. Domestic traffic will expand by 3.5% per year supported by growth in consumer income, an aging and more affluent and mobile consumer, and increased business travel. International-passenger traffic should expand by 5% per year. Solid growth in the U.S. economy and improving economic conditions in the rest of the world will provide support. Business travel between the United States and Asia and Latin America will exhibit the strongest growth. Growth in cargo traffic in the United States and worldwide will expand, as industrial activity and foreign trade continue to gain ground. Most recently, the weakness in Asian and other markets has taken a toll on outgoing traffic. We currently expect cargo ton-miles to expand by 5.5%–6.0% per year, on average, during the next decade.

Recent History

Air Traffic

Over the past decade, U.S. scheduled airlines have experienced an increase in passenger miles of over 46%, or average annual growth of 4.6%. Domestic traffic has expanded by 3.8% per year, while international traffic grew by nearly 7.5% per year. Passenger miles totaled 423.3 billion in 1988 and increased to 457.9 billion by 1990. The recession did take a toll on air travel and passenger miles slipped by 2.2% in 1991, with both domestic and international air travel declining 2.0%–2.5%. Air travel staged an impressive comeback the following year with an increase of 6.8% in passenger miles. Domestic travel rose 4.6%, but international passenger miles rose a whopping 13.2%. Over the next five years, 1993–1997, passenger miles expanded by nearly 5.5% per year. During this period, domestic and international traffic grew by 5.6% and 4.6%, per year, respectively. Solid growth in the U.S. and world economies provided the support. Last year, passenger miles grew by 2.3%. Domestic traffic rose by 2.5%. International traffic expanded by only 1.8% as a number of Asian countries went through a period of severe recession.

Through July of this year, U.S. scheduled airline-passenger traffic was running 3.2% ahead of its 1998 pace. Domestic traffic was up 3.5%, while international operations showed only a 2.4% increase.

Air cargo ton-miles grew by 88% during the past decade, 1989–1998. Domestic traffic increased by 42%, but international ton-miles more than doubled from 4.8 billion in 1988 to 11.1 billion in 1998. While it is true that air cargo traffic has experienced exceptionally strong growth during the past decade, it still accounts for a very small portion of total-freight traffic. As a share of both domestic intercity tonnage and ton-miles, air transport accounts for less than 0.5%.

System-wide cargo traffic was up 1.9% through July. Freight and express ton-miles were up 2.6%, offsetting a 3.7% decline in mail traffic. Domestic ton-miles were running just 0.3% below a year ago. The slight 0.3% increase in freight and express traffic was overwhelmed by the 3.6% decline in mail traffic. International cargo ton-miles were up 4.5% through July. Freight and express traffic, which accounts for 95% of the total, was up 5%. This more than made up for the 4% decline in mail traffic.

Airline Profitability

U.S. airlines have done very well on the profit front in recent years. In 1998, operating profits totaled $9.3 billion, up from $8.6 billion in 1997, $6.2 billion in 1996, and $5.9 billion in 1995. Operating profits in 1993 and 1994 totaled $1.4 billion and $2.7 billion, respectively.

The very impressive earnings performance experienced by U.S. carriers in recent years represented a dramatic departure from industry performance in the early 1990s, when a substantial amount of new capacity was delivered to U.S. carriers at the same time that traffic faltered. The combination of sluggish traffic and a huge influx of capacity drove down load factors (aircraft-capacity utilization measures) and severely weakened airline finances. U.S. scheduled airlines reported a load factor of 62.25% in 1989. The load factor averaged 60.8% in 1990–1991 and 62.19% in 1992–1993. The 47% jump in commercial-jet fuel prices in 1989–1990 only added insult to injury. As a result, during the 1990–1992 period, U.S. airlines reported operating losses of $6.1 billion.

Recent profitability has been driven by a number of factors:

- Strong demand for airline services has resulted in significant increases in RPMs and load factors. The load factor grew from 62.02% in 1993 to 70.18% in 1998.

- Fuel prices declined by more than 30% from 1991–1994. Prices inched up by 2.5% in 1995 and then surged ahead by almost 23% in 1996. However, this was followed by declines of 5% in 1997 and 27% in 1998. The price of commercial-jet fuel was actually 11.5% lower than it was a decade ago.

- Even with low fuel costs and record profits, airfares resisted downward pressure. From 1992–1998, overall consumer inflation rose by 2.8%. During the same period, airfares rose by 3.5%.

- Airlines also launched aggressive efforts to reign in labor and other operating costs. From 1992–1994, average hourly earnings in the air transportation industry grew by only 1.5%. Over the past four years, average hourly earnings have risen by 2.8% per year.

Industry Forecast

We expect US-scheduled airlines to report an increase in passenger miles of 4.1%. Domestic traffic should end up the year with an increase of 4.2% supported by healthy summer and holiday season traffic. International-passenger traffic will gather some momentum as the year wears on and finish the year with an increase of 3.5%.

Longer term, 2000–2008, passenger miles are slated to expand by roughly 4% per year, on average. Domestic traffic will expand by 3.5% per year supported by growth in consumer income, an aging and more affluent and mobile consumer, and increased business travel. International- passenger traffic should expand by 5% per year. Solid growth in the U.S. economy and improving economic conditions in the rest of the world will provide support. Business travel between the United States and Asia and Latin America will exhibit the strongest growth.

Growth in cargo traffic in the United States and worldwide will expand as industrial activity and foreign trade continue to gain ground. Most recently, the weakness in Asian and other markets has taken a toll on outgoing traffic. We currently expect cargo ton-miles to expand by 5.5%–6.0% per year, on average, during the next decade.

Airline profits should remain on solid ground, with healthy growth in traffic providing the foundation. While jet-fuel prices have started to turn up again, they are unlikely to surge ahead and cause the industry trouble. Finally, airlines should be able to raise fares, as demand remains strong.

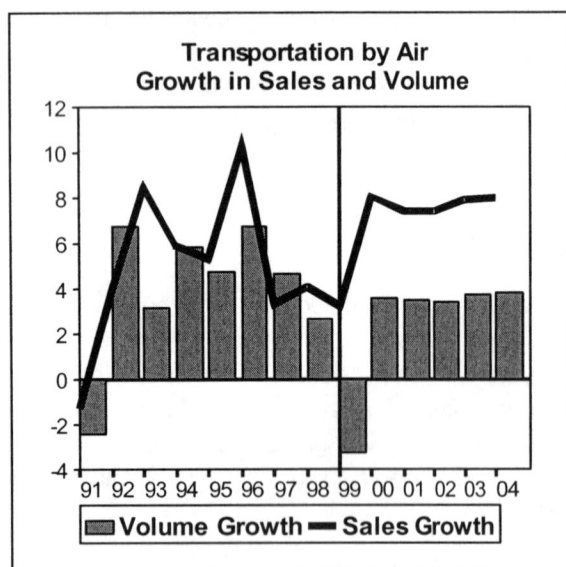

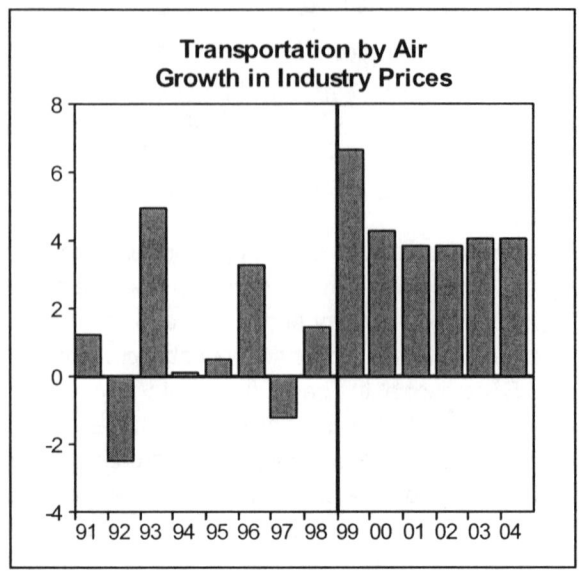

Transportation by Air

SIC 45

		1992	1993	1994	1995	1996	1997	1998	1999	2000	2001	Compound Average 88-98	Annual Growth 98-08
Sales													
	Billions of $	103.0	111.7	118.3	124.6	137.4	142.0	147.8	152.6	164.9	177.1		
	% Ch	4.0	8.4	5.9	5.3	10.3	3.3	4.1	3.2	8.0	7.4	5.8	7.3
Volume													
	% Ch	6.8	3.2	5.8	4.8	6.8	4.7	2.6	-3.3	3.6	3.5	3.7	3.0
Prices													
	% Ch	-2.5	5.0	0.1	0.5	3.3	-1.2	1.5	6.7	4.3	3.8	2.0	4.2
Production Costs													
Avg. Hourly Earnings													
	$/hr	13.43	13.55	13.78	14.13	14.45	14.93	15.34	15.73	16.26	16.83		
	% Ch	1.8	0.9	1.7	2.6	2.3	3.3	2.8	2.5	3.3	3.5	2.3	3.2
Input Price Index													
	% Ch	0.5	1.5	0.2	2.9	4.3	0.8	-4.0	0.4	2.7	2.8	2.0	2.6

Chapter 24:
Telecommunications

Telecommunications

The U.S. telecommunications industry remains poised for growth due to technological and regulatory change. The Telecommunications Act of 1996, which opens up the potential for genuine competition in local and long-distance markets, has created a stream of merger, acquisition, alliance, and restructuring activity, and will continue to re-shape the business landscape for the near future. Competition will lower prices and accelerate the transformation in services already underway.

Increased demand for mobile communications, toll-free and 900 lines, and the explosion of the Internet and on-line services, combined with the expected marriage of computers, television, and telephony, will provide the need for further investment in high-speed lines, cellular telephone networks, and faster transmission gear. Growth in the number of lines and the intensity of usage will offset expected rate decreases, yielding continued growth prospects for the industry.

The U.S. telecommunications industry, which serves more than 94 million households and 25 million businesses nationwide, is expected to have revenues of $273 billion in 1999. The industry can be analyzed in its constituent parts of local, toll, toll-free (800/888), and cellular services.

Local Service

Until recently, every local-exchange telecommunications market had one highly regulated monopoly carrier. This local-exchange carrier (LEC) provided service within its local-access area and was subject to both state and federal regulation. LECs included the seven regional Bell operating companies and their 22 sub-regional operating companies, as well as approximately 1500 independent operating companies, mostly rural cooperatives.

Under the Telecommunications Act, regulations are eased on the existing LECs, but their monopoly status is gradually eroded. Traditional long-distance carriers (AT&T, MCI, Sprint, and others), as well as other LECs, can compete for local customers. Competitive Access Providers (CAPs), companies that originally offered business customers special access services and interoffice transport services to long-distance carriers, can also enter the local-access market. In addition, nontraditional providers such as cable television and wireless companies can enter the local-access market.

Residential local-access revenues increased an estimated 3.5% in 1997, after increases of 6.3% and 6.0% in 1995 and 1996, respectively. The slower growth is tied to increased competition, which has increased the pressure on prices. Residential local-access revenue increases will continue in the vicinity of 3% through 2001. CAPs have

provided a measure of competition in the business local-access market since the mid-1980s. Consequently, business revenue increases, which have been more modest in recent years, will slow less dramatically and remain in the 3% range.

Long-Distance Service

The long-distance market is also heavily influenced by the Telecommunications Act. Just as long-distance players can invade the local-access market, so can local-access providers and CAPs enter the long-distance business. While AT&T remains the dominant force in this market, its share has steadily eroded from 81.9% in 1986 to 55.2% in 1994. MCI and Sprint, together making up over one-quarter of the market in 1994, have been the biggest beneficiaries of AT&T's decline; but a host of smaller firms, mainly resellers, have also sprung up.

Traffic is increasing in the long-distance market due to the various types of usage. Long distance now comprises data and fax traffic, as well as voice. Growth in international calling has been strong for several years, as the U.S. economy has become increasingly globalized. As video and Internet usage increases, demand for long-distance service will remain robust. Despite price moderation, revenues in the consumer market increased an estimated 7.2% in 1997 and will continue to grow in excess of 4% for the next several years. Due to aggressive competition for large corporate accounts, business revenue growth will be more subdued, averaging 4.6% annually through 2001.

800/900 Services

The 800/900 market (which now includes 888) is one of the fastest growing telecommunications markets. 800 service is an incoming-only line, in which the cost of the call is typically paid by the receiver. In contrast, with 900 services the caller pays for access for a specific service such as a sports score. Initially, mail-order sales and catalog establishments were the dominant users of 800 services. However, toll-free numbers are now widely used for customer service centers and centralized sales and marketing activities at non-direct-sale firms as well.

Portability of 800 numbers was required in 1993. Prior to that year, toll-free numbers were held by long-distance carriers, which made subscribers reluctant to switch carriers even for lower rates. Losing a prized number with a memorable mnemonic imposed significant business costs that lower rates would not offset. Portability increased competition, resulting in the lower costs that have been a major factor in the recent growth of the 800 market.

Technology has also fostered growth in this market. Originally, 800 numbers required dedicated-telephone lines, putting them out of the financial reach of most small establishments. The advent of switched inbound service allows 800 calls to be connected into a firm's existing telephone lines, significantly reducing costs. Growth was so rapid that the telephone system ran out of 800 numbers; and 888 was added as a toll-free prefix in 1995.

Toll-free revenues increased 9.0% in 1993 and 16.6% in 1994. Decreased availability of numbers in mid-1995 (until 888 came on-line) held 1995-revenue growth to 6.7%. However, toll-free revenues recovered, increasing an estimated 7.2% in 1996 and 6.7% in 1997, and are expected to grow in the 7% range annually through 2001. Toll-free growth will benefit from new applications for the service, such as remote data processing driven by increased use of personal banking, and finance options such as ATMs, credit card validation, and debit-card terminals.

Regulation of the 900 market has affected its growth adversely. FCC requirements that 900 providers describe the cost and nature of their services, especially for services marketed to children under the age of 18, and that disputed 900-call billings be charged back to the service provider have increased the cost of such services. This has led a number of services, particularly at the higher priced end, to quit the business. Also, 900 numbers are not yet truly portable, limiting competition across carriers. The net result is that 900 revenues in 1996 were estimated to be less than in 1991. While growth has returned to this market segment, it will not approach the attractiveness of the toll-free segment.

Cellular Service

By any measure, cellular service is the growth darling of the telecommunications industry. From an estimated 91,600 subscribers using about 350 cell sites and generating just over $350 million in revenues in 1985, this segment has mushroomed to an estimated 44 million subscribers utilizing 30,000 cell sites and spending over $24 billion on calls at the end of 1996. Annual growth rates in this segment were better than 30% in 1994 and 1995, falling to a still impressive estimated 24% in 1996. The increase for 1999 is expected to be around 12%.

The growth is coming from new subscribers. New users have been signing up at a rate of 28,000 per day, while the dollar amount of the average individual bill continues to drop. The wireless industry now directly employs in excess of 84,100 workers and reports a total capital investment since 1983 of $32.5 billion, $8.4 billion of that in 1996 alone.

With only 17% of the U.S. population estimated to use a wireless telephone in 1996, there is still plenty of room for growth. Once only the domain of the business elite, declining prices and the convenience offered by mobile communications is making cellular service an indispensable tool for sales personnel, as well as private individuals and families who are increasingly on the go. Despite anticipated competition from PCS and other mobile communications services, cellular telecommunications revenues should increase in the 12% range through 2001.

The Internet and Other Technological Opportunities (Issues to Watch)

The rapid rise in the popularity of the Internet and in other on-line services poses a unique opportunity for the telecommunications industry. From virtually no individual usage prior to 1994, growth in this area has exploded with about four million households subscribing to Internet Service Providers (ISP) in 1996 and an estimated 8.5 million in 1997. This is in addition to 13 million households subscribing to on-line services in 1996, up from less than one million in 1988. Clearly, some households have both Internet and on-line access. Estimates of Internet household penetration vary, but upwards of 24 million households may have Internet access by 2000. When business Internet use is factored in, the opportunity clearly becomes huge.

The current method used by most individuals for Internet access is via modem through a telephone line. Increased use of the Internet for e-mail, entertainment, and research has motivated many households to add a second or third telephone line dedicated to their computer. It has also fostered a tremendous increase in traffic on the existing telephone network. As Internet users demand ever more speed to push through large data files, such as video, telecommunications providers will either need to step up with more capital investment (e.g., fiber optic cable) or technological innovation (e.g., affordable ISDN, ADSL, etc.) or risk losing this business to cable or satellite–communications companies.

So-called collaborative technologies also offer opportunities for the telecommunications industry. These include video-conferencing, telecommuting, and other forms of data sharing, such as allowing doctors at different institutions to simultaneously view a patient's medical records. There were about 50,000 video-conferencing systems in use in 1995, compared with 5,800 in 1992 and 3,000 in 1989. The video-conferencing market posted revenues of $2.4 billion in 1994. Some market specialists believe a fivefold drop in the price of video-conferencing systems (from 1994 prices) is in store, leading to potentially dramatic increases in the demand for such equipment over the next few years.

$Million	1998	1999	2000
Residential — Local	27,623	28,490	29,345
% Change	2.9	3.1	3.0
Residential — Toll	53,428	55,628	57,817
% Change	5.4	4.1	3.9
Business — Local	27,845	28,747	29,637
% Change	3.0	3.2	3.1
Business — Toll	54,343	56,987	59,651
% Change	3.1	4.9	4.7

$Million	1998	1999	2000
Local Service	55,467	57,237	58,982
% Change	3.0	3.2	3.0
Toll Service	107,771	117,468	122,810
% Change	4.2	4.5	4.3
Toll Free (800/888)	13,357	14,374	15,386
% Change	6.9	7.6	7.0
Cellular Service	35,008	39,019	43,300
% Change	11.9	11.5	11.0

$Million	1998	1999	2000
Total – No Cellular	237,712	246,656	255,571
% Change	3.5	3.8	3.6
Total — With Cellular	272,720	285,675	298,871
% Change	4.5	4.8	4.6

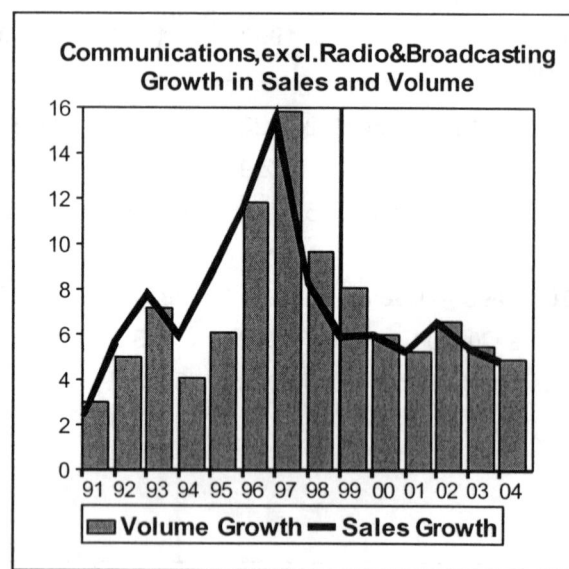

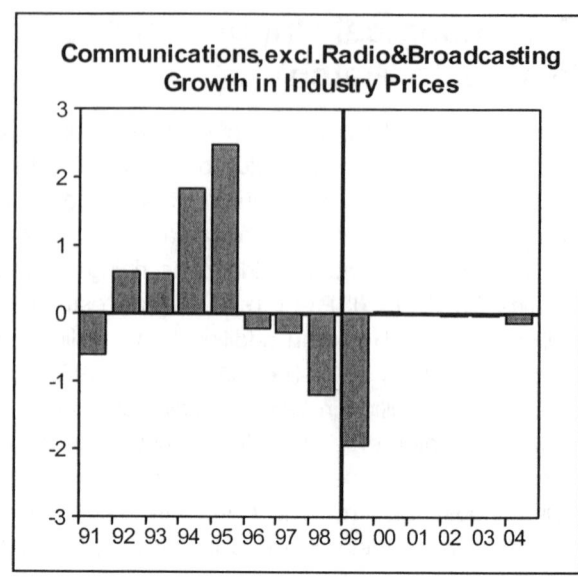

Communications, excl. Radio&TV Broadcasting

SIC 481

		1992	1993	1994	1995	1996	1997	1998	1999	2000	2001	Compound Average 88-98	Annual Growth 98-08
Sales													
	Billions of $	183.1	197.4	209.1	227.3	253.6	293.1	317.7	336.6	356.8	375.6		
	% Ch	5.7	7.8	6.0	8.7	11.6	15.6	8.4	6.0	6.0	5.3	6.6	5.4
Volume													
	% Ch	5.0	7.2	4.1	6.1	11.8	15.9	9.7	8.1	6.0	5.3	6.1	5.6
Prices													
	% Ch	0.6	0.6	1.8	2.5	-0.2	-0.3	-1.2	-2.0	0.0	-0.0	0.5	-0.2
Production Costs													
Avg. Hourly Earnings													
	$/hr	14.54	15.04	15.33	15.61	16.05	16.90	17.20	17.56	18.26	18.95		
	% Ch	3.3	3.4	1.9	1.8	2.8	5.3	1.8	2.1	4.0	3.8	2.7	3.6
Input Price Index													
	% Ch	1.1	1.2	1.8	2.7	0.6	0.8	0.5	0.1	1.3	1.4	1.3	1.3

Chapter 25: Utilities

Utilities

The electric-power industry is about to be turned inside out again. Just about every ten years, the power industry is jolted by a shift in public policy.

In the late seventies, it was PURPA—the Public Utility Regulatory Policy Act. PURPA was an administrative quagmire that resulted in artificial and contradictory regulations. Effectively, PURPA was repealed, but it led to the re-introduction of commercial and industrial cogeneration.

Toward the end of the eighties, regulatory reform (commonly referred to as deregulation) was begun. In process for more than ten years now, it is slowly making the industry more competitive, with its largest impact to date on the power production industry.

The power production industry is quickly becoming much more efficient due to these policy shifts, but it faces a daunting new challenge. The new public policy agenda may be even more disruptive than earlier policy shifts, and very expensive to achieve.

Preoccupied with SO_2 (2000) and NO_X (2002), the industry is facing a major change in environmental compliance with the proposed limit on particulate matter (PM) emissions to 2.5 microns scheduled for 2008.

The impact of the 2.5-micron standard for particulate matter will be tremendous—if fully implemented. Compliance will result in the replacement of more than 40% of coal capacity, predominantly with more efficient gas-combined-cycle units. Referred to as a "Marshall Plan" for the power-generation sector of the economy, the latest environmental challenge will recreate the power industry in the United States.

Near-Term Environmental Restrictions on SO_2 and NO_X

Today, there is intense competition in the electric power-generation industry. In the five years from 1993 through 1997, the system lambda—an inverse measure of competition—dropped by 20% or more in many regions. This cutthroat cost competition is expected to continue through 2002, when the capital spending mandated by the NO_X rules kicks in.

As shown in the table on the next page, to comply with the regulations on SO_2 and NO_X, power generators will have to make capital investments. Investment in Selective Catalytic Reduction will carry a total economic cost of approximately $6 per megawatt-hour (mWh). However, once the investment is made, the plants' dispatch costs—their variable costs—will increase only 31 cents on average. The supply curve will hardly move at all.

Although meeting the new NO_X restrictions will be expensive, it is affordable. The increase in costs will not cause the economic shutdown of most current assets. While their earning potential will be seriously impaired, and they may not be recovering any capital costs, they will keep running as long as they cover operating costs and earn a positive operating margin. These plants generate cash flow, although they may not be covering what we used to call the "fixed charges component of rates."

Most utilities are working hard to run more efficiently than ever. Due to deregulation, wholesale competition is improving management and operating practices and plant engineers are become expert at de-bottlenecking. Independent power operators have also de-bottlenecked their plants. The result is an increasingly competitive environment, which is lowering the price of electric energy.

Consumers may be happy, but many traditional utilities are frustrated by their low margins. Many have found it "strategic" to sell generating assets, often with unanticipated results. For example, one southern utility sold a plant to an industrial customer as "scrap steel". However, the industrial customer did not scrap it. Instead, the plant was carefully moved and reconstructed at the industrial facility. It is now generating power for the industrial customer and excess generation is sold back to the utility.

In summary, over the near-term, complying with near-term regulation of SO_2 and NO_X will increase the cost of producing power from coal and oil units. Although onerous, these costs will not force the economic closure of capacity-in-place. Rather, owners will actively work to reduce other costs as they compete against emerging market players with new, more efficient gas-fired units that limit the recovery of the capital required to comply with new environmental regulations.

The Cost of Complying with Environmental Regulations

	To Meet NO_X Restrictions 1998-2003	To Meet PM Restrictions 2003-2008	To Meet PM Restrictions 2008-2012
Tangentially-Fired Boilers	Install NO_X Burners & Overfire Air All-In Cost – $1.34/mWh Variable Cost – nil		Install Wet FGD All-In Cost – $6.60/mWh Variable Cost – $1.21/mWh
Wall-Fired Boilers	Install SCR All-In Cost – $4.50-$6.00/mWh Variable Cost – $0.31/mWh		Install Wet FGD All-In Cost – $6.60/mWh Variable Cost – $1.21/mWh
Cyclone Boilers	Install NO_X Burners, Overfire Air, SCR All-In Cost – $5.84/mWh Variable Cost – $0.31/mWh		Install Wet FGD All-In Cost – $6.60/mWh Variable Cost – $1.21/mWh
Coal Teakettles		Consider Re-powering as Combined Cycle/Fluidized Bed All-In Cost – $325-$375/kW Variable Cost – net reduction	
Gas-Steam		Consider Re-powering as Combined Cycle/Fluidized Bed All-In Cost - $325-$375/kW Variable Cost - net reduction	
Oil-Steam	Consider Re-powering as Combined Cycle/Fluidized Bed All-In Cost – $325-$375/kW Variable Cost – net reduction		

Mid-Term Restrictions on Particulate Matter (PM) Emissions

Over the mid-term, power prices will increase by one-fifth, as the industry adjusts to the new standards on particulates. An entirely new fleet of plants will be built made up of combined cycle gas turbines, with Selective Catalytic Reduction.

The only in-place coal plants that survive will be the largest and most efficient of the "flagship" plants. Their owners will make huge investments in SCR and FGD whenever they believe they can cover the $12/mWh total economic costs required to achieve compliance. Once again, however, the increase in their dispatch costs will be much less—their variable costs will be only $1/mWh to $2/mWh higher.

Looking at the EPA timeline shows that SO_2 and NO_X compliance is a walk in the park compared to compliance with PM regulations. Will it happen?

It's easy to argue that a 2.5-micron standard will not be implemented, but it is important to realize that every rule proposed by the EPA has been put in place. It is also likely that the full implementation will be delayed, and the analysis reported here assumes that implementation will be phased-in over the period 2008 to 2012. The fact is that environmentalists and the EPA want scrubbed coal. That means FGD, and that means a wholesale shutdown of coal plants.

Although the 2.5-micron rule will not bankrupt the industry, it is extremely expensive. The impact is incredible. Just in the Midwest alone, the most heavily affected area, WEFA estimates that 32 gW of older plants will be retired and replaced.

In our current analysis, WEFA has found that the state of Michigan will be hardest hit. Compliance with the 2.5-micron rule will lead to the retirement of 9.7 gW of steam capacity—virtually all of it coal, as the older, smaller, less-efficient plants are retired. That capacity will be primarily replaced by 13.1 gW of gas combined cycle equipment.

The capital costs in ECAR and MAIN alone will exceed $45 billion. The rest of the country is likely to spend another equal amount.

Environmental Timelines for Coal Powerplants

	1995	2000	2005	2008
SO_2	Phase I 105 plants 2.5 # SO_2	Phase II All plants >25mW 1.2 # SO_2	FGD phase-in	
NO_X	Low-NO_X Burners	0.4-0.54# NO_X		
Particulates	10 micron			2.5 micron
Air Toxics	None			

Forecast of Electricity Trends

Electricity Sales

Electricity retail sales are expected to continue to slow their advance in the coming years, averaging about 1.9% growth over the forecast period. This is lower than the 2.6% average annual increase of the 1980s and the 2.1% annual change of the first half of the 1990s, but still represents significant growth. Steady efficiency gains are projected to keep the rate of growth in total electric sales approximately 0.5% below the growth in the economy.

U.S. Electricity Sales Forecast
(Annual Avg. Growth Rates)

	1995–2000	2000–2005	2005–2010
Residential	2.4%	1.5%	1.9%
Commercial	2.7%	1.4%	2.1%
Industrial	1.2%	1.7%	1.4%
Total	2.0%	1.5%	1.8%

Capacity

With reserve margins still approaching 20% and with industry restructuring likely to push that number into the 16% range, there is still some excess capacity in the system to exploit before significant amounts of new capacity will be needed. WEFA's forecast calls for the addition of 13.5% more capacity in total to be added between 1995 and 2010, representing a compound annual growth rate of less than 1%.

This rate of projected capacity growth is lower than historical levels, and lower than our own forecasts were in years past. The changes in our thinking have been largely due to the changes in environmental policies. These policies will curb coal capacity in particular, and will benefit oil-gas capacity, especially natural gas. Nuclear and hydro capacity will remain effectively stymied as far as meaningful new growth.

Electricity Capacity Changes by Fuel Type
Net Summer Capability, Megawatts

	1995	2010	% change
Coal	300,609	277,292	-7.8%
Oil–Gas	207,000	349,163	68.7%
Nuclear	99,514	70,219	-29.4
Hydro	06,662	95,486	-1.2
Other	2,327	9,056	289.2%
Total	706,112	801,216	13.5%

Electricity Prices

Electricity prices will remain generally flat in real terms (after adjustment for the overall inflation rate of the economy). In spite of slightly falling real O&M (operations and maintenance) costs, fuel costs will rise slightly, while the capital component remains steady.

Conclusions

This analysis has endeavored to portray a rapidly changing, dynamic power industry in the United States and, through reasoned assessment, point into the directions in which it is headed. In an environment that is changing as quickly as this, it is difficult to single out the most volatile factors. Yet in the interest of attempting to provide an overall perspective as to the most significant risks, we have identified four key areas worthy of careful monitoring in the months and years ahead.

- **Natural Gas Prices:** Proponents of natural gas use claim improved finding rates and other technological advances ensure prices may never rise in real terms; but this is by no means certain. Gas prices will have an impact on the fuel choices made by utilities.

- **Environmental Changes:** All of the likely environmental changes now being considered will favor the use of natural gas. The speed and extent to which these changes are adopted will have a profound impact on future fuel choice decisions.

- **Public Sector Activity:** The evolving rules of the game favor competitive cost cutting over the more traditional regulation model values of reliability and safety. Will the ultimate result be cheaper power through more efficient resource use or lower rates due to safety concessions, as in the deregulated trucking experience?

- **Industry Structure:** The current merger mania has had apparent winners and losers. What is the optimum firm size, the optimum number of firms in the electricity market, and how close will the ultimate "competitive" result be to an optimum outcome (i.e., an outcome that minimizes price)?

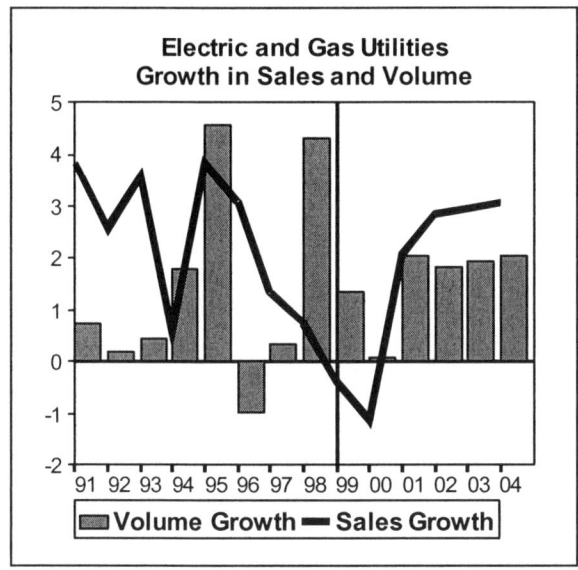

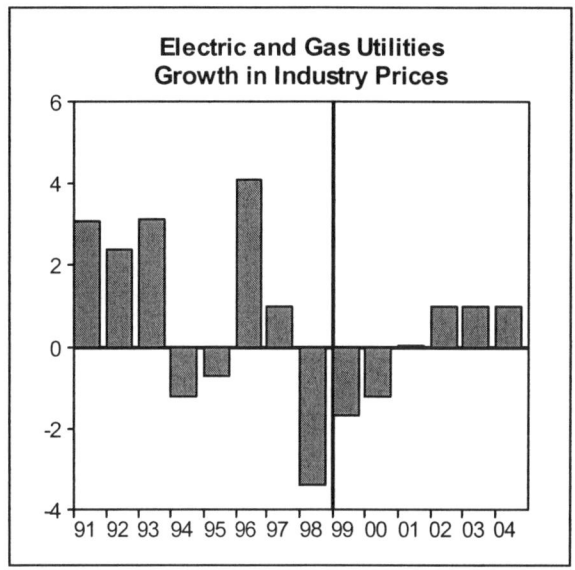

Electric and Gas Utilities

SIC 49

		1992	1993	1994	1995	1996	1997	1998	1999	2000	2001	Compound Average 88-98	Annual Growth 98-08
Sales													
	Billions of $	283.9	294.0	295.7	307.1	316.5	320.8	323.2	321.4	317.7	324.3		
	% Ch	2.6	3.6	0.6	3.8	3.1	1.3	0.7	-0.6	-1.1	2.1	2.5	2.3
Volume													
	% Ch	0.2	0.5	1.8	4.6	-1.0	0.3	4.3	1.2	0.1	2.1	1.2	1.7
Prices													
	% Ch	2.4	3.1	-1.2	-0.7	4.1	1.0	-3.4	-1.7	-1.2	0.0	1.3	0.6
Production Costs													
Avg. Hourly Earnings													
	$/hr	16.08	16.71	17.24	17.68	18.26	19.09	19.97	20.63	21.51	22.44		
	% Ch	2.5	3.9	3.2	2.5	3.3	4.6	4.6	3.3	4.3	4.3	3.4	4.0
Input Price Index													
	% Ch	0.9	3.0	-1.4	-1.6	8.5	3.6	-6.1	-2.5	3.8	2.7	1.2	2.2

Part 5: Wholesale and Retail Trade

Chapter 26: Wholesale Trade

Wholesale Trade

The wholesale industry is a large and diverse sector of the U.S. economy. In 1998, wholesale sales exceeded $2.5 trillion. Over the past decade, 1989–1998, wholesale sales of durable and nondurable goods have grown by 57%. The industry consists of a few large firms and many small ones. Employment stood at just over 6 million workers in 1998 and had risen to over 6.8 million by 1998. Currently, the industry employs nearly 7.1 million workers. Wholesale sales of durable and nondurable goods should increase by 4.5%–5.0% for all of 1999. Next year, slower growth in consumer and business spending and construction activity will dampen sales growth. Longer term, we expect growth in the U.S. economy of 4.5% per year, on average, in nominal terms. This should support an increase in wholesale sales of about 5.0% per year.

Sales and Employment

In 1998 wholesale sales were valued at $2.53 billion, an increase of 2% over the previous year. During the ten years from 1989–1998 wholesale sales increased by about 5.5% per year, on average. The wholesale industry employed over 6.8 million workers in 1998 up from 6.0 million a decade ago. Through July of this year, wholesale sales were running 5% ahead of their 1998 pace. The wholesale industry is currently employing nearly 7.1 million workers.

Wholesale sales of durable goods increased 3.5% in 1998 and 70% over the 1989–1998 period. Durable goods wholesalers employed over 4 million workers in 1998 up from 3.6 million a decade ago. Through the first-seven months of this year, wholesale sales of durable goods were up nearly 5%. Durable goods wholesalers currently employ nearly 4.2 million workers.

Wholesalers of motor vehicles and parts have done very well this past year as consumers have spent their income, increased their debt load, and reduced savings. Through July, wholesale sales were running 11.5% ahead of last year. In 1998 wholesale sales of motor vehicle and parts rose 3.7%. Over the past decade, 1989–1998, wholesalers of motor vehicles and parts have seen their sales rise 22%. Employment rose from 449,230 in 1988 to 518,010 last year. Currently, employment exceeds 539,000.

With consumers spending freely and new-home building strong, one would think wholesalers of furniture and home furnishings would have had another banner year. However, through the first seven months of 1999 sales were running just 1.8% ahead of a year ago. Sales in-creased 2.8% in 1998, and grew 59% during the 1989–1998 period. Employment rose from 151,360 in 1988 to 165,680 last year. Currently, employment stands at nearly 171,000.

With new home construction booming and the repair and remodeling business following along, wholesalers of lumber and construction materials have done well recently. Sales rose 7.3% in 1996, 5.3% in 1997, and 2.2% in 1998. Thus far this year, sales are running nearly 13% ahead of their 1998 pace. Over the decade from 1989–1998 sales increased 50%. Employment rose from 231,200 in 1988 to 263,600 last year. Currently, employment stands at 283,000.

Consumer spending has been strongly on the rise for a number of years. Wholesalers of sporting goods, recreational products, and toys have done well during this period. Sales jumped 6.8% in 1998, following increases of 7.1% in 1997, 10% in 1996, and 19% in 1995. Over the past decade, wholesale sales of sporting goods, recreational products, and toys have almost doubled. Thus far this year, sales have slowed, running just 3.7% ahead of a year ago. Employment rose from 746,000 in 1988 to 918,200 last year. Employment has continued to rise in 1999.

Wholesale sales of metals and minerals grew by 22% during the period from 1989–1998. Last year, sales fell by 3.9% following a 6.7% increase in 1997. Through July of this year, sales were running 5.6% below a year ago. Employment rose from 140,000 in 1988 to 152,500 last year. Currently, employment stands at 155,000.

Distributors of electrical goods posted a 3% increase in sales in 1998 following a 5.6% rise in the previous year.

Thus far this year, sales are running 7% ahead of last year's pace. Strength in new home construction, consumer spending, and business investment have provided the support. Employment rose from 498,130 in 1988 to 548,250 last year. Currently, employment stands at 555,200.

Strength in new home construction and home repair and remodeling has provided wholesalers of hardware and plumbing and heating equipment with a lift in recent years. Sales rose 4% in 1996, 6% in 1997, and 4.5% last year. Thus far in 1999, sales are running 5% above a year ago. Employment rose from 278,270 in 1988 to 306,000 last year. Currently, employment stands at over 310,400.

Wholesale sales of machinery, equipment, and supplies have posted impressive gains since we emerged from the 1990–1991 recession. Sales have been propelled forward by steady increases in U.S. business investment and expanding exports. Sales had fallen 6.7% from 1990–1991 and inched up by 1.6% in 1992. Since then, sales have risen by 9.6% in 1993, 7.7% in 1994, 9.5% in 1995, 6.8% in 1996, 8.6% in 1997, and 8.2% in 1998. Thus far in 1999, wholesales of machinery, equipment, and supplies are running just about equal with 1998. The demand for machinery and equipment in the United States has been mixed, and prices of high technology equipment have fallen sharply. Furthermore, export markets remain depressed. Employment rose from 746,000 in 1988 to 918,270 last year. Currently, employment stands at 990,000.

Wholesale sales of nondurable goods increased by just 0.6% in 1998. Over the 1989–1998 period sales grew by almost 45%. Nondurable goods wholesalers employed almost 2.8 million workers in 1998 up from 2.5 million a decade ago. Through the first seven months of this year, wholesale sales of nondurable goods were up nearly 5.5%. Nondurable goods wholesalers currently employ nearly 2.9 million workers.

Wholesale sales of paper and products increased 7.5% in 1998 and almost doubled over the past decade (1989–1998). Through the first seven months of 1999, sales were up 8.2%. Employment rose from 219,280 in 1988 to 278,860 last year. Currently, employment stands at almost 292,000.

The drugs, drug proprietaries, and druggist sundries segment of wholesale trade reported an increase in sales of 16% in 1998 to $124.2 billion. This has been the fastest growing segment of wholesale trade. Ten years ago in 1988, sales totaled $40.2 billion. Thus far in 1999, sales are running 17.6% ahead of their 1998 pace. Employment rose from 179,130 in 1988 to 238,380 last year. Currently, employment stands at 257,500.

Wholesale sales of apparel, piece goods, and notions barely increased at all in 1998 following 14.5% jump in 1997. Sales through July of 1999 were running 5.3% ahead of a year ago. During the preceding decade, 1989–1998, sales increased by 62%. Employment rose from 191,640 in 1988 to 224,300 last year. Currently, employment stands at 227,500.

Sales of groceries and related products rose 4.4% in 1998, following an increase of 4% in 1997. Over the past decade, 1989–1998, wholesale sales of groceries and related products grew by 47%. Thus far this year, sales are up 3.5%. Employment rose from 820,930 in 1988 to 921,550 last year. Currently, employment stands at 943,400.

Wholesale sales of farm products and raw materials dropped 13.5% in 1998, following an 8.8% decline in 1997. Sales were off another 6.9% through July of this year. The farm sector has been plagued by excess supply and weak crop prices. This has taken a toll on wholesale sales. Between 1997–1999, crop prices have fallen by over 12%.

Sluggish exports have taken a toll on wholesale sales of chemicals and allied products. Sales had increased 4.7% in 1997, but slipped by 1% last year. Thus far in 1999, soft exports are continuing to dampen sales, which were running 5% below a year ago through July. Employment rose from 125,000 in 1988 to 155,250 last year. Currently, employment stands at 162,500.

Weak oil prices depressed wholesale sales of petroleum and petroleum products in 1997 and 1998. Sales in those years dropped 2.5% and 16.9%, respectively. Rising crude oil prices have already had an impact on wholesale activities, with sales through July up 9.6%. Employment has declined over the past decade from 203,230 in 1988 to 155,860 last year. Currently, employment stands at 153,600.

Wholesale sales of beer, wine, and distilled alcoholic beverages rose 5.6% in 1998, following a 4.4% rise in 1997. Over the past decade, 1989–1998, sales have increased 43%. Through July of this year, sales were up 8.3%. Employment rose from 149,140 in 1988 to 155,860 last year. Currently, employment stands at 165,700.

Industry Structure

The products that wholesalers distribute to their customers are supplied by other firms in the manufacturing, mining, agricultural, and wholesale sectors of the economy. Wholesalers also distribute products that are produced outside of the United States and then shipped into this country. The wholesale industry has three categories—merchant wholesalers; manufacturers' sales branches and offices; and agents, brokers, and commission merchants. Of the three, merchant wholesalers account for the largest share of sales, employment, and firms.

Merchant wholesalers account for fewer than 60% of all wholesale sales, and at least 50% of all sales in each major product line, except motor vehicles and parts. Merchant wholesalers are distinguished from other types of wholesalers in that they actually take title to the goods. They may also sort, assemble, grade, and store them. Some also provide certain "value-added" services, such as packaging and labeling—a business strategy that is becoming increasingly important as thousands of wholesalers, selling products that are similar in quality and design, compete for customers.

Other wholesale transactions involve agents or brokers, who sell supplier-owned products primarily to retailers and other wholesalers for a commission or fee, and manufacturers' sales branches and offices, which sell the parent manufacturer's products mainly to retailers and industrial users. The Census Bureau collects its monthly and annual sales data based on the primary business of an establishment; therefore, wholesale activities of manufacturers' sales agents that are conducted out of larger facilities owned by the producer are not counted separately as wholesaling. However, benchmark reports are available every five years that distinguish between the types of wholesalers and better identify the non-merchant activities. Sales by manufacturers' sales branches and offices accounted for over one-third of all sales by wholesalers, while agents and brokers accounted for about 11%. Agents, brokers, and manufacturers' sales branches represent a similar proportion of total sales for each of the major wholesale product lines, with the exception of motor vehicles and parts.

Industry Trends

The wholesale-trade industry has been a fast-growing sector of the U.S. economy in recent years. During the 1990s, real value added in wholesale trade has grown at double or triple the rate of growth of the overall economy (measured by real Gross Domestic Product). Some of this added growth during the recovery was due to the fact that wholesalers concentrate in manufactured goods, which tend to be more cyclical than the economy overall. However, the sector's value added grew even during the last recession, indicating that wholesalers have increased their penetration in the distribution chain. This has been accomplished in large part through the addition of value-added services, assembly, and even customized production processes to their businesses. While these added activities may not fall into a strict definition of wholesale trade, the categorization of sales by establishment places them there.

Merchant wholesalers account for nearly 90% of all wholesaling firms and constitute the dominant wholesale distribution channel for each of the major product lines carried by wholesalers: bulk commodities, capital goods, and all consumer goods, except motor vehicles and parts.

Alternative Channels of Distribution

Despite the strong growth in sales of merchant wholesalers in recent years, those firms have been under increasing pressure from alternative channels of distribution. The most important alternative channels of wholesale distribution are direct manufacturer-to-retail arrangements, usually made by manufacturers under strategic alliances with major retail-chain-stores, warehouse clubs, discount stores, and home-center stores. Other alternative channels include mail order, catalog sales, and direct sales from manufacturer to industrial user or from retailer to industrial users. Shopping via the Internet is still in its infancy, but promises to be a very fast growing alternative channel.

The value of products distributed through these alternative channels are lost sales as far as most wholesalers are concerned. Thus, the size of the current and potential market for wholesalers has been diminished by the volume of products distributed through the alternative channels. This is one reason why wholesalers have expanded their service and value-added offerings in the markets where they still have a strong place in the supply chain.

Changes in the Industry

Intense pressures in the industry's competitive structure, in costs, and in other areas have caused significant changes in the wholesale-trade business in recent years.

For example, consumers and retailers are forcing changes in the beverage distribution system. Large retailers are demanding creative, contemporary, progressive changes to help them do a better job for consumers. Meeting these demands represents quite a change for beverage distributors, who historically have concerned themselves with delivery activities and have relied on their suppliers for marketing efforts. Now, a significant portion of the marketing burden has shifted to the wholesaler.

In another example of the ongoing changes in the wholesale-trade business, global competition among chemical manufacturers has brought about more work for chemical distributors, as customers call for blending, reformulating, bar-coding, and quality-control tests on top of repackaging. While manufacturers are working at cutting costs, enhancing efficiency, and concentrating on core business lines, much of this value-added business is passed on to distributors. While this redirects and expands opportunities for distributors, the greatest challenge lies in delivering the goods with the best service and at the lowest operating costs.

Chemical distributors used to be classic middlemen, buying in bulk and selling in parcels. Simple repackaging was the extent of their hands-on product. Today, distributors are not only repackaging as never before, but blending, reformulating (as manufacturers shift to less-hazardous products), bar-coding, testing, and performing other quality-assurance chores—even safety and regulatory training. At the same time, a major result of manufacturers' determination to wring out every possible supply-chain cost is to winnow the number of distributors to a minimum and add to the tasks of the survivors.

Outlook

Wholesale sales of durable and nondurable goods should increase by 4.5%–5.0% for all of 1999. Next year, slower growth in consumer and business spending, and construction activity will dampen sales growth. Longer term, we expect growth in the U.S. economy of 4.5% per year, on average, in nominal terms. This should support an increase in wholesale sales of about 5.0% per year. Wholesalers of consumer goods, high-technology products, such as computers, and drugs and medical supplies and equipment should experience the strongest growth. Wholesalers who are geared to the export market will generally do better than those with a domestic focus. Regionally, we would expect stronger sales among wholesalers serving the Southeast, Southwest, Mountain, and Pacific regions.

Merchant Wholesale Sales, 1994–1998, By Category
Billions of Dollars

	1994	1995	1996	1997	1998
Durable Goods	1091.9	1198.7	1241.7	1313.2	1359.4
Motor vehicles and auto equipment	188.7	189.1	192.5	195.4	202.7
Furniture and home furnishings	36.8	41.0	43.1	46.5	47.8
Lumber and other construction materials	79.4	79.3	85.1	89.7	91.7
Sporting, recreational goods, and toys	170.6	203.1	223.4	239.3	255.6
Metals and minerals, except petroleum	89.1	95.0	93.7	100.0	96.1
Electrical goods	163.5	193.0	194.5	205.4	211.7
Hardware, plumbing and heating equipment	63.4	67.2	70.0	74.3	77.5
Machinery, equipment and supplies	175.6	192.2	205.2	222.9	241.2
Miscellaneous durable goods	124.9	138.7	134.1	140.0	135.1
Nondurable Goods	977.0	1061.3	1134.5	1167.6	1174.5
Paper and products	66.4	79.8	79.5	84.1	90.5
Drugs, drug proprietors, and druggist sundries	76.5	83.8	93.7	107.1	124.2
Apparel, piece goods, and notions	72.3	70.3	74.7	85.5	85.7
Groceries and related products	293.4	312.6	319.1	331.8	346.4
Farm product raw materials	99.1	119.8	136.9	124.8	107.9
Chemicals and allied products	43.1	50.0	52.8	55.3	54.8
Petroleum and petroleum products	130.4	131.4	148.7	145.0	120.5
Beer, wine, and distilled alcoholic beverages	52.1	52.7	56.0	58.4	61.7
Miscellaneous nondurable goods	143.6	160.8	172.9	175.4	182.7
Total, all goods	**2068.9**	**2260.0**	**2376.2**	**2480.8**	**2533.9**

Chapter 27: Retail Trade

Building Materials and Supply Stores

The major retail group called building materials, hardware, garden supply, and mobile home dealers includes a segment called building materials and supply stores. The major group is dominated by building materials and supply stores, which account for half of all sales. Hardware stores generate an additional quarter of the sales in the major group. Mobile home dealers account for only a small fraction of this group.

The building materials and supply store category is the focus of this section. Building materials and supply stores are generally characterized as lumberyards and paint, glass, and wallpaper stores. Establishments that are engaged in selling lumber, building materials, paint, glass, or wallpaper to construction contractors and the general public are included in the building materials and supply stores category. The lumber they sell may include rough and dressed lumber, flooring, molding, doors, sashes, frames, and other millwork. The building materials may include roofing, siding, shingles, wallboard, paint, brick, tile, cement, sand, gravel, and other building materials and supplies. Hardware is often an important line sold by retail building materials and supply stores.

Sales at building materials and supply stores have benefited considerably from the boom in the residential construction and do-it-yourself market in the last several years. They will remain strong in the next two years, but growth is expected to slow. The aging of the population, combined with reduced population growth, will keep sales increases in a moderate range over the next decade. Prices will also grow moderately. They will be driven by lumber prices and a changing product mix reflective of environmental costs in this sector.

Demand Conditions

Building materials and supply stores sell to both professional contractors and do-it-yourself builders. Spending for do-it-yourself projects primarily comes from younger homeowners, while older homeowners tend to prefer to purchase professional services. Since professional home remodeling is a fragmented industry made up of many small firms, both types of home remodeling result in retail sales at building materials and supply stores.

Remodeling construction has been growing as a portion of total spending for residential construction. This trend will likely moderate in the near future, as the pent-up demand for remodeling and home improvements falls away.

An important demographic change is underway, however, which will affect the nature of sales in this market. Homeowners in the younger age brackets (25-to-34 years old) tend to do more work themselves, while older homeowners tend to purchase remodeling services. Many remodeling contractors purchase materials and equipment at retail building supply stores, but contractors' requirements are different from homeowners'. Building supply stores, thus, face the challenge of continuing to service their core business, while increasing their appeal to professional customers.

Supply Conditions

Stores in the building materials and supply category fall into two types. First are the major chains, such as Home Depot, Lowes, and Hechingers. Although these chains have grown, they still tend to be regional rather than national, and no one chain has more than a small portion of total sales for this industry. Total building materials and supply stores retail sales reached $116 billion in 1997 and almost $127 billion in 1998. Home Depot, the largest chain, is estimated to have a market share of approximately 15%. Even the larger stores, therefore, do not dominate a majority of the market. This category also has many small stores. As a result, the average sales volume per store is considerably lower than other store types like general merchandise and food retailing, where chains control a larger share of the market.

Small stores have been able to keep a larger share of the building materials and supplies market than have small stores in other sectors, such as grocery stores. An important difference between the two sectors is the existence of marketing agreements and cooperatives that allow independent retailers to enjoy the advantages of national purchasing and marketing, while maintaining financial independence. Chain stores will continue to move into this market aggressively, however, since there is evidently much scope for consolidation. Whether they can succeed in reducing the number of establishments in the face of the sector's unusual cooperative arrangement remains to be seen.

Retail Sales: Estimated Building Materials and Supply Stores Market Share

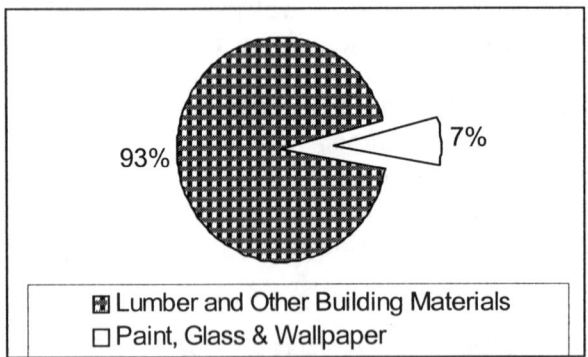

93%   7%

▓ Lumber and Other Building Materials
☐ Paint, Glass & Wallpaper

Industry Structure

Growth in retail sales at housing materials and supply stores tends to mirror growth in the residential real estate market and is reflective of the business cycle. Housing start activity in 1996 and 1997 was brisk. 1998 is showing signs of a banner year, aided by unseasonably warm weather early in the year, strong employment and income growth, and low mortgage rates. Retail sales growth at housing materials and supply establishments is expected to decelerate in the next two years and fall in a moderate range thereafter.

Over the last five years, the productivity of the U.S. economy grew, and so did per-capita income, which received an extra boost from the surge in the stock market. Workers have been spending a significant portion of this additional income on buying homes and on remodeling houses. As a result the year-to-year demand for the building materials increased sharply in 1996 by 7%, and continued to increase in 1997 by

9.9% and in 1998 by 9.4%. Our forecast indicates that the demand will increase 7.0% in 1999, with growth moderating to about 5.5% through 2001.

Building supply stores face a number of challenges on the environmental front. Their problem is not their stores, but what they sell and how it is used. These stores are the major supplier of most of the toxic materials found in a typical house, including paint, glue, cleaners, and home-building products such as insulation, drywall, and others. Even when used correctly, many of these products can be dangerous or harmful to the environment, and, if used incorrectly, they can be directly harmful to people. In addition, consumers may cause environmental damage through incorrect material disposal.

While courts have not typically found retail stores legally responsible for the environmental impacts of building products, some major retailers would like to address this problem. The retailers are concerned about the image of the sector as well as the image of their own stores. They are also concerned about possible regulation, which would add to retailers' costs.

Specific environmental issues that stores continue to face include the topics that follow:

- *Lumber and its substitutes*. While lumber is a renewable resource, different types of lumber may be more or less environmentally friendly. With lumber costs rising, retailers will likely need to substitute other types of lumber (including faster growing species), and steel and plastic products for traditional lumber.

- *Consumer education*. As consumers become more aware of environmental problems, retailers will need to supply more information about the environmental impacts of various products.

- *"Take-Back" items*. Stores that sell items that cannot be disposed of using normal methods will likely have to become collection points for the disposal of these items. Such items include used batteries, paint, and materials that constitute hazardous waste.

Environmental issues will pose a challenge in this competitive marketplace, because many stores will be unable or unwilling to invest in these areas if it will raise their costs above non-investing competitors. As a result, government regulation is likely to eventually cover this area.

Outlook

The aging of the population, combined with reduced population growth, will keep growth in sales at building supply stores very moderate over the next decade. The pent-up demand for remodeling and upgrading houses has largely worn off with the fast growth in home sales of the past few years. Therefore, the demand will fall marginally to 5.6% towards the end of 2000, and stay there until the end of 2001.

Trends & Forecasts: Building Materials and Supply Stores

	1991	1992	1993	1994	1995	1996	1997	1998	1999	2000	2001
Retail Sales (Bil $)	67.9	75.2	83.1	94.4	98.6	105.5	116.1	126.9	135.9	143.5	151.5
% Change	−3.5	10.7	10.5	13.6	4.5	7.0	9.9	9.4	7.0	5.6	5.6
Price Index % Change	3.2	1.2	1.5	1.8	1.8	1.3	1.8	-1.0	-0.0	1.6	1.4

General Merchandise Stores

General merchandise stores are defined as retail stores that sell a number of lines, such as dry goods, apparel and accessories, furniture and home furnishings, small wares, hardware, and food. General merchandise stores are broken down into three major groupings: Department stores, Variety stores, and Miscellaneous General Merchandise stores. This sector of retail accounts for approximately 12.8% of all retail sales.

With the massive restructuring undertaken by department stores in the 1990s, the general merchandise community has returned to good health. Variety stores are still in significant trouble, but the relatively small share of total sales, which they control, will limit their impact on the total for general merchandise stores. The miscellaneous merchandise stores are expected to climb back from their stagnant sales of the past few years. The combined performance of those three sectors is forecast to generate moderate sales growth for the overall industry in the near-to-medium term.

Demand Conditions

Each of the three subdivisions of general merchandise stores has a different significance to overall industry sales. Department stores, by far the biggest of the three, account for the majority of total employment in the general merchandise category, and almost 80% of total sales within this industry.

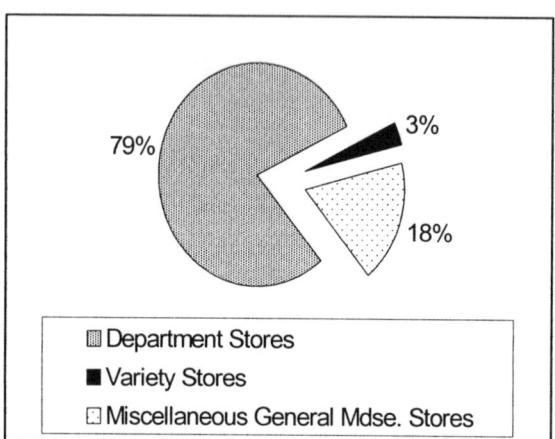

General Merchandise Market Share

A department store is defined as a retail store that carries men's and women's apparel, household appliances or other home furnishings, and various other lines. These stores are arranged in departments with individualized accounting. Department stores usually provide their own charge accounts, deliver merchandise, and maintain open stocks. In addition, department stores generally have more than 50 employees.

Establishments that carry a similar range of merchandise with less than 50 employees are classified as Miscellaneous General stores.

The third category of general merchandise store is a Variety store. Variety stores are primarily engaged in the retail sale of a variety of merchandise in the low and popular price ranges. Sales are usually made on a cash-and-carry basis, with the open-selling method of display and customer selection of merchandise. These stores generally do not carry a complete line of merchandise, are not departmentalized, do not carry their own charge service, and do not deliver merchandise.

Sales in general merchandise stores depend not only on specialization of the businesses, but also on the economic performance of the U.S. economy. Over the last several years, the economy has grown continuously and mortgage rates have remained relatively low. As a result, the demand for new and existing homes have surged ahead, thus boosting the sales of general merchandise products such as furniture and furnishings, appliances, carpets, house-ware, draperies, etc. Our forecast for the next two years indicates that the demand for these types of items will slow, as the housing market weakens, and general merchandise sales in all three categories will decelerate along with growth in the economy.

Sales at Department stores fell during the late 1980s due to the superior performance of specialty stores, such as The Gap, and the rise of superstores, such as Home Depot and Best Buy. From 1985 to 1992, department store sales were a drag on overall general merchandise performance. During that period, sales growth at department stores averaged 5.4%, while sales growth at all general merchandise stores was 6.4%. Since the beginning of the 1990s, however, department stores have been streamlining. Downsizing, product changes, and mergers with former competitors have created efficiencies that have encouraged more rapid growth of sales. Between 1990 and 1997, department store sales growth averaged 6.3%, compared to 6.1% for all general merchandise stores. In 1998, sales growth remained strong at 6.5%. Over the period 1999-2001, department store sales growth is forecast to moderate to an average rate of 4%, roughly in line with the expected increase for all general merchandise stores.

Variety stores sales have grown in fits and starts during the 1990s. Since the beginning of the decade, variety store sales have advanced at an average year-over-year rate of 5.1%, while sales in the overall general merchandise category grew by over 6.1% per annum. Although variety stores' market share rose from 2.7% in 1996 to 3.3% in 1998, they have not regained the strong presence they attained back in 1980, when their market share was 7.2%.

One of the major attractions of the variety store is a lower price. Since variety stores do not carry complete product lines, however, they are especially vulnerable to superstores, which carry every product in a category and have relatively low prices. Also, the proliferation of "dollar stores" is influencing the product mix within the category, and may be keeping total sales numbers down. Unlike department stores, which were hurt in the late 1980s and rebuilt themselves in the 1990s, variety stores are still struggling to survive. But, even if they have lost considerable ground in the last twenty years, their existence and sustainability in the changing U.S. economy has been surprisingly strong. Additionally,

faster growth could be within reach for the variety stores if this sector catches the merger fever that has swept across department stores over the past few years.

The final category under general merchandisers is Miscellaneous General Merchandise stores. Sales efforts at miscellaneous general merchandise stores continue to be a struggle. Sales growth averaged 12.9% from 1982 to 1993, but has slowed significantly to a 2.8% average growth rate since then. Miscellaneous general merchandise stores' market share grew from 11.5% in 1980 to 20.7% in 1993, but has since slipped to 17.8% in 1998. However, in 1998 sales grew 6.7%, the best showing since 1993. Over the next three years, the forecast calls for a slower pace of growth, namely about 5% in 1999 and 2.5% per annum from 2000-2001.

Supply Conditions

Like many industries, general merchandise stores experienced a rash of mergers and acquisitions in the late 1980s and early 1990s. At this point, most financially distressed stores have been acquired by more stable competitors. In addition, department stores, in particular, have undergone a major overhaul in the 1990s. Many chains have greatly downsized by cutting employees and closing unprofitable stores. The total number of competitors in the general merchandise industry has dropped over the past ten years, and the industry itself is much more sound as a result.

The merger and acquisition activity has no doubt helped to improve supplier efficiencies. However, store-brand identification has become blurred during some mergers. This has resulted in some strange selections at newly merged stores that are apparently being stocked with "least common denominator" merchandise, while they try to establish a new store-product identity. Store loyalties are being tested during this identity crisis, and some general merchandise stores, especially department stores, are losing out to specialty stores where the customer is sure of the type and quality of the merchandise that will be available.

Prices

Fierce competition has kept prices at general merchandise stores under pressure throughout most of the 1990s. This situation is unlikely to change much in the years ahead.

The recent wave of mergers and acquisitions at department stores has been driven by a pressing need to streamline operations, resulting in job cutbacks and administrative savings. Competition has also inspired increased investment within the industry, particularly by department stores. Renovations and improvements to existing stores and the building of new stores in more profitable locations have greatly increased the net value of the industry's property and equipment. In addition, there has been heavy investment in introducing new technology. Technology is used at the point of purchase to reduce shrinkage and for inventory control. It is also aimed at reducing total costs associated with fraud, theft, and supplier snafus. Although the new technology is expensive, it has helped department stores to improve their margins in the face of weak prices.

Similar strategies at variety stores and miscellaneous general merchandise stores are also allowing these businesses to reduce their costs and cope better with the competitive pricing environment.

Outlook

With the massive restructuring undertaken by department stores in the 1990s, the general merchandise store community has regained some of its health. Further gains in productivity through the implementation of technology should continue to increase profitability. In the short-to-medium term, sales and profits for all general merchandise stores are expected to advance at a more modest pace compared to the last few years. Variety stores have had two good years recently—possibly three if 1999 is included, but their historic growth volatility clouds future growth potential. Sales growth in both department and miscellaneous stores is expected to moderate.

Trends & Forecasts: General Merchandise Stores

	1991	1992	1993	1994	1995	1996	1997	1998	1999	2000	2001
Retail Sales (Bil $)	226.9	245.4	263.8	281.6	297.9	312.5	331.4	352.9	369.8	382.2	393.7
% Change	5.2	8.2	7.3	6.8	5.8	4.9	6.1	6.4	4.8	3.4	3.0
Price Index % Change	3.0	1.8	0.9	0.8	−0.6	−0.5	−0.3	−1.5	-0.5	0.7	0.7

Trends: General Merchandise Store Categories
Retail Sales (Bil $)

	1991	1992	1993	1994	1995	1996	1997	1998	1999	2000	2001
Department Stores	173.0	185.5	199.2	216.6	230.9	243.8	261.4	278.4	291.4	302.0	311.7
% Change	4.3	7.2	7.4	8.7	6.6	5.6	7.2	6.5	4.7	3.6	3.2
Variety Stores	8.3	9.5	9.8	9.5	9.8	10.6	11.6	11.8	12.8	12.9	13.1
% Change	−0.2	13.9	3.6	−3.0	3.5	7.7	9.0	2.3	8.1	1.2	1.4
Misc. General Mdse.	45.5	50.4	54.7	55.4	57.1	58.1	58.8	62.7	65.7	67.4	69.1
% Change	9.8	10.8	8.5	1.3	3.0	1.8	1.2	6.7	4.7	2.7	2.4

Department Stores

A department store is defined as a store that carries men's and women's apparel, along with either major house-hold appliances or home furnishings and various other lines. These lines are arranged in separate "departments" with the accounting on a departmentalized basis. The individual departments are collectively held under central-ized management. In 1998, department store sales accounted for 10.2% of total retail sales. This share has been steadily increasing during the 1990s, primarily because of the growth of deep discounters such as Wal-Mart.

Department stores tend to be a significant source of sales due to the large variety of offerings, which allows for more convenience when shopping for more than one item. The lure of the department store is the convenience of one-stop shopping. On the other hand, one of the biggest problems facing the department store industry is the lack of depth in individual product lines. For the most part, department stores offer generality, not specificity. A shopper wishing to purchase a particular product from a particular line may find that department stores offer a va-riety of lines with very few products under each. Sales growth will likely moderate over the next few years as the economy slows.

Demand Conditions

Department store sales increased by 6.5% in 1998, fol-lowing a 7.2% rise in 1997. Department stores' 1998 sales performance was above the 6.2% average for the decade thus far. Retail sales, in general, increased by just 5.0% in 1998. Department store sales have been consistently robust since the recession in the early 1990s, and have exceeded overall retail sales growth during that period.

Department Store Share (%) of Retail Sales Has Risen Since 1990

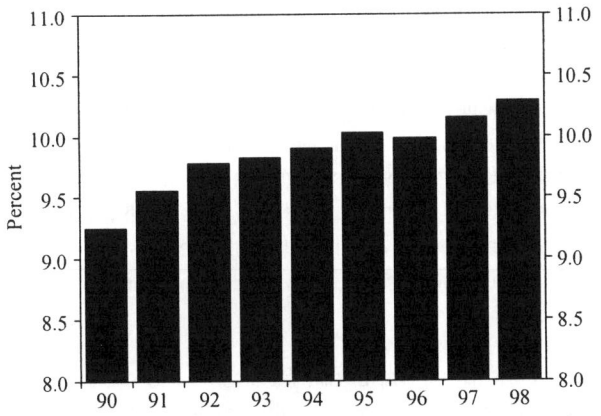

Department stores have greatly increased their market share over the past six years, after a disappointing per-formance in the second half of the eighties. In 1990, de-partment stores accounted for 9.3% of total retail sales.

Since then, restructuring within the industry has led to continued gains in market share. In 1998, department stores accounted for 10.2% of total sales. The rise of dis-count department stores played an important role in the direction of department store retailing. Discount depart-ment stores, such as Wal-Mart, have contributed to the overall growth of the industry by posting better-than-aver-age sales increases in every year of the 1990s.

Consumer spending at department stores is expected to remain healthy in the near future. The turnaround in sales brought on by various managerial changes has allowed the industry to become more competitive in the 1990s. Technology advances and continuing change will keep costs, and therefore prices, down, which should lead to strong sales in the future.

Industry Structure

One of the major reasons for stronger department store performance has been the consolidation in the industry. Many of the big names in the department store game not only downsized their operations in an effort to become more efficient and profitable, but also merged with other players in the industry. Federated Department Stores merged with rival giant R.H. Macy, at the time when Macy was under extreme financial distress. Many of the larger, more financially stable department stores have acquired or merged with less financially sound stores, improving poor profit margins and resurrecting the department store industry.

Department stores face stiff competition from various other forms of retail businesses. Entities such as QVC, the Home Shopping Network, mail order catalogs, and Internet retailing have an increasing ability to capture sales due to their unrestricted shopping hours and the convenience of shopping without leaving the house. Consumers no longer have to spend hours waiting in check-out lines, fighting traffic, finding parking, or jostling with the Saturday afternoon shopping crowd. Non-store retailers have greatly increased their sales revenues as shopper acceptance has increased.

Specialty stores are retail outfits that offer a collection of goods in a certain category line. One of the most popular and profitable areas is apparel. Stores such as The Gap and The Limited offer various lines of clothing, all with certain style and trend appeals that attract consumers who are conscious of fashion. Unlike in a department store, the lines of apparel at a specialty store are deep and well priced. Specialty stores helped boost apparel sales in 1992 and 1993, but have come under a lot of pressure recently from both department stores and the wave of new superstores.

"Category killers" or "superstores" are the latest trend in retail, and are a serious threat to department store sales. Home Depot, a large warehouse-like retail entity, offers anything and everything for the home, usually at prices much lower than its counterpart departments in department stores. These are called category killers because they sell practically every product offered in a particular retail category. Because they deal exclusively with one category of goods in large volumes, superstores can often acquire their goods more cheaply, and therefore have the ability to offer them to the consumer at lower retail prices.

In addition to the overwhelming number of products offered and lower prices, superstores have other attractions for the consumer. Barnes & Noble, a giant book superstore, offers food, music, and coffee. The stores attract customers based not only on their product offerings, but also on the atmosphere of the store itself. The potential of superstores is evident by their rise from zero sales and no market share in 1986 to $550 million in sales and a 33.3% share of the nation's retail revenue in 1996.

Seasonal Trends

Until recently, department stores relied heavily on the Christmas season (November and December) for much of their sales revenues. March and August, representing the Easter/spring clothing and back-to-school seasons, accounted for another large portion of sales. The seasonal nature of department stores is, of course, fairly similar to that of retail sales in general. The majority of spending is done near holidays or the change of seasons, when apparel sales are particularly strong.

Department stores have made attempts, however, to spread sales out during the year, and have succeeded to a small degree. December sales accounted for 16% of total yearly department store sales in the 1980s, and averaged 11.8% in 1998. Stores have begun introducing new items in January in an attempt to bring in more off-season business. In addition, department stores have spaced marketing efforts more evenly through the year.

Prices

Department stores have used pricing as a means to compete with the growing number of discount and specialty retail stores. In particular, in an effort to combat the low prices offered by superstores, department store prices have been increasing very slowly. During the 1990s thus far, department store prices remained relatively flat on an average per-annum basis. This compares to a level of price inflation for the retailing sector of 1.5% for the same period. Competitive pricing among traditional department stores and pressure from the share of discounting department stores have held the department store price index in check.

The competitive nature of the retail world suggests that price increases, if any, will be modest. The introduction of low-cost superstores necessitates the continued practice of discounting. Technological advances will help department stores lower overhead, with new processes that continue to lower costs and make industry employees more productive.

One of the most important factors in the resurgence of department stores has been the implementation of technology. Many stores intend to or already have implemented various technological strategies to help control costs and become more efficient. Electronic price-scanning equipment, point-of-sale computers, and automated inventory-control tracking systems are some of the ways department stores have become more efficient. Sales tracking allows management to discover which stores sell what products best, and allows them to revamp inventory and floor-space strategies to take advantage of the information. Inventory tracking keeps products properly stocked without expensive bookkeeping (which requires costly man-hours), and eliminates the need for unnecessary warehousing costs.

Productivity growth contributed greatly to the department store industry's turnaround in profit margins. This improvement is continuing, aided by ongoing investment in technology. The investment cost for technology can be large, but it cuts down on many costs in the long run, and makes employees much more efficient.

Outlook

Thanks to the reorganizations of the early 1990s and the growth in successful discount department stores, the department store industry has made a healthy contribution to the retail environment. The introduction of technology into management, sales, and administration will continue to make department stores more productive and more profitable in the future. However, department stores must constantly fight competitive threats from other retailers, especially superstores. Management must also take more steps toward matching offerings to consumer preferences, and making the shopping experience one that cannot easily be matched by another retail entity.

Trends & Forecasts: Department Stores

	1991	1992	1993	1994	1995	1996	1997	1998	1999	2000	2001
Retail Sales (Bil $)	173.0	185.5	199.2	216.6	230.9	243.8	261.4	278.4	291.4	302.0	311.7
% Change	4.3	7.2	7.4	8.7	6.6	5.6	7.2	6.2	4.7	3.6	3.2
Price Index % Change	3.0	1.8	0.9	0.7	−0.9	-0.6	−0.2	−1.6	−0.7	0.8	0.8

Food Stores

Industry segments classified as food stores include: grocery stores, meat and fish markets, fruit and vegetable markets, candy, nut, and confectionery stores, dairy products stores, retail bakeries, and miscellaneous food stores. Grocery stores account for about 95% of industry sales and nearly 90% of employment. Large chain-store companies operating supermarkets dominate the grocery store category.

Retail establishments categorized as food stores are primarily engaged in the distribution and sale of dry grocery items, canned goods, and perishable food items to the general public. Most food products are purchased for home preparation and consumption. Many establishments, especially chain supermarkets, also sell prepared meals, prescription drugs, tobacco products, small household appliances and housewares, health- and beauty-care products, pet-care products, and seasonal merchandise.

In 1998, retail sales at food stores were over $440 billion, a gain of 3% over 1997 levels. Sales (which include food and nonfood items) are expected to increase by 4% in 1999.

WEFA forecasts that retail food store prices will increase by an average of 2% per year over the period 1999–2001. The implication of this price gain, combined with average sales growth of about 3% per year over the same period, is that real sales volume is forecast to grow by only about 1% per year.

Trends in Consumption

Over the period 1990 through 1998, retail food sales grew at an annual average growth rate of 1.9%. Since 1998, that growth rate has exploded to 3.6% (through May 1999). As the U.S. economy continues at its robust pace, consumers have enjoyed substantial increases in personal income driving consumption expenditure categories higher. Food purchased for off-premises consumption has clearly participated in this recent growth spurt, although growth has been half that of consumer spending on purchased meals at restaurants.

Although population changes affect the sheer size of the market and the location of firms, income growth, lifestyle changes, and consumer tastes are the major determinants of the composition of purchased food and food-service demand. The dual-wage earning family is a mainstay of the social structure, and the opportunity cost of time looms large in consumer choice of foods and food services. Consequently, there is a continuing trend towards value-added pre-packaged ready-to-cook foods, pre-cooked food items, and bundled pre-cooked meals. Time saving has been an important reason behind the increased consumer demand for more goods and services, beyond the usual array of food and drug products, under one roof. There has also been proliferation of

information about food quality, health and wellness. Increased consumer information along with higher per-capita income growth has led to an expansion in market segments demanding fresh foods and produce, organically grown foods, and higher overall food quality. Indeed consumers have demonstrated a willingness to pay a premium for higher quality products, packaging, and additional services.

For the period 1999–2001, WEFA expects retail sales at food stores to increase at an average rate of 3% per year.

Short–Run Trends: Food Stores
Average Annual Percent Changes

	1990–1998	1999–2001
Retail Sales (%)	1.9	3.0
Price Index (%)	1.9	2.0

Industry Trends

As consumer demand has turned towards one-stop convenience, fresher and value-added pre-prepared foods and premium services, retail grocery stores have responded in kind with greater scale and scope. Increased physical store sizes have accommodated expanded individual food sections and, at the same time, permitted a wider diversity of products and services.

Grocery store size is increasing to accommodate changing consumer tastes. Produce departments have been the primary beneficiaries of expanded space. A greater allocation of square footage has allowed a greater diversity of fresh produce, including imported fruits and vegetables and more innovative marketing and packaging of items. Increased space has also allowed for the expansion of existing deli and meat departments in providing pre-packaged, ready-to-cook meats and an entire range of pre-cooked items and meal bundles. The former product extension has focused on the high-quality premium segment. The latter product extension has permitted retail grocery stores to enter the more traditional fast-food market, competing with branded take-out chains such as Boston Market, KFC, etc.

Increased store size has also permitted a greater array of non-traditional products and services that target convenience–minded customers. One of the major innovations in many newly constructed supermarkets is an in–store bank. While the bank's business is of course not included in the calculation of food store retail sales, this new kind of branch bank has created an added sense of convenience at the supermarket. Also, large supermarkets have set up in–store service counters (delis, snack shops, bakeries, flower shops, etc.) with separate checkout stations to speed up purchases of prepared take-out foods and other value-added products and services. Indeed, like branch banks, often these kiosks are subcontracted arrangements with branded vendors.

In addition to changes in store format, technology initiatives in inventory management and new merchandising techniques have been aggressively deployed to reduce costs and raise productivity. Better management of the supply chain continues to be the focus of most store operators. With an eye toward generating improved financial results, firms have been investing in more efficient systems to improve accounting and better coordinate supplier deliveries. Finally, though still a short way away, on-line shopping/home delivery services will be a new wave towards appealing to time-efficient consumers and garnering store loyalty.

Price Trends

Over the last several years, retail food prices have increased close to 2% on average. This is slower than the 5-to-6% increase experienced during the 1989-1990 period. At the same time, wholesale prices for food and kindred products have declined. To some extent this was part of a global trend in commodity and agricultural prices that have been endemic to the industry since 1997. Nevertheless, the price movements indicate that despite declining food costs in the agricultural industry, there are sufficient margins in the marketing and retailing side of the industry to support new services and profitability.

The central pricing issue facing the industry is the movement toward an everyday low pricing strategy at several large retailers. Consumers continue to demand value from retail operators and appear increasingly unsatisfied with the advertised (and unadvertised) sales promotions typical of traditional food retailing. Competition from discounters and warehouse clubs, which emphasizes low prices, has put pressure on food stores to adopt some form of low-price strategy. Stores' private-label brands can play an important role in a supermarket's low-price strategy. "House-brand" products sell for less than the national brands, providing shoppers with a low–price alternative. Stores continue to increase the shelf space devoted to private-label products, since they tend to carry fatter margins for retailers thanks to favorable supplier pricing.

Food stores have also instituted programs designed to generate customer loyalty and thwart wholesale clubs' attempts to increase their share of food sales. Many food stores now issue "clip-less" coupons or "frequent-buyer" cards, which customers present at the check–out counter to receive special pricing on featured promotional items. These frequent shopper cards are used to collect marketing information about consumers. If harnessed by food stores, in addition to creating customer loyalty, the customer profiles could also be used for targeting marketing campaigns designed to maximize the satisfaction of their loyal customer base through personalized sales specials.

Finally, the increasing emphasis on higher value-added products and services, particularly pre-packaged and pre-cooked items, has served to enhance profitability since these products typically carry a premium price relative to cost.

WEFA expects retail food store prices to increase an average of 2% per year over the period 1999–2001. The implication of this price gain, combined with sales growth of 3% over the same period, is that real sales volume is forecast to increase by just 1%.

Industry Structure

The retail-food industry is composed of food stores, independent grocery stores, and grocery chains. Firm size increases in quite the same order, with food stores characterized as the smallest entities in terms of share of industry sales and asset values. Independent grocery stores, grocery firms having no more than a dozen stores, tend to have a greater market presence within a more local geographic market. Grocery chains are the largest organizations in the industry by sales and assets. Most chains are corporate entities that hold more than one retail property and tend to span several regional markets. Top retailers include Kroger, American Stores, Safeway, Giant Food, and Winn–Dixie.

For several decades, the industry has shifted towards larger chains, away from smaller grocery outlets, as scale and scope have become important sources of economic profitability. The merger and acquisition wave of the 1980s continues today as firms continue to seek strategic advantage by expanding their presence geographically. Moreover, with the de novo entry by large membership club stores (such as Sam's), scale and scope has become paramount to maintaining industry position. The proliferation of warehouse clubs has proven problematic for the chain-grocery stores over the past ten years. Membership clubs have used a combination of low prices, a diversity of products in large-quantity sizes, and a "no-frills" atmosphere to appeal to many value-conscious shoppers. Fortunately for the big chain supermarkets, overbuilding and consolidation in the buyers club industry has slowed new warehouse club construction. At the same time, grocery chains have become much more innovative in garnering customer loyalty by issuing store cards as

well. These enable customers to realize discounts not available to non-cardholders.

The appearance of super-center stores that sell general merchandise and food has created a new entrant into the grocery business. These new food/drug/consumer product combination stores average more than 150,000 square feet (more than four times the size of the typical supermarket) and offer a wide variety of food and other merchandise. These retailers—like Walmart and Target—provide a diverse mix of products in a one-stop shopping experience. Despite the sheer size of the corporate entities, the relevant product market is still food, and therefore the grocery component of the super-center competes in the local market with more specialized grocery stores. It is not clear that corporate size will extend advantages to local grocery outlets. Nor is it clear that the ability to buy other retail goods in the same location will enhance the repeat-buying nature of grocery shopping.

Interestingly, while merger and acquisition activity has led to a decline in the number of firms in the industry, and market share has shifted to larger chains, industry concentration has not increased. Indeed the industry remains quite price competitive, indicating that smaller chains have garnered cost-efficiencies to remain profitable. Concentration in the local geographic market has shown the converse, with concentration increasing in most geographic markets. Margins on most grocery remains slim, but increased scope allows greater diversity in products, particularly higher-value products.

Food retailing will continue to be quite competitive but the outlook for the industry appears bright. New merchandising strategies and successful efforts to reduce costs should enhance profitability and offset the effects of only modest increases in core food purchases in the years ahead. Expect further consolidation in the industry as chains look for scale and scope. Smaller grocery chains will continue to focus on local market advantages including different store formats for different local markets, wider product choices, and more store services.

Trends & Forecasts: Food Stores

	1991	1992	1993	1994	1995	1996	1997	1998	1999	2000	2001
Retail Sales (Bil $)	374.9	376.1	384.3	397.2	407.9	420.4	429.9	443.0	460.8	474.5	488.7
% Change	1.7	0.3	2.2	3.4	2.7	3.1	2.3	3.0	4.0	3.0	3.0
Price Index % Change	4.2	1.6	1.5	1.8	2.0	2.8	2.0	1.3	2.2	2.0	1.7

Trends: Food Store Categories
Retail Sales (Bil $)

	1989	1990	1991	1992	1993	1994	1995	1996	1997	1998	1999
Grocery	307.2	328.1	348.2	354.3	358.1	365.7	378.6	389.1	401.8	410.2	421.7
% Change	6.8	6.8	6.1	1.8	1.1	2.1	3.5	2.8	3.3	2.1	2.8
Meat & Fish	6.4	6.1	5.8	6.0	6.0	6.1	6.0	6.0	6.1	–	–
% Change	2.4	−4.7	−4.9	3.5	0.0	1.7	−1.6	0.0	1.7	–	–
Fruits & Vegetables	2.3	2.7	2.7	2.1	2.2	2.2	2.1	2.3	2.4	–	–
% Change	23.6	17.4	0.0	−22.2	4.8	0.0	−4.6	9.5	4.4	–	–
Candy & Nuts	1.2	1.3	1.3	1.4	1.4	1.6	1.6	1.7	1.6	–	–
% Change	−12.1	8.3	0.0	7.7	0.0	14.3	0.0	6.3	−5.9	–	–
Retail Bakeries	4.8	5.2	5.5	5.7	5.7	6.1	6.5	6.7	9.2	–	–
% Change	−4.1	8.3	5.8	3.6	0.0	7.0	6.6	3.1	37.3	–	–
Other (1)	4.2	4.9	4.9	3.8	4.3	4.7	5.2	5.9	—	–	–
% Change	11.4	16.7	0.0	−22.5	13.2	9.3	10.6	13.5	—	–	–

Notes: (1) Includes dairy product stores, retail poultry stores, and miscellaneous establishments

Gasoline Service Stations

Gasoline service stations are retailers whose revenue comes primarily from the sale of gasoline. Many gasoline stations sell convenience-store (c-store) goods as well. In 1998, BP Amoco had the largest number of branded retail gasoline outlets at 15,500. Citgo, Motiva Enterprises, Equilon Enterprises, Exxon, Chevron, and Mobil were other big players. Motiva was formed last year by the joint venture of Shell, Texaco, and Saudi Refining Company. Separately, Equilon is the joint venture of Shell and Texaco.

Gasoline prices have begun to resurge in 1999, but on the whole, gasoline service stations' profits are squeezed. Convenience stores and affiliations and mergers are methods employed by gasoline service stations to improve the bottom line.

Demand for Gasoline

Consumer demand has been the driving force behind the steady growth in demand for gasoline throughout the 1990s. Consumer expenditure on gasoline fell by close to 12% to $112.1 billion in 1998, after increasing for six, preceding years. A fall in price was the key: prices dropped last year on approximately the same scale as spending. Consumer expenditure on gasoline is shrinking as a percentage of disposable income, from 4.9% in 1980 to 1.9% in 1998. This trend is expected to continue. There are offsetting factors at play in gasoline demand growth. While rising population and increasing number of vehicles have tended to increase the consumption of gasoline, other factors, especially more fuel-efficient vehicles, have mitigated it.

Motor-gasoline prices were exceptionally weak last year. A flood of supply kept domestic prices low. The mild winter in 1998/1999 also pressured prices downward. Strong demand in the peak driving season of spring and summer 1999 and crude oil production cuts have reversed these trends, shifting inventories down and pushing up prices. Gasoline stocks fell to a ten-month low in August 1999. According to the U.S. Department of Energy, the average U.S. city retail price for motor gasoline, including taxes in the second quarter of 1999, has sparked up 8% from its level a year earlier. Demand for transportation services will expand during the decade on both an aggregate and per-capita basis, and both consumer and business demand will grow.

The total vehicle miles traveled increased from 1,521 billion miles in 1980 to 2,619 billion miles in 1998, a 72%

increase. To a large extent, this was the result of a sharp increase in the number of vehicles registered over the past two decades. Automobile and light-truck sales have also boomed recently, with over 12% growth registered in the last five years. The number of registered vehicles increased from 140 million in 1980 to 205 million in 1998, a 46% increase.

Several factors contributed to such a dramatic rise in vehicle ownership. First was the growing size of the adult population. Second, the proportion of families owning more than one vehicle was 52.7% in 1980, 57.9% in 1990, and is still on the rise. 1999 is no exception. WEFA expects exceptionally strong, light-vehicle sales in the United States, increasing by a healthy 7.4%.

Consumption Expenditure on Gasoline and Oil

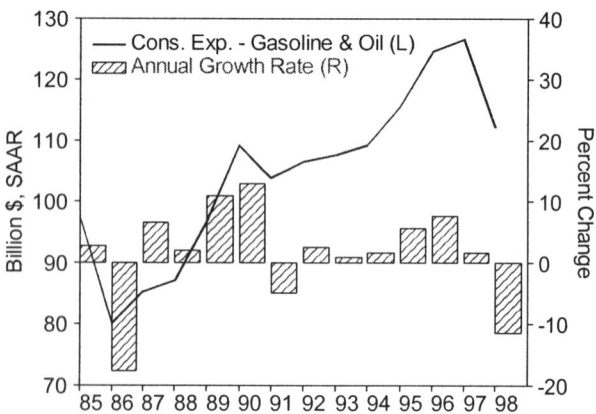

Also contributing to the rising vehicle mileage were demographic and geographic shifts. More people live in the sprawling suburbs today than in the previous decade, and tend to favor personal means of transportation to public transit. The impact of rising vehicle-miles traveled was mitigated somewhat by better-fuel efficiency of the vehicles produced. The fuel-economy standards for new automobiles is 27.5 miles per gallon (mpg), compared with 20.7 mpg for light trucks. The average fuel economy for 1998 model year cars was 28.7 mpg. 1998 light trucks averaged 20.9 miles per gallon. In both categories, imports were more fuel-efficient than domestically produced vehicles.

Consumer expenditure on gasoline and oil will gradually increase, averaging close to 3.2% per year. The bulk of this rise is estimated to come this year, with slower growth to follow in 2000 and 2001. A measure of additional consumer expenditure will come from the growing, less-fuel-efficient, light-truck sector. At 20.9 miles per gallon in 1998, light trucks' average-fuel economy is less than that of passenger cars almost two decades earlier. The share of light trucks in total-vehicle sales in the United States should reach 49% this year, compared with 22% in 1980 and 33% in 1990.

Industry Structure

Gasoline stations face a number of challenges. First, the industry is intensely competitive and still relatively fragmented despite a rash of merger activity among oil companies. The global-gasoline industry is becoming more concentrated: some of the largest mergers have occurred in this global industry. The joint company, British Petroleum (BP) and Amoco, has created the number-one branded gasoline retailer. When it was formed in 1998, the combination was the largest industrial merger to date. Two large industry players were created by joint ventures of Shell and Texaco, one of which also included Saudi Refining Company. A large, U.S. behemoth will be created by the proposed merger of Exxon and Mobil in 1999. BP Amoco and Atlantic Ritchfield Company (ARCO) also proposed a combination. Some companies have developed particular dominant positions by geographic region. This is often a key hurdle for approval of mergers by anti-trust regulators.

Fortunately for consumers, there is intense competition at the retail level among the major brands and between them and independent marketers— outlets affiliated with major suppliers but not owned by them. Independent-station owners must buy gasoline at the best possible price in a local or perhaps regional market; and then they must sell that product to car drivers at a profit, while competing with gasoline stations as close as next door. Since gasoline is a commodity, retailers cannot differentiate their product to boost sales, so they have to compete with lower prices and increased services, a combination that hurts profitability.

U.S. gasoline stations are among the most productive in the world. Retailers in the United States typically employ fewer people and sell a greater number of gallons of gasoline, compared to retailers in Japan, for example. However, prices are much lower in the United States than in Japan, and profit margins from gasoline retailing are tiny.

Components of the Price of a Gallon of Gasoline

Crude Oil	34.0%
Operation Costs	30.7%
Taxes	35.2%
Profit	0.1%

Source: Petroleum Marketers Association of America

Since gasoline stations are marginally profitable, two distinct trends are occurring to increase their profitability. First, gasoline stations have started to diversify into other types of businesses like convenience stores (c-stores) and fast-food restaurants. Second, many major brands have chosen to merge or form alliances at the retail level to reduce costs by eliminating redundant administrative expenses and pooling prime-real-estate assets.

Convenient stores have become an integral part of many gasoline service stations, generating between one-quarter and one-third of total revenue on average. Tobacco and soft-drink sales are particularly good for the bottom line. Another trend negates the advantages of the c-store approach, however—the proliferation of self-service pumps at gasoline stations. In fact, the bulk of gasoline stations now have self-service pumps. Although self-serving drivers may not generate large margins, they help to turn inventory faster. As a result, the combination of self-service pumps with a c-store is more profitable than the traditional full-service format.

Many gasoline retailers are also embracing cobranding, which pairs a branded-food emporium with the gasoline service station. This cobranding technique, like the c-store, tries to exploit the synergy that exists between fast food and gasoline retail. Car washes, quick lubes, and other services are seen as emerging profit centers, as well. Other nontraditional add-ons are planned for gasoline service stations of the future. Anything from e-mail access to ordering fast food and groceries at the pump is being tested in pilot programs. Currently, Mobil has a mechanism to remotely pay for gasoline through their Speedpass service.

Consolidation in gasoline retail has gained pace recently. Intense competition and stringent environmental regulations have eroded gasoline stations' profits and forced many independent-gasoline marketers to go out of business and many branded retailers to consolidate. Fortunately for the industry, government regulators have become more lenient toward vertical integration. Consequently, a record number of mega-mergers and alliances has been announced.

Environmental Issues

Gasoline usage has important environmental implications, and thus, its sale is heavily regulated. Environmental regulations affect every aspect of gasoline retailing including production, transportation, storage, and distribution, and these regulations are becoming more stringent and costly.

The most important environmental regulation affecting gasoline service stations is the 1984 law requiring the Environmental Protection Agency (EPA) to monitor underground-storage tanks (UST). USTs create health hazards because they can corrode, allowing gasoline to leak and contaminate soil and underground water. In 1988, EPA issued regulations setting minimum standards for new tanks and requiring owners of existing tanks to upgrade, replace, or close them by December 22, 1998.

Meeting the UST requirements is very costly for gasoline stations, at $125,000 to $150,000 per tank for clean-up. Where there is ground-water contamination, the cost can escalate to $1 million. The upgrade cost may be partly financed by the government through the Leaking UST Fund (LUST). Although now past the 1998 deadline, some tanks do not meet the guidelines. The EPA's Office of Underground Storage Tanks reports that progress on non-compliant tanks being upgraded, replaced, or closed is moving forward.

Apparel Stores

Apparel stores are specialty stores that sell men's, women's, children's and families' clothing, as well as all types of shoes. Apparel stores are generally located in malls and strip–centers. The top apparel chains in the United States include: The Limited, TJ Maxx, The Gap, Melville Apparel, Burlington Coat, Ross Stores, American Retail Group, Eddie Bauer, and Petrie Stores. Woolworth closed its U.S. general-merchandise operations in 1997. Sales at these stores represent approximately one-quarter of total industry sales.

In 1998, retail sales at apparel stores totaled $124.1 billion, a gain of 5.2% over 1997 levels. Sales gains will likely moderate in the short run. Demand for apparel will be supported by solid income growth, high levels of consumer confidence, and relatively stable prices, but slower employment growth will impede consumers' ability to increase spending at rates experienced in 1998. Over the longer run, demographics and consumer buying habits will determine the demand for apparel. The aging population and its relatively more frugal buying habits mean that growth in spending will be restrained in the years ahead.

Demand Conditions

Apparel store revenues totaled $124.1 billion in 1998, an increase of 5.2% compared to 1997. 1998 revenue growth was the second strongest of the 1990s and significantly exceeded the average growth of 3.4% experienced during the decade to date. High levels of consumer confidence, robust income growth, and solid employment gains drove the exceptional growth of revenue.

While revenue growth surged, employment in the retail apparel industry fell by 0.6% in 1998. The main reason for the decline in jobs is the changing nature of the apparel business. Increased competition has forced apparel stores to cut costs and increase productivity. That has meant streamlining the apparel workforce, either through layoffs or by complete closure of apparel businesses.

The retailing of apparel goods can be broken into several categories—men's and boys', women's, children's, family, footwear, and miscellaneous. Retail sales at women's clothing and accessory stores make up 26% of total apparel sales. Men's and boys' clothing stores account for 9% of retail sales in the apparel market.

Fashion products, which take 35% of the market, have an average of 10 weeks of product life. Seasonal products, with a 20-week product life, make up 45% of the market. Basic products sold throughout the year constitute about 20% of the market.

1998 Retail Sales: Apparel Market Share

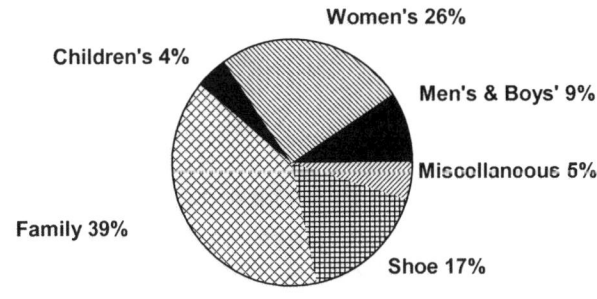

Although spending at apparel stores has increased every year during the 1990s, it has been declining as a fraction of disposable income. In 1998, apparel store spending accounted for 2.1% of disposable personal income, down from 2.3% in 1990. In fact, the share of non-durable spending in overall consumption has shown a downward trend, although spending on apparel has declined at a slower rate than spending on total non-durable goods. The discrepancy between rising consumer spending for apparel and apparel's falling share of disposable income is the result of two counteracting forces. Growing population and rising income have pushed up spending, but changing consumption patterns due to demographic shifts and consumer preferences have dampened it. Recent evidence shows that the latter has had a greater impact.

Apparel spending as a percentage of disposable income has fallen because of changing consumer habits. During the recession of 1991, apparel stores sharply marked down prices to get rid of excess inventories. Consumers took this as a permanent decrease in price and continued to expect low prices. Since apparel stores were facing intense competition from discount stores, they could not raise prices even after the recovery was well underway.

In the short run, demand for apparel will be helped by income growth and consumers' confidence in the economy. The recovery that began in the early 1990s continues and consumer confidence is strong. These positive factors may be tempered by rising levels of consumer debt. Although interest rates are not expected to increase much over the next year or two, slower employment growth may hinder consumers' ability to pay for new goods. As a result, apparel sales will likely grow by around 3% in 1999, but by about 2.5% in 2000. Over the long run, demographics and consumer buying habits will determine the demand for apparel. The aging population and its relatively more frugal apparel-buying habits signal subdued apparel-spending growth.

Supply Conditions

Specialty apparel stores are facing twin challenges. Personal consumer expenditures on apparel are not increasing as quickly as in the 1980s—the increase in size of the apparel "pie" has slowed. Increased competition from discount stores, sidewalk stalls, mail order, and now Internet sales have, in addition, limited the apparel stores' share of apparel retail sales—apparel stores' piece of the "pie" is growing slower than the overall apparel "pie." The market share held by specialty apparel stores has been declining over the past few years, falling from 21% in 1992 to less than 15% in 1998. Most of the share was lost to discount stores.

Intense competition has forced apparel stores to consolidate. Smaller and less financially sound apparel stores have either gone bankrupt or merged with larger and more financially secure chain stores. Publicly traded specialty-apparel retailers continue to grow faster in total sales than the industry as a whole, indicating a significant decline among independents and other privately held apparel retailers.

While consolidation has weeded out weaker stores, it has not led to a significant rise in the market share for stronger ones. This is because apparel retailing is notoriously segregated geographically, with one or two chains dominating each region. Entrants face not only dominant retailers, but also an overcrowded marketplace. Although entry is not difficult, many firms go out of business before they are established.

One of the major challenges faced by apparel retailers is the growing trend to "casual Fridays". Employers are now letting employees dress how they wish on Fridays and in some companies workers can dress how they please on any day, as long as they are not meeting clients. Casual Fridays mean that demand for suits, ties, and dresses is on the decline and retailers that sell this type of product will have to alter their product line to stay profitable.

Consumers have continued to be extremely price-conscious about purchases, despite the recent healthy income growth. Discount stores have recognized this trend and have successfully exploited it by making bargain hunting more popular. In the process, they have lured price-conscious consumers away from specialty-apparel stores. Sales at upscale-apparel stores, like Saks Fifth Avenue and Nieman Marcus, however, have not been affected by all of this bargain hunting. They have retained the loyalty of high-income customers, who tend to be more brand oriented than price oriented.

Middle-market apparel stores have begun to confront those challenges by targeting either bargain hunters or the brand hunters. For instance, Gap Inc. has remodeled its Banana Republic stores to make them more upscale and has increased the size of the chain by almost 50% in the past five years. At the same time, in order to compete with discount stores, it has promoted a low-end chain, the Old Navy outlets. Old Navy has been among the most productive apparel stores the last few years.

In the short run, specialty-apparel stores will follow a twin strategy. First, increase market share through mergers and acquisitions, exploiting the economies of scale. Second, arrest their declining market share in apparel at all levels of quality. Gap has provided a successful model for confronting both the discount stores and the high-end retailers. More specialty stores are expected to follow Gap's lead.

Prices

Apparel prices at the retail level fell 1.6% in 1998 after a 0.3% rise in 1997. Prices of apparel have declined four out of the last five years. Throughout the 1990s, apparel prices have increased at an average annual rate of 0.6%, 0.9% less than the 1.5% average annual increase in all retail goods prices.

Price Changes for Apparel

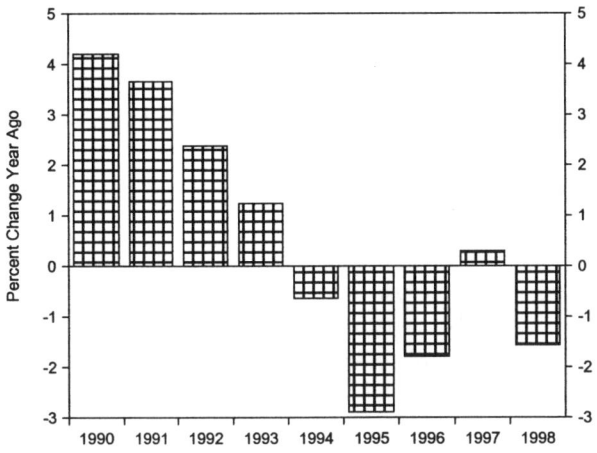

There are three reasons why apparel prices have increased less rapidly than overall retail prices. **First**, the prevalence of efficient inventory management has reduced the inventory costs. Equipped with Electronic Data Interchange (EDI), today's stores can communicate with manufacturers instantly and manage inventories more efficiently. Inventories are often purchased with credit, incurring costs to stores that rise with higher interest rates. Keeping inventories lean is best for profits, and stores have made progress toward that goal.

Second, apparel imports are taking over the market. Almost half of the apparel bought in the United States is foreign-made, with China and Mexico the largest suppliers. Low labor costs and virtually no import duties have reduced the purchase price of apparel. So has a rising American dollar. Growing competition among foreign manufacturers has aided in keeping apparel prices in check. The Asian financial crisis has also helped reduce the prices of imported apparel, as those economies look to exports for their recovery.

Third, consolidation in the industry has created giant retailers who exercise great buying power with manufacturers, keeping down purchase prices. The low purchase prices have been passed along to consumers, since intense retail competition has made any significant price increase risky for retailers.

Apparel prices will likely decline further in 1999 because the strong value of the dollar will reduce import costs but could pick up modestly in the next two years if the dollar weakens.

Trends & Forecasts: Apparel Stores

	1991	1992	1993	1994	1995	1996	1997	1998	1999	2000	2001
Retail Sales (Bil $)	97.6	103.5	107.1	109.5	110.9	114.6	118.0	124.1	128.2	131.3	135.0
% Change	1.8	6.1	3.5	2.2	1.3	3.3	3.0	5.2	3.3	2.4	2.8
Price Index % Change	3.7	2.4	1.2	−0.6	−2.9	−1.8	0.3	−1.6	−1.5	0.7	0.8

Furniture Stores

Furniture stores are defined as establishments primarily engaged in the retail sale of household furniture. These stores may also sell home furnishings, major appliances, and floor coverings. Furniture includes beds and springs, cabinetwork, kitchen cabinets, outdoor furniture, and waterbeds, in addition to more standard living room and dining room furniture. In 1998, furniture stores accounted for 2.6% of total retail sales and this percent has been fairly constant during the 1990s.

Consumer spending on furniture will remain strong over the next few years because of favorable interest rates and a recent spurt in housing. But when housing construction weakens, competition for retail furniture dollars will become more severe. The intensified competition will lead retailers to seek new efficiencies; therefore, cost cutting and consolidation should continue and price increases will be weak.

Demand Conditions

Furniture retailing is a cyclical, competitive industry, in which tight margins and a desire for increased efficiencies have led to a surge of consolidation. Furniture stores also face competition from a broad scope of other retail establishments, including department stores, warehouse stores, and discount clubs.

The industry appears likely to experience solid growth over the next few years with gains of 6.1% likely for 1999 and 2000. Growth in retail sales at furniture stores tends to mirror growth in the residential real estate market. Housing start activity in 1998 was brisk, and 1999 is likely to be another banner year, aided by high consumer confidence, strong income growth, and low-mortgage rates. Retail sales growth at household-furnishing establishments is expected to moderate after 2000, as new-housing construction weakens.

Not so long ago, the retail furniture industry was dominated by small local retailers and crafts people. In the first half of the 1990s, on the other hand, more than one-third of the industry's sales were recorded by the top-100 furniture stores. Furniture consumers today are increasingly savvy when it comes to finding the best value—tracking down the best prices from across the country and having their dream furniture shipped, all for less than what they would pay around the corner. In addition, the entry of large-chain discount-furniture stores into the market continues to attack the market share of smaller local retailers. Large retailers use their size advantage to put pressure on suppliers to keep prices low. After shrinking during the first three years of the 1990s,

employment at furniture stores started on the long road to recovery. Job rolls increased 2.6% in 1998. However, current trends in the industry suggest a turning point in the expansion of retail furniture jobs, as consolidation leads to fewer employers.

Pricing

Furniture retailers have jumped on the "every day low pricing"' (EDLP) bandwagon in recent years. EDLP is designed to counter consumer perceptions of large fluctuations in furniture prices, and therefore lead to a steadier stream of customers. However, EDLP has led many retailers into extremely tight profitability positions, which can then lead to price wars for market share. In such a tight margin environment, firms must always keep sales volume up in order to survive.

Continued cost cutting by both producers and retailers has led to the application of just-in-time inventory management in home-furniture stores. This practice has been in place since the beginning of the 1990s, causing the sector's ratio of inventories to sales to fall by almost 10% from 1990 to 1995.

Debt is a double-edged sword for furniture retailers. On one side, lower profit margins have forced many retailers into compromising debt situations. On the other side, many retail furniture purchases are made with credit. The use of store-specific credit cards and in-house financing may prove to be the new frontier of furniture price competition. The ability of furniture retailers to succeed in the land of debt will depend in large part upon their ability to keep their own financial houses in order.

Outlook

Competition for retail furniture dollars promises to be fierce for the foreseeable future as the industry contin-

ues its recent consolidation. Consumer spending on furniture is likely to be robust in the short term as households who recently bought new homes in record numbers now want to furnish these houses. However, as the housing market loses steam, so will furniture sales. Because of consolidation, downward pressure on prices is likely to continue.

Trends & Forecasts: Furniture Stores

	1991	1992	1993	1994	1995	1996	1997	1998	1999	2000	2001
Retail Sales (Bil $)	49.5	52.3	54.7	59.0	60.8	63.9	67.5	71.4	75.8	80.4	84.2
(% Change)	−2.1	5.8	4.6	7.8	3.0	5.1	5.7	5.7	6.1	6.1	4.8
Price (% Change)	0.8	3.4	2.4	3.8	1.1	1.4	−0.1	−0.2	0.8	1.3	1.4

Household Appliance Retailers

Home-appliance retailers sell major appliances (stoves, refrigerators, and laundry equipment), as well as smaller appliances such as electric irons, coffee machines, and sewing machines. These stores often sell related items, such as radios, televisions, and home computers. In 1998, appliance stores accounted for 2.5% of total retail sales and this share has been increasing during the 1990s.

Home-appliance stores have been under competitive pressure from other retailers and will remain under strain over the next few years. Competition from department stores, catalog operations, and general merchandise stores will keep margins low and prices down. In addition, sales growth will be moderate as the economy slows. As a result, the sector will likely see continued consolidation, including even takeovers by chains outside the sector.

Demand Conditions

Retail sales of large durable goods, such as refrigerators, ranges, washers, and dryers, are driven by general macroeconomic conditions such as interest rates, income growth, and employment growth. Trends in retail sales of household appliances are also correlated to shifts in the residential-housing market.

Retail sales in household-appliance stores were up 11.0% in 1998, but are expected to advance 5.6% in 1999, 4.4% in 2000, and 4.0% in 2001. This moderation of growth during 1999 and the forecast period reflects conditions in the housing market. Residential starts surged in 1998, but are expected to rise only slightly in 1999 before falling in 2000 and 2001. In addition, the pent-up demand for durable goods was very strong in 1998 and now that this pent-up demand has been satisfied, consumer spending on appliances will grow more in line with the economy.

Other economic factors also point to slower growth in the appliance sector. Interest rates have been creeping up and this increases financing costs for big-ticket items. In addition, employment and income growth is likely to weaken as the economic expansion enters a maturer phase. Since appliance demand is quite income sensitive, this will tend to moderate growth. Finally, consumer confidence, although remaining high, is unlikely to increase further.

Supply Conditions

Home-appliance stores operate in a competitive environment where most competition comes from outside the specialty. These stores accounted for less than half of all consumer purchases of household appliances in 1998. That may even be an overstatement of their influence in the household-appliance market, since they include sales of other items as well, such as computers, televisions, and radios.

Home-appliance stores held their own in the 1970s and early-1980s against the competition from department stores and others. In 1985, home-appliance stores accounted for 43% of total consumer purchases of home appliances. By the late 1980s, however, they started losing market share, and that trend has continued, albeit at a slow rate in recent years, through the present. The major competition comes from certain department stores (especially those with catalog operations), home centers, and a variety of other outlets, depending on the type of appliance. Small appliances are often sold at drug stores, while large appliances may be found at furniture stores, or bought through a contractor.

Appliance stores include both chain stores and independent stores. If catalog/department stores are included, it is evident that appliance sales are generally dominated by very large national chains. Sales within the narrow retail classification, however, are more evenly distributed, as chains that sell appliances only remain relatively small. The average household-appliance firm has 1.16 outlets, according to the *1992 Census of Retailing*; while the average retail firm has 1.21, the average building supply firm 1.22, and the average department store firm more than 24.

In spite of the loss of market share, appliance stores have been increasing their share of total retail sales primarily because sales of appliances have grown much faster than other retail sales in the 1990s.

Appliance Stores Sales as a % of Total Retail Sales

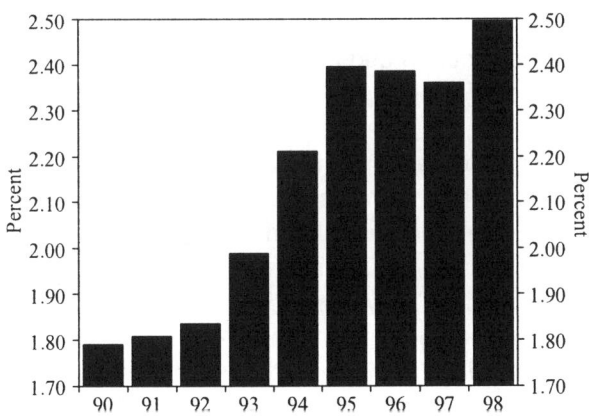

Price Trends

Home-appliance prices have risen more slowly than inflation over the past few years, and have even fallen in some years. The business is very competitive, and manufacturers are constantly adding features to items in what is a mature marketplace. Competition at the retail level has intensified as well, with the growth in the non-appliance share of sales.

Pricing strategies in household-appliance stores are progressively moving towards competition based more on financing and after-purchase service than on base prices.

Outlook

Home-appliance stores will remain under a constant competitive strain over the next few years. Although demand for household appliances will be fairly healthy over the next few years, home-appliance stores are especially vulnerable to sudden shifts in the economy, without the cushion that more diversified sellers enjoy.

Major investments such as durable goods purchases are usually put on hold in uncertain times, even if interest rates and unemployment are low. U.S. stock-market jitters could well result in consumers taking a pause to consider their current and future financial position before committing significant family resources to a new range. With few plans for new ranges, fewer trips to the home-appliance store will result. Foot traffic is not a common characteristic of the appliance-store category. Competition from department stores and general merchandise stores, both of which have the advantage of foot traffic, will keep margins low and prices down. As a result, the sector will likely see some consolidation, including even takeovers by chains outside the sector.

Trends & Forecasts: Household Appliance Stores

	1991	1992	1993	1994	1995	1996	1997	1998	1999	2000	2001
Retail Sales (Bill $)	33.6	35.8	41.4	49.7	56.6	59.8	61.7	68.5	72.3	75.5	78.5
(% Chi year ago)	1.6	6.7	15.6	20.2	13.7	5.7	3.3	11.0	5.6	4.4	4.0

Eating Places

Establishments classified specifically as eating places include full-service restaurants, limited-service restaurants (fast-food outlets), commercial cafeterias, social caterers, and ice-cream stands. Sales of prepared food at hotel restaurants, supermarket deli-counters, sports complexes, and certain types of institutions are excluded. Sales of food and beverages at drinking places (pubs, bars, and taverns) are also excluded. Retail sales in drinking establishments account for about 5% of the combined sales of eating and drinking places.

Sales are nearly evenly divided between full-service restaurants and fast-food outlets. Together these two segments comprise approximately 95% of sales at eating places.

In 1998, retail sales at eating and drinking places reached $247 billion, a 4.4% increase over 1997 levels. Sales growth is expected to average close to 4% over the next two years.

Demand Conditions

Aside from the sheer size of the U.S. population, which makes a very promising market for restaurant development generally, there are characteristics of the population that are important in assessing trends in consumer consumption. A key attribute of the U.S. population is that it is quite mobile, both nationally and within regional borders. Job search and placement is at the heart of intercity relocation, and commercial and residential growth corresponds to the expansion of localities and metropolitan areas within broad regions of the United States. The geographic extension of the population in growing communities continues to fuel the growth of independent and franchise restaurateurs. Indeed, movements in new restaurant establishments mirror the general trend in new housing. An expanding travel and leisure market is fundamental to restaurant growth within key regions. An overriding factor that, after several decades, continues to drive restaurant expansion is job growth and particularly the growth in the dual- and multiple-earner family. The share of the population that is employed outside the home is at an all-time high, and still growing. The labor force participation rate for the United States, defined as the civilian labor force divided by the population between 18 and 65 years old, is 67% and has steadily risen in the past twenty years. It is primarily affected by the trend in women working outside the home, but is also increasingly subject to decisions at the retirement margin. Increased hours at work and fewer hours for meal preparation translate into a strong demand for prepared meals brought into the home or consumed outside of the home.

Demographic trends in the population are reflected in the tastes and choices of consumers. Consumer choices over type of food and eating environment are affected in turn. Market information suggests that as consumers age they tend to switch to table-service restaurants and away from fast-food outlets. Some evidence also indicates that the frequency of restaurant visits declines with age. Sixty percent of 18- to 24-year olds are restaurant patrons on a typical day, while only 30% of adults over 65 are daily patrons. As the population—and average household—has aged, there has been a shift towards prepared food items and whole family-style meals as well. This shift has been accompanied by a marked interest in health, wellness, and a shift in tastes away from foods that are high in fat content. Consumers have come to demand a wider variety of fast foods, as well as prepared foods that incorporate healthier attributes.

Finally, the robust U.S. economy has generated increasing income growth, as well as record employment growth. Higher personal disposable incomes have stimulated the demand for higher quality foods and greater ambiance in restaurant establishments. In the face of these dramatic demographic shifts over the next decade, the product and marketing strategies of the retail food and restaurant industries will be tested.

Supply Conditions

The growing demand for diversity in restaurant foods has been matched by the scope of retail establishments in the industry. A wide set of foods and environments are offered through independent full-service restaurants, fast-food chains and franchises, full-service chain restaurants, and a variety of other suppliers including grocery stores, delicatessens, and small caterers. Indeed the market has been quick to respond to the spectrum of consumer tastes across each product-type, quality-price segment. At the national level, large chains have been expanding their portfolio of restaurants along the whole quality spectrum, adding entities with a higher quality-price product to other lower-end products. In local markets, grocery stores, delicatessens, and small caterers have found it easy to enter into the prepared-food/meal segment, competing with larger chains such as KFC and Boston Market, for example. The rivalry has led to substantial price-cutting and unbundling of products on the part of the larger chains, with less than desirable effects on profitability.

Fast food and larger restaurant chains have adopted a variety of new technologies to improve product quality and delivery, and to reduce costs. The use of computer systems to link sales and inventories has become widespread in the chains and is a direct source of corporate-cost reduction. Large chain investments in new production equipment and processes are being put in place to improve product quality. More famous among these are innovations in oil for fried foods and equipment to replace warmers for cooked product.

One of the problems in the industry continues to be overbuilding. Operators and franchisees blame the over-capacity on the big fast-food chains. A battle for market share is shaping up, and a shakeout is likely. Currently, one in four retail outlets across the country is an eating or drinking place.

Price Trends

With the plethora of restaurants in local markets and the relatively easy entry into the industry, price competition is generally quite strong. Labor costs and wholesale food costs are primary inputs in restaurants' costs, which in turn affect margins. Consequently, both influence markups and menu prices. Wholesale food costs have been quite benign and the retail food industry has enjoyed substantially lower costs as a result. Wholesale prices have in fact been declining since mid-1997, as global effects have driven world food prices down, affecting not only import prices but domestic prices as well. There is no reason why food prices should be expected to rise sharply even as the world economy begins to recover, since food commodity supplies remain ample.

Eating and drinking establishments, as a whole, account for over one-third of payroll employment in the retail sector and have accounted for over half of the payroll growth over the decade. Labor costs are a principal component of cost in the industry and wage growth has been quite strong. The growth rate in average hourly wages in the industry peaked in mid-1998 at 5.9% annually. This was about two percentages above the national average. Strong demand has made for a very tight labor market generally, and in the service sector in particular. Nevertheless, wage pressure has subsided somewhat since July of 1998, with wage growth at just above 4% annually, which is still about a half-percentage point above trend, and measuring in at $6.57 per hour. The effect of federal minimum wage hikes on eating-places appears to be smaller than anticipated thus far, although another hike may be on the horizon.

Over the past few years, many eating establishments adjusted marketing strategies towards building volume through lower menu prices. This tactic was workable in the absence of food-cost pressures. Food-cost increases put pressure on restaurant margins and led to selected price increases. Large chains have responded with initiatives aimed at lowering development costs for new sites. If successful, these cost reductions would ease the burden on new franchisees entering an already crowded market and allow expansion into smaller markets. Another tactic the industry has used to hold down costs and expand menu selection is construction of dual-branded outlets. The aim is to attract a broader mix of diners without the cost of two free standing stores and a blurred menu identity.

The customer response to many of the large chains' everyday "value pricing" plans is somewhat mixed. Most programs have emphasized price cuts on selected items or meal bundles. While these programs may build volume, they represent a threat to profits. Still, firms may have no choice, since consumers have displayed limits on their willingness to pay, and price increases have cost business unless supported by more creative, aggressive marketing strategies.

Industry Structure

For the most part, eating places are small businesses, unaffiliated with national restaurant chains. The two major market groups, full-service (or table-service) restaurants and fast-food outlets, have very different degrees of specialty concentration.

Data taken from the 1992 Census of Retail Trade (the latest available) indicate that fast-food outlets are dominated by hamburger and pizza shops. These two categories accounted for nearly half of the outlets in the fast-food segment and almost 60% of sales. In contrast, the top two segments in the table-service category (Chinese and Italian restaurants) together accounted for only 19% of outlets and 14% of category sales.

In the restaurant industry, sales growth comes from construction of new outlets, acquisitions, and increases in existing sales. Given the overbuilding in many segments of the market, WEFA expects firms to emphasize programs that aim to bump up same-store sales. Promotional tie-ins with movie studios and toy manufacturers have enjoyed a fair degree of success in the past. Unfortunately, for every hit promotion there seems to be at least one that falls short of expectations.

Outlook

Trends: Eating Places
Average Annual (Year Over Year) % Growth

	1994–1998	1999–2001
Retail Sales (%)	3.3	4.0
Price Index (%)	2.3	2.1

Note: Price index and retail sales include drinking establishments.

The outlook for food-service providers and restaurant operators is a bit cloudy. A battle for market share looms, as overbuilding in certain segments will keep prices low and profit margins under pressure. Successful operators must be able to squeeze more costs out of their budgets and formulate a successful marketing strategy to differentiate them from the pack.

Trends & Forecasts: Eating Places

	1991	1992	1993	1994	1995	1996	1997	1998	1999	2000	2001
Retail Sales (Bil $)	1945	199.9	210.5	217.0	222.2	227.8	236.5	247.0	258.5	268.9	278.1
(% Change)	2.2	2.8	5.3	3.1	2.4	2.5	3.8	4.4	4.7	4.0	3.4
Price Index % Change	4.1	2.2	1.9	1.8	2.2	2.5	2.7	2.1	2.1	2.1	2.2

Note: Retail sales and price index includes drinking establishment

Drug Stores

Retail establishments classified as drug stores are primarily engaged in the distribution and sale of prescription and non-prescription (proprietary) medicines, health- and beauty-care products, and seasonal merchandise. Many establishments also sell snack foods, beverages, tobacco products, small household appliances, and housewares. Industry retail sales figures do not include the value of prescription drugs provided through in-hospital pharmacies or supermarket pharmacies.

In 1998, retail sales at drug and proprietary stores totaled $105.7 billion, a gain of 7.6% over 1997 levels. Revenue growth will remain solid but moderate over the next two years. Although an aging demographic profile will boost sales, growth of managed-care facilities will restrain overall revenue gains. Market consolidation and implementation of new technologies will continue.

Demand Conditions

Drug store revenues totaled $105.7 billion in 1998, an increase of 7.6% over 1997. 1998-revenue growth was weaker than the 8.9% gain registered in 1997 but exceeded the 5.9% average growth rate experienced during the 1990s. The growth in revenue was supported by robust income growth, solid employment gains, and demographic developments favorable to increased drug sales.

Consumer spending for items sold in drug stores is driven by outlays for prescription drugs, non-prescription medications, healthcare, and beauty products. The rate of spending growth for these items has generally surpassed average nominal-income growth over the past ten years.

Demand for prescription drugs, a key-expenditure category, is driven primarily by physicians, and therefore indirectly by the health and demographic profile of retail consumers. Direct-to-consumer pharmaceutical advertising, recently allowed by the FDA, has increased the role of retail consumers in generating demand for certain prescription drugs. Health insurance companies and health maintenance organizations (HMOs) increasingly impact demand for prescription drugs as well.

The segment of the population that is older than 65 years of age will be one of the fastest growing population cohorts in the United States over the next decade or two. The medical community has come to depend on drug therapies, often stretching over long periods of time, as the first line of treatment in many situations that previously required surgical procedures. Older Americans tend to spend more on prescription and over-the-counter products, as they age and become dependent on long-term, health-maintenance regimens. The aging demographic profile will have a positive impact on drug store retail sales in both the short and long term.

During the summer of 1997, the FDA changed its stance on direct-to-consumer pharmaceutical advertising of prescription drugs. Previously, the FDA allowed television advertising that featured either a product's brand name or its indication, but never both in the same piece. This changed last summer when the FDA decided to allow direct-to-consumer television advertising with both the product name and indication, as long as the commercial also explained the main contraindications and side effects, and provided a telephone number or website where more complete information was available.

Due to the increasing presence of managed care in many states, demand generated by the new advertising may not result in additional sales at the retail drug store level. Since managed-care plans have varying degrees of control over formulary decisions, and thus brand selection, the direct-to-consumer strategy may not be successful in every market. Although spending in drug stores experienced very strong growth in 1998, much of the prescription sales was predetermined by health plans, and were not selected directly by the consumer. Expansion of health insurance coverage may drive sales higher in some areas of the United States. The movement of Medicaid patients into managed care opens up a new market for drug stores.

Healthcare spending in the early 1990s grew approximately 10% per annum in the United States. As the nation jumped on the Managed Care bandwagon, economy-wide growth in health spending slowed to an average annual rate of about 5.0% over the last 5 years. WEFA predicts that healthcare spending will start to accelerate once more to an annual rate of 6.3% over the next ten years. Prescription drugs will be the main reason behind the accelerating healthcare spending. Depending on the restrictive nature of the Managed Care situation in a particular region, especially in the prescription drug category, healthcare spending and, indirectly, growth in spending at drug stores will vary considerably on a regional basis around the national average during that time.

Demand for healthcare and beauty products is another factor in the drug store sales equation. The retail consumer's aging demographic profile is an advantage for the drug store category. The post-World War II baby boom generation's desire to cheat the aging process, combined with demand for nutritional supplements, should continue to boost sale gains in the future.

Shifts in consumer shopping habits, particularly the desire for convenience and one-stop shopping, provide an additional opportunity for store owners to boost sales by selling snacks and other expanded merchandise lines to pharmacy patrons.

WEFA forecasts nominal sales growth at drug stores to exceed 5% in 1999, but fall to the 4% range in 2000. This growth rate is lower than the average annual revenue increase over the last five years. Sales growth will be constrained by the cost savings associated with moving to managed-care plans as well as slower income growth.

Supply Conditions

In line with customer pleas for convenience and a new merchandise mix, drug store retailers are changing store layouts to accommodate drive-through pharmacies, expanded snack food shelf space, and value-added services such as one-hour photofinishing. And it is not just the layout of the typical store that is changing; store location decisions are also being affected. The hunt for new, more convenient locations has resulted in a migration away from smaller shopping mall stores towards larger, free–standing stores.

Technology continues to play a critical role in firms' efforts to increase efficiencies and reduce costs. Pharmacy computer systems are usual targets. The implementation of automatic prescription-refill systems, establishment of computer links between doctors' offices and pharmacies, and the computerization of patient records and reordering procedures are designed to impact the bottom line by increasing the speed of customer access to prescription supplies and by reducing human error. It also frees pharmacists for customer counseling and interaction, which are intended to create customer loyalty and increase sales of particular brands (or generics) that are more profitable for the store.

Technology initiatives have also focused on supply chain management issues: vendor delivery coordination, store stocking, and inventory control. In recent years, the industry has also undertaken a large investment campaign to outfit checkout counters with the latest in scanning and point-of-sale payment equipment.

Price Trends

Drug store prices at the retail level rose 1.7% in 1998 after a 1.3% increase in 1997. Inflation at the drug store level has tended to moderate as the 1990s progressed, falling from 7% during the 1990–1991 period to an average of 1.6% over the last five years. Throughout the decade, drug store prices have increased at an average annual rate of 3.3% versus 1.5% for all retail store prices.

Growth in the cost of items sold in drug and proprietary stores is driven in large part by the price of prescription products. Life saving, high-technology advances in the rigorous research, development, and testing stages of new prescription products have resulted in many innovative submissions to the FDA recently. Fast track approval by the FDA of new, cutting-edge therapies over the past few years resulted in a large number of ground-breaking pharmaceutical launches in 1997. The astronomical investment in technology, education, and pure research that is required in order to continue to further the development of advanced prescription products drives the retail price of prescription products in the market today. The expansion of managed care and the efficiencies that have resulted from standardization at both the retail and wholesale level due to market consolidation have held back retail drug store prices recently. Managed-healthcare plans will continue to grow. Nevertheless, as they target members of other plans to add to their membership rolls, many HMOs are beginning to differentiate themselves based on selection of services and outcome

Price Changes for Drug Stores

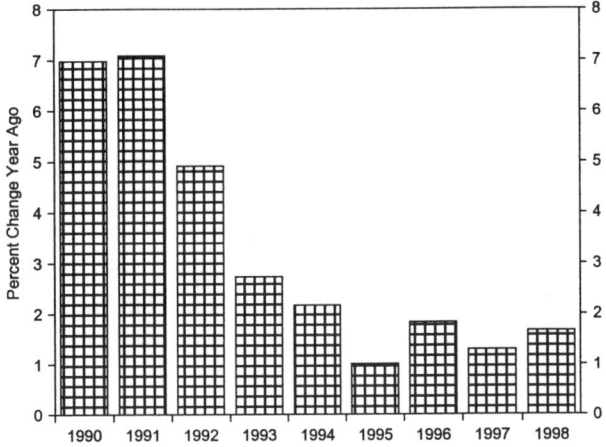

data, instead of focusing so much on base price as a selling point.

Outlook

The retail drug store industry is increasingly dominated by large retail chains. Top-chain retailers include Walgreen, Rite Aid/Thrifty Payless, Revco/CVS, Eckerd/Thrift, and American Drug Stores. The business environment is highly competitive. The large retailers try to increase their share of the drug store market, while at the same time trying to grow the size of their market by going after pre-scription and healthcare sales in supermarkets, mass merchants, small independent pharmacies, and regional drug store chains.

Supermarket operators Kroger, Safeway, Winn-Dixie, and Albertson's have posed the biggest threat to traditional drug stores using combination food/drug stores to take advantage of the link between nutrition and health. The supermarket retailers have also learned to leverage foot traffic to increase sales of health- and beauty-care products. Mass merchants like Walmart and Kmart have extensive pharmacy networks in their stores, and would rank among the top-ten drug chains in terms of pharmacy sales were they classified in that category. Mass merchandisers, discounters, and supermarket-combo stores have been particularly hard on small, independent drug stores whose owners neglected to introduce new technologies and expand merchandise. Some small drug stores have fought back by returning to the core pharmacy function of counseling in the hopes of carving out a high-service niche.

The forecast is for solid, but somewhat slower sales growth in the drug store sector. The aging demographic profile of retail consumers will help sales, but revenues will be held back by the cost constraints imposed by managed care. Look for further consolidation and development and implementation of new patient and pharmacy technologies to increase efficiency in the market.

Trends & Forecasts: Drug Stores

	1991	1992	1993	1994	1995	1996	1997	1998	1999	2000	2001
Retail Sales (Bil $)	75.6	77.7	79.3	81.3	84.9	90.2	98.2	105.7	111.6	116.4	121.4
(% Change)	7.1	2.7	2.2	2.5	4.4	6.3	8.9	7.6	5.6	4.2	4.3
Price (% Change)	7.1	4.9	2.7	2.2	1.0	1.8	1.3	1.7	1.9	1.5	1.7

Catalog and Mail Order Houses

Catalog sales are generally made by sending or selling catalogs to prospective customers, taking orders by mail or telephone, and shipping goods directly to the buyer. Although some businesses specialize in catalog sales, many other retail companies maintain catalog divisions that may only account for a small portion of sales. Official statistics for this industry include only sales of firms primarily engaged in catalog sales. Catalog sales by firms that primarily sell through other channels are not included in the official statistics. Other direct-marketing methods are not included in this specific industry. These include television sales, direct-telephone marketing, and electronic sales through the Internet.

In 1998, catalog and mail order accounted for 2.7% of total retail sales, and this ratio has been growing throughout the 1990s. The immediate outlook is positive as well, as mail order sales will show double-digit gains in 1999 and 2000.

Demand Conditions

Mail-order sales totaled more than $73 billion in 1998. Sales have grown at an average rate of 12.2% throughout the 1990s, as catalog retailing became popular for convenience and as key catalogers gained reputations for known quality. Catalog sales now account for 2.7% of total retail sales versus 1.4% in 1990.

Mail Order Firms' Share of Total Retail Sales Grew in the 1990s

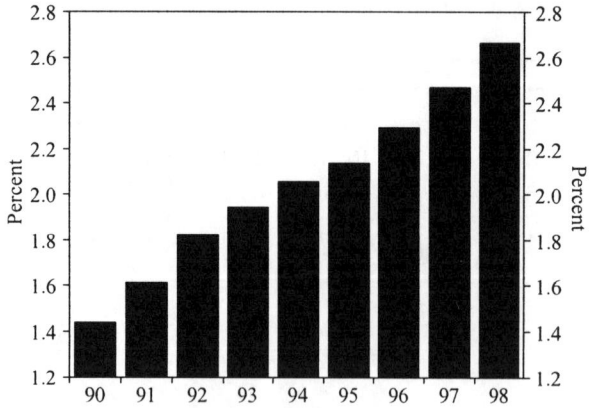

A significant additional amount of retail-catalog sales is chalked up by retailers that are not primarily catalog houses. The share of these retailers has been on the rise in the last several years, as more non-catalog companies have established catalog and sales-by-mail divisions in attempts to capture some of the sector's rapid growth.

J.C. Penney and three computer companies (Dell, Gateway, and DEC) run the largest catalog operations by revenue. It is clear that many of the important businesses engage in more traditional retail selling, but have a division devoted to catalog sales. Even the biggest traditional retailers have catalog operations. Federated Department Stores, for example, owns a small catalog operation called Bloomingdale's by Mail.

Pricing and Costs

The catalog-sales industry is very dependent on printing and publishing costs, and mailing costs. Printing costs rose more quickly than other prices in 1993 and 1994, reducing the industry's competitiveness with traditional retailing. In addition, the industry was hit with a 15% postal rate hike (for third-class bulk mail) in January, 1995. Mailing rates have proven to be a particular problem for the industry, since they have been rising faster than inflation in the 1990s. Over the past ten years, bulk-mail rates have risen at more than double the overall inflation rate.

Catalog companies have responded in two ways to these cost pressures. First, they have reduced mailings and searched for ways to make mailings more effective through the use of more careful targeting and use of demographic information, for example. Second, some companies have begun charging for catalogs, while allowing the catalog buyer a discount equal to the price of the catalog if an actual purchase is made. The price of these catalogs may be substantial; charges of $3.00 to $5.00 are typical. Charging for catalogs is more common among specialty retailers than among the largest companies (neither L.L. Bean nor Lands' End charge for catalogs), and it does not occur in the important electronics sector.

What They Sell

Catalog retailers account for about 60% of total catalog sales. Other industries that maintain a strong catalog sales presence include auto dealers and service stations, specialty retailers, and food stores. Consumer-catalog sales are concentrated in apparel and home goods, which typically account for half or more of all consumer catalog sales.

Outlook

Total catalog sales will continue to grow in the next few years at rates faster than the rate of growth of all retail sales. Growth will be slower than in the past, however, since total consumer-spending growth will not be as strong, and because catalog penetration may be reaching a saturation point. The portion of catalog sales accounted for by the catalog houses will remain on a declining trend as non-catalog retailers continue to establish and grow catalog subsidiaries.

Competitive Threats

Catalog companies face challenges from three other direct marketing methods: telephone sales, direct television sales, and Internet sales.

■ Telephone sales represent a threat, although they do not generally compete directly with catalog operations. Consumer telephone sales have been con-

centrated in services — financial or other services — and have placed less emphasis on the goods that catalog companies generally sell.

■ Direct television sales include the home shopping networks, "infomercials" of various lengths, and traditional direct-sales television commercials. Direct television sales to consumers are about 25% of the size of catalog sales to consumers. Most television sales are for retail goods, with services accounting for a relatively small proportion of total sales.

■ Internet sales (electronic commerce) are on a fast track, although still relatively small in size compared to catalog sales. Nevertheless, the traditional catalog industry has responded by establishing a presence on the Internet, and is even using it aggressively in marketing.

Sales of "other direct marketing" methods are likely to grow faster than catalog sales over the next few years. The Internet appears to be the only medium that directly competes with catalogs, however. The Internet shares several characteristics with catalogs that distinguish these sales methods from television and telephone sales:

■ Both require a similar investment in the presentation of the merchandise, either for the catalog or for the Internet page. Television and telephone sales present merchandise in very different ways.

■ The customer controls when and how to shop in both catalog and Internet sales. By contrast, television and telephone sales techniques involve control by the seller.

Neither television nor telephone provides a likely serious alternative to catalogs in the near future. The Internet, however, will be an important alternative to catalog sales, and both catalog and non-catalog retailers can be expected to continue to expand resources on testing and improving Internet sales.

Trends & Forecasts: Mail Order Houses

	1991	1992	1993	1994	1995	1996	1997	1998	1999	2000	2001
Retail Sales (Bil $)	30.0	35.5	40.5	46.2	50.4	57.4	64.6	73.2	82.0	90.2	96.5
(% Ch year ago)	12.7	18.6	14.0	14.0	9.1	13.9	12.5	13.2	12.0	10.0	7.0

Part 6: Finance, Insurance, Real Estate, and Services

Chapter 28: Finance, Insurance, and Real Estate

Financial Services

The financial services industry is comprised of firms that provide some type of financial service to consumers, businesses, or government. These services may be related to the payment system and involve such specific products as checking accounts, electronic deposits or payment arrangements, and credit cards; the credit markets, including any of a wide array of specific types of loans; and savings and investments, including all of the various forms that these may take. Historically, different types of financial services have been associated with different types of firms—depository and lending services have been associated with commercial banks and thrift institutions, for example, while services related to the issuance of and investment in financial securities have been associated with investment banks and securities brokers and dealers.

The traditional sharp distinctions between different types of firms providing different types of financial services have been disappearing rapidly in recent years, however, as a result of changes in regulations and technology. Banks now offer services traditionally offered only by securities firms, for example, and vice versa. Rapid advances in technology have even resulted in firms from totally different industries offering financial services; for example, when software firms become deeply involved in the payments system via developments in "home banking", through which people pay bills using personal computers. While the transformation of the financial services industry continues at a rapid pace, blurring the distinctions between traditionally very different types of firms, those distinctions are still significant enough for it to make sense to look at different categories of firms. In the following, commercial banks, thrift institutions, credit unions, securities brokers, and mutual funds are reviewed.

Commercial Banks

After suffering through a difficult period in the early 1990s as a result of large loan losses concentrated in the real estate area, commercial banks recovered strongly by the middle of the decade. At the same time, as a result of regulatory and other changes enhancing economies of scale in the industry, banking has been rapidly consolidating in recent years.

In 1998, insured commercial banks earned a record $61.9 billion, up 4.7% from 1997. The industry's basic measure of profitability, return on assets (ROA), declined slightly in 1998, to 1.19%, down from 1997's record high of 1.23% and back to where it was in 1997. In addition, return on equity declined to 13.95% in 1998, down from 14.68% in 1997 and the lowest since 1992 (when it was 12.98%). In the late 1980s and early 1990s, bad loans and weak performance plagued banks. This situation has since turned around and 1998 marked the sixth consecutive year of strong earnings. In all likelihood, bank earnings will register another good year in 1999.

Profits and Profitability of Insured Commercial Banks
1988 — 1997, annually

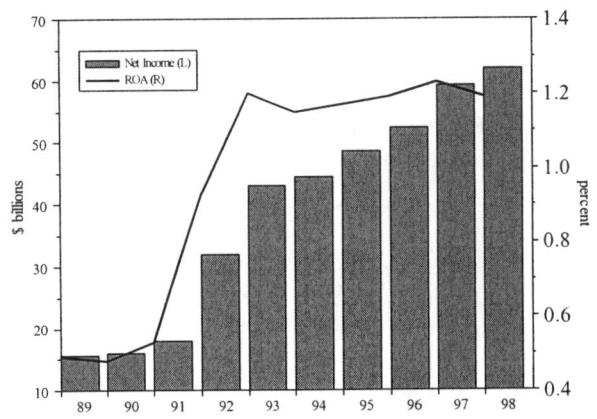

Total commercial bank assets increased by 8.5% in 1998, down from 9.5% in 1997. However, loan volume increased by 9.1%, up sharply from 5.2% in 1997. Real estate loans increased by 8.2% and commercial and industrial loans by 12.9% in 1998, while loans to individuals increased by only 1.7%, after declining slightly in 1997. It is the latter category of loans (which includes credit card loans) that has been the most troublesome for banks in recent years and they have significantly tightened lending standards for such loans as a result. Commercial bank assets are likely to continue to grow faster than the economy as a whole in the years immediately ahead.

Asset quality showed signs of weakening in 1998. Although noncurrent assets plus other real-estate owned as a percent of assets edged down to 0.65% from 0.66% in 1997, the dollar volume of noncurrent loans increased by $2.7 billion, the first increase since 1990. In addition, the volume of loan charge-offs increased by 13% in 1998, while net charge-offs as a percent of loans increased to 0.67%, up from 0.64%, and the highest since 1993 (when it was 0.85%). At their peak in 1991, bad loans that were written off by banks amounted to 1.6% of total loans on the books. Charge-offs of commercial and industrial loans increased to 0.43% in 1998 from 0.28% in 1997, and charge-offs of credit card loans increased to 5.19%, up from 5.11%.

As another sign of the much-improved health of the banking industry in recent years, the number of banks classified as "problem banks" has declined drastically. At the end of 1998, there were 69 institutions so classified, down from 71 a year earlier and 144 at the end of 1995. This also represents a 93% decline from the 1,016 banks classified as problem banks at the end of 1991. Even more dramatic has been the drop in assets represented by problem banks, as they have declined from $528 billion (equal to 15.4% of total bank assets) in 1991, to only $5 billion per year during 1996–1998. In 1998, that represented just 0.1% of total bank assets.

Assets of Problem Banks
1990 — 1998, annually

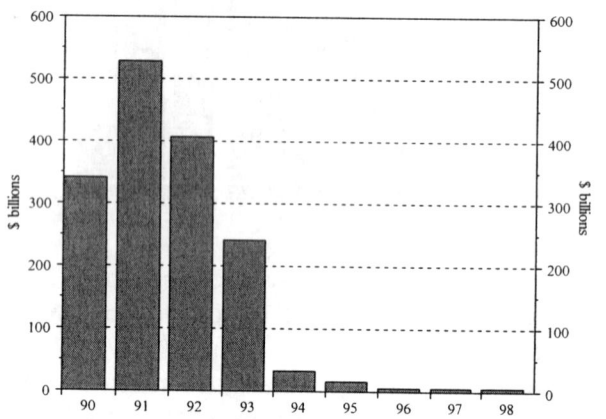

Consolidation of the banking industry continued in 1998, with the number of banks declining by 368 mainly because the number of independent institutions eliminated

through mergers (557) continued to significantly outpace the number of new banks chartered (190). Since 1985, the number of banks in the United States has declined by 39%, from 14,417 to 8774. This trend of consolidation reflects fundamental changes in the regulations and technology affecting the banking industry, and it can be expected to continue in coming years.

Number of Insured Commercial Banks at Year-End
1970 — 1998

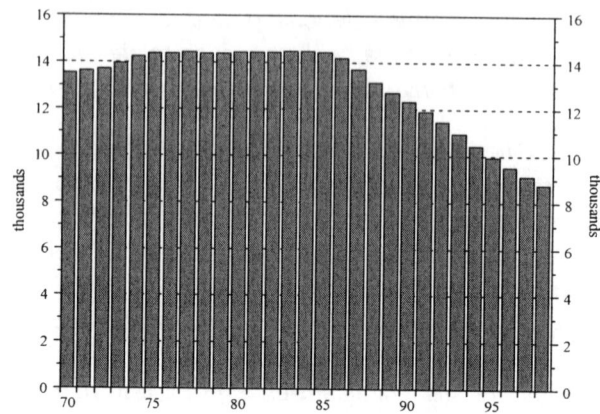

When they occur, bank mergers usually result in significant job losses as duplicative positions are eliminated. Even so, while the number of banks has dropped by 39% since 1985, mainly as a result of mergers, employment by banks has increased by 62,000, or 4.0%, over that same interval as overall bank services have increased.

Thrift Institutions

The "thrift crisis" of the late 1980s and early 1990s officially ended in 1995 with the closing of the Resolution Trust Corporation. In the seven years of its existence, the RTC sold or liquidated some 747 failed thrifts, representing approximately $450 billion in assets. Somewhat incredibly, following so close on the heels of that debacle, the thrift industry had returned to a remarkably healthy state by the late 1990s. Although the industry was considerably smaller than it was in the mid-1980s, in terms of both the number of firms and their total assets, not only had earnings recovered strongly but other key measures of industry health also registered highly favorable readings.

Total earnings of all insured savings institutions in 1998 were a record $10.2 billion, up 16% from 1997. In terms of profitability, the return on average assets in 1998 increased to 1.01%, up from 0.93% in 1997, and the first time since 1946 that it exceeded 1.0%. Return on equity increased to 11.36% in 1998, up from 10.84% the year before. As long as interest rates remain relatively low, and the economy generally healthy, thrift industry earnings should remain strong.

Net Income of Insured Savings Institutions
1984 — 1998, annually

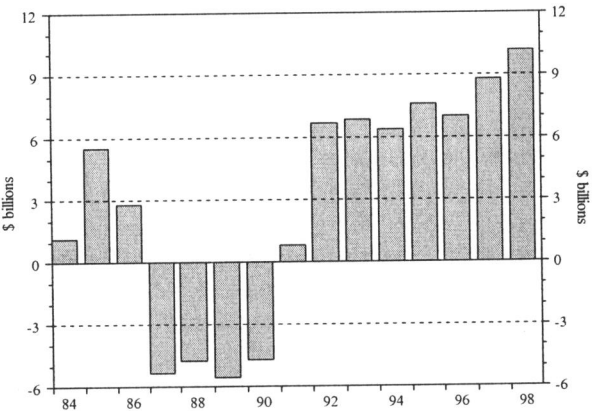

Balance-sheet measures also track the return to health of the thrift industry by 1998. Noncurrent assets plus other real estate owned as a percent of assets declined to 0.72% by year-end 1998, down from 0.95% a year earlier, marking the eighth-straight year of decline in this ratio. In 1990, it was 3.98%. Also, net charge-offs as a percent of loans declined to 0.21% in 1998, down from 0.25% in 1997, and less than one-third of 1993's figure of 0.65%. Moreover, by the end of 1998, the number and size of institutions classified by the regulatory authorities as "problem institutions" had diminished greatly. Whereas at the end of 1990, there were 480 such institutions, at the end of 1998 that number was only 15, down from 21 at the end of 1997. Moreover, those problem institutions that remained tended to be relatively small; altogether, their assets represented just 0.6% of total savings insitutions' assets. This constitutes a dramatic improvement from 1990, when the assets of problem institutions represented 23.7% of total savings institutions' assets. Also, there were no savings institution failures in 1998, which was also true in 1997—and that was for the first time since 1959.

Assets of Problem Savings Institutions
1990 — 1998, annually

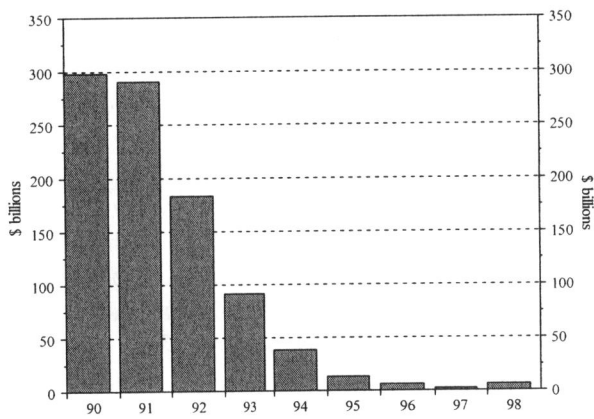

Although the savings institution industry was quite healthy in 1998, like the commercial banking industry, it continued to consolidate in terms of the number of institutions, which declined by 5.2% to 1,687. Over the past ten years, the number of savings institutions has dropped by more than half—in 1987, there were 3,622 institutions. Much, but not all, of that decline has been the result of consolidation within the industry through mergers and acquisitions. That trend of consolidation reflects some of the same factors underlying consolidation in the banking industry and, as such, can be expected to continue in coming years. At the same time, the size of the thrift industry has shrunk in terms of its total assets, with some thrift assets written off and others acquired by commercial banks and other financial institutions. Although total savings institutions' assets increased by 6.0% in 1998, since 1987 they have fallen by 28%.

Number of Insured Savings Institutions
1987 — 1998

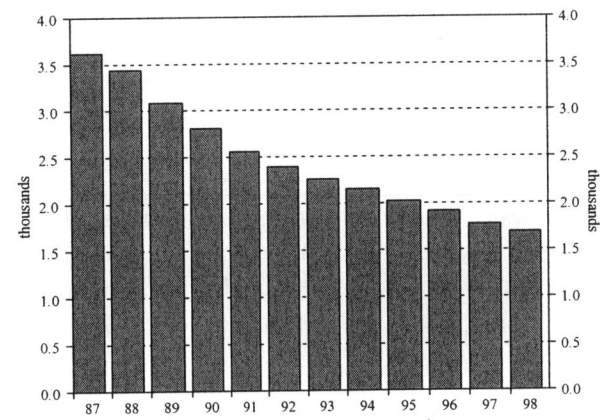

Credit Unions

Credit unions are cooperative financial institutions that provide saving and lending services to their members. In addition to basic services, large credit unions offer checking accounts, automated teller machines (ATMs), credit cards, individual retirement accounts (IRAs), and other services. The National Credit Union Administration (NCUA), an agency of the Federal Government, insures approximately 11,400 credit unions that hold more than 95% of all credit union assets. NCUA examines and regulates most federally insured credit unions to ensure their safety and soundness. Approximately 500 credit unions are insured either privately or by states. State agencies regulate these state and privately insured credit unions.

Credit unions represent a relatively small share of the total financial services market. Of the total lending by commercial banks, savings institutions, and credit unions, for example, credit unions represented just under 6% at the end of 1998. Credit unions are most important in the market for consumer installment loans, such as personal, auto, and credit card loans. In that market, credit unions accounted for approximately 12% of total loans outstanding at the end of 1998. Although credit unions represent a relatively small share of the total financial services industry, they have gained market share in recent years as regulations restricting their membership have been eased, and as they have charged lower fees and offered to pay higher interest rates than competing institutions.

Securities Firms

Securities firms perform various functions related to maintaining markets in financial securities, including short- and long-term debt instruments issued by governments and corporations and equity issues of corporations. Their two principal functions are investment banking and acting as securities brokers and dealers. Firms that provide investment-banking services assist businesses and governments in raising funds needed to finance capital expenditures and other spending, selling newly issued stocks and bonds to individual and institutional investors.

In recent years, an important new type of debt issue has been for the purpose of "securitizing" mortgages and other types of otherwise illiquid loans (such as credit card receivables and car loans). Such issues effectively remove these illiquid assets from the books of commercial banks, thrift institutions, and other originators through selling them to investors.

While investment-grade debt generally represents the largest dollar amount of offerings, substantial fees are also typically earned from high-yield bonds and equities. These latter instruments generate larger fees per dollar of issue sold, as they are generally riskier for investment banks to hold and also require more sales effort. While investment-grade debt might earn 50 cents in revenues for every $100 of issue value, comparable revenues for high-yield bonds might be $2, and for stocks $6.

The volume of all new securities (stocks and bonds) issued by corporations has increased substantially in recent years. During the five-year period, 1994-1998, corporations issued an average of $693 billion per year, versus $395 billion per year during 1989–1993, an increase of 75%. In recent years, new bond issues have accounted for about 85% of all new issues of corporate securities. As long as the economy continues to expand, the volume of new security issues is likely to remain large, and could even rise further.

New Securities Issued by U.S. Corporations, All Public Issues (stocks and bonds)
1988 — 1998, annually

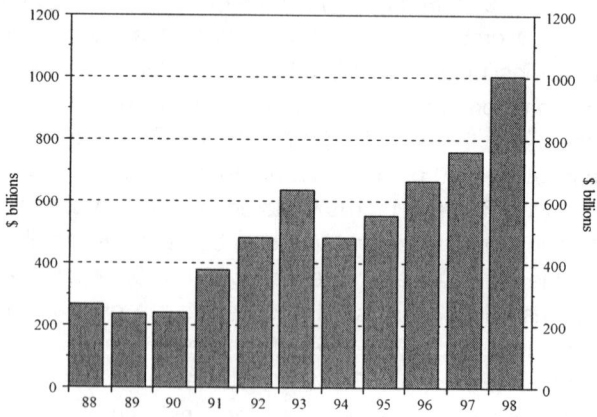

Securities dealers and brokers provide a "secondary" market for previously issued securities, bringing securities buyers and sellers together. These firms maintain active markets for all kinds of marketable securities, including debt obligations of state and local governments, as well as those of the federal government and corporate stocks and bonds. In recent years, as the volume of investments in financial securities has generally soared, so has trading activity in the securities markets. Trading volume on the New York Stock Exchange, for example, soared from an average of approximately 170 million shares per day during 1987–1991 to about 526 million shares per day in 1997. As the volume of retirement savings continues to grow, and as competition in the investment field intensifies, financial market activity is likely to continue rising in coming years.

Average Daily Trading Volume on the New York Stock Exchange
1988 — 1998, annually

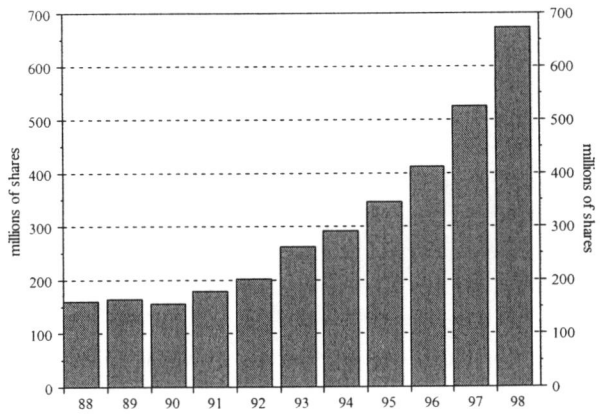

Mutual Funds

A mutual fund is a company that invests in financial securities on behalf of its shareholders. By combining the financial resources of shareholders, mutual funds offer small investors the ability to economically achieve the goals of professional money management and investment diversification. Professional money managers invest the fund's assets in a variety of stocks, bonds, or other securities selected from a broad range of industries, government agencies, and authorities. In effect, each mutual fund shareholder owns a percentage of the diversified portfolio created by the fund's money managers. The advantage of diversification is that, generally speaking, diversified portfolios of investments tend to be less risky than portfolios that are not diversified and are comprised of only a relatively few specific investments.

Mutual funds have stated investment objectives that are given in a fund's prospectus. The fund's managers select securities that they believe best meet their fund's objective. Investment objectives are usually described in terms of one or more main goals—such as "stability" (protecting shareholders' investment from loss), "growth" (increasing

the value of shareholders' investment), or "income" (generating a regular stream of income through dividends).

The mutual fund industry consists of investment companies, each of which sells shares in one or more mutual funds. Investment companies sell shares directly to the public or through agents. Registered representatives of brokerage firms, insurance agencies, and financial planning firms, among others, sell shares in mutual funds as part of their overall-financial service to clients. These funds usually add a sales charge, or "load," to the sale to compensate agents for their work and generate revenue for them. Organizations such as unions, associations, and retail stores also market mutual funds.

Many investment companies, however, sell shares in mutual funds directly to investors by mail and by telephone. These shares are often sold "no load"—that is, with no sales charge or only a nominal sales charge. Revenue for investment companies from these funds is usually provided by management fees based on size of assets or performance, or both. Some expenses, such as marketing and distribution, can be covered directly by assets of the funds if these funds conform to government regulations.

Mutual funds must meet specific regulatory requirements. A mutual fund must register with the U.S. Securities and Exchange Commission (SEC), issue a prospectus giving a detailed report of its operations, and adhere to strict rules concerning accounting and valuation. A number of regulations exist to prevent conflicts of interest among officials of investment companies. State regulations and securities laws also govern mutual funds. Because of the fiduciary nature of mutual funds, their operations are subject to regulatory scrutiny.

As incomes of many households have risen to levels that can support significant saving, and as pension plans have shifted away from traditional plans entirely financed by employer contributions to plans (such as 401K) that require contributions—and investment decisions—by employees, investment through mutual funds has soared in recent years. Moreover, when that trend is combined with sharply rising stock prices, which was the case in recent years, the result has been explosive growth in mutual fund assets.

Specifically, in the 10-year period from 1988 to 1998, total net assets of mutual funds have increased nearly seven–fold, soaring from $809 billion at the end of 1988, to $5.5

trillion at the end of 1998. As spectacular as that growth has been, the growth of equity funds over that period has been more than twice as fast, as their net asset values have increased more than fifteen-fold, rising from $195 billion at the end of 1988 to $3.0 trillion at the end of 1998. As a result of that explosive rise, equity funds have become far-and-away the dominant type of mutual fund, whereas in 1988 investments in both bond funds, and in taxable money market funds, were greater than those represented by equity funds. Moreover, as investments in mutual funds have soared in recent years, so has the number of mutual funds. The number of mutual funds nearly tripled between 1987 and 1997, jumping from 2,708 to 7,314 with new equity funds accounting for more than half of that growth. All indications are that, with the growth of defined-contribution retirement plans, and of the working-age population, rapid growth in this industry will continue in coming years.

Total Net Assets of Mutual Funds

1988 — 1998, annually

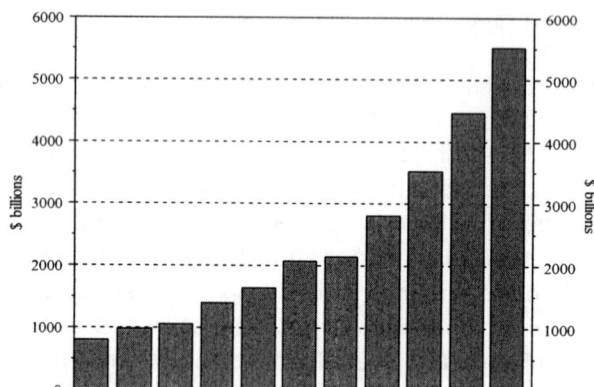

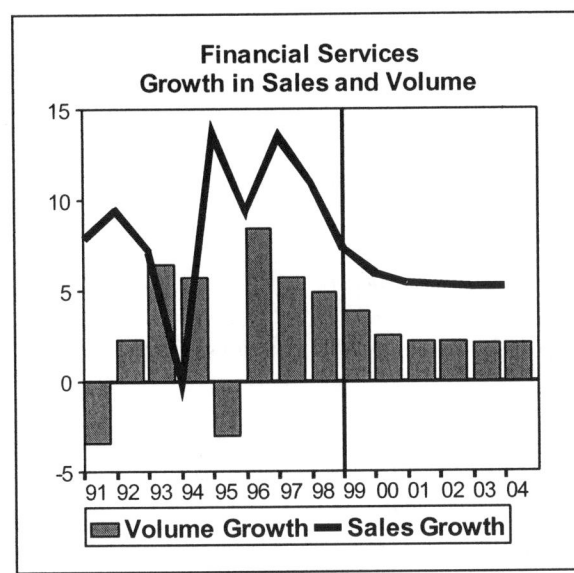

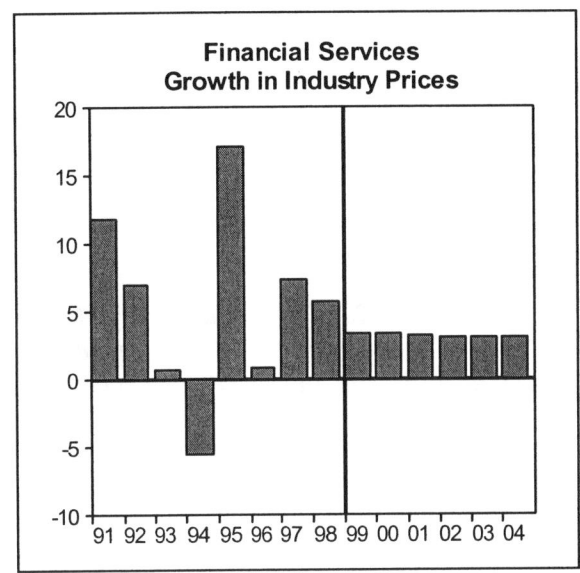

Financial Services

SIC 60-62,67

		1992	1993	1994	1995	1996	1997	1998	1999	2000	2001	Compound Average 88-98	Annual Growth 98-08
Sales													
	Billions of $	386.4	414.2	413.9	470.4	514.5	583.9	647.7	695.2	736.5	776.4		
	% Ch	9.4	7.2	-0.1	13.7	9.4	13.5	10.9	7.3	5.9	5.4	9.0	5.8
Volume													
	% Ch	2.3	6.5	5.8	-3.0	8.5	5.8	4.9	3.8	2.5	2.2	2.8	2.5
Prices													
	% Ch	7.0	0.7	-5.5	17.2	0.8	7.3	5.7	3.4	3.3	3.2	6.0	3.3
Production Costs													
Avg. Hourly Earnings													
	$/hr	9.33	9.68	9.95	10.16	10.53	11.03	11.69	12.29	12.82	13.39		
	% Ch	3.3	3.8	2.8	2.1	3.6	4.7	6.0	5.1	4.3	4.4	3.9	4.3
Input Price Index													
	% Ch	3.6	1.6	-0.5	7.5	2.0	4.1	3.8	2.9	2.9	2.9	3.8	3.0

Insurance Services

The primary sectors in the insurance service industries are life insurers, property-casualty (PC) insurers, and health-maintenance organizations. This sector is becoming increasingly intertwined with other financial businesses through the process of cross-industry mergers and acquisitions.

Consumer spending on health insurance increased by 1.8% in 1998 to $59.1 billion. A decade ago, insurance spending had totaled $23.8 billion. During the first half of the past decade (1989–1993) spending grew by 136%. During the past five years (1994–1998) spending has risen by only 10%. Medical- and hospital-insurance outlays account for about 80% of total health insurance spending.

For the aggregate of all insurance providers, we expect annual increases in sales of 6.0%–6.5% per year over the next ten years. This is about three-fourths of the growth achieved during the previous decade. Prices should rise by roughly 4% per year over the decade, versus 5.3% during the previous decade. Thus, volume growth in the insurance industry runs 2.0%-2.5% per year, on average, versus growth of almost 3% in the previous ten years.

Overview

The insurance industry reported sales of $466 billion in 1998, an increase of 9.9%. This followed a jump in sales of 15.7% in 1997. During the past decade, sales have increased by 8.4% per year, on average. Prices during this period rose 2.9%, yielding real growth in the insurance industry of 5.3%.

Last year the insurance industry employed 2.34 million, an increase of 3.5% over 1997. A decade ago, the insurance industry employed just under 2.1 million. Employment in the insurance industry has increased in all but one year in the past decade. In 1992, employment slipped by less than one-half-of-one percent. Average hourly earnings in the insurance industry increased by 5% in 1998, maintaining the same growth rate as during the past decade.

Property–Casualty (PC) Insurers

Both homeowners and commercial PC insurance have proved to be a pretty unprofitable business over much of the past decade due to earthquakes, hurricanes, floods, winter ice storms, and fires. Losses from catastrophes during the 1989–1998 period totaled approximately $80 billion. Companies with a heavy exposure in high-risk states, such as Florida, the Carolinas, California, and the Northeast, have had the more difficult time over the past

ten years. 1992 was a particularly bad year due to hurricane Andrew with claims totaling $15.5 billion. This was followed by 1994 with claims of $12.5 billion due to the Northridge, California earthquake. Property and casualty insurers had a relatively disaster-free year in 1997 with claims valued at only about $2.5-3.0 billion. However, in 1998, the industry was plagued by a number of disasters throughout the country leading to another year of red ink, as claims rose to $10 billion. The Atlantic storm season alone saw hurricanes Bonnie, Earl, Georges, and Mitch. Tropical storms Charley, Frances, and Hermine added to the damage.

The top-50 insurance companies reported homeowner PC-insurance premiums valued at almost $29 billion in 1998, an increase of 7.8%. Over the past decade, net premiums written by the top-50 insurance companies have grown by almost 70%. Last year, the top-four states for homeowner premiums were California at $3.2 billion, Texas at $2.5 billion, Florida at $2.3 billion, and New York at $2.1 billion. Together these states accounted for 34.5% of the direct premiums written by the top-50 insurance companies. Not surprisingly, these are also the four most populous states in the country accounting for 31.7% of the total population of the United States. The top-five companies in the homeowner-insurance business last year, measured by direct premiums written, were: State Farm, $7.0 billion; Allstate Insurance Group, $3.6 billion; Zurich Insurance Group, $2.2 billion; Nationwide Corp., $1.3 billion; and Citigroup (Travelers), $1.1 billion.

The top-50 insurance companies reported commercial PC-insurance premiums valued at over $20 billion in 1998, about equal to the previous year. Last year saw the slowest growth in premiums in six years. Over the past decade, net premiums written by the top-50 insurance companies have grown by only 7.5%. Commercial PC insurance is viewed as a commodity and pricing pressure has been extremely intense. Last year, the top-four states for homeowner premiums were California, $2.9 billion; New York, $2.0 billion; Texas, $1.2 billion; and Florida, $1.2. billion. Together these states accounted for 35.4% of the direct premiums written by the top-50 insurance companies. The top-five companies in the commercial PC insurance last year, measured by direct premiums written were: Citigroup (Travelers), $1.1 billion; CNA Insurance Group, $1.4 billion; Zurich Insurance Group, $2.2 billion; and Hartford Fire & Casualty Group and State Farm, about $1billion each.

Y2K Property-Casualty Exposure

The property/casualty insurance breathed a sigh of relief in early July 1999 when Congress approved a bill limiting the exposure of technology companies in Y2K problem-related suits. The bill established a 90-day period within which technology companies could fix the problem before the client filed a suit. Punitive damages were capped at $250,000 or three times compensatory damages, whichever is less, for small businesses. Small businesses are defined as having 50-or-less employees. For larger software companies, there was no cap on punitive damages. Class-action suits involving claims of $10 million or more or 100-or-more claimants would be handled in federal court. In general, the bill limited defendants' damage exposure to their share of the loss. The bill did allow damages to triple in cases where a technology failed to try and correct Y2K problems or misled clients about their efforts. Finally, damages could rise to twice the amount in cases involving multiple defendants where some had gone bankrupt. In these cases, solvent companies might have to pay for those that are insolvent.

PC insurers are entirely off the hook for Y2K-related problems. GTE filed a claim of $400 million against Allendale Mutual Insurance Co., Allianz Insurance Co., Affiliated FM Insurance Co., Industrial Risk Insurers, and Federal Insurance Company to recover the cost of meeting Y2K requirements. Zurich Insurance filed a lawsuit against Xerox Corp. to avoid paying the roughly $185 million Xerox expected it to cost to become Y2K compliant.

Life Insurers

Life insurers experienced good years in 1997 and 1998. Most or many of the positive factors that sparked this performance continued in 1999. Insurers have been consolidating, gaining the earnings of other companies through acquisition. Interest rates are still relatively low, despite the recent fed hikes. This is good for life insurers because it makes it unlikely that policyholders could borrow against the cash value of their policies at lower-than-market rates. Profits have generally been strong on variable-annuity products. In fact, annuities remain the key growth area in the life-insurance business.

Health Insurers and Health Maintenance Organizations

Consumer spending on health insurance increased by 1.8% in 1998 to $59.1 billion. A decade ago, insurance spending had totaled $23.8 billion. During the first half of the past decade (1989–1993), spending grew by 136%. During the five years 1994–1998, spending rose by only 10%. Medical- and hospital-insurance outlays account for about 80% of total health insurance spending. The remaining 20% is split between private workmen's compensation (15%) and income-loss insurance (5%).

Spending on medical and hospital insurance increased 2.9% in 1998 and 154% during the 1989–1998 period. During the first half of the decade (1989-1993), spending grew by 136%. During the five years 1994–1998, spending rose by about 8%.

Workmen's compensation spending has risen from $2.6 billion in 1988 to $8.7 billion last year. Income-loss insurance has increased very modestly, 17.5%, over the past-ten years, from $2.5 billion in 1998 to $3 in 1998.

Insurers and Health Maintenance Organizations (HMOs) play an important role in the American healthcare system. These organizations pay a large part of the medical and pharmacy bills on behalf of consumers. Traditional insurance plans allow consumers to purchase healthcare from any provider. The consumer, then, either directs the provider to bill a specific insurance company or requests reimbursement after paying the provider. In general, such plans allow the consumer freedom in choosing healthcare options.

HMOs typically provide services directly. These organizations may even have their own staffs of physicians and other professionals, and their own hospitals. In other cases, the HMO contracts with certain providers, and the consumer must obtain healthcare through those providers. HMO providers must follow specific rules in treatment and referral; the rules vary among HMOs. HMO payments to providers may take the form of salaries, with bonuses for cost containment, or *capitation agreements*, in which the provider (hospital or professional partnership) agrees to a fixed price per patient, regardless of the actual treatment.

There are also hybrid HMO insurance schemes, in which certain providers are preferred because they have contracted agreements, but consumers may obtain partial reimbursement for treatment by non-preferred providers, for example.

The health insurance market is divided between for-profit and not-for-profit providers. HMOs are mostly private, but some of the not-for-profit insurers have created HMO subsidiaries. HMOs have been growing rapidly in recent years, and they have gained market share in both the private and public sector. In the private sector, HMOs have proven to be able to keep costs from growing quickly, and have thus attracted the attention of corporate purchasers of health insurance. The public sector has found HMOs to be useful cost controls in both the Medicare and Medicaid programs. Some elderly are now covered through Medicare payments to HMOs, a procedure that is designed to reduce costs to the federal government. States are moving aggressively to contract Medicaid services, especially those for poor families, to managed-care providers. There is evidence that this is both cheaper and results in better health outcomes for this population.

As in the hospital sector, the health insurance/HMO sector has been undergoing consolidation. This has taken several related forms:

- Mergers between health insurers, including mergers between traditional-insurance companies and HMOs.

- The sale of not-for-profit health insurers to for-profit entities. This generally entails the creation of a foundation to hold and spend the surplus value earned by the not-for-profit partner in the transaction.

- The merging of roles as HMOs and traditional insurers begin to take on similar functions.

Outlook

Risks to PC insurers include, as always, unforeseen catastrophes like Hurricane Andrew in 1992. Compounding this ongoing risk is the fact that traditional sources of reinsurance (insurance bought by a property-casualty insurer to help reduce its risk for catastrophe payouts) have mostly dried up since Hurricane Andrew. In addition, should the investment markets turn negative for any reason, those PC insurers that have pursued written premiums too aggressively by pricing the business too low could find themselves in serious financial trouble rather quickly.

The potential that the year-2000 (Y2K) computer bug could have caused various kinds of product and systems failures raised quite interesting issues for the insurance industry. Some insurers modified policies to exclude coverage of losses resulting from Y2K failures, while others view the problem as a new, if temporary, opportunity for the industry.

Insurers are also at risk to the health of the financial markets. Poorly performing markets will directly affect life insurers' profitability. An upward spike in bond yields—which would lower the value of the industry's bond portfolios—would severely erode investment income for life insurers.

For HMOs, the possibility of Medicare reform and/or cuts in provider payments presents an ever-present threat to the status quo. The House plans to vote on managed-care-reform legislation late in September. In California, the legislature approved bills limiting health-plan liability, requiring coverage of physician-requested second opinions, establishing an independent review system, creating a department of managed care to oversee health plans, and mandating mental-health benefits parity for several conditions. Enrollment growth is also critical for HMO success, but this need is in conflict with the need to hold the line on prices. Such conflicts will fuel further consolidation. The California Medical Association recently reported that 34 out of 300 California medical groups could fail by the end of the year due to inadequate premiums and capitation.

For the aggregate of all insurance providers, we expect annual increases in sales of 6.0%–6.5% per year over the next ten years. This is about three-fourths of the growth achieved during the previous decade. Prices should rise by roughly 4% per year over the decade, versus 5.3% during the previous decade. Thus, volume growth in the insurance industry runs 2.0%–2.5% per year, on average, versus growth of almost 3% in the previous ten years. Insurance-industry employment is slated to expand by 0.5%-1.0% per year, on average. Average hourly earnings should increase by 4.5% per year, down from 5% per year in the previous decade.

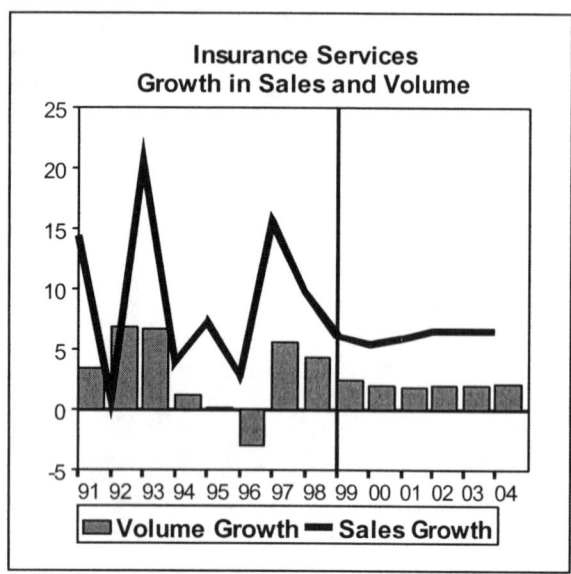

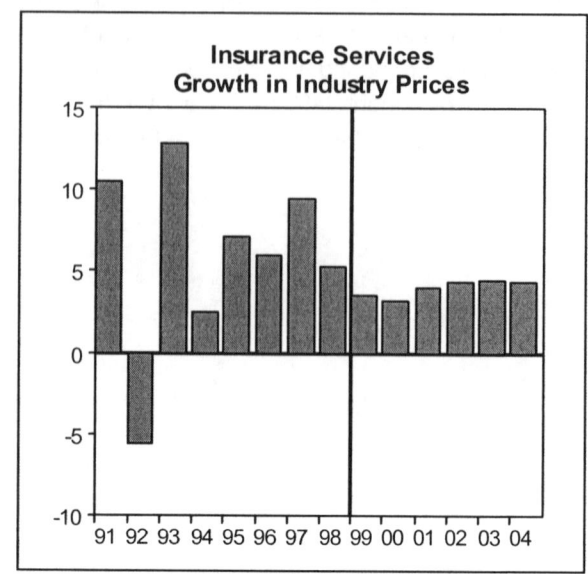

Insurance Services
SIC 63-64

		1992	1993	1994	1995	1996	1997	1998	1999	2000	2001	Compound Average 88-98	Annual Growth 98-08
Sales													
	Billions of $	264.9	319.4	331.8	356.3	366.8	424.3	466.1	494.9	521.8	553.1		
	% Ch	0.9	20.6	3.9	7.4	2.9	15.7	9.9	6.2	5.4	6.0	8.4	6.3
Volume													
	% Ch	6.8	6.8	1.3	0.2	-2.9	5.7	4.4	2.6	2.1	1.9	2.9	2.2
Prices													
	% Ch	-5.6	12.9	2.6	7.1	6.0	9.5	5.3	3.5	3.3	4.0	5.3	4.1
Production Costs													
Avg. Hourly Earnings													
	$/hr	12.37	13.14	13.97	14.82	15.34	15.82	16.64	17.06	17.66	18.39		
	% Ch	5.4	6.2	6.3	6.1	3.5	3.1	5.2	2.5	3.5	4.1	5.0	4.5
Input Price Index													
	% Ch	-1.8	8.1	1.6	6.8	4.4	7.1	4.6	3.2	3.0	3.5	4.6	3.6

Real Estate Services

The real estate service industry has exceeded expectations during 1998 and 1999. Home sales of existing units grew over 13% in 1998, and another 2% has been estimated for 1999. Home completions increased close to 5% in 1998, and 1999 is estimated to grow 10%. Furthermore, office rentals have increased significantly, and new commercial property has gained a great deal of interest. This is the direct result of an expanding U.S. economy. It is also the result of stable interest rates.

The real estate sector is, however, in a transition. With the expectation that the U.S. economy will slow, the real estate industry should enter a period of moderation. WEFA does not anticipate a major drop in the industry similar to what occurred in the early 1990s. Instead, we look for an adjustment from the fast pace of the last couple of years. This will likely result in business-practice changes.

Demand

Real estate agents and managers are engaged primarily in renting, buying, selling, managing and appraising real estate for others. Their business is closely tied to the economic health of the country, and they contribute a major part of GDP. The value of production of real estate services was $1322 billion in 1998. Brokers' commissions on the sales of residential structures accounted for slightly more than 4.0% of this. The real estate services industry employs roughly 1.5 million people dispersed throughout all states in the union.

Real estate is an industry that is quite regional in nature. Vacancy rates in New York may be very different from those in San Francisco. Additionally, the housing industry in the Southeast and Southwest is fast paced, while New England may be slightly slower. However, the economic health of the United States, overall, still has an impact on all real estate activity. Employment growth and consumer confidence are the primary factors affecting the industry. Furthermore, job creation and the number of new business entities have an impact on office rentals and vacancy rates.

WEFA expects real estate activity will change significantly in 2000 and 2001. By current market standards, it may be surprising that we look for a slowdown in the real estate service industry. During 1998, the sales of existing homes were slightly more than 4.96 million units. In 1999, existing-home sales are expected to reach 5.05 million units, still an increase of 1.8%. The sales of new homes, which have also been quite strong in the last two years, are estimated to reach 889,000 units in 1999. How-ever, we expect the fundamentals of the market to lose steam over the next couple of years, which will cause sales of both new and existing homes to weaken. Employment is slated to increase by only 0.4% in 2000 and 1.2% in 2001, compared to an estimated 1.9% increase in 1999. Furthermore, GDP growth is likely to slow to a modest pace of growth in 2000 and 2001 ranging between 2% and 2.5%. In contrast, a 3.9% rate is estimated for 1999.

Office-building vacancy rates nationwide peaked at 20.5% on an annual average basis in 1992. The rental market has been on a road to recovery since then. After 1995, the national vacancy rate dropped below 15%. In 1999 vacancy rates in many cities have plummeted; New York City and Chicago are especially tight markets.

WEFA expects stability in the office-building sector over the next few years as the U.S. economic expansion ages further. One key commercial-space tenant, the retail-trade industry, continues to consolidate, which tends to reduce space requirements. Rent increases on retail space have proven modest. Given expectations of continued market-share gains by the giant discount retailers at the expense of smaller operators, this sector should prove a sluggish source of demand for a few years yet.

Supply Conditions

The nonresidential real estate firms that have survived the shakeout of previous difficult real estate years follow "lean and mean" practices and promote more stability within the industry. The next two years will also require them to use their skills in a slowing sector.

Forecast

Inflation-adjusted gains for the overall real estate service industry are likely to average slightly less than 1% per year during 2000 and 2001. The long term also strongly suggests a flatness in volume demand.

For real estate agents and managers, the corporate emphasis on lean operations and cost reduction will continue to result in fewer employment opportunities, in fewer company transfers and, therefore, fewer sales of existing homes. Competition will continue to put pressure on commission rates, squeezing the incomes of agents and managers.

One of the major risks to real estate agents is interest rate. When rates rise, new housing sales slow or decline. This reduces sector employment or starts a contraction in the industry. The same risk holds for non-residential building operators. Higher interest rates squeeze some tenants and put a portion of their revenue at risk.

One supporting factor in the industry is mobility of families in the United States. Employment transfers and general movement around the United States has been very commonplace. The real estate industry has been a big benefactor of today's mobile workplace. Just about every time a home is sold or purchased, a real estate agent is involved in some form. As the U.S. labor market maintains its flexibility, look for real estate services to be on the receiving end in a beneficial way.

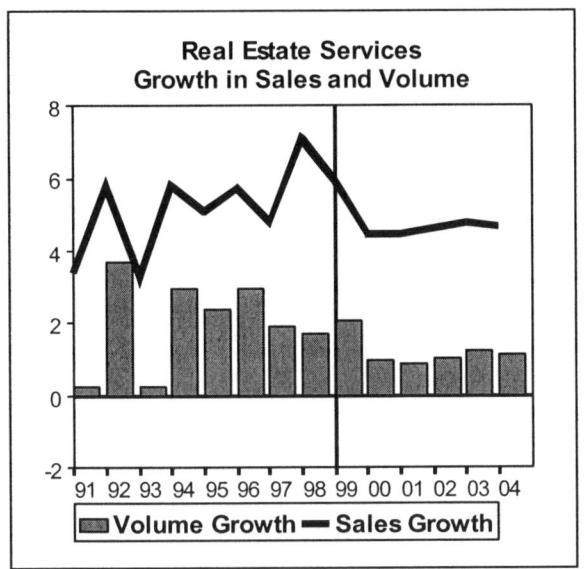

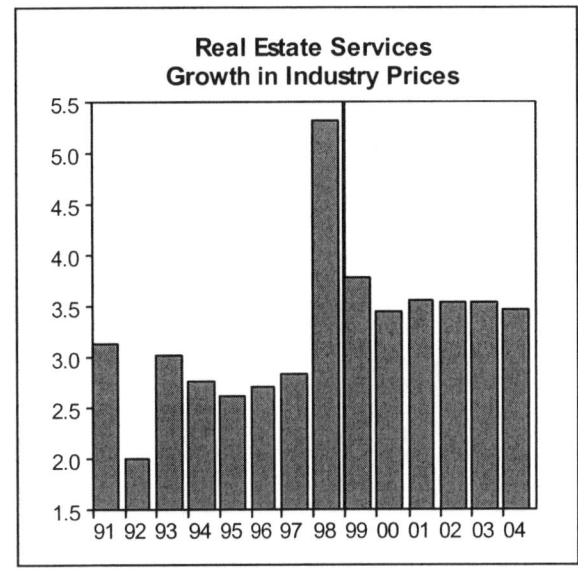

Real Estate Services

SIC 65

		1992	1993	1994	1995	1996	1997	1998	1999	2000	2001	Compound Average 88-98	Annual Growth 98-08
Sales													
	Billions of $	970	1002	1060	1114	1178	1234	1322	1401	1463	1529		
	% Ch	5.8	3.3	5.8	5.1	5.7	4.8	7.1	5.9	4.5	4.5	5.5	4.5
Volume													
	% Ch	3.7	0.2	3.0	2.4	2.9	1.9	1.7	2.1	1.0	0.9	2.0	1.0
Prices													
	% Ch	2.0	3.0	2.8	2.6	2.7	2.8	5.3	3.8	3.4	3.6	3.4	3.5
Production Costs													
Avg. Hourly Earnings													
	$/hr	10.82	11.35	11.83	12.32	12.79	13.33	14.06	14.61	15.14	15.70		
	% Ch	4.1	4.9	4.3	4.1	3.8	4.2	5.4	3.9	3.6	3.7	4.5	3.5
Input Price Index													
	% Ch	1.7	4.0	2.6	4.4	2.9	3.9	3.8	3.4	3.2	3.2	3.6	3.3

Chapter 29: Services

Hotels

The hotel service sector is an $878 billion industry in the United States. Dependent on both business and leisure patrons, the industry has historically known volatile profit margins, the result of the mixture of cyclical occupancy rates with high-fixed costs. The domestic-hotel industry has been consolidating recently, with an accelerating pace of both mergers and acquisitions. Marked improvements in its "breakeven occupancy" rate, coupled with strong demand for hotel services, have helped the industry experience exceptional profits over the past several years.

Demand

Solid personal-income growth due to the consistent expansion of the U.S. economy and accompanying stock market gains is providing for a strong year for the U.S. hotel industry. The number of domestic-person trips will expand over 7% this year. This will translate into a sales-volume increase of over 5%, as the majority of trips will involve a hotel stay. Travel to Europe from the United States has been temporarily subdued in 1999 as a result of the Kosovo crisis, which resulted in containing a larger share of U.S. resident accommodation expenditures to the domestic market.

Travel to the United States has not been as robust this year. Economic downturns in Latin America have stifled arrivals from Brazil and Argentina for the first six months of 1999. The beginnings of recovery in Asia have stopped the severe decline of Asian visitors to the United States, but it will be at least another year before the numbers climb back to where they were in mid-1997.

However, the vast majority of U.S. hotel demand is from U.S. resident leisure and business travelers. As a result, hotels have experienced solid growth in profitability in the last seven years, measured by both occupancy rates and room rates.

Supply Conditions

The hotel industry has been consolidating aggressively through mergers and acquisitions in recent years, with M&A climbing to $33.4 billion in 1998 from $11.2 billion in 1997. This has contributed to a drop in the average occupancy rate at which a hotel's expenses and revenues are equal. This rate, known as the "breakeven occupancy" rate, has consistently declined over the past five years.

The decline in the breakeven rate reflects a containment of fixed costs and other efficiency gains, as well as higher prices. Room rates have risen at a rate well above that of overall inflation over the last three years, while the industry's input costs have risen more slowly. Another factor that has contributed to lowering the breakeven rate for the industry is a shift in emphasis to room revenue from revenue from lower margin operations, such as food and beverages.

The decline in the breakeven occupancy rate, combined with exceptional demand and profitability, has sparked a new construction spree. While demand growth is expected to continue, occupancy rates are likely to fall a bit, as the increase in supply (through new construction) will outpace demand growth by a small margin.

Outlook

Revenue growth will slow slightly in 1999, as foreign demand remains stagnant and prices increase at a slower rate. However, domestic demand remains strong and the medium-term outlook for inbound tourism to the United States is robust. Over the forecast period, WEFA expects continued strong demand, slightly declining occupancy rates, and continued profitability. The FAA (Federal Aviation Agency) projects overall enplanement growth—a measure that includes domestic travel—of approximately 4.5%, which translates into an additional 100 million trips through US airports. Foreign-visitor arrivals contracted almost 3% in 1998. WEFA forecasts this market to regain some of these losses with 1.3% growth in 1999. However, the United States will experience steady international demand in the new millennium, with arrivals averaging over 3.5% growth on an annual average basis.

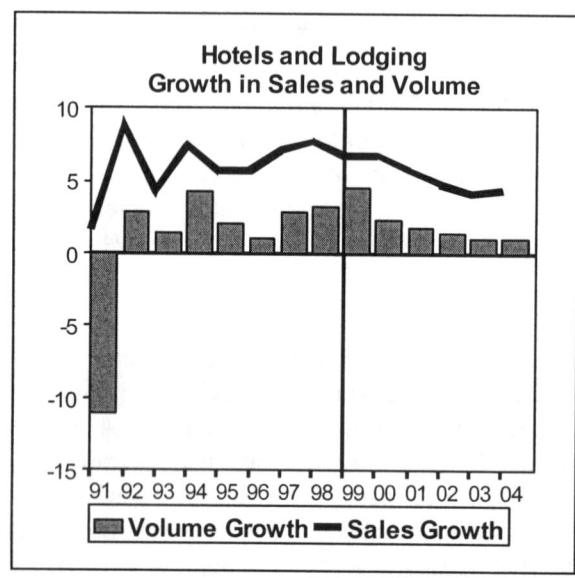

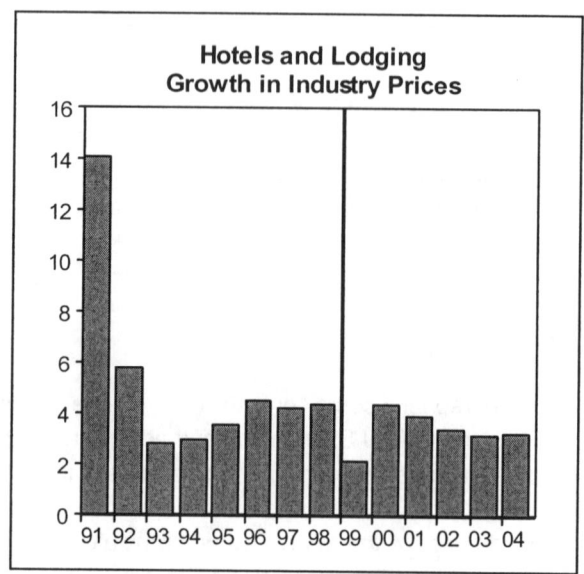

Hotels and Lodging

SIC 70

		1992	1993	1994	1995	1996	1997	1998	1999	2000	2001	Compound Average 88-98	Annual Growth 98-08
Sales													
	Billions of $	56.16	58.59	62.93	66.49	70.29	75.32	81.15	86.61	92.50	97.85		
	% Ch	8.8	4.3	7.4	5.7	5.7	7.2	7.7	6.7	6.8	5.8	5.8	5.0
Volume													
	% Ch	2.8	1.5	4.3	2.1	1.1	2.8	3.3	4.5	2.4	1.8	0.2	1.5
Prices													
	% Ch	5.8	2.8	3.0	3.5	4.6	4.2	4.3	2.1	4.3	3.9	5.6	3.4
Production Costs													
Avg. Hourly Earnings													
	$/hr	7.38	7.57	7.76	7.94	8.16	8.56	8.93	9.21	9.54	9.88		
	% Ch	3.3	2.6	2.4	2.4	2.8	4.8	4.3	3.1	3.6	3.6	3.3	3.5
Input Price Index													
	% Ch	2.6	1.9	1.3	4.1	2.5	2.6	1.7	1.8	2.6	2.6	2.8	2.7

Business Services

Business services are an extremely broad and encompassing sector of the economy that includes everything from photofinishing laboratories to security systems to trade-show arrangement. The largest and most rapidly growing categories within the sector are the computer-related services industries, including Internet-related companies. Other industries that are growing at a rapid pace include credit-reporting agencies, personnel supply services, building services, and miscellaneous equipment rental and leasing.

Apart from computer and data processing services, the largest category of business services is personnel-supply services, which include employment agencies (about $4 billion in revenues per year) and temporary help agencies (about $26 billion in revenues per year). Building services ($10 billion) and advertising ($8 billion) follow in size.

WEFA expects demand growth for the business services industry to exceed the general U.S. industry average over the forecast horizon. Prices should also increase by more than the overall inflation rate.

Demand Conditions

Computer programming and other computer-related services remain one of the growth leaders of the business-service industry. Their unprecedented growth has touched all aspects of industrial manufacturing, services, and the U.S. economy. Customized and prepackaged software, as well as computer and integrated systems design are included in this category. The growth of companies such as Microsoft, Netscape, Novell, Adobe, and America Online is evidence of how large this field has become. In addition, computer-hardware support and maintenance has grown in response to the specialization of many service areas. Cost-reducing pressures have led to cutting full-time employment positions and outsourcing as much as possible. This has also led to the growth of many other areas such as consumer credit and reporting, direct mail, secretarial, building cleaning and maintenance, and other types of services. There are a number of other benefits to outsourcing that make these industries grow.

- Outsourced contracts usually cost less than hiring an internal full-time staff.

- Outsourcing usually goes toward firms that specialize in particular areas of business. Specialization is a way of increasing efficiency.

- There is minimal expense in eliminating outsourced services.

With the intense pressure to reduce costs, we expect that the business-service industry will continue to see excellent growth in real terms. WEFA looks for an average annual pace of 3.9% through our forecast period. The proportion of U.S. workers who are employed by business-service firms will continue to rise. This should happen even if overall-employment growth slows or declines. The trend toward greater use of outsourced services will be standard corporate-business practices.

Employment agencies have also experienced major growth in renascence in recent years. The tight labor market in 1998 and 1999 has made many small firms scramble for employees. This has kept many headhunters and employment agencies extremely busy. Many agencies focus on hot areas of the labor market, such as computer-processing professionals, or they find other ways to provide value to clients. Competition within the industry remains intense and 1999's strong demand for specialized personnel has led to aggressive tactics.

The advertising sector remains strong in selected areas. Robust markets in both the real estate and employment sectors have led to significant gains in newspaper ads. Classified ads should also do well in 2000 and again in 2001. However, while continued growth is expected in newspaper advertising in the years just ahead, the rate of growth will be slowing. Look for more modest advances in the years just ahead.

Supply Factors

The supply of business-service firms will continue to expand as the demand for outsourced jobs continues to grow. As the demand for temporary employees becomes more specialized, more technical, and more professional, the need for business-service firms to provide training for employees will increase.

Outlook

The nature of the American workplace has changed. Emphasis on productivity and cost reduction has been relentless for at least a decade. However, the "Year 2000 Problem" (Y2K) with computer programs offered opportunities in the outsourcing and specialized business-service industry in 1999. Whether there will be residual interest in 2000Q1 remains to be seen. However, there should be a substantial slowdown in the employment growth of these services in 2000 and 2001.

Therefore, look for somewhat of a changed business environment in the next millennium.

The key risk for the business-service industry is economic in nature. The strength of the employment market drives the demand for many specialized business services. Both employment and temporary-help agencies are provided to numerous industries and types of business, so anything that slows employment growth is likely to negatively impact business services. Higher wages would slow business demand for workers, as would higher interest rates. The same can be said for advertising: anything that slows the economy and employment growth is likely to have a negative impact on advertising expenditures. The automobile industry and retailing are important segments of demand for advertising services, and both are quite sensitive to overall consumer and economic trends. These business segments have grown over 13% in 1998 and 8% in 1999. Further growth deceleration to the 7% range is likely in both 2000 and 2001.

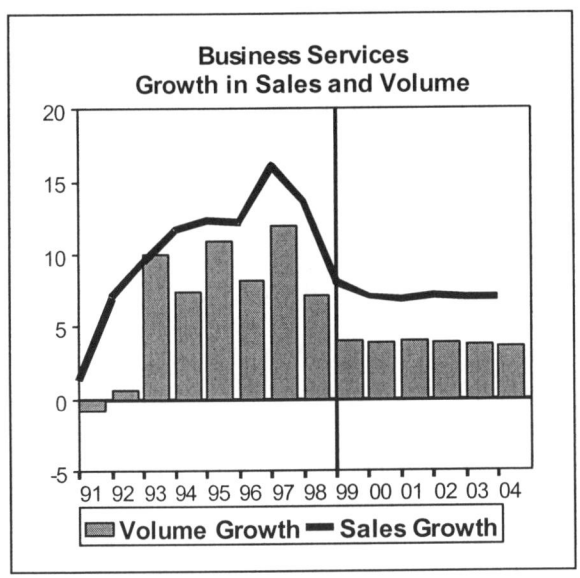

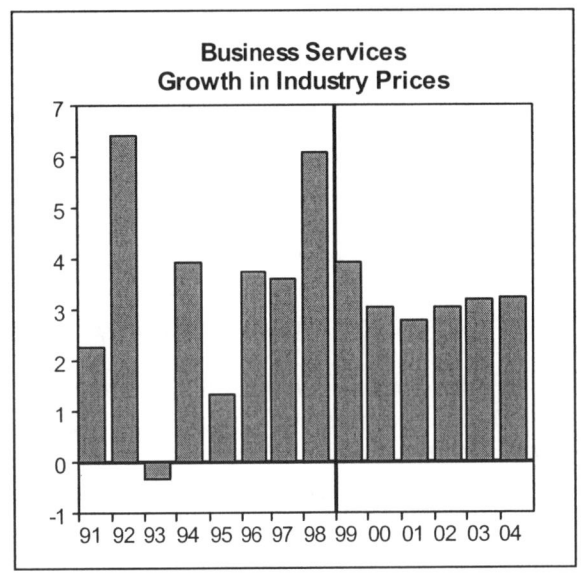

Business Services

SIC 73

		1992	1993	1994	1995	1996	1997	1998	1999	2000	2001	Compound Average 88-98	Annual Growth 98-08
Sales													
	Billions of $	312.0	341.9	381.7	428.9	481.2	558.2	634.3	685.4	733.8	783.9		
	% Ch	7.0	9.6	11.6	12.4	12.2	16.0	13.6	8.1	7.1	6.8	10.4	7.2
Volume													
	% Ch	0.6	9.9	7.4	10.9	8.1	12.0	7.1	4.0	3.9	3.9	6.7	3.8
Prices													
	% Ch	6.4	-0.3	3.9	1.4	3.8	3.6	6.1	3.9	3.0	2.8	3.4	3.3
Production Costs													
Avg. Hourly Earnings													
	$/hr	9.97	10.12	10.31	10.70	11.22	11.82	12.55	13.11	13.51	14.07		
	% Ch	2.2	1.5	1.9	3.8	4.9	5.3	6.1	4.5	3.0	4.2	3.8	3.8
Input Price Index													
	% Ch	2.2	1.3	1.8	2.9	1.8	1.8	2.2	2.1	2.5	2.6	2.3	2.7

Computer Programming, Data Processing, and Related Services

The computer programming industry is comprised of companies that provide computer programming services on a contract or fee basis. Such companies often provide additional services including software design and analysis, modification to custom software, and training of clients.

Companies that provide computer processing and data preparation services are included in the data-processing industry. Data-processing services could include partial or full preparation of reports, data entry, or timesharing of computers. The existence of these separate industries illustrates that participating firms can often perform specialized business services for clients more cheaply than the clients can in-house. Economies of scale and specialization are two reasons that outsourcing such operations often present cost savings for the firm.

The computer programming and data processing service industries have developed more fully over the last decade. Future growth is contingent on continued corporate outsourcing and on business' need for technical assistance. Companies will seek expertise with purchase decisions and support and training functions, as the world of hardware and software becomes increasingly complex. Preparations for the Year 2000 gave a substantial boost to the programming market: demand for software fixes increased before the new millennium. For the combined industry, WEFA expects revenue gains of nearly 15% in 1999, gradually slowing in 2000, and settling into a mature growth rate near 8%.

Demand Environment

The 1980s saw rapid growth in contract programming, but some of this was supplanted in the early 1990s by prepackaged software. This change echoed the hardware evolution that continues to bring more and more powerful desktop computers into offices and enables functions formerly possible only on mainframe computers. Nonetheless, the computer programming and data-processing businesses remain healthy. By industry estimates, customized software, or programming services, took the largest share of the overall software industry in 1998. Several important trends are at work to keep programmers busy.

- First, to hire permanent staff to keep current with rapidly changing technology is expensive. Often it is cheaper to contract programming and data processing work outside the company. This would include payroll as one example. Many information technology (IT) professionals now work on a consultant basis to client companies.

- Second, the widespread deployment of electronic mail and networked computers has increased the need for computer systems expertise. Only the largest firms can justify this as an internal cost.

- Third, January 1, 2000. In the new millennium, many existing computer programs had the potential to malfunction due to a programming convention that drops the "19" from four-digit dates to conserve computing memory. This "time bomb" boosted the short-term demand for programmers.

- Finally, as businesses increase communication, supply chain management, and other transactions with partners, IT will only become more important. In turn, support and other programming and data services needs are increased.

There is a force counteracting the boost that new software will lend the computer programming, data processing, and related services. The increased sophistication and range of industry-specific applications, including computer-assisted design (CAD), engineering tools, and graphic user interfaces, have also slowed demand for custom-programming services. Growth in prepackaged software will not let up. We imagine a wealth of new directions and niche markets for software to address. On balance, circumstances that require specialized knowledge provided by these service industries will sufficiently expand to produce growth. WEFA expects strong revenue gains for the combined data-processing and custom-programming industry in the neighborhood of 15% in 1999.

As the world leader in the field, U.S. custom programmers are also in demand overseas. The export of these services continues to offer excellent prospects. In 1999, much of the external demand may have been due to Year 2000 (Y2K) preparations. In general, these were thought to be progressing more slowly overseas than domestically. The tight domestic supply of capable programmers put a cap on growth, however.

Demand for timesharing services—including sharing processing power and storage—has decayed. Networking hardware and software has supplanted this need. Some of this lost business may be redirected to other parts of the combined industry: A switch from timesharing may be a switch to outsourcing of an entire data-processing function. The outsourcing decision is not without hassle. In lieu of production issues, managerial resources, quality control, and other issues arise.

Supply Factors

In the mid-1990s, it was estimated that there were more than 4,000 companies and many more sole proprietorships in the United States offering computer programming and related services. Since this business requires a relatively small capital outlay, there are few barriers to new market entrants. However, small start-up operations also have high failure rates, due to intense competition and small emergency funds in reserve.

During the same time period, about 7,000 data-processing services were in operation. These ranged in size from one-person shops to corporations employing several hundred people. The dynamic environment created by rapidly changing technology has allowed both industries to support a great number of companies, including many of small sizes. Constant pressure from clients to contain prices will keep competitive pressure keen. Data processing services areas will be particularly

affected. Industry consolidation may occur if the pace of technology slows, in order for companies to maximize efficiency.

In the run–up to the Year 2000, the supply of programmers and IT professionals became quite tight. Employment in the total U.S. computer programming and data services industry grew by an annual average of 9% in the past ten years, and by 13.5% in 1998. The active labor market was due, at least partially, to programming readiness for the Year 2000.

The Year 2000 Problem

In the past, computer programmers used a two-digit dating convention to conserve memory. This had the potential to malfunction at the turn of the century, when computers began to read 00 instead of 99. Solving the Y2K problem required either repairing old software and hardware, or replacing them with new products capable of handling the Year 2000 correctly. One solution was to accelerate purchase of new software and hardware. The other involved fixing existing products. The latter relied more heavily on custom programming services.

Correspondingly, the market was quite tight in 1998–1999 for domestic programming expertise. Over the past ten years, computer-programming employment grew by a compound annual rate of 11.5%, compared with growth in business services employment as a whole of 6.3% over the same period. In 1998 alone, computer-programming employment jumped by 15%. Wages have also been bid up. A post-2000 letdown in demand for programmers may also occur. This would especially affect programmers who specialize in older programming languages.

Key Forecast Trends

Despite the trend toward standardization and pre-programmed software, business continues to turn to outside programming and data processing professionals. It has simply become too expensive for some, particularly smaller concerns, to afford the staff and constant training required to keep pace with ever-changing technology. Labor markets for programmers are also very tight, which makes outsourcing more attractive, as well as detours around the bottlenecks of recruiting and hiring.

This industry is likely to face some softening in pricing power over the next ten years. Firms typically find it somewhat more difficult to negotiate down the cost of purchased services as compared to goods, and the tight labor markets crucial to these industries adds to upward wage pressure. However, pressure to cut costs has pervaded even the programming and data processing industries. Faced with cost-conscious clients, consolidation among programming and data processing companies will increase economies of scale and ultimately lend help to the bottom line.

Outlook and Forecast Risks

Payroll and other data processing functions for business are highly dependent on the state of the economy. A growing economy means a greater number of payroll checks, invoices, and business. The U.S. economy is expected to see close to 2.5% growth per year on average over the next five years. This represents a slowdown compared with the last five years. Growth in the data-processing industry is likely to follow suit. Custom programming will mature in growth also, but is a bit more independent of economic ups and downs.

Longer term, corporate computing via networks and communication via the Internet may present a risk to the health of the data processing and programming industries. Heightened user friendliness and shaved costs of networking and web functionality may coax companies to bring outsourced work back in-house. The skills gap would need to be closed and a greater pool of workers with appropriate technical skills would need to be available for this eventuality to occur.

Computer Software and Networking

This industry includes establishments engaged in the design, development, and production of prepackaged computer software. The software typically takes one of three forms: operating system software, which determines how a computer operates; applications software, including word processing, spreadsheet and e–mail programs; and utility software, which is designed to perform support functions for operating systems and/or applications. This software can be used on computers from personal (PCs) to mainframes.

Computer software and networking are rapid-growth businesses in the United States and worldwide. Preparations for the Year 2000 programming bug lent additional short-term support to software and networking demand. Some of this extra growth is borrowed from sales that would have occurred after January 1, 2000. WEFA expects strong gains of nearly 15% in 1999, a somewhat slower year in 2000, transitioning into a more mature rate of growth in the high 7%-to-8% range thereafter.

Demand

Prepackaged software sales have grown explosively in recent years, along with the dramatic gains in the speed and memory capabilities of personal computers (PCs). Prepackaged software is written for mass distribution. Total worldwide revenue for packaged software in 1998 is estimated between $130 and $140 billion, which indicates a double-digit increase from a year earlier.

Applications

Word-processing, spreadsheet, and e-mail applications were designed for the workplace. E-mail, in particular, however, has transcended this role and is prevalent market-wide. Games and reference software are typically designed for home use, and subject-specific and skill-enhancing software is marketed to schools.

Many businesses have decided that writing software programs in house is not cost effective. Thus, these businesses add to prepackaged software demand. Packaged applications specific to financial or human-resource functions are widely available. Enterprise resource planning (ERP) software, which includes these two functions plus many others, is another choice for business. SAP's R/3 and PeopleSoft are ERP software examples. Computer-Aided Design (CAD), other engineering applications, and supply-chain-management software offer packaged solutions to address target-market needs. On the negative side, however, software

has been penetrating the market rapidly. Many users now own the bulk of the computer and software capability they need. Future growth will depend more heavily on new product development and the entrance of computing into new business areas. The large replacement market will also be a force in the industry.

Increasingly, personal or desktop computers can perform tasks once feasible only on larger minicomputers or mainframes. As PCs have become more powerful, software sales to mainframe and minicomputer users have stalled. The most important applications for these larger computers have been accounting and database-management varieties. Reorientation of mainframes to a role in client/server technology has stimulated sales of mainframe software for this application. The proliferation of networks raises demands for packaged software makers to offer products able to run in varied operating systems and network configurations. Networking is also a boon to PC-utility vendors: networked PCs require additional functionality to harness maximum efficiency.

Database management software, used to store and manipulate data records, continues its strength. Oracle8, Sybase, and DB2 are popular database-management products.

In the home and school markets, the lines between entertainment and educational software are blurring. Entertainment software sales are often lumpy, whereas those to education present a more stable cash flow.

Synergy between the two camps makes business sense and is a natural fit: entertainment software vendors feel pressure to increase the educational content of games, and educational software makers are trying to reach younger audiences.

Operating Systems

In the PC market, the transition of most users from Microsoft's Window 3.x to Windows 95/98 and Windows NT operating systems continues to generate demand for software products that provide consistent applications and utilities. Computer viruses, often transmitted via e-mail, have gained in frequency and visibility, as they have become a more pervasive problem. This has translated into a boon to sales of virus-checking programs and diagnostic utilities. The large installed base of Microsoft Windows users provided a ready market for these conversions and upgrade products, and Year 2000 compatibility issues accelerated short-term sales.

In the client-server market, network-operating systems (NOS) enable sharing of files, applications, and network devices—such as printers, faxes, and modems, and other protocols. As such, servers and network-operating systems form the backbone of many corporate environments. In networks of PCs, Novell's NetWare has a large installed base; however, Windows NT and UNIX are the large players. When Windows NT and UNIX are compared, Windows NT has the advantage of a lower price tag. UNIX is widely installed on hardware other than PCs, especially workstations and servers, and is preferred for its robustness, which is a necessity for high-capacity hardware. The large number of applications and communications UNIX supports is another benefit. Linux is a UNIX-based entrant to the operating-systems market, with a small, although rapidly growing, market share. It is popular with Internet Service Providers as an operating system to host Web servers. Operating system, Windows 2000, is on the horizon.

During the recession of the early 1990s, business continued to invest in new software, particularly in that which it believed would reduce costs or in some way make the firm more competitive. Economy-wide pressure to contain costs, along with the pressure on profits produced by low inflation, have not eased. Instead, these pressures have intensified, creating a steady demand for software that is perceived to enhance productivity.

The real question is whether technology will ever sit still long enough for the market to mature. Each time it appears that the market for a current application is becoming saturated, new applications and expanded-hardware capabilities pull the industry in yet another exciting direction.

Supply Factors

The United States is a leader in the development and production of original software. Competition among prepackaged software makers has not receded, and the price of hardware continues to fall dramatically. These developments have allowed considerable price reductions on commercial software. One method of surviving in this competitive environment is for companies to merge or participate in joint ventures or other combinations. The result is that the software industry is becoming more concentrated over time. One example is the situation in the home- and school-software markets. Entertainment, media, and cable-TV giants are becoming a bigger presence in the entertainment software market. Small vendors are increasingly turning to merger and acquisition activity to compete against the deep coffers and brand-name leverage of these heavyweights.

Downward price pressure on software and networking products will continue. The correlation between hardware and software prices illustrates the similarities between the two industries. In both cases, each new wave of technology causes the price of the old to tumble. Such variability in the ground rules makes doing business in such industries treacherous.

The Year 2000 Problem

The Y2K computer programming problem occurred because computer programmers have, in the past, often used only two digits to represent the date in computer programs. This practice began in the early days of computing, when memory and storage space were scarce and expensive. When the year 1999 turned to year 2000, however, the two digits for the year changed from 99 to 00. Many computer programs, including those embedded in hardware, could have performed incorrectly or even failed when presented with this change. Almost any piece of software or hardware that deals with dates or time could have been at risk.

Much of the early concern about software centered on the so-called "legacy code" written in the 1960s and 1970s, primarily in languages like COBOL. This software is still in use in many organizations. More recently, hardware issues also surfaced as a Y2K concern. The so-called "embedded chip" problem could have affected devices ranging from process controllers in an oil refinery to programmable coffee makers.

Solving the Y2K problem required either repairing old software and hardware, or replacing these with new products that would handle the Year 2000 correctly. Both possible solutions were expensive and required significant engineering, programming and management resources. Repairing old software is labor-intensive and relies on scarce programming skills. On the other hand, replacing large, software systems requires time, budgetary and managerial allocations. Any fixes subsequently call for extensive testing. Such preparations were necessary, but subtracted from profitable activities of the firm.

Many organizations chose the latter option, where possible, and accelerated hardware and software purchases to fall before the new millennium. The information-technology industry may see a corresponding slowing of growth in 2000 as firms absorb the new technology purchases of 1998 and 1999.

Outlook and Risks

Technology continues to expand at a dizzying pace. The path toward convergence of PCs and TVs, the infusion of the Internet into business and the consumer domain, and the growing hand-held computing segment are forces driving the development of software and networking into the 21st century.

Corporations will continue under their mandate to cut costs in order to remain competitive. Firms will also increase the amount of information sharing and other communication between the firm and its partners. These trends will insure the health of the software and networking industries. As the market for computers becomes more saturated, savvy software producers must stay on the leading edge of what the market wants in order to prosper. Where software and networking industries can enable advances in business productivity or efficiency, they will gain revenue.

The Internet offers tremendous business potential as e-commerce expands. The number of people worldwide who access the Internet from home or business at least once per week was pegged at 147 million last year and is expected to top 300 million by next year. Still, this is a fledgling business in terms of software development. The Internet is also a natural forum for software sales: electronic sales of software in 1998 was estimated at $3.5 billion dollars by the International Data Corporation. This figure is forecasted to see exponential growth in the next three to four years. With the expansion of electronic commerce, the issue of Internet security has been brought to the forefront. Internet security is another fledgling market from the perspective of software development. Such windows of development opportunity should be recognized and seized quickly, however, because they will not remain open for long.

In the past, risks to the software business have been industry-centric, rather than dependent upon an economic cycle. The benefits of computerization were thought valuable enough that firms were inclined to move forward with hardware and software purchases despite a soft economy. Due to increasing computer penetration, the marginal benefits of new technology may be smaller now. Therefore, a future recession may have a more pronounced effect on the markets for hardware and software, as customers find it easier to delay new purchases. This would create a more cyclical industry than we have seen to date.

The most serious risks to companies in these industries are the speed and the bumpy path of technological change. For example, operating systems can generate a wave of migration to new platforms when these are released. The same might be true of new versions of popular-application suites. Substantial business losses may be incurred by delaying a new product, entering the market even slightly too late to capitalize on a new trend, or by remaining concentrated in older technology, which sells at a steep discount.

Equipment Leasing

Leasing is a method of obtaining the use of an asset without actually owning the asset. The length of time and cost involved in a lease agreement is predetermined. Finance leases and operating leases are the two most common methods. In a finance lease, the leasing company recovers all costs incurred plus a rate of return, with the lessee responsible for maintenance, taxes and insurance. Operating leases are usually short term, and the lessee acquires the use of equipment for a small portion of its economic or useful life. Other variations include: the leveraged lease, where the leasing company provides an equity portion of the equipment cost and lenders provide the balance; and the sale-leaseback, where a leasing company purchases equipment from the company that owns and uses it and then leases it back to that company.

Leasing volume in 1998 was estimated to be between $180–$185 billion. The top-50 U.S. bank-affiliated leasing companies reported assets of $82.6 billion in 1998, an increase of 22.4%. Equipment leasing volume will expand at a faster pace than overall investment in new equipment. There are inherent advantages to leasing that companies will continue to take advantage of. Furthermore, we expect the strongest growth in the next decade to come in areas where leasing is already very prominent, such as computers.

Background

Roughly 80% of U.S. companies lease all or some of their equipment. One-third of all equipment acquired in a given year by business in the United States is through leasing. Leasing volume in 1998 was estimated to be between $180–$185 billion. Leasing can cover something as small as a fax machine and as large as a co-generation facility. Computers are the most commonly leased piece of equipment. Roughly 50% of all commercial aircraft are leased. Companies acquire equipment through leasing by: ordering equipment and then approaching a lessor for financing, working with an equipment vendor or manufacturer that has its own leasing subsidiary, or obtaining the equipment directly from a leasing company.

Leasing is particularly attractive to small and start-up companies that may not have the financial wherewithal to purchase equipment, since it allows for rental payments that are more in line with financial capability. It also provides access to equipment for companies that want to focus on their core business and view the ownership of certain types of equipment as distracting. Full-service leasing provides operational and maintenance support. Finally, leasing is also an excellent way to satisfy unusual equipment needs during peak periods of demand. Two common types of leases are the operating lease and the finance lease, but there are other leasing "products" as well.

- Capital Lease: A type of lease classified and accounted for by a lessee as a purchase and by the lessor as a sale or financing if it meets any one of the following criteria: (a) the lessor transfers ownership to the lessee at the end of the lease term; (b) the lease contains an option to purchase the asset at a bargain price; (c) the lease term is equal to 75% or more of the estimated economic life of the property; or (d) the present value of minimum lease rental payments is equal to 90% or more of the fair market value of the leased asset less related investment tax credits retained by the lessor.

- Finance Lease: A full-payment, noncancellable agreement, in which the lessee is responsible for maintenance, taxes, and insurance.

- Full-Payout Lease: A lease in which the lessor recovers, through lease payments, all costs incurred in the lease plus an acceptable rate of return, without any reliance upon the leased equipment's future residual value.

- Leveraged Lease: In this type of lease, the lessor provides an equity portion of the equipment cost (20%-40%) and lenders provide the balance on a nonrecourse debt basis. The lessor receives the tax benefits of ownership.

- Master lease: A contract where the lessee leases currently needed assets and is able to acquire other assets under the same basic terms and conditions without having to negotiate a new contract.

■ Net Lease: A lease wherein payments to the lessor do not include insurance and maintenance, which are paid separately by the lessee.

■ Open-End Lease: A conditional sale lease in which the lessee guarantees that the lessor will realize a minimum value from the sale of the asset at the end of the lease.

■ Operating lease: Any lease that is not a capital lease. These are generally used for short-term leases of equipment. The lessee acquires the use of the equipment for just a fraction of its useful life.

■ Sale-Leaseback: An arrangement whereby equipment is purchased by a lessor from a company owning and using it. The lessor then becomes the owner and leases it back to the original owner, who continues to use the equipment.

There are approximately 2,000 companies in the United States providing equipment leases. They include banks, independent leasing companies, and industrial finance companies. Equipment lessors own equipment worth between $400-$500 billion. Smaller companies tend to specialize in a certain type of equipment, but major leasing companies have a very broad equipment portfolio. Leasing companies are particularly active in the aircraft, computer and telecommunication, industrial and manufacturing, medical, construction and material handling, and rail and on-highway equipment markets. Captive leasing, that is leasing that is done by an arm of the equipment manufacturer, is common in agricultural equipment, construction machinery, commercial trucks and trailers, and office equipment.

The top-50 U.S. bank-affiliated leasing companies reported assets of $82.6 billion in 1998, an increase of 22.4%. This followed an increase in assets in 1997 of 24.6%. The top-five bank-leasing companies in 1997 were Citicorp Global EF ($8.3 billion), NationsBanc Leasing ($7.3 billion), First Union Leasing ($6.2 billion), Bank America Leasing ($4.8 billion), and KeyCorp Leasing ($4.7 billion).

The bank-affiliated leasing business saw some changes in 1998. Last year the top spot went to Bank America Leasing and Capital with assets of $12.8 billion. This company now includes the assets of NationsBanc Leasing. The number two spot went to Citigroup Global EF with assets of $10.5 billion, an increase of 26%. First Union remained in third place with assets of $7.4 billion, up 18.6%. Banc One leasing moved up from eight in 1997 to fourth last year with assets of $6.2 billion, an increase of 15.4%. Banc One now includes the assets of First Chicago and NBD leasing. Holding at number five was Key Equipment Finance with assets of $5.9 billion, an increase of 26.1%.

Among the top-50 U.S. bank-affiliated leasing companies, the biggest increases in assets in 1998 were reported by People's Capital & Leasing Corp., +441.7%; SunTrust Leasing, +137.6%; MBC Leasing, +83.6%; Citizens Leasing, +77.2%; and M&T Financial, +64.6%.

Other major non-bank leasing companies include GE Capital, Associates Commercial, AT&T Capital, Caterpillar Financial, Heller Financial, and Copelco Capital.

Outlook

WEFA forecasts that business spending for machinery and equipment will expand by over 9% this year, in real terms, to approximately $850 billion ($92). In the longer run, spending should grow by roughly 3% per year, on average, exceeding $1,100 billion by 2008.

■ We expect computers and related equipment to post the strongest increases during the next ten years, driven by declining prices and a steady stream of new and more capable products. Growth in communication equipment will remain healthy, driven by efforts in the public and private sector to improve voice and data communication systems. Spending for computers and communication equipment is expected to expand by over 7% per year.

■ The current buying cycle in commercial aircraft is winding down, and deliveries will decline for a few years beginning in 2000. However, another buying cycle will begin before the middle of the next decade triggered by pressure to replace older aircraft and expand the fleet in selected air corridors.

■ Replacement demand and the need to expand capacity to meet the growth in traffic will stimulate demand for commercial trucks and trailers during the next ten years.

- Rail-equipment purchases will be influenced by expanding traffic, technological change, and the need to improve rail-industry efficiency.

- Growth in spending for industrial equipment will reflect anticipated growth in manufacturing volume of about 3% per year, which will trigger some industrial capacity expansion.

- Finally, growth in corporate demand for passenger cars and spending for construction and farm equipment will be modest.

In real terms, equipment leasing volume will expand at a faster pace than overall investment in new equipment. There are inherent advantages to leasing that companies will continue to take advantage of. Furthermore, we expect the strongest growth in the next decade to come in areas where leasing is already very prominent, such as computers. Additional support will come from the aircraft, rail, and over-the-road transportation markets where leasing already plays a major role. In addition, there will be steady growth in the leasing of medical equipment. Technology is allowing the development of highly sophisticated diagnostic instruments, which usually carry a hefty price tag; and the population is aging and requiring more medical care. The result is that the demand for medical equipment will continue to expand at a healthy clip.

Equipment leasing is part of a global industry, with more than half of the business now conducted in Europe and Japan. The recent economic slump in Japan and many of the other Asian economies took a toll on leasing companies in those markets. However, over the long term, WEFA expects leasing activity outside of the United States to expand rapidly, driven by favorable world economic conditions.

Motion Pictures

The primary products of the motion picture industry are motion picture and videotape production. These products include theatrical and non-theatrical/animated motion pictures and videotapes for exhibition or resale through motion picture theaters, cable/satellite-TV distribution networks, and through home-video sales and rentals.

Financial capital requirements are huge in the industry and in addition to traditional means of raising capital, mergers and acquisitions are commonplace. Indeed, with the market for video entertainment of all kinds expanding rapidly, along with the bandwidth capabilities of major distribution channels, a substantial degree of vertical, as well as horizontal, mergers have taken place since the 1980s. Technological changes on the producer and consumer sides of the market have enhanced production capabilities, provided lower costs of production, yet enabled new entry and new forms of substitute-video entertainment to be developed and marketed. Rapid expansion of multiplex cinemas is enabling theater attendance and receipts to sustain their rebound, which has continued since 1993. Despite overseas financial turmoil, non-North American revenue remains a major source of growth.

Videocassette recorders (VCRs) have become a commonplace possession, and this level of market saturation implies an ongoing slowdown in growth of video sale and rental activity. Digital-video production, with enhanced video and audio quality, has revived the old videodisc concept into a digital format. A substantial degree of growth in this consumer appliance is expected to provide new revenues in the coming decade. Revenue in the movie industry as a whole (the total in these three formats) has climbed more vigorously than expected—by about 8% in 1997. Revitalized popularity of theaters, along with an increase in ticket prices, underlies recent gains. These strong advances, we expect, will moderate gradually during the next few years, and revenue gains will settle at around 5% per year.

The Market and Industry

The topic "motion pictures" conjures up many diverse images: Hollywood glitz and glamour; artistic interpretation of culture; political issues and censorship; and huge amounts of money made under vast commercial conglomerates. These are the ingredients for an almost magical world filled with publicity, but in all other ways, just another industry. Like any other industry, the motion picture industry is, as it always has been, driven by economic forces, as well as creative forces. Bringing new pictures to the movie market requires an environment that fosters the creative process and the development of concepts and stories. The structure of property rights is therefore critical to the initiation of movie production. But it is not just creative genius that turns stories into movies. It takes a substantial capital investment and assumption of risk to set the stage for production and to keep production in motion. A vast distribution network, composed of a variety of media, is necessary to bring the final product to market—to the buyers of entertainment, viewers. What viewers want to see, and how much they are willing to pay, and when they are willing to pay and view movies, exert an equally powerful, economic force on what is brought to the viewers, when it is brought, and through what channel. What viewers want to see is largely driven by cultural tastes and alternative forms of entertainment, and often sets the stage for the trend of movies produced.

Like any other industry, the motion picture industry has been and will continue to be affected by several important factors: (1) access to large amounts of capital, (2) technological change on both the production side and the consumer side of the market, (3) demographic trends, and (4) new entry and alternative forms of video entertainment. The movie-production business is characterized by large investments in fixed capital, much like automobile production. These investments extend from acquiring or sharing economic rights to the creative content as well as the investment in specialized physical and human capital. Like the automobile industry and other oligopolistic industries that are similarly characterized by high fixed costs, motion picture production tends to be fairly concentrated in a few large studios. The top six are: (1) Sony Pictures (formerly Columbia Pictures and distributors of TriStar); (2) The Walt Disney Company (Buena Vista, Touchstone, and Hollywood Pictures); (3) Twentieth Century Fox Studios, (4) Paramount (Viacom, Inc.); (5) Universal (MCA, Inc.), and Warner Brothers (Time-Warner, Inc.). Success in the industry requires three things: a wide-distribution network, access to large amounts of capital, and the talent or luck to know what the market wants at the right time. The fortunes of rival-film producers tend to bob around with some volatility. A few blockbuster movies become blockbuster hits; other attempted blockbusters are duds; and sometimes low-budget "sleeper" films achieve wide popularity and exceptional returns on investment. The unpredictability of this range of outcomes is considerable.

Technology has engendered enormous change in movie making. Without computers, the audio and video experience of *Star Wars*, the realistic existence of dinosaurs in *Jurrasic Park,* and the creative animation of *Toy Story* would not be possible. Computer production, editing, and data-transmission capabilities permit multi-location production of movie segments by highly specialized small companies that are unaffiliated with the major studios except through contracts. While enabling the production of more realistic and elaborate sets at lower cost, new digital technologies have created an infrastructure of independent production-support firms within the industry (e.g., Pixar). Technology has changed the consumer side of the market as well. Indeed, the ubiquitous ownership of televisions, videocassette recorder/players, and increasingly digital videodiscs, has clearly opened new distribution avenues in replay markets. Innovations in digital audio and videography have enabled movie makers to push creative horizons and develop movies best experienced in movie theaters.

Population growth and growing disposable incomes, particularly in suburban rings, have spawned the development of large multiplex-theater chains. Movie-going is historically cyclical in nature. Nevertheless, the trend towards large theater complexes, housing arcades, restaurants, etc. is a new trend. These facilities permit a high volume of consumer traffic to view several movies within the first-run release. Large multiplex-theaters are therefore in the economic interests of producers and distributors. Having many theaters under one roof, with perhaps more than one being allocated to an expected blockbuster, gives the movie producers a greater chance of financial success because more viewers can be packed into the same release period, or viewing window. At the same time, having a greater capability to show a variety of movies permits theater chains greater scope.

While most of the films distributed in these mega-theaters tend to be films produced by major or minor studios, many independent films are produced and distributed outside of the majors. These independents tend to be smaller, self-financed operations that accumulate film rights, produce films often by renting larger studios facilities, and distribute films through separate, distribution agreements. Some small independents have specialized in merely acquiring rights to scripts and forming libraries of film rights.

In coming years, much of the growth in movie audiences and revenues will be outside the United States. In this segment, U.S. films continue to do well. For theatrical films released by Motion Picture Association member companies, 1997 foreign receipts rose by 6% over 1996. Japan, even in recession, is the top-export market for American films. Japanese have cut back markedly on higher cost, leisure pursuits such as golf—but more of them than ever are going to the movies. This may illustrate the reputed countercyclical nature of the less-expensive parts of the entertainment business.

The portion of the industry that includes the sale (but not the rental) of video tapes had been demonstrating strong growth recently, with a banner year in 1996, when sales reached $5.7 billion. However, video sales increased by less-than 3% in 1997. Meanwhile, despite surging returns for the dominant Blockbuster chain, 1997 video rentals were nearly flat at $2.6 billion after $2.5 billion in 1996. Movie-video sales and rentals combined totaled about $8.4 billion on the year, compared to $8.2 billion in 1996. This represents a rise of barely over 2%, sharply slower than the video sales/rental category's 11% growth in 1996.

Essentially, complete-market penetration by VCRs is one factor limiting expansion of the videocassette–based segment of the motion picture industry. Increasing concentration in the rental sector also plays a role, as small independently run shops close. With respect to video sales, superstore retailers such as Wal-Mart have reportedly opted to devote less display space to this product. On the other hand, Blockbuster, the nation's largest rental chain, has concluded that video sales do not cannibalize rental business nearly as much as previously feared; the chain is expanding its offerings of for-sale movies. Video sales still have growth potential, given their increasing affordability and the convenience of repeat-play features.

While video sales and rentals were basically treading water in 1997, theaters were a hot item. Ten large companies operate about half the movie screens in the United States, yet this accelerating concentration trend is also bringing a robust expansion in cinema facilities. Multiplex theaters with up to 24 screens are being built at a rapid pace in many areas. United Artists is the largest chain by number of locations, with 333 theaters. But its hard-charging competitor AMC has now surpassed it in number of screens. AMC operates 230 cinemas with an aggregate 2,489 screens, compared to United Artists' screen total of 2,201.

1997's top-grossing movie was *Men in Black*, with $250 million in North American sales. *The Lost World: Jurassic Park* came in second, at $229 million. No other film cracked the $200 million mark. However, skewing these results is 1997's seventh-place finisher, *Titanic*, which soon became the highest-grossing movie of all time. *Titanic*, released at the very end of the year, tallied 1997 receipts of $124 million. Within a few months, this amount swelled past $500 million. *Titanic*'s revenues from outside North America will certainly exceed its domestic gross; it is a billion-dollar-plus film. *Titanic*'s highly promoted release on video, moreover, is expected to revitalize moribund sales figures in this category.

Outlook

Technological change in production, distribution, and consumer appliances will continue to drive the trends in the industry in the coming decade. Specialization on the production side will continue to permit growth in a network of smaller support firms. Larger studios and holding companies will continue to integrate forward (e.g. Disney's acquisition of ABC/Capital Cities), particularly in Internet distribution, in order to ensure outlets and audiences for growing amounts of video content. And the reason is clear: success requires audiences and the larger the audience, the greater the success. This is so obvious as to be trivial, but in the context of new consumer patterns of viewing, movie (and indeed all video) producers must be nimble to meet consumer tastes, but have sufficient content across segments to be profitable.

Shifts in consumer tastes among entertainment media are already telling. Growing online-computer habits are clearly causing a substitution of consumer time away from TV viewing and creating new video-market segments. Technological change in consumer appliances and services (HDTV broadcasting, digital videodiscs, videostreaming capabilities, and growing bandwidth to the home) will make dramatic changes in the kinds of video entertainment and motion pictures that are produced, and how and when they will be distributed. The outcome is quite uncertain. What is certain is that there will be substantial change in video production and viewing habits; but perhaps not so dramatic as to render traditional-distribution media obsolete. We have seen this before. When the video industry was new, it was feared that the rental or purchase of movies on video would hurt theaters, but it seems to have simply broadened the market. Despite broad-based availability of affordable video sales and rentals, theaters continue to set records. Enhancing theaters' profitability, they have successfully established higher price points for both tickets and concessions.

Current windowing, the sequencing of releases, follows the path of the highest marginal-revenue channel to the least. Theaters are typically the initial market for full-feature films and animations, which then go on to videocassette sales and rentals, premium channels on cable television, and then traditional television stations and syndications. Interestingly, major TV-broadcast networks have shown a tendency to purchase more high-priced, recent-release movie rights lately. They are apparently scrambling to compete with cable TV's plethora of entertainment offerings. Producing an ordinary weekly series is an expensive proposition for TV networks, yet the endeavor not infrequently flops with the viewing audience. Conversely, airing an almost-first-run hit movie, though costly, virtually guarantees high ratings and ad revenues. A key development will be whether and how windowing will change with the advent of new distribution technologies.

Cable television is an important distribution channel for movies and will continue to be. Cable by most estimates pass roughly 90-plus percent of homes in the US and have upwards of 70% subscription rates. Given cable's ability to restrict viewing of premium events, it represents a vast medium for movie distribution. Indeed, many cable owners have integrated backwards to acquire access to content and movie production. (Turner's acquisition of MGM's library serves as one example.) Similar arrangements have formed to develop specially produced movies for networks like HBO. Expansion in the cable television industry has increased the demand for new movies and allows many smaller producers to make movies that would not otherwise come into being. Close to 700 movies are produced annually in the United States—substantially more than before the advent of cable. But, by some analyses, movie companies may be shooting themselves in the foot with this very abundance. Production and marketing expenses for a feature film are enormous. The confluence of circumstances in which a movie grosses $100 million yet loses money now occurs more and more often. Possibly, a surfeit of films has resulted in audiences overlooking quality productions that would stand out to better advantage amid a leaner field of contenders.

Cable-based, pay-per-view options remain a threat to video rentals, but not yet a large one. Pay-per-view viewing prices are equal to, or often slightly above, those for video rentals. They offer the convenience of eliminating the trip to the video store, but they have the drawback of offering only a single viewing with no pause options. In order for pay-per-view to become a serious threat to video rental, either prices will have to come down or flexible viewing options will have to become more widespread.

Sales of theater tickets (both domestic and foreign) and videocassette sales and rentals combined grew by about 8% in 1997, with the strongest gains occurring at the theater box office. Both video sales and movie rentals performed weakly during the year. WEFA expects a modest recovery in these segments. Movie-video sales probably have the best prospects to re-establish moderate growth. Even though the percentage of US households owning VCRs will rise very little from the current level, people will continue to start or expand home-film libraries. We expect overall revenues of the movie industry (the total in the three formats) to follow a moderating growth trend in the next few years. The current rate will settle down toward 5% per year.

Health Services

The health services industry is one of the largest sectors of the US economy. After adjusting for inflation, consumer expenditures on healthcare services accounted for 14.0% of total consumer expenditures and 9.6% of Gross Domestic Product (GDP) in 1998. By comparison, total consumer expenditures on motor vehicles and parts accounted for only 3.4% of GDP. Employment in health services establishments totaled 9.9 million, or 7.9% of total establishment employment.

Health services spending can be broadly divided into four categories: professional services (including physicians, dentists and other health professionals), hospital services, nursing home services and insurance services. Hospitals account for just over a third of all healthcare spending, and professional fees account for another 35%–40%. Nursing homes and insurance costs account for shares in the single digits of total health services spending. (Note that insurance costs in the chart below are net of payments by insurance companies to providers.)

Demand for Healthcare

In the United States in the past 20 years, the demand for healthcare services has been growing rapidly. After accounting for inflation, health services spending grew at an annual average rate of 3.2% from 1978 to 1998, considerably above the 2.8% growth in total real consumption expenditures. As a result, healthcare spending is growing in importance in consumption and GDP and, consequently, has become a target of major policy initiatives.

Three factors have driven the rise in healthcare spending:

- The Federal role increasing. The Federal government or the state portion of the Medicaid program finances over half of all spending for medical care. Health care spending is, therefore, closely associated with US budget issues, and many of the risks to this industry's outlook are derived from efforts to reform the Federal medical entitlement programs.

- Technology. Medical research has progressed substantially in the recent past, providing cures for conditions that were fatal only a decade ago. The amazing ability of medical science to diagnose and treat illness has been accompanied, however, by a rise in expenses. Many of the new procedures and drugs are very costly.

- Demographics. Older people use medical care more. The average consumer aged 75 years and older

spends close to three times more on healthcare than the average 25-to-35-year old. As birth rates fall and technology extends people's lives, the proportion of Americans who are older is growing steadily.

The growth in demand for healthcare services has slowed during the very recent past. After growing between 1980 and 1992 by almost 4% per year, spending adjusted for inflation on healthcare services slowed to less than 2% per year from 1993 through 1996, and accelerated to just 2.2% in 1997 and 3.3% in 1998. The slowdown in the growth of the elderly population, as well as the massive changes in the industry are to blame. In the near future, the inflation-adjusted growth rate of spending for healthcare services will likely remain between 2.5% and 3.2% per year. In a few years, the impact of managed care will fade as the portion of the population aged 65 and over starts to rise more quickly. Technology and higher incomes will continue to drive spending in healthcare over the next 10 years.

Supply

Healthcare supply is divided into market segments: the supply of professional workers, the supply of hospital beds, and the supply of insurance and management services. In the 1980s, all sections expanded quickly as healthcare spending grew rapidly. Their fate in the 1990s, however, has differed.

Supply of Professionals

Perhaps more than in any other industry except education, the delivery of healthcare services demands highly trained professional workers. Physicians and nurses are the major categories of professional healthcare workers. The supply of other types of workers, including occupational and physical therapists and physician's assistants, are growing rapidly, but these workers still constitute a relatively small portion of the total professional workforce.

The number of physicians and nurses has been increasing quicker than the overall population. The number of practicing physicians grew by 3% to 3.5% in the 1970s and 1980s, although this growth has slowed to about 3% in recent years. (Figures for physicians by specialty are from the American Medical Association, *Physician Characteristics and Distribution in the US*, annual.) Most of the growth in the number of physicians has been in specialists.

The number of registered nurses has been growing faster than the number of physicians, averaging about 4% annual growth over the last twenty-five years. The growth in the number of nurses is slowing a bit, but remains in the still-rapid range of 3% per year, despite an increasingly unstable job market in hospitals.

Supply of Hospital Beds

The second major category of healthcare service is hospitals. Hospital capacity is usually measured by the number of hospital beds and by occupancy rates. The number of hospital beds fell significantly in the 1980s, and has continued to decline at a slower rate in the 1990s. The number of hospitals has also declined, but much more slowly, and the average size of each hospital has fallen.

The decline in the number of beds is a result of technology and pressure from health insurers. Both factors have contributed to turning inpatient procedures into outpatient procedures. Technological advances allow safer, less-invasive surgery, and quicker recovery from surgery. Insurers have questioned the length of stays generally required for many procedures, and in some cases, have refused to pay to keep a patient in the hospital for longer than the insurer's physician advisors believe necessary. As a result of these trends, both the number of procedures performed and spending on surgery and hospital procedures have risen at the same time the number of hospital beds has declined.

Of more immediate importance to the industry is the consolidation of hospitals (and, to some extent, professional practices) into larger provider networks. For hospitals, this generally occurs through mergers. The number of hospital mergers and joint ventures has accelerated in the past few years, as organizations rush to achieve economies of scale in providing healthcare services. The results are twofold: first, the number of independent, community hospitals is declining; and second, the line between for-profit and non-profit hospitals is becoming blurred. For-profit hospitals remain a small segment of the market, accounting for only about 10% of the revenues of all community hospitals. However, this number has been slowly growing and for-profit hospitals can be expected to continue to play a crucial role in the current shakeout of hospital capacity.

Insurers and Health Maintenance Organizations

Insurers and Health Maintenance Organizations (HMOs) play a unique role in the American healthcare system. These organizations pay much of the actual bill on behalf of consumers. Traditional insurance plans allow consumers to purchase healthcare from any provider. The consumer then either directs the provider to bill the insurance company, or requests reimbursement after paying the provider. In general, these plans allow the consumer freedom in choosing healthcare options.

HMOs typically provide services directly. These organizations may even have their own staffs of physicians and other professionals, and their own hospitals. In other cases, the HMO contracts with certain providers, and the consumer must obtain healthcare through those providers. HMO providers must follow specific rules in treatment and referral. HMO payments to providers may take the form of salaries, with bonuses for cost containment, or *capitation agreements*, in which the provider (hospital or professional partnership) agrees to a fixed-price-per-patient, regardless of the actual treatment.

There are also hybrid HMO-insurance schemes in which certain providers are preferred because they have contracted agreements, but consumers may obtain partial reimbursement for treatment by non-preferred providers, for example.

As noted above, less than 10% of total health services expenditures pay for the services of these organizations. This is measured as the difference between the revenues of the insurance companies and HMOs, and their payments to providers. These services include the cost of salaries and wages for the clerical, management, and professional workers in the companies (except those involved in direct patient care), rents and other expenses, and the profits of the insurance companies and HMOs.

Similar to the hospital market, the insurance market is divided between for-profit and not-for-profit providers. HMOs are mostly private, but some of the not-for-profit insurers have created HMO subsidiaries. HMOs have been expanding rapidly in recent years, and they have gained market share in both the private and public sector. In the private sector, HMOs have proven to be able to keep costs from growing quickly, and have thus attracted the attention of corporate purchasers of health insurance. The public sector has found HMOs to be useful cost controls in both the Medicare and Medicaid programs. Some elderly are now covered through Medicare payments to HMOs, a procedure that is designed to reduce costs to the federal government. States are moving aggressively to contract Medicaid services, especially those for poor families, to managed-care providers. There is evidence that this is both cheaper and results in better health outcomes for this population.

As in the hospital sector, the insurance/HMO sector has been undergoing consolidation. This has taken several related forms:

- Mergers between health insurers, including mergers between traditional-insurance companies and HMOs.

- The sale of not-for-profit health insurers to for-profit entities. This generally entails the creation of a foundation to hold and spend the surplus value earned by the not-for-profit partner in the transaction.

- The merging of roles as HMOs and traditional insurers begin to take on similar functions.

Pricing

Healthcare price increases have moderated in recent years, but now they may rise again. Managed-care organizations are facing pressures: doctors and hospitals want more money; patients are rebelling against restrictions on drugs and specialists and expensive new treatment techniques; and lawmakers are considering "patients' rights" bills that would make lawsuits easier. As a result of all of these pressures, healthcare costs for employers are expected to increase by 9% this year, according to William M. Mercer, Inc., a leading benefits consulting firm, after rises of 6.1% in 1998, 0.2% in 1997 and 2.5% in 1996.

Overall, reported medical-care inflation fell during the 1990s as health-maintenance organizations put the squeeze on doctors, hospitals and drug companies to lower costs (see **Figure 1**). While the quality of care might have declined as a result, no downward quality adjustments, which would have raised inflation, were incorporated in the consumer price index. Now, consumers have rejected many techniques that once controlled costs, such as restricting access to specialists. These types of limits are being gradually abandoned. Instead, new plans are being introduced that require co-payments from employees. This approach hands the spending decisions back to individuals, but is a form of cost-shifting that asks consumers to pay more for what they want.

Figure 1
Consumer Price Index for Medical Care

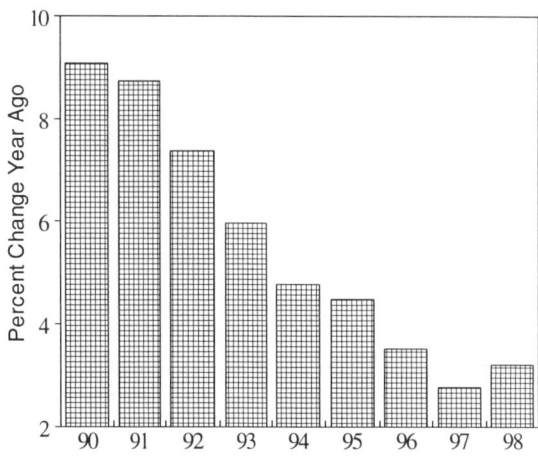

Medical spending accounts for about 14% of total output in the economy, but comprises just 4.7% of the consumer price index. Employers and government pick-up most of the tab, but the CPI is weighted by past consumer outlays, which typically include just deductibles, insurance, and "over-the-counter" self-treatment. Consequently, increases in medical costs will tend to squeeze profits, but their inflation impact will be under-reported in the overall consumer price index.

In the longer run, households will have to decide whether they are prepared to spend a bigger share of their disposable income on healthcare for the sake of unrestricted choice and the latest expensive technological advances. Employers, who through the 90s benefited from HMO cost cutting, will probably be unwilling to shoulder a return to rising employee healthcare costs of a magnitude that depresses profits.

Industry Structure

Changing Organization of the Healthcare Sector

The healthcare sector has traditionally been very fragmented, with professional partnerships, hospitals, managed-care companies, insurance companies and many others providing service, sometimes in overlapping pieces. The current wave of mergers among all types of health care organizations is creating two broad classes:

- *Healthcare provider networks* are based around hospitals. Often the lead hospital is a tertiary care and teaching facility in a large urban area, but a for-profit hospital chain may take this role as well. Through ownership and partnerships with community hospitals and professional practices, the network becomes a complete provider of all healthcare services, from simple family practice to the most complex surgical procedures. These large provider organizations can obtain the benefits of economies of scale in management and marketing.

- *Healthcare management organizations* are based around insurance or managed care organizations. Their purpose is to police the provider networks, insuring that costs are kept under control and quality is maintained.

WEFA expects the future to bring continued rationalization in the healthcare sector as provider networks and management organizations become larger and perhaps start to merge into enormous healthcare-supplier organizations. The industry is sufficiently fragmented that this process will take a considerable time.

In this streamlined healthcare system, the consumer, who is the final user of healthcare, remains removed from the provider. The consumer typically obtains health insurance from his or her employer, who has contracted with a management organization. The management organization, in turn, contracts with one or more provider-networks and pays the bills. As a result, the basic third-party payment problem, in which the users do not pay marginal cost, will remain a serious issue in healthcare.

Future structural changes in the industry will concentrate on this aspect of the industry. The healthcare management companies can be expected to intensify the following strategies to solve this problem:

- More careful review of payments.

- Oversight of providers' treatment decisions, and treatment guidelines based on cost. This will likely involve prohibiting certain procedures for certain people, essentially rationing healthcare.

- Additional co-payments by patients.

From the patient's perspective these actions cost more on an out-of-pocket basis, reduce the choice available to consumers, and substitute bureaucratic rule making for the traditional physician-patient relationship. The public will view such rationalization, therefore, as a deterioration in the quality of healthcare. This creates the largest risk in this industry: the risk that public pressure will increase government regulation and oversight of this entire sector.

The Important Role of Government

A major risk for the industry continues to be government regulation. The failure of the Administration's health proposal in 1994 probably doomed the idea of a major, systematic overhaul of the healthcare system. Nevertheless, the logic of cost reduction will continue to collide with political reality, as consumer/voters who are removed from the financial realities of healthcare perceive a deterioration in the quality of healthcare services.

Politics enters the health care industry in two ways:

- Both the state and federal governments heavily regulate healthcare. State-regulatory authorities include professional licensing boards, hospital authorities and insurance regulators. The Food and

Drug Administration and other organizations enter the scene at the federal level.

- State and federal governments pay a large portion of healthcare costs, and as a consequence, are important players in the market. For example, federal decisions about Medicare payment rates play an important role in medical services pricing. The movement by states toward managed care in Medicaid has had profound implications for the providers who serve this population.

Frustrated consumer/voters are likely to turn to the political process to prevent cost cutting from affecting the choice of physician and procedure inherent in the traditional insurance schemes. Pressure for government intervention in the industry can be expected to rise as more people enter HMOs. Predicting exactly how or when such intervention might occur is impossible. However, politics remains to be the most important risk facing the industry.

Outlook for Healthcare Services

Over the next ten years, spending for healthcare services will grow substantially faster than the economy. Healthcare services spending in 1992 dollars will be driven by the growing population of the elderly and continued adoption of new technology, and will average about the same rate of growth as in the past ten years. We estimate that the population aged 65 and over will grow at about 0.9% per year over the next ten years, and healthcare spending adjusted for inflation will grow 3.4%. "Usage intensity" (*per-capita* use of healthcare services) will therefore grow at about 2.5%, a rate similar to that seen in the past ten years.

Prices will be kept down in the near future by changes in the healthcare system. At an average rate of 3.5%, healthcare inflation will remain below the 3.9% rate recorded in the last ten years. Continued efforts by healthcare management companies to keep costs down will help put a lid on healthcare prices. The greater the ability of the management companies to control costs, however, the greater the risk of government intervention in the form of more regulation or a government-led reorganization of the industry.

Major Healthcare Sector Indicators: Annual
Percent Change

	1990	1991	1992	1993	1994	1995	1996	1997	1998	1999	2000
Real Consumer Spending on Health Services	4.7	3.1	4.0	1.3	1.0	2.0	1.7	2.2	3.0	2.7	3.2
Nominal Consumer Spending on Health Services	12.7	9.1	10.3	7.6	5.2	6.1	3.9	4.5	5.3	5.1	5.7
Medicare Spending	10.3	9.5	11.8	10.8	10.2	8.7	7.7	7.6	4.1	5.2	7.7
Medicaid Spending	20.2	32.4	21.1	13.4	9.0	8.9	6.5	6.9	3.7	8.4	11.6
Employment, Health Services Establishments	4.7	4.7	3.7	3.1	2.7	2.6	2.7	2.4	1.5	1.2	1.1
CPI, Medical Services	9.1	8.7	7.4	6.0	4.8	4.5	3.5	2.8	3.2	3.5	3.3

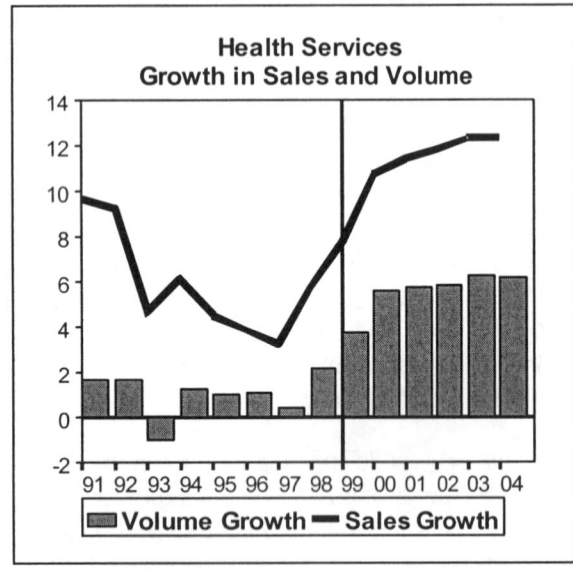

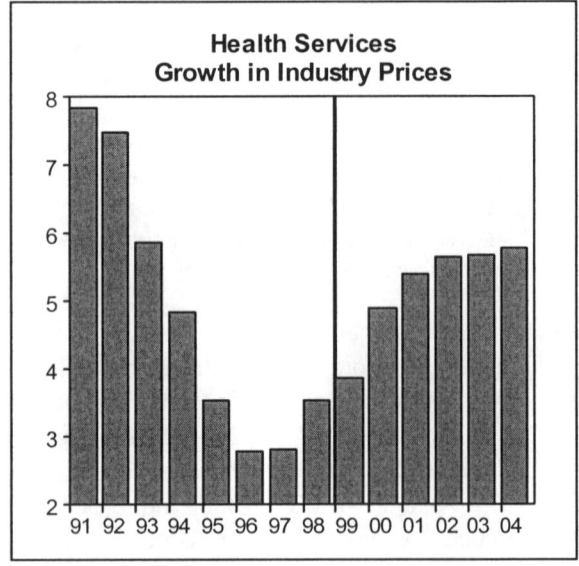

Health Services

SIC 80

		1992	1993	1994	1995	1996	1997	1998	1999	2000	2001	Compound Average 88-98	Annual Growth 98-08
Sales													
	Billions of $	544.7	570.5	605.5	632.9	657.5	679.0	718.1	774.0	857.3	955.3		
	% Ch	9.3	4.8	6.1	4.5	3.9	3.3	5.8	7.8	10.8	11.4	6.9	12.4
Volume													
	% Ch	1.7	-1.0	1.2	1.0	1.1	0.4	2.2	3.8	5.6	5.7	1.3	6.1
Prices													
	% Ch	7.5	5.9	4.8	3.5	2.8	2.8	3.5	3.9	4.9	5.4	5.5	5.9
Production Costs													
Avg. Hourly Earnings													
	$/hr	11.39	11.78	12.10	12.45	12.85	13.26	13.72	14.19	14.75	15.42		
	% Ch	3.9	3.4	2.7	2.9	3.2	3.2	3.5	3.4	3.9	4.5	4.1	4.4
Input Price Index													
	% Ch	2.1	2.1	2.0	3.2	2.1	1.7	1.7	1.7	2.7	2.8	2.6	2.9

Legal Services

A variety of establishments perform legal services in the United States. Private lawyers, representing more than an estimated three-fourths of the total number of practitioners in the legal profession, include firm sizes ranging from single to large corporations hiring hundreds of attorneys. The second group of legal services is comprised of providers of public legal assistance, who work either as public defenders or in legal-aid offices set up to assist those who can't afford the high cost of private legal counsel. The third group is made up of government lawyers who work for state, local or federal government agencies, and deal primarily with laws and regulations involved with government service. The last group is lawyers who work for nonprofit organizations and provide legal counsel in matters that relate to their particular organization's interests.

During the 10 years ending in 1998, revenues of legal services firms rose 5.9% per year, on average. While price increases are expected to decelerate over the next 10 years, annual growth in revenue is likely to be slightly higher. WEFA anticipates considerably more volatility and dispersion of performance among the industry's sub-sectors with increased competition from non-traditional law firms.

Demand for Legal Services

A negative effect on the growth in demand for legal services has resulted from the trend toward consolidation in many American industries. The smaller number of firms and increased cost consciousness at those firms has limited the market to some degree and led to heightened-price sensitivity. Many clients balk at rates for legal services that range from $150 to $600 per hour, depending on the location and the service provided. This price sensitivity has also led to increased demand for fixed-fee structures, particularly for the less complicated legal services. The high-fee structure and above-average fee inflation that the profession has enjoyed in the past is largely to blame for the emergence of a strong wave of competition in the legal- services industry.

A rather dramatic surge in consumer bankruptcy litigation has offset the falling demand for legal services in support of Chapter 11 corporate restructuring. Future demand growth areas for legal services tend towards sexual harassment suits, sophisticated estate planning and other types of elder law.

WEFA expects a modest increase in real terms in the rate of growth in legal service revenue over the next decade. During the 10 years ended in 1998, industry revenues rose an average of 5.9% per year, while prices charged increased 4.7%. Over the next 10 years, annual growth in revenue is likely to average slightly more than

6%, while price growth will decelerate to just under a 4% pace. WEFA anticipates considerably more volatility and dispersion of performance among the industry's sub-sectors with increased competition from non-traditional law firms.

Industry Structure

Emerging as a key supply-side issue within large, traditional-law firms, cost control has caused some firms to re-evaluate their way of business. The fast-track route to partnership has slowed, and lower-cost paralegal professionals are being given more assignments that were previously reserved for lawyers. In fact, demand for paralegals should rise rapidly over the next decade, as this trend extends throughout the industry.

Another supply-side development has been the spread of franchise law firms, which are often set up as storefronts in commercial strips or shopping malls. These firms are designed to handle basic, standardized-legal service at fixed fees that are well below those charged by the traditional partnerships.

A new brand of competition in the market for legal professionals and their services is the rise of legal temporary services. The attractive features of temporary legal help include no benefits, no hourly fees, and no long-term commitment after a short-run problem is resolved. One such firm, headquartered in Sacramento and owned and operated by marketing professionals rather than attorneys, has opened several offices in California.

The prepaid legal service, which is the legal equivalent to a health-maintenance organization, is another new form of legal services. This is a particularly attractive option for small firms that have a hard time affording traditional legal services. Members of the plan pay a modest monthly fee to have unlimited telephone access to legal professionals. When they need to hire legal counsel for litigation support or other projects, the rates are considerably lower than traditional fees. Montgomery Ward has such an operation that provides legal insurance for individuals.

Outlook

Also affecting the legal services industry is the aggressive cost cutting that has become so widespread in US corporations in order to preserve margins in the face of low inflation and a more competitive environment. Traditional law firms have encountered more competition from franchise and temporary firms in recent years, and will continue to do so in the foreseeable future. WEFA also expects clients to increasingly resist the billable-hour format for purchasing legal services. Trends in the workforce will include increased usage of paralegal employees, as well as a longer and more difficult track from law school graduation to firm partner. Finally, better automation achieved through increasing use of computers and improved management practices will provide law firms with some cost relief.

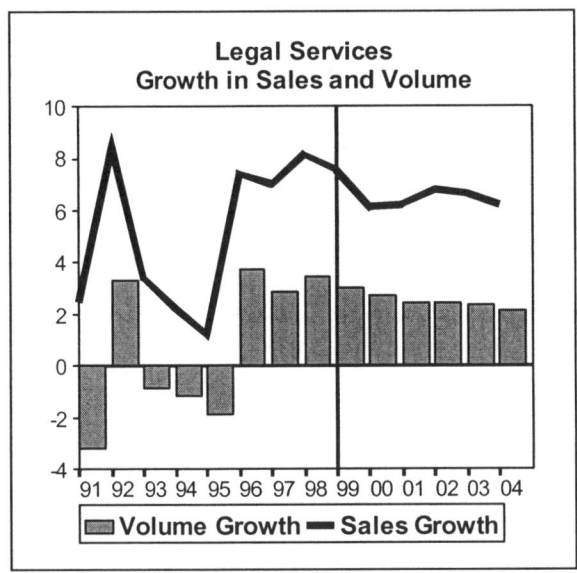

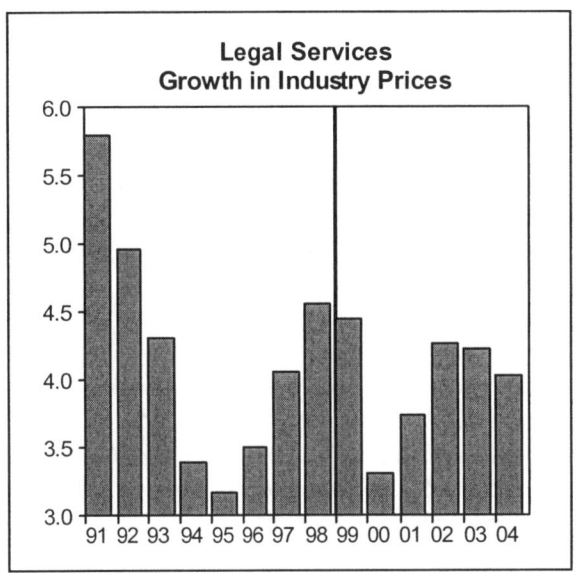

Legal Services

SIC 81

		1992	1993	1994	1995	1996	1997	1998	1999	2000	2001	Compound Average 88-98	Annual Growth 98-08
Sales													
	Billions of $	115.6	119.5	122.2	123.7	132.9	142.2	153.8	165.4	175.5	186.5		
	% Ch	8.4	3.4	2.2	1.2	7.4	7.0	8.2	7.6	6.1	6.2	5.9	6.2
Volume													
	% Ch	3.3	-0.9	-1.1	-1.9	3.8	2.8	3.4	3.0	2.7	2.4	1.1	2.4
Prices													
	% Ch	5.0	4.3	3.4	3.2	3.5	4.1	4.6	4.4	3.3	3.7	4.7	3.8
Production Costs													
Avg. Hourly Earnings													
	$/hr	14.96	15.20	15.56	16.06	16.58	17.29	18.04	18.83	19.50	20.24		
	% Ch	3.1	1.6	2.4	3.2	3.3	4.3	4.3	4.3	3.6	3.8	3.6	3.7
Input Price Index													
	% Ch	2.5	2.2	2.1	3.2	2.6	2.4	2.5	2.5	3.0	3.0	3.0	3.0

Educational Services

Educational services include both public- and private-educational activities. These comprise: education at the elementary and secondary levels, both public and private; colleges, universities and professional schools; vocational schools; educational courses by mail; and miscellaneous schools like music schools, drama schools, language schools and exam-preparation schools.

The historic wave of students jamming the nation's classrooms is moving from the elementary schools to the high schools, bringing with it increased costs of new schools, added problems in finding qualified teachers and potentially enormous higher education costs. Ongoing dissatisfaction with public schools— not only in terms of educational quality, but also in terms of drug availability and the personal safety of students—will spark renewed interest in the private-school option during the coming decade. Vocational and trade schools are likely to continue to do well over the next decade, particularly those providing training and skills in the computer field and electronics and other areas where the occupational outlook is favorable.

Demand Factors

In the Fall of 1999, the number of students stepping in to classrooms hit a record for the fourth consecutive year. Public- and private-school children in kindergarten through 12th grade reached 53.2 million, up a half-million from the previous record set the year before. College enrollment also hit a record with 14.9 million students in the Fall of 1999. This increase in school enrollment mainly reflects the "echo boom" of the children of the post-war Baby Boom generation, but is also the result of increased immigration and the fact that more students are staying in school longer.

School enrollment has been rising since 1985 and is projected to continue to climb until 2006, when it reaches a plateau. At that point, increases will start to be seen in the early grades because of rising birth rates, as the cycle begins again with growth rates first seen at the early grades, before moving up to the advanced grades.

During the current enrollment boom, most of the growth up to this point has been at the elementary-school level. Enrollment in elementary schools (grades K–8) increased from 31.2 million in 1984 to 37.3 million in 1996, an average annual gain of 1.5%. On the other hand, enrollment in high schools (grades 9–12) decreased from 13.7 million in 1983 to 12.5 million in 1990, before rebounding to 14.1 million in 1996. However, over the next few years, this experience will

be reversed as the bulge of elementary-school children moves on to high school. Elementary-school enrollment is projected to increase only 2% by 2008 from 1996, while enrollment in high school is projected to rise to 16.2 million in 2008, an increase of 15% from 1996.

For the ten-year period ending in 1995, private schools performed poorly. In the elementary area, where total school population advanced the fastest, private elementary-school enrollment rose only 5.6%, while public-school enrollment advanced 20%. This may have reflected affordability factors more than anything else. For high-school-age children the gap was even larger, as private secondary-school enrollment fell by almost 7% during the decade ending in 1995. This slump in private enrollments will probably reverse in the future, and growth should be roughly equal to public-school enrollment growth. Ongoing dissatisfaction with public schools—not only in terms of educational quality, but also in terms of drug availability and the personal safety of students—will spark renewed interest in the private-school option during the coming decade.

College enrollment has advanced strongly the past few years and will continue to expand at a robust rate for the foreseeable future. The number of college students is expected to reach 16 million by the year 2008, an increase of around 12% from 1996. The increase will in large part be due to the 18-to-34-year-old population, which is projected to increase 18% by 2008. This increase in the young-adult population is expected to more than offset the anticipated decline in the number of 25-to-34-year-olds enrolled in college.

Women have accounted for a disproportionate share of college-student growth, increasing their numbers from 6.4 million in 1983 to around 8 million in 1996, a rise of 25%. Enrollment is expected to surge to more than 9 million by the year 2008. College enrollment of men went from 6 million in 1983 to an estimated 6.3 million in 1996, an increase of only 5%. This number is projected to grow to 6.9 million by 2008, a 10% increase from 1996. As a result, the percentage of college students being female rose from 52% in 1983 to 56% in 1996. Female college students are expected to further raise their share to 57% in 2008.

There are approximately 3,000 vocational school establishments, a large majority of them controlled by corporate entities. Most of these institutions do, however, qualify for some form of government-education funding. The demand for vocational-school services is likely to continue to grow in the years ahead. With the continuing trend of corporate downsizing, the elimination of layers of management and acceptance of a generally less-secure employment agreement at most companies, degrees in many typical-business areas, such as marketing or general-business administration, no longer offer the assured route to occupational success they once did. While a college education still pays off in the long run, there are clearly occupational categories, especially those with a high-tech orientation that will pay off with more certainty. Training for some of these high-tech occupations is available from vocational schools, and this will help them in the future.

In addition, there is some demand for vocational and trade-school retraining for displaced workers in a variety of both blue- and white-collar occupations. Overall, look for many vocational and trade schools to continue to do well over the next decade, particularly those providing training and skills where the occupational outlook is favorable.

Supply Factors

Modest growth in elementary school enrollment will make it easy for those school systems to adjust. The bulge in high-school students, however, will be a more difficult problem to deal with. But, the severity of the problem will vary greatly among the states. For example, fifteen states will see a 15% increase in the number of public high-school graduates. Nevada tops the chart, expecting 77% more high-school graduates over the next-10 years, followed by Arizona with 56% and North Carolina with 40%. With the country's population shifting from the Northeast to the South and West, it is no coincidence that these states are experiencing extremely high-growth rates in school enrollment.

These figures give more credence to the Clinton administration's bid to hire new teachers and increase school construction. The White House proposals have met with stiff opposition from the Republican-led Congress, however, which prefers that federal money be sent to states and local-school boards to use on their own projects.

Whatever happens in Washington, new construction will be required. The push for increased spending on school construction and repair has already begun, as it reached a record $17 billion in 1998.

Finding enough qualified teachers is another issue that will continue to grow in importance, as class sizes swell and the demand for better education from the public intensifies. As a result, the public and private school teaching force is anticipated to rise by 75,000, or 6% in the next decade.

Therefore, look for a combination of new high-school buildings and expansions, increasing pupil-to-teacher ratios and even greater criticism of school safety as over-crowded high schools inevitably raise tension levels between students.

Social and Membership Services

Social and membership services cover a wide assortment of service organizations, including institutions providing welfare payments, job training and retraining, residential care for children and senior citizens, as well as re-election funds. Business and professional associations that promote the interests of their members and religious organizations are also included in this area.

WEFA expects a slowing of revenue growth over the next 10 years for the groups within the social and membership services industry. This industry's revenues advanced an average 9.4% per year in current-dollar terms during the decade that ended in 1998. However, over the next decade, we expect a slower rate of increase of about 6%, due to tight budgets at the consumer, business and governmental levels. Service fees charged by the various social and membership services groups increased at an average annual pace of 3.8% during the 1988–1998 period. Look for the pace of growth in those fees to decelerate over the forecast horizon to about 3%.

Recent Developments and Outlook

Individual and family social services include family counseling and welfare services. The number of people on welfare has surged since the beginning of the decade, and annual expenditures have averaged growth of just above 10%. This growth has strained the system's finances. Single mothers accounted for roughly half of this increase, and many of them are teenagers. There appears to be no right solution to this problem in sight. However, it does seem that any workable future solution—given projected numbers of recipients, expected financial resources available, and the political environment for the reform of public-assistance programs—will require that some kind of work be done in exchange for most benefits.

Job-training vocational-rehabilitation services include manpower training and vocational rehabilitation, and habilitation services for the unemployed, handicapped and anyone with a job-market disadvantage due to a lack of education, job skills or experience. Job retraining will continue to require substantial resources since the technical skills necessary for success in the job market are changing rapidly. Those remaining on the job, however, will also need continuous training in order to keep their skills up to date. As competition for highly trained technical employees heats up, firms that don't keep employment attractive and workers' skills up to date will lose those employees to other firms. Look for

continued health in this sector of the industry over the forecast period.

Demand for child-daycare services should slow a bit over the next 10 years from its recent rapid growth. This is because the population under-five years of age will actually fall through 2000, and then rise only modestly by 2005. Continued increases in the share of families with both parents working will offset the decline in the population pool. In many areas, the market for daycare services is currently tight. Consumers of daycare services are unhappy with the high rates of turnover in the industry caused by low wages, but are unwilling to pay more for services.

Residential care includes personal care for children and senior citizens, where intensive medical care is not a major element. Rising demand for these services has squeezed budget-constrained government facilities at the same time that private nursing homes and rehabilitation chains are doing reasonably well. Demand for residential care for senior citizens will remain largely unchanged over the next decade as the percentage of the population over-seventy years of age remains about the same. Beyond 2005, however, this percentage will begin to rise rather rapidly, and so will the demand for residential-care services.

Another segment of the industry includes other kinds of social services, such as advocacy groups, anti-poverty boards, community action and development groups, councils for social agencies, and regional planning organizations. Although the fund-raising efforts of this segment of the industry were assisted early in the decade by prominent entertainers, it has been one of the slower growing areas of social services, with revenues generally growing by less than 5% per year in current-dollar terms. Scandals over the misuse of funds, as well as concerns over political affiliation, have hurt contributions, as has the mood of American consumers who continue to be concerned about future employment and income despite the strength of the job market.

Business associations and professional-membership organizations include organizations engaged in promoting the business interests of their members, whether an industry or an occupation. These groups have increasingly developed ties to government and have established avenues to influence legislation in the direction they believe is beneficial to their members. About 40% of these organizations have at least one lobbyist and one PAC (Political Action Committee) fund. The number of trade, business and commercial associations rose strongly during the first half of the 1980s and then flattened out before actually declining during the first half of the 1990s. Only modest increases are likely in the number of those organizations going forward, and revenues within existing entities will rise slowly as members—both individuals and businesses—continue to experience increasing competition for their dollars.

PACs dominate political organizations. The Federal Election Campaign Act of 1971 brought PACs into existence in order to allow the pooling of funds and influence by a group. Given the rising cost of campaigning for office, PACs have increasingly come to dominate congressional elections and also provide a significant advantage for incumbents, who receive a majority of PAC funds. This has given rise to some concerns that PACs influence legislation in an unfair manner. Business PACs donate more than three times the amount of funds to election coffers than labor PACs contribute. These contributions are likely to continue to grow in the years ahead, unless campaign-finance reform is enacted that changes the ground rules under which these organizations operate.

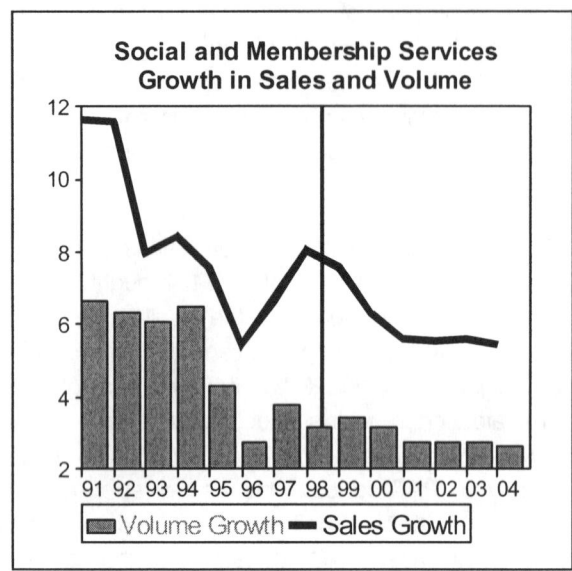

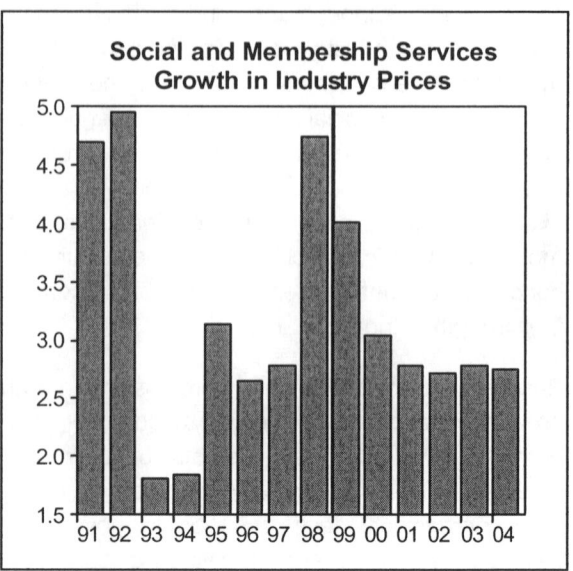

Social and Membership Services

SIC 83-84,86

		1992	1993	1994	1995	1996	1997	1998	1999	2000	2001	Compound Average 88-98	Annual Growth 98-08
Sales													
	Billions of $	197.6	213.3	231.4	248.9	262.4	279.9	302.5	325.4	345.8	365.1		
	% Ch	11.6	8.0	8.4	7.6	5.5	6.7	8.0	7.6	6.3	5.6	9.4	6.0
Volume													
	% Ch	6.3	6.1	6.5	4.3	2.7	3.8	3.2	3.4	3.1	2.7	5.4	3.0
Prices													
	% Ch	4.9	1.8	1.8	3.1	2.7	2.8	4.7	4.0	3.0	2.8	3.8	3.0
Production Costs													
Avg. Hourly Earnings													
	$/hr	6.51	6.65	6.84	7.05	7.31	7.54	7.89	8.24	8.61	8.96		
	% Ch	3.5	2.1	2.9	3.1	3.8	3.1	4.7	4.5	4.4	4.2	3.5	3.8
Input Price Index													
	% Ch	1.8	2.4	1.8	3.8	2.7	2.0	1.8	2.0	2.9	2.7	2.7	2.9

Engineering, Accounting, Research, and Management Services

This industry includes a broad variety of professional services that are supplied predominantly, although not exclusively, to business. The two largest components are engineering services and accounting services. The engineering services sector includes civil, mechanical, electrical and electronic, chemical, sanitary, industrial, petroleum, mining, aeronautical and marine engineering, and comprises almost 30% of total industry revenues. Accounting services represent somewhat less than 20% of total industry revenues. Other important industry subgroups are architectural services, research and testing services, management services and management-consulting services.

The growth in professional business services will likely be on of the highest of all industries in the United States over the next ten years, as it was over the last ten. Growth in sales is expected to moderate from the 8.4% per year averaged over the ten years ending in 1998 to 6.8% per year over the next decade. This still allows for healthy forecasted growth of 3.4% per year in real terms versus GDP growth of about 2.5%. The most rapid growth within the industry is likely to come in the accounting and management consulting sectors. Future demand for highway and bridge architectural services is also likely to be strong, as federal transportation spending receives a significant boost from the Transportation Equity Act for the 21st Century (TEA–21).

Recent Developments and Outlook

Engineering services were the hardest hit of the professional services included in this industry, during the first half of the 1990s. In addition to the cyclical forces of recession and the secular forces of downsizing and foreign competition, the engineering profession also suffered from severe cutbacks from one of its most important clients—the defense industry. Cutbacks in procurement spending and in weapon development have taken a toll on these services, forcing many engineers to switch their focus to civilian industries. The ongoing revolution in information technology, which has shifted the base of economic growth away from physical commodities toward information, is an additional problem for some engineering service firms. While this shift is good for electronic engineers, it is not beneficial to most of the rest of the profession.

During the first half of the 1990s, revenues accruing to engineering service firms rose an average of only 2% per year. Education and training for engineers in many foreign nations have made great strides, and these professionals are finding it easier to compete with US firms. In the future, growth will be healthy in certain types

of electronic engineering and in environmental protection processes. However, the profession's other challenges will continue, and overall, WEFA forecasts only modest gains for this sector.

In contrast to engineering services, accounting, auditing and bookkeeping services grew rapidly during the first half of the 1990s, seemingly oblivious to the fact that a recession took place. Indeed, revenues rose modestly in both 1990 and 1991, the years when many other professional-service businesses were losing sales. Large accounting firms have broadened their range of services well beyond traditional-accounting services. Small firms, on the other hand, have found it productive to specialize in more narrow fields where they can be more efficient and compete effectively with the large firms through lower overhead. Middle-size accounting firms, in contrast, have been pinched between the big firms, which offer services the mid-size firms cannot, and the small firms, many of which have become very competitive in narrow-niche areas. There is still strong demand for accounting services. A strong market for initial public offerings and ongoing merger and acquisition activity creates demand for accounting services. In addition, there are institutional and knowledge-based barriers to imports of accounting services. Moreover, outsourcing will continue to help accounting services firms grow.

Over the forecast horizon, management and management-consulting services will also do well. The sales of these firms rose almost as fast as that of accounting services over the last five-to-ten years, and have, in-fact, probably out-performed accounting firms somewhat since 1993. Management consultants provide operating counsel and assistance to the management of private, nonprofit and public organizations. Strategic planning, financial planning and budgeting, information systems planning and design, production planning, human resources, and marketing counsel are some of the services offered. The economic trends that propel accounting services also help management services and consulting. Hiring a consulting firm is quite often less expensive than maintaining in-house staff, and it is temporary. This favorable trend in the industry should continue for the years ahead.

Architectural service firms were hit hard during and immediately following the recession of 1990–1991. The downturn in demand for architectural services in the early 1990s was not just a cyclical slump, but also reflected the unwinding of the overbuilding in commercial construction that occurred in the late 1980s. Demand has recovered from this slump, with commercial construction up again in the last five years. Activity in this market is expected to grow only modestly in the future. However, future demand for highway and bridge architectural services is likely to be strong as federal-transportation spending increases, as does demand for services related to hazardous-waste projects and environmental facilities in general. Key to the outlook for federal transportation is the Transportation Equity Act for the 21st Century (TEA–21). At $217 billion, TEA–21 is the largest public works measure ever authorized by Congress. The Act is scheduled as a six-year commitment through fiscal year 2003.

The growth in professional business services will likely be above average over the next ten years, as it was over the last ten. Growth is expected to moderate from the 8.4% per year averaged over the ten years ending in 1998, to 6.8% over the next decade. This still allows for healthy forecasted growth of 3.4% per year in real terms versus GDP growth of about 2.5%.

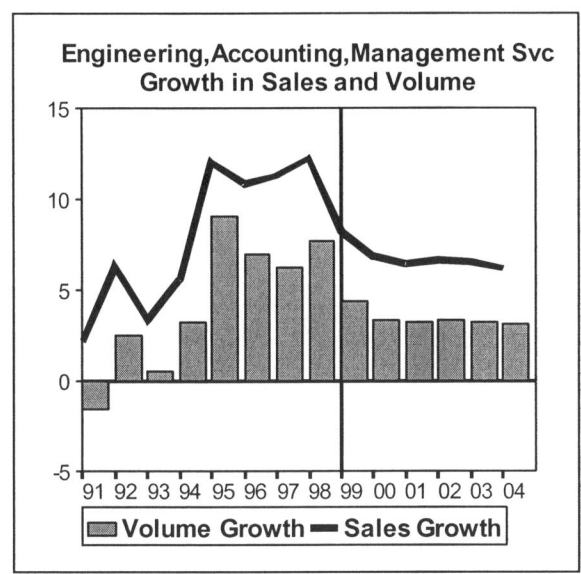

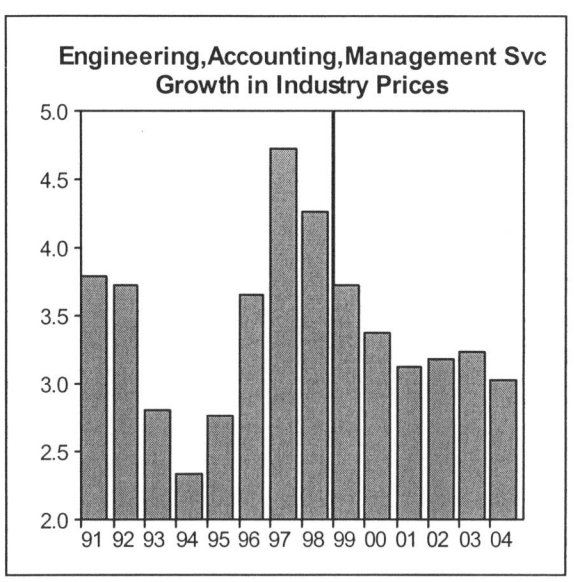

Engineering, Accounting, & Management Services

SIC 87

		1992	1993	1994	1995	1996	1997	1998	1999	2000	2001	Compound Average 88-98	Annual Growth 98-08
Sales													
	Billions of $	242.0	250.1	264.1	296.0	328.2	365.4	410.1	443.9	474.4	505.0		
	% Ch	6.4	3.4	5.6	12.1	10.9	11.3	12.3	8.2	6.9	6.4	8.4	6.8
Volume													
	% Ch	2.6	0.6	3.2	9.0	7.0	6.3	7.7	4.4	3.4	3.2	4.5	3.4
Prices													
	% Ch	3.7	2.8	2.3	2.8	3.6	4.7	4.3	3.7	3.4	3.1	3.8	3.3
Production Costs													
Avg. Hourly Earnings													
	$/hr	14.60	15.01	15.36	15.79	16.36	17.14	17.86	18.47	19.23	20.06		
	% Ch	3.7	2.8	2.3	2.8	3.6	4.7	4.2	3.4	4.2	4.3	3.8	4.0
Input Price Index													
	% Ch	3.3	1.6	2.2	2.6	2.6	2.8	3.5	3.0	2.9	2.9	3.0	3.0

Chapter 30: Environmental Technologies and Services

Environmental
Technologies and Services

Investment in equipment and technology for pollution control and abatement has increased at a fast pace over the past three decades. The Clean Air Act of 1970 started the ball rolling. Amendments to this act expanded clean air standards and regulations. The Clean Water Act of 1972 put the pressure on factories, cities and towns to reduce dumping of industrial wastes and sewage and improve water quality. Significant pressure has also been brought to bear by the EPA to reduce the output and improve the handling of wastes, toxins and pesticides. EPA regulations have also come into play in the area of noise pollution, which has had an impact on such diverse areas as jet engine and leaf-blower noise reduction.

During the 1990s, capital expenditures for pollution-abatement equipment rose an average of about 6% per year. Looking ahead, WEFA expects domestic expenditures for this equipment to advance in the 5% to 6% range on average per year. Spending on water-pollution systems should expand at a faster pace than air-pollution systems. We expect continued robust growth in spending to restore polluted sites to their prior condition.

Export opportunities for US manufacturers of pollution-control equipment are bright. Air and water quality in developing countries in Latin America, Asia and Eastern Europe are far worse than they ever were in the US. In addition, little has been done in these areas to address the problems of solid-waste management. US producers of pollution-control equipment will benefit, as countries in Latin America, Asia and Eastern Europe become more concerned about their quality of life and launch programs to improve their environment.

Recent History

Investment in equipment and technology for pollution control and abatement has increased at a fast pace over the past three decades. The Clean Air Act of 1970 started the ball rolling. Amendments to this act expanded clean-air standards and regulations. The Clean Water Act of 1972 put the pressure on factories, cities and towns to reduce dumping of industrial wastes and sewage and improve water quality. Significant pressure has also been brought to bear by the EPA to reduce the output and improve the handling of wastes, toxins and pesticides. EPA regulations have also come into play in the area of noise pollution, which has had an impact on such diverse areas as jet engine and leaf-blower noise reduction.

Of the three major areas of pollution equipment—made to treat air, water and solids—spending during the first half of the 1990s was concentrated in air-pollution equipment, which increased at an average annual rate of almost 14% per year. Much of this spending was in response to the Clean Air Act Amendments of 1990, which required substantial reductions in the emissions of a wide variety of hazardous air pollutants. Expenditures on solid-contained waste equipment rose rapidly early in the 1990s, only to fall off toward the middle of the decade. Water-pollution equipment was the laggard, as spending remained relatively flat throughout the first half of the 1990s.

In the second half of the 1990s, the demand for pollution-control technology has increasingly been focused on proactive, environmental management rather than direct compliance with regulations. The comprehensive environmental-management systems that have been adopted by many businesses include waste-minimization and pollution-prevention technologies, demand-side management, and accounting techniques that identify the environmental cost of each operation.

Air Pollution

Over the last thirty years, since the nation passed the Clean Air Act, air quality in the US has improved dramatically. The private and public sectors became more aware of the damage that had been done to our air quality and invested aggressively to first stem the tide of air pollution, and then reverse its effects. During the past three decades, total emissions for five major pollutants (lead, ozone, sulfur dioxide, carbon monoxide and particulate matter) declined dramatically. Increased coal burning at power plants resulted in an increase of nitrogen-oxide emissions into the mid-1990s, but regulations have been stiffened and the course has been reversed once again.

Expenditures on air-pollution abatement equipment have been on a downward trend since 1990. Shipments of air-pollution control equipment were valued at $825 million in 1990, but by 1997, the latest data, they had fallen to $722 million. This represents a decline of 12.5%.

Shipments of particulate-emissions collectors increased 11% during this period. Major types of equipment performed as follows: electrostatic precipitators –21%, fabric filters +21%, and wet scrubbers +77%. In order of their importance, the major buyers of particulate emissions collectors include chemical and fertilizer production facilities, pulp and paper mill operations, electric-utility steam-power plants, iron and steel mills, cement manufacturing, foundries, and grain milling and handling.

Shipments of gaseous-emissions control devices declined 14% from 1990 through 1997. Shipments of catalytic-oxidation systems increased from $15.4 million in 1990 to $34.4 million in 1997. Shipments of scrubbers increased from $16.1 million in 1990 to $23.1 million in 1997. These increases were offset by sharp declines in shipments of thermal and direct-oxidation systems and other equipment.

Water Pollution

Water quality has certainly improved as a result of the Clean Water Act of 1972, the Safe Drinking Water Act of 1974 and other EPA regulations. Efforts to reduce pollution and improve water quality have included increased investment in filtration devices and pumps and pumping equipment. Concerns about the dumping of industrial wastes and sewage, and oil and chemical spills have also triggered increased investment in a wide range of equipment used to contain, transport and monitor these materials.

Recent surveys of national water quality indicate that private and public sector efforts to reduce water pollution and improve water quality have been successful. However, they also indicate that there is more work to be done. This suggests that the demand for water-treatment and pollution-control equipment will remain strong.

The most recent Index of Watershed Indicators indicated that 16% of the nation's watersheds had good water quality; 36% had moderate water-quality problems; 21% had more serious water-quality problems; and sufficient data was lacking to fully characterize the remaining 27%. Finally, 1-in-14 watersheds was vulnerable to further damage from pollution.

Approximately 65% of the nation's rivers, lakes and estuaries are clean enough to allow basic uses, such as swimming and fishing. However, this still leaves about 35% that are too polluted for such uses. We are continuing to lose wetlands to residential and commercial development. However, the good news is that the rate of decline has slowed. Groundwater contamination from leaking underground storage tanks, landfills, septic systems, and fertilizer and pesticide applications, remains a major concern.

Waste, Toxic Materials and Pesticide Pollution

The US generates a huge amount of waste and the management of this waste has spawned an entire industry.

Over the past thirty years, US solid waste production has grown from 3.3 pounds per person per day to over 4.5 pounds per person per day currently. The industrial sector currently manages in excess of 260 million tons hazardous waste and about 8 billion tons of non-hazardous waste. The EPA has identified more than 650 chemicals and chemical products that represent the greatest threat to our air, water, and land quality. As recently as 1992 industry released over 1.6 million tons of these materials into the environment.

Over the last decade we have made significant progress in dealing with waste, toxic materials and pesticide problems. Recycling of trash has been on the rise, while the use of landfills has been declining. We have also seen an increase in recycling of hazardous wastes such as solvents. Chemical spills and releases of priority chemicals have been on the decline. Chemical releases such as forcing liquid wastes into deep wells, and releases to land (landfilling) are also on the decline. Regulations regarding underground storage tanks have been tightened.

The Comprehensive Environmental Response, Compensation, and Liability Act (CLERCLA) of 1980 of "Superfund" created a program to clean up abandoned hazardous-waste sites throughout the US. "Superfund" clean-ups started off very slowly, but have been accelerating in recent years. Of the roughly 1,300 sites of the list of worst sites, about 95% have clean-up operations underway and about 350 have been completely cleaned up.

Outlook

The growth of air-pollution control expenditures in the US is not expected to accelerate in the future. However, concern about the impact of air quality is not expected to subside. In fact, it is more likely that we will see efforts to improve air even further in the future. We have already seen an acceleration of regulations governing diesel-engine particulate emissions and a further tightening of emission rules is expected. As the southeast and southwest regions of the US continue to expand, the threat of increased air pollution, due to population and industrial growth and energy requirements, will trigger additional investments in air-pollution control devices, processes and equipment.

Spending on water systems is expected to increase. Concern about water quality in major urban areas will support strong investment in water-purification systems. The fast-growing regions of the Southeast and Southwest will have to wrestle not only with water-quality issues, but also water-supply problems as the population in those areas increases and industrial demand for water rises as well. New wastewater-treatment technologies will continue to replace, where feasible, conventional activated carbon absorption and air-stripping systems that merely transfer pollutants from one medium to another.

Waste management encompasses products for collecting and transporting solid waste, landfill policies, treatment and disposal of toxic wastes, and recycling. The trend in US sanitary landfill practices is for fewer but bigger solid-waste sites. Landfill sites today require sophisticated design and construction procedures, quality assurance/control oversight and documentation, and rigid monitoring and reporting of site operations. Small landfill sites are being closed down because of the difficulty in complying with increasingly complex regulations. Consequently, solid waste is being hauled longer distances to larger disposal sites.

In the hazardous-waste area, look for more investment in processing and disposing. The use of technologies such as putting waste through high-temperature electric arcs and ionizing remediation will increase. Bioremediation is also likely to gain importance as a method of solving toxic-waste clean-up problems. Bioremediation programs are currently in operation under federal and state regulatory authority at more than 150 sites in the country.

During the 1990s, capital expenditures for pollution abatement equipment rose an average of about 6% per year. Looking ahead, WEFA expects domestic expenditures for this type of equipment to advance in the 5% to 6% range on average per year. Spending on water-pollution systems should expand at a faster pace than air-pollution systems. We expect continued robust growth in spending to restore polluted sites to their prior condition.

Export opportunities for US manufacturers of pollution control equipment are bright. Air and water quality in developing countries in Latin America, Asia and Eastern Europe are far worse than they ever were in the US. In addition, little has been done in these areas to address the problems of solid-waste management. US producers of pollution-control equipment will benefit, as countries in Latin America, Asia and Eastern Europe become more concerned about their quality of life and launch programs to improve their environment.

Index

(Chapter names are in bold.)